Oswaldo Payá's Journey

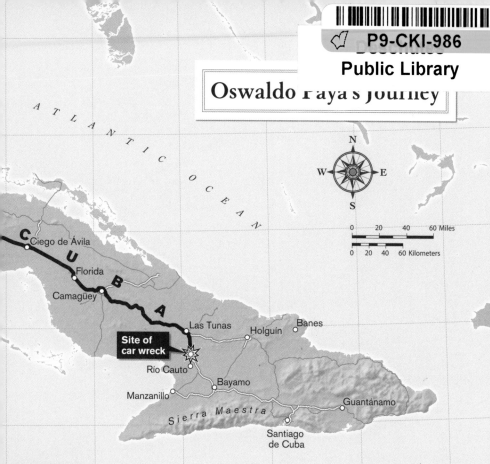

ATLANTIC OCEAN

N
W E
S

0 20 40 60 Miles

0 20 40 60 Kilometers

Ciego de Ávila
Florida
Camagüey

C U B A

Las Tunas
Holguín
Banes

Site of car wreck

Río Cauto
Bayamo
Manzanillo
Guantánamo

Sierra Maestra

Santiago de Cuba

Timeline

1940
Cuba adopts democratic constitution

1952
Fulgencio Batista coup

Oswaldo Payá born in Havana

1959
Fidel Castro takes power

1961
Failed US Bay of Pigs invasion

1962
Cuban Missile Crisis

1969
Payá sent to forced labor camp

1980
Mariel boatlift

1985
Payá delivers "Faith and Justice" speech

1986
Oswaldo Payá and Ofelia Acevedo Maura are married

1987
In *Ecos del Sínodo*, Payá urges Cubans to overcome "fear and repression"

1988
Pueblo de Dios appears

Payá launches *Movimiento Cristiano Liberación*

1991
Soviet Union collapse

1994
Thousands of *balseros,* or rafters, flee to Florida

1996
Payá creates the Varela Project, a citizen initiative seeking democracy

1998
Pope John Paul II visits Cuba

1999
Todos Unidos is launched

2002
Payá submits 11,020 Varela Project

signatures to National Assembly

Payá receives Sakharov award from European Parliament

2003
"Black Spring" arrests and prison sentences

Payá submits another 14,384 Varela Project signatures

2006
Payá presents sweeping plan for democracy, *Todos Cubanos*

2012
Oswaldo Payá killed in suspicious car wreck

ALSO BY DAVID E. HOFFMAN

The Billion Dollar Spy:
A True Story of Cold War Espionage and Betrayal

The Dead Hand:
The Untold Story of the Cold War Arms
Race and Its Dangerous Legacy

The Oligarchs:
Wealth and Power in the New Russia

GIVE ME LIBERTY

THE TRUE STORY OF OSWALDO PAYÁ
AND HIS DARING QUEST FOR A FREE CUBA

DAVID E. HOFFMAN

SIMON & SCHUSTER

NEW YORK   LONDON   TORONTO   SYDNEY   NEW DELHI

Simon & Schuster
1230 Avenue of the Americas
New York, NY 10020

First Simon & Schuster hardcover edition June 2022

SIMON & SCHUSTER and colophon are
registered trademarks of Simon & Schuster, Inc.

For information about special discounts for bulk purchases,
please contact Simon & Schuster Special Sales at
1-866-506-1949 or business@simonandschuster.com.

The Simon & Schuster Speakers Bureau can bring authors to your live event.
For more information or to book an event, contact the
Simon & Schuster Speakers Bureau at 1-866-248-3049 or
visit our website at www.simonspeakers.com.

Interior design by Ruth Lee-Mui
Map design by Kate Thorp
Havana map data from OpenStreetMap

Manufactured in the United States of America

1   3   5   7   9   10   8   6   4   2

Library of Congress Cataloging-in-Publication Data is available on file.

ISBN 978-1-9821-9119-1
ISBN 978-1-9821-9121-4 (ebook)

To Carole

Contents

PART IV

THE BLACK SPRING

We can't be just the spectators of our own history. We must be the protagonists.

Oswaldo Payá,
Pueblo de Dios, No. 7
1987

Prologue

Bleary-eyed, Oswaldo Payá had been up all night, waiting for his daughter to come home. Rosa María was twenty-three years old, a university graduate in physics, lively and strikingly attractive, with a rebellious streak very much like her father. That she had been out all night, Oswaldo could do nothing, but he waited for her, worried about her safety, agitated, unable to sleep. She had promised to join him before dawn for the long and dangerous journey, staying one step ahead of state security.

Where was she?

Oswaldo was sixty years old, with thick, wavy hair the color of charcoal and a swirl at the peak of his forehead. He had deep rings under his eyes and worry creases sometimes rippled across his brow, but his brown eyes were soft, understanding, and patient. Oswaldo dressed casually, in jeans and a short-sleeved checkered shirt, the collar open wide, his shirt buttons absentmindedly askew. His voice had a slight nasal tone. He was a practiced orator, clear and articulate. He had a lot to say, and did.

By day, Oswaldo was an engineer who specialized in medical electronics, troubleshooting life-saving equipment at Havana hospitals. He worked with oxygen tanks, ventilators, and incubators. He took great satisfaction when he could help save a life.

But his great passion was to change Cuba, to unleash a society of free people with unfettered rights to speak and act as they wished. He called it liberation. He had devoted many years to the cause, shared with his wife, Ofelia Acevedo. At this moment she was away, visiting her parents, but she knew he was taking another step into the unknown. She sensed he was rushing toward something. She wondered why he was taking the chances, hurtling into the darkness once again.

Ofelia and Oswaldo had made a promise to themselves as newlyweds years before: their children would live in a free country. They would fight for it and never flee Cuba. Oswaldo had spoken out against Fidel Castro's despotism since his own days in high school. He wrote dozens of manifestos and declarations, published underground handbills, formed a prodemocracy movement, and championed the Varela Project, a citizen initiative demanding free speech, a free press, freedom of association, freedom of belief, private enterprise, free elections, and freedom for political prisoners. He had never run from his values.

But lately, fear was choking him. The secret police, Seguridad del Estado, or state security, threatened his family. In fleeting encounters on the street, strangers came up to him and said simply, "Be careful, or your children could be hurt." Oswaldo knew that state security could cause an accident, a bicycle run off the road, or a careless driver running a red light. They could plant drugs in a boy's backpack, then haul him off to prison. They could detain and sexually assault a young girl. They could do anything. The thoughts were unbearable.

Oswaldo, shaken, had taken his three children, Oswaldito, Rosa María, and Reinaldo, to a convent of the Sisters of Mary Magdalene near their home in Havana. With assistance from the nuns, he showed them a hidden entrance leading to a concealed room. This was their refuge, he said; if he were ever arrested or if they were in serious trouble, they should come here, and the nuns would harbor them. The children thought it was a lark, but Oswaldo was serious. Another time, he turned to a visitor from Sweden and asked point-blank: What would it take to get asylum for my family?

Finally, in desperation, Oswaldo and Ofelia made a tough decision.

The time had come to send their children out of Cuba. The two oldest, Oswaldito and Rosa María, applied for and were admitted to the University of Amsterdam. They were to go in August. The youngest, Reinaldo, might go to Spain. It was agonizing for Oswaldo and Ofelia to think about being apart from their children, to abandon the vow they had made to build a free country for them, but they felt they no longer had a choice. They sensed the dangers were growing.

Where was Rosa María?

Oswaldo was heading to Santiago de Cuba, 540 miles to the east, to train young activists and organize local committees for the Movimiento Cristiano Liberación, the democracy movement he founded nearly twenty-four years earlier. He started it with friends in the parish of El Salvador del Mundo in Havana, where four generations of his family had anchored their Catholic faith. The *movimiento* had grown to more than a thousand members across the island, a civic and political movement, nondenominational but driven by the values of Christian democracy that had confronted fascism and communism in the twentieth century.

At this point, Fidel, almost eighty-six years old, had relinquished power to his brother Raúl, who eased up slightly on the economy but maintained a hard line against any dissent, continuing the Castro dictatorship of more than five decades. Members of the movimiento were frequently jailed, harassed, interrogated, and pressured to become informers. State security kept Oswaldo under surveillance, and his name was blacklisted. He could not travel by plane, train, or bus without being immediately spotted. The trip to Santiago de Cuba would set off alarms if he took public transportation. Yet, from years of experience, Oswaldo had developed a clandestine method to evade surveillance. He could move relatively unseen in a rental car driven by tourists. State security might spend a few fruitless days looking for him. In this case, the "tourists" were two young men, from Spain and Sweden, both eager democracy activists who had arrived in Havana two days before.

The only problem was that they arrived unexpectedly early, and now he had to rush the trip, which had been planned for later. On July 26, in four days' time, a holiday marked the anniversary of Fidel's 1953 attack on the Moncada army barracks in Santiago de Cuba, the first armed assault of his guerrilla war. State security was on alert. To reach Santiago, a day's drive, and get back, Oswaldo would have to hurry. He decided to leave before dawn, while darkness cloaked the streets.

Just before 6:00 a.m., Rosa María cracked open the front door.

Oswaldo was waiting in their tidy living room, with pale yellow walls and black-and-white checkered floor tiles. Rosa María steeled herself for his reproach. But as soon as he saw her, his anger melted away. She was safe. There was no time for questions. He had to leave before the sun rose. She had planned to go with him but was exhausted. She didn't dare ask him to wait for her. She knew he couldn't.

Oswaldo crossed the room and kissed her good-bye.

He grabbed his backpack. He motioned to Harold Cepero to grab his own overnight bag. Cepero was Oswaldo's protégé. While waiting for Rosa María, Oswaldo had spent the night talking with Harold about God, Cuba, democracy, and dictatorship. Oswaldo ranged over these topics naturally and passionately. With boyish good looks, tousled hair, faded jeans, and a white T-shirt, Cepero, thirty-two years old, was Oswaldo's hope for a new generation of activists. He was helping Oswaldo train young people to fight for their rights, and he and Rosa María were preparing a youth magazine. The first edition was almost ready. As Harold stepped toward the door, Rosa María rushed up to him and put her hand on his shoulder.

"Be careful," she admonished him. Cepero flashed back his wide, generous smile.

Oswaldo opened the front door of 221 Calle Peñón and cautiously stepped into the predawn darkness.

The air was pleasant and the skies clear. To his left he could see the knurled boughs of the old *álamo* trees that shaded his childhood playground, Parque Manila. The house where he had grown up, at 276 Calle Peñón, was directly across from the park. The house was a boxy two-floor structure of sun-washed masonry, with an oversized portico thrusting out toward the curb. Oswaldo was the fifth of seven children, and when he was a boy, the park was his second home. Next door, at 280

Calle Peñón, stood a similar but smaller house where Oswaldo's aunt Beba lived. She was his father's sister, with no children of her own. For as long as Oswaldo could remember, Beba was a presence in his family, often walking him and his brothers and sisters to Sunday Mass or taking them by the hand to the movies.

In recent years, Beba helped him once again. Her house became the nerve center for his ambitious and daring political quest.

Oswaldo turned to the right, away from the park. He and Cepero walked silently down the slope of Calle Peñón, past slumbering households, with dogs and roosters milling about behind gates and fences. Oswaldo looked warily for any cars in the shadows. Over many years, state security stationed their surveillance vehicles near the park, and they paid informers in nearby houses to keep an eye on him. Oswaldo hoped the darkness would cover their departure, giving them a head start.

El Cerro was once a neighborhood of luxury villas built in the 1800s by the upper classes seeking to escape Old Havana. Back then it was a refuge of spacious homes, with perfumed flowers and flickering gas lanterns. Even today, remnants of that era were visible on Calle Peñón: balconies of elegant stone balusters, decorative archways, and elaborate cornices along the rooftops. But over the decades, El Cerro slowly crumbled; concrete exteriors turned dingy, and once-breezy open windows were now shuttered behind rusty iron grates.

Oswaldo passed a forbidding, tall cinder-block wall. Six years earlier, the regime had painted a threatening slogan. "In a besieged fortress," it declared, "dissidence is treason."

A few blocks beyond, they reached the Calzada del Cerro, on most days a busy avenue. Now it was quiet. Oswaldo could barely make out the graceful colonnades that flanked the street, faint reminders of the city's lost grandeur. Just around a corner, a block off the Calzada, stood the parish church with a bell tower that was at the center of Oswaldo's faith. But it was not the church or the colonnade that commanded his attention.

He peered into the shadows, looking for a rental car.

•   •   •

At 6:15 a.m., a blue Hyundai Accent pulled up to the curb. Oswaldo recited a brief prayer, softly but audibly, and climbed into the rear seat on the driver's side. Harold climbed in the back on the passenger side. Two foreigners were in the front. Oswaldo had met them two days earlier. The driver, Ángel Carromero, twenty-six, led the Madrid youth wing of Spain's ruling Partido Popular, or People's Party. Next to him was Aron Modig, twenty-seven, who headed the youth organization of Sweden's Christian Democrats in Stockholm. They had come to Cuba expressly to assist Oswaldo, and rented the blue Hyundai to drive him around, evading state security.

Carromero was in flip-flops. Modig wore a T-shirt with navy and white stripes, and blue shorts. Their trip had been arranged somewhat hastily. Both knew the risks of the long drive, and Carromero was nervous about it, but they were eager to prove useful.

Oswaldo gave directions out of Havana toward the east, and onto the *ocho vías*, a broad eight-lane highway, almost empty at this hour. Carromero glanced at the rearview mirror and saw no one trailing them. Soon the sun was up and the road straight and wide.

Oswaldo talked for a long time, never tiring, full of memories and pent-up hopes, a lifetime of visions pursued and yet never quite fulfilled. As a boy he had witnessed the seizure of his father's business as Castro's revolution confiscated private enterprises in 1965. As a teenager he had protested the crushing of the Prague Spring with Soviet tanks in 1968 and was sent to Castro's forced labor camps. Later, as a member of the laity, Oswaldo demanded that Catholic Church leaders stand up for human rights and democracy, but, weakened by decades of repression, they chose reconciliation rather than confrontation. When Oswaldo published a popular newsletter, full of his essays demanding basic rights for the Cuban people, the archbishop insisted that he stop. He could not. By the 1990s, when Cubans were plunged into economic despair with the collapse of the Soviet Union, Oswaldo had become a prominent voice of the opposition.

As Oswaldo talked, the sun rose higher and they rolled down the windows. The morning air was already warm and fragrant.

Oswaldo recalled how they had launched the Varela Project, challenging Castro's dictatorship with a citizen petition for democracy. The project was named after Félix Varela, a nineteenth-century priest, philosopher, and Cuba's most illustrious educator. Oswaldo loved to recount how the movimiento had doggedly collected the signatures, door to door, over four years, then surprised Fidel and state security by submitting 11,020 signatures to the National Assembly in 2002, and another 14,384 signatures the following year. More than 10,000 additional signatures were still hidden by the nuns. Nothing like it had ever happened before in Cuba.

But Oswaldo and his movement paid a heavy price. He was thrust into the crosshairs of state security, a hardened secret police who were trained in the methods of East Germany's Ministry of State Security, the Stasi. In Cuba, state security harassed and intimidated dissidents and opposition figures using wiretapping, subversion, threats, detention, and fear. Payá took the brunt of it for years. After the first wave of Varela Project signatures were submitted, state security arrested and imprisoned seventy-five of his movimiento activists and independent journalists. They were given prison terms of up to twenty-eight years for nothing more than collecting signatures. Oswaldo was not arrested, but subjected to a different torment, a relentless psychological warfare. The threats he dreaded most were conveyed in exactly the same words, "You will not outlive Fidel."

When a US diplomat visited his house on Calle Peñón, Oswaldo was insistent. "People aren't taking seriously enough the threat that they'd liquidate me," he said.

He confided to a friend, "I see very few chances of getting out alive."

As Payá and the young activists drove deeper into the Cuban countryside, few cars were on the road, only people riding bicycles, and occasionally a horse-drawn cart. Oswaldo told the visitors about the hardships of day-to-day life on the island. Sugar and tobacco production—once mainstays of the economy—were lower than in the 1950s. Since 2010, Raúl had allowed a nascent private sector to grow, but for most of Cuba's eleven million people, living conditions were dire, salaries paltry, food and goods scarce.

Several hours into their trip, Carromero, the driver, noticed something. A car was following them, far behind, but steadily.

Anxious, Carromero started smoking, holding the cigarette between his fingers at the open window. A red Lada, the Soviet-era boxy auto fashioned after the Fiat, was on their tail, but still distant. The road was getting worse, and Carromero slowed. Carromero mentioned the red Lada to Oswaldo, who told him, "Do not give them any reason to stop us."

Carromero asked Oswaldo whether it was normal to be followed in such a remote place. Yes, Oswaldo replied. But he urged Carromero to remain calm. The tone of his voice was reassuring. He said that state security often did this to show who was boss, "Don't forget, we are here." They wanted everyone to live in fear.

Carromero pulled over for gas. The station was painted in a candy-red and white, with a sign, "Black Gold Servicecenter Sputnik." It added, "Welcome to Camagüey," a major city in central Cuba. They had been driving for five hours. Modig, who had been dozing in the car, snapped a photo of Cepero and the gas station at 11:09 a.m. The red Lada stopped too, and the driver eyed them from afar. Carromero looked back, uneasy.

On the road again, as they headed southeast, the red Lada peeled away. At midday they found a place for lunch, another gas station with a bar. They were hungry and wolfed down ham and cheese sandwiches. A boy was selling music CDs. Cepero bought two: one was a compilation of the Beatles, the other a Cuban artist.

Back on the road, a hot breeze rushed through the car windows. Oswaldo pointed out swaths of uncultivated land, fertile fields once devoted to sugarcane, now overrun by the invasive *marabú*, or sickle bush.

Carromero slipped the Beatles CD into the slot and turned up the volume. Oswaldo loved the Beatles. There were many hit songs on the disc, and he knew the lyrics. He was particularly fond of the *Abbey Road* classic "Oh! Darling."

The Cuban countryside rolled by, scenes of hay and grassland.

The music and warm air lulled Modig to sleep again, while Payá and Cepero sang their hearts out.

Then Carromero noticed something in the mirror.

Another car was tailing them, newer than the red Lada, and it was closing in, stubbornly. Carromero saw two men in the car.

Payá and Cepero turned around, too. "The Communists," Cepero said with a tone of scorn, referring to state security. The car license plate was blue, a government vehicle. Carromero asked what he should do.

Payá responded once again, *Don't give them any reason to stop us. Just keep going.*

The car drew closer. Carromero could see the eyes of the driver.

The other car seemed to leap forward. It charged at the Hyundai.

Carromero felt a powerful shudder. He heard a dry, metallic sound. Both cars were traveling in the same direction, so it wasn't a collision, but Carromero felt the shove.

He lost control of the Hyundai.

Modig had been dozing but suddenly awoke. He curled his legs up in a protective fetal position.

Oswaldo Payá was born ten days before Fulgencio Batista seized power in Cuba on March 10, 1952, establishing a brutish autocracy. Oswaldo was nearly seven years old when Fidel Castro ousted Batista. From his guerrilla outpost in the Sierra Maestra mountains, Fidel had once promised, "We are fighting for the beautiful ideal of a free, democratic, and just Cuba. We want elections, but with one condition: truly free, democratic, and impartial elections." But once in power, Castro built a dictatorship based on an overarching ideology, a single party, a secret police, total control of communications, and the elimination of civil society. His ambitions were totalitarian, to corral all of Cuba inside his revolution; as he put it, "within the Revolution, everything; against the Revolution, nothing." Still, the revolution was not airtight. Despite the police state, freethinking bubbled up from the grassroots, especially in the 1990s, when the loss of subsidies from the Soviet Union led to hardship and misery, unleashing waves of discontent.

Oswaldo devoted a lifetime to opposing Castro's repression. Oswaldo believed the rights of every person are God-given and cannot be taken away by the state. Yet for most of his life in Cuba, those rights were stolen, tarnished, and denied. Even something as innocent as hanging a *"Feliz Navidad,"* or Merry Christmas, sign on the bell tower of his church was considered subversive. Defiant, Oswaldo hung the sign anyway. He never lived in a state of liberty, but liberty lived in his mind and drove his fight for it.

His most daring challenge to Castro was the Varela Project, a citizen petition printed on a single sheet of paper creased at the half fold. At the top were five demands for freedom and democracy. Those who signed their names also gave their addresses and identification numbers. They stood up to be counted. Oswaldo had no modern tools of communication to mobilize the Cuban people—he had no access to radio, television, or print, and the online world barely existed—yet he was joined by tens of thousands of people demanding the right to choose their own destiny.

The Varela Project should have triggered action by the National Assembly, a referendum, a free and fair election, and a chance at a new, democratic Cuba. But Fidel Castro held a monopoly on power and was intolerant of any challenge to his authority. He ignored the petitions.

However, Castro could not extinguish the spirit of the Varela Project. When massive anti-government protests broke out in Cuba on July 11, 2021, some demonstrators raised their thumb and forefinger in Oswaldo's familiar "L" for *liberación*. Nearly all those who spontaneously crowded the streets that day shouted the same demands for *¡libertad!* that Oswaldo had championed two decades before. Many still remembered how Oswaldo had braved persecution and death threats, how he had urged them to overcome their fears.

Significantly, Oswaldo's quest grew from the soil of Cuba. The Varela Project was based on Cuba's existing constitution and had its roots in the nation's greatest democratic experiment, the 1940 constitution and the years that followed it. With nothing more than pen and paper, Cubans took the risks to sign and collect the Varela Project petitions. It was not a product of the Miami exiles or the US government, so often reviled by Castro as the enemy. When some of Oswaldo's relatives urged him to depart for Florida during the 1980 Mariel boatlift, he refused. "I believed for this entire time that Cuba had to be liberated from within," he insisted. The Varela Project was that cry from within.

How do people gain the right to think and speak freely, advocate their views, follow their conscience, worship or assemble as they desire— without persecution? How do they secure the right to choose their leaders and set the course for their own future? What does it take to attain such freedoms? These questions are at the heart of this book, the story of one man's journey into the whirlwind of dictatorship.

Oswaldo did not want to be called a dissident. He thought it applied to those who had once been inside Castro's revolution and then turned against it. Oswaldo never set foot inside, not from the day he was born. He preferred to be called opposition. He fought a lifelong challenge to a relentless and repressive machine. This book explores where he found the ideas and inspiration, the courage, faith, and persistence against impossible odds.

Throughout Cuba's volatile history, people rose to demand the right to rule themselves freely. A thread of tragedy and loss runs through their struggle. They were dreamers who dared wish for more, whose visions were cut short, whose pursuit of liberty was lost, then resurrected again by a new generation. Oswaldo Payá inherited these dreams, and turned them into action.

To understand Oswaldo's life and his quest, it is necessary to begin in the first half of the twentieth century, when Cuba was newly independent from Spain. Liberty did not come easily. Political corruption and violence took a toll. The United States cast a long imperial shadow. But in 1940, the Cuban Republic surmounted its difficulties and gave birth to a new, democratic constitution. It was the work of many, but especially Gustavo Gutiérrez, a jurist, politician, and thinker who harbored a vision of Cuba as a modern republic built on democratic values and constitutional rule.

The vision did not last. The 1940 constitution was later torn up. Dictatorship prevailed.

But Gutiérrez had planted a seed.

PART I

SEARCH FOR LIBERTY

ONE

AGONY OF THE REPUBLIC

The man of law rose in the temple of law.

Gustavo Gutiérrez wore a tropical suit of white linen, known as the *dril cien*, stylish and cool in the summer heat. He stood at a mahogany desk trimmed in bronze on the floor of Cuba's House of Representatives. At forty-five years old, Gustavo's black hair was already receding from a broad forehead. He had brown eyes and a penetrating gaze under thick, dark brows that curved in large arcs. Six feet tall, with an athletic build, he was stern and reserved, a member of the House, a politician, and a lawyer. He was an imposing figure, impatient with those who dithered, "black and white in speech and action," recalled his eldest daughter. He disliked the boisterousness and chicanery of politics, but he believed deeply that politics was necessary, that from politics came laws, the only way a democratic society could avoid chaos.

An enormous frieze, cast in bronze, was draped across the front of the House chamber. On the left, it depicted Cuba's struggle for freedom, and on the right, the benefits of liberty. In the rear of the chamber was a second-floor public gallery framed by a colonnade of eighteen Corinthian columns that rose to a soaring, skylit ceiling. Above the columns, another frieze displayed sepia motifs on themes ranging from mother-hood to literature, from work to equality, from justice to freedom.

These were the lofty ideals of the republic. But on this afternoon in July 1940, Gustavo knew that the reality below was darker. Since independence from Spain, the republic's history had been marked by tumult, violence, corruption, and disappointment. The promise of freedom had never been fully realized. Gustavo's generation was the first to come of age in this fledgling republic. He had run with a crowd of bright young intellectuals and artists, amassed wealth, political stature, and prestige, and then witnessed a terrifying fall into dictatorship.

He tried to right the ship, to establish the pillars of democracy.

They stood—for a while.

Gustavo was born on September 22, 1895, in Camajuaní, a small town in central Cuba. Only months before, the war for independence had begun.

His father, Miguel, an immigrant from Santander in northern Spain, had arrived in a vast stream of migration subsidized by Madrid after 1868 to flood the island and tamp down independence fervor. The immigrants were known as *peninsulares,* often young and destitute but strong-willed and determined to succeed. Miguel became a prosperous tobacco grower and packer. He was a tall fellow, with a large mustache that curled up at the ends. His wife, María Sánchez de Granada, was a strict disciplinarian known as "Mamabella." Gustavo was the second of their five sons and a daughter.

When Gustavo was born, one of the first family friends to come by with congratulations was Gerardo Machado, twenty-four years old. Machado and his father had once been cattle raiders; now they were in the tobacco business, like Miguel. The families were very close. Gerardo had been injured working in a butcher shop in Camajuaní and had only three fingers on his left hand.

Machado cradled the infant Gustavo in his arms. Then he went off to fight with the rebel army.

•   •   •

The first Cuban war for independence from Spain, the Ten Years' War, 1868 to 1878, had ended with a treaty that was supposed to be followed by reforms and autonomy, but promises went unfulfilled and Cubans remained under the Spanish boot. The Spanish captain general in Cuba had absolute authority: he could ban public meetings; elections were corrupt; critics could be exiled. The peninsulares prevailed at the polls and dominated politics. They held majorities in the colonial government, provincial and city governments, the military, and the clergy, as well as judges, magistrates, prosecutors, solicitors, court clerks, and scribes.

To throw off Spanish rule, a ragtag rebel army began fighting anew in early 1895. It was a conflict of steel ripping flesh, charred fields, and ghastly death camps. General Máximo Gómez, the commander of the rebel army, waged guerrilla warfare against Spanish troops that outnumbered him five to one. Determined to deny Spain the rich bounty of Cuba's harvests, Gómez destroyed the economy of the island he was defending, wrecking Cuba's sugar plantations and mills. He targeted the big planters, manufacturers, mining operations, and lines of communication. Bridges and rail lines were dynamited. Tens of thousands of workers lost their jobs, with no choice but to join the rebel forces or become refugees. One night on the battlefield, Gómez wrote by candlelight that "Cuba's wealth is the cause of her bondage" to Spain, thus the rebels "are determined that everything must be destroyed." His rebels had no uniforms, small rations, and old rifles, shotguns, and pistols. By legend, their most fearsome weapon was the machete, a large, heavy-backed knife with a sharp edge about two feet long, a curving blade and thick wooden handle, ideal for sugarcane harvesting. While the machete was terrifying, it was more symbol than combat weapon. Far more lethal were the well-aimed sharpshooters in the rebel ranks. While the first war had been fought in the east, this time the rebels, led by Antonio Maceo, a veteran of the Ten Years' War, spread what one historian called "flame and misery, pillage and plunder" to the west and across the whole island. Slavery had ended in 1886, but Cuban society continued to be deeply divided along racial lines. Black and mixed-race Cubans joined the rebel army en masse, many harboring dreams of a better place for themselves in a free Cuba.

Spain fought back with its own scorched earth tactics. General Valeriano Weyler, a veteran of the Ten Years' War, forced a million Cubans into crude garrison towns and guarded encampments surrounded by barbed wire. Death was the penalty for escape. Both soldiers and civilians succumbed to waves of yellow fever. Starvation set in. More than 100,000 people died—perhaps up to 170,000—in the policy of "reconcentration." Even after the policy ended in 1897, hundreds died every day in the major towns and cities, many interred in mass graves, or their bodies left stacked by the roadside for wild dogs and birds. "The country was wrapped in the stillness of death and the silence of desolation," wrote a former congressman, William J. Calhoun, on visiting Cuba at the request of President McKinley in 1897.

The USS *Maine* was sent to Havana to signal concern for the substantial US economic interests in Cuba. On several occasions, the United States attempted to buy the island from Spain, and groups in both Cuba and the United States had sought annexation. When the ship was destroyed by a blast in the Harbor of Havana on February 15, 1898, killing 266, a war cry erupted in the United States, fueled by sensationalist journalism that blamed Spain, although no proof was ever found. Twelve weeks after the United States declared war, following the Battles of San Juan and Kettle Hills and the destruction of the Spanish fleet in the Port of Santiago de Cuba, a weary Spain surrendered Cuba, its last colony in the New World. The formal handover to the United States came on January 1, 1899.

The island's fields were blackened, pastures barren, fruit trees bare. Two generations of Cubans had embraced the fight for independence; many had devoted the better part of their adult lives to the cause and were now impoverished. The island was deeply divided; more than 60,000 Cubans had served on the Spanish side in various auxiliary capacities during the war, far exceeding the 40,000 rebel troops. Cuba's population was 1.5 million at war's end, a devastating loss of some 300,000. The island was a smoking ruin and not yet entirely free.

The United States established a military occupation of Cuba from January 1899 to May 1902, building hundreds of schools and improving public health. Cuban doctor Carlos Finlay's discovery that mosquitoes transmitted yellow fever was verified, leading to improved sanitary conditions. At the same time, the US occupiers arrived with a haughty sense of superiority. Leonard Wood, the second military governor, ordered Cuban schools reorganized, "adapting them as far as practicable to the public school system of the U.S." Cuba's new draft constitution was patterned on the United States' separation of powers. Wood, a general with a medical degree from Harvard University, had commanded the Rough Riders, the volunteer cavalry unit that fought to expel the Spanish, with Theodore Roosevelt as his second-in-command. He believed that after a brief period Cubans would want to be annexed by the United States. He looked down upon them as needing "new life, new principles and new methods." He wrote President McKinley in April 1900, "The people here, Mr. President, know that they are not ready for self-government." He wrote to Secretary of War Elihu Root, "These men are all rascals and political adventurers whose object is to loot the Island." This attitude was held widely in the United States, too. In newspaper cartoons, Cubans were portrayed with racist, humiliating tropes, as infants; rowdy, undisciplined youths; and out-of-control gun-toting delinquents, all requiring constant guidance and tutelage from North America. The rebel army, which fought for three years before the United States intervened, was not even acknowledged in the peace treaty with Spain and was excluded from the signing ceremony. When one of their most senior and revered commanders, Major General Calixto García, passed away, the United States organized a military parade on February 11, 1899, to carry him to Havana's Colón Cemetery. But due to a misunderstanding, the rebel fighters were told to march in the rear. Indignant, they abandoned the procession. The rebel army was disbanded later that year.

The war marked the first US territorial expansion outside the North American continent: the Philippines, where rebels fought for independence for several years; Guam, which fell under US control; Puerto Rico, which became a US territory; and Hawaii, which was annexed by the

United States. What to do with Cuba? In 1901, in exchange for ending the military occupation, Cuba's first constitutional convention was forced to accept a provision that gave the United States "the right to intervene" in the island's affairs for "the maintenance of a government adequate for the protection of life, property and individual liberty." This was the Platt Amendment, named after Senator Orville H. Platt, Republican of Connecticut and chairman of the Senate Committee on Relations with Cuba, who insisted that the United States had a duty to preserve stability on the island. The amendment, largely based on a memorandum written by Root, was approved as a rider to an appropriations bill and signed by McKinley on March 2, 1901. It was a fateful decision. Cuba was hamstrung from signing treaties with other countries, and severely limited in taking on debt. Despite serious misgivings, the Cubans accepted the terms in June; it was made clear to them that they had no choice. The Platt Amendment became an appendix to Cuba's 1901 constitution. The island became a quasi-protectorate of the United States, putting it in a legal and political chokehold that would have consequences for decades.

Tobacco rebounded quickly after the war, and Miguel Gutiérrez survived the devastation. In 1900, he moved his family to Havana, which had fared better in the war than most places in Cuba. A photograph shows Miguel seated outdoors in a wicker chair and holding a rolled document. Mamabella is nearby, surrounded by five of their children, including a skinny Gustavo, his arm around a younger brother.

Gustavo was sent to Cuba's best schools, including the prestigious Jesuit preparatory academy Colegio de Belén. The Jesuits placed a heavy emphasis on classic literature, Latin, and Greek. He had been bookish as a young boy and was smart and a quick learner.

When Gustavo was twelve years old, the United States returned to rule Cuba in a second intervention. Political forces behind the island's first president, Tomás Estrada Palma, had committed fraud in his re-election campaign, prompting his opponent, the popular war general José Miguel Gómez, to organize an armed insurrection. Estrada Palma resigned, leaving Cuba rudderless. President Theodore Roosevelt sent in the marines and installed a civilian administrator, Charles Magoon, from 1906 to 1909, another potent reminder of the Platt Amendment. In 1912, the Partido Independiente de Color, a political party of Black Cubans who were seeking to take part in upcoming elections, staged an armed protest out of fear of being excluded. The government responded with brutal force, killing hundreds. The United States landed troops again, on a smaller scale; and once more in 1917 to protect US sugar plantations at a time of unrest.

Gustavo's parents sent him to the United States for a year, attending St. Ann's Academy, a Marist Brothers school in Manhattan, to sharpen his English. On his return to Cuba, he prepared for university at the Instituto de La Habana, the equivalent of a high school. Lanky but muscular, he excelled in baseball, traveling to Cincinnati to play in US youth leagues. Gustavo was an exacting catcher. A friend later wrote, "When I close my eyes, I can see a thin, athletic Gustavo standing tall, always minding his position, paying close attention to everything, fully involved in the contest, impeccably framing the pitch, remaining completely calm, not squabbling with his rivals; in short, foreshadowing what would later be his typical demeanor throughout his life: somewhat reserved, somewhat cold."

Gustavo entered the University of Havana, Cuba's only center of higher learning. Fewer than one adolescent in twenty at the time went beyond six years of public schooling. At the university, the schools of law and medicine were the largest, overshadowing almost all others, because they were valuable stepping-stones to professions. The university, neglected at the end of Spanish rule, had been reinaugurated after the war, and moved to a hilltop location in Havana's Vedado neighborhood. It was still plagued with problems, however, including no-show professors on the payroll. Gustavo graduated in 1916 with a *doctorado* degree in civil law, and a year later with a second *doctorado* in public law, both with honors.

From his late teens, Gustavo had single-mindedly courted María Vianello, the vivacious daughter of a tobacco planter. Like Gustavo, María received the best schooling of the day, studying French at the prestigious

El Colegio Francés de Leónie Olivier in Havana, traveling to Paris, and later studying piano, mandolin, and painting. They married in 1918, living for a while with his parents.

The dean of Havana's legal establishment, Antonio Sánchez de Bustamante, spotted Gustavo as a smart young law student. With a distinctive white mustache and neatly trimmed beard, Bustamante was Cuba's most respected legal mind. He gave Gustavo an internship in his law firm when he was twenty years old and still a student, then a lawyer's job, for a year, upon graduation. Bustamante held a chair in international law at the university. When he was sent as Cuba's diplomatic representative to the Paris peace talks in 1919, he appointed Gustavo to teach his classes. When six new assistant professorships were created—the school desperately needed qualified faculty—one went to Gustavo to teach international public law. He soon became secretary-treasurer of the Cuban Society for International Law, of which Bustamante was president. Bustamante's law firm represented foreign companies and banks in their expansive interests in Cuba. Gustavo was exposed to the nexus of money and influence, and the sizable share of the economy that was dominated from abroad.

Gustavo's circle of friends were lively young intellectuals and artists who gathered for hours of intense criticism, debate, and camaraderie. On Saturdays, they often assembled at the offices of *Social*, Cuba's premier cultural monthly magazine, founded by Conrado Massaguer, a caricaturist, illustrator, and satirist whose elegant drawings graced the cover of each issue. After meeting at *Social*, Gutiérrez and his friends moved to the cafés. A favorite was the popular café at the Teatro Martí, a complex with patios and gardens, pomegranates, and orange and banana trees. Here Gutiérrez was joined by the leading lights of a restless new generation: the literary editor of *Social*, Emilio Roig de Leuchsenring, a graduate of Belén and the university's law school; the poet Rubén Martínez Villena; the author and thinker Jorge Mañach, a Harvard graduate; and writers Juan Marinello and Enrique Serpa. The poet and journalist Andrés Nuñez Olano recalled the café was where "we would tirelessly discuss with each other; we would bring up something we had recently written or read, throwing it out there as if it were a challenge; we would lay into people and their reputations; we would fiercely critique each other; we would drop names, waving them high like banners or trampling upon them like rags; we would outwardly express, in the same tones, what enraged us, what excited us, what disappointed us . . . in short, we magnificently lived out our remarkable youth."

All of them were in their twenties and deeply discouraged by Cuba's direction. They were passionate about the need for a wholesale "rejuvenation," or "regeneration." The great promise of independence—dramatic change, a free and sovereign Cuba—had faded. They blamed the generation of the independence war, especially Cuba's second, third, and fourth presidents. As historian Lillian Guerra put it, the war generation had "presided over the stillbirth rather than the birth of a republic."

After the US intervention, the second elected president was José Miguel Gómez, an attractive figure with cattleman gusto who rose to major general in the rebel army. He took the presidency in 1909 as a poor man and left in 1913 as a millionaire with a new marble palace in Havana. When visitors came seeking favors, he was said to genially offer them cigars, in a box, into which they were expected to put the bribes. The third president, Mario Menocal, who had been a major general in the war, looked the other way at substantial stealing by his friends and relatives. The fourth and current president, Alfredo Zayas, who took office in 1921, was a perpetual political striver, lawyer, and poet who had formed his own party. Zayas was not a battlefield war hero but had been outspoken for the rebellion and was captured by the Spanish and deported. He was a slight man, timid, with bad teeth and a yellowish complexion, but brilliantly clever, and known as someone who never hesitated to take the smallest graft. On the eve of his inauguration, a columnist in *Social* compared Zayas to an eel: slippery.

It was painfully evident to Gustavo and his friends that, as historian Luis A. Pérez Jr. wrote, "Almost everything turned out different than the way it was supposed to be." Much of Cuba's wealth and opportunity were beyond the reach of the Cubans themselves. Foreigners prevailed over production and property; sugar, banks, railways, public utilities, and other enterprises were dominated by interests from the United States and elsewhere. Also, fresh waves of Spanish immigrants surged to Cuba after the independence war. Some seven hundred thousand arrived between 1902 and 1919, mostly young, ambitious, poor, and in pursuit of riches. They controlled retail commerce and made up more than half the merchants on the island. They were strongly represented in the professions, education, and the press, and the Catholic Church remained substantially a Spanish Church. This meant that Cubans were squeezed into one area where they could succeed and survive, government and politics, where the levers of power dispensed patronage and graft. The public treasury became the largest employer of the middle class. "Corruption developed into a pervasive presence in Cuban public life," wrote Pérez. "Graft, bribery, and embezzlement served as the medium of political exchange." A job in Cuba's bureaucracy was called *un destino*, "a destiny," or a salvation, and election campaigns celebrated as the "second harvest," after sugar. Public office-holders rewarded their families and supporters with money, land, licenses, contracts, franchises, and concessions. By one estimate in 1921, Cuba's government spent $15 million a year on *botellas,* or no-show jobs and sinecures.

At the café where Gustavo met his friends, there was much soul-searching. How had the ideals of independence gone off the rails? Cuba seemed unable to govern itself. Not only in politics; the social sphere was also a mess. "Cuban society is disintegrating," warned the respected anthropologist Fernando Ortiz. More than half the population could not read or write and, alarmingly, illiteracy was growing. Although Cuba's population had doubled since the independence war, school enrollment fell. In 1900, seventy-five students per thousand residents were in classrooms; now it was fifty per thousand. Even more alarming, the school dropout rate was abysmally high. "So," said Ortiz, "our poor little Cubans leave school, when they have attended it, at the age of thirteen or fourteen, with an education of age eight or nine." Cuba, he said, was becoming a "twentieth-century republic with mid-nineteenth-century mentality and habits."

Gustavo and his friends witnessed a culture of impunity. Legislators enjoyed constitutional immunity from criminal prosecution; at the same time, amnesty bills were routinely passed, setting aside past convictions, and pardons were granted by the thousands. Fully a fifth of all candidates for political office in the 1922 elections had criminal records, Ortiz lamented.

Black Cubans and those of mixed-race heritage, a third of Cuba's population, had been promised social justice and political equality after independence but received neither. After the war, nine-tenths of the sugar and tobacco production was white-controlled, as was most of the livestock, while Black Cubans mostly held small farms. In the professions, Black presence was very small. In 1907 there were only four Black lawyers and nine doctors on the island. But Cubans of color were predominant as laundresses, dressmakers, builders, shoemakers, woodcutters, tailors, musicians, domestic servants, bakers, and barbers. By 1919, among Black males twenty-one years old and over, the illiteracy rate was more than 48 percent, compared to 37 percent for whites. A total of 10,123 Cuban white men more than twenty-one years old had received professional or academic degrees, compared to 429 Black Cubans.

In January 1919, Gustavo took the café debates to a wider audience in a speech he delivered to the Cuban Society for International Law. He was just twenty-three years old, but a protégé of the respected Bustamante. His words reflected the worries of many. He decried Cuba's "great national evils" but said they were partially rooted in the people themselves. "The incompetence of the governors," he declared, "befits the indifference of the governed, the passivity of the Congress, the foolishness of the voters, the lack of direction of our international politics, and the disorder of our inner life." He then insisted that Cuba must begin a wholesale change in its political culture. "Start over," he said. "This is what we have to do." It was not enough to create laws and institutions, he insisted. Citizens had to be taught about honor and the meaning of good government. Someday, he predicted, a generation would come of age with "public servants known for their integrity and admired for their skill," with judges "who always try to get to the bottom of the issues" and democratic presidents "who live by the people and for the people."

"Liberty can be gained," he concluded, "but never given up." It was an appeal to Cubans not to retreat. But the situation was about to go from bad to worse.

They called it the "dance of the millions."

After World War I, Germany's sugar beet crop was decimated. The United States ended war price controls. As a result, the price for Cuban sugar skyrocketed. The 1919 to 1920 crop brought in an astounding $1 billion, more than all the harvests from 1900 to 1914.

Bank deposits soared, luxury goods flooded the stores, and property values zoomed. Cubans and foreigners engaged in speculation, price fixing, bank manipulation, and credit pyramids. A luxurious residential area, Miramar, spread out to the west of Havana, with elegant avenues bordered by flowering trees and shrubs. In the evenings, limousines cruised up and down the seaside Malecón Boulevard, the women in dresses designed in Paris, with billowy scarves and sparkling jewels. New casinos opened, famous opera stars performed, world-champion boxers fought, horses raced for staggering purses. Money cascaded down to the cane workers and farmers known as *colonos*, who could buy their first necktie or patent leather shoes or put money down on a phonograph. All of it was built on a dizzying expansion of credit, borrowed on sugar.

Then it all crashed. As competing supplies of sugar from elsewhere began to enter the world market, prices collapsed. In Cuba, unemployment, strikes, and shortages broke out. The domestic banking system nearly failed. In 1920, foreign banks held only 20 percent of the total deposits in Cuba, but by 1923, more than 76 percent were in foreign banks. One result of the crash was that even more sugar mills were taken over by US banks when they defaulted on loans or went bankrupt; National City Bank took over nearly sixty mills after the owners went bust.

Despite the crash, sugar remained the most powerful engine of Cuba's economy. In the first twenty-five years after independence, when Cuba became the single largest producer in the world, national income quadrupled. Sugar demanded land, labor, and capital. For land, vast *latifundios* were created, estates with, as Ortiz, the anthropologist, put it, "territories so large that in other countries they would be provinces." For labor, Cuba began importing tens of thousands of workers from Haiti and Jamaica, and many stayed on, to find jobs in the cities.

For capital, the main source was the United States. Although the statistics are imprecise because of hidden ownership, by 1919 mills owned by US interests produced 51.4 percent of Cuba's sugar. The Cubans had 22.8 percent, and Spanish interests were 17.3 percent. There were prominent exceptions, such as Havana sugar king Julio Lobo. The US sugar mills, however, were far more efficient than others, and US interests also controlled the railroads, the phone system, the docks, and the banks.

In the aftermath of the crash, Gustavo and his friends again asked: What went wrong?

Their discontent led them to rediscover José Martí.

In the first years of the republic, Martí was not widely known on the island, regarded as a faded revolutionary martyr. But Gustavo and his generation found more and more about him to admire.

Martí was born in Havana in January 1853. His father, Mariano, was a Spanish sergeant who later became a police inspector. His mother, Leonor, came from a Spanish military family in the Canary Islands who immigrated to Cuba. Although Mariano would later encounter economic troubles, when José was born they were a relatively affluent military couple, living a few blocks from the sea on the outskirts of Old Havana. José was a precocious student, tutored by a famous poet and educator, Rafael Mendive. Imbued with his teacher's rebellious spirit, Martí formed a young "revolutionary" club in school, and when he was sixteen years old he wrote a letter urging a former classmate, a Spanish military cadet, to desert. When the letter was discovered, Martí was charged with conspiracy, and after a trial, sentenced to six years of forced labor, including at a limestone quarry. The quarry was a hellish scene for prisoner 113: massive walls of limerock; the sun's fierce heat; prisoners excavating with picks and sledgehammers; quicklime burning their feet; and a fine, white powdery dust choking their lungs. Martí's ankles were rubbed raw by the prison chains, his eyes burned by the blinding whiteness. In the quarry he saw the horrors of political imprisonment in Cuba, and it left him with a deep loathing of Spanish colonial rule. After six months, he was released, thanks to lobbying by his parents and the intervention of a friend of his father. He was exiled to Spain at age seventeen, where he unenthusiastically studied law. He was more attracted to philosophy and literature. Four years later, he sailed to Mexico to join his parents, who had settled there, and was drawn into politics. "Except for literature, nothing interested him so much as politics," wrote biographer Jorge Mañach. "The art of making a people and ruling them impressed him as something magical. . . ." After protesting a regime in Mexico installed by a military coup, Martí taught for a year in Guatemala, and in 1878 returned to Cuba, where he became active in the underground resistance, and was banished again to Spain. Soon he arrived penniless in New York City, and, still restless, traveled to Venezuela, where a dictatorship again forced him to depart. Back in New York in 1881, he began an extraordinary fourteen years of journalism—and activism for an independent Cuba.

He worked from a tiny room in a New York boardinghouse. "A good part of the day and night he spent at the table in a sea of newspapers and magazines, filling sheet after sheet of copy paper with a handwriting made almost illegible by intellectual drive," wrote Mañach. He earned money as an accountant by day, and by night wrote poems of lyric intensity for a new book, *Versos Libres*. In 1882, he began writing for the great Buenos Aires daily *La Nación*, and his reputation for reportage and commentary spread across Latin America. Martí was an observant witness to the rise of the American experiment. In his dispatches, he denounced the materialism, prejudice, expansionist arrogance, and political corruption he found in the United States, but he embraced the love of liberty, tolerance, egalitarianism, and the practice of democracy there. In New York he worked as an editor, translator, secondary-school teacher, university professor, diplomat, and playwright while tirelessly squeezing in time to advocate independence for Cuba. A political thinker and revolutionary, a prodigious writer, teacher, poet, and tireless organizer, Martí laid the foundations for Cuba's war of independence.

Martí possessed an almost mystical faith in democracy. "There isn't a throne that can compare to the mind of a free person," he wrote. "As the bones to the human body, the axle to the wheel, the wing to the bird, and the air to the wing, so is liberty the essence of life. Whatever is done without it is imperfect." Martí was convinced that the next drive for Cuban independence should be a people's uprising, a wave of civilians. The war was just the starting point, he thought; it had to lead to the republic of tomorrow, free of dictatorship. He was alarmed that Máximo Gómez—whom he needed to lead the battle—remained a stubborn authoritarian. In 1884, Martí met Gómez and Antonio Maceo in New York. The two great military chieftains looked down on Martí; Gómez thought Martí was a better poet than revolutionary, and Maceo thought Martí was unlikable and unreliable, a schemer rather than a soldier. At one point, Gómez brusquely told Martí to "limit yourself to obeying orders." In protest, Martí wrote a long letter to Gómez in which he warned against swapping "the present political despotism in Cuba for a personal despotism, a thousand times worse." Martí added, "One does not establish a people, General, the way one commands a military camp."

Martí was an intense, slight man, with quiet magnetism and persuasive sincerity, always wearing a black coat and bow tie, with a high forehead, receding boyish curls, and black mustache. Despite ill health and the severe strain on his family, Martí became an irrepressible organizer. He founded the Cuban Revolutionary Party in 1892 and managed to draw in the sizable and fractious Cuban exile community in New York as well as raise money from the poor tobacco workers of Tampa and Key West, Florida.

Martí's writings and speeches expressed a romantic, amorphous vision for Cuba. He imagined a country with justice for everyone and a government that would abolish social and racial inequalities. "With all, and for the good of all" was his simple, powerful pledge.

He repaired the breach with Gómez. They met at Gómez's home in the Dominican Republic in March 1895 and signed a joint manifesto declaring that "Cuba returns to war with a democratic and educated people" who bear "no doubts about Cuba or its ability to obtain and govern its independence." Their goal, they declared, was to overthrow the "corrupt and provincial monarchy of Spain and its sluggish, vice-ridden wretchedness." Martí and Gómez landed in Cuba on April 11 amid rough seas in a dinghy at night, near Baracoa on the far eastern end of the island. On May 5, at a ruined sugar mill called La Mejorana, they joined Maceo to plan the course of the new war. Once again, they argued. Martí recorded in his diary that Maceo wanted to govern Cuba with "a junta of generals," creating a nation that would be subordinate to its army. By contrast, Martí wanted a democratic, elected government. Maceo wanted Martí to go back to New York and raise money and arms; Gómez had earlier pressed Martí to do the same, but acquiesced to Martí's desire to see combat first. The tense meeting at La Mejorana broke up, unsettled. Maceo took off with his men on horseback in one direction, Gómez and Martí in another. Martí had been through weeks of hard marching in the Cuban bush, and his physical condition was frail, but his diary entries were full of optimism. From an encampment amid cedars and shrubs at Dos Rios, about forty miles northwest of Santiago de Cuba, Martí penned a letter by candlelight on May 18 to an old friend from Mexico. Despite the turmoil with the generals, Martí wrote with clarity and serenity. "I am now, every day, in danger of giving my life for my country." His mind was racing beyond the battlefield to a more distant future for Cuba. He worried about the power of the United States, seeing a giant rousing itself to empire, fearful that it might swallow up Cuba, the Antilles, and more. Martí declared that it was his "duty" to resist the threat of US expansionism by establishing Cuba's absolute independence. "I lived in the monster, and I know its entrails," he wrote of his time in the United States. "And my slingshot is that of David."

Martí was interrupted that night at the camp; he never finished the letter.

The next day, Martí and Gómez spoke to the troops. "We rallied the troops and Martí spoke with genuine ardor and a warrior's spirit," Gómez noted in his diary. Another witness wrote that Martí spoke "with the fervor of an apostle." Then a battle erupted with Spanish forces who had tracked them down. Martí, on horseback, was shot and killed. Much about his death was later spun into a myth of glory and martyrdom, that

Martí charged heroically into battle when Gómez had urged him to stay back. What is known for sure is that his bloodied body was carted away by the Spanish troops.

To Gustavo's generation in the 1920s, the Martí story sparked imagination and curiosity. They were drawn by his martyrdom, by his political thinking and organizational skills, by his faith in democracy and his expansive pledge of a Cuba "for all."

They were also drawn by Martí's prescient warning of domination by the United States. "To change masters is not to be free," Martí had declared. This danger seemed to Gustavo to be right in front of their eyes in the early 1920s—the power in Cuba of one man, Major General Enoch H. Crowder of the US Army.

Crowder was well known in Cuba. He had served in the first US intervention after the independence war, then again in the second intervention under Magoon. Crowder was principally responsible for Cuba's codes of administrative law and visited Cuba frequently. He had devised and implemented the US military draft in World War I, served as judge advocate general in the army, had written a legal code for the Philippines, and came to Havana in 1919 to help Cuba rewrite its electoral code. He was considered a tremendous administrator, and the task of helping Cuba in its troubled times appealed to his sense of altruism. Once Zayas took office as president in 1921, Crowder became a proconsul, with unparalleled access to the palace.

After the "dance of the millions," Cuba was broke, and desperately needed a loan from the United States. Before any loan, Crowder insisted that Zayas must carry out reforms. He pressed for a "moralization" program and wrote fifteen lengthy memorandums to Zayas over six months, making detailed proposals to clean up the government regarding electoral reform, graft, auditing, the lottery, and eliminating no-show jobs. Under pressure, Zayas listened. He appointed a new cabinet, five of them recruited by Crowder and dubbed the "honest cabinet."

Crowder's raw power led one editorial cartoonist in Cuba to depict Zayas signing a paper with Crowder holding his hand, and Zayas asking, "Which name shall I sign, Crowder's or mine?" To Gustavo and his friends, it was an irritating reminder of the grip the United States had on Cuba. Gustavo wrote, "General Crowder's actions in Cuba could not have been more offensive to Cuban sovereignty." A wave of nationalism was rising in Cuba, not so much anti-American—as most of Gustavo's friends had a good impression of the United States—but rather a desire to see Cubans making decisions about Cuba. The nationalism was also fueled by restive winds from abroad: the Mexican Revolution and the constitution of 1917; the more distant Russian Revolution; and the effect of the university reform in Córdoba, Argentina, in 1918.

Zayas secured a $50 million loan from J. P. Morgan & Co. in 1923, and Crowder was named US ambassador to Cuba. But Zayas no longer needed Crowder's advice. He fired the honest cabinet and went back to the old ways. He put fourteen members of his family on the government payroll, including his son in charge of the corrupt lottery, which authorized special "collectors" to sell the tickets and keep a fat slice of the revenues. Politicians made a fortune by possessing multiple lottery collectorships. In the Christmas lottery of 1923, a man buying a ticket asked for his traditional wager on the number 4444. He was told he could not have it because Zayas's wife had asked for it. The "four fours" ticket "won" second prize of $200,000, or about $2.9 million today. The depth and breadth of corruption offended the sensibility of even those who were long inured to it.

At the time, a nascent civil society was rousing itself in Havana. Gustavo was at the forefront, organizing the Association of Good Government in early 1922, a group of young professionals and businessmen who launched a campaign against corruption and graft. Cuba also enjoyed a vibrant press, with thriving periodicals such as *Bohemia*, *Social*, and *Carteles*, among others. By one count, there were thirty-seven daily newspapers in Havana alone. Many survived only due to political graft and subsidies, but taken together there was a plethora of voices.

Then in 1923 came a wave of open rebellion.

In March, a gathering of writers issued a manifesto denouncing Zayas, his corruption and Cuba's "delinquent rulers." While Gustavo did not sign the document, his café friends did, led by Martínez Villena and joined by Mañach and Marinello. They came to be known as El Grupo Minorista. Separately, an elite group of scholars published a shocking and detailed account of corruption under Zayas, written by the anthropologist Ortiz. It echoed what Gustavo had said a few years before—it was time for a complete overhaul. Next, a student protest broke out at the university, seizing several buildings. The leader was one of Gustavo's law students, Julio Antonio Mella, a powerful speaker who organized demonstrations against the miserable quality of the university faculty, demanding free tuition and autonomy for the university. As a result, more than a hundred professors—many of them no-shows—were fired. The students formed a new, powerful force, the University Students Federation, or FEU, and unleashed still more anger at the government and the powers that be.

Gustavo played a direct role in the largest and most serious protest, which erupted in August. The Zayas government neglected to pay pensions for veterans of the war—a grave insult. A protest group, the Veterans and Patriots Association, sprung up with unruly rallies in Havana theaters. The group's manifesto called for repeal of the corrupt lottery, proper collection of taxes, abolition of the botellas, honest elections, competitive bidding for government contracts, an independent judiciary—and more. The Veterans and Patriots movement captured the public's imagination, including many young professionals. Gutiérrez became one of the association's two secretaries and part of the inner council. The Veterans and Patriots embraced the refrain Gustavo had used in earlier years, "For the Regeneration of Cuba," but they resisted his suggestion that they become a full-fledged political party. Zayas launched a crackdown. Eventually the Veterans and Patriots protest faded.

If Gustavo was the angry young man in 1923, over the next few years he turned more pragmatic and amassed wealth, prestige, and political stature. No small reason for this change was that Gerardo Machado, who had once cradled him in his arms, rose to the presidency.

Machado, a brigadier general when the independence war was over, returned to Santa Clara and became mayor. In one of his first acts, he burned down a court building containing records of his father's cattle raiding. He also served under Cuba's second president, Gómez, as inspector general of the army and secretary of Gobernación, essentially the chief of national law enforcement. Then he worked with a succession of US companies, becoming a successful vice president of the firm controlling the whole of electric and phone utilities in Havana, and he built a personal fortune with other companies as well. In 1924, the Liberal Party nominated Machado for president. With a heavy six-foot frame and tortoiseshell-rimmed glasses, he never failed to flash a smile, giving him a certain magnetism. "*Chico*, come and see me!" he said to everyone, taking them warmly by the arm, a campaign approach that worked. Gustavo had joined the Liberal Party, made up largely of workers and veterans, including many mixed-race and Black Cubans. He remained at heart a liberal populist. But politics in Cuba was driven more by personality than party. Politicians shifted allegiances more often out of self-interest and the rewards of office than any ideology.

Machado's campaign slogan was simple: "water, roads, and schools!" He called for a "platform of regeneration." He vowed to end political corruption, build local industry, and serve only one term, not "one single day longer." In Cuba and Latin America, reelection was seen as the first step toward dictatorship, so Machado's promise resonated. He had backing from the United States, especially companies with business interests in Cuba. No one expected him to be totally clean. Vote-buying, bribery, and coercion went on during the campaign, but on election day 1924, Machado won five of the six provinces.

For Gustavo, the election seemed to herald the coming of a reform era. Two leaders of the Veterans and Patriots movement joined the new government, and Machado won the endorsement of Ortiz, the scholar who had written the scathing critiques.

In 1925, Machado appointed Gustavo as counselor to the secretary of state, the government's foreign relations legal adviser. This was precisely where Gustavo's own interests had taken him, into international law. He had just completed a book about the League of Nations. He was now inside the government, not sitting outside in the cafés.

In September, the literary editor of *Social*, Emilio Roig de Leuchsenring, began to profile a new generation of Cuban intellectuals. He selected Gustavo to be the first, praising him as an "eloquent speaker, a profound writer, a tireless fighter" in the "intellectual and political order" of Cuba. In the same issue, Gustavo wrote an essay about global affairs. He titled it "The Need for a New World." He was an unalloyed idealist, declaring that all humanity was entering a "new era" of progress, including the benefits of modernity—electricity, aviation, chemistry, and radio. He described the globe as more interconnected than ever. He was a true believer in Woodrow Wilson's vision of a liberal, democratic world order. He declared that Cuba must not be left behind.

At the time, US finance and business interests were stronger than ever in Cuba. Machado was probusiness and traveled to the United States to offer assurances of his cooperation. At home, Machado proposed the most ambitious public works program ever seen in Cuba, including the construction of a 733-mile-long central highway from Santiago de Cuba in the east to Piñar del Rio in the west. The contract went to a company controlled by Machado and cronies, and they gained an estimated $30 million from it. But to many Cubans, these projects signaled progress after years of drift and inaction.

The president also launched construction of a new national capitol, and he refashioned Havana, extending the seaside Malecón Boulevard. For the capitol, Machado demanded a crash construction effort. The contracts were signed in 1926, and the capitol was finished in three years and fifty days at a cost of about $20 million, a huge overrun, by some accounts more than half of it graft. In the rotunda stood "La República," the fifty-foot-tall Statue of the Republic, an imposing symbol of Cuban statehood depicting a woman standing with a pointed lance in one hand and a shield in the other. Sculpted by the Italian artist Angelo Zanelli in Rome, thin robes of plated gold covered her muscular, bronze body, and she wore a Phrygian cap, an emblem of liberty often associated with the French Revolution.

Somewhat later, Machado launched another lavish architectural and design project, to build the Hotel Nacional, a four-hundred-room luxury resort intended to rival other grand hotels around the globe.

Gutiérrez became wealthy from these projects. He earned legal fees estimated by his family at $125,000 over several years, or about $1.8 million today. Although as a young man he had bristled at US economic dominance over Cuba, Gustavo was nonetheless adept at making connections with US banks, architects, and engineers. He also traveled to Spain and elsewhere in Europe and had sophisticated taste in art and architecture.

Gustavo built a mansion in Miramar, the lush neighborhood west of Havana. He created a storybook palace, resembling a Spanish castle with Italian accents. A turret and tower rose in the center. Inside, a mahogany curved staircase climbed to the second floor under a cupola; an Italian-themed salon was illuminated with a chandelier of Murano glass, the walls covered in blue silk. Gustavo's third-floor library contained more than five thousand volumes on shelves that reached the ceiling. The house was named El Castillo Bellabrisa, or the castle with the beautiful breezes. Gustavo and María had four daughters, and it echoed with the sounds of a bustling family.

In his library, where he did much of his thinking and writing, Gustavo kept a quote from Abraham Lincoln under the glass on his desk: "I do the very best I can, I mean to keep going. If the end brings me out all right, then what is said against me won't matter. If I'm wrong, ten angels swearing I was right won't make a difference."

Soon he would need those ten angels.

TWO

TO TYRANNY AND BACK

In early 1927, President Machado sent a message to Gustavo Gutiérrez. He wanted to talk to the young lawyer.

Machado's presidency had begun with a surge of goodwill. He seemed a man of the people. He strolled in the streets, gave $100 to a beggar, and donated a piano to a rural school. After a few months in office, Machado had become the most popular president Cuba had ever had.

But beneath the surface, there were flashes of trouble. Just three months after his inauguration, in 1925, an opposition newspaper, *El Día*, published a series of cartoons, one of which hinted that his daughter was a lesbian. On August 20, the editor of the paper, Armando André, a veteran of the independence war, was shot and killed while turning the key to his front door. Just days before, witnesses recalled hearing Machado at a club say he regretted "the necessity of having to kill him."

Machado had pledged as a candidate to deal harshly with labor, and upon taking office, he did. Alfredo López, leader of the newly formed labor federation, was abducted on a Havana street, tortured in prison, and subsequently killed. In early 1927, Chester Wright of *International*

Labor News reported that Machado's forces had killed no fewer than 147 people. Mella, the fiery student leader expelled from the university, led the formation of a Communist Party. After calling Machado a "tropical Mussolini," Mella was arrested on phony murder charges. He staged an eighteen-day hunger strike, was released—and fled to Mexico.

In response to Machado's invitation, Gustavo went to the presidential office. Also invited were two prominent lawyers: Ricardo Dolz, former president of the Senate, and Octavio Averhoff, who later became rector of the university. Both were of Machado's generation, had taught Gustavo in law school, and since formed a law firm with him. Machado hinted at something sensitive to discuss; he knew all three would give him honest advice.

He told the lawyers that, despite his earlier promises, he wanted a second term. He might have to change the constitution to do it. He didn't feel like waging an election campaign, but he desired more time in office.

Machado asked for the lawyers' advice. Dolz and Averhoff said that Machado need not worry about a contest—the people of Cuba knew how much he had done.

Machado then looked at Gustavo. "Well, I don't have to ask you because I know you're with me," the president said.

But Gustavo was not. "Mr. President, my opinion is that you shouldn't reelect yourself."

Machado, furious, slammed the table. A lock of hair fell into his eyes. He was not expecting any opposition from the son of Miguel Gutiérrez, a family he had known for decades. "You are the one who opposes it? The one I lovingly held in my arms when you were an infant?"

Gustavo did not back down. "Don't do something which you will seriously regret," he said.

Machado did not listen. He confided his intentions to Crowder, the US ambassador to Cuba. Crowder reported to Washington that Machado was "savoring of dictatorship." The United States decided to look the other way. When President Coolidge came to Havana in February 1928 to address the Sixth Pan-American Congress, he declared that

Cuba's people were "independent, free, prosperous, peaceful, and enjoying the advantages of self-government." This was hardly true. At that time, four students accused of being Communists were arrested by police for putting up posters. They disappeared; their families could get no information. After Coolidge left town, portions of one student's body were found in a shark's belly. Another decomposed body washed ashore, prison chains still attached, half consumed by sharks. It appeared that the old Spanish custom had been revived of releasing prisoners from a chute in Morro Castle into the warm, shark-infested waters.

Machado was unrestrained. Using fear and bribery, he co-opted the Conservative Party to join the Liberal Party in backing him, along with the smaller Popular Party, in an arrangement to squelch competition. It was called *cooperativismo*. He distributed enough largesse to subvert them all. Then he cooked up a scheme to amend the constitution, making the Cuban president's term six years instead of four, without chance for reelection. A handpicked Constituent Assembly, meeting in April and May 1928, created the new six-year presidency, then declared that Machado was eligible for the new term—the full six years. Machado of course was happy to oblige.

Gustavo was bitterly disappointed. The power grab dashed his hopes for genuine constitutional reform that would include suffrage for women, a cause of his wife, María. To make matters worse, Bustamante, his mentor, served as chairman of the Constituent Assembly.

Machado was dangerously intoxicated with power, and Gustavo knew it, but he found reasons not to abandon the president. Machado was the leader of the Liberal Party. The Machado and Gutiérrez families were close. Gustavo had business ties to the government. He long had wanted Cuba to be run by Cubans, a principle he had not abandoned. He felt a sense of duty to the larger good; he couldn't just go into exile or give up.

At the same time, university students erupted in fury at Machado's plan to remain in office. A small but active group formed the Directorio Estudiantil Universitario, or university student directorate, to oppose the regime.

The students wrote pungently phrased manifestos and pamphlets against Machado, denouncing his power grab as "a disastrous precedent that would threaten the stability of democratic institutions" and turn the constitution into "a useless piece of paper." In 1927, students in the *directorio* were expelled and the university closed. It was reopened—and then closed again, in 1928.

On November 1, 1928, Machado, nominee of all three parties, was elected to the new six-year term, unopposed. It was a farce, not democracy.

A few weeks later, Gustavo heard shocking news from Mexico. Early on the evening of January 10, 1929, assassins gunned down Mella from behind as he walked down a street. The evidence pointed to a hit job ordered by Machado.

In the center of Havana, the magnificent Capitolio neared completion, its cylindrical dome soaring three hundred feet high. On May 20, Machado took his oath of office at the Capitolio for a second term, wearing a top hat and morning coat. A photographer snapped a picture of him standing amid the granite columns on the portico. The photograph was used by Cuban painter Enrique García Cabrera to draw the scene, which was then forged into a bronze bas-relief square panel and affixed to the main entrance doors.

In late 1929, Gustavo started something entirely new. He and María traveled extensively in Europe and filled their home with art and artifacts from Italy, France, and Spain. Gustavo was an internationalist. He wanted Cuba to be connected to the world he had experienced, not an isolated backwater. He liked to say that Cuba needed to "catch up to that car of progress and modernity that has gotten a little ahead of us." With this idea, he founded a monthly journal of culture and intellectual thought, *Revista de La Habana*, to advance his vision of an educated citizenry. The first edition of the *Revista*, with an Art Deco cover, appeared on newsstands in January 1930 for 20 cents, with an opening editorial essay signed by the editors but clearly written by Gustavo titled "Toward a Culture in Pursuit of Truth." He expressed the deep disappointment his generation felt coming of age in the new republic. He bemoaned a "lack of truth" in Cuban life, a "lack of honesty," and a "brazen lack of education." His writing was urgent, impatient, and resentful that the war-hero generation had led the country into a dead end. Now it was time, he insisted, to look ahead. "We must align our literature, our arts, and our sciences with modern ideas. We seek to be in sync with this age of radio, air travel, and machinery, which demands speed, elegance, simplicity, and above all, strength." A sign of the times: the magazine listed sixty-one radio stations in Cuba and where to find them on the dial.

When the Great Depression struck, Cuba was undergoing a profound demographic shift. Gustavo's generation was reaching the age of peak economic productivity. Nearly 750,000 young people had entered the labor force. Soon many were jobless and deeply frustrated. Sugar prices fell, and the US stock market crash of October and subsequent economic collapse inflicted a terrible blow. Wages in the sugar harvest fell to rock bottom; salaries were slashed for public employees. Factories closed. Some 250,000 heads of household were totally unemployed, representing about 1 million people in a total population of 3.9 million.

In this environment, opposition to Machado spread among lawyers, doctors, engineers, teachers, accountants, and other professionals. Machado could have responded tactfully. Instead, armed thugs invaded the bar association, the federations of doctors, dentists, pharmacists, the society of engineers, and the academies of science and history, and installed Machado's desired officers. The president outlawed all public demonstrations by political parties or groups not legally registered.

On September 30, 1930, police opened fire on a march of university students, killing Rafael Trejo, a leader of the directorio. Machado immediately sealed the university, nailing the doors shut and stationing guards. The student directorio—enraged by the killing—published a manifesto on October 29 declaring that they had no alternative but to fight for "the deep social transformation that our present moment requires."

Gutiérrez reprinted their entire manifesto in *Revista*, then he printed his own letter to a fellow professor, written in a soulful tone, lamenting that the university, now dark, would be seriously damaged if dragged into the political conflict. "To bring a problem of this nature to the heart of the university is, in my opinion, to do politics, and politics of the worst kind." He wondered if the lights would ever come back on. The closure of the university was the final blow to his law professorship.

Machado next closed high schools all over Cuba, then closed teacher training colleges. In November 1930, constitutional guarantees of rights were suspended—a declaration of martial law. Lifted briefly, it was reimposed in December for the whole island. Army units in full combat dress took over police functions in the cities and towns; army tribunals replaced civilian courts. Military censors gagged the newspapers; editors complained that they constantly had to redraw the front pages. Machado forced the closure of the Havana Yacht Club, a playground for the aristocracy, on grounds that it was being used by "conspirators" against the government. Gustavo's parents had joined the club in 1909, and he often took his family there.

In December 1930 *Revista de La Habana* ceased publication, in part due to the Depression, but also the political uncertainty.

Machado had created a secret police and specialists in torture. But perhaps the most horrific group was a government death squad, the *porristas*. They were organized by Leopoldo Fernández Roz, a teacher, to carry out private, unlawful acts. Provided with arms, ammunition, and identification cards, they took orders directly from Machado. They killed, assaulted, and tortured. Machado also used prostitutes to create a female force provided with knives, razor blades, and gloves tipped with steel claws to rip the clothes off women protesters on the streets. The death squads used the dreaded *ley de fuga*, an old Cuban custom. A prisoner is taken to a selected spot and told to run. If he runs, he is shot; if he does not, he is shot; and the report is written: "killed while trying to escape." Ruby Hart Phillips and her husband, John, who was the Havana correspondent for the *New York Times*, witnessed it once outside their Havana apartment. "We saw a youth come running," she wrote. "He was alone in the street, his shadow the only other thing moving. He was weaving wildly from side to side, as if he did not know where he was going. Then I saw him halt, raise his arms, and wave them. In the still hot afternoon, his voice was perfectly audible. . . ." The man cried, "Don't shoot anymore." Then several men on a cliff nearby opened fire. "The first fusillade struck him in the back. He stumbled, falling. The second smashed through his head and shoulders. He fell in front of the huge stone statue erected to former president General José Miguel Gómez."

Machado also used hardened criminals to do his dirty work. At about 8:00 p.m. on December 30, 1931, approximately a hundred imprisoned convicted criminals carrying blackjacks, knives, and hammers were let into Gallery No. 2 at the Príncipe Fortress, a dank prison in Havana. Some seventy students were being held there, shivering on small canvas cots, many held for nothing more than opposition to Machado. The thugs beat and slashed them savagely.

A fragmented opposition struggled to confront Machado, and a grim war played out on the streets. The most violent resistance came from a clandestine organization known as the ABC, working in secret cells of seven members each. A cell leader knew only the six others on the team, and one director from another team. They were organized in a hierarchy of levels A, B, C, and so on, so that if one cell was arrested, the whole organization would survive. The ABC soon attracted more and more young professionals and intellectuals. The group proposed an extensive political, social, and economic program, but its real impact was terrorist attacks against members of Machado's government in reprisal for the bloody repression of the opposition. The ABC used a system called *chequeo* in which they carefully monitored a target's movements before an ambush. They killed Miguel Calvo, the hated chief of Machado's special torture unit, at 7:30 a.m. on July 9, 1932, when he passed by the cliffs near the Hotel Nacional, as he did every morning. Two months later, the president of the Senate, Clemente Vázquez Bello, was returning home from a morning swim at the beach when he was cut down by youths holding sawed-off shotguns. Machado retaliated. On September 29, Gonzálo Freyre de Andrade, a friend of Gustavo and former law professor who defended students resisting Machado, was brutally butchered at home in Havana, along with two brothers.

Havana echoed with bomb blasts. On April 14, 1933, seventeen bombs went off. Machado moved about only in an armored car with a phalanx of guards, guns bristling.

Gustavo's university classrooms were closed, his hopes for reform dashed, his *Revista de La Habana* shuttered, and Machado, the friend of his family from Camajuaní, now ruled as a despot. The Great Depression and Machado's dictatorship cast a long shadow over Cuba. Hungry mothers with small children begged in the doorways of vacant houses in Havana. This was the kind of despair unseen since the days of the *reconcentrados* during the independence war. Weeds choked the flowers and shrubs in Miramar's once-glorious parkways.

During these desperate days, Gustavo made a decision that is difficult to explain. On June 26, 1933, he accepted Machado's appointment to be secretary of justice, a cabinet position responsible for upholding the rule of law at a time when Cuba was drowning in lawlessness. One day after the job had been offered, a government car was waiting to take him to the ministry. The driver accidentally slammed the door on Gustavo's hand. It was painful, and as María tended to it, Gustavo said aloud it was a bad omen; perhaps he should refuse the position. But she encouraged him to do his duty. In his swearing-in remarks, Gutiérrez said, "I am taking over this department with certain concerns, but without any trace of hesitation." He did not say what the concerns were, but the streets were engulfed in violence. Gustavo felt loyalty to Machado, a sense of duty, and thought it better to be working from the inside, with a slim possibility that he could effect change.

When President Franklin Delano Roosevelt took office in March 1933, Gustavo saw a glimmer of hope. Roosevelt recognized the need for a change. His approach to Latin America would be the "good neighbor" policy, so he did not want to start with intervention in Cuba. He dispatched Assistant Secretary of State Sumner Welles as ambassador, with an implicit mandate to get rid of Machado.

Cool, lean, and handsome, immaculately dressed, and a friend of Roosevelt since they were at school at Groton, Welles had experience in Latin America and had written a two-volume history of the Dominican

Republic. He arrived in Havana on May 8 and organized negotiations between Machado and the opposition, including the ABC and the university professors, but not the directorio. Gustavo brightened when he learned that Welles had come with a goal of reforming the constitution and electoral laws, then holding new elections. On July 26, Gustavo delivered an important early concession to the opposition, releasing hundreds of political prisoners. But despite Welles's intense effort, the negotiations stalled.

Then came a wave of strikes. Bus drivers quit working; streetcar motormen and taxi drivers walked off the job, as did stevedores, ferrymen, longshoremen, and newspaper workers. Soon the country was paralyzed with a general strike. Food ran short, as did gasoline.

On August 2, Gutiérrez abruptly resigned as secretary of justice. He had been in office just thirty-eight days.

On August 7, a huge crowd gathered in front of the Capitolio. The crowd was told—falsely—that Machado had quit. It went wild with enthusiasm. But then Machado's plainclothes police and porristas drove through and opened fire, killing 28 and wounding 168. Havana was gripped by fear in the days that followed. Shots echoed across the city, murders were reported daily, and frightened residents cowered behind closed doors.

On August 11, Welles demanded that Machado take an immediate leave of absence, and his cabinet resign. Next, Machado was told of a revolt by the Aviation Corps. In disbelief, he went to headquarters to face down any rebellion. When he marched in, officers told him he must resign or there would be bloodshed.

He realized it was over. The next day, Machado boarded a seaplane at the airport outside of Havana and flew off to the Bahamas, never to return.

Hungry looters ransacked a large store of supplies in the presidential palace in Havana, staggering into the streets under loads of coconuts, canned foodstuffs, stalks of bananas, and office equipment. Even fragments of furniture were taken as souvenirs. All the plants were pulled up, windows smashed, and an improvised sign "For Rent" was hung on the palace, to cheers.

Mobs began a violent spasm of revenge. The founder and more than a dozen of the porristas were killed by avenging hordes. The assassin who was alleged to have slain Mella in Mexico was found by students and killed. The mansions of Machado's cabinet members were ransacked. Doors were ripped off and rooms looted, one by one.

At the Capitolio, three main entrance doors leading to the rotunda were made of bronze, each decorated with ten square bas-relief panels portraying a scene from Cuban history. On the panel depicting Machado's 1929 inauguration, the president was standing on the portico, looking out toward the people. The students scratched off Machado's face. On a second panel, showing Machado with the other presidents of Cuba, he was defaced with deep, angry slash marks.

Gustavo was terrified and went into hiding. The threat of mob violence was everywhere. One unruly crowd appeared near their house but then detoured to ransack a police station. "Gustavo and I were sitting on the porch of our house . . . with our daughters," María recalled. "A large group of young men passed by, yelling and calling us 'rats,' which is what they called Machado's supporters. We had to go inside. There was a terrible spate of looting and robberies. We got a phone call saying that they were going to tar and feather G.G. and parade him around the city."

Gustavo's priority was to protect María and his four daughters. He had no idea whether he would be targeted. After show trials by students, he and other professors were ousted from the University of Havana because of their association with Machado. Bustamante was expelled from the law school.

Out of work, Gustavo could not meet the mortgage payments on the mansion and was forced to sell it. He moved his family to a dingy, low-rent, two-bedroom apartment in Old Havana. At night the area was known for noisy bars, cabarets, and restaurants, not the ideal neighborhood for his daughters. But María kept their spirits lifted. In their darkest days, when the commotion on the street was too much, María pulled out her mandolin and played it for the family.

Cuba fell into a vortex of upheaval. Sentiment for dramatic change swept the island, not only in the political and intellectual classes of Havana, but also among working people in the countryside, where strikes were breaking out. People wanted a break with the Machado dictatorship but also with the corruption and misery of the old political system. The tenor was nationalistic and sought to free Cuba from the influence of the United States.

Initially, Welles handpicked a provisional president, Carlos Manuel de Céspedes. He was the son of a Cuban revolutionary hero and had been Cuba's ambassador in Washington and Paris. But he was largely unknown to the Cuban people, lacked decisiveness, and seemed to be a puppet of the United States.

Two distinct forces rose to take power.

The first came from the army, where officers were still largely Machado supporters. In early September, disgruntled sergeants and enlisted men revolted, forcing out about five hundred officers. The rising was led by Fulgencio Batista, thirty-two, a sergeant-stenographer who exuded personal charm and can-do hustle. The sergeants' revolt was intended to stave off rumored troop reductions and pay cuts. Batista took control of the military.

The second force was the radical students of the directorio. Their leader was Ramón Grau San Martín, a patrician doctor and professor of physiology at the University of Havana, who had a fashionable private practice. Grau was among Cuba's most accomplished physicians, had been dean of the university medical school, and was a prolific scholar. He was imprisoned once, six years earlier, while protesting the expulsion of university students. A tall and gawky bachelor, Grau, forty-six, had a finely clipped mustache and wore elegant suits. He was by nature a pragmatic man, and a reformer.

The students and the sergeants joined forces and Céspedes was removed in a bloodless coup on September 5. Grau and Batista, and several hundred supporters, went to the presidential palace, where Grau told the president calmly, "We have come to receive from you the government of the nation." Céspedes abandoned his post without formally resigning. Briefly, an executive committee of the students and sergeants took charge, but after five days, Grau became provisional president.

Thus began what is called the revolution of 1933. Grau, with the impatient students at his back, issued a blizzard of progressive and reformist decrees. Some of them dated back to unfulfilled hopes of the Veterans and Patriots movement a decade before. Grau set a minimum wage for sugar cutters and an eight-hour day for all workers; established voting rights for women; granted autonomy to the university; created a program of agriculture and land reform; and ordered all businesses, factories, and farms to employ at least 50 percent Cuban-born workers. Grau dissolved all political parties that had cooperated with Machado, including the Liberals. His government promised to hold elections for a constitutional convention the following April, which would lead to a new constitution.

Significantly, the despised Platt Amendment was abrogated, ending thirty-four years of US hegemony over Cuba. Gustavo and his generation felt this was long overdue.

The United States refused to recognize Grau's government, which undermined his chances for success. Welles had multiple reasons for opposing Grau. He saw him as a product of a mutiny, beholden to the students and sergeants, and attempting a leftist social overhaul, including land reform that would threaten US interests. Moreover, Welles had seen his own choice, Céspedes, forced out.

Grau's rapid-fire decrees led to near anarchy. More than eighty labor strikes were under way. The historian Luis Aguilar wrote that "the appearance of the government, with the coming and going in the Presidential Palace of armed young men shouting for the urgent enactment of some decree, was not reassuring." The newspaper *El Mundo* asked, "Who is ruling Cuba?"

On October 2, about three hundred of the deposed army officers staged an armed uprising at the Hotel Nacional, a monument to Machado and luxury. They barricaded themselves inside the hotel, refusing Batista's orders to return to barracks as privates. A firefight broke out between them and the army, positioned outside. The army shelled the hotel and sprayed it with gunfire, while the deposed officers, many of them crack riflemen, returned fire from balconies and windows. As many as one hundred soldiers were killed and dozens wounded; at some point eleven unarmed officers were massacred near the tennis court. The elegant hotel was a shell-pocked, bloody mess. The surviving officers eventually surrendered.

Grau and Batista had barely talked to each other, and their alliance collapsed. Batista pushed out Grau on January 15, 1934, and Grau left Cuba on a steamer bound for Mexico five days later. In just 127 days in office, Grau had become a torchbearer for ideas of social change that remained alive in Cuba for decades. The student directorio disbanded, but some members were convinced after the bitter experience of 1933 that they needed a political party to carry forward Grau's vision. That new party, the Auténticos, was founded on February 8.

Batista was now indisputably in charge. A week after Grau was ousted, Cuba was again recognized by the United States. Batista, who was of mixed-race heritage, had cut sugarcane as a young man and grasped the plight of the poor. He remained the ruling military strongman behind the scenes for the next seven years as presidents and politicians came and went. Constitutions were torn up, reinstated, revised, and torn up again. Elections for a new constitutional convention were promised, scheduled, delayed, and delayed again. Balloting for president and Congress was held but the reins of power remained firmly in the hands of Batista. Three men held the office of Cuba's president in these years, but all were puppets of Batista. Political parties were banned, reinstated, and dozens of new political groupings appeared, many of them youthful, aggressive, and revolutionary, including the Auténticos. But for the most part, these groups were still searching for a solid footing or were driven underground. The real center of power was the military, which Batista steadily expanded so that by the end of the 1930s, the army had taken control of the lottery, customs, and other agencies. Batista mostly ruled by canny maneuvering, but he resorted to brutality at times, suppressing a general strike in March 1935 in which a dozen or more people were killed. Less than two months later, the army confronted and killed Antonio Guiteras, who had served as interior minister in Grau's short-lived government but now was plotting a socialist revolution and violent uprising against Batista. The jails filled with political prisoners, opposition parties struggled to survive clandestinely, and periodic beatings of journalists and the occasional discovery of the corpse of a political opponent with a bullet in the head "made it even clearer how far Cuba was from anything resembling democracy," wrote Batista's biographer Frank Argote-Freyre.

Within a year or so of losing his mansion, Gustavo managed to move his family back to a rented house in Miramar. It was not Bellabrisa, but he found time to think and write. He did not know how long the resentment over Machado would linger. His experience must have led to some personal soul-searching. Gustavo had served in Machado's government, but he also saw clearly the horrors of Machado's despotism and believed his ouster in the revolution of 1933 was justified. In a moment of reflection a few years later, Gustavo wrote that in the spirit of "loyalty and personal decency" he would accept responsibility for having served in the Machado cabinet, however briefly. Machado, he said, ruled with "great achievements and great errors." But "no one can force me" to accept blame for acts in which he did not agree, nor take part.

The public hysteria subsided. What Gustavo had seen in the past few years—the despair and desperation of the mobs, the unchecked power of Machado, the revolutionary cries under Grau—all led him to conclude that a new system must be built for Cuba and that he could help create it. A new system was the only way to permanently end the cycles of corruption and dictatorship.

To do this, Gustavo would have to rebuild the constitution. And to do that, he would have to climb back into the political arena.

In the summer and autumn of 1934, he began to write a new constitution for Cuba. He hoped to rescue the Liberal Party from the ignominy of the Machado dictatorship. He was brimming with strong emotions and ideas. The Cuban people, he concluded, had been worn down "by the most ruthless economic crisis in recorded history" and were "lost in an endless labyrinth of myriad hatreds and ambitions." Gustavo wrote that Cuba had only three choices: a constitutional system with elections, anarchy, or a dictatorship. He believed the only way forward was electoral struggle, "so that it is the people, and only the people, who decide."

By October, Gutiérrez had drafted a new constitution, and a new platform for the revitalized Liberal Party. He was working with Ramón Vasconcelos, a journalist and polemicist who headed the party. Vasconcelos was a man of contradictory and ambiguous views; once a critic of Machado, he had become a spy for him in Europe, sending back reports on radical student exiles. After Machado's ouster, Vasconcelos returned to Cuba. Briefly banned, the Liberals were reinstated by 1935, but the party began to break up into splinters. Gustavo and Vasconcelos clung to one of them, still called the Liberal Party, but reduced in size and influence from the old days.

Gustavo's draft constitution was profoundly influenced by the deprivations of the Great Depression. He was smitten by Roosevelt's New Deal and the idea of social democracy and activist government, and fashioned his program after it.

But Gustavo also inserted a provision in the draft constitution that reflected his democratic spirit and idealism.

"Sovereignty resides in the people," he wrote, "and all governmental authority comes from them." To give those words heft, he added:

> The right of legislative initiative belongs, first and foremost, to the people, who can exercise this right by submitting popular messages or bills to Congress, provided that they have been duly signed by no fewer than 5,000 voters and written in a legible and respectful manner.

For the next few years, Gustavo lobbied hard for a new constitution containing this kernel of hope. In October 1936, he presented a draft to the Cuban Senate. He had reduced the number of required signatures for a citizen initiative to a thousand people, adding a requirement that the signatures be notarized. Gustavo then worked as an adviser to a Senate special commission studying the new constitution. By December, it had

hammered out a fresh draft, and made it public. This time, the requirement for a citizen initiative was ten thousand signatures, but eliminated
any requirement that they be notarized.

At a Havana convention of the Liberal Party in August 1937, held at
the elegant National Theatre, Gustavo implored party members not to
dwell on their past troubles. He urged a "new route," toward social democracy, inspired by the New Deal, quoting FDR. Gustavo was elected
to the House from Havana in 1938.

The idea of a new constitution had been in the air since Grau's brief
presidency. All the provisional governments under Batista supported it
but did not act. In mid-1938, acting out of self-interest, Batista gave new
life to the idea, promising elections for a Constituent Assembly to write
a new constitution. The United States was pushing him to accept civilian rule. To retain power, he realized he would have to win a legitimate
democratic election. Batista's support for a new constitution was critical
to Gustavo's hopes; without it, the new charter may never have come
about.

Batista proceeded to transform himself, at first by creating an alliance
with Cuba's Communist Party, which had been growing in popularity,
although banned for many years. The party was small, well organized,
and took orders from Moscow. Batista, long despised by the party, legalized the Communists in September 1938. He was being pragmatic,
hammering together whatever planks he could to build a civilian political coalition, including some former supporters of Machado. Gustavo's
Liberal Party was part of this Batista alliance.

The opposition force was the Auténticos, led by Grau, the doctor
and professor who returned in December 1938 from four years of self-
imposed exile in Miami. He wasted no time building a challenge to Batista with an alliance that included the ABC radical opposition group
that took shape during the battle against Machado. The Grau forces
were committed to civilian control of government, in contrast to what
had been years of Batista's military-backed *caudillo* rule.

By the spring of 1939, all the political players had agreed on the
need to elect the delegates to a Constituent Assembly—essentially, a

constitutional convention. The balloting on November 15, 1939, was the fairest in the history of the Cuban republic. This was the genuine pageant of democracy—people making the choices—that Gustavo had longed for over the years. In a stunning result, Grau's forces won a victory over Batista and his allies, taking forty-one of the seats, to thirty-five for Batista. Most importantly, Batista accepted the outcome, and did not use troops or thugs to rig the balloting. For Batista, the constitution was a stepping-stone; his larger goal was to win the presidency. On December 6, he resigned from the army—a major step in his transformation— and announced he was running as a civilian.

Cuba faced a blizzard of political pressures in 1940. The Constituent Assembly would meet to write the new constitution from February to June, divided between the Batista and Grau blocs. At the same time, a national election campaign would be under way, with Batista facing off against Grau. The vote was set for July 14.

The constitutional convention opened on February 9, 1940, in the marbled House chamber of the Capitolio. The hall was electric. Gustavo recalled that the public gallery was packed with "working men and women, peasants, professionals, businessmen, landowners and soldiers, teachers, elegantly dressed ladies of the most exclusive social circles, politicians of all affiliations, revolutionaries of all leanings. It was a melting pot come to a boil, nervous and passionate." Gustavo felt the diverse crowd "gave a stamp of extraordinary grandeur" to the moment. A flag that had once covered José Martí's tomb was given to the Assembly as a gift, a reminder of his ideals. A US diplomat who attended the opening ceremony reported that the public gallery was packed with Auténticos, who cheered when Grau appeared but loudly booed when Batista's name was mentioned.

Outside, the whole country followed by radio. Cuba's most popular magazine, the weekly *Bohemia*, published a running chronicle in every issue. There was an atmosphere of high-mindedness as the convention opened. The participants realized that Cuban society was demanding more than the usual politics. Grau, elected president of the Assembly at the outset, declared, "The rivalries, hatreds and factions that have so far separated us must not exist in this assembly. . . . This assembly represents the destiny of Cuba."

Jorge Mañach, who had taken part in the café debates with Gustavo and was a former ABC member and one of Cuba's leading intellectuals, called the convention "the consummation of a nation's prolonged, dramatic yearning. . . . If we are here today, it is because the people willed it, and we are here for what the people want."

José Manuel Cortina, a lawyer, politician, and journalist, implored the Assembly, "Here, we must dampen self-serving passions." He offered a simple slogan for the work ahead: leave the parties outside! Bring the nation in!

Nonetheless, the Assembly was plagued by trouble. One session went nineteen hours and an older delegate collapsed from illness; Grau stopped to take his pulse and prescribe medicine. The drafting process fell behind. It was performed in *secciones*, or committees that worked almost entirely in secret. To overcome delays, the Assembly created a seventeen-member umbrella coordinating committee, led by Cortina, to pull together the drafts from the secciones. But the coordinating committee also fell behind. At one point the coordinating committee threatened to give up, caught in a bitter dispute over taxation of large plantations and the rights of small farmers. The committee was persuaded to keep working. On April 25, the public gallery in the chamber was filled with law students who had come in hopes of witnessing history. When they looked down on the floor, it was empty. There was no quorum.

Then a dirty deal nearly derailed everything. A small political faction led by Mario Menocal, the third president of Cuba, who was at this point an aging patriarch, was lured to switch from Grau's coalition to Batista's in exchange for political plums, including the right to pick candidates for vice president, the mayor of Havana, and other positions. "Cuban politics is pretty rotten," the US ambassador, George Messersmith, who had just arrived, wrote to Washington. The deal shocked the country and shifted the balance of power to Batista—giving him control of the convention in midstream—a stinging setback to Grau. When Grau tried to resign in protest, it was rejected by the convention. Then, on May 17, Grau submitted a "formal and irrevocable" resignation, potentially throwing the convention into chaos.

José Manuel Cortina rose to the moment and reminded Grau of the pledge they had made at the outset to avoid "fanatical, self-serving political partisanship and pigheadedness." Grau stayed on.

After the Machado dictatorship and Batista's strongman rule, the new constitution was written expressly to limit the power of the executive, creating the post of prime minister and giving Congress power over cabinet ministers. A president was limited to one four-year term and could not run again for eight years. The Assembly debated the death penalty, habeas corpus, equality before the law, labor rights, agribusiness, and religious freedom.

Democracy seemed imperiled by Hitler, and Cuba had been awash in Nazi propaganda. In May, debate flared over an amendment, proposed on the spur of the moment, to outlaw organizations with "totalitarian tendencies." Was it right to impose limits on speech and assembly in a free society? The proposed amendment was revised to guarantee freedom of assembly, but it also declared that groups "contrary to the democratic representative system of government," or those that seek to subvert the state, would be unlawful. It was approved.

In the same vein, Joaquín Martínez Sáenz, who had been a founder of the ABC movement, proposed an amendment drawn from his experience fighting Machado's dictatorship with bombs and violence. It declared that "appropriate resistance" could be used by citizens defending the rights guaranteed in the constitution. Some members questioned whether it was necessary, but Martínez Sáenz recalled how Machado had used the ugly porristas. The new amendment, he argued, would protect the right of people to resist with force. The amendment was approved and became Article 40 in the new constitution, with important ramifications in the years to come.

The Assembly rushed to finish. Of the total 286 articles, 236 were approved in only 14 sessions. The new constitution was more than twice as long as the 1901 charter, in part because it included 61 sections on social and economic matters such as family, work, and culture.

For once, bickering parties, the politicians, and schemers all came together to accomplish something larger than their narrow self-interests.

The constitution, finished on June 8, included the provision for a citizen initiative that Gustavo had first authored years before. It became Article 135, Section F, which provided that laws could be proposed by congressmen and senators, government officials, courts—and by citizens. "In this case," the constitution declared, "it will be an indispensable prerequisite that the initiative be exercised by at least ten thousand citizens having the status of voters." It was not a panacea. A proposed law would still require approval by Congress and have to be carried out. But it meant that citizens would have a voice, a chance to shout "Enough!" Had it existed earlier, Gustavo believed, Cuba's citizens might have expressed outrage at the Machado dictatorship, the violent porristas, or the corrupt lottery. They might have slipped the leash of the Platt Amendment or the grip of Batista.

Now, four decades after independence, they had the power of initiative—a key to their own destiny—if they chose to use it.

On July 5, 1940, Gustavo joined the throngs gathered at the Capitolio for what he hoped was the dawn of a new era. Crowds swelled before the palace of white limestone and granite with a striking dome that rose above Havana's jagged rooftops. From the portico, lined by towering columns, Gustavo could see a red carpet snaking down the broad main steps, flanked by a rippling sea of summer suits and floral dresses. Invited dignitaries were escorted up the red carpet by an honor guard. Beyond, spectators jammed small balconies and filled the canopied storefront sidewalks.

At the top of the main steps, leaders of the political factions that made up the Constituent Assembly stood shoulder to shoulder, facing the crowd, every one of them wearing a dril cien.

The new constitution they had created was truly democratic. It laid out separation of powers among executive, legislative, and judicial branches, with an independent judiciary. There would be both a president and a prime minister, a "restrained" executive, as Gustavo had put it, to prevent the rise of another caudillo, or strongman. The constitution declared that all Cubans were equal before the law and prohibited discrimination of any kind. It contained strong guarantees of individual rights, including habeas corpus; freedom of thought, speech, press, conscience, assembly, and religion; inviolability of the home; and privacy of correspondence. Elections were to be based on a popular vote. The constitution was bulging with promises of social justice. It had sections on family, culture, property, and labor—with a provision, for instance, that the monthly salary of a primary school teacher must be at least one millionth of the total national budget—all of which was unusual for a constitution. Gustavo knew there was a risk that if the social benefits did not materialize, disenchantment would erode trust in the document. The new constitution also carried many provisions that were stated only as goals, and would require legislation to become reality, such as a new electoral code. But even with imperfections, Gustavo felt the constitution was a genuine blueprint for social progress, democracy, individual rights, and an activist state. It was a fresh start, finally leaving behind the flawed 1901 constitution, which gave the United States a protectorate over Cuba that undermined its first decades of independence.

On the portico at exactly 5:00 p.m., an army cornetist sounded a call to attention. Carlos Márquez Sterling, a university law professor, who became president of the Constituent Assembly when power shifted, stepped up to a small table. In remarks that boomed over the loudspeakers and were broadcast live on radio, he declared that the new constitution "broke the spirit" of the old Spanish colonial era and demonstrated "we are beginning to enjoy our life as a responsible nation." He acknowledged that the document had flaws but said it was a product of Cubans working together with maximum effort. He avowed that the constitution would close the book on years of improvisation, uncertainty, and provisional governments. "Law has prevailed over force," Márquez Sterling stated. "Justice over arbitrary judgments. Liberty over chaos."

Márquez Sterling declared the constitution of 1940 formally promulgated, the last act of the Constituent Assembly. Applause welled up from the steps and the streets beyond. At the Plaza de la Fraternidad, adjacent to the capitol, cannons fired a twenty-one-gun salute. The army band played the national anthem, "La Bayamesa," with lyrics written in 1868, when Cuba's first war for independence had begun.

In the presidential election that followed eleven days later, Batista won, defeating Grau 58 to 42 percent, with an expensive, all-out propaganda campaign in which he used the army to muscle and intimidate voters.

On November 21, Gustavo was chosen to be Speaker of the House of Representatives. He was optimistic that Cuba had turned a corner. As Speaker he could shape legislation to turn the new constitution into everyday reality. In early 1941, he drafted and introduced an electoral code. The law eliminated an old system that resembled an electoral college, based on each region, and put into practice direct popular election for the presidency, which would boost the prospects of populist parties, including the Auténticos.

But Gustavo's optimism did not last. Batista did little to create the semi-parliamentary system that Gustavo and others had envisioned. A backroom deal, made earlier, meant that Congress was overcrowded with both incumbents who were in office before the new constitution, and those elected since. Many stopped coming to the Capitolio altogether. By autumn 1941, Gustavo could not summon a quorum in the House chamber. Legislation was languishing. Disenchanted, he stepped down.

But he was not finished with public life. Gustavo was an internationalist. Back when he was debating his friends in the cafés, Gustavo had written a book on the League of Nations, optimistic about the power of international law to prevent war. The rise of Adolf Hitler shattered those illusions. During World War II, he began writing another book. Published in February 1945, *La Carta Magna de la Comunidad de las Naciones* described the horrors of Nazi Germany and demanded that the world adopt a new, more aggressive approach to protecting human rights. Gustavo drafted what a global bill of rights might look like, drawing from the US Constitution, among others, and from his own experience in writing the 1940 constitution for Cuba. He emphasized the importance of free expression, free assembly, equality before the law, and the sanctity of human dignity. He declared "it is essential to insist upon the advantages of democracy as the system of political organization of nations for the enjoyment of equality, liberty, and justice."

His ideas proved influential in the first years of the United Nations. Cuba's diplomats were at the forefront in pushing for a global declaration of human rights. They prepared a version that closely paralleled the provisions proposed by Gustavo. When the formal drafting of the Universal Declaration of Human Rights began under Eleanor Roosevelt, the documents submitted by private individuals, and studied in the preparations, included Gustavo's proposed global bill of rights. He went on to become Cuba's deputy ambassador and then full ambassador to the United Nations, where he led the General Assembly's committee on economics. He also headed Cuba's national economic council; served at the UN Relief and Rehabilitation Administration, helping displaced war victims; and represented Cuba at global trade negotiations. He was a mandarin—a diplomat, jurist, and scholar.

Gustavo's greatest contributions were the constitution of 1940 and the citizen initiative. But after all his work, he was discouraged. Cuba had not yet established public faith in democracy and honest government; violence and corruption persisted. The constitution was important, a set of rules, but it was only a piece of paper. To succeed, it must be accepted by the society it governed. Gustavo worried constantly about losing the people's faith in laws and democracy. By 1944, he felt the constitution was in danger of becoming "ineffective," and said so in a public speech warning of the drift.

As it happened, there was a mesmerizing voice on Cuba's most popular radio network with the potential to sweep away the old maladies and defend democratic ideals.

It belonged to Eddy Chibás. He would take the baton.

THREE

"BITE, ROOSTER!"

On August 5, 1951, Eddy Chibás began his Sunday as usual, with *café con leche*, bread and butter, double portions. From the top floor of an Art Deco apartment tower in Havana, he eagerly read the newspapers and magazines, then dug into clippings and documents sent to him by friends and supporters from all over Cuba. He checked to make sure the pencils on his desk were sharpened. He started to write on sheets of paper, slowly, in a firm hand. As the hours passed, he skipped lunch, engrossed in his script for the evening radio show, his outrage building and spilling onto the pages.

He was forty-three years old, short and stubby, nearsighted, and wearing thick glasses that gave the impression he was always squinting. He had never married. He could be erratic and distracted. He had been known to rummage through his address book and telephone a woman with an invitation to lunch, only to be reminded that it was already 5:00 p.m. He would pace absentmindedly on the phone as the cord twisted into a knot around him. He raced around Havana in a Packard convertible, ignoring traffic signs and speed limits, probably because of his poor eyesight.

He had one preoccupation: to clean up Cuba's soiled politics and dysfunctional government. The obsession began as a radical student at the University of Havana, grew intense in the struggle against Machado, and deepened during the Constituent Assembly, to which he was elected, outpolling every politician on the island except for ex-president Grau. On the radio, Chibás regularly defended the 1940 constitution against disrespect and neglect. He was determined to shame the grafters, gangsters, and enemies of democracy, and he did so every Sunday evening on CMQ radio, Havana.

In his normal routine, the radio script was typed by his devoted personal secretary, Conchita Fernández, while Eddy wrote by hand. Later, a few close friends would arrive at the López Serrano building, the tallest residential apartment tower in the city, crossing the terrazzo sunburst floor in the lobby, and take the elevator to the penthouse apartment with a view of the Gulf of Mexico. They would read the scripts silently, then comment; Eddy was impatient and attentive. He wanted to know what worked—and what didn't. He usually left for the studio at about 7:45 p.m., in a white dril cien suit, smoking a Chesterfield, greeted by a throng on the street. He would walk or drive his Packard convertible to CMQ Radiocentro, five blocks away, where another crowd of fans waited.

It was the heyday of radio. By 1949, there were more than half a million receivers in Cuba, and the island was more tuned to radio than elsewhere in Latin America. The most powerful station was CMQ, with a twenty-five-thousand-watt transmitter, state-of-the-art headquarters, and an enormous audience. The airwaves in Cuba were a cacophony of talk, zesty entertainment, and advertising that produced rich rewards for the owners. For years, CMQ had been associated with the Cuban soap manufacturer Crusellas, a subsidiary of Colgate-Palmolive in the United States. Cubans got far more news, culture, and entertainment from radio than from newspapers. Radio was much easier for the large number of Cubans who were illiterate.

In 1947, Eddy's weekly radio broadcast at 8:00 p.m. scored the highest rating for a single show in Cuban history, surpassing the wildly popular *radionovelas*, or soap operas. A *New York Times* reporter described Eddy as a "reporter, crusader, gossip and muckraker" who provided listeners with a half hour of "verbal fireworks." Chibás brought a natural charisma and theatricality to radio, passionate and messianic. When he came on the air, people stopped what they were doing. Visitors to Havana walked down the empty streets and heard Eddy's broadcast from open windows. In villages and small towns, multiple families gathered around a radio set, cheering him on with whoops of *"¡Pica, gallo!"* or "Bite, rooster!" when he went after someone. Chibás spoke a language they understood. He was sometimes called *El Loco*, or the crazy one, because there was something over the top about Eddy.

At the core of it was a deep-seated moral outrage. Chibás was flamboyant in his manner, compared to the sober Gustavo Gutiérrez, yet both were champions for an honest Cuba, devoted to eradicating the stains of corruption and democracy's failings. Gustavo's quest had been a relatively quiet one, writing laws and a constitution. Eddy's crusade was a hectoring one, full of drama. He understood the immediacy of radio and mobilized people as no one had before him.

Chibás was the son of a wealthy engineer, Eduardo Justo Chibás, who owned sugar and coffee interests in Oriente Province, and served as the director of tramways and electricity in Santiago de Cuba. The younger Chibás was educated at the Colegio de Dolores in Santiago and at Belén in Havana, the two most famous schools on the island, as well as a boarding school in the United States. He enjoyed a privileged life: travel across the ocean on a steamship, vacations in the Swiss Alps, touring Paris and Venice, and membership in the Havana Yacht Club. In 1924, his father built a luxurious Italianate mansion in the Vedado neighborhood of Havana. But the youthful Eddy gravitated as a student to radical politics, inspired by the fiery rhetoric of Julio Antonio Mella at the university, and enthralled by Professor Grau, who stood up for the students and the directorio. When Grau became president in the revolution of 1933, Eddy began hosting a radio program extolling him, *La voz de las Antillas*, or the Voice of the Antilles. In the years that followed, Eddy's popularity grew. He played a major role in a general strike against Batista in 1935, and was imprisoned for six months. After serving as a member of the Constituent Assembly in 1940, Chibás ran as an Auténtico for the House that year and won easily. He captured a Senate seat in 1944. With Eddy's support, Grau won the presidency in a landslide, which Chibás hailed as a "glorious journey." Chibás hoped Grau would at last redeem his brief, turbulent presidency of a decade earlier. Grau inherited a wave of prosperity; sugar prices soared at the end of the war, and Grau's campaign slogans included "Let there be candy for everyone." Chibás was an unabashed and eloquent propagandist for Grau. He arranged to buy a thirty-minute program on CMQ radio to speak about the Auténticos and the new president.

Before long, Eddy's enthusiasm for the "glorious journey" ran aground. The president, who had always projected an image of puritanism, turned out to be tolerant of the most blatant graft. In December 1946, Chibás reported on his radio show that the education minister, José Manuel Alemán, was siphoning off sugar tax money meant for schools and diverting it to Auténtico candidates. "What have you done, bandit, with the funds destined to buy paper, pencils and other material for public schools?" Chibás demanded in a rage. Later he denounced cabinet members for profiteering by selling goods such as rice, lard, and flour, which were in shortage and under official price controls, on the black market. In a brazen heist, Alemán and a cohort of aides took a convoy of trucks to the Treasury building, walked past the guards without interference, loaded suitcases with bundles of currency, and drove to the airport, where a chartered DC-3 was waiting. They flew to Miami, where the money was transferred to Alemán's business headquarters, a cool $19 million.

Eddy's whole experience in politics was shaped by the revulsion to Machado's power grab. The constitution of 1940 was written to expressly prohibit two consecutive terms for the presidency, so Chibás was stunned to learn that Grau was thinking of seeking a second term by changing the constitution. This was the worst that could happen: his idol, his mentor, violating the provisions of the constitution they had written together. Chibás wrote a twelve-page letter to Grau urging him to end the corruption of his ministers and not seek another term. Eddy asked Grau why he had "opened his arms to the old politics." Grau ignored him. Soon, Chibás broke with Grau entirely. Chibás said Grau was transformed from an "apostle of honesty" to the "apostle of the black market, botellas, and corruption."

In May 1947, Chibás began organizing a new party that split from the Auténticos. The Cuban People's Party, known as the Ortodoxos, pledged to follow the original Auténtico program—guided by the revolution of 1933—before it was tainted by corruption and backroom deals. The informal emblem was a broom, to sweep away corruption. Its slogan was *vergüenza contra dinero*, which roughly translates to honor or dignity versus money. The party vowed not to make any bargains or pacts with others. These pacts were a basic element of Cuban politics, but Chibás loathed them and believed they had watered down the Auténtico program.

At an early meeting, a tall, twenty-year-old university law student showed up out of curiosity. His name was Fidel Castro.

Grau eventually gave up his second-term ambitions. In 1948, the Auténticos nominated Grau's labor minister, Carlos Prío Socarrás, for president. But Chibás jumped into the race with a last-minute, breakneck campaign. In May, he sold his father's mansion in Vedado and used the 25,000 pesos to finance it. He had only three weeks, but drew large, enthusiastic crowds. He came in third, with 16.4 percent of the vote, nothing short of a miracle considering how briefly he campaigned. His 320,929 votes were almost double the number of registered Ortodoxo voters. The results marked Chibás as a "rising star in the island's political firmament," wrote his biographer Ilan Ehrlich. "His unique style of politics, one that had demolished all formal barriers between candidate and voter, was clearly popular."

Prío won the presidency in 1948. His campaign was buoyed by vote-buying, but there was no military intervention, as in the past. Prío had been a fellow student radical with Chibás in the 1920s and general secretary of the directorio fighting Machado. Prío had mellowed since then. As the new president, he was handsome, well-meaning, and democratic. He had worked on the 1940 constitution and was a founder of the Auténtico Party. Always smiling, he came to be known as the "cordial president." As historian Hugh Thomas put it, Prío "loved liberty, though it was unfortunately difficult for him to distinguish between liberty and license."

On the radio, Chibás was unsparing in his criticism of Prío. He alleged the president was the secret owner of Manhattan high-rise buildings, a sensational charge that Chibás never substantiated but that resonated widely. In another jaw-dropping case that Chibás highlighted on the radio, this one about Grau, a judge had issued indictments charging ministers under Grau with embezzling large sums from the state and accusing Grau of tolerating the thievery. Evidence files in the sensitive case were held in the judge's chambers, with two guards who were instructed not to open the door to anyone. On July 4, 1950, they opened the door, armed bandits charged in, seized 6,032 file folders containing the evidence, and disappeared. The files and the thieves were never found, and the case never came to trial. Someone had covered up for Grau in spectacular fashion.

Power and money were a volatile mix in Havana, but another disease was also threatening democracy and the rule of law. Armed gangs and their leaders were everywhere.

Called "action groups," the gangs had their roots in the violent student organizations opposing Machado in 1932 and 1933. Many had lost any ideological motivation by the 1940s, but survived as small, murderous squads that sought to extract botellas, the no-show government jobs; pursued deadly rivalries; and engaged in lucrative rackets. They infiltrated the Auténticos. When Grau took office in 1944, there were at least ten groups working, some as Grau's bodyguards; the leader of another was appointed chief of police in Havana in return for election support. A gangster group, the Unión Insurreccional Revolucionaria, or UIR, left a grim calling card—a note saying "Justice is slow but sure"— beside the body of a victim. The University of Havana, off-limits to the police because of its unique autonomy, became a gang haven. They monopolized textbook sales, peddled exam papers, raided the office of the bursar, and fought gun battles.

For a few years, Fidel Castro, who had been around weapons since his childhood and carried a pistol at the university, was immersed in this dangerous, gun-ridden climate on campus. He was loosely implicated in several assassination attempts, but charges were dropped. He was affiliated with the UIR for a while and was friends with its leader, Emilio Tró, who later died in a shoot-out. Fidel was more a foot soldier than a chieftain. But his world was filled with grandiose notions of violence and uprising. He joined an ill-fated plan to invade the Dominican Republic and overthrow the dictator Rafael Leónidas Trujillo; after training for a month, the operation was blocked by the Cuban navy. In April 1948, Fidel took part briefly in a violent mass protest in Bogotá, Colombia. That September, in Havana, he organized student protests against a bus fare increase—which was rescinded after buses were burned.

Drawn more and more toward politics, especially toward Chibás, Fidel created a political splinter group, Acción Radical Ortodoxo, not formally affiliated with the Ortodoxos, but parallel to the larger party. He was listening to and learning from Chibás.

Chibás sought change through legal means, such as the courts and elections. He believed that words on the air could be as powerful as weapons. Once a student radical, he now opposed insurrection or any form of armed struggle. By contrast, Fidel's offshoot was inclined toward insurrection, and welcomed members from the UIR gang. This created tension between Chibás and Fidel. On one occasion, at a public event, Fidel tried to climb into Eddy's Packard and was ordered out. Chibás, asked later what happened, replied, "Nothing, but I don't like people to see me with a gangster in my automobile." Still, Fidel campaigned for Chibás in 1948. Fidel may have been tolerated because his wealthy father controlled valuable votes in Oriente Province. The young Fidel was also absorbing a great deal from the Chibás methods—bombastic propaganda, manipulating symbols, and most importantly, how to mobilize people. In May, Fidel had introduced Chibás to a massive campaign crowd in Santiago de Cuba, saying, "We are in the presence of a great man!" Chibás addressed the rally from the top of a truck, and with the applause still rippling through the crowd, supporters clamored for him to jump into their arms. Chibás dove headfirst. The frenzy left an impression on Fidel.

Chibás became the most powerful opposition voice in Cuba, regularly denouncing gangsterism and corruption. Chibás often went to the radio studio accompanied by several of his Ortodoxo colleagues. At least once when Chibás was at the microphone, those present included the admiring young Fidel.

Free speech thrived on radio in Cuba during the 1940s. But under fire from Chibás in 1950, Prío responded with censorship. The president issued a decree that allowed anyone who felt injured by a radio broadcast the right of reply. It was a thinly veiled attempt to gag Chibás and clearly unconstitutional. Chibás went on the air to protest what he called Prío's "gravest" error. "Whenever you attempt to violate public liberties," he vowed, "you will have to confront me, your incorrigible adversary."

Prío later promised the owners of CMQ that the decree would not be implemented. But in early 1951 it was invoked by a notorious gangster, Rolando Masferrer, who demanded equal time against Chibás and got it.

That summer, Chibás fought a verbal duel with Prío's education minister, Aureliano Sánchez Arango, claiming that the minister had used school funds to buy real estate in Guatemala. Sánchez Arango had rid the ministry of the gangsters and botellas, yet Chibás pursued him. On July 21, Chibás vowed to bring proof of his claims to the Sunday radio show. "I shall be ready," he declared, "to open my portmanteau and show the nation the proofs of the embezzlement . . . to prove that this government of Carlos Prío is the most corrupt in the history of the republic." Eddy asked for extra airtime on July 29, and anticipation ran high. But when he emptied his briefcase, Chibás did not have the proof. He recycled some other charges but could not substantiate the central claim.

Chibás may have fallen into a trap, perhaps offered the information by someone who didn't deliver. In the days that followed, he was taunted on the street by chants of "The briefcase, the briefcase," which stung his pride. Chibás clung to a hope that, even without proof, he would be proven right.

On August 5, 1951, Chibás prepared in the morning for his Sunday radio show. Late that afternoon, he was joined in the apartment by Luis Conte Agüero, Ortodoxo Party secretary and a friend who would read over the radio scripts.

Eddy possessed a Colt .38 pistol, and at one point asked Luis, "Listen, which one is the safety lock?"

"You don't know?" responded Agüero incredulously. He showed Eddy how the gun functioned, sure that Chibás was joking with him.

Eddy suggested they try it out, aiming out the bedroom window at the sea in the distance. But Luis said it wasn't a good idea—the bullet might hit someone. True, Chibás said, holstering the weapon.

That evening he headed out in a white linen suit with a cigarette in his hand. A crowd of fans awaited him. He took a car to the CMQ Radiocentro building and went to Studio No. 3.

Once again, he hammered the theme of corruption. "Cuba needs to wake up!" he said, lamenting that his previous radio show did not generate as much reaction as he had hoped, that "my knocking was not, perhaps, sufficiently strong."

Power to the microphone was cut—Chibás had gone over his allotted time. Listeners heard an advertisement for Café Pilon.

"Onward, fellow members of the Ortodoxo movement!" Chibás continued, audible only to those in the studio. "Let us fight for economic independence, political freedom, and social justice! Let us sweep the thieves out of the government! People of Cuba, stand up and move forward! People of Cuba, wake up!

"This is my last knock on your conscience!"

With his left hand, he slammed the desk. With his right, he fished in his pocket and suddenly there was a shot.

No one saw him squeeze the trigger, but Eddy Chibás slumped over, wounded, and his .38 fell on the floor.

He had shot himself in the stomach. He survived another eleven days. He died in a hospital after emergency surgery in the early morning hours of August 16.

His listeners never heard the "last knock," and the suicide has never been fully explained. Chibás may have been distraught at lacking the proof, or embarrassed that he let down his audience. He may have attempted only to injure himself, a stunt to call attention to his crusade.

Either way, he had been a conscience of the nation in his own throbbing, insistent manner.

Fidel Castro held an unwavering vigil outside Eddy's hospital room. When Chibás died, Fidel stood by the open bier at the university's Aula Magna, or Great Hall, for twenty-four hours as part of the honor guard, in the front row.

Huge throngs followed the cortege to burial at the Cristóbal Colón cemetery, where radio stations had set up microphones for tributes to Chibás. Fidel prepared five separate speeches, one for each station.

He spoke longer than anyone else.

PART II

FIDEL

FOUR

THE FIREBRAND

Fidel Castro set out to fill Eddy's shoes as a crusader against corruption. He had learned a great deal from watching Chibás: how to campaign and mobilize people; how to use radio as a weapon; how to gather accusations and proof. He also wanted to erase the taint of his gangster past. Eager to make himself more widely known before the 1952 elections—he was still a relatively minor figure in politics, at twenty-five years old—Castro set his sights on the biggest target, President Carlos Prío. He spent several months digging into Prío's finances, uncovering evidence the president was corrupted by money and gangsters.

Prío owned farms in a tobacco-growing region outside Havana, Santiago de las Vegas. Trained in the law, Fidel sifted through land records and found that Prío had acquired farms as a payoff for the pardon of a wealthy businessman convicted of raping a nine-year-old girl.

Castro went public with his first exposé on January 28, 1952, in the daily newspaper *Alerta*. The headline read "I ACCUSE" and it was accompanied with a photograph of Fidel. Next, Fidel disguised himself as a gardener. On the grounds of Prío's *finca* outside Havana, he took photographs of the elegant appointments: fountains, a shooting range, a waterfall roaring into a swimming pool. On February 20, *Alerta* published his second exposé under the words, "This is the way the President lives with the money he has robbed from the people."

A third exposé, on March 5, revealed a seamy underside of the *pistoleros*. The pistol-packing Castro had once been a foot soldier among them. He knew Prío had been paying off gangster groups with botellas or no-show government jobs in ever-escalating amounts, a dubious bribe to reduce violence. Castro calculated that there were more than 2,120 sinecures given to the gangsters, and on top of that, cash payments were being made directly from the presidential palace to each of 60 gangs, enclosed in envelopes bearing the seal "President of the Republic."

Fidel's revelations came at a critical moment. A leadership vacuum enveloped Cuba before the 1952 vote. Political power had often come from outsized personalities. Grau had taken the Auténticos from nothing to the pinnacle of power. Chibás, considered the front-runner for president, hoped to take the Ortodoxos on the same trajectory. Now he was gone. No one else stood out. The former president, Batista, a senator, had returned to Cuba after living in Daytona Beach, Florida, and ranked in third place in public opinion polls. The parties, by themselves, remained chronically weak.

Fidel was too young to run for president, but he ran to be an Ortodoxo Party delegate from a Havana district, relying on local political clubs in poor neighborhoods of warehouses and tenements. He waged a vigorous grassroots campaign, speaking three or four times a night, wherever he could find listeners, and sending out a flood of personal notes. Conchita Fernández, who had been secretary to Chibás, recalled how Castro summoned crowds by standing before them and waving copies of *Alerta*. He was passionate and charismatic, audacious and appealing, and the crowds applauded "deliriously."

Who was this curly-haired, imposing firebrand, and what did he believe?

Fidel's father, Ángel Castro y Argiz, was a Galician who fought with Spanish forces during the independence war and returned to Cuba in December 1899. Working hard, like so many peninsulares, he started with manual labor but found success in business. He cultivated sugar, settling in Mayarí, a dusty town of shacks sustained by the United Fruit Company. Ángel later owned a sawmill and was able to purchase Las Manacas, a plantation near Birán, which eventually expanded to twenty-six thousand acres. Fidel was born there on August 13, 1926, the third of seven children by Ángel and Lina Ruz González, a peasant girl who began working in Ángel's household as a servant when she was four-teen. Ángel was married but at some point separated from his first wife, María Luisa Argota Reyes, a teacher. When Fidel was five years old, he and his siblings were sent off to Santiago de Cuba to be tutored by the family of Ángel's friend Louis Hibbert, the Haitian consul in Santiago de Cuba. Fidel recalled this as a desolate time, when he was often hun-gry and received no lessons. He displayed a bullying, angry streak. Two years later he was enrolled as a first-grade boarding student at La Salle, a Catholic school in Santiago de Cuba. This was better, but he was still a fighter with a temper and, after getting into some scrapes, was expelled. Then Ángel sent him to a prestigious Jesuit school, Colegio Dolores, in Santiago, where he began fifth grade in 1938. Classmates recalled that he arrived with the toughness of a farm boy who developed a zeal for debating, history, and sports, playing basketball and baseball. He went on to Havana's exclusive Belén High School in 1942. Outclassed by bet-ter athletes, Fidel plunged into a frenzy of self-training, persuading the priests to set up a lightbulb for him on a court outside so he could shoot baskets at night, eventually making the team. Fidel possessed a near-photographic memory, and played a game with other students: they would ask him what was on a particular page of a textbook, and he would recite it back, usually accurately. He was heavily influenced by the Jesuit teachers at Dolores and Belén. They were almost all conserva-tive Spaniards in those years, emphasizing order, discipline, and loyalty; some were followers of the Spanish dictator Generalissimo Francisco Franco. According to his biographers, Fidel was fascinated by the rise of Fascists in the 1930s. He read Hitler's *Mein Kampf*, mimicked Musso-lini speeches in front of a mirror, and followed the progress of the Axis armies on a map on his wall. Above all, his modern hero was the Spanish

Falangist José Antonio Primo de Rivera, a caudillo who founded the Spanish Fascist Party, while his hero from the history books was Alexander the Great. Fidel never witnessed a working democracy, only a "rural spoils system, with everyone in on the take and the winnings going to the strongest," wrote biographer Georgie Anne Geyer. He watched as his father opened the family safe to pay off politicians to buy votes.

In April 1943, Ángel Castro divorced his first wife and married Lina Ruz, and later that year legitimatized their children. For most of his boyhood, Fidel had been named Fidel Casiano Ruz González, after his mother. He now became Fidel Alejandro Castro Ruz. He enrolled in the law school of the University of Havana in the autumn of 1945. "Those of us who did not have anything to do went to law school," Fidel later recalled. Indifferent about his studies, Fidel rarely attended classes. He married Mirta Díaz-Balart, daughter of a United Fruit Company lawyer, in 1947, and spent two and a half months in the United States. On returning to school, he crammed just before exams with his prodigious memory. He graduated in 1950 and formed a small law office with two classmates, but most of his work was for poor farmers and workers with paltry earnings. His father, Ángel, loaned him money for the rent.

If democracy was Cuba's brass ring, by the spring of 1952 it seemed tantalizingly within reach. The presidency was transferred peacefully and under the constitution three times—in 1940, 1944, and 1948. While imperfect, elections were democratic. "We were growing accustomed to living within the constitution. For twelve years we have been without enormous blunders, in spite of common errors. Civic peace cannot be achieved except through great effort," wrote young lawyer Fidel Castro. As president, Prío began to implement some neglected provisions of the 1940 constitution, including a vital step, creating the National Bank and a monetary system. He also cooperated with Congress to pass legislation on many fronts, including budgets, which Batista and Grau had imposed by decree, allowing for significant corruption. At the same time, the toll of the gangsters, Grau's corruption, and Prío's indiscretions had deepened public cynicism. Prío attempted early in his presidency to end political violence with a law against gangsterism. Then it was revealed he was paying off the gangsters. It seemed no political leaders could be trusted.

Cuba was ripe for the television age when it dawned in the 1950s. Middle- and upper-class Cubans had money for luxury goods such as television sets. Many had visited the United States and watched television. Even before they owned a set, audiences in Cuba were reading about programs and entertainers in newspapers and magazines. On top of that, advertisers for beer, tobacco, and particularly soap and other household products were searching for new audiences. One of the first two Havana television stations, started by Goar Mestre and his brothers, who owned CMQ radio, went on the air December 14, 1950, and became Cuba's dominant television network. A year later, Cuba had six operating television stations, with fourteen more planned. The number of TV sets, mostly in Havana, soared from six thousand in 1950 to more than a hundred thousand three years later; Cuba had the highest penetration of television sets per household in Latin America. CMQ broadcast opulent musical productions that re-created the big stage spectacles of Havana's nightclubs, and popular *telenovelas*, soap operas that consisted of 150 to 200 one-hour episodes a year. Television showcased a consumer and capitalist cornucopia, and Cuba's commercial television was deeply influenced by the United States—production, programming, and advertising practices all came from the north. One of the most respected and prestigious shows in Cuba was *Ante la Prensa*, a Cuban version of *Meet the Press*. CMQ carried programming from NBC in the United States, including *Alfred Hitchcock Presents* and *The Adventures of Rin Tin Tin*.

Television would also prove to be a boon—even more powerful than radio—for the next self-appointed savior of Cuba, Fidel Castro.

Newspapers and magazines were also plentiful. In the late 1950s a dozen daily newspapers were published in Havana, only two fewer than in London, a city nine times its size. Most were in the pocket of special interests or supported by government subsidies, what one study called "an intricate system of official bribery." No more than six or seven met their entire costs based on advertising and circulation. But there was a plurality of voices, and Cuban journalism had high standards compared to other countries in Latin America.

At about 4:00 a.m. on Monday, March 10, 1952, the phone rang at Gustavo's residence in the Miramar section of Havana. He was now fifty-seven years old, had represented Cuba at the United Nations, and was head of the government's national economics board. He was wrestling with economic problems such as Cuba's dependence on sugar and the need for more housing.

Who would be calling at such an hour?

Soon Gustavo was shouting, startling his wife and daughters awake. "I can't believe it!" he declared. "We have lost fifty years of the republic!"

The caller informed him that at 2:43 a.m., former president Batista had carried out a coup against Prío with the support of disaffected junior military officers. The next presidential election, scheduled for June, would not happen.

The officers, mostly middle class and educated at military schools in the United States, were seething at being passed over for promotions, better living quarters, and pay. In January they approached Batista, but he put them off, thinking he had a chance to run again and legitimately win the presidency. In March they told him: a coup now or never. By this time, running behind in the public opinion surveys, Batista realized he'd lose the election, so he joined them. He showed up in a leather bomber jacket at Camp Columbia, the headquarters base that housed about two-thirds of Cuba's military forces, and assumed command without a single shot.

Soon after, Batista sent word to Gustavo, asking him to become the new secretary of state. Gustavo refused. In his twenties, he had spoken out about the need for more enlightened citizens; in his thirties, he had bluntly advised Machado not to grab power; in his forties, he drafted a new constitution for Cuba. Now democracy was fading before his eyes. He was angry and despairing. But at the same time, he retained a sense of duty, that he should serve Cuba as best he could. He was a top economic policy maven.

Batista's forces seized radio and television stations. Prío drove to the Mexican embassy and requested asylum. Three days later he left the country for Miami. Havana went about its business in the weeks that followed. Shops, theaters, businesses, casinos, and restaurants remained open. Many businessmen and merchants supported the coup, hoping for more stability. There were no riots. People were cynical and fatigued.

Batista started out with a relatively enlightened set of economic policies, attempting to diversify Cuba beyond sugar, and stimulate growth with government subsidies. He was a populist and hoped prosperity would suffice to keep a hold on imaginations—and power. But he had no public mandate. He suspended the 1940 constitution and replaced it with new statutes that allowed him to lift rights to free speech, assembly, and press for forty-five days at a time, which he did repeatedly. Congress was terminated (although he promised to keep paying members' salaries for six months), and the prime minister and vice prime minister offices were abolished. Batista put off elections. When some members of both houses of Congress tried to assemble in defiance at the Capitolio, troops dispersed them with a few gunshots. Batista created an eighty-member "consultative council," stacking it with sugar magnates, union leaders, and others who would not give him trouble.

Batista could be brutal, if necessary, but to keep control he preferred to maneuver, using varying amounts of cunning, bribery, and subversion. He had always longed for popular legitimacy, even when his own actions destroyed the mechanisms of democracy. When Batista heard in April that students were planning a protest to symbolically bury a copy of the 1940 constitution, four of them were arrested and brought before him. He tried to ingratiate himself with the students. They could not bury the constitution, he implored them, because it had not died.

"Precisely," one of them answered. "It has been murdered."

Fidel Castro found his calling. Fighting Batista became his preoccupation. Three days after the coup, Castro published a bristling statement in a mimeographed pamphlet, accusing Batista of "tearing the constitution to shreds." Two weeks later, he filed a court complaint against Batista, claiming the coup had "demolished the constitution," and Batista should be punished with more than a hundred years in prison. The court dismissed it.

Castro gave up on peaceful protest. When the Ortodoxos staged a rally at Chibás's tomb on March 16, Fidel climbed atop a crypt and proclaimed that the time had come to overthrow Batista by force. The deposed president Prío organized an opposition conference in Montreal on June 2, 1953, but it was mostly talk. Castro wanted action and took up arms. Traveling around the island, he organized small, secret cells, carrying out military training in rural seclusion. For the most part, his men were recruited from peasant farms and working-class neighborhoods: busboys and street vendors, unskilled laborers and parking-lot attendants.

In early 1953, he began laying plans for his first attack. The target would be the Moncada Barracks, the largest military installation in Santiago de Cuba and the second largest in the country, after Camp Columbia in Havana. He rented a farm, "El Siboney," with a white stucco house, eight miles from Santiago, as a staging area. Fidel's plan was a shock assault on the military base. He believed the surprised soldiers would simply stand down, then he would seize the barracks, raid the weapons stocks, declare victory on radio, and wait for the population to rise in support. Fidel had prepared a victory declaration in advance. It was a recording of the final radio address by Eddy Chibás.

On Thursday, July 23, a manifesto titled "The Cuban Revolution" was typed up and preparations made to deliver it to the weekly *Bohemia* magazine and two newspapers on the following Sunday morning. The manifesto did not hint of the impending attack but read, "The Revolution declares its absolute and reverent respect for the constitution of 1940 and would reestablish it as its official code."

Two days later, Castro made his way toward Santiago, as did his fighters, some by car, others by bus. By midnight, 118 men and 2 women had assembled at the farmhouse. The women, Melba Hernández and Haydée Santamaría, sister of Fidel's deputy commander, Abel Santamaría, had smuggled guns out of Havana in a box marked "flowers" and acquired tan army uniforms for the fighters as disguises. Fidel delivered final instructions, relying on a rudimentary sketch of the Moncada Barracks. He broke out the uniforms. A tall man, Fidel pulled on his own—his wrists protruded from the sleeves, his ankles stuck out from the pants. But that was the largest on hand.

At about 5:00 a.m. on July 26, a caravan of cars packed with the fighters pulled out of the farm onto the dirt road toward the city. A separate group headed for Bayamo for a diversionary attack.

Four hundred soldiers were assigned to the Moncada Barracks, but Santiago was celebrating Carnival, and many were just staggering back from all-night partying. About three hundred were in the garrison, most asleep. The main building was a three-story, light-yellow structure wedged into a hillside. It had once been a Spanish citadel. Fidel and his largest group of fighters planned to surprise the guards at Post 3, one of several entrances to the barracks, then rush in. A second group, of about half a dozen, which included Castro's younger brother Raúl, was to take the adjacent Palace of Justice and shoot from the roof. A third group, of twenty-two, led by Abel Santamaría, including Haydée and Melba, were to seize Saturnino Lora Civil Hospital, on the other side of the barracks.

The attack was a disaster. The Moncada soldiers did not stand down. Alarms rang, and soldiers opened fire with a high-powered machine gun. Five of Fidel's men who got inside the Moncada thought they were heading toward the armory, but instead found themselves in a barbershop. The armory was one floor below. Raúl and his group abandoned their positions and melted back into the city. The rebels at the hospital quickly donned medical uniforms and impersonated doctors, nurses, and patients. The two women, Haydée and Melba, posed as mothers nursing their newborns. But the army soon captured them all.

In a chaotic retreat, exhausted and uncertain, Fidel and the surviving insurgents straggled back to the farm. Some of the fighters quit on the spot and turned themselves in.

Castro was audacious and reckless at Moncada. But what happened next was just as stunning. Panicked and furious, government soldiers went berserk. Captured rebels were interrogated and, with hands tied behind their backs, massacred with a .30-caliber machine gun in the target practice range at the barracks. The thirty-three corpses were repositioned around the fortress to make it look like they had died in combat—a crude cover-up. All told, sixty-one of Fidel's men were killed by Batista forces. Nineteen army soldiers were killed, and nine civilians. Over the next week, more dead rebels began to turn up elsewhere: three in a dry well; twelve more on a highway embankment and wooded area, shot through the head, execution-style.

Rumors and news reports about the bloodshed alarmed civic leaders in Santiago, including Archbishop Enrique Pérez Serantes, a friend of Fidel's father. Appalled by the wanton killing, the archbishop typed up a pastoral letter promising to spare the lives of any fugitives if they turned themselves in. Then he went looking for Fidel.

Hours after the onslaught, Castro left the farmhouse on foot for the mountains with nineteen men, some of them wounded. They hiked through the hills for days.

At dawn on August 1, a single-engine De Havilland Beaver plane flew low over a wooded area where Fidel and the rebels were hiding, dropping thousands of leaflets announcing that Pérez Serantes would mediate if they surrendered. Meanwhile, a Cuban army sublieutenant, Pedro Sarría, was leading a sixteen-man patrol in the area and surprised Fidel as he was sleeping on the floor of a peasant's hut. Fidel came out in his underwear with his hands up. When a soldier aimed a gun at Fidel, Sarría quickly deflected it, saying, "You do not kill ideas." Fidel owed his life to Sarría, and to Pérez Serantes, who drove and walked for miles in the mountain region, offering his personal guarantee of safety for those who surrendered. In the end, the archbishop did not find Fidel, but his efforts to stop the killing made a difference.

The Moncada bloodshed stained Batista, in power just over a year. It suggested a return to the days of terror under Machado. Batista imposed press censorship and emergency powers on August 2, followed by a repressive "public order" law on August 6 that the journalist Ruby Hart Phillips recalled "silenced the island." The law provided stiff penalties for *desacato*, the elastic offense of "contempt" of the government. Havana's principal newspapers eliminated editorials and published no comments about the government. Phillips wrote, "For centuries in Cuba the public has discussed politics in cafés, bars, buses and on the streets, but now no one dared talk."

Two trials of the Moncada attackers were held in Santiago. In the first, starting on September 21, Castro defended himself, theatrically changing into the black robe of a lawyer when acting in his own defense, cross-examining his accusers one minute, then taking it off when answering questions as the defendant. At the end, his brother Raúl and other leaders were given thirteen years; twenty others got ten years; and three men got three years.

Fidel had staged such a striking performance that it was decided to consider the case against him separately. The second trial began October 16 in a cramped room at the Civil Hospital. Before three judges, Fidel delivered an expansive defense of his actions. A reporter for *Bohemia* took notes, and Fidel later composed a lengthy document that he described as the text of his speech. However, the reconstruction is embellished.

Fidel's defense was that the attack was proper against a dictatorship. He insisted that he stood for "public liberty and political democracy." He vowed to restore "the Constitution of 1940 as the supreme law of the state until such time as people would decide to modify or change it."

Standing before the judges in the makeshift courtroom, Fidel painted a glossy picture of democracy in the Cuban Republic in the years before Batista's coup of 1952.

It had its constitution, its laws, its liberties; a president, congress, and courts. Everyone could meet, associate, speak, and write freely. The men in government did not satisfy the people, but the people could change them, and it was only a few days before they would have done so. . . . They were proud of their love for liberty and believed it would be respected as a sacred right. They had placed a noble trust in the certainty that no one would dare commit the crime of attacking their democratic institutions. They wanted a change, an improvement; they wanted to take a step forward, and they saw it near. All of their hopes rested on the future.

"Poor people!" he added. "One morning they awoke with a shock. . . . A man named Fulgencio Batista had just committed the crime no one expected."

Democracy was never quite as neat and clean as Fidel described. But it is notable that he paid tribute to democratic values and that he praised constitutional rule and the right of people to speak freely. Fidel claimed his Moncada assault was legally justified. He pointed to Article 40 of the 1940 constitution, which stated that "adequate resistance" could be used when defending constitutional rights. That article stemmed from the experience of the student radicals of 1933, who turned to armed rebellion in response to Machado's violent suppression of protests. Vague, Article 40 was one of the compromises made in those difficult, rushed days of writing the constitution. But now Fidel held it aloft as proof that he had the legal right to armed rebellion.

Castro's speech provides an important preview of what was to come. He did not want to turn the clock back to 1952, to the soiled politics before Batista's coup. Instead, he envisioned a much grander enterprise. He declared that "revolutions constitute a source of law." Upon taking power, the "revolutionary movement" would approve five laws, the first of which would reinstate the 1940 constitution "as the true supreme law of the state." The word "revolution" was shopworn. But in Fidel's mind it carried an important definition: a revolution would be endowed with absolute power. Fidel said the revolution would have to assume all the authority of a state, "such as the powers to legislate, to enforce the laws, and to judge." The revolution would be the "only source of legitimate power." Fidel was describing a revolution that would have supralegal rights, that would be the supreme power.

This was far from the democratic spirit or letter of the 1940 constitution.

Overall, in a trial that lasted a few hours, Fidel gave a bravura performance. He turned attention from the charges against him to charges he leveled against the state. He had become the victim, in his telling. He transformed the courtroom into a stage, upon which he cast himself as Cuba's savior.

"Condemn me, it does not matter," Fidel told the judges. "History will absolve me!"

The judges were not moved. Castro was sentenced to fifteen years in prison and sent to the Isle of Pines, forty miles from the mainland.

In prison, Fidel did not rest. He read books voraciously. He sent many letters to Naty Revuelta, the wife of a cardiologist in Havana with whom he was passionately infatuated, and later had a brief love affair. While in prison, his marriage to Mirta fell apart, and they divorced. Fidel wrote letters from the Isle of Pines using pencil, pen, and sometimes lemon juice as invisible ink, which would show up when ironed by the recipient. Fragments of smuggled letters were quickly retrieved in Havana and typed up by friends, bit by bit, re-creating the long, embellished version of his courtroom speech, "History Will Absolve Me." In June 1954, he wrote to Haydée and Melba that he hoped for a mass uprising, inspired as much by propaganda as by guns. "Our task now is to mobilize public opinion in our favor, to spread our ideas and win the backing of the masses of the people." In a separate letter a few weeks earlier, Fidel wrote to Melba, urging her to "[d]eal with the people artfully and with a smile. Follow the same tactic used in the trial: defend our viewpoints without making unnecessary enemies. There will be enough time later to crush all the cockroaches together."

The savior was coming back.

FIVE

THE GUERRILLA

Fidel walked free from prison on May 15, 1955, after just nineteen months at the Isle of Pines. He stepped out in a double-breasted suit, with a thin mustache. The other twenty-nine Moncada prisoners were also released, including Raúl, the result of an amnesty law approved by Batista, for which Fidel's friends campaigned for nearly a year. Castro made no concessions and wasted no time.

On July 7, he left Havana for the United States to organize and raise money, and then Mexico, where he assembled a guerrilla force for insurrection against Batista. The organization would be called the 26th of July Movement, after the date of the Moncada attack. In McAllen, Texas, Fidel collected a $50,000 donation from former president Prío. Next, he established a base on a secluded ranch outside Mexico City, where his fighters trained in ambushes, hit-and-run tactics, shooting, mountain climbing, and the making of Molotov cocktails, grenades, and booby traps. They also took long marches at night. One evening, Fidel met a doctor from Argentina, Ernesto "Che" Guevara, two years younger than Fidel, who had spent some years wandering the continent, most recently in Guatemala. He witnessed the CIA-backed coup to overthrow the elected government in Guatemala, and it radicalized him. He escaped to Mexico, where he and Fidel talked late into the night about guerrilla warfare tactics. Guevara took immediately to Fidel, and signed on to become the physician to Fidel's guerrillas.

In early October 1956, Fidel paid $15,000 for a seventy-five-foot yacht, the *Granma*, in bad disrepair, berthed at the Port of Tuxpan on the Gulf of Mexico. For a month, working at night, repairs were attempted on the diesel engines, but one continued to malfunction. The vessel was designed to carry ten passengers.

The fighters set sail on the *Granma* at 2:00 a.m. on November 25, in a severe storm. Eighty-two men clambered onto the boat, including Fidel, Raúl, and Che, as well as weapons, ammunition, and equipment. They were pelted by sheets of freezing rain and tossed by enormous waves. Water filled the keel and the pumps failed. The men bailed frantically with buckets. The *Granma* was supposed to arrive in Cuba on November 30, when a planned popular uprising would occur in Santiago de Cuba, spearheaded by Frank País. A youthful urban underground organizer, he had agreed with Fidel on the strategy, which they hoped would lead to a nationwide general strike.

Everything went wrong. In Santiago, the uprising began that morning with a rebel attack on the police, a customs house, and the maritime police, but government reinforcements arrived, people did not rise up, and País was arrested. The *Granma* was still at sea, and only reached Cuba on December 2. It ran aground at 6:00 a.m. near Las Coloradas Beach, south of the original target, missing a waiting party with food, weapons, trucks, and jeeps. Fidel and his men waded across two miles of swamp, holding their guns above their heads, forced to jettison backpacks, medical gear, a radio transmitter, and food to reach solid ground. Hungry, exhausted, and soaked, with some men missing, they were soon spotted by Batista's army, lunged for cover, and then marched for three days straight. On December 5, they set up a camp at Alegría de Pío, but neglected sentry posts or patrols. They were ambushed by the army; twenty-one were killed, thirty more captured, and others escaped in small groups.

When Fidel regrouped with his survivors a few weeks later, there were just seven weapons among them.

Quietly, to evade detection by the army, they slipped away to the mountains. On December 25, Fidel and a small group climbed the highest peak in the Sierra Maestra, the Pico Turquino, at 6,476 feet. Fidel exulted, "We have won this war!" But he had not won any war, not even fought one. Three weeks later, on January 17, a band of twenty-one Fidel fighters raided a Rural Guard army post at La Plata, seizing rifles, a submachine gun, a thousand rounds of ammunition, and food—their first victory. Another raid followed on a different post. But they were still a tiny band in a remote wilderness, and the next steps were not at all clear.

Fidel realized he needed to fight a different kind of war. As Chibás once said, words could be deadlier than guns. Batista's censors had blocked Castro's access to the Cuban press. No one on the island was hearing his words. Fidel turned to foreign journalists. Only a few weeks after arriving in the mountains, he sent an emissary to sneak through army patrols in the foothills, taking word to Ruby Hart Phillips of the *New York Times* in Havana. Fidel wanted a journalist from the United States to visit his mountain redoubt.

Batista boasted that Fidel had been killed, the revolt crushed. "It began to look as though the revolution was going to fail," Phillips wrote. But when she got the message from Castro, she realized Fidel had decided "to prove to Cubans that he was alive."

Phillips could not do it herself; a woman from the United States in the mountains would be immediately recognizable, and she might be deported afterward. But an editorial writer of the *Times*, Herbert Matthews, a specialist on Latin America, had been to Cuba before and was planning a vacation in Havana. Phillips cabled the foreign editor in New York and insisted that Matthews come immediately.

Arriving on February 9, Matthews soon was trekking into the hills with guides. Heavy rain turned paths into slick rivers of mud. Fidel's men communicated with each other in the night through soft, coded whistles. Eventually, reaching a rock crevice shielded by dripping leaves and boughs, Matthews was told to wait. At dawn, Matthews came face-to-face with Castro. "Taking him, as one would at first, by physique and personality, this was quite a man—a powerful six-footer, olive-skinned, full-faced, with a straggly beard." Castro was "dressed in an olive gray fatigue uniform and carried a rifle with a telescopic sight of which he was very proud.

"It seems his men have something more than fifty of these and he said the soldiers feared them," Matthews wrote of the gun.

Fidel talked for three hours. "The personality of the man is overpowering," Matthews wrote. "It was easy to see that his men adore him and also to see why he has caught the imagination of the youth of Cuba all over the island. Here was an educated, dedicated fanatic, a man of ideals, of courage and of remarkable qualities of leadership."

"Castro is a great talker," Matthews noted. "His brown eyes flash; his intense face is pushed close to the listener and the whispering voice, as in a stage play, lends a vivid sense of drama."

Fidel was also remarkably good at illusion. He had twenty men with him, but they marched by Matthews in repeat loops to give the impression he had many more. Castro said the army deployed groups of two hundred men, while his guerrillas fought in "groups of ten to forty, and we are winning." During the interview, Raúl approached Fidel and said the liaison from "column number two has arrived." There was no column number two. There were no groups of forty. Nor did they have fifty guns with telescopic sights. All of it was made up to impress Matthews, who did not spot the deception.

"He has strong ideas of liberty, democracy, social justice, the need to restore the Constitution, to hold elections," Matthews wrote of Castro. He quoted Fidel as saying, "Above all, we are fighting for a democratic Cuba and an end to the dictatorship."

When the story appeared on the front page on February 24, 1957, in the *Times*'s Sunday edition, with a photograph of Fidel holding the rifle with a telescopic sight, Batista's credibility was ruined. His defense minister issued a statement calling the story "a chapter in a fantastic novel" and claiming the interview did not take place. On February 28 the *Times* proved otherwise by publishing a photograph of Matthews and Castro smoking cigars during the interview.

Official press censorship in Cuba was imposed in forty-five-day increments by Batista. When copies of the *New York Times* arrived in Havana, a censor took pains to scissor out objectionable stories. By chance, however, a period of censorship ended just as the Matthews story appeared. Matthews published two more articles over the next two days. All had an immense impact in Cuba. Fidel was rapidly elevated to a major figure. Fewer than three months after the disastrous *Granma* landing, he was depicted as a savior—exactly what he wanted. He was waging psychological war against Batista.

He boasted to Matthews that "we have been fighting for seventy-nine days now and are stronger than ever." In fact, guerrilla morale was low. They marched slowly and were hungry and sometimes lost. Some of Fidel's fighters abandoned the hard life, returning to the cities. By one estimate he was down to only twelve rifles. Che Guevara was suffering asthma attacks that virtually paralyzed him.

In the year and a half Fidel spent in Mexico training his fighters, one last effort was made to negotiate a political settlement between Batista and the moderate opposition on the island. The president refused to give ground. Once these talks collapsed, the stage was set for the rise of an urban underground. As with Machado, students stepped forward and led a violent opposition. Matthews had gotten a taste of it. Before leaving Havana, he met clandestinely with one of the most important leaders of the urban underground, José Antonio Echeverría, president of the Federation of University Students and leader of the Directorio Revolucionario movement, devoted to armed revolt. Heavy-set, florid, with a mass of hair in a pompadour touched with gray, Echeverría, twenty-four years old, was every bit as persuasive and charismatic as Fidel.

On March 13, two weeks after the Matthews story was published, Echeverría's forces staged a headlong, armed attack on the presidential palace. Batista was in the palace but was not hurt. Echeverría and another group separately took over a radio station, where they announced that Batista had been killed. On leaving the radio station, Echeverría ran into a police patrol, which killed him, leaving him to bleed to death in the street. The attack had utterly failed. More than forty fighters were killed. A swift and violent government crackdown followed.

This left Castro with one fewer rival but not yet a revolution. He and his fighters were still tromping through the rain-slicked mountains, in what Robert Taber of the Columbia Broadcasting System (now CBS) recalled as "not so much a military campaign as a long, toilsome expedition through an interminable wilderness." Fidel was secure in the Sierra, but not a military threat to the regime. The Batista army rarely ventured into the mountains. Taber wrote to his editors that the urban underground was a disorganized, scattered force. "Yet the Batista regime, too, is confused, disorganized, inefficient, and, what is more, frightened."

Taber and cameraman Wendell Hoffman spent two months with Castro in the mountains. The CBS broadcast "Rebels of the Sierra Maestra: The Story of Cuba's Jungle Fighters" aired in the United States on Sunday, May 19. Seated on the mountaintop at Pico Turquino, Fidel declared "we have struck the spark of the Cuban revolution." He said his purpose was to restore the constitution of 1940 and called on the United States to stop sending weapons to Batista. On May 26, the influential magazine *Bohemia* published three pages of photos from the CBS expedition, as well as an article based on the cameraman's recollections. "They won't be able to defeat us," Castro insisted, quoted in a *Bohemia* headline. The edition sold out and another was printed. Once again Fidel's tactic of speaking to a foreign correspondent echoed inside the country.

"Suddenly, Castro appeared on television screens throughout the United States," Phillips recalled. "President Batista was much upset. He couldn't understand how all these reporters got through the 'ring of steel' which his army claimed had been thrown around the Sierra Maestra."

In May, Santiago organizer Frank País was released from prison, along with twenty-two members of the *Granma* expedition, after a ruling by Judge Manuel Urrutia Lleó, who said "all people have a right to take up arms against a dictatorial government." The court ruling echoed what Fidel had said in the Moncado trial about Article 40. Judge Urrutia earned Castro's favor by his decision. País was back in action. The mountain fighters desperately needed a supply line for food, new recruits, weapons, ammunition, and communications. País could do this, but he also proposed to restructure the overall movement to shift more control to those waging an underground resistance in the cities. Fidel thought the battle against Batista should be commanded from the mountains. "The proper order should now be: *All guns, all bullets, and all supplies to the Sierra,*" Fidel wrote to Celia Sánchez, daughter of a well-off physician in Manzanillo, a gateway to the mountains. Sánchez had become an indispensable coordinator for Castro, sewing and sending uniforms, relaying watches, boots, blankets, food, and medicine, and raising money.

With his guerrillas expanding to about two hundred men in July, Fidel once again declared that his intention was to establish a democracy for Cuba.

This time two establishment figures met Fidel in the mountains: Raúl Chibás, brother of Eddy, who led a faction of the Ortodoxo Party and was headmaster of a Havana military prep school, and Felipe Pazos, an economist and first president of the National Bank of Cuba. Once again, Castro was thinking about image and illusion—in this case, a veneer of respectability, stature, and importance. Photos were taken of the visit, and the film hustled down the mountain to the editors of *Bohemia*, which published a two-page spread featuring seven photos of Raúl Chibás and Fidel conferring "in the gloom of the virgin jungle." It was more psywar against Batista.

Fidel, with the visitors, drafted a statement of goals and ideas, dated July 12, that came to be known as the "Sierra Manifesto."

"We are fighting for the beautiful ideal of a free, democratic, and just Cuba," the document declared. "We want elections, but with one condition: truly free, democratic, and impartial elections."

The manifesto called for creation of a temporary government to replace Batista and "move the country toward democratic and constitutional normalcy." It proposed holding elections "for all offices of the state" at the end of one year, following the 1940 constitution, and "power will be given immediately to the elected candidates."

Moreover, the manifesto demanded freedom for political prisoners, "absolute guarantee of freedom of information, of the spoken and written press, and of all the individual and political rights guaranteed by the Constitution."

Fidel also vowed to bring about a social revolution in Cuba: radical change for schools, farms, and industry. The manifesto called for Batista's ouster and for the United States to suspend arms sales to the regime but contained no anti-American rhetoric or screeds. Robert Quirk, a Castro biographer, found that "the manifesto bore the unmistakable imprint of Castro's prolixity—it consisted of twenty-two handwritten pages."

The manifesto was published in full in *Bohemia* on July 28. The magazine, hugely influential, had a circulation nearing 500,000 in a nation of 5.8 million and was one of the most sophisticated and widely read in Latin America. It was also strongly critical of Batista.

Two days later, País, hiding out in safe houses in Santiago, was located and killed by the police, shot at point-blank range by one of Batista's police cronies. País was twenty-three years old. Thousands turned out for a funeral procession in which youths took down the Cuban flag and ran up the banner of the 26th of July Movement.

Batista's hold was weakening, and his regime was rotting from within.

Outwardly, Havana was still the moneyed playground of glitz and excess, a center of vice of all kinds, mostly underwritten by organized crime protected by Batista's police. Batista legalized gambling for hotels and nightclubs, prompting construction of new hotels, including the Riviera and the Capri. The Hotel Nacional opened a casino in late 1955, and soon casinos opened in the Sevilla-Biltmore and Comodoro Hotels, as well as in the Tropicana, Sans Souci, and Montmartre nightclubs. The big mobsters of the day—Lucky Luciano, Santo Trafficante, Meyer Lansky—sunk their teeth into Havana. Illegal drugs were plentiful; theaters and clubs showing pornography were expanding; and brothels multiplied through the early 1950s, with 270 in full operation by the end of the decade. Habaneros purchased more Cadillacs per capita than in any other city in the world. The Chrysler Imperial ranked second.

Over the Christmas holidays in 1957, Phillips described a city of light and luxury. "In every house, from mansion to hovel, there was a Christmas tree and the stores were filled with shoppers. The new Havana Riviera opened with a gala fiesta. Tourists arriving in Havana asked where the revolution was and were told it was only a minor disturbance seven hundred miles away." The government financed a grandiose new hotel and entertainment complex to be called the Monte Carlo. "Havana will be a magical city," Lansky told his driver one day in 1958 at the construction site. "Hotels like jewels. . . . Fabulous casinos, nightclubs, and bordellos as far as the eye can see."

But beneath the surface rippled powerful forces of change.

Sugar's power and curse still gripped Cuba. When Batista took power, more than half the arable land was devoted to sugar; the largest banks were devoted to financing sugar; and more than half the labor force was involved in sugar. World War II touched off a sugar boom, the largest since the "dance of the millions" in the 1920s. Cuba's per capita income was among the highest in Latin America. The economy was middle income, roughly equivalent to Argentina and Uruguay in Latin America, or Italy in Europe. But this sense of prosperity concealed a hidden trap. The economy was slowly stagnating. Each year an estimated 50,000 men reached working age, but between 1955 and 1958, only 8,000 new jobs were created in industry. An estimated 475,000 sugar workers, about a quarter of the total labor force, averaged less than 100 days of employment a year. Making matters worse, the sugar harvest hit a ceiling. The harvest was 5.6 million tons in 1947 and 5.6 million in 1958. The way out would be to diversify and industrialize, to create factories, jobs, and exports, to free Cuba from reliance on sugar.

Gustavo Gutiérrez believed this was the only solution. He had devoted more and more time to economics in the late 1940s as global trade was liberalized after the war, and Cuba sought to benefit from it. He became head of the Junta Nacional de Economía, the National Economic Council, and pushed for policies to modernize Cuba and end dependence on sugar. In 1953, Batista appointed Gustavo finance minister. The Cuban Treasury—which during Grau's presidency was raided in broad daylight—remained a chaotic mess, and he tried to clean it up. Gustavo found the job horribly difficult, constantly putting him at odds with Batista. Then Gutiérrez uncovered a fraud, and confronted Batista about it, saying he wanted to resign. Batista insisted he remain, needing Gustavo's credibility and the respect he commanded abroad. In response, Gustavo demanded his own ministry on the economy, based on the economic council he had previously directed, and he wanted unfettered authority as the minister, starting in 1955. Batista agreed and Gustavo became one of his leading economic advisers.

Batista recognized the need to diversify, but he was unwilling to break the sugar barony that controlled the industry in the early 1950s. Instead, he tried to work around it. The government borrowed heavily to fund state development banks, which then pumped loans and subsidies into projects ranging from rice farming to livestock, from coffee to tobacco. The subsidies brought Cuba new airplanes, cargo ships, and oil refineries—with help from international oil majors—and such construction projects as the Tunnel of Havana under the bay, new electricity plants, aqueducts, roads, and hotels. New hospitals, monuments, parks, schools, and public facilities cropped up. Tourism boomed. Foreign investment flooded in. The stimulus unleashed a spurt of growth, especially in 1956 and 1957. The ownership of the sugar business had changed, too. By 1958, two-thirds of the mills were controlled by Cubans. In this period of prosperity, Gustavo managed to repurchase the Bellabrisa castle too.

While Cuba was well off compared to most of Latin America, the comparison for many Cubans was the far richer United States. US culture and commerce had washed over the island for decades. The annual per capita income of Cuba, at $374, was but a third of the poorest state in the union, Mississippi, at $1,000, but Cubans were frequently tempted by a US lifestyle never far from their sight. "The United States is mirrored in every phase of Cuban life," observed Phillips. "The modern Cuban eats hot dogs, hamburgers, hot cakes, waffles, fried chicken and ice cream."

A stark disparity separated bustling Havana and destitute rural Cuba. In the countryside, children suffered malnutrition, and their schooling was a few hours each day in a one-room schoolhouse. Nationwide, while 180,370 children started first grade in 1949, only 4,852 made it to the eighth grade. Nearly half of Cuba's school-age children were simply not in school. However, for the middle and upper classes, and especially those in the cities, there were good private schools, mostly run by the Church. About 76 percent of the country could read and write in 1953, a high literacy rate for Latin America, but there had been virtually no improvement for two decades. Literacy was lopsided: more than 90 percent of Havana residents could read and write, but in the countryside, only 58 percent could, and in the depressed regions of the east—Oriente Province—it was below 50 percent. Similarly, the infant mortality rate was the lowest in Latin America, close to that of developed economies, but in rural areas, 80 to 90 percent of children suffered intestinal parasites. Only 15 percent of rural residents had running water, compared to 80 percent in the cities. In Havana, the doctor-to-population ratio was 1 to 227; in Oriente it was 1 to 2,243.

Batista's rule was mercurial and merciless. He was an illegitimate ruler who longed for legitimacy. He used a strong hand against any opposition, then relaxed it. He played groups off against each other. In particular, he gave the Cuban Communists room to operate while telling the United States he was a reliable anti-Communist.

Batista had been this way since his caudillo years of the 1930s, but the tactic no longer worked.

Violence consumed Cuba in 1957 and 1958. Batista faced a growing army of clandestine foes made up of professionals, journalists, skilled workers, teachers, mothers, and students, all known as *clandestinos*. They printed and distributed literature, set off bombs, plotted kidnappings, and derailed trains. While frequent acts of sabotage gave the impression of a tightly knit organization, historian Julia E. Sweig found much of it was spontaneous, a relatively easy way for people to repudiate the regime by cutting telephone wires or tossing a stick of dynamite. Thousands of young urban women took part in the anti-Batista effort, through public protest and clandestine militancy.

Batista tried to smash the underground. Hours after the failed attack by radical student leader Echeverría, security forces assassinated Pelayo Cuervo Navarro, a leader of the Ortodoxos. They caught and imprisoned Fidel's underground leadership. They found and killed the surviving directorio members. In one jail, prisoners were ordered to step on a scale to be weighed. The floor of the scale, a trapdoor, dropped like an elevator and landed the prisoner in the basement below. The basement was a torture chamber. It was just like the Machado years—feeding people to the sharks all over again.

Press freedom, another pillar of democracy, withered. Bribes and subsidies were doled out to the press, which was also subjected to censorship.

Corruption thrived. A weekly magazine, *Carteles*, revealed in 1957 that no fewer than twenty members of the Batista government owned numbered Swiss bank accounts, each with deposits of more than $1 million. Batista deposited millions of dollars in illicit payments from the burgeoning casino business in foreign bank accounts. "Not to be rich was a humiliation," a Batista minister once remarked. "It was not a scandal to sell oneself." All these factors led to a mood of anger and resentment that could not be masked by the glitz of Havana. Gustavo was thoroughly disgusted at the corrupt appetites of Batista and his privileged few, who siphoned off the country's resources, but he was committed to Batista's economic policy and remained in government.

Batista lavished money on the military and considered it the core of his support. But when he brought back old cronies to senior positions, discontent spread through the ranks, and there were a series of revolts, including a 1957 mutiny at Cienfuegos Naval Station. Then, on March 14, 1958, the United States announced suspension of arms shipments to Batista. Crates with 1,950 Garand rifles were held on the docks in New York. This was an ominous signal. Batista had been a reliable anti-Communist early in the Cold War, welcomed US investments in Cuba, and had been visited by Vice President Nixon. Now the United States was pulling back.

In the mountains, Fidel revved up the war of words. Andrew St. George, a freelance magazine writer and photographer from New York, came to the Sierra for a month in the spring of 1957 and returned for multiple two-month-long trips the following year. He did more than any other journalist to portray Fidel and his rebels as saviors of Cuba, a great moral force compared to the ruthless and corrupt Batista. Che Guevara remarked that the presence of a foreign journalist, preferably from the United States, "was more important to us at the time than a military victory."

St. George, writing in *Cavalier* magazine and later in *Look*, *Coronet*, and *Life*, amplified Fidel's message that his intention was to preserve Cuba's democracy. "Within a year" of victory over Batista, Fidel told him, the revolution "would hold a truly honest election." He wanted to "free immediately all political prisoners, restore freedom of the press, reestablish constitutional rights." Asked if his movement was inspired by communism, Fidel replied, "This is absolutely false." He told St. George, "We need a climate of freedom, in which we can develop democratic habits. This is never possible under tyranny." The story by St. George quoting Fidel was carried in *Look*, circulation four million.

In a February 1958 piece in *Coronet*, St. George wrote that Castro, on the day they met in the mountains, "was a free man and a triumphant one," a "lodestar of hope throughout restless Latin America," a "tall, forceful young orator with a dignified Roman face and great personal magnetism." The rebel army was "now over a thousand strong," and "their morale is high, their guerrilla tactics well learned." The article was illustrated with a romantic etching of Fidel with a scraggly beard, holding his rifle with the telescope sight, in front of a traditional peasant *bohío*, a thatched-roof hut. The magazine also published what it called "Castro's idealistic blueprint for liberty," an essay by Fidel titled "Why We Fight." All the evils existing in Cuba, Fidel wrote, "have a common root: the lack of liberty.

"The single word most expressing our aim and spirit is simply— freedom."

Marching and living with the rebels in the mountains, Andrew St. George witnessed the growth and expansion of the rebel army. By 1958, Fidel's forces opened new fronts—fighting groups—led by Raúl, Che Guevara, and others. On February 24, 1958, an electrifying voice was carried on shortwave radios across Cuba: "Here, Rebel Radio! Transmitting from the Sierra Maestra in Free Territory of Cuba!" Castro had launched a mountain transmitter, and with only brief interludes Cubans heard it nightly. Batista tried to jam the broadcasts in Havana, but the war of words went on.

As the historian Lillian Guerra has shown, the rebels sought to manage their own image as a superior *moral* force to the dictatorship. After a critical battle in the summer of 1958, Fidel's forces took 433 soldiers prisoner, and then released 422 to the Red Cross and the rest back to the army, an act of magnanimity. Raúl, however, took no prisoners and killed 140 in one week. St. George became part of the Fidel myth-making machine. "I felt like never going back to New York," he wrote, adding that "millions of people all over the world would see and get a clearer image from my pictures of these rebels *with* a cause."

But there was a darker side. The rebels established a merciless system of "stern jungle justice." Alleged bandits and spies were executed. Raúl also staged terrifying mock executions. The rebel army pounced on women and girls suspected of spying and executed them too. St. George and his editors found some of the images too awful to publish. St. George had misgivings, but he suppressed them in his reports.

By early 1958, Castro had set up a state within a state in the mountains. He had shoemakers, gun repairs, a butcher's shop, a bomb factory, hospitals, a bakery, and a cigar factory. But guns were still hard to get. On March 30, near dusk, a twin-engine Curtiss C-46 cargo plane flew low near the Sierra range, making a hard landing on a dirt road about seventeen miles south of Manzanillo. The plane roared to a stop, broke its landing gear, and fell limply to one side. The cargo was more than five tons of weapons and ammunition, including two .50-caliber machine guns, submachine guns, rifles, mortar shells, and a huge load of rifle bullets. The haul was the work of Huber Matos, a teacher in Manzanillo and former Ortodoxo Party member. He had smuggled the materials from Costa Rica. Fidel came out of the mountains to greet Matos, and later put him in charge of a rebel unit in Santiago. He became one of the top guerrilla commanders.

Castro and the urban underground planned a general strike to crip-
ple Batista's regime and force him to resign. Fidel vowed "total war." But
the strike, called for April 11, was a dud. A few factories closed, a few bus
lines stopped, but by late afternoon, Havana seemed back to normal.
The revolutionaries had made a series of logistical and political blunders
that left them without support of other key groups, or weapons sufficient to set off a popular revolt.

But Batista was losing ground. In a battle of singular importance on
June 29, Fidel's fighters surrounded the army's 11th Battalion, resting
in a valley at Santo Domingo. Fidel had three hundred fighters; they
took on nearly a thousand army soldiers. The army unit was decimated;
many were taken prisoner, and only a third escaped alive. Fidel's fighters
captured the army's communications code book, too. Soon more army
battalions collapsed, and Batista's high command panicked.

Almost the entire army withdrew from the Sierra Maestra. The
small band of guerrillas had the army on the run.

In December, Batista heard from his own generals that his army was disintegrating. Fidel's forces were advancing up through the center of the
island. A general told Batista, "Nothing more can be done."

Batista's children left Havana on December 29 for the United States.
He burned his private correspondence and other documents. Batista
summoned his top government officials and military commanders to
a New Year's celebration at Camp Columbia. At about 3:00 a.m. he resigned and headed for the airport, flying out of Cuba to the Dominican
Republic.

The Batista dictatorship was over. Fidel Castro promised to sweep
away the old maladies. He promised to bring a social revolution, a reform of schools, farms, and factories. He promised a "provisional" revolutionary government, giving way to a vote. What Cubans heard from
Fidel, from his manifestos and his interviews and his radio speeches, was
a return to the 1940 constitution, freedom of the press, guarantees of
individual rights, and honest elections.

That's what they were told.

SIX

"JURY OF A MILLION"

Fidel Castro came down from the mountains and spoke at 1:00 a.m. on January 2 to a crowd in Parque Céspedes in the center of Santiago de Cuba, a city of legendary defiance and resistance. He addressed them from the wooden balcony of the town hall, speaking without notes, youthful, with a grave face and straggly beard, using a tone that was an eloquent blend of counselor, father, and rebel, as the historian Hugh Thomas described it. For the first time, he was reaching a wide audience on live television. He promised a government by the people "and nobody else but the people." There will be "absolute freedom of the press and all individual rights in the country," he declared. The crowd roared its approval.

He then began a long, slow victory caravan toward Havana, snaking through the countryside and towns, accompanied by his bearded, bedraggled troops. He rode in an open jeep, followed by trucks, an armored personnel carrier, buses, more jeeps, and a Sherman tank. He made impassioned speeches everywhere. At Camagüey in central Cuba on January 5, he spoke for three hours until his voice grew hoarse, then he stood around for another two hours, making himself available to all who wanted to talk to him. He pointed to the journalists and vowed, "There will be no more censorship like that imposed by tyranny. Only a government with something to hide would censor news."

On the roads, people waited for hours for his caravan to arrive, then surged toward him. "Everyone wanted to see him, to hear him speak in person, to touch him, if possible, to shake his hand or kiss him," wrote biographer Robert Quirk. "Cubans of all classes acclaimed him as their country's liberator and savior."

Just two years before, Fidel had been hidden in the ravines and chasms of the Sierra Maestra. Now he was suddenly a superstar. The frenzy was like nothing he had ever known. He seemed to hardly sleep, his face creased with fatigue, speaking day and night as the caravan inched along.

He paused at Matanzas, about sixty miles outside of Havana. At 2:00 a.m. on January 8, inside the town hall, he gave an interview to television impresario Ed Sullivan for his Sunday variety show, seen by fifty million viewers in the United States. Fidel wore his US Army Ridgeway field cap and combat fatigues as his fighters jostled all around, a few rifle barrels sticking up in the rear. Sullivan asked Fidel about the long tradition of dictators in Latin America, known for enriching themselves, torture, and killing. "How do you propose to end that here in Cuba?" he asked.

Fleetingly, Fidel turned away from Sullivan, flashing a youthful face at the camera, then back.

"Very easy," he said in halting English. "Not permitting that any dictatorship come again to rule our country. You can be sure that Batista will be the last dictator of Cuba. Because now, now, we are going to improve our democratic institutions so that no one can"—a pause—"use the powers to bury our constitution and our law."

A few hours later, he entered Havana riding a tank. Crowds hoisted the red-and-black banners of the 26th of July Movement. Church bells pealed and factory whistles blew. Next to him on the tank were Huber Matos, who had smuggled the planeload of weapons to the rebel army, and Camilo Cienfuegos, a popular, ever-smiling rebel commander from the countryside. A live television broadcast captured Fidel's every move.

After years of violence and uncertainty, expectations soared that the *barbudos*, or bearded ones, would bring fundamental change. People saw them as honest, incorruptible, and youthful, almost reincarnations of the legendary heroes of the independence war against Spain, the *mambises*. Fidel wore a small medallion of Cuba's patron saint, La Virgen de la Caridad del Cobre, around his neck, visible at the open collar. Before the rebel army entered Havana, one of Fidel's men handed out rosaries to each fighter. Archbishop Enrique Pérez Serantes of Santiago, who once had helped save Fidel's life, praised him as an "exceptionally gifted man" with "tenacious commitment." Fidel made a symbolic stop at his old Jesuit school in Havana, Belén, kissing the flag.

In the evening, Fidel appeared at Camp Columbia, the military base where Batista had first declared the coup of 1952, and from where he had fled on New Year's Day. Castro again spoke without notes and made an adroit move. He knew that the revolutionary *directorio*, the student underground, was stockpiling weapons at the university. They were potential rivals for power. Facing the throng, Fidel demanded to know: Why stockpile guns? "*¿Armas, para qué?*" Fidel declared. "Arms, for what?" The huge crowd echoed, "*¿Armas, para qué?*" Just asking the question was enough. The *directorio* backed off. Fidel's words electrified the night air. As he began, several white doves fluttered about. One landed on his shoulder and stayed there, while two more alighted in front of him. The crowd was now mesmerized. Soldiers, some of whom had fought for Batista, removed their caps and stood at attention, hands over their hearts. Others fell to their knees in prayer.

"We cannot become dictators," Castro declared. "We shall never need to use force because we have the people, and because the people shall judge, and because the day the people want, I shall leave."

The next day, January 9, Gustavo Gutiérrez was tossing restlessly on a cot in the Argentine embassy in Havana. The Latin American embassies were swamped with requests for asylum from Batista's aides, ministers, and military officers, all fearing revenge amid talk of firing squads and plans by Castro's government to seize the property and bank accounts of the *Batistianos*. The embassies built sleeping bunks in their garages and constructed small shelters on the grounds until the asylum-seekers could fly out of the country under diplomatic protection.

Gustavo's family was ridden with anxiety and begged him to leave the country for his safety. At first he resisted, but then relented. On January 9, he wrote a letter to his third daughter, Yolanda. He was melancholy and defensive. "Good fortune has turned against us," he said, "but if it is for the good of the country, I accept it. What I don't accept is that the victors could teach us anything about honesty or anything of the sort. We have fallen victim to our loyalty and integrity. Lift your head high and defend yourself because we're innocent."

He sought asylum from Argentina. When it came time to depart on January 16, Gustavo's wife, María, came to the embassy. They agreed she would stay behind. Gustavo telephoned his four daughters one by one to say good-bye. He promised to return as soon as things settled down.

At the airport, he boarded the plane, but an angry mob was gathering, hoping to attack the plane and seize Eusebio Mujal, the Batista labor boss. In earlier times, he had been a member of the Constituent Assembly that wrote the 1940 constitution and an Auténtico. Mujal was a fickle character and a frequent target of Castro's 26th of July Movement.

Seated in the plane, Mujal was terrified. He feared he would be killed by the raging mob. Gustavo tried to calm him. He got up and spoke to the pilot, emphasizing the need to get going. Soon the plane was in the air.

Then came trouble: the pilot announced that the landing gear would not retract. They returned to the airport for repairs.

By then, the mob had reached the runway, thrusting pistols, rifles, bats, and sticks in the air, screaming for Mujal.

But one of Fidel's rebel army commanders, the charismatic Cienfuegos, who had provided a security escort to Gustavo and the others from the embassy to the plane, ordered his men to surround the aircraft, then jumped up on the wing.

A frightened passenger inside the plane panicked. "We're going to be killed!"

But Cienfuegos addressed the mob, not the passengers. "None of you take a step forward and no one is entering this plane."

The landing gear was hastily repaired and the plane took off.

Gustavo Gutiérrez, who had been among the idealistic reformers of the 1920s, who witnessed the raw underside of dictatorship with Machado and Batista, who drafted and redrafted the constitution of 1940, who had given Cubans the citizen initiative, and who had championed the idea of a democratic government, watched out the airplane window as the island slipped away.

He would never see Cuba again.

Fidel Castro was a committed nationalist, an anti-imperialist who resented the long economic shadow of the United States. He was a mesmerizing orator with a fierce rallying cry that Cuba—its independence, its dignity, its very essence—was a cause worth fighting and dying for. But what he most wanted was to bring about a far-reaching social revolution, to help the poor and the peasants and to address the stark inequalities in income, education, and health care between Cuba's relatively well-off cities and its haggard countryside. Castro was obsessed with eliminating the "underdevelopment" of Cuba, the shame of poverty, illiteracy, and disease.

At first Fidel called his ideology "humanist." He said "it differs from capitalism because it does not starve men," and is "different from communism" that "deprives men of their liberties." He added that "liberty with hunger is not liberty, we want liberty with bread." He soon began turning these words over at every opportunity: liberty with bread, bread without terror. He liked to say he was forging a third way that would shun the totalitarianisms of the twentieth century—fascism and communism—for democracy and freedom, in contrast to his single, oft-repeated epithet for Batista, la tiranía, the tyranny. But with all his speeches, manifestos, and promises, Fidel had never really said how any of this would work.

What would he actually do?

At the heart of democracy is competition: a contest of ideas, values, and proposals, and a method of accountability. Never perfect, the sturdy, underlying genius of democracy is the relentlessly spinning wheel of competition, freely held, dissent openly expressed, grounded in the bedrock principle that all those participating are committed to the outcome.

Fidel Castro abhorred this competition. He was self-centered in pursuit of power and could not share it. He was fearful of dependency on others. Perhaps it was his childhood, marked by deprivation, loneliness, and combativeness, or the later years as a guerrilla warrior and conspirator that made him so intensely self-reliant. In a guerrilla war, the commander needs discipline, confidence, and gut instinct. But when the war was over, Fidel did not change. Everything was intensely personal. He recoiled at criticism, perceived it as disloyalty, and disloyalty as treachery. He was impatient and unforgiving. He possessed none of the skills important in a democracy, such as the ability to accept defeat or compromise, to share power, or to follow rules set by others. It was not in his experience. His life had been spent fighting, in words and with bullets. His manifestos contained the words "liberty," "democracy," and "freedom," but he had never built anything like them. His leadership was thoroughly about himself, driven by his charisma.

Castro did not reach this point with a master plan. He would adapt as needed. He was a protean opportunist.

"What Fidel was thinking no one knew," recalled Carlos Franqui, who had run Fidel's rebel radio station in the mountains and became editor of the newspaper *Revolución*, the organ of the 26th of July Movement. Perhaps Fidel himself didn't know at the beginning what he wanted for the revolution beyond the rallying cries.

Soon his actions began to fill the void.

In January came the firing squads.

Batista's security forces had been cruel and merciless. More grisly evidence surfaced after he fled. The magazine *Bohemia* published three extraordinary "liberty" editions, one million copies each, all of which sold out. The magazine's success stemmed in part from its strong anti-Batista coverage in the recent past. Now, under publisher Miguel Ángel Quevedo, *Bohemia* printed shocking photographs of mutilated bodies and mass graves. Page after page of photographs fed a public furor. The magazine had kept a secret tally of an estimated ten killings a week in Havana alone in the Batista years, and published a grim timeline listing more than nine hundred victims, accompanied by thirty-five photographs of tortured men and one female survivor. *Bohemia* made an exaggerated claim that more than twenty thousand Cubans had lost their lives to Batista's forces. Fidel picked it up as fact, but later it was shown to be wildly inflated. The reality was probably two thousand to three thousand killed, no small toll.

Just as the photographs were published, Fidel set up revolutionary tribunals across the island to conduct trials of alleged Batista "war criminals." Many of those accused had committed atrocities, but the trials were carried out in a spirit of rage and revenge. Verdicts were delivered without a semblance of due process or appeal. One lawyer, who defended sixty-five cases in the tribunals, said he was usually allowed only five minutes before trial to look at the files; was often "venomously interrupted" by prosecutors; was "never allowed to bring defense witnesses"; and that there were "no real safeguards" for defense lawyers, who were berated for being "defeatist" and "counterrevolutionary." This lawyer recalled that hearings began at 10:30 a.m., then a lunch break was called, after which the lawyer returned to discover "the verdict had been passed and the appeal rejected." Those found guilty were executed by firing squad.

In early January in Santiago de Cuba, some seventy prisoners were lined up in front of a deep trench and mowed down by rebel forces with machine guns. On January 12, four military officers charged with torture and murder stood trial before a massive public gathering and were shot. The next day, reports said nineteen were tried and executed in Camagüey, eight at Manzanillo, and three at Colón.

Before long, criticism began to mount from abroad that Castro was presiding over a "bloodbath," as Oregon senator Wayne Morse, a Democrat, put it. Fidel was incensed by the criticism. On January 15, when he entered the Havana Hilton, the lobby was clogged with reporters and well-wishers. Asked whether there might be a US intervention, Fidel fumed. "If the Americans don't like what is happening in Cuba, they can land the Marines and then there will be two hundred thousand gringos dead," he said. The remarks made headlines around the world.

He did not stop there. On January 21 he staged another mass rally, in front of the presidential palace, before half a million people. Offices and factories were closed, flags flew throughout the city, and people carried banners such as "Cuban women demand execution of murderers." The rally cemented Fidel's grip on the popular rage. He declared, "All those who demand that gunmen be punished raise your hands." Hundreds of thousands of arms shot into the air, with a roar of approval. Andrew St. George took a photograph on the stage just as Fidel raised both of his own arms and turned to the rebel army officers behind him with a look of pleased astonishment.

"Gentlemen of the diplomatic corps, journalists of the entire continent," Fidel declared. "The jury of a million Cubans representing all views and social classes has voted."

Castro had unleashed a wave of passion that was only growing more intense. "Fidel's popularity bordered on madness," recalled Franqui. From the rallies, he drew his legitimacy—and mandate. If the jury of a million was with him in the plaza, he wanted nothing more. "To those who are democrats, to those who call themselves democrats," he declared, "I say that this is democracy!"

The next day, Fidel ordered a show trial in the Havana sports stadium for Jesús Sosa Blanco, a notorious Batista military commander accused of murders in Oriente Province in 1957 and 1958. In what he called "Operation Truth," Fidel invited foreign journalists to witness this exercise of revolutionary justice. Sosa Blanco was in handcuffs on a stage before seventeen thousand people, many shouting "bandit," "assassin," and "thug," and demanding "¡Paredón!" or "To the wall!"—the firing squad. The defendant carried himself with dignity, saying the televised proceedings resembled a Roman circus. He was convicted and later executed. Paul Bethel, the press attaché in the US embassy, wrote, "The one necessary ingredient, justice, was totally absent."

After the trial, other tribunals were no longer televised, but the gruesome executions went on. In Havana, Che Guevara served as judge and prosecutor at La Cabaña, a fortress across the bay from Havana where dozens were shot on a firing range. By May, about 550 Batista officers and soldiers had been executed.

In a sensational trial in Santiago, a tribunal met on February 13 to hear charges against forty-five members of the Batista air force accused of genocide, murder, and other crimes for some six hundred air attacks on populated areas in Oriente Province during the final month of the war. Before the trial, Fidel had called the pilots "the worst criminals of the Batista regime." After three weeks of testimony by some eighty witnesses, the court acquitted them, based on lack of evidence.

Fidel was incredulous. The next day he called the verdict "a big mistake" and the pilots "cowardly assassins." Fidel demanded a military "review court" reexamine the case, saying that revolutionary justice should not be based on legality but on the "moral conviction" of the people. The bar associations of Havana and Santiago, and the national association, all objected to the review court. It ignored the principle of double jeopardy and was without precedent in Cuban legal history. The rebel army commander Matos was in Havana that day with Fidel and recalled being stunned at Fidel's decision—it was absurd, arbitrary, and subverted the rule of law. But Matos also noticed that no one dared to question Fidel's judgment.

The review court found forty-three of the pilots guilty and sentenced them to prison terms of up to thirty years. Only two were acquitted.

Castro got what he wanted. He *was* the revolution.

In those early weeks of 1959, Manuel Urrutia Lleó was largely out of sight in Havana. The quiet judge from Santiago had ruled in 1957 that force was justified against the Batista regime. While still in the mountains, Fidel handpicked Urrutia as president of the revolutionary government. Taking office in Havana, Urrutia selected a cabinet of moderates, men with experience and skills, many drawn from the urban underground of the 26th of July Movement. At this point, Fidel needed competence; the rebel army could not provide the needed administrative leadership. Fidel reserved for himself the title of commander in chief and attended cabinet meetings rarely.

What happened in Urrutia's cabinet room was to destroy the pillars of the 1940 constitution that Fidel had pledged to preserve.

Those pillars were already damaged. Key legislation to implement the provisions of the constitution had never been passed. Batista's coup was another wrecking ball.

Fidel had promised repeatedly to restore the 1940 constitution. He had pledged to allow political parties, and to hold elections within eighteen months. But now, as key decisions were made, the voters, the elections—indeed, the whole democratic process—were nowhere in evidence. Urrutia simply announced that the revolutionary government was "interpreting the people's will and feelings" and thus taking upon itself all the powers necessary to write and enforce the laws.

Between January 5 and February 7, 1959, the constitution was gutted. It had prohibited the death penalty. The new government amended it so anyone associated with Batista could be executed, including retroactively for offenses committed in earlier times when the death penalty was banned, and the firing squad could be used for any "persons guilty of treason or subversion against the established order." This marked a dramatic change for Cuba. Revolution or counterrevolution had never been considered a crime punishable by death. Fidel himself had not faced the death penalty after the Moncada armed uprising.

The 1940 constitution proclaimed that property was sacrosanct and could not be seized by government, except by judicial authorities for a justified public reason. This was changed by the Urrutia cabinet so that property could be seized from anyone who had served under Batista. Later it was further revised to allow confiscation of property for Fidel's agricultural reform.

The 1940 constitution proclaimed that it was a crime to interfere with the participation of citizens in politics. That was changed so that participation was no longer guaranteed to anyone who had been associated with the "tyranny," meaning Batista.

The 1940 constitution guaranteed citizens the right of habeas corpus, meaning that they could not be detained and imprisoned without being brought before a judge or a court. The cabinet suspended habeas corpus for three months, and it was suspended again before the end of the year.

The bottom line was abolition of constitutional guarantees of personal freedom.

The 1940 constitution opened with a preamble that the framers were "invoking the favor of God." This was changed to "make possible the realization of the Revolution."

"God" was stricken from the text.

The democratic structure of the 1940 constitution was also gutted. It provided for a freely elected president and Congress, an independent judiciary, and separate branches of government, with checks and balances. The constitution declared that the president of the republic "shall be elected by universal, equal, direct, and secret suffrage, on a single day, for a period of four years." This provision was deleted. Instead, the new cabinet created a system in which the executive and legislative powers were *both* given to the Council of Ministers, appointed by the president. If the president was to resign, he or she would be replaced by decision of the Council of Ministers. It was an entirely closed loop that eliminated the voters.

There was a certain breathtaking cynicism to this. When Batista had arranged a similar structure after his coup in 1952, and claimed a revolutionary basis for law, Fidel ridiculed him as "monstrous, shameless, and brazen." Now Fidel was doing the same thing.

Other decrees abolished the old political parties, except for the Communists. Also abolished were elected city and regional governments, as provided for in the 1940 constitution. The Council of Ministers took over their functions. Another decree banned from political life all those candidates who had run in the elections of 1954 and 1958, under Batista.

All this was done in a feverish, revolutionary spirit. The Cuban people were never asked to approve the changes, nor did they demand to do so. The politics of the old Cuban republic were disparaged by the revolutionaries. "We finish with all the vices of the past, all the old political games," declared *Revolución*, the organ of Fidel's movement. Castro often vowed that he would not let *politiquería*, or political chicanery of the past, drag down the revolution.

Fidel had foreshadowed in "History Will Absolve Me" that he would do this. He had declared that "revolutions constitute a source of law" and that a revolutionary movement would approve its own laws. But he had solemnly vowed that the 1940 constitution would be restored as the "supreme" law of the land. In throwing out the "old political games," the revolution also threw out Fidel's promise to restore the constitution and thus destroyed the foundation of Cuba's experience with democracy, limited as it was.

On February 7, all the changes made by the cabinet were codified into a single document, published as the "Fundamental Law of 1959." This was a strange hybrid, containing the changes made by the cabinet, as well as other provisions copied verbatim from unchanged portions of the old constitution.

Untouched, and left in the law, was Gustavo's provision for a citizen initiative based on ten thousand signatures, with one difference. In the 1940 version, the citizens could propose laws and an elected Congress would consider them. Now Congress was eliminated. Any citizen petition would have to be submitted to the Council of Ministers, the revolution's unelected legislative and executive power.

Nine days later, Fidel became prime minister, having forced out José Miró Cardona, a lawyer and professor at the university. Everyone knew Fidel was the center of power so he might as well have the title, but his habits were maddening: meetings in the middle of the night, decrees piling up unsigned, no permanent office or home. He moved among his suite on the twenty-third floor of the Havana Hilton; the apartment of his loyal aide Celia Sánchez in Havana's Vedado district; the apartment of his former lover Naty Revuelta; a villa in Cojímar, a small fishing port twenty-six miles east of Havana; and a house near Tarará Beach where Che Guevara lived. Fidel sometimes conducted business sitting on a rumpled bed in his striped pajamas in the Hilton, or at midnight in a minister's apartment, or driving around the city. "His style has never really changed," recalled Franqui. "He never calls meetings to discuss what is to be done, or even to find out what is being done. He improvises and never shares power. At most he would spare us a few words as he walked down a crowded hall or as he sat in his jeep. Fidel kept moving, only communicating with us when he was surrounded by crowds." Teresa Casuso, who had been close to Fidel in Mexico and worked out of the Hilton as his press liaison, recalled that he was "incapable of managing himself," "lost in the labyrinth of power," and "pathetically unqualified to be a ruler." Once at the end of an interview, a television reporter asked Fidel how he felt after coming down from the Sierra, and he replied softly, with a faraway look, "I miss my mountains."

The *New York Times* journalist Herbert Matthews wrote to his wife from Havana in early 1959, "The whole trouble, to simplify it, is disorganization, amateurishness, and incompetence, and it all centers around Fidel and his character." Fidel, he added, was "too untrained, inexpert and impractical to grasp what has to be done and how to do it."

According to a biographer, Fidel "hated facing up to the responsibilities of running a country." But Fidel loved the crowds. His speeches were always impromptu and rambling. In March he addressed a fawning audience and mentioned his intention to break up the large plantations, which he warned would be met with opposition from the landowners. "They tell us a lot about the law," he declared. "Yes, but which law, the old one, or the new one?" He said the "old" laws were written by the vested interests, but he would respect the "new" laws of the revolution. "For the old law," Fidel declared, "nothing, no respect; for the new law, all respect!" The crowd cheered.

"Where does the constitution of the republic come from?" he asked. "Who makes the constitutions and who is the only one who has the power to change the constitutions?"

"The people!" they shouted back.

"Who has the right to modify the constitutions, the minority or the majority?" Fidel asked.

"The majority!" they shouted back.

"Who has the majority?" Fidel asked.

"The revolution!" they responded.

"The revolution!" Fidel affirmed.

Fidel told the crowd that constituent power—that precious license to make decisions for the people—was now held by the Council of Ministers. They were "representative of the immense majority of the people."

"Here governs a majority of the people, by the people and for the people!" Fidel boomed.

It was nothing of the sort. The Council of Ministers was not representative; no one had ever voted for them, nor voted to transfer constituent power to them. There was no competition, no elections, no accountability—just the power of Fidel.

Huber Matos believed in the revolution at the start. He was a middle-class schoolteacher with a small rice plantation near Manzanillo. Like Fidel, Matos joined the Ortodoxo Party. Later he was furious at Batista's 1952 coup. A small man with outsized determination, Matos brazenly smuggled the ammunition and guns to the rebel army. After victory, he was appointed by Fidel to be military commander of Camagüey, dominated by wealthy cattlemen and sugar growers. Matos was popular and a staunch anti-Communist.

In the early months after Fidel took power, Matos began to see disquieting signs that the revolution was not headed where he thought. The Communists were making their move for power.

Others heard similar footfalls. Not everyone understood what it meant at first.

By the late 1950s, the Cold War between the United States and the Soviet Union was a global contest of ideology, politics, culture, economics, and military might. In a policy of containment, the United States attempted to counter Soviet efforts to penetrate and subvert governments all over the world. It never escalated into direct combat between the superpowers but was fought in the shadows between war and peace. The singular focus on fighting communism during the Cold War led the United States to support some regimes that were undemocratic, ruled by dictators and generals.

The Soviet Union was a totalitarian state, officially atheist, with an

Orwellian thought police and all-powerful Communist Party. The toll of Joseph Stalin's great terror—the mass repressions of the late 1930s and beyond—became more evident after his death in 1953 and the return of many prisoners from the gulags. Despite Nikita Khrushchev's nascent thaw and revelation of some Stalin atrocities in his secret speech in 1956, the Communist Party of the Soviet Union was still monolithic, permitting no competition and no freethinking.

Cuba's Communist Party, the Partido Socialista Popular, or PSP, had flourished in its cooperation with Batista in the early 1940s. It was broadly popular in the labor movement, had elected representatives in both chambers of Congress, and its vote totals reached a peak in the 1948 elections. But the arrival of the Cold War bode ill for the party's influence in Cuba. By 1953, Batista made the Communists illegal, and the party was reduced to a hard core of disciplined members. Some leaders went into hiding, although they remained in Havana. Batista's efforts to suppress the Communists were perfunctory; few were ever arrested, and the party's propaganda mechanisms operated efficiently. The party received concealed inspiration and support from the Soviet Union.

In 1959, once Fidel arrived in Havana, the Communists sensed a new day. They "emerged from hiding," as a cable from the US embassy put it. They opened offices, and their newspaper, *Noticias de Hoy*, resumed printing. Other political parties and personalities from the Batista years were discredited and disappeared, but noticeably the Communists were allowed to operate in the open and the membership grew.

Miguel Ángel Quevedo, the publisher of *Bohemia*, who had a strong personal tie to Castro, heard the footfalls—and was aghast. "Against Communism," declared the large headline on an editorial in the first edition of the magazine in 1959. He called the Communist Party a "minority of minorities" in Cuba, yet warned that they were trying to infiltrate the revolution. He insisted there was no common ground between Cubans who just liberated the country from a despot, and the Soviet Union, which "crushed the liberties of a dozen European countries, machine-gunned the defenseless Hungarian people, and constitutes the greatest example of despotism in the world." Quevedo was sure that

Fidel, whom he ardently supported, would not let the Communists in the door. "Communism will have no justification nor be complicit with power here," he wrote. "The revolution that is inexorably advancing is Cuban and democratic in intention and heart. It has nothing to do with the enemies of freedom."

When Fidel went to the United States in April 1959, accepting an invitation from the American Society of Newspaper Editors to speak in Washington, DC, he repeated, "We are not Communists." He told the newspaper editors, "The first thing dictators do is to finish the free press and establish censorship. There is no doubt that the free press is the first enemy of dictatorship." On April 19, a Sunday, Castro met for three and a half hours, alone, with Vice President Richard Nixon in his formal office in the US Capitol. Fidel, speaking English, seemed nervous and tense. Nixon brought up the threat of communism, but Fidel brushed it aside. He said he had no fear the Communists would come to power in Cuba, that he could easily put them in their place. "He is either incredibly naïve about communism or under Communist discipline—my guess is the former," Nixon wrote after the meeting. "It was apparent," he wrote of Castro, "that while he paid lip service to such institutions as freedom of speech, press and religion, his primary concern was with developing programs for economic progress. He said over and over that a man who worked in the sugarcane fields for three months a year and starved the rest of the year wanted a job, something to eat, a house and some clothing and didn't care a whit about whether he had freedom along with it." After the meeting, Nixon urged President Eisenhower to begin preparations to overthrow Castro.

A few days later, in New York City, Fidel met in a hotel room with Gerry Droller, the CIA's top Latin America expert, whose conclusion was just the opposite: "Castro is not only not a Communist; he is a strong anti-Communist fighter." On June 30, a Special National Intelligence Estimate prepared by the CIA stated, "The Communists probably do not now control Castro, but they are in a position to exert influence in his regime, and to carry on further organizational work." Later in the year, the CIA's deputy director told Congress, "Our information shows that the Cuban Communists do not consider him a Communist Party member or even a pro-Communist. On the other hand, they are delighted with the nature of his government, which has allowed the Communists opportunity—free opportunity—to organize, to propagandize, and to infiltrate. We know the Communists consider Castro a representative of the bourgeoisie. Our conclusion, therefore, is that Fidel Castro is not a Communist, however, he certainly is not anti-Communist."

The US government was confused. President Eisenhower got a brief note about the Castro visit from Secretary of State Christian Herter. On communism, the note concluded that "Castro cautiously indicated that Cuba would remain in the western camp," but acknowledged Fidel was an "enigma."

At that point, Fidel was certainly not a Communist in the classic sense. He was too free-wheeling and impulsive to be restrained by a Soviet-style party with strict discipline. He had not espoused Marxist or Leninist ideology openly. He was primarily a nationalist and a social reformer.

But Fidel was also manipulative and nimble. Before he went to the United States he conferred secretly with Blas Roca, leader of the Partido Socialista Popular. Of course, Fidel didn't owe them anything. They had criticized the Moncada attack, refused to support the guerrilla war against Batista, and backed Fidel only at the very end, when it was clear he would prevail. But now Fidel needed the Communists to consolidate his power. His sprawling 26th of July Movement was a loosely formed conglomerate that included the urban underground and many anti-Communists who joined out of hatred for Batista. It was ill suited to become a pillar of Castro's rule. He needed organizers who could help him take control of youth, labor, and women's groups, and scores of local, neighborhood, and national associations. The remnants of the old political parties could not be much help either; they had "quietly disintegrated from lack of interest," as one study put it, and Fidel condemned them as discredited symbols of the past. The Cuban Communists were the answer. Fidel knew they would unhesitatingly salute him as the "maximum leader," shared his distrust of capitalism and imperialism, and remained well structured. The Partido Socialista Popular "had men who were truly revolutionary, loyal, honest, and trained. I needed them," Fidel said later.

Separately, Raúl Castro was closer to the Communists. He had met a Soviet KGB officer, Nikolai Leonov, in 1953 after attending a socialist youth conference in Europe. They became friends while sailing to North America when it was over. In April 1959, Raúl sent an emissary of the Cuban Communist Party to Moscow with a secret request for Soviet military advisers, which he got. Che Guevara was a Marxist but not a party man, although pro-Soviet. His anti-American views were deepened by the US overthrow of leftist president Jacobo Árbenz in Guatemala in 1954. In the early months of the revolution, Fidel was cautiously navigating through different power centers in Cuba. There was a fair amount of uncertainty. Would he follow the more pragmatic, moderate cabinet ministers working under Urrutia, or the more radical path of Raúl and Che? Did Fidel possess some hidden blueprint, or was he just making it up as he went along?

The full Council of Ministers met, but mostly to ratify decisions made elsewhere, especially by the powerful trio of Fidel, Raúl, and Che. As "maximum leader," Fidel could be deftly manipulative. For example, when he was developing his most far-reaching policy, the agrarian reform law, two plans were secretly drafted. One was the work of Humberto Sorí Marín, the minister of agriculture, which was relatively moderate and would have left intact many existing farms. Separately, at Che's beach house at Tarará, a more radical plan was drafted that would expropriate the largest landholdings and steer toward state ownership. Fidel was involved with both plans. The first plan was to buy time and calm the vested interests, according to Franqui, while Che's plan was much more to Fidel's liking, and the one he adopted.

Matos, the military leader of Camagüey, a province of plantations and ranches where resistance to the agrarian reform was strong, thought the law should have been subject to an open, democratic debate before it was adopted, but he observed, "We are not doing so." The proposal that came out of the beach house was announced by Fidel on May 17, and rubber-stamped by the Council of Ministers on June 2. It created the National Institute of Agrarian Reform, or INRA. This organization soon blossomed to become one of Fidel's major sources of unchecked power, a state within the state that oversaw highways, health, credit, education, and agriculture, with Fidel as its president.

At the same time, Fidel put Raúl in charge of military intelligence and a new security apparatus began to take shape, known broadly as the G-2. It would become both an internal force—a secret police—and carry out overseas intelligence activity. Raúl's cohort Ramiro Valdés was key in building the new service, as well as another veteran of the Sierra, Manuel Piñeiro, known as "Red Beard." Secret services had existed under Machado and Batista, too, and were responsible for some of the most egregious subterfuges and violent repressions of those turbulent times. Fidel, a conspirator much of his adult life, most certainly suspected that others were plotting against him, just as he had done; he needed spies inside and outside Cuba to detect and meet any existential threat to himself and the revolution.

Amid everything, Fidel dominated the show day by day. He was always the center of attention: savior, liberator, performer. Every third night or so he was on television, often speaking for several hours, continuing well past midnight, impromptu, relying on his prodigious memory, his eyes large and intense, his gestures captivatingly awkward, often engaging in what historian Jennifer Lambe called a "hypnotic dance of rhetorical jousting" with a panel of journalists. Fidel was the star of "blockbuster reality television," she concluded, and it captivated Cuba. The television age amplified Fidel like nothing that had gone before.

On live television July 17, Fidel turned against President Urrutia, who had been a leading voice of anti-communism. Fidel declared that such anti-communism was counterrevolutionary. By the time Castro finished speaking, several hours later, crowds had gathered demanding Urrutia quit. He submitted his resignation, and a new president was announced, a pliant and prosperous lawyer, Osvaldo Dorticós, who, as a member of the cabinet for revolutionary laws, had directly participated in the gutting of the 1940 constitution. Dorticós had once been a member of the Cuban Communist Party.

In the last week of July, hundreds of thousands of Cuban peasants flooded into Havana, mobilized by the 26th of July Movement, wearing khakis and *guayaberas*, and carrying their machetes in leather sheaths on their belts. They assembled in the Plaza Cívica to see and hear Fidel on the anniversary of the Moncada attack. Castro had shocked people earlier in the month by announcing his resignation as prime minister because he could not work with President Urrutia. When Fidel came to the microphone before the massive crowd, they cheered for ten minutes, machetes glinting in the air. Fidel promised he would return to office as prime minister because it was what the people wanted.

"This is democracy!" he declared. "Democracy is the fulfillment of the will of the peoples. Democracy is, as Lincoln said, the government of the people, by the people and for the people."

Fidel's popularity in these months was genuine. He had delivered important early economic benefits: slashing rents, drastically cutting telephone and electric rates, and negotiating pay raises in labor contracts. Health reforms, a literacy campaign, and unemployment relief would follow. In just a few months, hundreds of thousands of Cubans felt the impact of a significant redistribution of income. It was not sustained, but in the first year it was real.

A moody and unsettled Huber Matos came to see Fidel at the Hilton the day after the rally. Matos was unnerved by the expanding influence of the Communists. He realized that INRA was becoming a powerful superstructure, and in Camagüey it was run by the Communists. When he read *Verde Olivo*, a journal published by the military, it was filled with Marxist propaganda. He noticed Communist organizers moving into labor unions on the Camagüey docks. He found that some of his officers were being pressed to attend a military school for six-week political indoctrination courses with a Marxist tone. Matos confided his worries to Camilo Cienfuegos, chief of the general staff, who said he shared Matos's misgivings. "This isn't going where it's supposed to go," Camilo told him. But Cienfuegos was afraid to join Matos in protesting to Fidel.

Matos also shared his concerns with Pedro Díaz Lanz, a pilot and head of the air force, who had been to the military's political indoctrination courses and heard the Communist orientation firsthand. Díaz Lanz issued a press release from air force headquarters blasting communism, was personally called on the carpet by Fidel, then promptly defected to the United States, testifying before a US Senate subcommittee.

On June 8, Matos gave a speech in Camagüey to mark lawyers' day, saying that the revolution should not drift from its democratic principles. He didn't directly mention the Communists, but his remarks were a clear warning. The speech was then published in *Revolución*. Matos believed communism was toxic to democracy. He believed others shared this worry, but none of them could see clearly where Fidel was going: one day, he criticized the Communists; the next, he said their views should be respected. "Ambiguity reigned," Matos complained. When Matos approached Fidel directly, he was brushed off.

Matos decided that he had only one option left. He knew it might anger Fidel, but he sent in his resignation letter. Then he went to the Hilton to see Fidel, holding his breath. Surprisingly, Castro greeted him warmly and implored him not to quit. "We still have much to do."

"What you fear, that we're falling into the hands of Communists, you have to forget it," Castro told him, as Matos recalled the conversation. "You have to keep in mind that most of us aren't affiliated with the Marxists. There are a few Communists, which is inevitable in any revolutionary process, but I have it under control. With us, the Communists won't get very far." Fidel acknowledged that "Raúl and Che are flirting with Marxism and there are others out there" doing the same. "But that doesn't mean they are going to take control of the process," Fidel said. "I have everything under control."

Matos insisted that Communist influence was growing. But Fidel denied it. "We are neither to the left nor to the right," he said in a favorite slogan, but "against all totalitarianisms, because they curtail freedom, which is so dear to the people."

Castro was persuasive—for a while. Matos did not quit.

But Fidel reached a critical turning point in the late summer of 1959.

The exact moment is not known, but it is clear that he decided to take a more radical, strong-armed approach. He would pursue his revolution and yield none of his personal power.

From the summer onward, he never repeated the anti-communism that cropped up in his earlier speeches and private conversations. He stopped talking about "humanism," and he grew protective of the Communists. He said that anti-communism was "counterrevolutionary," and everyone knew what that meant: the enemy. Fidel was not openly embracing communism at this point, but he was giving its followers lots of room.

On October 1, a somewhat stooped Russian, with thick glasses and a big-boned body, arrived in Havana. Aleksander Alekseev's cover story was that he was a journalist from the Soviet news agency Tass. He was actually a KGB officer, experienced in Latin America, who in Moscow had been assigned a special mission to contact Fidel. For days he walked all over Havana, sitting in cafés and reading as many newspapers as he could. He attended Fidel's public speeches and listened carefully. It was a revolution like none he had seen elsewhere in the hemisphere, both anti-imperialist, with harsh criticism of the United States, but also anti-Communist. "I could not understand what kind of revolution this was, where it was going," he later recalled.

He found Che and asked him to arrange a meeting with Fidel. They met in the early morning hours of October 16 on the eighteenth floor of the INRA headquarters building, where the lights were still burning. Alekseev brought gifts: caviar, vodka, and an album of Russian music. Soon he and Fidel were talking about the first steps toward establishing relations between the Soviet Union and Cuba. A major Soviet trade exhibit was traveling the world. It was in Mexico City at that moment. Fidel asked the KGB officer if the trade show might make a detour to Havana. Alekseev said he would find out.

Later that day, Fidel abolished the existing Ministry of Defense and set up the new Revolutionary Armed Forces, installing Raúl as the head, giving him control over all the defense and intelligence services. Raúl's rise was a clear signal of Fidel's direction. The radicals were on the move.

The appointment of Raúl was too much for Matos. On October 19, he wrote a new resignation letter to Fidel. He wanted to leave quietly and go back to teaching. His letter was passive and reasonable but contained a subtle warning. "It is good to remember," he wrote to Fidel, "that great men begin to decline when they cease to be just."

Castro was enraged. He saw the resignation as disloyalty and ingratitude. One did not "leave" the revolution. In Fidel's mind, Matos was a defector. He dispatched Cienfuegos, chief of staff of the army, to arrest Matos in Camagüey.

Matos called together his military officers. "They have done me the injustice of calling me a traitor," he said. "All I wanted was to save the revolution."

Cienfuegos was an extremely popular figure, perhaps as well regarded by the public as Fidel. He wore a beard like the others, and a floppy cowboy hat. When he arrived at the barracks to make the arrest, Camagüey radio broadcasts had begun shrill declarations that Matos was a traitor. Camilo was pained by it all, and over coffee confided to Matos, "You know that we hold the same position on communism. I think Fidel is acting wrongly." Tense and disconcerted, Cienfuegos said he must arrest Matos.

His fury growing, Fidel flew to Camagüey. Thousands gathered to hear him speak. Fidel led them on a march to the Matos barracks, a mob scene that was televised. He took a microphone and accused Matos of being a "traitor" and an "ingrate," of leading a conspiracy to overthrow the revolution. Although the charges were patently absurd, Matos was taken into custody and brought to Havana, incarcerated at the military fortress in a small, dark punishment cell, three feet by ten feet, to await trial along with fifteen of his officers. In Camagüey Province, there was confusion. A sign was erected outside the high school saying, "We want this situation clarified—we do not want communism."

Later that day in Havana, the American Society of Travel Agents was meeting, a convention that Cuban officials hoped would spark a new surge of tourism. The Cuban Tourist Institute rolled out the red carpet at the big hotels, hoping to re-create the glamorous nightlife that had once appealed to US tourists.

Fidel flew back from Camagüey, and just as he alighted from a helicopter near the Havana seawall, a plane swooped low and released a cloud of leaflets. The plane, a dark gray twin-engine B-26, was piloted by Díaz Lanz, the former air force chief who had defected to the United States in July. The old plane had been found at a Florida airstrip. Díaz Lanz tossed out mimeographed leaflets, which he had signed, warning Cubans that Fidel was permitting the Communists to take over the revolution. Díaz Lanz repeated a claim, which he made previously, that he personally heard Fidel say he planned to deceive the Cuban people and introduce a Soviet-style system of communism.

Cuba's military scrambled planes and fired antiaircraft guns at the intruder, to no avail. Shooting and explosions echoed around the city that night. *Revolución* reported in large-type headlines that bombs had fallen. But there were no bombs. The Havana police chief blamed armed men in cars who sped through the crowded streets firing in every direction and tossing hand grenades. However, it seems likely that the Cuban antiaircraft fire was aimed low and inadvertently hit civilians on the ground. Two people were killed.

The shaken travel agents left for home, convinced that tourism to Cuba was a lost cause. Bookings plunged. Fidel went on television for four hours, saying that a "war criminal," Díaz Lanz, had "bombed innocent Cuban civilians." Castro delivered a vitriolic attack on the United States for allowing the plane to fly from Florida. He also attacked Matos, and claimed two independent Havana newspapers, *Diario de la Marina* and *Avance*, were part of the cabal, adding that he did not know how long "the people will permit these two newspapers to carry on a campaign against the government."

At Fidel's summons, the huge crowds—his "jury of a million"— returned to the streets. They assembled outside the baroque presidential palace on October 26. Some three hundred thousand people came, a vast sea of faces. Fidel's voice was hoarse; it seemed he had been talking for days on end, but his speech was one of his most combative ever. This was not the Fidel of humanism, doves, and democracy. He was now saying Cuba was under siege by enemies within and without. He wrapped the Matos case and the Díaz Lanz leaflets into the same threat. The bombing was like Pearl Harbor, he said; the Cuban people would fight to the last man in caves and underground tunnels if necessary to repel an invasion.

Fidel asked the crowd whether the revolutionary tribunals should be brought back. A sea of hands went up, and some shouted "To the wall!"

Then Fidel asked the mob: Should Matos be shot?

"Yes!" they shouted back. "To the wall!" The crowd echoed the chant again and again.

To the tension, one other factor was added: exiles based in Florida staged raids by flying small planes over Cuba, dropping flares to firebomb the sugarcane fields. On October 28, two days after Fidel's speech, an alert was declared in Camagüey that small airplanes were arriving to target the fields. A Cuban air force single-engine Sea Fury took off to intercept the intruders.

At precisely the same time, Camilo Cienfuegos prepared to fly to Havana, having finished his business in Camagüey. He was accompanied by an army sergeant and his pilot. They boarded a twin-engine Cessna 310 and took off.

Camilo's plane never arrived in Havana. It disappeared. Fidel jumped to lead the search, appearing everywhere on television and radio, examining maps, gazing at the sky, all to no avail.

The plane was probably shot down by the Sea Fury, mistaken for the firebombing intruders. It was never found.

What Matos had worried about privately—the influence of the Communists—was debated openly in Cuba. In May, Ruby Hart Phillips observed that Communist Party leaders had installed a modern printing plant for their newspaper, *Noticias de Hoy*, and "there seems no doubt from reading *Hoy* that the Communists are highly pleased with their progress under the Castro regime." Bethel, the US press attaché in Havana, recalled, "Communism was more than an important issue in Cuba by July of 1959; very little else was being talked about."

This alarmed the hierarchy of the Catholic Church. In the past they had been somewhat timid—and divided—when it came to politics. But the prospect of communism coming to Cuba, bringing with it atheism, galvanized the bishops. They were especially concerned about protecting Catholic religious education. They issued a call for a national conference, a public show of support. The response was stunning, far greater than they expected. On November 28 and 29 in Havana, despite cold and rain, nearly a million people crowded into Plaza Cívica, the scene of Fidel's great speeches. A US embassy official said it was larger than any audience assembled by Castro since his triumphal arrival in January. Fidel attended, along with his mother and sister, but he left early. A wooden image of La Virgen de la Caridad, Cuba's patron saint, was brought from El Cobre, a village near Santiago. Thousands of flaming torches lit up the night, reflected on rain-slicked pavements. Archbishop Pérez Serantes of Santiago celebrated a midnight Mass. On the surface, the event was about faith, but the undercurrent was about communism. Without confronting Fidel directly, the Church sought to show that it was steering the moral and ethical values of Cuba, leaving no room for a totalitarian ideology. Then, in the closing speeches on November 29, José Ignacio Lasaga, a leader of the Catholic youth movement, declared openly, "We want the whole of Cuba to hear very clearly today, and to know forever, that the Church everywhere is opposed to Communist and Marxist doctrines and, in general, to all those that advocate the subordination of man to the state . . .

"Totalitarian State, No!" he said. "Social Justice, Yes!"

The crowd broke into a prolonged cheer that lasted several minutes. The echoes would be heard far longer.

Right after the event, Fidel, somewhat stunned, met the KGB man, Alekseev, once again. "It's all bad," Castro said. He got cold feet about bringing the Soviet trade exhibit to Havana so soon. He needed to buy time. Please tell the Soviet officials to wait, he said. They agreed.

On December 11, Matos went on trial, accused of treason, to be judged by a military court handpicked by Fidel, who also selected the prosecution witnesses. Matos was not permitted to call any defense witnesses. He was calm and coherent, insisting he was neither a traitor nor a deserter. Raúl, however, called Matos a traitor and declared Matos would "die on his knees."

"We are not Communists," Raúl told the court. "I have said it a thousand times, if we were, we should say so. If we were, we would step forward and proclaim it, because we have fought for freedom of expression. But let me say it one last time, I am not a Communist."

On the last day of the trial, Fidel spoke for nearly seven hours. For the most part he went over the history of the revolution. He offered no evidence of any crime by Matos. But he said Matos had wounded the revolution by resigning. He was interrupted by shouts of "To the wall!" from the audience. Fidel finished at 2:00 a.m.

The prosecutor asked for the death penalty.

Matos was permitted a final statement. It was 5:35 a.m.

He said he would face the verdict, even death, without regret, because he acted to uphold his personal honor.

"A revolution such as ours cannot condemn anyone for his thoughts," he declared. "To do so would represent a denial of the same revolution. Martí has told us that the first duty of each man is to think for himself, and I have exercised that right in the ranks of the revolution. No one told me when we were in the Sierra Maestra that after we had triumphed we should have to keep silent or to say yes to everyone. You can take away a major's stars, but you can never remove the star of freedom that, as a soldier, I have carried in my breast."

Matos was found guilty. His only offense was that he angered Fidel by opposing the inroads of Communists into the revolution. He was sentenced to twenty years in prison. Fidel decided against the firing squad, which might turn Matos into a martyr. The official photograph of Fidel and the victorious rebels riding the tank into Havana in January was retouched.

The image of Huber Matos was airbrushed out.

SEVEN

THE SILENCING

At the dawn of 1960 in Cuba, boots and high heels pounded and clacked on military parade grounds. Tens of thousands of students, office workers, and peasants were organized, trained, and armed into new civilian militias. Ruby Hart Phillips witnessed patrols of youths marching under the supervision of military officers through Havana; teenagers were drilled in parks, joined by bank employees, commercial and industrial workers, bus drivers and conductors. Andrew St. George photographed a group of young girls, in white socks and skirts, marching on a Havana street as nearby army officers shouted orders. About thirty-five thousand Cubans had joined the civilian militias, and the number was growing. Some did it to identify with the barbudos and the revolution, but many others just sought to show loyalty and thus stay out of trouble.

At the same time, with Fidel's help, the Communists muscled their way into the leadership of Cuba's labor federation. They forced out elected chiefs in tobacco, hardware, construction, maritime, metals, agriculture, and electrical unions as well as those representing musicians, artists, and actors. A key tactic of internal control in the purges were strongarm militias, inserted in labor unions to keep workers in line. The government suspended the right to strike, postponed wage increases indefinitely, and took control of all hiring; other labor matters that had been subject to collective bargaining were assigned to the Ministry of Labor.

The old Cuba, capitalist and Western, was being dismantled. The Communists captured the professional associations, or *colegios*, of lawyers, doctors, pharmacists, and public accountants. These groups were a robust part of Cuba's independent civil society. They were being brought to heel by the revolution. The method usually was to air a vague accusation against the board of an association, then demand a new "revolutionary board," followed by purges of independent members. Sixty members of the Havana lawyers' association were thrown out. The medical society board was taken over; all other political forces in the medical profession were purged for the "sake of unity." Of course, "unity" meant no competition, no dissent, no independent thinking. The purges struck associations of journalists, radio announcers, theater artists, and engineers as well as benefit societies. The Communists had so thoroughly moved into public life that Phillips observed "now it is difficult to distinguish between devoted Castro followers and Communists."

Next, the Communists targeted the University of Havana, which had long guarded its autonomy. They used the same tactics: subverting the board of governors and appointing a new one. The historian Hugh Thomas says the university was easy prey because it had become so "rotten with politics and gang warfare." A strongly anti-Communist student leader, Pedro Luis Boitel, charismatic and promising, was edged out of an election to the University Students Federation (FEU) by Fidel, who directly intervened for another candidate. Boitel was subsequently arrested as a counterrevolutionary and died in prison. Visiting Havana at this time, photojournalist Andrew St. George observed, "A year and a half after Castro took power, Havana is a hive of Communist and Communist-front activity."

Then they punched out society's eyes and ears.

•   •   •

The newspaper *Información* was a staid, gray broadsheet. The editors purposefully kept their opinions off the front page—it was always full of news. The newspaper's presses usually began rolling at about 4:00 a.m.

The edition for Saturday, January 16, 1960, was almost ready. Then Ángel Fernández Varela, the editor, heard a commotion outside his office. The door burst open and five men strode in. They were tough militia members from the union of typesetters and printers who said they represented "the workers" of the paper. Their leader was pro-Communist. He waved two wire service stories in front of the editor. "You can't publish these!" he shouted. The two stories, by the Associated Press and United Press International, carried critical comments by members of the US Congress, expressing concern about Communist infiltration in Cuba. The stories were to be printed in the next day's paper.

"Who says I can't publish them?" Fernández Varela demanded.

"We do!" they replied, saying the material was an insult to Fidel and the revolution.

The editor reminded them that Fidel had promised censorship would never again be imposed on Cuba.

This was not censorship, the printers replied—they were patriots standing up for the country.

Soon, reporters gathered at the door, the arguments became heated, and the crowd swelled with typists, office clerks, and copy boys.

The printers insisted that they would insert a disclaimer, called a *coletilla* or postscript, under the two articles. It would say the articles were false.

Fernández Varela grew furious and demanded that the disclaimers not be printed. The printers refused to budge. The presses rolled. *Información* had the widest news coverage of the Havana papers. The front page that day contained articles about dangerous winter weather in Europe, a boundary dispute between China and India, the Fifth National Congress of Ophthalmology meeting in Havana, and a strange floating object discovered in the ocean near the Isle of Pines, off Cuba's southern coast. But the most explosive items in the paper were on page four. The two coletillas were almost unnoticeable amid the dense type. They said the paper's workers respected freedom of the press but they too had a right to speak, and wanted to state that the article above the coletilla "does not conform to the truth nor to the most elementary journalistic ethics."

The coletillas were a wedge of subterfuge, a provocation against the newspaper's management.

Conceived by a small group of Communists, they marked the beginning of the end of the independent press in Cuba. The next day, the management of the newspaper denounced the coletillas in an unusual front-page editorial. They said the disclaimers were published against their will, and through "procedures involving violence, coercion," a "serious attack on freedom of the press, perhaps as serious or more so than censorship."

At the end of the editorial, a coletilla.

In earlier years, the press in Cuba had not been pure, but it did enjoy a measure of freedom and was vital to democracy, even a nascent one. In Batista's dictatorship, newspapers eagerly accepted subsidies from the regime; of fifty-six papers, only five or six survived on their own revenues. The subsidies—clandestine, and intended to curry favor—amounted to $217,300 a month to various papers and $22,000 monthly to some individual journalists. In addition to the money, Batista wielded direct censorship, especially after 1954, with written rules about what was to be omitted from reports, including guerrilla activity, public opposition to the regime, and brutal repression of the opposition. Batista's censorship was punitive and used selectively, ignoring everything else.

On coming to power, the revolution eliminated the subsidies, which Fidel called "bloody money from tyranny." Fidel wanted cooperation, not on some things, but *everything*. He wanted newspapers, radio, and television to serve as megaphones for the revolution. At a ceremony for journalists, Dorticós, the president, said that "every Cuban journalist" must be "a rank and file soldier in this great struggle to diffuse our great revolutionary truth to the world."

When Castro entered Havana in January 1959, there were seventeen privately operated newspapers in Cuba. In 1960, they began to fall like dominoes.

The day after the coletillas were imposed on *Información*, the independent afternoon newspaper *Avance* fell.

The editor, Jorge Zayas, thirty-two years old, who had studied at Columbia University, was furious at the suffocating atmosphere in Fidel's first year in power. Zayas was an anti-Communist Catholic and, as he put it, an editor who "cannot conceive of true democracy without freedom of the press." By his own telling, he helped Fidel's rise to power, sending journalists to report on Castro's rebel camps, and working closely with the 26th of July Movement. When Castro prevailed, Zayas called it "a glorious day for Cuba." He took over as editor of *Avance* from his mother on the day Castro entered Havana. But his views changed as he saw the Communists march in. In December 1959, speakers at a labor convention urged that *Avance* be confiscated and the editors shot. Fidel was there and did not protest, calling *Avance* a "counter-revolutionary" newspaper. That was a death knell. Zayas sent his family out of the country, and he secreted away his possessions, including a cherished library. Then, after the *Información* debacle in January, Zayas took on the coletillas personally. He published an editorial denouncing them in *Avance* on January 18.

The next day, the newspaper was seized by the union militia—which meant the end of its independence—and Zayas fled to Miami. Soon *Avance* was put in the hands of the government. In mid-March two more newspapers, *El País* and *Excelsior*, were closed and converted to national printing offices.

By April there were only four remaining independent newspapers, including *Información*.

Among the four, *Diario de la Marina* was an institution, a conservative, Catholic, probusiness daily founded in 1827. According to Hugh Thomas, in January 1960 "the old papers of Cuba were at full blast in denunciation of the revolution, led by *Diario de la Marina*." The newspaper published a column titled "The Words of Fidel," which printed

Castro's promises verbatim—such as elections, a free press—and asked: What happened? The editors of *Diario* saw their circulation triple in four months, but they sensed danger. Worker militias around the country were staging events in public squares, burning newspapers, and they usually burned bundles of *Diario*.

Diario de la Marina had been struggling with the coletillas just as the other papers. But in May, 318 of the newspaper's 450 workers drafted a statement in *support* of the paper's management. Their letter was scheduled to be published May 10. Late the night before, a group of armed thugs entered the plant and held employees at gunpoint, smashing the printing plates containing the letter, and began ransacking the newspaper. Before dawn, *Diario* was fully occupied by two union militias leading the campaign to bring the Cuban press completely under Fidel's control. The last edition came out on May 12. The Rivero family, which owned it, fled the country. Fidel's supporters gleefully celebrated the demise of the daily with a symbolic funeral procession from the university to the Malecón, where a group of students, serving as pallbearers, dumped the "corpse" of *Diario de la Marina* into the sea. "The people will not cry," said Fidel.

The day after *Diario*'s demise, the largest-circulation newspaper in Cuba, the progressive *Prensa Libre*, printed a somber, uncompromising page-one essay by the columnist Luis Aguilar, warning that Cuba was entering a dark period. He said,

> There will be no disagreeing voices, no possibility of criticism, no public refutations. Control of all the means of expression will facilitate the work of persuasion, collective fear will take charge of the rest. And underneath the sound of the vociferous propaganda, there will remain . . . the silence. The silence of those who cannot speak. The implicated silence of those who, being able to speak, did not venture to do so.

On May 16, the management of *Prensa Libre* was forced out of the building. Within months, *Revolución* moved into the modern printing plant and turned its own printing plant over to *Hoy*. In June, *El Crisol*, a paper mostly composed of crime and sports news, closed. *Información* died by the end of the year.

Fidel had silenced all the major independent newspapers in months without firing a shot.

Television also fell at his feet. A major collision came with Castro's old friend Luis Conte Agüero, who had become a commentator and author.

Years before, Conte Agüero had been a close associate of Eddy Chibás, and was with him on that fateful Sunday, hours before shooting himself at the studio. Later, Conte Agüero became an official of the Ortodoxos, and for nine years had been close to Fidel. Castro had written him admiring letters from prison, praising his "intelligence," "valor," and "integrity," and Luis had campaigned for Fidel's amnesty in 1955.

Conte Agüero was a staunch anti-Communist and Catholic. His hopes for a free and democratic Cuba were shattered after Fidel's first year in power. He had written a biography of Fidel that Castro didn't like, and within hours of receiving a courtesy copy, Fidel ordered the entire publication confiscated from the presses.

In the spring of 1960, Conte Agüero began a series of anti-Communist broadsides on radio and television. Letters flooded into the studios of Radio Progreso, and to CMQ Television, where he was the host of *Conte Agüero Speaks*. He framed the conflict in stark terms, warning that democracy was at stake.

Fidel fired back one night, saying his old friend was "playing the game of the enemies of the revolution."

On March 24, Conte Agüero read an open letter to Fidel over the radio, declaring that the Communists were stealing the revolution. He then walked out of the studio toward the television center of CMQ, where he planned to read his appeal again on his regularly scheduled program. But outside the building were squads of Communist toughs and members of the rebel army in plainclothes, carrying brass knuckles and clubs. Conte Agüero fled. The CMQ television operation, owned by brothers Abel and Goar Mestre, was Havana's most important outlet.

The day after the debacle on the street, Abel Mestre went into a studio just before the popular show *Ante La Prensa*, on which Fidel had often appeared. He locked the door, and then announced on the air that he and his brother were giving up. They both went into exile, and the station soon fell under control of the government. All television and radio were then merged by decree into a state network.

Elections are the gears of democracy, the moment when ideas and candidates are finally chosen after all the sound and fury. Fidel had promised the revolutionary government would take power only temporarily, then hold elections—in one year, or eighteen months, or two years; it varied. But in fact, Fidel did not like the idea of elections. He may have remembered his father, Ángel, distributing cash to buy votes in Oriente Province, or recalled the sham elections of the Machado and Batista dictatorships, or the toxic mix of money and politics that had so outraged Eddy Chibás. Viscerally, Fidel did not want to compete for power. He was convinced of his own destiny and determined to never give up.

For the first time, at the May Day 1960 rally in Havana, he publicly acknowledged that he didn't want to hold elections. The rally drew a quarter of a million people to Plaza Cívica after a massive parade that included military units as well as the rapidly expanding unarmed civilian militias. The march featured Cubans in uniform, from six-year-old boys with toy shotguns to white-gloved infantrymen with automatic rifles. Speaking for three and a half hours, Fidel insisted that he had brought "real democracy" to Cuba, "unobjectionable democracy," "sincere and honest democracy," which was evident in the approval of the masses spread out before him. "Real democracy," he insisted, was "the Cuban revolution," giving land to the peasants, a degree to college students, a house for every family, a doctor for every sick person.

He said nothing about a ballot for every voter, and his tone became scornful when he brought up elections. "Why is it considered that the only democratic governments are those elected by votes?" he demanded. "A revolutionary government is brought to power not by a pencil but the blood of the people."

Elections, he said, had brought only fraud in the past. "We have thus exercised that direct democracy with greater purity, a thousand times greater purity, than that false democracy which uses every means of corruption and fraud to falsify the true will of the people.

"Our enemies, our detractors, ask about elections—" he began to say.

The crowd cut him short. "Revolution! Revolution!" they shouted. "*¿Elecciones para qué?*" or "Elections for what?"

"We already voted for Fidel!"

Then and there, Fidel tossed out all his earlier promises to hold elections. In the Sierra Maestra manifesto, just two years before, Fidel had written, "We want elections, but with one condition: truly free, democratic, and impartial elections."

Now he proclaimed "direct democracy." It was nothing more than frenzied mass rallies, with him as maestro and messiah. A real democracy would demand a free and fair mechanism for voters to choose their leaders, to hold those leaders to account, nourished by competition. Fidel's "direct democracy" contained none. Most importantly, it lacked any channel for a "no" vote—it was all "yes," a show of hands. He could never lose. All "no" sentiment was dismissed and stigmatized as "counterrevolutionary," illegal, and banished.

When the photographer Andrew St. George returned to Havana in the spring of 1960, he was "alarmed and appalled by what is happening to Cuba." He recalled Fidel's own article for *Coronet*, written two years earlier, which contained a straightforward pledge to create democracy. St. George said the article was now reappearing in the Cuban press "as a reminder of Castro campaign promises that have gone unfulfilled and ignored." The article, he said, was "a haunting image of the early high principles of a revolution that is unmistakably going wrong."

Fidel had eviscerated the 1940 constitution, abandoned the promise of elections, and destroyed the free press. But through all this, the Cuban people still did not rise in protest. Many were enraptured by Fidel, welcomed the revolution, and willfully gave up their rights. For those who were against, the avenues for protest were closing. Fidel had already built an effective secret police, the G-2, and they were hunting down "counterrevolutionaries." A mood of fear prevailed. A lawyer who studied in the United States and had once been a fervent Castro partisan told St. George, "Make no mistake, this is a dictatorship. We have terror in Cuba. It's *not* violent terror, *not* gunfire in the streets. It's in the decrees and statutes that could send a man to prison and to a secret firing wall for opposing the Government in any way at all."

No one could stop Fidel. "We're riding a train without brakes," a prominent journalist told St. George, discussing the growing hostility with the United States. Only two years earlier, the US had provided Cuba with $543 million of its $777 million imports, and Cuba sent $491 million of its $733 million in exports to the United States. Now Fidel launched a "furious political and economic war" against the northern neighbor, as St. George put it. The United States escalated tensions in return. Castro embraced the Soviet Union, which he had hesitated to do a few months earlier. On February 4, 1960, deputy Soviet premier Anastas Mikoyan arrived in Havana to open the delayed trade exhibition, laying a crown of roses with the Soviet flag in front of the statue of José Martí. Moscow agreed to buy a million tons a year of Cuban sugar for the next four years and provide a $100 million credit.

On March 4, the French freighter *La Coubre*, bearing eighty-nine tons of small arms and explosives purchased in Belgium, exploded in Havana Harbor, killing about a hundred people and injuring many others. Fidel blamed the United States, which denied responsibility. (The origins of the explosion were never determined.)

In late 1959, President Eisenhower had backed the financing and development of an anti-Castro opposition. In March, two weeks after the explosion, Eisenhower signed a secret recommendation by the Central Intelligence Agency to begin a covert action, training Cuban exiles for guerrilla warfare on the island. In April, Soviet oil began arriving on the island, and on May 2, Cuba recognized the Soviet Union. As Cuba's annual sugar harvest ended, the government began to nationalize the huge plantations, taking over 2.7 million acres, including those belonging to United Fruit and other US-owned companies. When Texaco, Shell, and

Standard Oil refineries refused to accept Russian oil that summer—at
the behest of the US State Department—they were taken over by the
Cuban government. In retaliation, Eisenhower cut the US 1960 sugar
quota by seven hundred thousand tons. Three days later, Soviet leader
Nikita Khrushchev vowed "the Soviet military can support the Cuban
people with rocket weapons." Khrushchev then committed to buy the
sugar the United States had left on the docks. In August, Fidel began a
wave of expropriation of American-owned businesses on the island.

Eisenhower announced a complete ban on exports to Cuba on October 13, except for some medicine and food, a trade embargo that would
remain in place for decades.

In response, Cuba took over 382 large private enterprises, including all the banks, and nationalized another 166 US enterprises, including Woolworth's; Sears, Roebuck; General Electric; Westinghouse; and
Coca-Cola, as well as hotels and insurance companies. The takeovers
were carried out by INRA, the state-within-a-state. But it was at the direction of Castro alone. Andrés Suárez, who was undersecretary of treasury in the government at the time, recalled that the nationalizations
highlighted how Fidel operated as a classic strongman. They "were not
preceded or followed by any meetings, demonstrations, or other public
expressions of the popular will," he said. "The Prime Minister simply
dictated an order."

Quevedo, the publisher of *Bohemia* who had done so much to pave
the way for Fidel's rise to power and who had bluntly warned about the
coming of the Communists, wrote, "The deceit has been discovered.
This is not the Revolution for which over 20,000 Cubans died. In order to
carry out a purely national Revolution there was no need to submit our
people to the hateful Russian vassalage. To carry out a profound social
revolution, it was not necessary to install a system which degrades man
to the condition of the state. . . . This is a revolution betrayed."

He went into exile.

Even as independent civil society in Cuba was collapsing in 1961, one
man stood fast. Enrique Pérez Serantes, the archbishop of Santiago

de Cuba, seventy-seven years old, a burly man with thick-rimmed eye-glasses and bushy brows, could not be pushed around, not by Castro and certainly not by the Communists.

He had personal ties to Fidel. Born the son of farmers in Galicia, Spain, Pérez Serantes was ordained a priest in Cuba in 1910, when the republic was still young. He became bishop of Camagüey in 1922, then archbishop of Santiago in 1949. He knew the wealthy landowners of eastern Cuba, including Fidel's father, Ángel. During the war with Batista, Pérez Serantes sent chaplains to join Fidel's rebel army; one of them, Father Guillermo Sardiñas Menéndez, became a *comandante* in the rebel army, with a backpack and an olive-green cassock. When Fidel appeared in Santiago de Cuba on the night of January 1, 1959, Pérez Serantes joined him on the town hall balcony; the archbishop declared that the Church and the revolution were allies. The cathedral doors on the square were thrown open so all could see the altar honoring the venerated Virgen de la Caridad.

Although the Church hierarchy had been divided over Batista, many priests and members of the laity enthusiastically backed Fidel's rebel army. His concern for the poor fit well with Catholic social doctrine. On his victory caravan to Havana, Fidel suggested he would allow religious education in public schools, a goal the Church had been seeking, without success, since the writing of the 1940 constitution. When he went to Washington, DC, that spring, Fidel confidently told senators that the "Catholic Church supports the revolution, as do 90 percent of the people." In March 1959, a group of eight Havana priests published an open letter in *Diario de la Marina* celebrating the shared values of the revolution and the Church: the dignity of all human beings, respect for life, the integrity and liberty of the individual, and a commitment to social justice.

But now, a year and a half later, those values were no longer shared. Fidel was a champion of the poor but not of freedom. Pérez Serantes was jolted by the growing presence of the Communists.

The Catholic Church in Latin America had tended to be allied with conservative elites, including wealthy landowners and the military, supporting undemocratic and authoritarian regimes. In Cuba, it never had the power or moral authority as it did elsewhere in Latin America. The Cuban Church remained closely tied to Spain. In the summer of 1960, four of the six bishops in Cuba were Spanish by origin, as were the majority of the clergy and those in religious orders. Franco still ruled Spain, and questions about loyalty of Spanish clerics to the dictator lingered in the background. Only a fraction of the Catholic population in Cuba was regularly observant. The Church concentrated its resources more on the white, middle, and wealthy upper classes than with the poor and Black Cubans, at least until World War II, after which a few schools for the poor began to appear. The Church was chronically short of priests, especially in impoverished rural parishes.

The population was also influenced by *santería*, a fusion of primarily the African Yoruba religion with Catholic elements that grew out of the slave trade in Cuba.

Still, the Church was resilient, the largest nongovernmental organization in the country, running the best private schools and many hospitals and charities. When the hierarchy wanted to act, it could mobilize people, not only from the pulpits but also with pastoral letters, widely heard and read. In many parish churches, simple mimeograph and printing machines could churn out leaflets and small publications. A sign of the Church's influence was the million people it turned out for the national conference in Havana. The only other person in Cuba who could do that was Fidel, and he noticed.

For Pérez Serantes and the Catholic hierarchy, the confiscation of *Diario de la Marina* in May 1960 was an enormous blow. The newspaper had been a semiofficial Church organ. Pérez Serantes was quoted in it as far back as 1914, when he publicly defended the right of workers to strike. Now he decided to act: to confront the revolution, to oppose Fidel on the rise of communism, and to do so directly, in pastoral letters.

Filled with indignation, Pérez Serantes composed the first letter, "For God and for Cuba," to be read on Sunday, May 22, but it leaked early in the two remaining independent newspapers, *Información* and *El Crisol.*

"We cannot say that our enemy is knocking at the doors," he wrote, "because he is already inside, speaking loudly and acting as though in his own kingdom."

"It is well known today that the great enemy of Christianity is Communism, always vigilant, always alert, always ready to take advantage of every situation . . ." Communism "is everywhere," he warned, and Catholics must have "nothing, absolutely nothing" to do with it. The revolution had expelled God, and "We want God in everything, everywhere and at all times . . . because without God, chaos!"

This passion was shared by a younger priest, Eduardo Boza Masvidal, forty-four years old, rector of the private Santo Tomás de Villanueva University, established by American and European Augustinians on the outskirts of Havana. A slight, soft-spoken man, he had already written articles in the progressive Catholic magazine *La Quincena* expressing an uncompromising and militant anti-communism. Boza Masvidal had been appointed auxiliary bishop of Havana in early 1960 and was fast becoming a voice of the streets. The year before, he signed the open letter in *Diario* celebrating the shared values between the Church and the revolution, but, like Pérez Serantes, he no longer believed it. In a speech at the university at the close of the semester on June 2, Boza Masvidal said, "The state has no right to control all means of expression, to impose thought control, foment class warfare or usurp private properties." A police state is not acceptable to Christian theology, he added.

The G-2 secret police had already detained hundreds of people for being counterrevolutionary, and the pace was quickening. So was opposition. Several groups, consisting in part of militant and dissident Catholics, organized an underground, armed resistance to the regime. One of them, the Movement for Revolutionary Rescue, amassed weapons in clandestine cells and carried out a campaign of sabotage and bombings in Havana in the winter of 1960–61 while its leader, Manuel Artime, was working with the CIA. Separately, two groups of armed rebels were still resisting Castro's regime in the Escambray Mountains.

Another opposition movement—more political—was established in November 1959, by José Ignacio Rasco, a Villanueva professor who had been a classmate of Fidel's at the Jesuit school Belén and earned a law doctorate at the University of Havana. Rasco joined the anti-Batista urban underground in the late 1950s and also became an executive and columnist for the newspaper *Información*. Rasco and his old classmate Fidel were on good terms at first. But Rasco sensed that Fidel was taking Cuba toward Marxism. Rasco in late 1959 formed a new organization, the Christian Democratic Movement. It began to attract students and young professionals with an intelligent critique of the revolution: strongly anti-Communist, demanding the immediate restoration of the 1940 constitution and the holding of elections. Rasco said if he had to choose between Lincoln and Lenin, he would take "the world where liberty does not perish."

When the movement was announced, Fidel called Rasco. "We are in a moment of revolution," Fidel said, "and we can't allow any kind of conflict." Fidel demanded that Rasco obey unconditionally. Rasco refused. The G-2 went on a manhunt for him. Rasco hid in Havana and then fled to Miami, where he joined US efforts to overthrow Castro.

All told, there were perhaps several dozen opposition groups, but their leaders were individualistic, proud, stubborn, and hopelessly divided. Daniel Braddock, chargé d'affaires in the US embassy, told the State Department in a cable that the opposition was "defeating its own purpose" by "division, confusion and weakness." In August 1960, after much internal hand-wringing and debate, the whole Catholic leadership spoke with one voice in a joint pastoral letter warning of "the increasing advance of communism." Tensions were running so high that Pérez Serantes was cautioned about threats to his life and decided not to personally read aloud the pastoral letter in Santiago. "We condemn communism," the bishops declared in the letter, describing it as a system that denied people their individual rights and imposed dictatorship "by means of police terror."

"Catholicism and communism respond to two concepts of man and the world that are totally opposed to each other and can never be reconciled," they wrote. "The Church is today and will always be in favor of the humble," they added. "But it is not now and never will be with communism." Their letter reflects the intensity of the Cold War confrontation, written just seven years after Stalin's death and at a time when the truth of his Great Terror was slowly coming to light.

Then on September 24, Pérez Serantes wrote a biting pastoral letter, "Neither Traitors nor Pariahs." He recalled that in Oriente Province, "all the people were mobilized" for the revolution against Batista. "For the revolution, for Fidel, its beloved leader, everything was given: money, clothes, prayers, sacrifices and all the men who were needed, who, with the greatest disinterest, with great fervor, like someone going on a Crusade, climbed the Sierra leaving everything, without looking back." These loyal followers of Fidel were betrayed, he declared. "While fighting for the Revolution, our people never thought, never did the Cuban people think, that the iron hand of communism would hang threateningly over our heads; nor that it would be the few devotees of Marx and Lenin who would try to snatch away the well-earned laurels of victory." He asked, pointedly: What did the Communists do for the revolution?

"Cuba, yes," he wrote. "Slaves, never."

Fidel answered with blustery rhetorical tirades, saying the priests were tools of "imperialism," meaning the United States, or "Falangists" representing dictator Franco's Spain. But Fidel could not easily silence the Church. He could not subvert the Catholic hierarchy from within, as had been done with journalists and lawyers. On August 31, Fidel told the new ambassador from the Soviet Union, Sergei Kudryavtsev, that the Catholic bishops' letters had "failed" and "the people were not listening to the clergy." But in truth Fidel was rattled and irritated. The pastoral letters were resonating. The Church was mobilizing people—creating voices in competition to his own.

Pérez Serantes personally wrote eight pastoral letters from May to December 1960, and signed two more by the entire Church leadership. In the end, the Church did not have the power to topple Fidel. But there was, separately, a powerful, existential threat looming over Castro.

The United States was planning to overthrow him.

In this jittery period, on September 28, having just returned to Havana from the United Nations, Fidel began a speech on the balcony of the presidential palace. It was just after 10:00 p.m. As he spoke, carried on live television and radio, a small explosion was heard nearby, and he stopped. "That little bomb," he said, "everybody knows who paid for it!" Once again, it was the fault of the imperialists—the United States—and he promised that Cubans would resist heroically. "The people are prepared to resist anything that falls, even atomic bombs!" The crowd began to chant "¡Paredón!" or, "To the wall!"—the firing squad. Two more bombs went off before the speech was over.

Fidel, crossing another threshold that would shape the revolution, then announced the establishment of "a system of collective vigilance." He added, "We are going to set up a revolutionary vigilance committee on every block so that the people can see what is going on." Soon, volunteers were organizing the network across the country to work shoulder-to-shoulder with the police, the army, and the citizen militias, carrying out denunciations, arrests, and imprisonment of people deemed counterrevolutionary. On October 10 they were named Committees for Defense of the Revolution, and the organization spread not only to neighborhoods but also factories, stores, offices, and schools. They kept an eye, too, on people who attended Catholic Mass. They turned every citizen into prying eyes and created a vast web of street-level informers. The committees were foundation stones of the police state, and resembled similar methods used by Stalin and Mao.

Raúl Castro told the committees, "You are supposed to keep an eye on everybody, and a hand grasping onto their neck."

Fidel's trademark cigar, clenched in his teeth, triggered ideas at CIA headquarters about how to kill him. Jake Esterline, deputy chief of the CIA branch running Cuba operations, kept a box of cigars in his safe that were laced with chemicals that would have caused Fidel to become disoriented. The plot was to trick Fidel to smoke one before a speech and make a public spectacle of himself. Another idea was to infuse the cigar, or perhaps Fidel's shoes, with a chemical that, once in contact with his skin, would cause his beard to fall out. Neither cigar was lethal, nor used. A more deadly scheme was to coat cigars with botulinum toxin, one of the deadliest substances known to man. Fidel would not have to smoke it—just put it in his mouth. A full box was prepared. All these plots were hatched in the waning days of the Eisenhower presidency.

The cigar conspiracy was never undertaken, but by the autumn of 1960, a secret assassination plan was put in motion. Botulinum toxin was fashioned into solid pills that would dissolve in water. The CIA worked through Chicago Mafia boss Sam Giancana to deliver three of the poison pills to Santos Trafficante, the Cosa Nostra boss in Havana. Trafficante supposedly had a contact in Fidel's office who could slip the pills into a drink. While the poison pills were delivered to the mobsters, they never made it to Fidel's coffee cup. The contact in Fidel's office, it turned out, was a disgruntled employee who had been fired months before. The CIA official in charge of these plots, Richard Bissell, was also in charge of the more ambitious plan to overthrow Fidel and his regime with a landing force of Cuban exiles. "Assassination was intended to reinforce the plan," he insisted. "There was the thought that Castro would be dead before the landing," making it "either unnecessary or much easier."

To overthrow Fidel, the CIA at first envisioned putting ashore small guerrilla bands that would work with opposition on the island to create a popular uprising. But in November 1960, just as John F. Kennedy was elected president, the Cuba operation was changed by the CIA. Instead of guerrilla bands, a decision was made to launch a sizable amphibious landing by Cuban exiles trained by the US military. A training camp was established in Guatemala.

The CIA also tried to cobble together a political committee that could become a provisional government after the "uprising," and created a propaganda radio station. But the CIA faced the reality that opposition leaders were fractious, and no one had sufficient standing to lead a popular uprising. Still, the propaganda station Radio Swan, based on Great Swan Island off the Cuban coast, went on the air, and the announcers included Fidel's onetime friend Luis Conte Agüero and the former *Bohemia* publisher Miguel Ángel Quevedo.

In late 1960, rising prices for food and clothing in Cuba, and shortages of foodstuffs that once were plentiful before the revolution, stirred popular dissatisfaction. In the countryside, Ruby Hart Phillips recalled "a growing feeling of discontent among peasants" about the huge government-run farms, called cooperatives, being created by Fidel's agrarian reform, and low wages. In Havana, housing had deteriorated, streets were dirty, and lines of people now formed in front of stores. The year-end celebrations of the past were gone, and so was Santa Claus, whom Fidel had banned.

Already, many of Cuba's middle- and upper-class citizens—the core of the Catholic Church—were fleeing. Thousands applied for visas to the United States every week. On departure, they were forced to leave their money and possessions behind. In addition, with support from the US government, thousands of children left Cuba without their parents, who were appalled at the Marxist indoctrination in schools. The airlift, which came to be known as Operation Pedro Pan, depended on a hidden network to obtain US student visas for the children and to finance the flights. It eventually brought 14,048 unaccompanied children out of Cuba between December 1960 and 1962; they often spent months or years with strangers before reuniting with their parents. Exodus and exile came to be as much a part of revolution as Fidel and the barbudos.

Miami swelled with a generation of Cuba's best and brightest. The adult refugees were overwhelmingly professionals and technicians: dentists, doctors, agronomists, teachers, and engineers.

On January 2, 1961, Fidel staged a massive display of armaments Cuba had purchased from the nations of the Eastern Bloc, primarily Czechoslovakia and the Soviet Union, including tanks, rocket launchers, artillery, and antiaircraft guns. In his speech Castro attacked the enemies of the revolution as *gusanos*, or worms. The crowd perked up at every mention. "The worms think the revolution cannot do away with them," Fidel declared, vowing that it could.

He then ordered the US embassy staff cut from eighty-seven to just eleven persons within forty-eight hours. "Kick them out!" he shouted. The crowd answered, "Kick them out!"

President Eisenhower broke off relations with Cuba the next day.

The war of words with the Church intensified as Fidel warned of an imminent "Yankee invasion." On January 6, civilian militias occupied

the San Francisco church in Old Havana and its adjoining buildings, and
the offices of the magazine *La Quincena*, which suspended publication.
Three Catholic seminaries in small towns outside Havana were seized,
as well as Catholic Youth headquarters. "An open battle against the religion of Christ has been started," warned Pérez Serantes in another pastoral letter.

On February 7, Raúl Castro appeared at a student rally in Havana
to respond to a strike call from an underground student organization.
Raúl called the strike organizers "war criminals in priests' robes." The
students, soaked in a driving rain, chanted,

Raúl, Raúl, the priests should cut cane,
And if they don't want to cut cane,
Let them go back to Spain.

Raúl responded that priests were trying "to poison the minds of our
children against the revolution."

The Bay of Pigs invasion was the worst-kept secret of 1961. The element of surprise was lost long before it began. Castro had been bracing for it for months. He received intelligence reports that identified
the exile training camps and an airfield in Guatemala run by the CIA in
preparation for a Cuba landing. The facts were in plain sight: workers
at the coffee plantations gawked at the base preparations; some disaffected trainees were sent back to Miami, awash in rumors of an imminent invasion. On January 10, the *New York Times* carried a front-page
headline, "U.S. Helps Train an Anti-Castro Force at Secret Guatemalan
Air-Ground Base."

Later, Kennedy told his press secretary that Castro "doesn't need
agents over here. All he has to do is read our papers."

Kennedy campaigned in 1960 saying that the United States could not
allow a Communist beachhead in Cuba, angering Vice President Nixon,
his opponent, who knew of the secret overthrow planning but was unable to reveal it. On taking office, Kennedy inherited a deeply flawed CIA

plan for an amphibious landing. Key elements were already under way. Repeatedly over the early months of his presidency, Kennedy struggled with his own doubts, but in the end, he approved it. His problem was not a failure to grasp Castro's direction. The State Department issued a thirty-two-page "white paper" on Cuba, which Kennedy had reviewed, that concluded Castro was establishing a "repressive dictatorship" on the island. Kennedy's problem was what to do about it.

From the start, the CIA plan was doomed. It contained a serious miscalculation that a landing by Cuban exiles could set off a popular uprising. Bissell, the chief CIA architect of the operation, had concluded there was no chance this would happen. But Bissell did not tell Kennedy.

A second significant error came in March after Kennedy got involved with the planning. He was uncomfortable with a highly visible landing near a populated area. He wanted the operation to look more like an internal guerrilla uprising. On hearing Kennedy's dissatisfaction, Bissell moved the landing zone from the town of Trinidad on the southern coast to the remote Bay of Pigs, farther west at the Zapata Peninsula, known for a vast swamp. The inhospitable and thinly populated terrain, it was thought, would slow the Cuban response and perhaps give the invaders cover. In actuality, it impeded the landing.

A third error was that the CIA estimated there were thousands of people who could be contacted and mobilized for internal resistance on the island, including three thousand in Havana. But they were not made privy to the invasion plans so were useless.

The operation began on Saturday, April 15, with an air strike, targeting Cuban warplanes on the ground. The CIA's attacking B-26 light bombers were painted to resemble Cuban air force planes, a camouflage to create confusion. They bombed three airfields, but some of Castro's planes were unscathed.

The air raids tipped off Castro that an operation was imminent. In a funeral oration the next day at Havana's Colón Cemetery for seven people killed in the raids, he declared that Cuba would defend its "socialist revolution." This was the first time he had publicly described the revolution as socialist, although he did not elaborate.

Kennedy canceled a second air attack, set for Monday, April 17, the day of the landing. This left the landing brigade dangerously exposed to Cuban planes that had survived the first raid. Cuba had a small air force, but it included T-33 training jets retrofitted to carry rockets and twin .50-caliber machine guns capable of firing seventeen hundred rounds per minute. The T-33 jets proved especially fast and deadly, seriously damaging two ships carrying ammunition and supplies for the invading brigade.

The brigade itself landed early in the morning of April 17 and secured a beachhead but became trapped without reinforcements or resupply after the ships were hit. "We are out of ammo and fighting on the beach. Please send help," the brigade's military commander, José "Pepe" San Román, radioed in the desperate final hours of April 19. "We cannot hold."

For Castro, word of the landing came soon after it began. He made a shrewd decision, ordering his air force into the sky at dawn. The Cuban Sea Furies and T-33 jets pinned down the brigade until the rest of Cuba's forces could reach the Zapata Peninsula. In the end, Castro's forces crushed the invasion. Of the 1,511-man force, 114 were killed and 1,179 captured. Others were evacuated or escaped. Some survived in the swamps for days by eating insects and the raw meat of chickens, lizards, crocodiles, and snakes.

Eisenhower wrote in his diary that the Bay of Pigs operation might have been called "Profile in Timidity and Indecision."

Kennedy remarked to a friend, "How could I have been so stupid to let them go ahead?"

At the same time, Castro immediately set out to crush any opposition from inside the country. The secret police began nationwide mass detentions. Tens of thousands of people were yanked out of their homes and offices—doctors were pulled away from operating rooms—and forced into overcrowded stadiums, prisons, and schoolyards. The total arrested has been estimated from fifty thousand to more than a hundred thousand. The rights of habeas corpus, contained in the 1940 constitution, had been stripped away in the early days of the revolution, so the detained had no legal protection. The Committees for Defense of the Revolution played a role, block by block, singling out people to be arrested. Although many of those detained eventually were released, the regime had made a grim, potent point that it could rule by fear and intimidation—and anyone could be subject to it.

Fidel was jubilant and boastful. Once again, he had survived, and it seemed luck was on his side. He went to the sports stadium to personally interview the captured brigade members, one by one, before the television cameras. He must have been surprised at the sloppy US planning and execution, but he was not taking any chances. Within weeks, the Soviet Union sent eight additional KGB officers and new equipment to Cuba to help bolster the G-2. Despite the disastrous outcome, the Kennedys did not cease planning to overthrow Fidel.

Fidel's fury at the Catholic Church reignited. The invaders wore shoulder patches that displayed a shield with a Latin cross in the center. Among those taken prisoner were three Catholic priests, regular clergy, all Spanish nationals who had lived in Cuba previously and served as chaplains to the brigade. The head chaplain, Ismael de Lugo, was carrying an announcement he composed to be broadcast to the Cuban people after the invasion.

"The liberating forces have landed on the beaches of Cuba," the statement declared. "We have come in the name of God, Justice and Democracy to restore the rights that have been abridged, the freedom that has been trampled upon and the religion that has been subjugated and slandered." The statement added that the brigade "is constituted by thousands of Cubans who in their totality are Christian and Catholic. Our struggle is that of those who believe in God against the atheists, the struggle of spiritual values against materialism, the struggle of democracy against communism. . . .

"Catholics: long live Cuba, free, democratic and Catholic."

Castro launched a wave of repression at the Church. An estimated 250 priests and monks were taken in the initial roundups, including Boza Masvidal and Evelio Díaz, archbishop of Havana, both confined in crowded cells at Villa Marista, a former seminary now turned into a G-2 headquarters and detention center. At the La Salle School in Havana's Vedado neighborhood, the brothers were forced into the infirmary, told to pray quickly, and to remove their cassocks. They were told they would be shot if a single incriminating piece of counterrevolutionary evidence was found in the school. This was cruel psychological warfare. Elsewhere around the island, Church tabernacles were defaced, chalices filled with beer, and sacred images smeared with excrement. In Camagüey, Marist brothers and priests were paraded through the center of the city single-file, hands raised, while being harassed by the population.

Pérez Serantes was not arrested; perhaps because, given his stature, the outcry would have been too great. But Pérez Serantes was forced to accept a military escort at all times. The escort commander, a friend of Raúl, seized papers on the prelate's desk, hunting for evidence of collusion with the invasion brigade. Pérez Serantes was subject to another pressure technique of the revolution. A mob of several hundred *fidelistas* demonstrated in front of the archbishop's office, shouting threats, including "*¡Pérez Serantes, Paredon!*" He took it in stride. According to the archbishop's biographer Ignacio Uría, his greatest anger was that a guard assigned to the escort stole his episcopal ring from his office; he filed a complaint, but never got a reply.

Boza Masvidal was transferred to the old La Cabaña fortress, where he was beaten.

Pérez Serantes was summoned one evening by Raúl, who had made his headquarters in Santiago at the mansion of a sugar baron who had fled. Raúl talked from 10:00 p.m. until 6:00 a.m., trying to persuade Pérez Serantes to organize a joint statement from the bishops denouncing the Bay of Pigs invasion. Pérez Serantes never did it. After all that had happened, he could not.

A crushing blow against the Church came in Fidel's May Day 1961 address in Plaza Cívica. He spoke in the evening, after a day-long succession of marches and parades in which his portrait was carried next to that of Karl Marx. He mocked the priests who had accompanied the CIA-backed brigade to the Bay of Pigs and read aloud the confiscated announcement the brigade planned to broadcast. When he reached the

sentence saying they were Cubans, Christian, and Catholic, Fidel ex-
claimed, "What a lie!" He accused the chaplains of being "friends of
Franco." Then Fidel announced that he would revoke permits for all foreign priests in Cuba, except those who could prove they supported the
revolution. The other priests "can begin packing." He declared that the
government was closing and nationalizing all private schools, including
Villanueva University, where Boza Masvidal was rector. These were devastating setbacks to the Church in Cuba because so many of the Catholic
priests were foreign, and the schools a vital part of their mission. Castro
was a product of these schools—La Salle, Dolores, and Bélen. From now
on, Fidel said, "They can teach religion, yes, in the churches they can
teach religion." The meaning of this was clear: religion had to be confined to the church, and teaching it in schools was prohibited, revoking a
protection for private schools that was in the 1940 constitution.

Fidel often boasted in later years that he had shown restraint—"there
was not a single priest executed." However, Fidel had other methods to
make them disappear. He forced them into exile.

On May 17, the *Covadonga*, a black-hulled liner, sailed from Havana
for Spain with 140 priests and nuns. More followed voluntarily, fleeing
the hostility. Many thought that they would soon come back to Cuba.
They were wrong.

Fidel's three-and-a-half-hour speech on May Day was one of his most
important. In his call-and-response style, he mocked the old political system. "What elections did they want? Those elections with vote-buying
carpetbaggers who had dozens of agents dedicated to corrupting consciences? Those elections in which poor working-class men and women
had to hand over their IDs so they would be given a job? . . .Those false
and prostituted elections . . . ?"

Fidel insisted that the revolution "has simply changed the concept
of false democracy, of pseudodemocracy as a means of exploitation by
the ruling classes, to a system of direct government of the people, by the
people, and for the people."

This was his jury of a million, spread out before him.

"Do the people have time now for elections? No!"

The crowd responded, "No!"

Left unsaid was another possible road Fidel could have taken: holding free and fair elections. But he never went that way.

Could the Cuban people have protested? Few dared. The fear of the G-2 was too great.

Fidel had promised to make the 1940 constitution the "supreme law of the land." Now he declared it dead. "To those who talk to us about the 1940 constitution, we say that the 1940 constitution is already too outdated and too old for us. . . . That constitution has been left behind by this revolution, which, as we have said, is a socialist revolution."

He promised to develop a "socialist constitution" that would provide for "a new social system without the exploitation of many by man."

On September 8, an important religious festival in Cuba celebrates La Virgen de la Caridad, the nation's patron saint. A procession was planned for 1961, as in the past. Then all religious processions were banned by the government. Boza Masvidal, out of prison, asked the government for permission to hold the annual procession two days later and permission was granted if it was held before 9:00 a.m. Boza Masvidal refused and called it off. Nonetheless, crowds came on September 10. About four thousand people gathered by late afternoon in Havana. Many had not heard of the cancellation or did not want to hear it. The mood was tense, the church densely packed. Soon the crowd began calling out "*¡Cuba sí! ¡Rusia no!*" and rolling chants of "*¡Libertad!*" followed by "Down with communism!" The chants were so loud that they drowned out the church bells.

When the restive crowd began to head toward the Presidential Palace, police opened fire, first over the heads of the crowd, but then into it, killing Arnaldo Socorro Sánchez, seventeen, who was carrying an image of the patron saint. Eventually the crowd dispersed, but it had been one of the largest-ever outbreaks of protest against the regime.

Boza Masvidal was arrested two days later in Havana and hauled off to the dreaded Villa Marista.

In April, Fidel had canceled permits of foreign priests. Now he ordered their formal expulsion. On September 16, a Saturday, some 135 priests and brothers from religious orders were escorted to the Port of Havana and forcibly boarded on the waiting liner *Covadonga*, which had taken priests and nuns away in May. Boza Masvidal was taken to the harbor in a car by four armed men. He had nothing but the clothes on his back and was without a passport or other travel documents. Both the passengers and the crowd on the dock cheered as Boza Masvidal boarded.

At the top of the gangplank, he turned and made the sign of the cross. The *Covadonga* set sail for Spain.

The next day, there were few celebrations of Mass in Havana or elsewhere in Cuba. After the expulsions and exodus, about 200 priests remained in Cuba of the approximately 800 before. Cuba had 520 parishes.

"The enthusiasm of the people for the Castro government has cooled," wrote Phillips of the *New York Times*. "From the wild bursts of joy at the overthrow of the Batista regime in January 1959, they have reached a state of sullen resentment today."

One of the few remaining bright spots was *Lunes*, the Monday culture supplement to *Revolución*, the newspaper mouthpiece of the revolution. The supplement was filled with free-thinking writers and widely read throughout Latin America. But in June, at a series of meetings held at the National Library, the editors were accused of publishing material that was subversive, decadent, and undermined the revolution. At the third meeting, on June 30, Fidel was the only speaker. He addressed the question they had been debating, whether artists could be free to express themselves. "Within the Revolution, everything," Castro said. "Against the Revolution, nothing."

There could be no competition.

Lunes ceased publication within three months.

On December 1, 1961, Fidel appeared on television as he had so many times before. The speech went on for three hours, but one line was different from what Cubans had heard before.

"I am a Marxist-Leninist," he said, "and I will continue to be a Marxist-Leninist until the last day of my life."

He then announced the process by which he would create a single revolutionary party, modeled on Soviet communism. All the revolutionary forces would be under one roof—there would be no competition.

Not surprisingly, in Castro's first three years, no one attempted to activate the citizen initiative created decades earlier by Gustavo Gutiérrez. It was still formally embedded in the fundamental law of 1959. But no one dared try it. After what happened to Matos, who would raise a hand of dissent? Anyone who circulated such a petition would undoubtedly be accused of disloyalty or treason and pay a heavy price.

The initiative required not only a provision of law; it also needed someone with the courage and conviction to carry the banner.

It would take time and hard lessons. But that person was coming.

PART III

GIVE ME LIBERTY

EIGHT

THE SECRET LIBRARY

The two brothers were well known. Alejandro and José Payá distributed newspapers, magazines, and books all over Havana. Alejo was the boss, and his right-hand man was José, known as Pepe. Wiry, gregarious, and full of energy, Alejo rose every morning at 4:00 a.m., when his wife, Iraida, made coffee. He liked it strong and griped when it was weak.

They lived at 276 Calle Peñón, a two-story house set back from the street, facing the tree-shaded Parque Manila. Each morning, Alejo left before sunrise to pick up the papers from printing presses around Havana, as well as the weekly *Bohemia*, other magazines, books, and anything else that could be printed and sold. Alejo then dropped them at kiosks, hotels, and shoe-shine stands. When he finished, he went home to nap, then rose again for the afternoon papers. It was a long, hard day, but Alejo made the most of it. He knew people at the printing houses, in the bars, and the doorman at every hotel.

Before the revolution, Alejo and Pepe's vehicles groaned with Havana's daily newspapers. When Eddy Chibás died, when Batista staged a coup, when Castro assaulted the Moncada Barracks, the headlines came tumbling out of Payá vans. They had inherited the business from their father, also named Alejandro. He was born in the Valencia region of Spain and had immigrated to Cuba in 1920. He worked long and hard, first with a shoe-shine stand, then later expanded to distributing the newspapers. The boys did well with the business, but it grew more difficult as capitalism withered after the revolution. Advertising dried up and newspapers were taken over or closed in the early 1960s. The brothers kept going as best they could. When the revolution published dozens of new propaganda texts, they distributed those instead of newspapers.

Alejo's wife, Iraida Sardiñas, also came from a family of merchants and landowners. Her father, Emiliano Sardiñas, built up a Havana bank as a young man, but lost it in the roaring 1920s, then ran a bodega in the center of the city. One of her uncles owned a ranch in Matanzas, about sixty miles from Havana.

Iraida and Alejo's first child was a daughter, Rosa. The next three children, almost a year apart, were all boys: Alejandro, Reinaldo, and Óscar.

On February 29, 1952, they welcomed a fourth son, Oswaldo José Payá Sardiñas. Another daughter, Marlene, and a son, Carlos Alberto, followed.

The older brothers kept a special watch over Oswaldo, who grew up to be scrappy, trouble-prone, and uninhibited. His oldest brother, Alejandro, recalled that Oswaldo "could not hold his tongue. He was funny, extroverted, witty, likable as a kid. Later, he talked back. He would never stay quiet.

"He didn't know the meaning of danger," recounted Alejandro. Once, the boys rented horses to ride for a few hours. They hoisted Oswaldo on his steed, and it took off. The horse would not slow when Oswaldo pulled the reins. He was lacerated as the horse galloped through trees, crossed a busy avenue, and kept on going. Oswaldo felt invincible and, even when his brothers finally caught up with him, did not want to dismount. They took him to the hospital for stitches. The Payá boys would also chase freight trains that rolled through a nearby railyard, hopping aboard the slow-moving cars. The younger Oswaldo, legs pumping, tried to keep up, although he often had to be lifted by his older brothers. Once, Alejandro and Oswaldo were at a local sports center when a gang approached Alejandro, who was four years older than Oswaldo but not particularly agile or strong. The gang demanded that Alejandro fight their leader. He turned around and ran home. Oswaldo stood fast, and the gang retreated.

Oswaldo was nicknamed *el Chivo*, or "the goat," by his childhood friends. The story was that it started with a prank one day at Parque Manila, where Oswaldo did a good imitation of a goat eating grass. But it may also have reflected his stubbornness and determination. Oswaldo's younger brother, Carlos Alberto, recalled that "he had a very strong and individualist kind of personality."

Once when helping their father load newspapers into the van, the brothers grabbed Oswaldo by the arms and hoisted him atop a throne of newsprint bundles, a moment of kinship he never forgot. They were a clan.

One day in 1965, when Oswaldo was thirteen years old, he was hanging around the back room of the house that his father used as a warehouse for the business. A militiaman burst through the door. "Step away from the desk and the cash register!" he told Oswaldo, who was skinny with a mop of jet-black hair in wavy curls that fell on his brow. He did as ordered. The revolution had come to Calle Peñón.

Fidel was in the midst of a campaign to persuade Cubans to adopt a socialist morality. Che Guevara said they should work for moral incentives rather than financial ones. In his speeches, Castro attacked vendors, businessmen, and capitalists as "parasites," "leeches," and gusanos, or worms. One by one, private businesses were being seized by the state in a campaign that stretched on for years.

On the day of the raid, Alejo was handcuffed and taken away. The militiamen ransacked the storeroom and carted off what they could. They confiscated Alejo and Pepe's vans. Then they came for the family cars. Alejo and Pepe had a 1948 Willys jeep and a 1950 yellow Chevrolet. "Where are the keys?" one of the militiamen demanded. The car keys

were in another room, always on the piano. "It was a very tense moment," recalled Marlene, Oswaldo's younger sister, who watched, petri-
fied. If they didn't get the cars, the militiamen threatened, Alejo would
go to prison for a long time. "My mother said, give them the keys. *Give
them the keys!*"

Alejo's arrest alarmed the Payá family, but they knew why it happened. Castro had cast himself as champion of the peasants and the
poor, a crusader for socialism, and destroyer of the old Cuban establishment that had prospered under capitalism. The Payá family was rooted
in this corner of Cuba's urban middle class: observant Catholics, entrepreneurial, and strongly anti-Communist. They sent their children to religious private schools, and they read the conservative *Diario de la Marina*
and the Church biweekly *La Quincena* until these publications ceased to
exist. They sensed that Castro was coming for them.

Che Guevara had promoted the dream of a Communist utopia, the
rise of a "new man." The state would provide for every need, and money
would eventually disappear. Material incentives—such as profit—would
become the "debris of the past." This ideology regarded with envy and
hatred all those who had enjoyed the fruits of capitalism. Small businessmen were arrested and their shops confiscated. In 1965 Fidel created a
new Communist Party of Cuba to control the island, absorbing the 26th
of July Movement and the old Partido Socialista Popular, among other
organizations. The newspapers *Hoy*, of the old Communists, and *Revolución*, of the 26th of July Movement, were merged into a single new daily,
Granma, a party propaganda sheet.

A sense of isolation and hostility weighed heavily on the Payá family and on their relatives and friends. Among Iraida's eight brothers and
sisters, the debate at every kitchen table was whether to remain in Cuba.
Fidel had closed and nationalized the Catholic schools, including Cham-
pagnat Academy, founded by the Marist Brothers in 1931, where Oswaldo
and his older brothers had been students. It was turned into a military
academy, and Oswaldo was sent to a public school, where he was taught
about Marx and Lenin. In fifth grade, he recalled, he was given a school
textbook that declared, "Science has shown that Jesus Christ did not exist."

In 1965, the year Alejo was detained, dissatisfaction spread throughout the island. Hundreds of desperate Cubans launched small, leaky boats or rafts trying to leave. On September 28, Castro announced that he would let anyone go who wanted to, designating the small fishing port of Camarioca as the departure point. Unexpectedly, hundreds poured into the port to embark.

The elder Alejandro, Oswaldo's grandfather, considered taking his family to the United States. In addition to his sons, he had a daughter, Josefina, known as Beba. The elder Alejandro lived with her in a house on Calle Peñón, next door to Alejo and Iraida. Beba was the only one of the three with a college degree, in pharmacology.

But the strongest voice belonged to Alejo, Oswaldo's father, who made the final decision to stay in Cuba. With his contacts all over Havana, Alejo often predicted, in private, that Castro would not last another six months. He kept waiting for better times. By contrast, five of Iraida's brothers and sisters fled. Each time one of them announced plans to depart, they were forced to immediately give up their property to the state. "It was a very rough time because they took everything from those people who left Cuba," recalled Carlos Alberto. "They did an inventory down to the last spoon." Jewelry was confiscated. The departing Sardiñas family members waited at Calle Peñón until the last minute. The house became a way station for heartbreaking separations.

The Payá family's oasis was the parish church, El Salvador del Mundo, which anchored the *parroquia del Cerro*, the parish of Cerro. The church, built in 1843, was a rectangular structure of thick stone walls, a high-ceilinged nave, and large doors opening at the front and sides, to keep cool in the tropical heat. Beautiful drawings, slowly fading, adorned the ceiling of the nave.

Every Sunday, Rosa, the eldest child, walked her brothers to church down the gently sloping hill of Calle Peñón, across the busy, colonnaded Calzada del Cerro, to a small square with a spreading ceiba tree. The church stood just beyond the tree.

For decades, the parish had been home to people of renown. José Martí and the famous epidemiologist Carlos Finlay, who discovered that mosquitoes carried yellow fever, had once walked these streets. In the late 1940s, the assistant pastor was Eduardo Boza Masvidal, who many years later was deported for leading Catholic Church resistance to communism. Alejo and Iraida were married at the church. Alejo was not very religious, but Iraida's faith remained steadfast even as church attendance declined and parishioners were jeered and taunted. Ramón Antúnez, who was Oswaldo's closest childhood friend, recalled that Iraida refused to be deterred by the harassment. She told the boys, "Move forward. Keep going forward. Faith is first. They can't stop us. They can't paralyze us. We're not doing anything wrong. We can't be scared." He added, "We kept going."

Iraida believed in humility and charity, was not impressed by vanity, and would never bow to power, money, or prominence. She put an enormous amount of energy into the seven children, insisting they live by their faith. The *parroquia* was their second home. After Mass, the boys playfully raced around, climbing the rickety wooden stairs up the bell tower, and running across the plaza. "We weren't saints," recalled Oswaldo's older brother Alejandro.

The family kept their distance from the revolution. Oswaldo was the only boy in his class who refused to join the Communist Party organization for young people, the José Martí Pioneers. The Payás were marked as outsiders by the regime, which viewed outsiders as disloyal. Being observant Catholics added to the stigma. In the seclusion of his own home, Alejo complained about the everyday problems: food rationing, shortages, the prying eyes of the Committees for Defense of the Revolution on every block. But Alejo griped only discreetly. In public, he eschewed politics and did not confront the revolution. He told his children to study hard and keep their heads down. Alejo had a saying that reflected this survival tactic: "You have to yield—in order to triumph."

The parroquia was made up of families—sprawling clans such as the Payás—that endured together. Parishioners were sometimes hit with stones as they walked to church; eggs were thrown at the sixteen-foot-tall entrance doors. The parish priest's car was defaced with *chapapote*, or black tar. On the Easter holidays, especially on Good Friday, the government stationed loudspeakers outside the church with festive music, or a noisy motorbike circled around and around to disrupt the Mass. Harassment was common and petty. Rolando Sabin, a family friend, knew of a five-year-old who had been called to the front of his classroom and interrogated in a humiliating way because he said he believed in God.

Oswaldo showed a devotion to the parroquia. He was an altar boy, and eagerly participated in religious ceremonies, festivals, and schooling. One day, Francisco Mascaró, the husband of Oswaldo's sister Rosa, noticed the church door was open on a weekday afternoon, and went inside to check. He found Oswaldo, then barely a teenager, kneeling and looking at the tabernacle in solitude. "What are you doing, Oswaldo?" he asked. The boy replied, "Praying. Don't you know that I am going to be Saint Oswaldo del Cerro?" He was being facetious and self-deprecating, but his faith was well established.

A week after the 1965 militia raid, Alejo was released. He was unshaven and unbowed. He had lost the business but not his confidence. Upon walking through the door, he told his overjoyed family not to utter a word of complaint. One of his sons, Óscar, said that Alejo may have been threatened by the authorities with another prison stint if he complained. So he was doubly determined to keep his head down.

Soon Alejo got a job at a state-run printing house that published sports magazines. His duties, at least nominally, were to create magazine covers for various sports and athletic events. But Alejo was entrepreneurial and had other plans. He had friends who controlled the printing presses. He began a clandestine business designing and printing small, colorful cards for children known as *postalitas*. The cards, illustrated by talented artists, recounted stories from popular radio and television shows for children, such as the tales of Zorro. They were numbered sequentially, resembling baseball trading cards. Alejo proceeded carefully, making a deal with the actors, commissioning the artwork, then printing the cards during off hours. His family wrapped and packaged them in a back room of their house, to avoid prying eyes. Soon Alejo had a thriving underground business, making a profit and defying the revolution.

The postalitas were hugely popular. Children played games with them and collected them. Oswaldo may have taken from his mother a deep faith and love of the Church, but from his father came a streak of determination.

Abruptly in 1968, the hammer fell on what remained of small businesses. On March 13, Fidel announced the state would seize all remaining private enterprises in Cuba, except for family farms. Castro denounced tradesmen, barkeeps—he had a special dislike of them, saying they made money "hand over fist." Every repair shop was a "base of immorality and crime," he declared. In fact, bars were a major source of scarce goods on the black market, and repair shops served a vital function, cannibalizing and improvising parts for cars and appliances at a time when the whole country was short of spare parts. Most cars had only one working headlight; the major cause of traffic accidents was faulty brakes because no one could find brake fluid, so they substituted water or shampoo. In what Fidel called a "revolutionary offensive," the government confiscated 55,636 small businesses, many of them family-owned and -run, including corner groceries, butcher shops, poultry and fish stores, vegetable and fruit stands, laundries, barbershops, boardinghouses, shoe and auto repair shops, bars, and restaurants, as well as all stores selling garments, shoes, hats, furniture, cigarettes, books, flowers, hardware, and appliances.

The result was catastrophic. Small businesses and the black market had filled the gaps in the inefficient state-run system. Without them, fruits, vegetables, and clothing soon disappeared from stores. Lines grew longer. The milk ration for adults in Havana was eliminated. "Capitalism has to be dug out by the roots, parasitism has to be dug out by the roots, the exploitation of man has to be dug out by the roots!" Fidel declared. The end of private enterprise was a "triumph of the revolution."

Oswaldo had turned sixteen years old that year. At church, families often gathered after Sunday Mass for a free-flowing discussion of their worries and concerns, at first just in the foyer, but later in the hall. Sometimes the conversations would be about a book that had been smuggled into the country, or about a news item that had been picked up on shortwave stations such as Voice of America, Radio Canada International, or Radio Exterior de España. Oswaldo listened intently and participated as time went by. In 1967, a new pastor came to the parroquia, Alfredo Petit Vergel, who had studied and been ordained in Rome and who spoke five languages. A family friend recalls that Petit brought three very strong personal characteristics to the parish. He was determined to search for truth without fear of consequences; he had a strict sense of austerity, with contempt for material goods, and never talked about money nor passed a collection plate; and he practiced "perseverance, elevated to the rank of virtue." Oswaldo's childhood friend Antúnez said Petit was "strongly anti-Communist," a "brilliant man" who "saw the rude reality of Cuba."

Petit encouraged open and free discussions. "At the church, we found a bubble that we didn't have on the street," said Oswaldo's brother Carlos Alberto. "We had access to knowledge they didn't give us at school." Petit was a mentor to an informal group of teens and preteens in the parish, who called themselves Vikings after a famous 1958 Kirk Douglas film. They were a rambunctious and mischievous group who raided the church refrigerator, played dominoes in the sacristy, and mercilessly chased wild cats in the square. They were also a constant presence in parish activities, under the watch of Petit, who often talked to them about being open and truthful. Oswaldo, a member of the group, was deeply influenced by Petit. At school, Oswaldo had also attracted a small group of friends who shared his rebelliousness. He was easygoing, with a certain magnetism. Oswaldo called his group the *contestatarios,* or the renegades. Their political consciousness was growing.

In the 1960s, young Cubans knew of the hippies and youth counterculture in the United States and Great Britain, but they had little opportunity to emulate the flower children of Haight-Ashbury. Fidel and his puritanical revolution mocked, and sometimes arrested, the young men with long hair and tight jeans—symbols of protest—and the Beatles were banned on radio and television. The novelist José Yglesias, who lived in the United States, was visiting Havana in 1968 and met at a café with a young poet he knew. "For young people there is a totally repressive situation, there is no way in which they can express their interests, no outlets for them," the poet told him.

Oswaldo Payá was no hippie, but in his own mind he was a rebellious outsider. His first real political revolt came in the summer of 1968.

On August 20, Soviet and Warsaw Pact troops invaded Czechoslovakia, crushing the Prague Spring, a movement led by Alexander Dubček, a party official seeking a more democratic and reformed socialism.

Strangely, Fidel Castro was quiet. He said nothing for three days.

Privately, Fidel was brooding over how Soviet leaders had sidelined and insulted him at the end of the Missile Crisis of 1962. The Soviet Union had deployed nuclear-armed missiles on Cuban soil aimed at the United States, triggering the most dangerous crisis of the Cold War. During the perilous days of October, Fidel, in a state of high militancy, commanded a Soviet air defense unit to shoot down a US U-2 spy plane. This horrified the Kremlin leaders. To make matters worse, Fidel wrote a letter to Nikita Khrushchev insisting that if the United States invaded Cuba, the nuclear-armed missiles should be launched—preemptively. Upon receiving the letter, Soviet leaders rushed to end the crisis. "They thought Fidel had gone mad," recalled Brian Latell, a former Cuba analyst for the CIA. Fidel was not consulted in the negotiations between Kennedy and Khrushchev that ended the crisis, and the Soviet withdrawal of the missiles from Cuba left Fidel feeling vulnerable and his pride wounded. "Cuba did not agree with the way the issue was handled," Castro told the Cuban Politburo in January 1968 in a secret speech confessing his anger six years later.

Now, not knowing of Fidel's long-simmering resentment of Moscow, Cubans waited for his reaction to the Soviet invasion of Czechoslovakia. Many thought Fidel might denounce it as an act of imperialism, a superpower dictating to a small neighboring nation. Hadn't Fidel spent much of his life railing against imperialism? On the other hand, Cuba relied on Soviet economic largesse. Fidel had embraced communism. On August 23, Fidel finally appeared on television, looking wooden and stiff. He announced that he supported the Soviet invasion, saying it was necessary because Czechoslovakia was "heading toward capitalism" and striving to leave the socialist camp. His decision marked a turning point. If Fidel had any doubts before about an alliance with Moscow, they were gone. The novelist Reinaldo Arenas recalled feeling a sense of no return. "There was no way out," he wrote. "The leader who had fought against Batista was now a dictator much worse than Batista, as well as a mere puppet of the Stalinist Soviet Union."

Oswaldo Payá was outraged by the crushing of the Prague Spring, in the way a teenager coming of age might be. His views were forming fast. He did not hold his tongue. The leader of the contestatarios delivered a harangue in the schoolyard against the Soviet invasion, explicitly criticizing Fidel's support for it. This was the first time he openly spoke out against Castro, and word of it probably spread. His childhood friend Antúnez recalled, "Czechoslovakia's very far away, but that bothered him."

At the same moment, Fidel was worried about signs of unrest in the younger generation. In a speech on September 28, he warned of "youths who have gone wrong" who sought "a revived version of Prague" in Cuba, and who were engaging in acts of protest around Havana. He warned that they would be "retrained" and declared firmly, "We are revolutionaries. We are socialists. We are collectivists. We are Communists."

Oswaldo turned seventeen years old in February 1969 and soon received a draft notice. Military service for three years was mandatory. Oswaldo went in May, joining hundreds of other young men gathered at the largest sports stadium in the country, the Estadio Latinoamericano, in El Cerro, the Havana district where Oswaldo had grown up. None of them was told where they were going. They were taken from the stadium to the central rail station, put aboard a train that pulled out of the city toward Cuba's rural heartland. Two other passengers on the train noticed something unusual—judging by the familiar faces, those put on this train were almost entirely religious Catholics, seminarians, Jehovah's Witnesses, Seventh-Day Adventists, Baptists, homosexuals, or young people who'd been caught trying to leave the country illegally. For different reasons, they were all outsiders, or, as the revolution put it, ideological "deviants."

At dawn, the train unloaded them onto flatbed trucks. Supposedly they were going to military training. But where?

Oswaldo could not keep quiet. He sensed something was wrong. He began to question whether they should escape. He organized an informal protest as the recruits were milling around the parked trucks. A few were sympathetic, but an older man whispered to Oswaldo that everyone would abandon him the minute soldiers came. When the soldiers got wind of the protest, they fired their weapons into the air. The young recruits all hit the ground in surrender. Payá was forced to the ground and kicked by the soldiers.

The trucks moved on.

During the summer of 1966, Paul Kidd, a Canadian journalist, had been roaming the Cuban countryside. Inexplicably, the government gave him a press credential that allowed him to go anywhere he liked, unaccompanied by officials. He knew Cuba and had visited for a decade. In Camagüey, the grasslands and lush sugar fields of central Cuba, near a rural hamlet, El Dos de Céspedes, he discovered a barbed wire fence around a compound with two long, white barracks.

The army guard at the gate was suspicious. "You are alone?" he asked.

Kidd had stumbled upon the expanding Castro police state. The barracks housed a forced labor camp, one of about two hundred across the country. Over nearly three years, they held more than thirty thousand men under armed guard. The formal name of the camp system was Unidades Militares de Ayuda a la Producción, or military units to aid production, otherwise known as UMAP. But the use of "military" was a camouflage to disguise the true purpose. The camps held those considered hostile, or "social deviants," or potentially disloyal to the revolution. Fidel had constructed a simple black-and-white choice: be loyal to the revolution, "integrated" into it, or be outside of it and suffer. One of the punishments was three years of hard labor.

The revolution had started punishing "social deviants" years earlier. In raids carried out in October 1961, police targeted thousands of people, including "homosexuals, vagrants, suspicious types, intellectuals, artists, Catholics, Protestants," and others, the propagandist and editor Carlos Franqui recalled. He protested to Raúl and Fidel, as well as to Ramiro Valdés, the interior minister and secret police boss. Valdés, he recalled, "was bragging about the success of the operation while the others laughed." Valdés said he had consulted Soviet, Vietnamese, Chinese, Czech, and East German security services and they recommended harsh measures against such people, including the firing squad, prison, and "reeducation camps." That same year, the regime's publishing house printed and disseminated fifty thousand copies of a text by Mao that declared "enemies are forced to work and become new men through work." This idea of forging a "new man" through hard labor greatly appealed to Fidel. A historian, Abel Sierra Madero, says that Fidel loved the metaphor of the steel forge. "With this logic, the concept of the 'new man' functioned as a mold and those who did not conform to this ideal were considered to be slag or waste of the forge, that is, counterrevolutionaries and 'softies.'" Raúl declared in April 1965 that the revolution would only reach its goals with "a youth with tempered character" that was "forged on sacrifice," away from "soft talk," and inspired "not by the dancers of twist or rock and roll."

The camps were created in 1965, first in Camagüey and later elsewhere. A clandestine system was set up to identify high school students and others considered "antisocial" or "deviant." The Committees for the Defense of the Revolution, which had grown into a vast network of informants, compiled lists and sent them to the military. The G-2 also played a role. Then, in November 1965 and again in June 1966, mandatory military conscription was used as a cover for the roundup. A young man would get a draft notice but, instead of being sent to army training, was switched to a labor camp. Fidel claimed they were sent to the camps "to help them improve their attitude. To change, to learn; it is about turning them into useful men in society." In reality, Castro had created an assembly line to feed the forced labor camps.

In Camagüey, Paul Kidd talked his way past the gate. He saw barracks that resembled cattle pens. Inside, hammocks fashioned out of strips of jute sacks were strung between wooden poles. The 120 inmates, all young men, had been active Catholics and Jehovah's Witnesses. They received $7 a month for working sixty hours a week, mostly cutting sugarcane. "The system of discipline was simple," Kidd wrote. "Inmates who didn't work didn't get fed."

That was not the impression given in the pages of the Ministry of Defense journal *Verde Olivo*, where the forced laborers were depicted as heroic field workers, with group portraits of each brigade, the captions listing their bountiful harvest yields. In fact, Castro faced a serious shortfall of agricultural workers in those years, and the forced labor camps bridged the gap. Behind the barbed wire, there was none of the idealism of the "new man." The reality was grim and miserable. Father Petit was sent to the camps in 1966 as a young Catholic priest, and one of his first tasks was to build barbed wire fencing until his bare hands were bloody. The worst abuses were aimed at Jehovah's Witnesses, a Christian sect that believes all authority rests in God. Based on their religious beliefs, they refuse to serve in the military. At the Manga Larga camp, on the plain of Camagüey, they were stripped naked, tied up, and strapped to a fence in the blazing heat for days at a time. In another camp, Jehovah's Witnesses who refused to march military-style were jabbed with bayonets, then hoisted into the air with sticks between their legs. In a third camp, a Jehovah's Witness was winched by his hands up a flagpole, an agonizing punishment. A medic, José Luis Llovio-Menéndez, appalled at the sight, insisted that the boy be rescued immediately, saying such barbarism was like that used by Batista. The youth was lowered down, his wrists bloody, and he fainted but survived the ordeal.

The forced laborers were transported to the fields in darkness and brought back in darkness, and often moved from camp to camp, disoriented and exhausted. At one camp, a guard told them, "You are going to rot here. You'll get out when you accept the revolution." At yet another, food was scarce, and a can of sardines was shared by four people—one sardine each. Another prisoner recalled scraping the common pot used to make rice for the camp, secreting scraps in his pocket to eat. As punishment, they were often tied to fences, left to the mercy of giant mosquitoes. Others were buried up to their necks for days.

A sign at one camp entrance read, "Work will make you men."

Fidel was scornful of homosexuals, saying they could never be "a true revolutionary, a true Communist militant." In a speech at the University of Havana in 1963 he said, "A lot of those idle dandies, sons of the bourgeois, go around wearing pants that are too tight"—the audience laughed—"some with their little guitars, acting as if they were Elvis. They've taken their lewdness to such an extreme that they want to go out to public spaces and put on their queeny shows out in the open." Later, homosexuals in the UMAP camps were subjected to electrode shocks and insulin-induced comas, barbaric attempts to modify their behavior, according to Sierra Madero's research. Two waves of psychologists and psychiatrists were sent to the camps, the first in 1966 to "research" homosexuals, the second in 1967 for "assistance."

After Paul Kidd's article describing the camp in Camagüey, other reports began to tumble out. Ramón Calvo, a twenty-year-old, escaped from a camp to Havana and then was smuggled aboard a freighter to Miami. He described UMAP camps surrounded by barbed wire guarded by the army, where the men worked harvesting sugarcane twelve hours a day. A human rights report by the Organization of American States in April 1967 noted that Castro's government had created a new prison system that "constitutes a system of exploitation equal to slavery." These are "real concentration camps," the report said.

Fidel, who boasted of the revolution's moral purity, grew defensive about the camps in 1966. Popular resentment was spreading, especially among families who discovered that their sons were incarcerated in horrid conditions. In August, Fidel suggested it was someone else's idea. "Do people want to turn this country into a concentration camp? When a new plan arises, all they can think of is the use of prisoners surrounded by a barbed-wire fence. No, the revolution does not mean slave labor." However, the camps went on for almost two more years.

The poet and novelist Heberto Padilla was courageous enough to speak out in public. In a 1968 essay in a Cuban magazine, he identified a location in western Cuba, at Guanahacabibes, where the regime had created one of the first camps. Padilla warned, "In the short life of the

Revolution, we have effectively had our miniature version of Stalinism, our Guanahacabibes, our dolce vita, our UMAP. . . . It is the future of our society that is in jeopardy."

Criticism also mounted from Fidel's admirers overseas. Graham Greene, the British novelist and author of *Our Man in Havana*, visited Cuba just after the June 1966 call-up. He warned that the UMAP camps were a "dark shadow" cast over the revolution, worse than the US blockade or food rationing. "The initials stand for forced labor camps controlled by the army," he wrote. This wasn't a small "tactical" mistake like those of the past, Greene said, but a "moral mistake" that "compromises the revolution." This must have stung Fidel, who had spent hours talking to Greene on his visit. In the summer of 1968, the UMAP camps were quietly phased out. Fidel was never held to account. Under the system he created, he could not be. He was, however, a canny tactician. He had responded to the discontent of Cuban families as well as international pressure.

But Fidel had not entirely abandoned the UMAP. The system lived on, without the name.

Oswaldo Payá was racing headlong into it.

Sugarcane stalks—green ribbons against the sky—towered over their heads as the young men clambered down from the flatbed trucks in the summer of 1969. They were in central Cuba, far from anywhere they had known. Oswaldo Payá had never cut cane in his life. He had grown taller since the militia raided his father's business, but he was still thin, and the harvest work was backbreaking. They wore long sleeves and improvised headgear, sometimes a rag wrapped under a straw hat, to ward off the mosquitoes. For two months, they hacked away at the endless rows of stalks, stripped away the leaves, and piled the rods, to be hurriedly carried to the mills before the sinewy core, the sucrose, could spoil. The long days began at 5:00 a.m. and ended at dusk. They constantly were drenched by rain, by sweat, and slogged through muddy fields. Their food was a chunk of bread in the morning and a piece of sweet potato and rice at night, brought by sympathetic soldiers. When that dried up, they ate from buckets of molasses left for cattle feed. Sanitation was miserable—no clean water—and many were sick. Payá was almost defeated physically by the strain, but he remained defiant. One day, fed up, he complained to the guards that the brigade had worked beyond endurance. A guard fired a gun into the air by Oswaldo's head and ordered him back to work.

Fidel had a grandiose ambition for the "atomic bomb of sugar," aiming for a ten-million-ton harvest in 1970, more than any *zafra* in Cuba's history. Long before, Fidel had correctly recognized the curse of Cuba's reliance on sugar. He pledged to diversify the economy, creating more industry, but the first five years of his revolution, in which Cuba abandoned capitalism and adopted Marxism, produced dismal economic results. With shortages and scarcity growing, Fidel swung back to reliance on sugar. To achieve the ten-million-ton harvest by 1970, the growing season began earlier, in the summer of 1969. Factories and offices were emptied of workers to cut cane, and the forced labor camps were deployed to the fields. Fidel was obsessed with the goal, a "point of honor" for the revolution. Billboards around the country exhorted, "What are you doing toward the ten million?" Fidel canceled Christmas celebrations so that people could work in the fields.

Payá carried a card that identified him as a member of sugar-cutting brigade no. 9. The card, with a large "10 million" emblazoned on one side, certified that he contributed "with his decisive effort" to the "historic harvest of 1970." Actually, he was trying to survive, trudging through fields until he could barely stand. Then, after a few months, the harvest was over. The young men were taken to an airstrip and flown to the Isle of Pines. It wasn't a paradise, but it was dry. There were no more towering sugarcane stalks. Instead, there was stone.

The thinly inhabited island, 1,181 square miles, lies about 40 miles off Cuba's southwestern coast. It is home to the Presidio Modelo, an unusual prison complex built by President Machado between 1926 and 1928 and made up of five panopticons—the cells are in a circular structure, with a watchtower in the center. When the tower is darkened, it is impossible for the inmates to tell if they are being observed. Fidel and

Raúl had been sent to the presidio after the Moncada convictions, but spent their twenty-two months there in a nearby infirmary. By 1969, the prison was closed, and guard barracks were used to house the new brigade straggling in from the sugar harvest.

The Isle of Pines was rich in marble and other types of stone. A capacious quarry not far from the prison provided raw material for prefabricated cement walls and building blocks used all over Cuba. Oswaldo's new forced labor duty was as rough as the last—he was breaking rocks.

At one point, Oswaldo escaped to nearby hills. He was unarmed and alone, fired up with anger. The unit commander, his patience stretched thin, called Alejo, Oswaldo's father, in Havana. Alejo traveled to the Isle of Pines and talked his son into returning to the camp.

Over time, the camp restrictions proved somewhat less onerous than the UMAP system. On weekends, the inmates were allowed to visit the small town nearby, Nueva Gerona, and encouraged to take night courses at a school there. Payá studied French. There was no barbed wire. Their group was called only *unidades de trabajo*, or work units, to avoid any association with the old UMAP.

But the young men still endured harsh conditions in the quarry ten hours a day, and they returned to the barracks at night blanketed in dust and grit. One day, Oswaldo played a trick on the guards. An old Russian radio was used for the morning wake-up call. Oswaldo sneaked into the command room and preset the dial to Voice of America. When the radio was turned on the next morning, the vacuum tubes took a few minutes to warm up, the guard wasn't paying attention, and suddenly "The Star-Spangled Banner" played over the loudspeakers.

The quarry work continued through August 1970, when the units were shifted to other projects, such as civilian construction sites on the Isle of Pines.

Suffering through common misery, the inmates made friends easily. In the isolated quarries, they talked freely, without the conformism necessary elsewhere. Oswaldo's friends included Andrés Cárdenas Machado, five years older, a hot-tempered amateur boxer. He had been sent to the camps because, during a meeting with a military recruiter, he refused to join the army, and had smashed the recruiter in the face. Another of Oswaldo's friends was Humberto León, who like Oswaldo had demonstrated a youthful streak of independence. Humberto had played in a popular rock band, Los Kents, that sang rock and roll in English, including songs by the Beatles and the Rolling Stones, music that was considered enemy propaganda by the Communist Party. Humberto had escaped from a regular military call-up and went home. He was thus marked for the camps and sent to the sugar harvest at the same time as Oswaldo.

Together, Payá and his friends eagerly explored Nueva Gerona. On the way into town, they sang the Beatles—particularly the love song "Something," one of Oswaldo's favorites.

The church on the town square, Nuestra Señora de los Dolores, was shabby and nearly abandoned. A priest came by every few weeks. Payá proposed to his friends that they spruce up the church—an act of charity, but also rebellion. They found the priest, who agreed and gave them the key. They scrounged up some paint, cleaned the pews, and washed the windows. They soon attracted a crowd of parishioners to Mass. One Sunday, Oswaldo, who was assisting the priest with Mass at the front of the church, saw the pews filled with people, a remarkable sight. It also attracted the curiosity of the local Communist Party chief, who came by during the service and was shocked. Andrés, who was standing near the door, told him to leave.

On weekends, the young men bunked in the church. This was permitted as long as they reported for work by 5:00 a.m. on Monday. Payá was their cook, in a small kitchen in the rear, and invariably made his friends a plate of boiled yucca and spaghetti.

Across the square from the church stood a small library. Andrés was the first to go there and crack open the door. Soon his friends filed in. Two young women were at the desk, both library trainees from Havana. One was tall, with green eyes, the other a pretty blonde. Andrés let his friends flirt with the tall one, while he zeroed in on the blonde, who was the director. Andrés told her he was searching for something serious to read.

He waved at the books in the front of the library. They were volumes about Marxism. "I need to *read*," Andrés said, "but not this trash."

"Shh," she said, holding a finger to her lips.

He shrugged, unafraid. "What else can they do to me?" he asked. "I'm breaking stones."

Then she took him to a door in the rear of the building, a storeroom. She unlocked it. There was a threadbare carpet, a comfortable couch, a few chairs, floor lamps, and a window sealed shut, with blinds closed. On the shelves, they found a gold mine: hundreds of books considered subversive or prohibited in Cuba, in Spanish and English, including world-class collections on philosophy, politics, religion, and art. They also discovered a large collection of music albums, and a record player that worked.

"Shh," the director said again. She told them to come back anytime. She left and locked the door behind her.

The young men were starved for knowledge. There was so much to read, to talk about, to debate—and the music was delightful, mostly classical recordings. They devoured a Spanish-language edition of George Orwell's *Animal Farm*, a commentary on totalitarianism. They pulled out the works of Pierre Teilhard de Chardin, a renowned Jesuit priest, paleontologist, and French thinker, including *The Phenomenon of Man*, his provocative essay on evolution, the universe, and the fate of mankind that the Vatican had warned should not be used in school classrooms. "It contradicted some of the teachings of the Church," Humberto recalled, "so for us it was explosive." They found *Tiberio*, a biography of Tiberius by psychologist Gregorio Marañon, who described the resentments and anxieties that drove the second Roman emperor. All of them spotted the parallels with Fidel. "Those months spent reading the books fueled our minds," Humberto said. They read Nietzsche; history works on Stalin, Trotsky, and the Russian Revolution; art books about van Gogh; and they all read and discussed Mika Waltari's novel *The Egyptian*. The shelves held Boris Pasternak's *Dr. Zhivago*, still banned in the Soviet Union, and a complete collection of the works of Spanish philosopher José Ortega y Gasset, who wrote about the role of the individual and the masses in society. For all of them, it was an eye-opening experience to be exposed to authors and ideas that had never appeared in their Cuban classrooms.

They argued and listened. They perched on the chairs, paced the carpet, and came back every weekend for almost a year.

In Havana, meanwhile, the revolution was slamming doors on writers and free expression. In March 1971, the poet Heberto Padilla, who had protested the UMAP camps, was arrested and detained for five weeks, then pressured into reading a public "confession" to win release. Padilla's "crime" had simply been his acid commentary on the revolution. In one poem, titled "Instructions for Joining a New Society," he listed what the state required of citizens:

> First, one must be optimistic
> Second: composed, willing, obedient
> (having passed all athletic tests).
> And finally, go about as each member does:
> One step forward and
> two or three steps back:
> but always applauding.

The person Padilla describes here is pretending loyalty—applauding the revolution, "obedient," but in turn falling behind. This kind of criticism was intolerable to Fidel's revolution by 1971. In May and June, following Padilla's arrest, according to documents unearthed by historian Lillian Guerra, the regime secretly decided to ban all books by foreign and domestic authors who took up Padilla's cause; they were to be subject to censorship inside Cuba, their works prohibited in libraries and erased from catalogs and other publications. The list included Jean-Paul Sartre, Mario Vargas Llosa, and Carlos Fuentes.

Fidel's revolution, born to fight Batista's "tyranny," was growing into a system with totalitarian ambitions. "Totalitarian" was first coined in the context of Italian fascism. A critic of Benito Mussolini invented the term, and Mussolini adopted it with enthusiasm. Mussolini defined it this way: "Everything within the state, nothing outside the state, nothing against the state." Fidel used nearly identical words in his command to intellectuals in 1961. In a definition created after

World War II, Carl Friedrich and Zbigniew Brzezinski said totalitarian regimes had at least five common elements: a dominant ideology, a single ruling party, a secret police force, a monopoly on information, and a planned economy. Castro had all five. There were still cracks in the system—Fidel may have been more totalitarian in aspiration than in practice. But his mind-set was totalitarian, backed by the use of fear and coercion.

At the same time, in Nueva Gerona, in a secret and forgotten storeroom, young men who were deemed outliers and social deviants, who had been sent to a penal colony to be reeducated, reveled in the freedom to think and talk. They took it in deep, satisfying gulps. During the days at the quarry, they were hungry, tired, and trapped. But on weekends in the library, their horizons expanded. They challenged each other and learned from each other. They returned as often as they could.

One Sunday, recalled Humberto, a member of the group posed a question: "If God is all good, how can he let bad things happen?"

Oswaldo jumped to his feet to respond—he had strong ideas about God and faith. Oswaldo gave them a rational and persuasive answer to their question, reminding them that man had created many of his own sins.

In those freewheeling discussions, they also learned that Payá had a singular, simple conviction: freedom is an essential attribute of every human being, endowed by God and not by the state. As Oswaldo put it, rights come from God, not from Fidel. "We were born with those rights," he said, "to be free."

The forced labor camps attempted to "reeducate" and "retrain" the outsiders, to coerce them to believe in the revolution. But for Oswaldo Payá, the experience was the opposite.

They had not conquered his soul. They had nourished it.

NINE

DEFIANCE

In a photograph, Oswaldo is wearing an open-necked khaki work shirt, too small for his gawky frame, the cuffs high above his wrists. It was taken outside his home on Calle Peñón after his return in 1972. He was thin as a rail. Rations had been meager on the Isle of Pines; lunch was sometimes a truckload of grapefruit dumped on the ground. But in the stone quarry, under the blue sky and with little else to lose, he and his friends lost their fear. They were open and honest with each other. No one told them what to think. Their sense of independence and defiance only grew. When they were sent to civilian construction projects on the Isle of Pines, Andrés, a former boxer, was selected for an interview by an evaluation team from Havana. The team, some in uniform, faced Andrés from across a table. The questions were asked by a psychologist. Andrés had a feeling he was expected to be humble. He wasn't. "You have educated me," he told them.

Then he paused. "I will be your enemy for life. You have failed."

Compared to the freewheeling days on the Isle of Pines, Oswaldo found Havana suffocating: the Marxist ideology, the incessant propaganda, and the pressure to conform. Cuba had become increasingly dependent on the Soviet Union. Thousands of Soviet technical advisers had arrived over the previous year. Small boys on the streets learned to say *"tovarishch!"* or "comrade!" in Russian, when begging.

Oswaldo took courses to finish high school and prepare for the University of Havana. He decided to enroll in theoretical physics. Two of his older brothers were studying to be medical doctors. Remembering his father's advice to keep his head down, Oswaldo hoped that physics would not be burdened by the heavy ideology that was present in areas such as law and journalism.

Before he could enroll, he had to undergo a long interrogation by leaders of the Communist Party youth organization. He braced himself.

"Well," began the first questioner, "do you believe in any god?"

"In any god, no. I believe in God."

"Okay, but that's a belief that you have, a definite belief like that, because you've heard talk of—"

"No, no," Oswaldo protested. "I believe."

"Well, is it something your parents taught you? Something you'll get over?"

"No," Payá insisted. "My parents taught me this, but I do believe, and there's no reason why I should get over it."

"Okay, but you don't go to church, do you?"

"Yes, I go to church."

"Well, look, you're going to have to learn dialectical materialism and the science of Marxism."

Oswaldo shot back: "Who said that Marxism is a science?" This touched off a long argument that went back and forth for several hours. In the end, the students allowed Payá to enroll.

The physics courses were rigorous, but Payá discovered the department was as political as the others. Fidel had ordered many officers in the military and security services to take university courses. They mingled with younger students. The whole campus was blanketed with party ideology. Students were encouraged to monitor, accuse, and denounce each other, as if "it was the most normal thing in the world," Payá recalled later.

His friend from the camps Humberto also enrolled in physics. "They were after me constantly to join the union of Communist youth," he remembered. "What they used to do was they assigned other Communist youth to work on you. To convince you. I was dodging the encounters." The most relentless were twin girls he had known in high school. "They'd wait for you at the entrance to the school. And they followed you all the way to the class, giving you a speech. Why didn't you become a member? What keeps you from becoming a member?"

Oswaldo felt isolated and ostracized. His family had been stigmatized for years as Catholics, but the hostility on campus was disheartening. Professors deliberately omitted his name from lists of assignments or classes; they looked past him when he raised his hand in class. In a seminar about Albert Einstein, Humberto was called upon to answer a question about the behavior of light waves. As he responded, the leader of the seminar interrupted, exclaiming, "But you're not a Marxist!" Humberto replied that of course he was not a Marxist, he was a Catholic. "And the guy opened his eyes wide and all those in front of me turned and said, 'Ah! What are you doing here?'"

A weekly meeting was held to scrutinize each student's ideological attitude. At first, Oswaldo tried to keep quiet, but after a while, he spoke his mind. Then he stopped going to the meetings. At the time, his girlfriend, Carmen, was also studying physics. She helped him with the lab work. The relationship was rocky—a friend recalls they broke up several times. But they shared antipathy toward the regime. Carmen's father, a political prisoner, was released while she was at the university. She asked Oswaldo to marry her and leave with them to Venezuela. Oswaldo refused. If anyone is going to leave Cuba, he declared, it must be Fidel.

After the Einstein confrontation, Humberto quit the physics courses. He didn't want to leave, but a school official warned him there would be more and more pressure. Oswaldo's situation also deteriorated. He was identified as an outsider who refused to conform. Finally, campus life was so miserable that he decided to leave the university. "They didn't kick me out," he recalled. "But they asphyxiated me."

•   •   •

Castro and the revolution began to face tough new challenges in the early 1970s. The sugar harvest came in at 8.5 million tons, nearly a record, but short of Fidel's 10 million tons. Fidel made a halfhearted offer to resign. "The people can replace us any time they wish—right now, if you want," he said at a rally. Cries of "No!" and shouts of "Fidel!" rose from the crowd. Of course, the people could not replace him, Fidel did not resign, and by his very makeup he could not relinquish power. But the harvest marked a turning point. The revolution had been a wild ride for a decade, a social, political, and economic upheaval largely held together by Castro's charisma. It needed a sturdier foundation.

Instead of allowing genuine civil society groups that would be autonomous and independent, Fidel fashioned "mass organizations" for peasants, women, students, laborers, and others that anyone could belong to. The idea was to give every person a stake in the revolution, but in fact the groups were loosely organized and passive, no substitutes for an active civil society. At the same time, Fidel kept his dictatorial whims and made even the most minor decisions. He spent an inordinate amount of time trying to breed a hybrid supercow that would make Cuba self-sufficient in milk production. He imported thousands of cows from Canada, and air-conditioned their barns against the tropical heat.

Growing popular discontent, shortages, and poor overall economic performance led Castro to accept the need for a more formal political structure. There was talk of "consolidation" and "institutionalization." The Soviet Union, now the source of 60 percent of Cuba's trade, pressed Fidel to delegate more decision-making. Cuba had been governed since the early days of the revolution by the fundamental law of 1959 as well as a blizzard of decrees. Now Castro agreed to prepare a new socialist constitution. A commission led by the old Communist Party chief Blas Roca drafted a new document, which was unveiled in 1975.

In its preamble, the constitution declared that Cuba would be guided by "the sociopolitical ideas of Marx, Engels, and Lenin," as well as José Martí. It declared Cuba is a "socialist state of workers" led by Fidel Castro with "the objective of building [a] Communist society." The Communist Party of Cuba, the constitution said, "is the leading force of the society and the state." The constitution offered guarantees of individual rights, but the language made it clear they were weak. For example, freedom of speech and the press must be "in keeping with the objectives of socialist society." None of the freedoms could be used in opposition to "the existence and objectives of the socialist state, or contrary to the decision of the Cuban people to build socialism and communism." A large portion of the language in the constitution came directly from the Soviet Union. Of the twenty-two articles in the new Cuban constitution that dealt with rights, a third were taken almost verbatim from the text of the Soviet constitution of 1936.

In a nod toward building institutions, the new constitution created an elected parliament, the National Assembly of People's Power, as well as provincial and municipal assemblies, to be more in tune with local problems. According to Castro's biographer Tad Szulc, there was a brief window for a genuinely democratic electoral system for the new parliament. Some drafters advocated that National Assembly members be chosen by direct election. But others wanted to avoid exactly that, and sought an indirect method of picking members from municipal assemblies and local elites to ensure that the Communist Party retained control. "So bitter was the internal dispute over this point," Szulc says, that the final draft of the constitution failed to spell out precisely how the members of the new legislature would be selected. Castro settled that later, inserting language that the members would be picked indirectly, giving the party control.

Nor was the process of writing a new constitution democratic. Unlike the elected body that wrote the 1940 constitution, no Constituent Assembly was created. Rather, the draft by the Blas Roca commission was published in the party organ *Granma*, inviting comments from the public that resulted only in minor adjustments, then approved by the Communist Party Congress in December 1975. In a national vote on February 15, 1976, the draft constitution was approved by 97.7 percent, a Soviet-style result.

The new constitution did not change the fact that Fidel remained Cuba's undisputed leader. He presided over the Council of Ministers and the Council of State, was first secretary of the Communist Party, and commander in chief of the Revolutionary Armed Forces. For all of Fidel's early boasting about direct democracy and the jury of a million, there was no direct mechanism for Cuba's people to vote for their leader.

In addition to the provisions borrowed from the Soviet Union, the new constitution contained portions that were simply cut and pasted from the fundamental law of 1959 and the 1940 constitution. One of them was Gustavo's citizen initiative, based on ten thousand signatures.

Perhaps Fidel did not notice it, or perhaps he concluded that no one would ever dare to use it. Until then, no one had. In the socialist constitution of 1976, it was enshrined as Article 86 (g).

This time it would not be neglected.

Later in 1976, a nascent human rights organization was formed clandestinely in Havana, the first of its kind under the revolution. One of the co-founders was Ricardo Bofill, who had been a young professor of Marxist philosophy in Havana in the early years of the revolution but had grown disenchanted. A slender man with a mustache and a mop of curly hair, he began lecturing about human rights. He wrote a manuscript sharply critical of Fidel's handling of dissent, titled *Points for a Critical History of the Cuban Revolution*. On October 8, 1967, Bofill and three dozen others—including some members of the old Communist Party—were arrested and accused of a disloyal plot against Fidel, which Castro called a "treasonous microfaction." Bofill was sentenced to twelve years in prison. He suffered a near-starvation diet and physical and psychological torture, including long periods of isolation. Feeling on the edge of madness, Bofill began to smuggle out of the prison a series of letters, which he called *balitas*, or little bullets, addressing them to foreign diplomats and statesmen.

Upon his release in 1976, Bofill created the Cuban Committee for Human Rights with Martha Frayde, a graduate of the University of Havana Medical School who had been close to Castro and originally supported the revolution, but also had grown disillusioned. They began to send information abroad about political prisoners and other human rights violations—sowing seeds that later came into full bloom.

•   •   •

After quitting the university, Oswaldo struggled for years to find work. He studied at night school to be a high school physics teacher. Political pressures were considerably less in such schools, which catered to manual laborers. But Payá was still ostracized. Every time he applied for a job, a file arrived, noting that he was a Catholic and contrarian, and he was rejected. "They wouldn't let me work," he later recalled. "When they saw I was a religious person, they rejected me. At the same time, there was an antivagrancy law, so you could be imprisoned for three to five years if you weren't working. But they wouldn't give me work." Finally, he found a job hauling trash and running errands for a state-run film studio. By July 1977 he earned a teaching degree. The new constitution had put schools in the hands of local municipalities. One school, desperate for a physics teacher, hired him no questions asked. Still, he was being watched. "Every class had to have ideological, political content," he said. "It was ridiculous. So they'd always observe me and always rate me poorly because I didn't praise the revolution." He started night school again, seeking another degree, this time in electrical engineering.

In 1979, Huber Matos was released after serving a full twenty-year sentence for warning of the coming of communism. He had suffered years in solitary confinement but never lost his dignity. He landed in Miami on November 3, vowing to pursue "a free Cuba."

At the time, in a clandestine negotiation with a group of Miami exiles who were coordinating with the Carter administration, Castro agreed to two measures. First, he freed about four thousand political prisoners. Second, he allowed once-unthinkable return visits to Cuba by those who fled to Florida in the 1960s. Perhaps he thought the exiles, whom he called gusanos, or worms, would be impressed with socialist Cuba. Perhaps he thought he could play on their nostalgia or their longing for family reunions. Certainly, for Fidel, part of the appeal was money they might bring. But the decision had a complex aftermath, not entirely as he planned. More than one hundred thousand exiles returned for visits. The worms were now called butterflies and were back for the first time, leading to poignant and often difficult reunions with relatives and old friends. Many of the butterflies were affluent, educated, and brought accounts of prosperity in the United States.

On April 1, 1980, six Cubans seeking political asylum crashed a bus through the gate of the Peruvian embassy in Havana. A Cuban policeman guarding it was killed. Infuriated, Fidel impetuously withdrew all the remaining guards. Within days, the country exploded. More than ten thousand Cubans desperate to leave spilled over fences and crowded into Peru's embassy. On April 21, Fidel announced that anyone who wanted to leave the island could do so by boat from the industrial port of Mariel, 25 miles west of Havana and 123 miles across the strait to Key West. Hundreds of small boats came from Florida to carry away family members and relatives. In what became known as the Mariel boatlift, 124,789 Cubans left between April and September. A small minority of those were prisoners and mental hospital inmates that the Cuban government put onto the departing vessels.

Boats came for Oswaldo, too. They were brought by his first cousins, who had left at the outset of the revolution. "They came to me and said, we know you are in a difficult situation, and you're a dissident, so you can leave with us!" Oswaldo recalled in a later interview. He told his cousins, "No, I am not leaving Cuba." They were stunned, he added. "What do you mean you're not leaving? We've spent a lot of money, we brought a boat to come and look for you."

Oswaldo later reflected, "Honestly, for me, that would be fleeing, and I believed—I won't deny that I was highly politicized—I believed for this entire time that Cuba had to be liberated from within." He wasn't sure how or when this liberation would happen. But, he said, "I had a fixed idea, which was struggling and working to put an end to this regime in Cuba, and in Europe too. I was younger. I always thought that first we would liberate Cuba and then we would help free Europe from communism."

The boatlift was tumultuous. The government prompted mobs to attack the homes of those departing, shouting denunciations, throwing eggs and stones, and painting slogans. Such an attack was known as an *acto de repudio*. Everyone in a school or workplace would be ordered to the streets to participate. When the demand came to the high school where Oswaldo taught physics to participate in one such act, he refused. Students and other teachers noticed. It was another black mark.

Oswaldo's youngest brother, Carlos Alberto, was about to graduate from high school. He too refused to attend an acto de repudio targeting a classmate. As a result, Carlos Alberto was cornered and accused of insufficient loyalty to the revolution. Oswaldo remembered that his brother exploded. "If you all are going to commit an acto de repudio and attack a church, I'll always be on the side of the church. I'll never be on your side. I'm against this revolution and I don't agree with the government's nonsense." Oswaldo came to his defense. "He protected me and got me out of there," Carlos Alberto recalled. His entry to the university was delayed for two years, but he eventually got into architecture school. However, after four years, he was summoned one day to the dean's office, where state security was waiting. Carlos Alberto recalled he was "trembling" as they pressed him with questions about his indifference to the revolution. In a graphic arts class, his team had created a US flag, a poke in the eye to the regime.

Carlos Alberto realized he needed to act; he went straight to the embassy of Spain and started to fill out paperwork to leave the country.

Andrés Solares had an inspiration. He noticed that Cuba's 1976 constitution included a provision allowing for a citizen initiative. He resolved to take advantage of it.

Solares, an only child, grew up in Havana. His father worked in a department store in the city; his mother was a homemaker. They sent him to private schools, where he gained a spirit of independence. For reading, his mother gave him the works of Martí. After high school, Solares enrolled in the University of Havana, at first studying physics, then civil engineering. He never joined the Communist Party youth organization and tried to skirt the ideological currents on campus. He graduated with an engineering degree in 1968, specializing in maritime engineering and ports. Cuba had lost many engineers in the exodus of the early 1960s. Solares's expertise was desperately needed.

Cuba's main island, with 3,570 miles of coastline, is pocked with harbors that are its gateways to the world. A quarter of the globe's sugar supply once crossed these docks. The waterways, harbors, and docks figured in many chapters of Cuban history, from the arrival of Columbus to the Bay of Pigs. In the 1970s, Solares surveyed the coast, examining the ports. What he saw was decay and neglect. He also saw the same dead end in Cuba's Soviet-style political system.

For a year after graduation, Solares remained an instructor at the university, hoping to train a new generation of engineers and technicians. Then he was awarded a scholarship to study abroad by the United Nations Educational, Scientific, and Cultural Organization, UNESCO. He enrolled at the University of Wales at Cardiff, his first time ever outside of Cuba. In June 1970 he earned a diploma in port and shipping administration and began studying for a doctorate. During his time in Britain he traveled widely, seeing ports there and throughout Europe, including Rotterdam and Antwerp. When he returned to Havana for a break, the contrast was a shock. "Everything was going backwards at full speed," he recalled. "Everything was worse than the day before."

The Cuban government insisted he stay home, and not return to Cardiff to finish his doctorate. This rankled him. He managed one return trip before being forced to remain in Cuba, his degree unfinished. In Havana, he grew restless. In 1975, he tried to organize an independent union of port workers and engineers. When state security heard about it, he was detained, interrogated, and given a blunt warning: union organizing was prohibited.

Solares worked on construction projects, including building an airport, but could see the economic troubles all around him. In 1980 he began teaching a postgraduate course on economics at the Ministry of Transport. In his classes, he openly discussed the problems with Cuba's economy, using statistics and theory. The classes were well attended; Solares was telling it like it was, in the year of the Mariel exodus. But the government wasn't pleased. When it came time for a second year, his classes were canceled.

Andrés felt he needed to protest, that something more had to be done. He decided to establish a new political party in Cuba, called the

Cuban Revolutionary Party, the same name used by Martí. The goals of the new party were to create "a fully democratic society," with direct elections, free speech, freedom of association, freedom of the press, and an emphasis on improved living conditions. He called for "full, unrestricted enactment of all of the principles set forth in the UN Universal Declaration of Human Rights." The far-reaching 1948 UN declaration had been forged with input from Gustavo Gutiérrez many years before.

Solares was a technocrat who had a substantial library of books at home. He looked up the text of the 1976 constitution and found the provision that said ten thousand people could petition the National Assembly through a citizen initiative.

"It is possible in Cuba to apply for a new political party, based on what's written in the constitution," he told his wife, Adriana, an architect. She gave him a skeptical look. "Be careful."

Andrés set out to collect ten thousand signatures. With informants everywhere, he concluded it would be reckless to behave clandestinely. So he did not try to hide. He worked slowly, meeting people one by one, creating small cells of supporters. He mailed a brief description of the new party principles to Senator Edward Kennedy, Democrat of Massachusetts; President François Mitterrand of France; Carlos Andrés Pérez, a former president of Venezuela; and a cousin in New Jersey. In the four letters, Solares said Fidel's system had become "dictatorial, corrupt, and repressive." Next, he printed blank petitions, with the name of the party at the top, and about a dozen lines for signatures. He reassured people, *It is legal. It is in the constitution.*

He had not yet collected a signature when there was a knock on the door on December 22, 1981.

State security had intercepted his letters. They arrested Solares, searched his house, and confiscated all his papers and documents. He spent weeks locked up in Villa Marista. They interrogated him relentlessly.

A month later, Solares was put into the backseat of a police car and handcuffed to a nervous young man, Juan Manuel Cao, a twenty-year-old student at the Cuban Art and Film Institute. The car sped out into the night.

In the car, Cao told Solares he had been arrested for writing "enemy propaganda." He was composing an essay defending Solidarity labor union leader Lech Walesa and criticizing the Communist government of Poland. Cao had not published it, but someone informed on him. Solares, who was just days from his thirty-sixth birthday, told Cao that he had insisted to his interrogators that what he was doing, seeking signatures, was legal under the constitution. At first, they denied it. Then they looked up the constitution. Yes, the provision was there. Solares said they warned him, "Okay, go get one signature. Then get another. But when you get the third, we will be waiting for you."

The police car stopped. It was late at night. Solares remembered thinking, *Oh shit*. They were at the doors of the Havana Psychiatric Hospital, known as Mazorra. Both were forced to change into hospital clothing, then locked in a ward with dozens of mental patients. Some had committed crimes, others suffered severe mental illness. Frightened, Solares and Cao huddled on a bunk and watched hospital aides administer electroconvulsive therapy—electric shocks—to one of the patients. Cao suffered an asthma attack and had no medicine. Solares convinced someone in the hospital to call his wife. She rushed to Mazorra and was allowed to see him for one minute. "You can imagine," Solares later recalled, "one day you are a normal person, and one day you disappear. Your family doesn't know where you are. And then your wife learns you are in Mazorra." A few days later, Solares and Cao were sent back to the secret police headquarters. The nerve-rattling trip to Mazorra was meant to intimidate them.

Cao was sentenced to three years in prison. Solares was imprisoned for several months at the notorious La Cabaña prison. He was inmate 736238. After a short trial where he once again protested his innocence— that collecting signatures was legal under the constitution—Solares was convicted on May 13, 1982, of writing "enemy propaganda" and sentenced to eight years.

The first attempt to use Gustavo's citizen initiative had ended in disaster.

TEN

"FAITH AND JUSTICE"

Oswaldo Payá greeted Christmas every year with a special joviality, even in hard times. When he was a boy in the 1950s, Havana was wrapped in sparkling light. But Fidel had eliminated the public displays. Now there were no lights, no Christmas trees. The city was darkened by a revolutionary patina of shortage and sacrifice. Still, Oswaldo brightened on the holiday. As a gift each Christmas season, his friend Rolando Sabin gave him a cassette tape of Christmas carols, which Oswaldo cheerfully sang.

One season, Payá had an inspiration about how to light up his church. Although people could celebrate inside homes and churches, outdoor decorations were not officially sanctioned. Oswaldo wanted to poke through the veil of darkness. He spent weeks creating—out of scrap wire and discarded parts—a small sign that said "Feliz Navidad," with alternating lights that illuminated an image of a manger. Then, along with Rolando and another friend, he hauled the sign to the church, with a ladder.

The bell tower on El Salvador del Mundo church was like none other in Cuba. Perched at the front of a rectangular stone building, it was distinctively round, like a silo, and topped by a conical roof and a cross. Of the three church bells, two hung freely in arched, open-air portals, and the third, the largest with the deepest sound, was embedded in the thick wall of the tower. To reach it, Oswaldo first had to climb to the choir loft, push open a small wooden door, and climb creaky stairs to the base of the tower. Long ago, a wood platform offered a place to stand, where the bell pulls could be reached, but it was rotted. Oswaldo and his friends brought the ladder inside the tower and steadied the ladder. Oswaldo climbed it, higher still, to reach the arched portals and the bells. He gingerly hoisted the illuminated sign through one of the portals and suspended it on the outside of the tower, facing the square below.

Then he slipped.

"¡Rolando, cojones, que se cae!" he shouted. *Rolando—shit!—it's falling!*

Oswaldo gripped the sign and the ladder. Everything held. Then he heard voices on the street, in the square.

"Rolando!" they chanted playfully. "¡Rolando, cojones, que se cae!"

Payá and his friends broke out laughing. They climbed down and went out into the park to see the sign and to listen to the reactions of people passing by. In the darkness, the message "Feliz Navidad" shone through, with flashing lights, although people could not always see the manger. Some said the silhouette was a sheep; others said a cloud.

No matter, they had pierced the veil.

As a high school physics teacher, Oswaldo was surrounded by teenagers. Santiago Cárdenas, a doctor and his friend, asked him to assist with a church program to advise parents about teenage growing pains, a day-long event titled "Adolescence: Realities and Challenges." Santiago began with a talk about physiological and psychological aspects. A priest then discussed pastoral issues. Oswaldo took the third session, to talk about teenage life from the street.

In Cuba's history and culture, there was always a special place for oration. Public speaking was an admired trait, taught in the best schools, such as Belén. Fidel had mastered it. So had Eddy Chibás, whose voice on the radio stopped the country in its tracks. But as a public speaker,

Oswaldo was modest and soft-spoken. His voice was slightly nasal or reedy. He was sincere but not soaring.

Oswaldo spoke from his heart and soul that day, unafraid, raw, and insistent, talking about his own teenage years. He recalled being treated as an outcast because of his Catholic faith. He urged his listeners to understand it was not easy being a teenager in revolutionary Cuba, up against the propaganda and ideology of an omniscient state that frowned on the Beatles and "Yellow Submarine," that crushed every youthful, creative, and rebellious urge. It was not easy being an adolescent in a world that attempted to impose absolute control and conformity, where the Committees for the Defense of the Revolution watched every block, where loyalty to the revolution is demanded in every classroom.

The room was full. Many in the audience had privately harbored the same thoughts. They applauded, then stood and applauded more. Some were in tears. It was the first time Santiago had seen Oswaldo draw such an emotional reaction from a crowd.

Payá saw that many people felt the same chest-tightening suffocation in a Cuba without rights and freedoms as he did.

At church on a Sunday, Oswaldo was greeting parishioners at the door. A man wearing the white clothes of a *santero*—an Afro-Cuban religion—entered the foyer.

"Friend," Oswaldo greeted him, "how can I help you? Do you need any explanations?"

"Do not insist, young man," the man replied. "My relationship is directly with God, and I know how to handle it. It is a personal encounter between Him and me. I don't need any intermediaries. Thank you."

Payá often retold the story, saying he never imagined how the faith of people could be so simple yet mature. He might have been speaking of himself. His Catholic faith was a steady keel on which he centered his life, and it gave rise to his bedrock principle for social action: the rights of man are bestowed by God, not the state. This grew almost entirely from his experiences living the Catholic faith in the persecuted Church. "We must resist and also confront everything that dehumanizes people," Payá said, vowing to fight "any attempt to disfigure the human being as God created him: free, dignified, full, beautiful, with every opportunity." For Payá, religious faith gave rise to this "seed of unquestionable freedom" and was inseparable from the struggle against dictatorship. He found it simply intolerable that a totalitarian regime could take away the inviolable rights that had been given to each human being by God.

This idea, commonly called natural rights or natural law, has run through centuries of thought. The French scholar Jean Gerson declared in 1402 that all humans possessed individual rights "as a gift from God." Natural law was an important part of Enlightenment thinking in the late seventeenth and eighteenth centuries and was championed by Thomas Hobbes and John Locke. More broadly, human rights became powerful new weapons of American and French revolutionaries who battled for political democracy and religious freedom. The Roman Catholic Church had, for much of the nineteenth century, rejected the radical Enlightenment idea of rights, but it changed dramatically in the late nineteenth and early twentieth centuries, embracing human rights and eventually championing them around the world. The Catholic thinker Jacques Maritain crystallized many of the ideas in natural law and insisted on the bond between Christianity and democratic values. After World War II, Christian democratic movements in Europe were at the forefront of confronting communism, declaring that every human was unique, and not to be lumped into faceless class struggles, as in Marxism, or hammered into some "new man." Christian democracy also spread to Latin America—especially Chile, Venezuela, Peru, and El Salvador—but not to Cuba. The revolution had snuffed it out.

Oswaldo Payá would have been at home with all these ideas and was familiar with many of these thinkers and their works. But as a practical matter, he was isolated in Cuba. For many years, the revolution treated religion and democracy as subversive. Payá had little access to Western thinking, no library to enrich himself, nothing like the back room on the Isle of Pines. There was simply no model to draw from except what was smuggled from abroad by visitors. What books did fall into his hands, he read avidly. An influential volume was *Cristo y las religiones de la tierra*, or *Christ and the World's Religions*, an encyclopedic history by the Austrian cardinal Franz König, translated into Spanish in three volumes. Oswaldo possessed only the last volume, a 760-page tome, *The Great Non-Christian Religions in Existence Today*. His friend Rolando Sabin held another volume, and the priest Alfredo Petit held the third. Oswaldo was deeply interested in the Spanish Civil War and read José María Gironella's trilogy, starting with *Los cipreses creen en Dios*, or *The Cypresses Believe in God*. Payá was a huge fan of G. K. Chesterton and possessed several of his works, including his biographies of Saint Thomas Aquinas and Saint Francis of Assisi. He also kept at close hand Carlo Carreto's *Letters from the Desert* in which the Catholic activist recounted a spiritual odyssey that took him from Italy into the Sahara. Payá savored and often talked about *A Thousand Days* by Arthur M. Schlesinger Jr., a memoir of the Kennedy years, and was also strongly influenced by a book about India's independence from Britain, *Freedom at Midnight*, by Larry Collins and Dominique Lapierre. Sabin obtained a copy of a film, *The Mission*, about Jesuit missionaries in eighteenth-century South America, starring Robert De Niro, whose actions defending an indigenous tribe raise profound issues of good and evil. Watching the film in private at Antúnez's house, Payá and his friends debated it almost until dawn.

Payá was not an abstract philosopher. Rather, he was a thinker of the street who drew his conclusions from the everyday life in Castro's revolution.

After years of study at night school, Oswaldo earned a degree in electrical engineering in 1983. It opened new possibilities. He went to work at a state-run enterprise that maintained and repaired medical equipment in Havana's hospitals. The job gave him a sense of purpose; he was often summoned at odd hours for emergencies. When Oswaldo arrived, often on his bicycle, hospital workers greeted him warmly, since they had to constantly cope with equipment breaking down. His skills were specialized, in demand, and he liked engineering, which generally steered clear of political ideology.

Late one evening in June 1984, Oswaldo visited Humberto León, his friend from the Isle of Pines. Humberto had just completed four years as a political prisoner in La Cabaña prison. He was accused of creating and disseminating "enemy propaganda" at a time when state security was rounding up intellectuals seen as disloyal to the regime. The evidence against him was nothing more than short stories he was writing, seized at the time of his arrest. Now free, Humberto decided the time was ripe to leave. He was to catch a flight to Costa Rica early the next morning. Oswaldo came to say farewell. They went to the roof, to talk freely, fearing that Humberto's apartment was bugged. A friend of Humberto joined them.

In a wrenching conversation, Humberto insisted that Oswaldo should leave too. Oswaldo refused and said he had been thinking of ways to change the situation inside the country. Humberto was skeptical. He knew Oswaldo was a person of faith and strong convictions but not a confrontational type who was going to "open his shirt and show his chest and say, okay, shoot me!" Humberto recalled, "He was so laid back in that sense."

Payá reassured Humberto that he was thinking of a peaceful path. "Let's try to bring with us people that will go out and at least hold a placard and say, 'I want to be free,'" he said. Oswaldo added it might be possible to use the regime's own rules against it. He mentioned the 1976 constitution, a possible "crack in the wall." Oswaldo didn't elaborate.

Humberto thought the whole idea of fighting Fidel was delusional. "Look, I don't want to tell you to quit," he said, "but I don't think these people are going to open their hands very easily. They're not going to give you a chance."

Payá said he wanted to try.

"It is going to be hard," Humberto replied. "You'd better leave."

"I'm not leaving," Oswaldo insisted. "They are the ones who have to leave."

Nine days later, Payá received a letter on rough brown paper. The message raised his hopes. It was from Jaime Ortega, the archbishop of Havana. Ortega was the son of a sugar worker and was born in 1936 in the mill town of Jagüey Grande, in Matanzas Province. Ortega had not been interested in religion as a young man. By his own account, he memorized the words of prayers but didn't pray. The picture of the Sacred Heart in his family living room was just another ornament. "God, faith, religion were outside the horizon of my life," he later recalled. Then, at thirteen or fourteen years old, he had an awakening that dramatically changed him. He became an observant Catholic, attending Mass daily, studied for the priesthood, and was ordained in 1964. Two years later, he was sent to the UMAP camps and was released in 1967 after serving eight months. He became a parish priest in his hometown and later in Matanzas. There were so few priests in Cuba that each assignment meant being responsible for several churches at once. In 1978, he was appointed bishop in the western Cuba province of Piñar del Río, and then in 1981, Pope John Paul II appointed him archbishop of Havana, traditionally the most influential Church leadership position in Cuba.

By his own reckoning, Ortega always exhibited a "sad smile." When he took over his new duties in Havana, he had every reason to be melancholy.

The Church was in dire straits. It had never recovered from Fidel's crackdown after the Bay of Pigs. Archbishop Pérez Serantes, who led the resistance to communism in his eloquent pastoral letters, died in 1968, never having written another. "All the Church's institutions were gone," recalled José Conrado Rodríguez, an outspoken Cuban priest from Santiago de Cuba. "All of its charitable institutions. All of its service institutions. The Church had almost disappeared." The 1960s came to be called by some the age of "the Church in the Catacombs." The phrase came from Pope Paul VI, who in 1965, at the catacombs of Domitila in Rome, a place symbolizing the first Christian martyrs, expressed grief for "those parts of the Church that still live in the catacombs today," for the Church that "now toils, suffers, and barely survives in countries with atheist and totalitarian regimes." Cuba was such a country. In the 1970s, the number of seminarians in Cuba dropped to all-time lows. At the end of the decade there were 221 priests in Cuba, not many more than in 1961. Before the revolution, there was a priest for every 8,848 people in Cuba, but by 1980 there was a priest for every 45,248. There had been 2,553 nuns in Cuba before the revolution, but only 195 or so remained.

Some priests tended to 3 or 4 churches at once; some even to 11 or 12 churches. Just as damaging, the Church had lost its voice on radio, television, and in print and lost its vital educational backbone, the schools.

Fewer than 1 percent of Catholics on the island were practicing. They were a small, committed band of faithful, so tiny that everyone knew almost everyone else from parish to parish. The Church's resources were so scarce that Catholic parishioners were known to filch paper and ink from workplaces and bring them to church for printing leaflets. A parishioner rationalized that stealing from the state-owned enterprises, not uncommon in the years of shortage, was carried out in the name of God. To atone for it, a priest blessed the leaflets.

To rescue the Church in Cuba, the bishops turned to Ortega. He knew the problems: empty pews, dilapidated churches, indifferent Catholics. He also saw a larger peril. In Latin America, the Catholic Church was going through a period of self-reflection. Yet the Church in Cuba was isolated and being left behind.

The Second Vatican Council, from 1962 to 1965, had transformed the attitudes of the Church toward human rights, democracy, and social justice. In a series of sweeping new doctrinal statements, the Church came to endorse many of the same principles it had rejected a century before. It opened the way for local bishops and clergy to enjoy more autonomy, and elevated the role of laypersons, urging them to take part in local and national affairs. The Church was no longer to be a passive accomplice to authoritarian regimes but a powerful advocate of democratic change and human rights. A bishops' conference in Medellín, Colombia, in 1968 took the lessons of Vatican II and sought to apply them to Latin America. The bishops called for a dramatic shift for the Church away from the wealthy elites, to serve the needs of the poor. At the same time, the movement known as liberation theology gained popularity. Liberation theology claimed that the problem of the poor was not just an individual one requiring welfare within the existing social system; rather, it was a structural problem requiring profound change in the institutions that cause poverty, including liberal capitalism and multinational corporations. In some cases, liberation theology borrowed Marxist language.

When the Latin American bishops met again in January 1979 in Puebla, Mexico, with Pope John Paul II present, they were deeply polarized. John Paul urged them to reject liberation theology, calling it overly political and ideological, with echoes of Marxist class conflict. Debates flared over human rights, economic oppression, and the mission of the Church. But the significance of Puebla for the Cuban bishops was their own irrelevance. Those who attended went home with nothing useful to offer their dwindling parishioners. The Puebla texts did not reflect Cuba's reality, said Fernando Azcárate, retired auxiliary bishop of Havana.

Six months later, Azcárate stood at a meeting of Cuban priests and challenged them to revitalize the Church. They unanimously agreed, but the project got off to a fitful start. The Mariel boatlift interrupted everything. The Church grew alarmed that both clergy and laity were thinking of leaving and appealed to them not to flee. Then Azcárate became ill.

The bishops turned to Ortega to take over the project in 1983. He discovered that he could hardly begin without confronting the question of Fidel, who overshadowed all else. Could there be a reconciliation with a regime that denied the existence of God and had sent Catholic young men to forced labor camps? Could the Church accept what Fidel had done to the schools? Could the Church embrace the man who had driven Christianity to the margins, removed "God" from the constitution, and ditched freedom of conscience, religion, and speech? Would a serious rapprochement bring tangible benefits, or was it better not to rock the boat? There was clearly a yearning for better times among Catholics on the island, but also widespread fear. Since the tumult of the early 1960s, the Church and the revolution had settled into an uneasy détente, but it was more a truce than anything else, in which the Church was weak.

No one in Cuba could fail to grasp the meaning of Pope John Paul II's pilgrimage to his native Poland, ruled by a Communist regime. In 1979, the former cardinal Karol Wojtyla of Krakow drew thirteen million people into the streets, a third of the country's population. John Paul's visit frightened the Communists. Before the trip, the Polish Communist

Party sent out secret instructions to schoolteachers, saying "the pope is our enemy" and is "dangerous." When he came, the pope challenged and undermined the moral premises of the totalitarian system in a careful and deliberate way. The future of Poland will depend, he said in Krakow, "on how many people are mature enough to be nonconformist."

"Things that people had believed for decades, but could not affirm publicly, John Paul had affirmed," recalled the pope's biographer George Weigel. "Things they had wanted to say, he had said." The pope's pilgrimage paved the way less than two years later for the rise of the Solidarity labor movement, led by Lech Walesa.

The challenge of the Polish pope to communism was certainly an inspiring drama—but was this a course for Cuba? Was there a leader to galvanize Cubans as John Paul had done in Poland? In fact, after so many years of Fidel's domination, no one could really challenge him. Moreover, Fidel would never allow it. But there was another path. The Church could make peace with Castro. Under Pope Paul VI, who led the Church from 1963 to 1978, the Vatican negotiated directly with Communist governments under a policy known as *Ostpolitik*. The architect was Augustino Casaroli, considered the most accomplished member of the Holy See's diplomatic service. For years, Casaroli, often wearing nondescript civilian clothes, had pursued cautious rapprochement with Communist governments in Eastern Europe, usually bargaining for concessions to protect the Church, defend its autonomy and property, and ensure its continued survival. "There are enemies of the Church," Casaroli liked to say, "but the Church has no enemies." In 1974, Casaroli had brought Ostpolitik to Cuba, where he saw the dire condition of the Church, but also sensed the bishops' desire to end their long and painful marginalization. Casaroli met with Fidel and urged the bishops to engage with the government, to insert themselves into the existing social reality—the revolution—and to use "loyal and willing cooperation for the common good" without compromising their principles. This was a far cry from the pastoral letters of Pérez Serantes, who warned of the "iron hand of communism." But it was Casaroli's classic formula: work with Communists to help the Church.

In April 1979, Casaroli was named Vatican secretary of state by John Paul, the pope's chief operating officer and principal adviser. The appointment signaled that the Vatican would go in two different directions at once: the pope would continue his high-profile campaign on behalf of the persecuted Church, stressing human rights and religious freedom, as he had in Poland. Casaroli would continue to quietly nurture his contacts in the Communist world, including Cuba. Casaroli may have played a role in the selection of Ortega as archbishop; they were likeminded. Ortega wanted to see Catholics going about their lives as a part of Cuban society, no longer ostracized, the kind of modest, pragmatic goal that Casaroli had pursued elsewhere.

Ortega proceeded cautiously at first. He needed help after becoming archbishop in 1981. He turned to the Catholic laity. The role of laypersons had expanded in Cuba during the lean years of the 1960s and 1970s. In Vatican II, under the rubric of *Pueblo de Dios*, or People of God, the laity were given elevated status, encouraged to assume a more active role, and to exercise more freedom of expression. In Cuba, the laity was especially important within the Church, given the shortage of priests.

Seeking someone he could trust, Ortega turned to the Sardiñas family that he'd known as a priest in Matanzas. He asked one of Iraida's sisters to suggest someone reliable to assist him with his pastoral council, a group of his close advisers. The recommendation came back: her nephew Oswaldo Payá was young, a teacher, and would work hard. Ortega was known for the practice of giving promising lay Catholics an opportunity to work in the Church, as a secretary or assistant. Oswaldo jumped at the chance to serve as Ortega's assistant. When the archbishop wanted to visit a community or a youth center, Payá contacted people and set it up. He took notes when Ortega spoke, turning them into a report for the archbishop. Ortega may have known Oswaldo was a nonconformist, but they got along. Oswaldo was well suited for this kind of work, knowledgeable about Catholic life on the island.

Three years later, the letter from Ortega on July 9, 1984, carried an invitation to Payá to join a new, larger pastoral council. Although it would meet only once a year, a smaller, inner group would be at Ortega's side to prepare his ambitious reexamination of the Cuban Church, to be called the *Reflexión Eclesial Cubana*, or REC. Payá would be in the thick of it—and he hoped it might be a way to bring about peaceful change.

His hopes must have risen even higher in the autumn of 1984 and early 1985. Across Cuba, in every parish, candid debates broke out. The reason was a key decision by Ortega for the REC. The traditional method of European theology had been to look first at established Church dogma and then see how it might apply to the way people were living. But Ortega brought in a bottom-up method prevalent in Latin American Catholicism, known as *ver-juzgar-actuar*, or see-judge-act. People were encouraged at the outset to speak about their daily hardships and experiences rather than listen to some predetermined prescription. The method put priority on everyday reality, not abstract theological principles. It had been used at Medellín, giving bishops a shocking picture of Latin America's poverty.

In Cuba, the process unleashed a flood of restiveness and complaints. Much of it reflected the energy of a new generation who had grown up with the revolution—and had much to say. Historian Petra Kuivala, who reviewed the handwritten notes taken at many meetings, found a remarkable spirit of openness as people concluded they could air their grievances candidly in meetings convened at their church. In Piñar del Río, parishioners found they could talk "without restrictions nor fear" and in a "spirit of liberty." Their laments concerned not only religion but also economics, jobs, health care, and discrimination. Many Catholics had abandoned their faith, or hid it, or were silently faithful, not practicing but still feeling a connection. In Matanzas, one report concluded, "There are many, countless, anonymous Christians in Cuba: those who host sincere beliefs but are afraid of expressing them." On top of this, many Catholics described being ostracized—criticized at work, losing their jobs, blocked from careers. These findings resonated with Ortega, who dreamed of coaxing the faithful out of the shadows. Oswaldo also grasped the significance. It echoed his own family's experiences.

Ortega dispatched Payá to each of Cuba's seven dioceses to listen, take notes, and handle a blizzard of survey questionnaires. Payá actively took part in the REC process, which included meetings, producing reports, and then more debate at open assemblies. Payá became the secretary of the new, larger pastoral council that Ortega created in 1984. At one of the meetings, a group of young women was listening to Ortega when he turned to Payá, who was sitting off to the side of the rostrum.

"Oswaldito," he asked, "did you get that down?"

The women whispered to each other. Among them was a young engineer, Ofelia Acevedo Maura. She asked the others, "Who is that?" "Oswaldo Payá," they said, describing him as the archbishop's *cachanchán*, or loyal sidekick. Later, Ofelia glimpsed him again milling about in the hallways. She recalled he was brash and unafraid. He was telling a circle of friends that nothing he could ever say or do would be accepted by the Castro government. Joking, Oswaldo said that even if he killed Ronald Reagan—the diabolical Reagan!—he would not be forgiven by the Cuban regime. Ofelia was introduced to Oswaldo and soon they were dating. Santiago Cárdenas, Payá's friend from those days, said Ofelia was "the perfect soul mate, who dazzled him with her fine spirituality, magic smile . . . caramel eyes," and her dignity.

Ofelia's father, Orlando Acevedo, had served in the Cuban armed forces in the 1940s and early 1950s, then worked at the national bank. He was an outspoken Democrat, never happy with the government. Ofelia's mother was a pharmacist. When the revolution came and Che took over the national bank, Orlando lost his desk job. They said he wasn't loyal enough to the revolution. He found work rolling cigars in a tobacco factory.

Ofelia and Oswaldo shared a passion for change in Cuba. She remembered her father's words at home, always furious at the dictatorship. In the summer of 1985, when Oswaldo began to put his own fury into words, Ofelia was at his side.

On a rainy May 23, 1985, Carlos Alberto Christo, a Brazilian priest who had met Fidel in earlier years, arrived at 9:00 p.m. at the presidential palace in Havana. Christo was known as Frei Betto, a Dominican brother, and an enthusiast for liberation theology. He was ushered into Fidel's office. Dressed in his olive fatigues, Fidel began to reminisce about his childhood. It was the start of twenty-three hours of interviews about Castro's views of religion that unfolded over the next few days.

"I never really held a religious belief or had religious faith," Fidel told Betto. He conceded that he was influenced by his Jesuit teachers, by their values and discipline. But he said, "Nobody could instill religious faith in me through the mechanical, dogmatic, irrational methods that were employed. If somebody were to ask me when I held religious beliefs, I'd have to say, 'Never, really.'"

Betto's questions were admiring. He never pressed Fidel sharply on anything. Perhaps responding to Betto's empathy, Castro recalled how his father, Ángel, handed out cash at election time. When it came to questions about persecution of the Catholic Church, Fidel was disingenuous. "No churches in Cuba were ever closed down—none of them," he said. And what about the expulsion of the priests? That was not his fault, Fidel said, but due to "the militant political attitude taken by some priests—especially the Spanish ones." The expulsion was done "only once," he added, claiming that "after that, relations were normalized." This was just one of his many distortions and elisions. "Some years ago, we had difficulties with the Catholic Church," Fidel declared, "but they were solved, and all the problems that existed at a given moment disappeared."

Fidel made no apology nor even acknowledged the harsher aspects of his treatment of the Catholic Church. But that was not the purpose of talking to Betto. Rather, Fidel was laying the groundwork to bring the Catholic Church into his arms.

On October 11, 1985, Oswaldo received another letter on the same rough brown paper from Ortega. It confirmed that he had been elected to represent the Havana archdiocese as one of the 173 delegates to the final conference on the future of the Cuban Church, known as the *Encuentro Nacional Eclesial Cubano*, ENEC, or the Cuban National Ecclesial Encounter. The conference, set for February 1986, was to be the culmination of the reexamination Ortega had launched. As a delegate, Oswaldo would again be in the thick of change, a participant in the most important national Catholic gathering since 1959. In the months before the conference, Ortega had set up a drafting committee to hammer out the language of a final document, as well as a separate commission, known as the presidency, to oversee the ENEC conference itself. The drafting committee worked on the document through autumn.

Out of sight, in private meetings, Ortega and Castro began to choreograph a reconciliation, a wary embrace between the persecuted Church and its chief tormentor. Carlos Manuel de Céspedes, secretary of the Episcopal Conference of Cuba, a priest and a trusted ally of Ortega, played a key role in the secret discussions, which continued through the summer of 1985. In November, Ortega led the seven Catholic bishops in their first direct group meeting with Fidel.

When Betto's book on Fidel was published in December, it touched off a sensation. Lines formed around the block from bookstores to get a copy. Some six hundred thousand were printed, a huge run in a country of ten million people. What Fidel had told Betto was not revelatory, but the content was not the point. The significance was the mere fact that it was about Fidel and religion, published by the state, in the open. "For the great majority of Cubans, the book marked a return of religion to the public sphere," said historian Kuivala, who added that the biggest surprise was that "it was Fidel himself who broke the silence." Ortega was as pleased as Fidel about it. "It has brought the subject of religion out of a somewhat taboo, reserved area," he told a journalist. The book marked another step toward the embrace of Castro and Ortega.

In late 1985, delegates from Havana gathered to prepare for the ENEC conference and share ideas with Ortega. The delegates knew Ortega placed a great deal of importance on the event. Oswaldo and Ofelia were now engaged. They went together to the preparatory session, held at Peñalver, the house of the Salesian sisters in the Guanabacoa neighborhood of Havana.

Oswaldo carried the text he had written with Ofelia's help. All the other texts had begun with the word "faith," such as "Faith and Culture." Oswaldo titled his "Faith and Justice."

At his turn to speak, his voice was confident. Many in the room knew Oswaldo personally, or knew others in his large family, a mainstay of the parroquia. They were respectfully attentive.

At the upcoming conference, Oswaldo declared, the argument should be made that the Church in Cuba must be a temple of freedom. The rights of every human being were a gift from God, and thus the Church itself was the instrument of liberty. He appealed to the Church to rise to its great mission. He was summoning and imploring but not hectoring.

Yet his words also carried an unmistakable message. He was challenging Fidel's authoritarian rule.

Catholics, he said, must have the right to speak out, to write, assemble, read, and think as they chose. They must be allowed to remedy injustice, to seek freedom for the hundreds of political prisoners locked up for their beliefs. Catholics must no longer be marginalized, de-Christianized, or squeezed into the periphery of society. Payá emphasized the principle of being able to speak the truth. Catholics must at last be themselves, not coerced into submission by the state, no longer fearful of expressing their faith, no longer passive conformists.

The delegates sat in a stunned silence. "Everybody was in shock at that moment," recalled Dagoberto Valdés, a member of the Catholic laity from Piñar del Río who knew Oswaldo well.

Two delegates swiftly jumped up to denounce Payá. One insisted Oswaldo's proposal was counterrevolutionary. Oswaldo had heard this often over many years and was not surprised.

But what happened next, neither he nor Ofelia had anticipated. Ortega stood and, his voice rising, told Oswaldo his document could not be presented at the conference. He grew angry and, out of character, pounded the table to make his point. Ortega realized that Payá's appeal for democracy and respect for people's rights would probably infuriate Fidel; it would be seen as a dagger aimed at the heart of the revolution.

Ortega put Oswaldo's "Faith and Justice" to a vote then and there, among the Havana delegates. Most voted "no." Five people voted "yes," among them Oswaldo, Ofelia, and Oswaldo's older brother Alejandro.

Oswaldo's proposal was rejected. Oswaldo and Ofelia were stunned. A Jesuit priest, Father José Manuel Miyares, rose to speak. "One day when this history is written," he said, "I want it noted that at least once somebody spoke the truth—as Oswaldo did."

But these words could not mask the break between Payá and Ortega. Oswaldo and Ofelia left the hall, shell-shocked.

In the weeks that followed, Ortega refused to drop the matter. He wanted to be doubly certain that Payá did not submit the text. Soon after the meeting, the archbishop summoned José Conrado, the outspoken priest from Trinidad on Cuba's southern coast who was originally from Santiago de Cuba. Conrado was a member of the presidency, the small group Ortega had established to oversee the conference. He was also a friend of Oswaldo and respected his ideas.

When Conrado and Ortega met, the archbishop was "totally out of his mind, screaming," Conrado recalled. Ortega feared Oswaldo's "Faith and Justice" text would sabotage his plans for the conference. "He blamed me, that Payá would have gone to this extreme," Conrado said. "The truth is that the government was very worried" about the upcoming conference. "The Church was starting to walk a tightrope. Jaime was feeling very directly the pressures from the government. He thought at that moment that it could end in some violent way. Jaime practiced a sort of realpolitik. That is the crossroads we were at."

Ortega instructed Conrado, "This cannot be allowed. This cannot come out. You've let something like this slip by—it's going to be a serious problem for us."

Another member of the presidency was Dagoberto Valdés. Valdés recalled that Payá's speech came up at a meeting of the presidency just before the conference. Ortega didn't specifically criticize Oswaldo's ideas, Valdés recalled, but firmly said, "Now is not the time."

The presidency rejected Oswaldo's text, as Ortega wanted. Ortega did not personally tell Oswaldo, but sent an intermediary to inform him. Oswaldo was told that he could speak from the floor instead. Payá agreed to withdraw the text out of respect for the institution. "He was incapable of doing any harm to the Church," Valdés recalled.

What Payá did not know was that Ortega had, at the same time, established a back channel to Fidel. In advance of the conference, Ortega had sent a draft of the ENEC document, without Oswaldo's "Faith and Justice," to Fidel for his approval, another step in the embrace. This document was a blueprint for the future of the Church in Cuba, and Fidel was being given an advance look. The text was carried to Fidel by Carlos Manuel de Céspedes, Ortega's close ally in the negotiations with Castro. Fidel sent it back with approval.

Fidel was invited to but did not attend the conference. He left shortly after for a Communist Party congress in Moscow.

On February 17, 1986, Oswaldo and Ofelia took their place among the delegates at the opening of the ENEC held at Casa Sacerdotal, which bears the name of the Cuban thinker and priest Félix Varela. It is an elegant, colonnaded former Jesuit seminary with a spacious interior courtyard unlike any other in Cuba. The conference culminated with Mass at the Havana cathedral on February 23. Valdés recalled that Oswaldo spoke up for his ideas during the proceedings. He also carried a copy of his text, which he had renamed "Christ, Truth, Justice, and Freedom." Oswaldo spotted the visiting Vatican representative, Cardinal Eduardo Pironio of Argentina, president of the Pontifical Committee for the Laity, who was personally urged by John Paul to attend. Oswaldo handed Pironio a copy of his text. "Please," he said, "give this to the pope." Pironio, who had been at both Medellín and Puebla, responded with sympathy. "Oswaldo," he said, "you know that what we are talking about here is not the nature of Marxism. It is not the nature of Christianity. What we are talking about is how the Church can come out of the catacombs without having its head cut off."

To achieve this, Ortega hoped to send a clear signal to Castro that the Church was not an adversary or competitor, that it would never again bring a million Catholics into the plaza, as in 1959. The final ENEC report accepted that Cuba was a socialist state. It drily reviewed the basic facts of the 1961 conflict but laid blame on "both sides" and appealed for "steps toward a dialogue" with the government. As Christians, the report declared, "we must practice forgiveness and be willing to overcome the insults coming from both sides in the past, with a constructive attitude that looks to the future." The report declared that the Church wanted to "fully participate in building a better world in our country." But it did not include the restive, raw commentaries of Catholic believers that had spilled out in the earlier REC meetings.

The report contained a few contorted sentences about Marxism, noting that some aspects are the "complete opposite" of "the Christian view of man and the world," but also claiming that Marxist values are "in part coincident, partly convergent, and partly contradictory to our cultural tradition." Valdés wrote this section, and he knew the logic was tortured. It was certainly true that advocates of liberation theology had drawn parallels between Catholic social doctrine, concerned for the poor and downtrodden, and Fidel's focus on peasants and the poor. But did Catholics share values with a Marxist ideology that was atheist? Hadn't Castro persecuted the Church in Cuba for years? The point here was not to speak about these painful questions. Rather, it was rapprochement. Ortega essentially decided that to save the distressed Church, he had to make concessions.

The conflict between Payá and Ortega was profound and irreconcilable. Ortega felt responsible for keeping the Church alive and was willing to deal with Fidel. He wanted to restore some of what was lost in 1961. The Catholic Church was the most significant charitable institution on the island, and the well-being of people rested on its ability to survive. Ortega thought that to begin a long climb back, dialogue with Fidel was essential, and could be carried out without compromising basic principles. By contrast, Payá felt that any compromise of freedoms and rights—including a decision to remain silent about them—was a road to serfdom. Payá certainly felt the pain of what the Church had lost under Castro, but he believed it was senseless to talk about stolen goods with the thief.

The archbishop "really had strong feelings" about Payá, not entirely critical, but wary, according to Conrado. "He appreciated Payá. Payá was one of the faithful who really had helped him and collaborated with him. But as Payá started to feel his political ambitions, Jaime thought that he was using the Church and the Christian community for a political project. And that could create very serious problems for the Church. So Jaime would say, 'Don't hide yourself behind the Church and don't remain confined to the Church.'"

However, Payá did not see it that way. In his mind, he was summoning the Church to uphold its own highest values. The demands for truth and natural rights were hardly a vanity project, but a cry for the Church to do what it had been talking about for so long. Oswaldo felt as invested in the Church as Ortega, and was stung by the rejection for long afterward. His disappointment was in the positions taken at the conference, but Oswaldo did not abandon his faith. He continued to serve on Ortega's pastoral council.

In earlier years, Oswaldo read books about religion, at least those he could find. Now, in 1986, he started looking for books, and ideas, about politics.

He would have to find another way to change Cuba.

Oswaldo and Ofelia were married on September 13, 1986, at the church where he had knelt and prayed as a boy, where he had listened to Petit talk about liberty, where he had hung the "Feliz Navidad" greeting on the bell tower. Oswaldo wore a blue three-piece suit with a maroon tie, and Ofelia a flowing white bridal gown with a sheer lace overlay, her veil held in place by a crown of lace flowers. She clutched a bouquet of small white blossoms. It was a Saturday and the pews were jammed with adults and children of the Payá and Sardiñas clans, as well as friends and coworkers. Ofelia's father, Orlando, looking distinguished in his suit and tie, walked her down the aisle. At the reception, the newlyweds shared a classic three-tiered wedding cake, a gift from Oswaldo's childhood friend Ramón.

For the wedding day, one of Oswaldo's older brothers hired a limousine to take Ofelia and her father from their home to the church. When she arrived, Ofelia and her father went directly inside. Her friends had brought a large floral arrangement and some presents, and Ofelia told them to put the flowers and gifts in the limousine.

During the ceremony, the chauffeur and limousine disappeared, and all her wedding gifts too, never to be seen again. Oswaldo's brother later learned that state security had quietly substituted one of its officers for the chauffeur. It was a message to Oswaldo and his bride.

The wedding hall was missing one family member. Carlos Alberto, Oswaldo's younger brother, had been under pressure from state security at the university, and was eager to leave Cuba for Spain. He was hunting for a ticket on an outbound flight. At the time, he had composed music for Oswaldo's wedding and was looking forward to the celebration. But a flight came available the week before the ceremony. Carlos Alberto asked his brother what to do. Oswaldo urged him to grab the seat. Carlos Alberto left for Spain and never returned to Cuba.

From Oswaldo's days as a teenager, the church foyer was always filled after Mass with informal discussion about events of the day. Now, Oswaldo attempted to turn these Sunday gatherings into something more organized, a club. It was risky. Fidel's government had left little room for alternative ideas or freethinking, nor for independent clubs and organizations. Information was rigidly controlled in the official press. But Cubans could sometimes hear shortwave radio broadcasts from the United States and Spain, and they would talk about them. When Payá began to organize the club, he was taking a chance that state security would notice. He went ahead anyway. He created *Peña Cristiana del Pensamiento Cubano*, the Christian Club of Cuban Thought, meeting weekly at the church. As Oswaldo explained it, the club was unofficial, independent, and intended to look at Cuban society "with a free, critical point of view."

The first sessions were devoted to Félix Varela, the priest who, from 1812 to 1822, became Cuba's foremost philosopher and educator. Varela's legacy had been neglected by the revolution—as had all Cuban Catholic thought from the nineteenth to the twentieth centuries. The club debate would bring him alive, Oswaldo hoped, in open discussion of the kind that Varela had once championed.

Born in Havana in 1788, Varela was orphaned by age six, and reared in St. Augustine, Florida, where his grandfather was a commander of a

Spanish troop regiment. His grandfather wanted young Félix to become a military man. But on coming of age, Varela solemnly told his grandfather he did not want to kill men—he wanted to save their souls. He returned to Cuba to study for the priesthood and was ordained in 1811. He was slight, sallow, and long-featured, with shining dark eyes and a high forehead. Varela became a professor of philosophy at the College and Seminary of San Carlos in Havana, which had a faculty of eight and only thirty-nine students. The energetic young professor soon revolutionized the study of philosophy, and went on to add new fields of study. "He virtually lived in his classroom, his laboratory, and his study," reported biographers Joseph and Helen McCadden. "He caused learning to become vital and pertinent and fashionable in Havana."

Varela believed that philosophy should not be dictated solely by the canons of the past but must be adapted to the present, based on the power of the individual to see the real world and draw conclusions about it. "The best philosophy of all," Varela wrote in 1812, "is the eclectic, in which we do not swear by the word of any one man, but are led by reason and experience, learning from all but clinging . . . to no one." Oswaldo saw parallels with his own faith and values.

Varela became known to generations of Cubans as the "first who taught us to think." His books ranged across grammar, human understanding, poetry, deductive and inductive reasoning, ethics, and a famous essay on the faces of patriotism. He pioneered explicative teaching instead of rote memorization, and secured the acceptance of Spanish instead of Latin as the language of instruction. He also insisted that students learn not only from books but also from hands-on experiments in the laboratory. He personally initiated the first modern science courses in Cuba, including experimental physics and chemistry. Varela was a "born teacher," according to his biographers. "Tirelessly he walked" among students, "peering with them into microscopes, helping them perform chemical miracles, exhorting them to challenge ancient conclusions and to observe for themselves." This, too, struck a chord in Oswaldo, a former high school physics teacher.

Varela left for Spain in 1821 to represent Cuba in the Cortes Generales, the parliament, during the *Trienio Liberal*, the three liberal years when King Ferdinand VII was sidelined. Active as ever, Varela pushed autonomy for Cuba and advocated abolition of slavery. When Ferdinand reclaimed the throne in 1823 and disbanded the liberal Cortes, Varela sailed to New York aboard a freighter. He had once idealized Spain, but the Cortes had exposed him to the monarchy's underside. "Spain is a cadaver," he wrote. In the United States, Varela became a champion of Cuban independence, publishing the magazine *El Habanero* from Philadelphia and then New York. Smuggled into Cuba and circulated widely, it infuriated Cuba's Spanish governor, who hired an assassin to get Varela. The killer went to New York and reportedly was talked out of it—by Varela himself.

Varela's political goals were democratic and nonviolent. He never favored armed rebellion. He thought that the right ideas, energetically disseminated, could triumph without the use of guns.

To help with the club's first meetings, Oswaldo's close friend Rolando Sabin had found a tattered biography of Varela, and Varela's original texts, at a bookseller of old volumes in Havana. After the first sessions, word of the freewheeling *peña* in Cerro began to spread. Anyone could walk in. Some of them, Sabin thought, looked suspiciously like undercover officers of state security.

One year after the Havana conference on the future of the Church, Ortega asked a difficult question: What had they achieved by the reconciliation gesture to the socialist state? In a lengthy homily in February 1987, he admitted that expectations had been "excessively enthusiastic." Any positive signs were "timid." Socialism was rigid, "difficult to modify." Ortega was certain that his course was right, but the Church was growing frustrated and impatient. The Church wants dialogue, he said, and the state seems to want dialogue. But will it happen? He declared once again that the Catholic Church could function "in Cuba with its socialist organization."

That autumn, Sabin heard on Vatican Radio that Pope John Paul II was about to convene a synod of bishops on the role of the laity in the Church. A central question was whether laypeople could act independently of local bishops. This was an important question in Payá's conflict with Ortega.

Taking another risk, Payá and Sabin decided to launch their own weekly newsletter about the synod, to be called *Ecos del Sínodo*, or *Echoes of the Synod*. The idea was to spread word of a major Vatican event throughout the parroquia and the city. There was only one Church publication at the time, and it was usually months behind the news. Starting an independent publication was subversive. The revolution controlled all the news. The mere suspicion that Oswaldo was trying to mobilize people through an independent newsletter would invite trouble from state security. Ortega, too, would see it as a challenge to his authority.

Nonetheless, Oswaldo took the chance. He was joined by Sabin, who had helped him hang the "Feliz Navidad" sign on the church; the doctor Cárdenas; and his childhood friend Ramón Antúnez. They planned their newsletter at the church, or at Antúnez's house. Sabin took notes on the Vatican events by listening to the radio. Oswaldo wrote opinion pieces. Sabin edited everything. Each issue came out on a Sunday to be distributed at Mass. Much of the newsletter was devoted to everyday information, such as how to tune in Vatican Radio on shortwave. Sabin wrote an article about how the pope had once been a lay Catholic in his native Poland. The most striking article was signed by Oswaldo and printed on the first page of the second issue. "We live under a regime that is trying to de-Christianize every aspect of society," he wrote, while at the same time many Catholics are "concealing their faith." The next week, Oswaldo criticized "inhibition, silence, or retreat," or giving in to atheism. Some Catholics have proposed a "certain adaptation" to the revolution, Payá wrote, "and to insert ideology in the Church's message, as an astute way of survival." This was a direct jab at Ortega. "This would deny the Christian vocation for the truth," Payá insisted. "It would be like giving to Caesar what is God's. It would be the antithesis of Christian incarnation."

The following week, Payá wrapped his message in flowery language of good Christian intentions, but lurking in the bouquet were words of steel. Oswaldo asked Cubans to overcome "fear and repression," work and fight for "justice," proclaim individual rights, and pronounce hope that "God's love will bring freedom, which can't be taken away."

All these messages were conveyed on nothing more than a smudgy handbill, printed on two sides of one piece of paper. Oswaldo and Sabin had discovered, cleaned, and repaired a broken mimeograph machine in the church. Sabin typed the articles. He scrounged up stencils for the mimeograph, and packages of bagasse paper, made from a by-product of sugarcane processing, very rough and not durable but good enough.

Five issues of *Ecos*—about three hundred copies of the first, then more later—were distributed throughout Havana on Sunday mornings in October and November 1987 by the four friends. Ramón and Santiago each had a car. They arrived at churches before Mass and asked that *Ecos* be distributed afterward. The newsletter was well received; people were hungry for news, waited for *Ecos* every Sunday, and asked for more.

Ortega was alarmed by the appearance of *Ecos del Sínodo*, perhaps fearing that Payá was spreading views that would further endanger his rapprochement with Fidel. Céspedes, the priest who was Ortega's intermediary with Castro, sent a letter to the church demanding an end to the newsletter. The parish priest brought the letter to Oswaldo and his friends. They agreed to halt. At this point, the Vatican synod was over. But Oswaldo's rebellion was not.

ELEVEN

THE MOVEMENT

Tremors shook the Communist world to its foundations in 1988. Mikhail Gorbachev struggled to breathe fresh air into the wheezing Soviet Union. In Czechoslovakia, a playwright, Václav Havel, became a leading icon of the opposition. In Poland, the outlawed Solidarity labor movement led renewed strikes and protests. In Cuba, Oswaldo Payá and his friends devoured Spanish-language issues of *Sputnik*, a digest of the Soviet press that was once rather dreary but was now filled with exciting news of change. They listened to anything they could get their hands on, including shortwave radio broadcasts and magazines smuggled in from the United States.

It was a time of promise. The first child of Oswaldo and Ofelia, a son, Oswaldito, was born in February. The couple vowed they would not leave Cuba and that their children would live in a free country. That summer, Ofelia was pregnant again.

Oswaldo's imagination was stirred by Lech Walesa, the beefy ship-yard electrician from Gdańsk who led the Solidarity labor union in a long underground struggle, facing constant surveillance and pressure from the Polish government. Payá admired Walesa's gritty courage, wearing a cross on his chest, mobilizing thousands of workers, peacefully defying the authorities. Oswaldo wondered: Could they create a Solidarity labor movement in Cuba? Fidel had crushed independent unions in his first years in power, but radical change was in the air. So much seemed possible. "It can be done," Payá told his friend Santiago Cárdenas. They met with a group of trade unionists and dockworkers who had organized themselves informally through the Church and were looking for allies. The contact was made through parish friends, a trusted word-of-mouth network. Cárdenas knew that discussions about mobilizing the public could be risky; Fidel believed that "the streets belong to the revolution." But Payá and Cárdenas went ahead with the meeting regardless. A week later, a teenage son of one of the workers came back to tell Cárdenas, in a terrified low whisper, that his father had been arrested and his house searched.

The idea of a Cuban "Solidarity" labor union was shelved. "We are definitely not Polish," Cárdenas said.

Oswaldo kept searching for a way to change Cuba.

The plight of political prisoners in Cuba began to get more and more attention, including from Oswaldo. Two former Cuban political prisoners, now in exile abroad, had published searing memoirs that drew attention to those who remained in jail for their beliefs. Armando Valladares, freed in 1982 after twenty-two years, wrote *Against All Hope*, describing squalid living conditions, forced labor, and punishing isolation in dark cells. Jorge Valls, released in 1984, authored *Twenty Years and Forty Days* about his long journey through Cuban prisons. Both men had been incarcerated in the panopticon prison on the Isle of Pines. Valladares broke rocks in the same quarry where Oswaldo had once labored. Valladares told harrowing tales of guards descending on the prisoners in the circular cell block. "Howls of protest and anger filled the Circular," he wrote. "The guards were making a butcher shop out of the stairways. There was a hail of blows with chains, bayonets, and truncheons. They were breaking heads and arms."

Andrés Solares, the engineer jailed in 1981 for preparing to collect signatures for a new political party, was still behind bars at the Combinado del Este, the maximum-security prison outside Havana. He performed an amazing feat: in cramped hand, on small sheets of paper, he secretly wrote the name and sentence of each prisoner around him, taking pains to record those who were sick or abused. He then folded the lists into tiny paper packets and slipped them to his wife, Adriana, who was permitted to visit once every six months. She took them to foreign embassies in Havana. The information eventually made its way to the human rights groups Amnesty International and Americas Watch.

Fidel's police state operated in the shadows, with snooping, infiltrators, and informants, constantly generating a sense of fear and dread. Political prisoners were tangible evidence of the dictatorship at work. While the government did not talk about them, family and friends sometimes learned where the prisoners were held, and thousands of former prisoners knew how the system worked. A substantial amount of anecdotal evidence was available to those who sought it. Ricardo Bofill, gaunt and bespectacled, the onetime philosophy professor whom Castro had jailed three times for a total of nine years and branded an "enemy of the revolution," was living in a Havana apartment directly above the local Committee for the Defense of the Revolution. He diligently collected information on political prisoners, arbitrary arrests, torture, restrictions on travel, and limits on publications and the press. Bofill had a particularly good network among relatives and friends of those locked away.

Their plight inspired Oswaldo to write one of his first appeals beyond the Church, an impassioned and provocative two-page open letter he distributed in 1987. The jailers, he wrote, subjected prisoners to torture and isolation, but the prison manuals "didn't say anything about man having a soul." That's when "the men in power and the persecutors lost the battle," he wrote. The prisoners' souls could not be destroyed. It was a gutsy declaration.

Halfway through his second term, President Ronald Reagan decided to call attention to Cuba's political prisoners in 1986. In his anti-Communist crusade against the Soviet Union, Reagan had raised the plight of dissidents and Soviet Jews being denied permission to emigrate. Yet in Latin America he often ignored human rights abuses by right-wing military regimes and dictatorships that were fighting Marxist insurgents. In one especially egregious case, an elite military unit in El Salvador, trained by the United States, murdered hundreds of men, women, and children, yet Reagan certified to Congress that El Salvador was making a "significant effort to comply with internationally recognized human rights"—and US aid continued. Reagan saw the world first and foremost through the Cold War prism of fighting communism. In his diaries, he wrote of El Salvador as a besieged ally, but Cuba was orchestrating a "Communist takeover" of Central America. The brutality in El Salvador was ignored, but Cuba's was called out.

Reagan appeared with former political prisoner Valladares at the White House in December 1986 and condemned the "horrors and sadism" of the Cuban prison system. The president wrote a personal letter of encouragement to Bofill in June 1987, saying the United States would press for international investigations of human rights conditions in Cuba. "This should bring hope to the thousands of men and women cruelly and unjustifiably imprisoned in Cuba," Reagan wrote. The US ambassador to the United Nations, Vernon Walters, began a campaign to pressure Fidel on the prisoners, saying Cuba represented "one of the worst cases of massive violations of human rights in the world." Walters said Cuba had some fifteen thousand political prisoners. His estimate was true in the 1960s, but the numbers had come down since, to about a thousand.

The Reagan administration's campaign was amplified by the rising power of Jorge Mas Canosa, a Cuban exile and wealthy Miami businessman who founded the Cuban American National Foundation. The organization spearheaded a new type of vigorous and effective anti-Castro lobbying by the exile community in Washington, DC, and Mas Canosa was a force behind the creation of Radio Martí, a US-funded station opened in 1985 to transmit prodemocracy broadcasts and anti-Castro propaganda to Cuba. His foundation reprinted the critical Amnesty International report on Cuba's prisons.

Reagan appointed Valladares head of the US delegation to the forty-three-member UN Human Rights Commission. After more pressure from the United States, the commission, meeting in Geneva in March 1988, agreed to send a delegation to Cuba to examine the charges of human rights abuses. Castro had resisted such an inquiry previously, but now accepted it, perhaps thinking he could easily finesse a visit. In a televised interview with Maria Shriver of NBC, he insisted, "There is no revolution in the world, no country in this world that has been stricter in its respect for human rights than ours has been."

But his actions spoke louder than words. After the Geneva decision, he immediately sought retribution against Bofill. When Bofill staged a low-key, independent art exhibition and used the gathering to call attention to torture in Castro's jails, state security created a mob scene on the street. Next, the regime tried to tar Bofill in the state-controlled press. From March 16 to 23 he was described as a *fullero*, or a cheat. He was called a *pícaro,* or rogue, from birth, a petty thief who eventually became a master schemer, a "chameleon," and an informer. When asked about Bofill in the television interview with Shriver, Castro denounced his group as "an organization of liars and cheats."

Bofill, a slight man, was beaten up three times by plainclothes officers from state security. But the campaign against him backfired in one important aspect. Now the words "human rights" were mentioned in public. Fidel's interview on NBC was twice aired on Cuban television and reprinted in full in a special supplement to *Granma*. And later in the year, the United Nations was sending a delegation to investigate human rights.

Oswaldo knew about Bofill's group and could feel the quivers of change. But how could he be part of it?

He found an answer in the weeks that followed, along with his three friends Rolando Sabin and Santiago Cárdenas, both doctors, and Ramón Antúnez, a law student. The four remembered how people had snapped up their smudgy, one-page *Ecos del Sínodo*. They decided to try again, despite the archbishop's opposition. They spent weeks working out the details of a brash, independent new publication.

Starting a newsletter, even a single-page sheet, would expose them to possible arrest. But so much was changing, they decided it was worth the risk. They named it *Pueblo de Dios*, or *People of God*. This was the same rubric under which Vatican II had encouraged a more active and robust Catholic laity in the 1960s, and by taking the name, Payá and his friends signaled the archbishop: do not interfere. "At this point, Oswaldo was in fighting mode," recalled Antúnez. "He said we have to do something, because the Church was going ahead with its own politics of getting closer to the government, and everybody else was quiet."

Antúnez added, about Payá, "He was always rebellious. But he wasn't one of those loud-mouthed, raucous rebels, full of hate. He never mentioned Fidel. Never. He would say, 'It will end. It will pass.' He didn't have hatred. It was a curious thing. [He would say] 'Something has to be done . . . that will win popular opinion. You have to move people.'"

They would move people with *Pueblo de Dios*—with words.

The first issue promised it would "proclaim and defend the rights of the people" and do so with the "truth." These two words—"rights" and "truth"—were at the core of Oswaldo's beliefs. The publication, they said, would promote "freedom of conscience" and would insist that no one takes the place of God.

No one could mistake the meaning of this statement. They would not worship Fidel.

When the articles for the first issue were ready, Sabin typed them on stencils for the duplicating machine, using typewriters at his house, from the church, and from friends, trying to give a little visual variety to the text. The first issue carried a brief, punchy essay by Payá, questioning why Cubans were afraid to use the expression "thank God," or "God bless you" or "God willing." The reason was fear of being labeled as religious. "People think twice, or look around before mentioning the Lord's name." Payá suggested: let's not be afraid to say "God" out loud.

They printed the first issue, drove out to distribute the copies on Sunday before Mass, and the old enthusiasm came rushing back. People waited, passed them around, and asked for more.

The Church hierarchy was alarmed. The parish priest at Cerro,

Father René Ruiz, approached Cárdenas after the second issue. "Look-ing at me seriously," Cárdenas recalled, the priest asked, "Are you going to keep publishing the little sheet?" Ruiz said Ortega was distressed.

"Yes," Cárdenas replied. "We'll go on."

No changing course, no going back?

"No, Father. We're still in the middle of it."

Ruiz left them alone, but they knew Ortega would not. They were forced to stop using the old church mimeograph. Once they even sneaked into Ortega's own offices, with help from a friend, and printed copies. Then they switched to a Baptist church in Mariel, twenty-five miles away. Sabin recalled that in the middle of a print run there, "We were surprised by the pastor, who lovingly but firmly told us we could not go on."

Pueblo de Dios was printed in several hundred copies, distributed widely, hand-to-hand, one person to the next, well beyond Havana. The project was illicit, and that boosted its appeal among people hungry for independent information. Soon they were printing almost a thousand copies.

With the fourth issue, the editors decided they would dare to give a copy to Ortega. Sabin was assigned the delicate task. He approached the archbishop after Mass and put *Pueblo de Dios* in his hands.

"Can you come to my office?" Ortega said.

Sabin and Ortega spoke for two hours. Ortega asked the group to stop publishing. Sabin explained Oswaldo's vision and reasons, but Ortega would not hear of it. At one point he grew angry—as he had at the meeting before the ENEC—and slammed his hand on the table. He asked Sabin to inform the others that he was demanding, as their bishop, that they stop publishing. Sabin told his friends.

Ortega also met privately with Payá one Sunday, in a remote place, according to Oswaldo's friend Cárdenas. Again, the archbishop asked Oswaldo to stop. Ortega interrogated Payá. *Who put so many strange and wrong ideas in your head?*

The fifth issue came out in July 1988. In the past, *Pueblo de Dios* had always carried a disclaimer that articles were the opinion of the author.

This time, a "clarification" was added, saying, *"People of God* does not speak for the diocesan Church or any part of it." And it added that "all opinions are debatable."

On the front page, Payá spoke from his soul. Two years had passed since Ortega's reconciliation with Fidel. Payá did not mention either of them but delivered a devastating verdict. If Ortega had hoped that reconciliation would improve the lot of Catholics on the island, the opposite had happened. Based on "the experience of the people themselves," Oswaldo declared that pervasive discrimination still existed against religious Catholics, in jobs, schools, all institutions, all leading to "marginalization, being watched, and sometimes the use of coercive measures." He had experienced it personally. "The lack of rights," he said, "affects many Cubans who hide their faith."

Payá insisted that religious freedom and freedom of conscience must be established permanently, something that "can't be taken away."

Still, out of respect for the Church, Oswaldo and his friends agreed to heed Ortega's demand to stop *Pueblo de Dios*—for a while.

In the spring of 1988, Andrés Solares learned that he would be released, six and a half years into his eight-year sentence for intending to collect signatures and start a political party. Amnesty International had named him a prisoner of conscience and, with others, had pressed Castro for his freedom.

On May 13, the door to his cell opened, and Andrés was taken directly to the airport to be sent into exile. Once there, he saw his family arrive, carrying a bag of his clothes and a box of family heirlooms, including his diplomas, his grandfather's patent for a sugarcane machine, and an album of old cigar stamps collected by his father.

At the airport, a guard attempted to confiscate the box. Solares was furious. He loudly protested on the spot, insisting that it was his right to take the box. More officers arrived, from state security and immigration. Solares declared he was not leaving Cuba without the box. He would rather go back to prison.

It was nearly midnight, and the other passengers were boarding.

Three of them were just-released prisoners eager to leave. Finally, at about 2:00 a.m., the guards relented and Andrés was able to board the plane to Miami with his family and his box. When he stepped on board, the passengers applauded.

In the box, sticking up from all the rest, was a treasured copy of *Constitutions of the Republic of Cuba*, a compilation by the Academy of History of Cuba, which Solares had consulted when preparing to start his new political party. The large-format book, with a torn, blue leather cover, contained the text of the 1940 constitution.

What Solares had barely begun before he was jailed—to use the citizen initiative—Bofill now attempted. On July 20, 1988, he distributed a press release, passed hand-to-hand in Havana, announcing he was forming an independent political party. The same risky endeavor had landed Solares in prison.

When Julia Preston, a foreign correspondent for the *Washington Post*, wanted to interview Bofill, she first had to elude the Cuban state security minders, who followed correspondents. Once free, she found Bofill in his darkened, hot apartment on July 23. He had no air-conditioning, only a rocking chair in an empty room. But Bofill had a surprising intensity and spoke a rapid-fire Cuban Spanish. The purpose of the new group, to be called the Pro–Human Rights Party, was to collect ten thousand signatures to force the Cuban government to add the 1948 UN Universal Declaration of Human Rights to the preamble of the Cuban constitution. Bofill's plan was audacious and probably impossible. He told Preston that he had already gathered some two thousand signatures. "We have to start with ambitious goals," he said. Sometimes Bofill had been accused of hyperbole, Preston wrote, but no one questioned "his tenacity in the face of relentless pressure by the Cuban authorities."

When she left Bofill's apartment, the state security minders followed her for several hours through the streets of Havana.

Bofill had touched a raw nerve. Fidel was not about to allow a new political party to spring up. "We must say here, once and for all, that we don't need more than one party . . . just as Lenin didn't need more than one party to carry out the October Revolution," Castro declared. "I say this so those who think we are going to start allowing pocket-size parties to give up their delusions. . . . No, there is only one party here."

"We got a few thousand signatures," Bofill recalled years later. "It was not that many." When people were asked to sign, they were afraid of state security, so Bofill did not get far. But the mere idea had given Castro a fright. "Fidel was afraid of everything that had to do with opposition," Bofill said. "Fidel would not tolerate it."

And with that, the second effort to realize Gutiérrez's dream of a citizen initiative was extinguished.

Change in the Communist world was now unfolding at breakneck speed. Reagan went to Moscow, strolled with Gorbachev in Red Square, and declared that the Cold War was over. Gorbachev presided over a party congress in which he proposed to create a new presidency based on democratic elections. In Havana, the weekly *Moscow News*, published in Spanish and filled with stories of *glasnost* and *perestroika*, was in so much demand that vendors kept it off display and tucked away for special customers.

But Fidel was having none of it. In July 1988, the word *glasnost* did not appear in print nor on radio or television in Cuba's state-run media. After tolerating limited ventures into free enterprise early in the decade, Fidel reverted to socialist orthodoxy in 1986, embarking on a program he called "rectification." He shut down independent farm markets when he heard about a Cuban garlic farmer who earned a profit selling at his own prices, not those dictated by the state. Castro was determined not to give an inch to Gorbachev's economic and political reforms. "We must not play or flirt with capitalist things," he said. "This is complete garbage."

However, Fidel could not stop the winds of change from reaching Cuba. The *Washington Post* correspondent Preston discovered there was an emerging interest in human rights. A Cuban journalist was publishing a newsletter about religion that covered human rights topics. The circulation was only thirty copies, but the fact that it existed at all was a sign of changing times. Elizardo Sánchez, once an enthusiast for Castro's revolution, who later worked in the Foreign Ministry and then became a professor at the University of Havana, turned to dissent and, after repeated jailings, announced the formation of a new human rights group in Havana.

Oswaldo Payá had faced his share of obstacles—his text had been rejected for the ENEC conference and his popular newsletters had been shut down twice by the archbishop. In the summer of 1988, with a spirit of new times in the air, he decided to start something more ambitious. He was fascinated by the events in Moscow, especially Gorbachev's demolition of old Soviet ways of thinking. "This began to tear down the myth that communism was an eternal and unshakable power," he said.

Payá was inspired yet again by Félix Varela. According to Sabin, "Studying Varela opened up a world of ideas for Oswaldo that shaped everything that was going on in his head." Payá had acquired Varela's *Cartas a Elpidio,* letters Varela wrote from New York and Madrid to his young friends in Havana between 1835 and 1838. The letters stressed the importance of a constructive, positive, forward-looking religion that valued individuals as the core of a just society. This resonated deeply with Payá's own convictions. Varela warned against demagogues who feed on people's lack of faith or moral purpose, or who play on superstition, ignorance, and fanaticism. For Payá, the letters brimmed with lessons for his own time. Varela placed a high value on liberty and a free society and believed religion should not be isolated from it. So did Oswaldo.

Castro was in many ways what Varela had warned against: atheist, demagogue, and despot. Varela advised his young Cuban friends to always stay on the high road. Payá grasped the lesson.

Payá pondered often: What kind of organization or action would bring about genuine change? Bofill's new political party was snuffed out. A labor union would be swiftly crushed. "We had passed the stage of talking. What we knew was that we had to do something concrete," recalled Antúnez. "But we had a problem that, if it was too visible, they would quash it. We had to find something that would be allowed within the very narrow range of what the government permitted."

They met one day at a house that Oswaldo had moved into on Calle

Santa Teresa. It was narrow, with a pink stucco exterior, around the corner from Calle Peñón, where he had grown up.

Oswaldo raised the idea of establishing an amorphous, loose-knit popular movement that, by its indistinct structure, could not be easily shut down. A movimiento would be like the morning mist, people with a common idea but not easy to arrest.

Cárdenas, who was ten years older than Oswaldo, cautioned him that it was risky.

"Aren't you afraid?" Cárdenas asked. Payá responded that yes, some days when he looked at his son Oswaldito in his bed, "I feel a cold that paralyzes me." But he stubbornly would not be deterred, "like the goat that he was," Cárdenas said.

Oswaldo and his friends argued over what to call the movement. At first they preferred just Liberación, or Liberation. "One simple word, simple and fast, like Solidarity," said Cárdenas. But according to Ramón, "Liberation sounded a little bit like liberation movements in Latin America, with more of a socialist style. And we wanted to make sure we were distinguishing ourselves from that."

Payá proposed adding "Christian" to the title. Although they wanted overall to create a nondenominational, secular civic movement that would embrace people of different faiths, he argued, they were inspired by Christian values and Catholic social doctrine. Oswaldo often repeated the verse of St. John from the New Testament, "And ye shall know the truth. And the truth shall make you free."

But his friends pushed back, saying the use of "Christian" in the title would mark the movement as religious and cause confusion.

One Saturday, Payá invited his friends back to the house, instructing them to dress as bricklayers, as if they were to repair the patio, so as not to attract attention from state security. Once gathered, he whispered that the time had come for "the baptism" of the movement by name. Oswaldo proposed Movimiento Cristiano Liberación, or Christian Liberation Movement. Antúnez voted yes. Cárdenas voted no. They had two other friends present. One voted no, and the other yes. Oswaldo had prevailed, 3–2. The movement was born.

Although they added *Cristiano,* they still intended to remain independent from the Church hierarchy. Also, Oswaldo was careful to distinguish between himself and Elizardo Sánchez, who was trying to form a
new human rights group. Oswaldo called Sánchez a dissident—a former
insider turned critic. Oswaldo had never been inside the revolution. He
was not a dissident, but the opposition.

Oswaldo began to write a manifesto for the movement. He wrote
in longhand, slanting to the right as if the letters were being blown by
a stiff wind, across page after page of thin paper. He wrote in a tone of
declamation and drew from his years of thinking about liberty—from
the rock quarry on the Isle of Pines to the pews of Cerro.

Nosotros los cubanos, he began, "We the Cuban people, proclaim before the world our determination to achieve freedom and the full dignity
of man, restore sovereignty to the people, and build a new nation for
all . . ." Payá insisted that Cubans will "reclaim the freedom that God
has endowed us" with "the most authentic rebellion of all: a rebellion
of the soul."

The thirty-five-point manifesto was a repudiation of all that Castro
had wrought. "Marxism is alien to our common roots," Oswaldo wrote.
"It has no connection to the birth of our nation. It is neither morally nor
spiritually linked to our culture or our struggles for liberation." And, he
said, "With this outdated ideology, and against our national character,
a system has been imposed on our society which has made us regress.
It has damaged Cuban society culturally, economically, as well as morally, suppressing the foundations of the respect for human dignity. That
system, whether called socialism, communism, or the Revolution, has
sown distrust among the Cuban people . . . imprisonment and estrange-
ment have touched every household."

Payá decried the Castro "lifelong, absolutist autocracy" that "ignores
the will of the people" and has "attacked all of our nation's values and
traditions, they have repressed our religious beliefs, and they are trying
to de-Christianize society and destroy the family."

He lamented the loss of real unions, authentic student organizations, a free press, independent courts, and legitimate legislatures.

"This system has failed in Cuba," he declared. "It failed because it cannot win over the Cuban people's hearts or consciences."

"Now, it is the people's turn, and the people will give freedom and democracy a try."

Payá was careful to point out that he did not want to go back to the 1950s, "but we shall also not remain trapped in the current decade. Today we will give birth to a new era for Cuba."

He urged the Cuban people not to wait for the regime or some foreign power to deliver the rights to which they are entitled. Those rights included "our freedom of expression, our freedom of assembly, our freedom of association, our right to strike, our freedom of artistic expression, and our right to protest."

A copy of the manifesto was smuggled to Miami and delivered to Radio Martí, the US-sponsored, anti-Castro station aimed at Cuba.

On September 8, the holiday that celebrates Cuba's patron saint, Payá and Ofelia went to the beach with Antúnez and his family in Ramón's black 1951 Buick. They had a Zenith shortwave radio and crowded around it at the hour of the news broadcast from Radio Martí. They were electrified to hear the announcer report the creation of a new movement in Cuba, "being run by Oswaldo Payá Sardiñas." So far, it was just a few people.

Before long, state security took notice.

Fidel boasted to Maria Shriver in February that there were no human rights problems in Cuba, but the visit by the UN Human Rights Commission showed otherwise. They arrived on September 16, 1988, and set up at the Hotel Comodoro in Havana. Over 10 days, they took testimony from 87 people, about 30 of them from nongovernmental organizations. They met with Fidel and Archbishop Ortega as well as government ministers. They inspected the old prison on the Isle of Pines, and the maximum-security prison Combinado del Este, where Solares had been incarcerated. The panel was inundated with about 1,600 written statements, of which 1,183 people said they had been denied the right to emigrate or return to Cuba; hundreds more detailed violations and

abuses of the right to due process, work, freedom of expression, association, religious belief, and more. The panel spent several months working
on a report. The fact that 1,600 people were courageous enough to approach the UN delegation suggested clearly that human rights concerns
had not disappeared. Although Bofill did not personally meet the UN
delegation—he was afraid of being physically attacked again—his group
did and provided a 110-page report detailing government abuses.

Soon thereafter, Bofill packed his bags. He left Cuba on October 5
for a speaking tour in Europe and never returned. Before he left, however, he met Oswaldo and conveyed his experience, the struggle to mobilize people and collect signatures for a cause. "He was a persuasive
person," Bofill recalled of Payá. "I told him to act with the power of
persuasion that he had."

The day after Bofill left Cuba, Payá heard surprising news from
Chile. A national referendum resulted in the ouster of the right-wing
military dictator, General Augusto Pinochet. Nearly four million people
voted "no," opposing another eight years in office for Pinochet. The
"no" campaign featured testimony from victims of torture and relatives
of those who had disappeared under Pinochet. The vote showed how a
people's referendum could change the course of history, peacefully and
profoundly.

Everyday life in Cuba was increasingly grim. A military intelligence
officer from the German Democratic Republic, a Communist dictatorship helping the Castro government, was appalled by what he saw. In
a lengthy cable on November 1, 1988, the officer reported that Cuba
seemed to be coming apart at the seams.

Shortages were everywhere, he wrote: potatoes, rice, meat, vegetables, fruit, milk, eggs, beans. It was hard to find toothpaste, toilet paper,
lightbulbs, spare parts of all kinds, paint, plaster, tools, nails, screws,
and wood. Transportation was in a catastrophic free fall, people waiting an hour for a city bus and paying double for the fare, while tons
of goods piled up at the Port of Havana because trucks were broken
down, short of batteries, tires, and spare parts. Sixty-eight cargo ships
carrying 495,000 tons of freight were waiting to offload. An official "port

transportation emergency" was declared. Many apartments were over-crowded with three generations, some families living in garages, but the officer observed that authorities were unable to solve the housing problem and unwilling to try. "Water is allocated by the hour, and power cuts occur." All of Fidel's appeals to people to work harder were falling on deaf ears. Due to the deteriorating conditions, the crime rate had soared; theft and burglary were running rampant, including an armed robbery of all the passengers on a bus. "More and more people are wondering why such conditions exist in the thirtieth year of the revolution." The officer reported that Fidel was losing his exalted status and becoming more a butt of quiet, knowing jokes. In Cuban cinemas, when the films showed Castro, some people defiantly hummed *"Ese hombre está loco,"* or "That man is crazy," the title of a Cuban pop hit by the singer Tanya Rodriguez. "There is a growing unease and mistrust among the population toward the political leadership," he added. "The miserable mood is mostly carried by people from thirty to forty years old, but is beginning to spread to the elderly, and they are by no means counter-revolutionary." In addition to the negative mood among the people, the officer wrote, "a kind of helplessness is also noticeable among leading and midlevel officials."

The cable, titled "Signs of crisis in the main areas of social life in the Republic of Cuba," was important information to the East German bosses. Their own regime was troubled by shortages and dysfunction. The cable was soon passed to the defense minister, and then went all the way to Erich Honecker, general secretary of the Socialist Unity Party of Germany, or SED, who presided over his own secret police agency, known as the Stasi.

Nothing in the report was secret to people on the streets in Cuba, including Oswaldo Payá. He was still thinking about the surprising success of Walesa in Poland, and he grew a big walrus-like mustache, in silent testament to the Solidarity union leader who was challenging communism from within.

TWELVE

THE STASI LESSONS

In Havana, Oswaldo and his friends kept watch for a thin fellow with light eyes and graying hair who called himself Edgar. That wasn't his real name, but he gave no other. He was an officer of state security, and he drove a cream-white Lada, the boxy little Soviet-made sedan that was the signature car of the secret police.

Edgar was keeping an eye on them. He began watching them in the late 1980s. Occasionally his car would be spotted near Payá's church, then suddenly swerve out of sight down a side street.

Edgar was the point, and behind him was the spear.

Cuba had a long history of informants, subterfuge, and secret police. Machado and Batista relied on brute force and torture. In Castro's revolution, coercion was taken to a different level: the mind. Castro had been steeped in conspiracy for most of his adult life, from the university gangs to the Moncada attack, from the Mexico guerrilla training to the *Granma* landing and his Sierra Maestra bastion. As a guerrilla leader, he knew that spies and informants were a force multiplier, allowing a small, outnumbered band to triumph over a much larger force. Manuel Piñeiro, known as *Barbaroja* for his flowing red beard, who was intelligence chief for Raúl in the Sierra Maestra and later Fidel's cunning but urbane overseas spy-master, explained it this way: Castro and his *compañeros* never forgot they were once just a besieged gang of fighters hiding from Batista's army in sugarcane fields. They never lost sight of how they had gone so far—survival was their life, and intelligence was their means of survival.

In power, Castro lavished personal attention and scarce resources on espionage, counterintelligence, and the secret police. His spies caught wind of the Bay of Pigs preparations in Guatemala in 1961—as did journalists—and had never stopped; three decades later Cuba had built one of the half-dozen best foreign intelligence agencies in the world. In a feat of audacity, Castro planted twenty-eight double agents with the CIA, compromising intelligence collection about Cuba for many years until they were unmasked in 1987. The Cuban exile community in Miami was a major target of Castro's spies as well as providing cover. Eventually, Castro's officers recruited and planted a mole, Ana Belén Montes, deep in the US Defense Intelligence Agency.

The regime's intelligence prowess was all the more extraordinary because it rose from an impoverished island, plagued by shortages of foodstuffs and spare parts.

The Committees for the Defense of the Revolution had informants on every block, a grassroots intelligence and snooping network. Each block committee had two sources who reported to the Departamento de Seguridad del Estado, or state security. Castro's former bodyguard Juan Sánchez recalled state security "had octopus-like tentacles that reached everywhere. Every industry, institution, ministry, and school, even in the tiniest village, was infiltrated or controlled by agents." State security was part of the Ministry of Interior, which also included foreign intelligence and counterintelligence branches. State security employed ten thousand to fifteen thousand staff, headquartered at Villa Marista, a former Marist Brothers school in southern Havana. Villa Marista was, for anyone detained, a dreaded destination. The compound was an inter-rogation center and contained basement cells, each two by three meters, with a metal or wood bunk bed and a hole in the floor for a toilet.

In December 1979, jolted by another wave of popular unrest and economic trouble, Castro told the National Assembly, "We are sailing in a sea of difficulties." He responded by turning to hard-liner Ramiro Valdés to take over the Ministry of Interior and the security agencies. Valdés, a veteran of the Sierra Maestra, had founded the ministry after the revolution.

Tensions ratcheted up with the United States. Relations soured in the second half of President Carter's term, primarily over Cuba's military deployments in Angola and Ethiopia. After Carter, Reagan's fierce anti-Communist ideology put Castro on guard. Fidel was also uneasy about Solidarity's challenge to the Communist regime in Poland. In June 1981, the Cuban Ministry of Interior hosted the East German secret police for a ceremony in Havana. The deputy Cuban minister, Brigadier General Pascual Martínez Gil, reassured an East German minister that what happened in Poland "would never be possible in Cuba." He added, "Counterrevolution would never be allowed to raise its head. At the first sign, the authorities would resort to decisive repressive measures."

Fidel was not so confident. His intelligence services had long used subversion, deception, informers, and psychological pressure tactics. But he wanted to find new ways to suffocate any opposition in Cuba. As it happened, the Stasi, the Ministry of State Security in the German Democratic Republic, had been refining their methods to detect opposition and nip it in the bud. The Stasi had created an operational technique known as *Zersetzung*. It meant "decomposition."

Soon it would be brought to the streets of Havana.

During the Cold War, a drab campus that could not be found on any list of higher educational institutions stood in the small municipality of Golm, nestled in the Potsdam district of East Germany, about a half hour southwest of Berlin. It was called the Juristische Hochschule Potsdam, or Potsdam University of Law. The main purpose of the school was not law, but to train secret police. Self-contained and off-limits to outsiders, it was centered around a wide parade ground, a legacy of the days when it was a Nazi air intelligence base. Now the students piled out of dormitories for exercise at dawn, had breakfast in a cafeteria, and were in uniform and in class by 7:30 a.m. They stood at attention at the end of every class. The school, run by the Ministry of State Security, or Stasi, trained senior and middle managers and young recruits just out of high school in secret police methods for "combating the enemy," as the Stasi documents often put it.

In 1981, an unusual student arrived at the gates. He was Jacinto Valdés-Dapena. He was thirty-nine years old, had studied in Pennsylvania in the 1960s, later passed his exams in Spanish language and literature at the University of Havana, and worked as a language teacher in German and Czech. He was also a first lieutenant in Castro's counterintelligence directorate of the Ministry of Interior. Valdés-Dapena was one of five foreigners ever admitted to the Potsdam school. He came to learn the latest methods of East Germany's secret police, including how to use psychological intimidation against dissent and opposition.

The Stasi was originally modeled on the Soviet KGB. Its insignia resembled that of the KGB, styling itself as the shield and sword of the party, the SED. Valdés-Dapena could not have missed the parallels between the East German Communist regime and that of Castro. The East German ruling party blamed its problems on "the work of vermin," just as Fidel blamed gusanos, or worms. Both regimes were paranoid about Western "enemies"—the East Germans treated West Germany with as much hostility and suspicion as Fidel regarded the United States. Critical opinions, unconventional lifestyles, and dissident behavior were regarded by the Stasi as signs of "hostile-negative elements," as the textbooks put it. Everyday life in East Germany was plagued with consumer goods shortages, and people tried desperately to leave. About 2.7 million fled the East between 1949 and 1961, crossing the border from East Berlin to West, until August 1961, when the authorities sealed the border and built the Berlin Wall. The Cuban people, too, were forbidden to leave without the regime's permission, and attempts to flee could be punished by jail. Many Cubans risked their lives in small boats and rafts, just as East Germans risked theirs to scale the wall. Both the Stasi and Cuba's state security maintained their own interrogation centers. The Stasi had seventeen jails, run from the main one in Berlin-Hohenschönhausen, with damp, cold bunker-like cells, each with a wooden bed and a bucket toilet. Both the Stasi and Cuban state security were hard-wired into a Moscow-based network known as SOUD, which contained data on perceived enemies of socialism, including dissidents, journalists, and foreign intelligence officers.

The Stasi patrolled the border against escapes—at least 138 people died trying in the Berlin sector—but its duties extended far and wide to spot dissent early and prevent it from taking root. A Stasi principle was *Vertrauen ist gut, Kontrolle ist besser*—trust is fine, but surveillance is better. The Stasi kept central card file indexes: the "F16" file contained 5.4 million records, and the related "F22" cards contained separate entries on why the Stasi was interested in each person. The Stasi was skilled at the technical aspects of surveillance. In the city of Karl-Marx-Stadt (now Chemnitz), three hotels were organized so that any room could be monitored with a video camera from an adjoining room. In Leipzig, the Stasi had 120 employees to open 1,500 to 2,000 letters a day. In East Berlin, 600 operatives worked on mail censorship across an entire floor in the main railway station. Since the 1950s, the Stasi had relied less on physical repression and more on fear and surveillance, but they knew the techniques of coercion and violence, including assassination by staging a car wreck.

All these were timeworn instruments of secret police under dictatorship. Many were taught at Potsdam. But Valdés-Dapena was likely most interested in something else, the crown jewels of Stasi methods.

The most important pillar of the Stasi was an army of unofficial workers, *Inoffiziellen Mitarbeitern*, known as the IM, which eventually reached a total of about 189,000 people in East Germany. Always undercover, they were much more than informants. The Stasi had spread them throughout society, to infiltrate cultural institutions, workplaces, and schools. They could be found on a factory floor or in the director's suite. The goal was not only to listen for dissent, but to penetrate any group that might have unorthodox or critical ideas, identify the ringleaders and other participants, subject them to pressure, and steer everyone away from opposition. The Stasi had put increasing emphasis since the 1960s on spotting dissent at the earliest stage, sparing the costs and messy aftermath of using force—searches, arrests, and imprisonment. The Stasi handbooks contain repeated and stern instructions to use "preventive" and "damage-preventing measures" to catch "incipient" protest. This required constant manipulation of the entire society. The Stasi wanted to know everything about everybody.

The shelves of the Potsdam school held extensive blueprints for how to do this. The Stasi prepared guidelines and handbooks, the latest of which, *Guideline 1/79*, had been issued the year before Valdés-Dapena arrived. The guideline was devoted to building and running the IM network and stamped "secret classified information." The goal of the IMs was to gather "information about plans, intentions, measures, means, and methods" of all sources that might launch "subversive attacks" against the East German state and party. The potential "enemy forces" feared by the regime were many: from overseas intelligence services to homegrown artists and intellectuals who dabbled in freethinking and those few courageous souls who might seek to flee the country.

The Stasi guidelines and handbooks revealed a system for infiltrating a society so deeply that the slightest murmur of dissent could be snuffed out. The Stasi preferred not to crack heads if they could quietly get inside people's minds—and manipulate them. Among the twelve major subjects studied at the Potsdam school was "operational psychology."

The core of the Stasi system of repression was carried out by Department 20, or HA XX, which was responsible for fighting "political-ideological diversion" and "political underground activity." The department scrutinized the state bureaucracy, churches, cultural groups, sports, and the political underground, and in the 1970s spied on peace, environment, and human rights groups in East Germany, among many others. It targeted forty-five organizations in the arts and culture, thirty-three in mass media and publishing, twenty-nine in public health, twenty-six in sports, twenty-four in friendly political parties and mass organizations, sixteen units of post office and telecommunications, fifteen offices in central government, thirteen in education, and churches. Critical to controlling them all was the undercover IM force, whose job was described as "disinforming, disorganizing, paralyzing, and crushing" any hostility to the state or party. The Stasi had strict rules that meetings with the IM had to be held in safe houses. These were known as "conspiratorial flats," and in one Berlin district, Prenzlauer Berg, near the Berlin Wall, the apartments were nestled every block or two. Most of the IM were twenty to forty years old, and there were six times more men than women. They were trained to exert "constant self-control," pose in "realistic and lifelike action," and avoid at all costs revealing what the Stasi was up to.

The Stasi officers lectured the IM operatives on how to systematically collect information using eight questions or principles: "when, where, what, how, with what, why, who, to whom"—and the handbooks repeatedly posed the most important question to be answered: "who is whom" among the targets of surveillance.

In the Potsdam school, Valdés-Dapena had access to the mother lode: a massive handbook, *No. 200/79*, comprising 4 volumes and 805 pages full of the accumulated experience of Stasi officers on the street. The handbook provided a full blueprint for Zersetzung, covert psychological warfare against people who might be hostile to the regime. In the words of the handbook, the Stasi wanted to "fragment" people and "paralyze" them.

Zersetzung was intended to make them come apart at the seams—to make their head explode.

The methods of psychological warfare against possible targets included "systematic discrediting of public reputation . . . and prestige" based on a "mixture of true and verifiable, as well as untrue but believable, personal details"; the "systematic implementation of professional and social failures to undermine the self-confidence of individuals"; the "purposeful undermining of convictions" about role models and ideals; "creating mistrust and mutual suspicion" within a group; "reinforcing rivalries within groups by exploiting the personal weaknesses of individual members"; and wrecking groups by destroying the ability of members to meet and communicate.

How to do this? Suspects were put under constant surveillance.

Phones were tapped, cameras installed, and IM watched them at work and play. Targets could then be unnerved by the spread of "letters, telegrams, telephone calls, etc., compromising photographs . . . or compromising documents." There was also "targeted dissemination of rumors about certain persons in a group." The goal, according to the handbook, was to "raise doubts in people," to "provoke fear," to "cause panic and distress" that they might get in trouble with the authorities, to "stir up disappointment," and "to get them to break away from the group" voluntarily.

The Stasi handbook stressed the value of focusing on relationships and group dynamics, to exploit "envy, jealousy, contempt, misjudgment, and degradation, which then have to be broken open and sharpened" by the secret police. The Stasi gave an example of a church member who was outspoken against the state. The Stasi found that members of his family were alcoholics and used church cars for their own purposes. So the Stasi sent fake letters about him to the church leadership purporting to be from "among the faithful," and the church member was removed by the church leadership itself. The Stasi left no fingerprints.

Valdés-Dapena also had access to Stasi forensic tricks for Zersetzung. For example, when the Stasi had learned a dissident was preparing to mail a three-hundred-page manuscript to people inside the country and beyond, with different packaging so it could not be easily tracked, an informant told the Stasi where the original manuscript could be found. The Stasi secretly marked it with radioactive tracking material and then, when sent, confiscated it in transit so it never reached the recipient. The Stasi also maintained a huge central file of every typeface from typewriters around the country, to unmask those who wrote anonymous protest letters. Chemicals were used for tracking people's movements, and clandestine photography for recording who was at a certain meeting. A Stasi minicamera could be concealed in a pocket with a small hole for the lens, and a remote shutter release hidden in another pocket. The Stasi had a special "scent archive" in which it obtained smell samples of suspects. Specially trained dogs could then recognize the suspect's smell on objects and in places.

Zersetzung was a gradual, mental grinding down of the target. In the case of a Berlin dissident, Wolfgang Templin, whom the Stasi labeled "Traitor" or just "T.," they discovered his couriers to the West. Those people were searched and marked at every border crossing they made. The freelance work of Templin was disrupted, then he was summoned— unknowing what was happening—to be given a specific job by a local district council. The job was actually selected by the Stasi so they could watch him closely. A contact in Templin's building snooped on his family's behavior, looked for minor infractions, such as failure to display the flag. His finances were secretly examined, as well as his mother's. He was summoned by the army for a mandatory medical exam to detect real or made-up medical issues with which to discredit him in political underground groups "and cause his isolation." Then the Stasi circulated fictitious stories suggesting Templin was under investigation by the Stasi, to create suspicion among his compatriots. A plan was drawn up to assign a "suitable" IM to start an extramarital affair with Templin's wife "to shake up the foundations of the T.'s marriage." The Stasi goal was to "cause T. to be preoccupied with himself so that he has little time to focus on his hostile activities" and to "discredit him within the political underground."

Six months after the campaign against him began, an IM reported to the Stasi that Templin had developed a "persecution mania."

"He believes he is constantly watched and is convinced that the MfS is behind it," the undercover collaborator observed, using the acronym for the Ministry for State Security. He "increasingly displays pathological delusions of conspiracy," checking every room, unplugging phones, and raising doubts among friends of his mental condition.

Valdés-Dapena made several visits to Potsdam, but wrote his 210-page dissertation in Cuba. He absorbed the Stasi lessons in full. His thesis incorporated material from the handbooks and guidelines. He distilled them into a plan to use the undercover IMs to infiltrate and wage psychological war against dissident groups in Cuba. He also embraced the Stasi method to jump on a case "immediately when the first signs of politically subversive activity appear."

At his doctoral defense on November 25, 1983, at the Potsdam school, Valdés-Dapena was the toast of two dozen Stasi officers, as well as his teachers and several Cuban intelligence officers. A first lieutenant when he arrived in Potsdam, Valdés-Dapena was now a captain in counterintelligence. His doctoral thesis was titled "The Counterrevolutionary Plans and Intentions of US Imperialism to Create and Inspire Enemy Bases and an Internal Opposition Movement in the Republic of Cuba. The Requirements for the Political-Operative Fight Against the Hostile Plans and Intentions of the USA Imperialism by the Cuban Security Organs." The long-winded title paid tribute to Castro's view of the United States. But it also reflected the goal of the captain's work, to absorb lessons from the Stasi about how to extinguish internal opposition.

In his oral defense, Valdés-Dapena emphasized the importance of creating undercover agents and infiltrating them silently into the opposition. This must make it "impossible for the enemy to set off its subversive acts," make their "plans and intentions fail," promote "demoralization," and create "conditions for destroying" the opposition. All drawn from the Stasi blueprints. The Stasi tutors were pleased with their Cuban student. They submitted eight comments on his thesis, all laudatory. One of the reviewers, Lieutenant Colonel Wolfgang Grunow, hailed Valdés-Dapena for having grasped the most essential lesson, to infiltrate the minds of targets and figure out where they were headed. This meant picking up signs of "wavering" and "negative political-ideological understandings and behaviors," then "fundamental questioning" of Marxism-Leninism, followed by "antagonistic beliefs" and underground activity.

Paul Kienberg, who for nearly two decades had run Department 20, responsible for fighting "political-ideological diversion," wrote a glowing review of Valdés-Dapena's thesis, calling it "clear, logical and practice-oriented" and saying it would be valuable for state security when he got home. Kienberg urged Valdés-Dapena to always strive to understand: "Who is the enemy, who must be counted as among the enemy's assets, who is politically unstable and misguided, and who can we rely on?" He said churches were being used as "free space for dissenters" and had become "a reservoir of these persons . . . and their ideologies, which are alien and hostile to socialism."

The school conferred on Valdés-Dapena a doctor of laws degree magna cum laude. But the laws that he had mastered were mostly about how to curb dissent.

In the four-volume Stasi handbook, the secret police officers made a list of suspicious targets to watch out for. The list included:

People who distribute and publish literature critical of Marxism and hold discussions about it.

People who criticize decisions of the party and the government.

Those who see a gap between what was promised and the real conditions of socialism.

People who write and think about how to change socialism internally in an evolutionary way to a more democratic socialism.

Those who congregate in schools, universities, and religious communities.

The artistic intelligentsia "who produce or discuss literature with antisocialist content."

People who look at political upheavals or coups, seeking to identify parallel mechanisms to dismantle the existing power structure.

Near the end of the list, the Stasi warned about people who plan, prepare, or carry out "collections of signatures" against the party and government.

Every one of these was a tripwire for the secret police. And every one could be applied to Oswaldo Payá.

In the years after Valdés-Dapena earned his degree, Fidel set out to emulate the Stasi. Earlier, with the Committees for the Defense of the Revolution, he had turned every Cuban into a potential informant. Fidel had once said, "Who can make a move without the CDRs knowing about it? Not even an ant!" But Fidel yearned for more—especially sophisticated technology for snooping and spying. It is not fully known how Fidel got more information or the methods of training his secret police; certainly the Soviet Union must have helped. But the East German regime, part of the Soviet bloc, was one of his closest allies and suppliers. They taught the Cubans in earlier years how to forge documents, including passports, and shipped to Havana all the printing equipment.

The Cubans alerted the Stasi in 1982 to sophisticated satellite communications that were being used by the CIA; neither Cuba nor East Germany had knowledge of or experience with satellites. At one point in the 1980s, Cuba requested from East Germany two hundred tiny microphones that could be implanted in walls or doors; sixty miniature tape recorders that could be hidden on a body; and photography equipment such as concealed miniature cameras. Separately, in a clandestine operation code-named "Royal Palm," the East Germans shipped a Russian heavy truck, two five-ton trailers, and a container to Cuba in 1985 to create a listening station to intercept all US communications at Guantánamo Bay. The Stasi ran Royal Palm but shared the intercepts with the Cubans, who had no way to crack the US communications on their own. The grateful Cubans meanwhile raided embassies in Havana and stole communications ciphers from other countries, which they shared with the Stasi. The Cuban Ministry of Interior also turned to the Stasi for technical help in creating a computer database to track 1.5 million people in Cuba, a monitoring system of anyone considered suspicious. A document describing the system said it would contain information on all targets of the secret police, including everyone considered a counterrevolutionary, and "religious activists with positions contrary to the Revolution."

Oswaldo Payá was one such activist.

THIRTEEN

REBELLION OF THE SOULS

When the new year of 1989 dawned, the Communist world began to disintegrate. Oswaldo found the pace of events exhilarating. In Poland, Lech Walesa and the Communist government held roundtable talks on political and economic reform that led to the legalization of Solidarity. In the Soviet Union, the first relatively free election since the Bolshevik Revolution was held for a new Soviet legislature, the Congress of People's Deputies. In Prague, protesters shouted "Freedom! Freedom!" in Wenceslas Square despite police attempts to squelch the demonstration. The police arrested Václav Havel, a move that elevated him to a national figure as a daring anti-Communist.

Ofelia and Oswaldo celebrated the birth of their second child, a daughter, Rosa María, in January. Again, they vowed that their children would live in a free country, and they would fight for it.

Fidel Castro stood against the winds. When Gorbachev came to Cuba in early April, at the peak of his drive for *glasnost* or openness, Fidel was disdainful. In a speech to a special session of the parliament, Castro insisted that Cuba could not follow Gorbachev's example. "Anyone can understand this is absurd," Fidel declared. "Anyone can see this is madness."

On June 14, Fidel made an extraordinary move that stunned the whole country. A popular general, Arnaldo Ochoa Sánchez, a veteran of the Sierra Maestra and one of the most decorated officers in Cuba, was arrested and accused of corruption, along with three other officers. The general, who had commanded Cuban troops in Angola and Ethiopia, five years earlier had been awarded the title Hero of the Revolution, Cuba's highest military honor. Ochoa was subsequently accused of overseeing cocaine smuggling from Colombia, but it seemed unlikely he could have done so without Fidel or Raúl knowing about it. After a televised show trial, Ochoa and the other three were executed by firing squad near dawn on July 13. The reasons for his downfall are still murky. He clearly became disenchanted with the revolution. He also appears to have been protecting drug smugglers, and Castro may have thought he went too far and used the case as a pretext to eliminate a rival. Andrés Oppenheimer, a *Miami Herald* journalist, wrote that Castro was signaling to the armed forces, the Cuban people, and the world that "Cuba would not tolerate the 'new thinking'" of Gorbachev. "The executions made it clear that there would be no independent thinking—let alone dissent—permitted on Castro's island," he wrote. The aftermath led to an important power shift. Raúl, who was already in charge of the Ministry of Defense, took additional control over Cuba's security services. The interior minister at the time, José Abrantes, who had worked extremely closely with Fidel, was arrested in parallel with Ochoa, accused of covering up the smuggling, and sentenced to twenty years in prison. The Ministry of Interior had long enjoyed more access to lucrative foreign deals and imported goods than the military. Now Raúl and the military would call the shots.

In June, the Communist crack-up seemed to accelerate. In Poland, Solidarity won elections to the new parliament. In Moscow, the Congress of People's Deputies met for the first time, and the nation was spellbound by proceedings broadcast on television that broke new ground in freedom of speech.

In China, student protests in Tiananmen Square called for democracy and reform. On June 4, Chinese troops massacred hundreds, and perhaps thousands, of the demonstrators.

The Tiananmen massacre left Oswaldo with a sense of dread. He feared it could be the harbinger of more violence—that a transition to democracy might awaken animal spirits and ignite mass protests and killings. He often talked about the difficult steps of transition, saying it had to go peacefully, "from the law to the law."

In July, Oswaldo and his friends again published *Pueblo de Dios*, their most potent way to reach people. They printed it clandestinely. The entire front page of the issue, no. 6, was devoted to an essay by Payá with a striking tone—clear, unabashed, and principled. Oswaldo wrote that *Pueblo de Dios* was halted in 1988 because it was "misinterpreted" by the archbishop. But they could restrain themselves no longer. People of God was back—to fight for religious freedom, to defend the poor, to denounce injustice, and "to remind all that nobody has the right to take away the freedom that God gave us so lovingly." The purpose: "In a nutshell, to give voice to those who don't have a voice."

Oswaldo was incensed by a government statement that the Church and the Cuban state were now enjoying good relations. He responded that the Church as an institution was cozying up to Castro's regime while believers were still being persecuted. "The decades-long campaign of de-Christianization of our society continues," he wrote. Before anyone talks about building socialism, he demanded, "we need to speak about freedoms of conscience and religion . . . which presupposes freedom of speech and association."

The newsletter was a direct challenge to Fidel and to Ortega. A friend had loaned Payá and Sabin the use of a computer and a printer. They set the new edition in a nice type and printed about a thousand copies. But before distributing them, Oswaldo and Rolando had a moment of panic. Very few people in Havana had a computer—could state security track down the fonts and discover their source? Out of an abundance of caution, Rolando retyped the issue on a standard typewriter, printed another thousand copies, and hid the incriminating edition in the church.

The revived newsletter was grabbed quickly in churches all over Havana on a summer Sunday morning.

On August 6, Ortega came to Payá's parish church to celebrate the Feast of the Transfiguration. Oswaldo, Rolando, and Santiago were all present. The pews were full.

Ortega did not mention names, but his homily was aimed directly at Oswaldo and his friends. In a tone of annoyance, Ortega said the parish was proving too radical and wayward from the hierarchy. Ortega almost always spoke with an easy smile and a soft manner, but on this day his mood was darker and his face betrayed little warmth. He warned that if the rebelliousness continued, there could be consequences. "We realized the whole homily was about us. He didn't say *Pueblo de Dios* or the names of its authors, but it was about the laity and the movement," Ofelia recalled. Ortega was clearly under pressure from the government over *Pueblo de Dios,* and he bridled at the blatant disregard of his own demand to stop publication.

Ortega never took any concrete steps to punish them, but his warning foreshadowed more pressure to come.

In September, issue no. 7 of *Pueblo de Dios* was published, carrying only a two-page essay by Oswaldo. He summoned Cubans to take matters into their own hands, a bold suggestion in a dictatorship. "We can't be just the spectators of our own history," he insisted. "We must be the protagonists."

Oswaldo floated a new idea that he called a "national dialogue."

"We propose that all Cubans search together for a path to the future," he wrote. "Only in an environment where everyone can propose ideas and be heard with respect and serenity will we be able to find what is best for Cuba." The references to "serenity" and "dialogue" were Oswaldo's reaction to the Tiananmen Square massacre and his desire to avoid chaotic change in Cuba. But inside the velvet glove was a steel hand. His essay demanded that *everyone* be allowed to decide Cuba's future, not just Castro and his government. Payá then laid out what such a dialogue would require, including release of all political prisoners and an end to coercion and retaliation against government critics. In such a national dialogue, he wrote, Fidel could not dictate the outcome. "No system, ideology or party, no matter how fair or impartial, can be above the nation," he insisted. He quoted José Martí, "Our homeland is an altar, not a pedestal."

"Sovereignty, the people's right to decide their own destiny, can exist only in pluralism and democracy," Oswaldo wrote. "We Cubans are a modest people," he added, "but we don't know how to live without liberty."

At the bottom of the page, he drew an insignia with a capital "L" in the middle for Liberación.

On November 9, the Berlin Wall fell, twenty-eight years after it was erected. The Cold War in Europe was over. West and East Germany would be unified. The Stasi was disbanded and the school in Potsdam closed. To Oswaldo, the wall coming down was confirmation that communism was finished. Although Castro tried to cut off information about the events, Payá and others heard it on Radio Martí and other foreign stations.

Fidel refused to give any ground. "Giving up is for cowards," he declared. The "red flags of our revolution will never be lowered from their masts."

Raúl Castro had been even more devoted to Marxist orthodoxy than Fidel. In the autumn months, he choreographed a purge of the Cuban security services and Ministry of Interior. By December, all heads of departments and most officers and staff of the ministry were replaced by Raúl's military loyalists. His takeover of the security services meant only one thing: even less tolerance of dissent.

Rolando Sabin had not taken part in the last edition of *Pueblo de Dios* because he was studying for his examinations in internal medicine and personally felt he should follow the archbishop's request. But very early in the morning on Monday, March 12, 1990, he heard a knock at the door. He opened it to find a large group of police and security officers. For the next five and a half hours they searched his apartment. They picked up a book titled *Prayers of the People of God* and passed it around as if it were incriminating evidence. Then they handcuffed Sabin and took him to the police station on Infanta Street, Havana. He was left alone in a single cell.

Santiago Cárdenas was arrested that morning too, and then state security came to Oswaldo's house. Ofelia, still in bed, realized what was happening, and grabbed from a drawer the text Oswaldo had been composing the night before. She concealed it under bedsheets, then sat their one-year-old daughter, Rosa María, atop the sheets. The text was never found by state security, which overturned the rest of the house before taking Oswaldo away.

Sabin was closely interrogated about *Pueblo de Dios*. The last edition, with Oswaldo's powerful essay, had been distributed in the narrow streets around the cathedral in Old Havana, and someone turned a copy over to state security. The point of the arrests, Santiago recalled, was "to liquidate *Pueblo de Dios*."

Oswaldo and his friends had anticipated this day. They had agreed that if arrested, they would tell the truth. "And so I did," Sabin recalled. But state security mistakenly believed that Sabin was the group leader, when he had never joined the movimiento nor taken a role in producing the last edition.

The formal accusation was "clandestine printing and illegal distribution of printed matter," Cárdenas recalled, "to which was attached a warning that we would go directly to prison without a trial if we repeated the offense." Oswaldo received a similar threat.

After more than thirty hours in detention, they were all released to their homes and instructed not to leave without permission. They all promptly ignored the warning. Sabin met with Oswaldo at the church soon after their release. Cárdenas recalled Oswaldo freely pedaling around town on his bicycle.

But something had changed. After the arrests, they were watched constantly. "At any moment, anywhere, a white Lada car was following, or Edgar appeared," Sabin recalled. Cárdenas said that "it was evident day and night. There were interrogations in the workplace, monitoring on the streets, telephones cut off, outrages and insults every day. We would receive visits from state security before anniversaries or important holidays, telling us to stay at home and warn us that we could not go out on those days into the streets. Something similar to round-the-clock house arrest."

Edgar approached Sabin one day, still under the mistaken impression that he was the group leader. The state security officer tried to persuade Sabin to become an informant and threatened to blackmail him if he did not. On this day, Edgar said, "Tell your friend Oswaldo that he rides his bike all over Havana, and one day he might have an accident."

Sabin did not tell Oswaldo. He refused to be a tool of Edgar's intimidation. But as a precaution, he told Oswaldo's older brother Alejandro.

Sabin was a medical doctor and worked at a hospital in Havana. One day, Edgar told the hospital director that Sabin had been arrested for treason. This immediately cascaded into trouble. The director called Sabin into her office. She said she would not expel him from his post, but from that moment on, whatever difficulty that emerged in the hospital would be his fault. Out of fear, some of Sabin's friends and coworkers stopped talking to him.

Oswaldo was indignant about the detentions and refused to be intimidated. But the experience also led him to conclude that they needed more than a movement. They needed something concrete to carry out. "Inactivity kills us," he told Cárdenas. "We can't go on like this. We have to find a goal, so that people will move and work. And find it soon."

The answer came from Antúnez. A law student, he mentioned to Oswaldo that the 1976 constitution allowed for a citizen initiative based on ten thousand signatures. It was the successor to Gustavo Gutiérrez's provision in the 1940 constitution.

Both Solares and Bofill had tried to use it and failed. Payá remembered Bofill's ordeal and futile quest.

In the summer of 1990, Oswaldo decided to try again. The initial gathering of signatures by the movimiento would be very low-key, practically underground, to avoid reprisal. But as Payá worked it out in his mind, they would expand and eventually collect ten thousand signatures to propose a law that would lead to an honest referendum, a national dialogue—and after that, fundamental change.

Occasionally Oswaldo slipped into a Franciscan monastery in Havana. He knew a young friar there, Juan Rumin, who had a hard-to-find photocopy machine. The Franciscans had bought it on the black market and it was highly prized. Oswaldo entered the monastery with an empty briefcase, made hundreds of duplicates, and walked out with a full briefcase. He was printing documents for the movimiento, and sometimes he made a large number of copies of the UN Universal Declaration of Human Rights.

On November 20, Payá formally submitted to both the National Assembly and the government a proposal for a "national dialogue" and referendum. It called for creating a "round table" such as the one Walesa had pursued in Poland, with representatives from every corner of Cuban society. Oswaldo signed the proposal, then waited for a response.

He was met with stony silence. By the end of 1990, all he had was a receipt from the Council of State that his submission had been received. When someone from the movimiento checked with the government about the legality of his proposal, the reply was: it is legal. But there were other signs of displeasure. On December 24, Edgar approached Santiago Cárdenas and tried to intimidate him for being involved. Two days later, he approached Ramón Antúnez. On January 27, 1991, another state security official questioned Oswaldo. Meanwhile, the government and the state-controlled press ignored Oswaldo's proposal.

"They *never* answer you, they don't respond," Ofelia recalled. "Neither yes nor no. They never say anything. They just ignore you. Nobody dared to make any decisions. The Communist Party controlled all institutions of the media, the policy was to silence people. It has always been that way, to silence people." Oswaldo also took his proposals to the Catholic bishops. But after all that had happened with *Pueblo de Dios*, they ignored him too. "They don't want any communication," Oswaldo later commented about the bishops. "When we send them documents asking for support, they don't even read them."

"Oswaldo never got tired," Ofelia added. "He was convinced that we could fight against this regime. He was aware of what could happen. He would say it was a rebellion of the souls. They wanted to crush the person. But they can't crush the soul."

By the spring of 1991, the Communist world was in its death throes. Gorbachev had lost his luster, and ethnic nationalities were pulling the Soviet Union apart. Boris Yeltsin was elected president of the Russian Federation and championed a drive toward free markets and democracy. The Soviet Union that had been Castro's benefactor and ideological guiding light for three decades was reeling. The values of democracy and free markets that Fidel had resisted for so long were now in ascendancy. And the United States went to war in Iraq and ejected Saddam Hussein from Kuwait with an impressive new generation of precision-guided conventional weapons.

Cuba was sinking into a morass. A *Washington Post* correspondent, Lee Hockstader, found lines and shortages at bakeries, grocery stores, and pharmacies. Canned foods, automotive parts, and machinery from Eastern Europe already had grown scarce as former allies turned their backs on socialism and on Cuba, but by 1991 the shortages were closer to home. Cuban rum and beer were rationed; pork was hard to find for Christmas, bananas and eggs scarce. With food rationing, residents of Havana got five pounds of rice a month, ten ounces of red beans, twenty ounces of lentils, a half pound of cooking oil when available, four pounds of sugar, and three small cans of condensed milk.

Castro declared Cuba was entering a "special period in a time of peace," a country on a wartime footing. But the words were hollow—and mocked—as Cuba slid into depression, its lifeline severed from the sinking Soviet *Titanic*.

In March, Cuba's seven Catholic bishops, led by Ortega, privately wrote Fidel a scathing letter that called for a more open political system. They were responding to Castro's own request for suggestions. The letter, never made public, was far more critical than Fidel expected.

Oswaldo, still haunted by the Tiananmen massacre, worried about the impact of so much hunger and misery in Cuba. In a public message of the movimiento, he expressed fear that the shortages and tension could lead Cubans to "kill each other over a slice of bread." What could follow? "Catastrophe, chaos, repression."

In June 1991, Oswaldo and members of the movimiento began distributing a handbill that for the first time openly appealed to the public for signatures. Signed by Oswaldo, it emphasized that the petition was legal and based on the constitution. "Therefore, no citizen should be afraid of exercising their right," he wrote. The handbill called for collecting ten thousand signatures to back legislation for a referendum, then a national dialogue and changes in the constitution, as he had proposed in November. The process was left vague in the handbill, but Payá sensed that people were fed up. "We appeal to your Christian conscience, to your Cuban conscience," he declared, warning people not to remain "passive and anguished" about their plight. "Now there is time," he said. "Later it may be too late."

Payá announced in the handbill that starting on June 16, 1991, the petitions could be signed at his residence, Calle Santa Teresa 63, in El Cerro. The house was where the movimiento had been born, just around the corner from where he had grown up on Calle Peñón.

On June 10, Oswaldo brought a press release announcing the signature campaign to the major state-run Cuban newspapers and radio stations. They all ignored him. But word spread anyway. Twenty or more people a day began to show up at the house, asking to sign. State security noticed.

In the early morning hours of July 8, Payá took a phone call from San Juan, Puerto Rico. The call was from Julio Hernández, a businessman. Born in Havana in 1939, the son of a newspaper editor, Hernández had studied at Villanueva University and later the University of Havana, was active in Christian democratic youth politics, and became a young anti-Castro militant. At one point he had worked with the CIA bringing weapons into Cuba before the Bay of Pigs invasion. After the invasion failed, Hernández was caught and interrogated but let go. He left Cuba in June 1961. In later years he remained involved with the Christian democracy movement and built textile businesses in Florida and Puerto Rico.

Hernández said he heard that Oswaldo was collecting signatures and asked whether he could help.

Oswaldo was expansive and candid on the phone. He repeatedly emphasized that he feared "a bloodbath," and was acting to avoid it by proposing a peaceful process for change. His petition was "an attempt to save the life of the nation, the lives of the many people who could die, and give them a future with rights. We don't think that a truly liberating process involves bloodshed."

Payá emphasized that he was not seeking to oust Fidel, just "going to the people so they will say what type of change they want and how they want it to happen."

How was his security? "It's true," Payá said, "that we've been under pressure." He and others had been questioned and detained for short periods. But he insisted it was legal to collect ten thousand signatures. Even the state security officers admitted as much during the interrogations, he said. "It's true there are a lot of rumors going around, but we say it is yet to be proven that they won't respect the law."

Three days later, the government gave its answer.

On July 11, the front door to the Payá house was shut, held by a latch. Payá's friend Dagoberto Capote, one of the five founders of the movimiento, was in the house to answer questions should people come to sign the petition. They had not collected a large number. Some signatures were in the house and another two hundred or so were hidden. Oswaldo and his family were staying at his childhood home, around the corner. The Santa Teresa house had some repairs under way.

At 5:00 p.m., three men broke down the door, knocking over a table with the signatures, scattering a copy of the constitution, and smashing a bust of José Martí on the floor.

The men then shoved Dagoberto against the living room wall, threatening and insulting him.

Within minutes, one of Payá's neighbors, Roberto Cabeiro, who lived at no. 59, arrived and began slugging Dagoberto in the chest. "You maggot, I won't let you collect signatures!" he shouted.

Speaking to the other intruders, Cabeiro declared, "This one needs to have his head bashed in."

Another man rushed in, whom Dagoberto did not know. He searched the entire house, took papers, and disappeared.

A small mob crowded inside, overturning furniture and pushing Dagoberto into the street. Cabeiro and the others came outside and encouraged the crowd to attack Dagoberto. "You need to be finished off!" Cabeiro shouted.

Dagoberto appealed for help from another neighbor, an off-duty policeman who was in plainclothes. The officer turned away.

Two policemen arrived and took Dagoberto to the local precinct, saying it was for his own protection.

The mob then painted graffiti on the front of the house that translated to "Payá, you worm," "CIA agent," and "Long live Fidel."

Soon Edgar arrived at the local police precinct and returned Dagoberto's bicycle, which had been at the house. Edgar had "directed, down to the last detail, the preparations for the 'spontaneous' harassment," Santiago Cárdenas later wrote. "We had seen him lurking in his cream-colored Lada" weeks before the onslaught. The mob attack was an acto de repudio, a government-orchestrated tactic of mob intimidation often used against Fidel's foes. The mob had arrived on a bus, neighbors said.

The third attempt to use the citizen initiative was in shambles. Cárdenas recalled that "it showed our opposition was serious and real."

One evening after the attack, Payá and Fernando Avedo, one of the five original members of the movement, were riding their bicycles in Havana. It was dark—the city was under another of its periodic blackouts—and a truck with its lights off swooped down on them, forcing both into a ditch, then sped away. Oswaldo was unhurt, but Avedo was bruised and his bike destroyed. There were no witnesses.

On September 8, Oswaldo and Antúnez went to El Cobre, a small town near Santiago de Cuba where a basilica houses the revered likeness of La Virgen de la Caridad. This was the feast day of the revered saint. At her feet, they placed an appeal headlined, "Now, Freedom!" in which they called for Fidel to "clear the way for a democratic, pluralist process." Oswaldo vowed not to lose hope but admitted that the movement's demands for peaceful change had been met with "scorn, threats and displays of force." They had been jailed and harassed, and even riding a bicycle was dangerous. He kept riding.

"There will be socialism—at any price!" a defiant Castro declared October 14 before a crowd in Santiago de Cuba. His voice sometimes near breaking, Castro vowed that Cuban Communists "will seek ways to save the country, to save the revolution, to save socialism."

The Soviet Union collapsed on Christmas Day 1991. The seven-decade Communist experiment was over in the place where it began.

Castro was adrift. Cuba's economy nosedived.

Oswaldo did not immediately return to collecting signatures. He pondered what had happened and how to overcome the obstacles.

The movimiento "had to start from scratch several times," he recalled. He started again.

By early 1992, Oswaldo concluded that his citizen initiative was missing something. It was a petition drive, but seeking what? In the handbill, he kept the goals vague: national dialogue, a referendum, a new constitution. But clearly these were not enough.

He decided to write out a full road map for transition to a new society. He often wrote at night, sitting in bed with a board on his lap, scratching away in longhand. Maybe, he thought, this detailed plan would help persuade people to make the leap, help them see that it was possible.

In writing the transition plan, Oswaldo was attempting to climb a very high mountain. He had to find a way to transform a desperate people and devastated economy into something more promising and free. He was a physics teacher and a medical technician with high ideals, not a legal draftsman. He simply wanted to sketch out a bridge to a new world that would be sufficiently sturdy—and believable—that people would follow him over it.

The same questions were being asked all over the former Soviet bloc: How do nations weighed down by decades of central planning and one-party rule suddenly turn themselves into a free market democracy?

Poland went for "shock therapy," a rapid shift to capitalism. Yeltsin was going down that road too. At the same time, almost none of the former Communist states were attempting to punish or prosecute the former regime. The Stasi officers largely just melted away as East Germany was absorbed into the West. The emphasis was on reaping the riches of new-found capitalism. However, there was a crucial difference. The European nations were already free of communism. Cuba was not. Payá was writing a transition plan for—someday.

Gustavo Gutiérrez would have understood Oswaldo's difficulty. In many ways, Oswaldo was single-handedly repeating what had preoccupied Gustavo and his generation, culminating in the constitution of 1940, a blueprint for an entire society. As Gustavo wrote back then, a constitution itself was not enough; people must have faith in democracy for it to work. This was still an enormous gap. After thirty-two years of Fidel's charismatic and dictatorial spell, Cubans had very little memory of or experience with democracy.

Still, Oswaldo produced an extraordinary document, called *Programa Transitorio*, or Transition Program, brimming with sound principles and optimism. He repeatedly affirmed the right of all Cubans to decide their fate, to "practice democracy," to assure "freedom of expression," to protect rule of law, to enjoy "balanced dialogue, justice, freedom and accountable participation."

If approved in a plebiscite, it would steer Cuba from the Castro revolution to a new society without "power vacuums, disorder or lack of control." It was based on the principle of separation of powers, including independent courts. The plan, forty-six pages and nine chapters, ranged over economics, education, health, the military, the press, and law, including a national council of the transitional government to carry it out, and smaller commissions to oversee departments and sectors. From the very start, Oswaldo insisted, "freedom of expression and association, including the establishment of political parties, unions and student organizations, will be guaranteed by law." It would be a total reversal of the revolution.

In contrast to Fidel's harsh siege mentality, Oswaldo wrote in dulcet tones of harmony, envisioning a "civilization of love" in which people would regard each other "as the brothers and sisters they are as children of God." Oswaldo was fond of such rhetorical flourishes, but he was also acutely aware of the dark side of human behavior. He worried often about "social explosion," about Cubans killing each other over a piece of bread.

To cope with the heavy baggage of the past and avoid retribution, Oswaldo proposed creating the National Commission for Dialogue and Reconciliation, and he imagined that smaller panels would be formed "at all places of work, barracks, neighborhoods and schools." There would be "amnesty for everyone," and no prosecution of Castro's regime or those "who committed abuses, crimes, betrayals and other actions" against the people and the nation. "We will look to the future, and not to the past," he wrote. Oswaldo did not want to repeat Fidel's show trials in the sports stadium, followed by firing squads.

But there was one exception. Fidel Castro must go. "No man or political position can be above the people, institutions and the law," Oswaldo declared, "even when some people attribute exceptional virtue to that man or when a very charismatic person is in that position." Every single Cuban is equal in rights and dignity to Fidel, Oswaldo insisted. The country was more than just one man and would no longer be ruled by him.

In March 1992, Carlos Aldana, a Communist ideologue and Politburo member, made a surprising comment in an interview with the German news agency Deutsche Presse-Agentur. He claimed dissidents and opposition members could run for seats in the National Assembly if they ran as individuals, not members of a party. Until then, candidates for the rubber-stamp parliament were largely handpicked by local assemblies.

Oswaldo decided to test Aldana's offer. He wanted to press the government by using its own laws. "It is a way to remove their mask," he told Cárdenas. On March 19, he announced in Havana that he would run for parliament to represent Cerro in elections set for October. He introduced himself as a "teacher and engineer," a specialist in electronic medical equipment employed by the Ministry of Health, a father of three small children, a Cuban Catholic. He pledged to "work peacefully" through the laws and pursue change toward "reconciliation and full justice." He mentioned that he and others had been collecting signatures for a plebiscite, but "we have constantly been repressed and threatened by the authorities."

"We do not yet know the procedure to run" for office, Oswaldo added. If Aldana was serious, "my decision to run is also serious. The only thing lacking is the commitment of the government to respect laws." In a phone call to reporters in Miami a few days later, Oswaldo said, "By running for office, I'm putting the government on the spot."

After the announcement, people stopped him on Calle Peñón and promised to vote for him.

Then the police came. He was taken to a local office of the Committees for the Defense of the Revolution. From inside, he could see his mother, Iraida, on the street, worriedly looking through a window to see what was happening to her son.

"There, they threatened me, saying there would be blood if I ran. The party, state security, the police, the Committees for Defense of the Revolution, the people who had assaulted my house—they were all there."

In July, the National Assembly modified the constitution, supposedly to allow direct elections. However, the system was rigged—only those candidates approved in advance by local commissions and municipal assemblies could run. When those groups met to select candidates, the government dispatched armed guards to make sure no one entered who was unwanted.

Oswaldo did not run for parliament, but the experiment encouraged him to think he could use the existing laws to fight the dictatorship. This became a pillar of his political quest in the years ahead.

State security hunted for Oswaldo's accomplices in the movimiento. In June they arrested three men in Santiago de Cuba who had earlier collected signatures and accused them of distributing "enemy propaganda." Oswaldo's friends and supporters in Havana, too, were summoned by the police, one by one. They were told that Oswaldo was a "CIA agent" and a "counterrevolutionary," a "racist," and an "alcoholic."

Edgar had struck again. State security was grinding Oswaldo down.

FOURTEEN

RAFTS OF DESPAIR

He drank coffee, nothing else. There was nothing else.

Oswaldo's mornings were hard. He was hungry, but he worried more about his young children. When he got a few bread rolls with his ration card, he saved them for the children. He had lost weight, and the sleeves of his shirts hung limply from his arms. The Lech Walesa–style mustache drooped from his thin face. He rode his bicycle more than nine miles to work and back every day. Ofelia, pregnant with their third child in early 1992, could not ride with him. They were living with her parents in the La Lisa neighborhood, on the western edge of Havana. She left the house three hours earlier, in the darkness, to wait for a bus to the city center. The bus system had nearly collapsed for lack of fuel and spare parts. When the bus did come, people were crammed on board, sometimes four and five abreast in the aisles, arms flailing out the windows. Dreaded electricity blackouts, to save fuel, rolled across the city every day.

When the Soviet Union disappeared, so did Cuba's lifeline of food and fuel. It was a time of want and fatigue.

Soviet bloc trade accounted for more than 70 percent of Cuba's imports and exports. When it vanished, Cuba could not produce enough food to feed itself. The Soviet bloc had provided 100 percent of Cuba's condensed milk, butter, cheese, and wheat flour; 87 percent of its wheat and lard; 63 percent of canned meat; and 57 percent of corn. The bloc provided Cuba 100 percent of its lumber, most of its fertilizer, and more than 80 percent of its autos and parts for agricultural equipment. Almost overnight, Cuba was forced to buy food, fuel, and manufactured goods on the world market using hard currency, which it did not have. Trade collapsed. The economy shriveled. The US trade embargo, imposed more than three decades earlier, remained in place.

Hunger was widespread; thousands of people suffered neurologic damage, including impaired eyesight. Ofelia's father, Orlando, roamed the streets of Havana looking for anything to feed his family. A friend in the countryside brought them what he could salvage from the fields. In a Havana bakery, a shipment of bread arrived, but when it wasn't distributed right away to people who had lined up outside since dawn, they invaded the bakery, shouting "We're hungry!" The lost imports after the Soviet collapse accounted for 44 to 57 percent of Cubans' caloric intake, and food rations were reduced sharply. The per-person monthly allotment of rice fell from 5 to 2.5 pounds, sugar from 4 to 2.5 pounds, and coffee from 4 ounces to 1.

Struggling to cope, one cook invented a "steak" made from grapefruit rind, boiled three times, seasoned heavily, breaded, and fried in hot oil. The government published and distributed to households *The Family Book*, a 430-page do-it-yourself survival guide that carried chapters on tending gardens and family nutrition, how to make soap and candlesticks. But there was also more extreme advice. "Survival is a tough ordeal," it said. The book assured readers that all parts of a plant are edible: "roots and other subterranean parts," "sprouts and stems," as well as "barks." Also, "the immense majority of animals that have fur can be eaten; likewise birds, large snakes, some small snakes, lizards, frogs, and even insects." In an emergency, they added, "All mammals are edible, among them dogs and cats." There were instructions for how to skin them.

After their third child, Reinaldo, was born in February 1992, Ofelia resumed riding a bike to work with Oswaldo. Without fuel or spare parts, almost nothing in Havana moved, not buses or trains or cars. Cuba bought 1.23 million surplus bicycles from China, labeled "Flying Pigeon," "Forever," and "Phoenix." They were the only way to get around. Even the military tried to adapt the bicycles, mounting a machine gun on one model and turning another into a stretcher-bearing ambulance.

Oswaldo rigged bicycles with basketlike seats on the front and back so the whole family could be ferried together to visit relatives. Oswaldo took the two boys, and Ofelia their daughter. Ofelia was terrified the kids would accidentally get a small foot stuck between the spokes. It happened once to Oswaldito, and he bled profusely as they rushed him to the hospital.

Jaime Ortega, the Havana archbishop, led Cuba's bishops in a cry of distress. In September 1993, they issued an extraordinary seventeen-page pastoral letter that declared, "There is discontent, uncertainty, despair in the population." The food shortages are "extremely serious," they said. "The beautiful and fertile soil of our island, the Pearl of the Antilles, has ceased to be the mother earth," no longer the bountiful source of "pumpkin and cassava, malanga and corn," and "the people wonder how it is possible that these things are scarce." Ortega now sounded the themes so long championed by Payá. The pastoral letter directly criticized Fidel's wearisome ideology, his monopoly of the press, the incarceration of political prisoners, the controlling nature of state security, and, most fundamental of all, the disappearance of truth. "The unhindered search for truth is a condition for freedom," Ortega wrote. Payá had written much the same in *Ecos del Sínodo* six years before.

Ortega's changed perspective was driven by what all the bishops were feeling across the island, a sense of desperation. Church attendance in Cuba was surging, a sign of people in despair. The quotidian deprivations, lack of simple basics such as soap or toothpaste, were eroding people's confidence in the revolution. They were still aware that they lived in a police state that often detained them for such offenses as "social dangerousness," for holding US dollars, or for selling produce to scrape by. But they were no longer quite as fearful. They had to survive.

In a drastic move, Fidel legalized the holding of US dollars in July 1993. Later he allowed the return of private farmers' markets, selling surplus vegetables. But neither measure changed the darkening mood. Black markets thrived and dollar prices were astronomical, creating more bitterness. "Down with Fidel!" graffiti appeared. A few days after Fidel's decision on the dollars, Brian Latell, the CIA's top analyst of Latin American affairs and a Cuba specialist, appeared in a rare open meeting of the US Senate Select Committee on Intelligence. "Castro's government is in acute distress," he said. "The impact of the economic crisis on the population has been devastating." The situation was so fragile that the CIA began to identify potential future leaders on the island, those who might play a leadership role if the regime were toppled. The fall of the Berlin Wall had surprised Washington. This time they wanted to be prepared.

While Cubans suffered, Fidel did not. He enjoyed a private life of bounty, according to his former chief bodyguard, Juan Reinaldo Sánchez, who had served at Castro's side for seventeen years. In a memoir written after he left Cuba, he said Fidel often spent summer weekends on a ninety-foot yacht, visiting his private island, Cayo Piedra, ten miles off the southern coast of Cuba. There, Castro would go deep-sea fishing, laying out on the dock lobsters, bream, skipjacks, and dorados he had caught. With "the barbeque coals already glowing bright red, Fidel would indicate which fish he wanted grilled immediately," he said. "The private life of the *comandante* was the best kept secret in Cuba."

When Sánchez decided in 1994 that he wanted to retire, "a tad disenchanted with all I had seen, heard and experienced," he was thrown in prison.

Six miles east of the Malecón seawall in Havana, at the fishing village of Cojímar, hundreds of Cubans gathered on the beach in the summer of 1994. Up and down the coral-covered shoreline, they assembled makeshift rafts to carry them away. Kevin Hayes of the *Hartford Courant* ran into a twenty-eight-year-old physical education teacher, Orestes, who had just finished building a raft for six people, including his wife, Carmen. Five inner tubes were wrapped in burlap and tied together with thin laundry cord. They would be joined by a cook, bus driver, house painter, and welder. Just a few hundred yards away, a raft carrying five people was pushed into the sea. As it hit the water, hundreds cheered wildly from the beach, and from windows and rooftops nearby, people waved good-bye and shouted words of encouragement.

The raft capsized in the high waves and churning water. Soon it was pulled grudgingly back onto the beach.

These were the *balseros*—the rafters, desperate to escape. More than five hundred a day were landing in Florida. An unknown number died at sea.

The balseros were another sign to Oswaldo that Cuba was a powder keg.

A spark came in May when 122 people broke into the Belgian ambassador's residence, seeking asylum. "We have nothing left to lose," they wrote in a statement to foreign journalists. "Our country is true hell." In June 21 people smashed through the gates of the German embassy with a truck. Then 8 people occupied the Chilean consulate. All were risking everything they had to get out.

In the early morning hours of July 13, Frank González Vázquez, who was twenty-two years old, stepped aboard a tugboat, the *13 de Marzo*, in the Harbor of Havana, along with 71 others, mostly women and children. González hunkered down in the space under the stairs in the machine room. At about 3:15 a.m., the old tug shuddered and left the docks, most of its passengers hidden belowdeck. Only the planners of the operation were above. They had hijacked the boat and were heading to Florida.

Out of the harbor and into the bay, larger tugboats of the same Cuban government maritime enterprise that owned *13 de Marzo* pursued the runaway vessel. One rammed it hard, and González was thrown against the engine. But the tug kept moving. It was seven miles from the Cuban shoreline when two more government tugs boxed it in. Others began shooting pressurized water onto *13 de Marzo*. In the machine room, Frank was up to his knees. People tried frantically to bail with jugs.

The other tugs began to ram *13 de Marzo* every few minutes. "They hit us so many times that many tables in the machine room fell over completely, and every time the boat turned or moved, the water came in with greater force," González recalled. The water reached his waist. The crowd belowdeck panicked. Some fainted.

Then one of the tugs crashed into *13 de Marzo* with enormous force, climbing onto the stern, cracking the tugboat in half.

González jumped into the dark waters. The tugboat sank in less than two minutes in a whirlpool of terror. Frank felt himself being pulled down about twenty-five feet before he managed to return to the surface. Forty-one people drowned, including women and children.

Those who survived were bobbing in the water. The government eventually hauled them aboard a rescue raft, and then a military tugboat. Later they were handcuffed and taken ashore. Women and children were released but men were taken to Villa Marista. González was shown a false confession, which claimed the entire disaster was the fault of the lead organizer of the operation, who deliberately forced the collision. He signed it, desperate to get out of jail.

"I know it was wrong," he recalled, "but I was traumatized after what had happened."

In a ten-day period that followed, three more Harbor of Havana ferries were hijacked. Then on August 5, a hijacked ferry was recovered. As it was returning to port, a crowd of thousands gathered on the seaside at Malecón, shouting angry antigovernment slogans. They were met by police with clubs and responded with a hail of rocks. Dozens were injured in the furious protest, which came to be called the *maleconazo*. Fidel toured the scene later and, as always, blamed the United States. He said he would no longer prevent people from leaving. "We are not opposed to anything, to letting those who want to leave, leave," Castro declared.

This opened the floodgates.

Thousands of balseros appeared on the beaches, lashing together inner tubes, scraps of wood, Styrofoam, and cloth, and spreading black tar on the raft bottoms.

They usually left at night, shoving flimsy ships of hope into the dark, roiling sea. In total, during the entire balseros exodus, more than thirty-two thousand people fled Cuba. So many were landing in Florida that President Clinton on August 19 rescinded a long-standing policy to admit to the United States any Cuban who made it ashore. Those who were picked up by the US Coast Guard were taken to Guantánamo Bay Naval Base and held for months—but most eventually found their way to the United States.

In the August exodus, a raft with ten people departed from the beach one night. The weather was clear. In the early morning hours, they were rescued by the US Coast Guard. The crew told everyone on the raft to leave their belongings behind, but Lizbet Martínez Lorenzo, twelve, who spoke no English, protested that there was one thing she could not abandon. An only child fleeing with her parents, she pulled her sole possession, a violin, out of a plastic bag.

In the dark, bobbing waters of the Straits of Florida at 4:00 a.m., she began to play "The Star-Spangled Banner."

With every step, Oswaldo looked over his shoulder. Edgar was still there. Oswaldo's movement—the Movimiento Cristiano Liberación—expanded, but gradually and carefully.

The movement created small, clandestine "base" groups, or teams, often in a Catholic parish church, working from person to person, one trusted friend leading to another. Oswaldo visited the teams after work or on weekends. "I was afraid all the time," Ofelia recalled, "because the persecution against Oswaldo was also increasing. I thought that one day he would not come home. They were always trying to get Oswaldo to make a mistake" so they could charge him with a crime and put him in jail. "At that time a person with a bag with three malangas, or a bit of wheat flour, rice or powdered milk to feed his children, was accused of theft or embezzlement, and ended up in jail."

A decade after Oswaldo had strung the Christmas decor on the church tower, his old friends were headed off in different directions. Santiago Cárdenas left for exile in Miami. Rolando Sabin remained the Payá family doctor and Oswaldo's friend, but he had not joined the movement. Ramón Antúnez, Oswaldo's childhood pal and one of the movement's founders, remained close to him but would leave Cuba in 1998. Payá needed to find more people to help manage the movement. He wrote to José Ignacio Rasco, who had founded the Christian Democratic Party in Havana back in 1959 and was now a professor in Florida, asking for materials to train his members in civic activism.

One of the movimiento base teams took root in Lawton, a poor Havana neighborhood just south of Cerro. At a church there, a rebellious young man, Regis Iglesias Ramírez, read a wrinkled copy of *Pueblo de Dios* that had been passed from hand to hand. He was intrigued by the ideas. He wondered who had written it.

His father, Carlos, had been a believer in the revolution, a journalist working for Prensa Latina, the Cuban official news service, which sent him to Beijing in 1976 as its correspondent. Tagging along as a young boy, Regis was exposed to the world beyond Cuba, and it glittered by comparison to the poor and backward life he knew. Flying to Beijing and back to Cuba, his family stopped in Prague, at airports in Madrid, Gander, and Shannon, and Regis was transfixed by the shiny glass display cases with toys—alluring metal trains and cars—that he had never imagined possible. He began to question why Cuba was so poor. Regis also spent days with his parents in East Berlin and Moscow, cities that looked terribly shabby. Was this the future? He asked his father, "Is this the kind of socialism we are building in Cuba?" His father wrote a book critical of the Chinese Communist Party leaders titled *Walls of Democracy*, which Regis read in manuscript form. It was mostly an indictment of the Chinese Communists and said nothing about Cuba. Nonetheless, the Cuban authorities never allowed it to be published—far too controversial and critical of another Communist system.

After Beijing, Regis returned to Havana, where he became a fan of rock music, mostly collected on cassettes that he played in his father's car: the Beatles, Pink Floyd, the Eagles, the Rolling Stones, all considered subversive. He began to wear his hair over his ears. He was defiant and edgy, an aspiring rocker. Then, when he was fifteen, his father was sent to Tokyo by Prensa Latina. To see Japan at the peak of its economic glory in the 1980s impressed Regis still more. He witnessed the start of MTV, saw the glittering citadel of capitalism, and returned to Cuba with an armful of albums. He became even more rebellious, styling his hair in spikes to look like Rod Stewart, for which he was ejected from school. He refused military service, another protest. He and his friends used to hang out at a park with a music player, a makeshift power cable feeding off a streetlamp. The police periodically roughed them up. Once, Regis was arrested and he loudly cursed Fidel as he was being led to a jail cell. His father had become an editor at Prensa Latina but lost his job when he edited and released a story about the rise of the Solidarity labor movement in Poland.

Regis found a safe harbor in the parish church, Santa Clara de Asís, which stood on a slight hill. The choir loft was ideal for catching radio broadcasts from Florida. The parish priest, a charismatic fellow who'd been imprisoned by Fidel, encouraged the youth to talk freely. Regis and his friends gathered there after Mass to listen to radio broadcasts, play rock music, and debate politics. They talked about Gorbachev and Walesa, Havel and Mandela. Regis started to devour *Sputnik* magazine, describing the waves of change sweeping the Communist world.

In the choir loft, Regis heard about "a guy in Cerro who is talking about liberation." Soon, a base group for the Movimiento Cristiano Liberación was set up in Lawton. They would only meet at the church, or in parks. On the phone, they would use code names such as "the baker" in case state security eavesdropped. Their first contact in the movimiento was Dagoberto Capote, who had been beaten at Oswaldo's house when it was mobbed. Regis asked to meet the leader of the movement. In an early evening in a park, when Regis first saw him, Oswaldo walked with a casual saunter, a bit of sunburn on his face and that drooping Walesa mustache. He did not seem to Regis like a radical. In a long conversation as the sun went down, Oswaldo described what he meant by liberación, and his fervent hope that Cuba could avoid violence. He also described his own journey to the opposition: from protesting the Prague Spring in 1968, to the Isle of Pines camps, to the frustrated quest for change in the Church, and finally the establishment of the movimiento.

Regis had a burning question. Many people were starting to talk about "human rights" so they could be recognized as political refugees and win a visa to the United States. "Is this about leaving the country?" he asked. "I can't follow somebody who's just going to use me as a vehicle for leaving the country."

"I'm not going to leave," Payá replied.

Antonio Díaz Sánchez also was driven toward Payá by a sense of disenchantment. He was short, with wiry hair, a decade younger than Oswaldo. His father had been a general in the Cuban army before the revolution. After Castro came to power, his parents decided, like the Payá family, to steer clear of the revolution. Tony was prohibited by his parents from joining the José Martí Pioneers, the Communist Party organization for young people. When he was eighteen years old, during the Mariel boatlift, his teachers demanded that he join classmates in an acto de repudio against a departing family. Tony refused. He was later called on the carpet at a party meeting and barred from attending the university. He wound up cutting sugarcane for three years in a military brigade. When he got out, the only schools he could attend were technical or vocational. He became an electrician, but he still seethed with rebellion. He was among the sixteen hundred Cubans who presented complaints to the UN Human Rights Council when it came to Havana in 1988. He was sure that showing up in person put him on the state security blacklist. Later, he organized a rare public protest in Marianao, a Havana municipality, over a government decision to charge citizens in dollars for the fees to obtain documents to leave the country. To protest, Tony went door to door collecting signatures. Although he was ignored, it provided a useful experience in collecting signatures for a cause. He also did a short stint working for a dissident human rights group in Havana.

By day, Tony labored at a construction site, a single building project that, typically in the socialist economy, was plagued by shortages and dragged on for years. A friendly worker at the site took him aside one day and said, "Have you heard about Oswaldo?" Tony had not, but he volunteered for one of the base teams of the movimiento. He met Oswaldo after the 1991 mob attack and they hit it off, bouncing ideas back and forth. Tony was impatient. He thought that change in Cuba might come overnight—just as the Berlin Wall had fallen suddenly. Oswaldo warned that if change came too abruptly, violence would follow. They had to slowly build a bridge, Oswaldo said, from one system to the other, from "the law to the law," without falling into the raging river below.

Tony owned a motorcycle, and soon he and Oswaldo were riding it every weekend to visit others in the movimiento. Tony drove, and Oswaldo held on tightly.

Oswaldo sensed that hardship and hunger had created a desire for change. He felt it in the people he knew, in his neighborhood, on the streets. But he was still searching for ways to harness it. The regime controlled all the means of mass communication—the radio, the television, the newspapers. The streets belong to the revolution, Fidel often declared. No competition was tolerated.

One night Oswaldo pulled out his board for writing in bed, along with a pencil and scrap paper he salvaged from work. He began to write about the "new spirit" among people, "a change of heart," a "clamor for change." He sketched out yet another plan for Cuba. This time he called it *Foro Cubano*, or the Cuban Forum. He envisioned a "great meeting that allows us to work together for the good of all, to meet in a great forum." But the plan was weighed down by complexity. He filled page after page with lists—different subforums, tasks, and goals. Oswaldo always wanted to be precise about how things should work. On behalf of the movimiento, Oswaldo and Tony announced the plan March 25, 1994. Oswaldo had become a leading opposition figure by this time, one of half a dozen on the island, but Foro Cubano didn't catch on. No one in the opposition offered a word of support. Nor did it find any traction in a population suffering hard times. What captured their imagination more was getting out—the rafts.

Oswaldo and other opposition figures met with a visiting diplomatic delegation from Spain on November 10, 1994. No sooner had the Spanish group departed than Oswaldo and others were arrested. Oswaldo was locked up at the police station on C Street and Zapata Street in Havana's Vedado neighborhood. The dungeons of the station were known as *el tanque*, or the tank, where hundreds of prisoners were jailed, generally for common crimes, and was often so overcrowded that some had to stand. When Oswaldo was thrust into el tanque and the guards shouted that he was a "child rapist," it was a signal for other prisoners to beat and kill him.

Oswaldo stood against the closed gate in darkness. He could hear the breathing of the men coming toward him. He pleaded with them: he was not a child rapist, he was a defender of human rights, but they kept coming. Suddenly a voice shouted, "Stop!" Oswaldo felt a man approaching him, ahead of the throng. "Do you remember me?" he said.

Oswaldo recognized him as one of the neighborhood kids he knew in Parque Manila in El Cerro. Over the years, Payá had helped him when he was unemployed.

The man turned to the prisoners and told them he had known Oswaldo since he was a child. It was true—he defended human rights. The guards had lied.

The atmosphere changed radically. The prisoners gave Oswaldo precious space in the dark cell, and they ended up talking all night.

The "clamor for change" that Oswaldo saw at the time was genuine, a restless churning. Soon, independent groups began to coalesce. People were pursuing their own interests beyond the state's control. Doctors, lawyers, journalists, economists, religious believers, environmentalists, and tradesmen gathered in a nascent civil society. Pioneering independent libraries appeared, usually just a few shelves in someone's living room holding volumes long considered subversive or unattainable. This awakening was fueled by desperation, necessity, and improvisation—and a sense that risks were worth taking.

The new mood reverberated in an upstairs room at the home of

Ricardo González Alfonso, a former television producer. He became disillusioned when the government censored a children's show he was writing. In his proposed script, parents were driven by economic despair to steal from their workplace and barter goods to survive. It was real life; the censors slashed it. González left television, and for a while sold peanuts on the street. Later, eager to join the tide of change, he established in his house a small school, a library, and a center for independent journalism, which was considered illicit. He was joined by Raúl Rivero, one of Cuba's most acclaimed writers, a poet and journalist who once worked for *Bohemia* and later was the Moscow correspondent for Prensa Latina. They began to teach and practice journalism with a simple goal, telling the truth.

Rivero's personal journey had taken him from the heights of the official state media to total rejection of the revolution. In the 1980s, writing for Prensa Latina, "I realized that I was beginning to report things that were false. It is difficult to accept that. It is difficult to accept that you are lying. It is difficult to realize you are portraying a version of reality that is not correct." He tried a job in book publishing, but everything there also "seemed to be a lie." He abandoned the revolution and all its organizations. "I went from indifference to indignation. What I wanted to do was real journalism." He wanted to tell stories of "what they were not saying in Cuba."

He and González formed Cubapress, an independent news agency, one of five that existed in 1995. Like the libraries, they were small, scrappy, and breaths of fresh air. Twice a week, the upstairs room became a classroom for six or seven aspiring reporters. Rivero managed to secure textbooks from Reporters Without Borders, which promotes a free press around the world. Rivero taught his reporters to steer clear of ideology and focus on reality. "What I used to say in those classes was that you don't have to write that Fidel is a son of a bitch. What you have to report is, the children in Cuba cannot eat. The type of journalism that people would believe in." He urged his reporters to write articles about everyday problems Cubans faced, such as "you could get only one pair of shoes every three years."

Bypassing the government, reporters for Cubapress sent dispatches to the Inter American Press Association, or Sociedad Interamericana de Prensa, which redistributed them to newspapers around Latin America. The reporters waited for a trusted contact in Miami to phone them, and hurriedly dictated. They also made sure to give a backup copy to someone else sitting at another phone in Havana, to be called again from Miami if the line went dead. It happened often. The journalists struggled with few resources. They were paid in cash when it could be brought in. "We made very little money," Rivero said, "but we worked with a lot of passion." Their dispatches were soon being read on radio broadcasts, including the US-funded Radio Martí. This flow of independent journalism back into Cuba—where the only official journalism was state and party propaganda—was extraordinary. All five news agencies were harassed by state security. The Cuban government considered them illegal. Fidel had once declared that everything within the revolution was permitted, and everything outside was not. The independent journalists were outside—testing the boundaries of the possible.

Another independent voice surfaced in Piñar del Río, at the far western end of the island. Dagoberto Valdés, who had participated in the church's ENEC process with Payá, started a magazine for the Catholic laity named *Vitral*, or Stained Glass. The magazine was often sharply critical of the government. Valdés also founded a small cultural center, giving lessons on how citizens can build a democracy.

Payá told Valdés one day, "This is our first Cuban Spring."

At this point, in 1995, the Movimiento Cristiano Liberación was one of the largest independent groups on the island, with hundreds of members, but many others were emerging. In October, Leonel Morejón Almagro, a Black Cuban activist and lawyer, began to organize a single event that would bring together the various fragments of civil society.

As a law student in 1986, Morejón founded a group that combined environmental concerns with pacificism, called NaturPaz. It was not an opposition group, and at the time, he still supported the revolution. But for his activism, he was arrested and the government threatened to expel him from law school, effectively destroying NaturPaz. He grew disenchanted, and as a lawyer began to defend the rights of dissidents. He joined Corriente Agramontista, a group of lawyers seeking to reform Cuba's legal system from within, a dissident practice that was harassed by the authorities. In 1995, Morejón was fired from the Law Office of Marianao, a state enterprise, on a trumped-up technicality, and then ejected from the bar association. This was a devastating blow, a "total destruction of my life and dream." His path to becoming a lawyer had been full of obstacles. He came from a poor, Black family; unlike other law students, who after class "went home to drink beer and dance," Morejón worked in construction and as a milkman to put himself through school.

After being disbarred, Morejón became a legal adviser to several opposition groups and soon came up with the idea of forming *Concilio Cubano*, or the Cuban Council, to bring together the disparate opposition groups. Elizardo Sánchez, the former professor who had become a leading dissident, played a key role. Oswaldo joined and helped frame the agenda. When the founding document was published in the autumn of 1995, it bore the markings of Oswaldo's thinking. It called for a peaceful transition to democracy, unconditional amnesty for political prisoners, a process of "legal transformation" to protect human rights, and inclusion of all Cubans, including those in exile.

The list of Concilio member groups started with a few dozen and exploded to 130 in weeks. The green shoots of civil society had surfaced. Some groups were no more than two or three people, others larger. The list ranged from the Pacificist Movement for Liberation to the Cuban Civic Current, from the Feminist Forum to the Pro Human Rights Committee, and included the Association of Cuban Engineers, the Independent Medical Association, NaturPaz Ecological and Pacifist Movement, Corriente Agramontista—and dozens more. "Ten years ago, there were fewer than ten dissidents in Cuba," said Sánchez. "Now we are thousands."

In yet another precedent-shattering moment, the Concilio asked Castro's government for permission to hold its first conference, in the open, early in 1996. No such gathering of opposition forces had ever been permitted inside Cuba under Fidel's rule.

"It would be a miracle if they allowed it," Sánchez said.

Fidel was in no mood to allow it. Soon Edgar and state security began to go after the leaders of the council. The lessons of Zersetzung—adopted from the Stasi—were applied methodically. State security officers infiltrated the Concilio, figured out "who was who," then frightened or discredited the leaders.

In one sabotage operation, state security sent about twenty forged letters to families of political prisoners, claiming Sánchez was stealing money sent to them from a charity in Miami. The "charity" was a fake, but the families didn't know that, and angrily confronted Sánchez, who told them it was untrue. The scheme was a classic Stasi gambit.

Morejón was approached by a Cuban official who had infiltrated the Concilio and offered what Morejón called a "dirty deal," seeking to recruit him as an informer in exchange for material goods and legalizing NaturPaz. The infiltrator suggested Morejón go on television and denounce Concilio as a project of Miami exiles. He sent the official packing with a stern "no."

The other leaders of the Concilio were individually detained, repeatedly, a few hours each time. The strategy was to unnerve them and break their resolve to hold the conference.

Edgar had a particular strategy to use against Oswaldo.

On January 13, 1996, two Cessna 337 civilian planes took off from Opa Locka Executive Airport near Miami and flew toward Havana's coastline. One of the planes was piloted by José Basulto, a Miami exile and veteran of the Bay of Pigs who had become an advocate for nonviolent change. Basulto was a cofounder of Brothers to the Rescue, a humanitarian project to identify the balseros from the air and alert the Coast Guard to their location. Over the years, Brothers to the Rescue flew more than a thousand missions and saved thousands of rafters from drowning. But the balseros exodus had tapered off, and Basulto was looking for new ways to promote democracy. On this day, he made a provocative gesture. The two planes dumped a half million leaflets that fluttered on the winds into Havana. On one side of the leaflets, printed in blue and red, were bold letters: "I am the change!" and "Not comrades, Brothers!" and "The streets belong to the people." On the other side was printed one of the thirty articles of the UN Universal Declaration of Human Rights. Basulto called the fly-over "Operation Dr. Martin Luther King." The planes returned home safely.

On the ground in Havana, police frantically tried to scoop up the leaflets, and so did many residents of the city. One of the independent press agencies, Habana Press, reported on the fluttering leaflets to Miami radio stations.

The airdrop did not go down well with Fidel.

In the days that followed, state security detained Oswaldo for questioning. In the interrogation room, they pushed across the table one of the leaflets. Look, they said—*your words are on the flyer!* They were pointing to the UN human rights declaration. "You are the inspiration!" Oswaldo stayed calm. He sensed that state security agents were trying to threaten him, perhaps hoping to charge him with a crime over the airdrop. It was a ludicrous but revealing tactic, Oswaldo thought, showing how the regime was shaken by the simple leaflets. Oswaldo was released without charges, but he had an uneasy feeling.

The Concilio conference was set for February 24, although they still didn't have permission or a venue.

State security swung into action. Morejón, the founder, was arrested in mid-February, along with four of the five members of the Concilio secretariat. More arrests followed, targeting leaders of the many participating groups. Each time, they were warned of danger to their families, and threatened with criminal and terrorism charges if they persisted.

A day before the scheduled conference, Morejón was summarily tried and convicted on charges of "disobedience" and "disrespect" and sentenced to fifteen months in prison.

With the leaders in jail, the Concilio conference was called off.

At 1:11 p.m. the next day, Saturday, February 24, three Cessna 337 planes from Brothers to the Rescue took off from Opa Locka Executive Airport and flew toward Cuba. One of them was piloted by Basulto. The group had announced a humanitarian flight to search for rafters—they had no leaflets this time—but Basulto was also hoping to show solidarity for the Concilio. He had sent the coalition several thousand dollars and thought there might be demonstrations that day. It was a holiday marking *El Grito de Baire*, the declaration proclaimed at the village of Baire, near Santiago de Cuba, that began the independence war in 1895.

Two of Castro's spies had infiltrated Brothers to the Rescue. One had abruptly left Florida early Friday and was already in Havana. The Brothers had announced in a press release on Thursday that they would fly a humanitarian mission over the Straits of Florida that Saturday. Castro probably knew, one way or the other, about Basulto's plans.

The sky was picture-perfect and the seas calm and glassy. As the unarmed Cessna planes approached Cuba, a pair of Cuban Air Force jet fighters, a MiG-29 and a MiG-23, took off from a base outside Havana at 2:55 p.m.

Basulto's plane dipped inside Cuba's twelve-mile territorial limit for a few minutes but the other two Cessnas were over international waters, looking for rafters. Within the next half hour, without warning, the Cuban warplanes shot down the other two Cessnas with heat-seeking air-to-air missiles. Four crew members—three of them U.S. citizens, one a permanent resident—were killed. Basulto's plane barely escaped back to Florida. The shootdowns were cold-blooded killings, condemned around the world.

Oswaldo and Regis had both been warned by state security on Saturday morning not to leave their homes. They disregarded the order and met later in the day at Regis's grandfather's house. The collapse of the Concilio, the arrests, and now the shootdowns cast a dark cloud over the first Cuban Spring. "The Cuban opposition was in a lot of shock," Payá recalled later. "There was a lot of confusion."

FIFTEEN

THE VARELA PROJECT

In early March 1996, Oswaldo Payá was forced to rest at home, recovering from minor surgery. He had time to reflect. He had just turned forty-four years old. The change he sought for Cuba had been elusive. Fidel's revolution, despite all the shocks and deprivations, had proven unyielding. The events of February—the loss of the Concilio and the shootdowns—were discouraging.

Oswaldo started again.

He suspected that state security had put an eavesdropping device in his house. When he needed to talk privately, he often walked next door to his aunt Beba's house. Ever since he was a toddler, Beba had doted on Oswaldo. Oswaldo was stretched out on Beba's couch one day when his friend Tony Díaz stopped by. Oswaldo was writing. Tony asked how he was feeling. Oswaldo replied but did not look up. He kept writing, by hand, the pen scratching across the paper. The socialist constitution of 1976 was unfolded on the couch.

Oswaldo looked up and handed Tony the paper. "A project for change," he said.

It was not long—just five points. But Tony realized it was different than before, simpler and more direct. The proposal called for guarantees of freedom of speech, press, and association, amnesty for political prisoners, the right to own private businesses, unhindered voting under a new electoral code, and a referendum followed by new elections.

It did not mention Fidel. Previously, in the Programa Transitorio, Oswaldo had called for removing Fidel. But he realized it was futile to knock heads with Castro. Nor did it make sense to beg the government for change—they would never give an inch. Rather, Oswaldo had concluded he must maneuver around Castro, to create an independent mechanism in which people could be mobilized as the agents of change. It was an almost impossible dream. "We didn't think the government was going to give in easily," Tony later recalled. "We had to come up with a plan they couldn't stop. We were in a political give and take, to try to win the battle and represent the people."

Oswaldo was learning by trial and error. He realized his earlier documents were too long. He needed to simplify, to be more of a preacher with a sermon than an electrical engineer with a complicated wiring diagram.

His main strategy to bring about change, which he had been thinking about for a long time, was to use the system against itself. He wanted to use the existing laws, and especially the 1976 constitution, which retained the citizen initiative.

The plan had risks. The constitution existed on paper, but Fidel set his own rules. He once defended the 1940 constitution, then destroyed it during his first months in power. He was the law, the maestro of the masses; he was the revolution.

Henrik Ehrenberg, a Swedish democracy activist who worked with Oswaldo for many years, recalled that Fidel recoiled at anyone who might rival him for the attention of the masses. Mobilizing people was his purview alone. "That's why they don't like the Church or independent unions. They don't even want independent chess clubs. Because if you mobilize you have structures parallel to the state. That's why they always crack down very hard on people such as Oswaldo that mobilize people. Most of the opposition in Cuba did not mobilize . . . they send out press releases, go to meetings, do interviews, they don't try to create movements, organizations. . . . Oswaldo had a completely different idea. . . . It has to do with the signing of the petitions, the whole idea was very Christian democratic, to give people back their dignity, use their human rights, their freedom of expression. That is a very *mobilizing* idea."

Oswaldo had lived with Castro's regime a long time. He knew his plan risked arrest, a prison term, losing a job he enjoyed, and that it could endanger his family. He could have given up at any point. He could have gone into exile. Or he could have been satisfied with talk and no action, just issuing press releases. But he decided to do more. He and Ofelia had promised that their children would live in a free country. He was determined to act on it.

The new project needed a title. Miguel Saludes, another member of the movimiento, suggested naming the project after Félix Varela, the priest and thinker whose writings had long inspired Payá. Oswaldo immediately embraced the idea. Later he asked Tony about naming it the "Varela Project." After all, Oswaldo insisted, they were doing exactly what Varela had once advised—taking the high road in a nonviolent quest for democracy and rights.

Tony wasn't sure. He recalled the name Movimiento Cristiano Liberación had led to confusion about whether they were a religious group. But Payá had made up his mind.

It would be *Proyecto Varela*, the Varela Project.

At first they worked on it quietly to keep Edgar from finding out. How to collect ten thousand signatures without being detected, infiltrated, and crushed by state security? All the signatures would be worthless if confiscated and destroyed. Moreover, Edgar and state security were growing more active, not less. Through 1996, more than two hundred people connected with the Concilio were either interrogated, detained, or jailed by state security.

"It was hard," Payá recalled. "It wasn't well understood. There was a lot of fear."

The gloom deepened with the arrest on July 16, 1997, of four dissidents: economist Marta Beatriz Roque, former fighter pilot Vladimiro

Roca, lawyer René Gómez Manzano, and professor Félix Bonne. As an informal political group, they had been pressing for peaceful internal change, and publicized a paper calling for reforms titled "The Homeland Belongs to Us All." They had warned, "It is impossible to continue leading the nation to its ruin without expecting an uncontrolled awakening of the populace." Roca, a social democrat and dissident, was the son of Blas Roca, the Cuban Communist with whom Fidel had conspired in the early years of the revolution. The message of the arrests was: don't trifle with Fidel.

Early that same year, Oswaldo endured a personal crisis. His eldest son, Oswaldito, suffered a potentially grave hepatitis infection. The boy recovered, but then was hit with a new illness and potential liver failure. Cuba could not provide a life-saving transplant. "We were scared," Ofelia recalled. Oswaldo turned to Sister Fara González, who was then superior general of the Daughters of Charity, a widely recognized and respected order. The nuns had been close to the Payá family for many years. Sister Fara was known for her intense humanitarian efforts and proved decisive in getting permission from the government for Oswaldo and Ofelia to rush their son to a Miami hospital for treatment. Archbishop Jaime Ortega also intervened to help. The treatment was successful and the boy did not need a transplant. It was the first time Oswaldo had been outside of Cuba. He had one political meeting, to explain Proyecto Varela to Julio Hernández, José Ignacio Rasco, and a few other Christian democrats. Then he and Ofelia took their son to Disney World.

Back in Havana, Payá decided to gingerly confront the Castro regime with an experiment. He would try to run for the parliament as an independent, as he did in 1992.

The constitution stated that the parliament is "elected through a free, direct, and secret ballot by the voters, in the proportion and according to the procedure that the law establishes." However, in practice the process was not free, direct, or elected. Candidates were handpicked by special local commissions under the control of the regime. No outsiders ever got on the ballot. No races ever had more than one candidate. There wasn't even a "yes" or "no" vote for the appointed candidate. Just a "yes."

Oswaldo's experiment was to challenge the closed system with a peaceful, legal campaign. Ten members of the movimiento ran as independent candidates for the parliament, including himself, Regis, Tony, and Miguel, each running from their own section of Havana. They collected about 120 to 140 signatures each and announced their candidacy with a crude flyer that included short biographies and a small photograph. The rebellious Regis, his hair still long, appeared in a coat and tie.

They filed their paperwork on November 25, but days later the answer came back: no places on any ballot. "For people to really decide, there must be options and choices," Oswaldo complained. "This would be the legitimate and democratic thing to do."

The elections, Oswaldo said in a December 10 letter of complaint to the parliament, were "not a decision made by the people." His letter was met with cold silence. The experiment confirmed, in Oswaldo's own mind, the importance of holding free elections early in any transition to democracy. He had a bedrock faith that, given a genuinely free and fair choice, people would vote for democracy over Castro. But he was still a long way from such a vote.

Oswaldo printed the first signature petitions for the Varela Project. On a single page were the five points, with room at the bottom for ten signatures, each with a line for an address and an identification number. To get ten thousand seemed daunting. "I have to confess there was a time and a moment when I lost my faith" that it could be done, Tony recalled. "It is really hard. But Oswaldo had blind faith that we were going to reach those ten thousand signatures and that it would change the history of Cuba."

In December 1997, the Castro government allowed Christmas to be celebrated as an official holiday for the first time since it was banned in 1969. This was an important signal.

Oswaldo's spirits lifted. A friend was coming.

The first pope to ever set foot on the island, John Paul II landed in Havana on January 21, 1998, a hot and humid afternoon. The visit promised to bring Castro the kind of legitimacy he had long craved. Fidel greeted him at the stairway of his plane in a double-breasted blue suit, not his usual military fatigues. In welcoming remarks, filled with anti-American broadsides, Fidel acknowledged "difficulties" between the regime and the Church, but insisted "the revolution is not to blame." This was a blatant whitewash of the truth. In his remarks, John Paul did not answer Fidel. The pope spoke softly, but had brought a powerful message of his own. To the Cubans, he said, "You are and must be the protagonists of your own personal and national history." For the rest of the visit, he confronted Fidel's dictatorship only indirectly. But John Paul stole the show.

Oswaldo was put under state security surveillance for the entire visit. He was not invited to any of the meetings with the pope. But Payá was thrilled at what he heard, which echoed his own words in "Faith and Justice," in *Pueblo de Dios*, in the founding declaration of the Movimiento Cristiano Liberación. Payá did not entirely invent the message—for a long while, he had been listening to, and admiring, the Polish pope.

In his first papal Mass, in Santa Clara on January 22, the pope challenged the Cuban regime's monopoly on education—the takeover of religious schools in 1961 that had dealt a devastating blow to the Church. John Paul said that parents, and not the state, should be allowed "to choose for their children" the schooling they most desired, including teachers, civic content, and religious training.

The next day, John Paul celebrated an open-air Mass in Plaza Ignacio Agromonte in Camagüey, attended by two hundred thousand cheering youths and broadcast on state television across the country. The pope summoned the youths—singing, dancing, jumping up and down, and waving Vatican and Cuban flags—to seek a freer life inside Cuba, rather than fleeing it. "Do not look outside for what is to be found inside," he declared, adding, "Do not leave for tomorrow the building of a new society in which the noblest dreams are not frustrated and in which you can be the principal agents of your own history."

The pope's message in Camagüey echoed Oswaldo's impassioned plea in the final issue of *Pueblo de Dios*. "We can't just be the spectators of our own history," he had written. "We must be the protagonists."

More than a slogan, it was the essence of all that Oswaldo believed in and worked for.

That evening at the University of Havana, John Paul addressed intellectuals and cultural figures, an audience selected by the government. The pope paid tribute to Félix Varela, whose ashes are interred in the Great Hall, "the foundation stone of the Cuban national identity," who had taught Cubans how to think—and think freely. The pope added that Varela "spoke of democracy, judging it to be the political project best in keeping with human nature, while at the same time underscoring its demands."

In four paragraphs of speech text about Varela, without even mentioning the revolution, "John Paul had laid out the framework for its replacement by an authentically Cuban system of freedom," according to the pope's biographer George Weigel.

For Oswaldo, this was a reaffirmation. The pope's speech was wind in his sails—the Varela Project was ready.

In Santiago de Cuba, on January 24, the pope made a plea to release political prisoners. He also defended the Church's long pursuit of religious freedom, which Archbishop Pérez Serantes had once championed so intensely, insisting the Church would not become a slave to Fidel's communism. Exultant crowds began chanting "We are not afraid!" and then "¡Libertad! ¡Libertad!"

At the close of the visit, in Havana on January 25, in the square where a million Catholics gathered in 1959 and where Fidel had vast rallies for the revolution, the pope celebrated a final Mass, with Fidel and Raúl Castro present. The pope again returned to the idea of freedom, saying Cuba's problems were the result of a system that denied the dignity of the human person. He called for a state that "enables every person and every religious confession to live their faith freely."

Oswaldo and Ofelia were in the crowd, but got separated. Oswaldo tied a rope to the pant leg of his youngest son, Reinaldo, so as not to lose him in the crush, while Ofelia moved closer to the front with Rosa María. They were reunited just as the pope was talking about liberación. The pope declared that attainment of freedom "is a duty which no one can shirk. . . . This liberation cannot be reduced to its social and political aspects, but rather reaches its fullness in the exercise of freedom of conscience, the basis and foundation of all other human rights."

The crowd began chanting, "The pope is free and wants us all to be free!"

John Paul replied, "Yes, free with the freedom to which Christ liberated you." The square filled with mushrooming chants of *"¡Libertad! ¡Libertad!"*

The square shook with the words and ideals Oswaldo and Ofelia had shared ever since they met in a Church conference hallway. They were ecstatic.

Then Oswaldo looked behind him and to each side. He was surrounded by state security officers.

In the days after, Payá publicly launched the Varela Project, taking advantage of the excitement John Paul had generated and a sense that all the restlessness and energy of recent years could be harnessed for good. The petition was printed under a title at the top:

"VARELA PROJECT. CITIZEN PETITION. SUPPORTED BY OUR CONSTITUTIONAL RIGHTS."

The petitioners, it said, request the National Assembly to put five basic proposals to a popular referendum. They were:

1. The right of freedom of association for "social, political, economic, cultural, trade union, student, religious, humanitarian, and other associations and organizations." Also, "the rights to freedom of expression and the press."
2. An amnesty for "all those who have been arrested, punished, and imprisoned for political reasons," who have not taken part in acts that directly threatened the lives of others.
3. Citizens will be guaranteed the right to set up private companies, and work under new laws governing contracts and economics.

4. The establishment of a new electoral code that allowed for genuinely free elections to parliament and guaranteed plurality and democracy.

5. New elections between nine months and a year after the referendum.

Oswaldo told a friend a few weeks later that Fidel's hold on the country was based on coercion and intolerance. "In other words," he said, "it is like keeping our hands tied while the ship sinks. And we Cubans must free our hands, to break the rope."

In the past, Oswaldo had never collected more than a few hundred signatures at a time. Now, by comparison, he was setting his sights on a colossal task. He knew how the regime wielded fear, how it caused Cubans to shrink into a pretend mask of conformism, to stay out of trouble. Who would break the ropes and break the fear?

Alejandro González Raga would.

González grew up in Camagüey in a family that lived the revolution. His father was a Communist Party member, and his mother held a job in the Ministry of Interior. González went to a military school at his father's insistence and served in the Cuban Navy as a telegraph operator. When he got out, he shared the usual rebelliousness of youth at the time—he liked the Beatles, idealized America, and found the lack of opportunity discouraging. He held odd jobs in a warehouse and on the docks. Finally, during the "special period," he settled into more entrepreneurial work, carving up old tire treads to make sandals for sale. Later, he made money by ferrying wood furniture and ceramic floor tiles from craft shops in Camagüey to be sold outside Varadero, Cuba's fancy tourist beach resort, where dollars and foreign visitors were driving an expansion.

Through these odd jobs he met Ángel Sardiñas Díaz. They worked together, hauling furniture and floor tiles from one city to another, load after load, but after a while the profit dwindled. González went back to making sandals. His friend Ángel desperately wanted to flee Cuba. All his previous efforts had failed. Once during the balseros exodus, he bought a boat, but it sank. Another attempt to get legal exit papers through a sister in Mexico also failed.

One day, Ángel invited González to his father's small cattle farm. He confessed, "I'm making a raft, and I want you to come with me."

González told him he would not leave Cuba. "I'm not going to risk it, not with these conditions on this little raft. The most I can do is go with you to the beach and help you to the shore."

The raft was made of two tractor tires sewn together with ropes, lined with tarps and sacks. Two wooden beams held it all together lengthwise, while a metal plate supported a small gasoline engine that powered a propeller. They moved the raft from Camagüey to a village on the northern shore, Boca de Camarioca, just 101 miles south of Key West, Florida.

On August 12, 1998, they found a farmer with a tractor and flat trailer who, for $30, would ferry the raft from a concealed spot to the shoreline under the cover of darkness. The path to the shore was rough. Ángel was taking three others with him on the vessel. They loaded gasoline, water, and food, then piled branches over it for camouflage, all concealed under a tarp. The other three passengers and González hid under the tarp. Ángel stood on the tractor fender as captain and lookout, grasping an upright pipe. He gave instructions to the farmer. They hauled the rig cautiously toward the shore. It was dark, and Ángel told the farmer to turn off the tractor lights and step on the gas down the final stretch toward the shore. He thought there might be police nearby.

The tractor groaned, and accelerated with a surge.

Then it hit a huge berm of dirt that the farmer did not see. The tractor shuddered and balked. The trailer jackknifed and buckled.

Ángel was savagely smacked by the pipe he had been grasping, and thrown to the road.

The pipe had pierced his neck.

A frantic effort to save his life followed, and a nearby car stopped to help them rush Ángel to the hospital.

He died on the way in González's arms.

The days that followed were difficult. González was jailed for two weeks and interrogated.

He was haunted by the memory of the raft, the accident, the sight of Ángel so close to his dream, and yet so far.

"Why do people have to leave?" González asked himself. He decided, "I am going to do something so that other people don't have to go through this."

Soon after, González joined the Varela Project. He collected signatures, he said, so he could live in a country where people did not have to die dreaming of escape on a raft.

Fredesvinda Hernández grew up on an isolated farm, the daughter of poor peasants in the foothills of the Escambray Mountains, 160 miles southeast of Havana, where the only path to the farm was on horseback or donkey. Her family worked the land to survive—vegetables, tobacco, and farm animals. They were people of faith. After the revolution, her father became a believer in Jehovah's Witnesses, an early Christian sect that eschews government and political involvement and does not serve in the military. Young male Jehovah's Witnesses in Cuba were persecuted severely in Castro's UMAP camps.

For years after 1959, the Escambray region was a hotbed of armed resistance to Castro. Rebels, some backed by the CIA, roamed widely. Fredesvinda remembered hearing volleys of gunfire across the hills; it drove her mother to distraction. By 1965, Castro's forces had extinguished the rebellion. Fredesvinda's family, however, was not left in peace. Her father was arrested three times because, once he became a Jehovah's Witness, he refused to grow tobacco for religious reasons and health concerns. Her brother refused to salute the flag. They lost the farm in the revolution's confiscations and moved to a small town.

Fredesvinda, who dropped out of school after the fifth grade, married another Jehovah's Witness. At their wedding, the groom's father vanished. He had been taken away. Starting in 1971, the regime decided to systematically round up thousands of male peasants in the region who were known rebels or rebel sympathizers. They were transferred to undeveloped locations to work the fields and build housing that became new towns, all on a sort of permanent probation that prevented them from leaving. Fredesvinda's father-in-law was taken to López Peña, a settlement in Piñar del Río Province. A few years later, Fredesvinda and

her husband were resettled there. The "captive towns" for the Escambray families were guarded by militiamen. The roads were muddy and
no one owned a car. Fredesvinda arrived in 1975 and bitterly called it a
"concentration camp." Her anger simmered.

By the early 1990s, she was ready for change. Travel restrictions
eased. She joined an opposition group made up of political prisoners and
their children who wanted to recover farmlands the revolution had confiscated. Fredesvinda was good at networking and felt defiant about her
family's treatment. She began working as a stringer, or assistant, to Victor
Arroyo, an independent journalist in nearby Piñar del Río. He took her
reports and messages from the towns and published or broadcast them.

Once he gave her ten Varela Project petitions to take to the captive
town. All ten were filled out in just two days.

Then he gave her fifty petitions. She was persuasive. "What we were
asking for was freedom," she recalled. "When people knew, they would
sign. This is what we had been waiting for."

Fredesvinda's transportation was a bike owned by an older gentle-
man; he gladly ferried her around, like a taxi. One day he had dropped
her in a town she did not know well. She noticed that state security began
to question him. She briskly walked up to the back door of a neighboring house, opened it, tossed thirty signature petitions on a countertop,
then walked—or nearly ran—in the other direction. A woman who lived
there was in the yard, and she remained silent.

The state security officers abandoned the bicycle, grabbed Fredesvinda, and demanded that she give up the petitions. She said she had
none, and they let her go.

A few weeks later, she returned to the house. The woman in the
yard—acting on her own—had taken the petitions around town and collected the signatures. She proudly handed them back to Fredesvinda,
completely full.

Andrés Chacón first heard about the Varela Project in Santiago de Cuba,
on the far eastern end of the island, where he taught anatomy in medical
school and was also in charge of a tissue transplant bank at a local hospital.

As a youth, he had come to question the misery and sacrifices of life in Cuba. An aunt in the United States who was in frequent touch with his family reminded them that life was better beyond. "She would talk to us very clearly," he recalled, and as a result, he began to question everything. "I never agreed with the revolution. I saw what we had, and what we did not have. Why couldn't we have it? There was something wrong."

Chacón earned a medical degree in Santiago and was teaching first- and second-year anatomy students when a friend of a friend brought him the Varela Project petition. Chacón was forty years old, always mingling with the students, working as a tutor for those in the first two years of study. The atmosphere was always "effervescent," he remembered. The town was like that; Santiago de Cuba was the cradle of Cuba's independence war and of Castro's revolution.

Chacón read the petition only once. "I signed it immediately," he recalled. The friend gave him fifteen petitions, figuring he would come back and pick them up eventually. Chacón's medical students snapped them up and signed. They began to share with their friends, and soon they were beating a path to Chacón's door. As a tutor, "I would stay after hours to help them," he recalled. "That attracted a lot of students. That's when I used my ability to again tell them about the Varela Project."

But Chacón also realized that somebody else was watching. State security had spies among the faculty. The dean called him in and asked why he was attracting so much attention compared to the other teachers. "It's just my personality," he explained. "You know how I am."

Later, when they found out he was collecting signatures for the Varela Project, Chacón was regularly called in by state security, often once a week. "They kept asking me, 'Why are you doing this? Who was ordering you to do this?' And I always responded, 'I am ordering myself to do it.'

"I would tell them it is not just going to be beneficial to me, it's going to be beneficial to you too, as an official, as a state security officer. It will benefit you because you have a family. And you have children. And this is going to help them."

State security kept up the pressure. "I know I was being followed. I was being watched," Chacón said. He managed to keep his job at the local hospital only because of his responsibility for the tissue transplant bank. People were surprised at his nerve. "Yeah, I would tell people, I have an ongoing weekly meeting with state security right there in the hospital, where they had an office."

Chacón met Oswaldo in Santiago one afternoon. Oswaldo approached quietly. A runner knocked on Chacón's door, saying, "There is someone who wants to see you." Chacón nodded "yes" and the runner went to get Oswaldo. As they drank coffee, Oswaldo came across as mild-mannered and pleasant. They both worked in hospitals and had much in common. Oswaldo wanted to know if Chacón was being harassed for collecting the signatures. "I told him yeah, but it wasn't a problem for me. I was going to keep doing it." Oswaldo asked Chacón to become his coordinator in Santiago de Cuba. "Let's work on this," Oswaldo told him, as Chacón recalls it. "But you have to take care and protect yourself from the enemy. This is something that really strikes hard at the Cuban government. And for that reason, we have to be very careful. They have a lot more power than we do, and they are going to try to eliminate us."

Oswaldo fought a war of nerves with Edgar. State security tried to break down and break into the Varela Project. They looked for cracks or weaknesses, hoping to infiltrate meetings, recruit informers, and pressure members. Chacón was constantly on the lookout for false signatures in the petitions signed at the hospital, submitted by state security officers posing as doctors, to contaminate the lists. He usually caught them.

Oswaldo was naturally loquacious and easygoing. But he began to adopt a harder shell to protect himself and the project from prying and infiltration. State security was tough, and he had to be just as tough. He became more guarded, more suspicious of others, and yet it caused a gnawing dilemma. He needed other people, lots of people, all over Cuba, to help collect signatures. But there were enemies lying in wait, people he could not trust, land mines planted by state security. Oswaldo kept a vigilant watch for infiltrators. He had to step carefully, to be shrewd, skeptical, and hard-nosed. Ricardo Zuñiga, a US Foreign Service officer who served in Havana and knew Oswaldo during this period, recalled that state security was a formidable adversary. "They had multiple tools to aim at you: to dissuade, to co-opt, to show up at your work, to harass your children. They weren't going to kill you, just make your life miserable." Each target of state security, such as Oswaldo, was assigned one officer—in Oswaldo's case it was Edgar. He had been assigned to Oswaldo and the movimiento for years now.

The Swedish democracy activist Ehrenberg had volunteered as a driver for Oswaldo on many trips to the island. The very first time, Ehrenberg showed up with a red Nike baseball cap. "Take it off!" Oswaldo commanded, worried it would stand out. "I know they are monitoring me, I know they are tracking me."

"Every meeting was a risk," Ehrenberg recalled. "State security was sometimes one step ahead of us. They would hear he was coming somewhere and go around the day before, threatening people not to come." Oswaldo took evasive action, postponing a meeting, warning his people so they could stay out of trouble.

"This is for real," Oswaldo often told small groups, soberly describing the dangers ahead. He met them in rooms with blinds drawn. He instructed them how to keep state security from seizing the petitions— and how to protect the people distributing them. The Varela Project was legal under the constitution, he reminded them, but they were also going up against Fidel.

State security always seemed to be on a higher state of alert when Castro went abroad. Oswaldo noticed their cars arrived early in the morning outside his house. "I'd leave on my bicycle to go to work, and they'd follow me. After I went into the office, my work often required me to go to hospitals, sometimes in a company car. Security forces in cars with walkie-talkies would follow me. If I went to a hospital . . . treatment room, four or five agents would stare at me through the windows. They'd surround the hospital. Later, if I left on my bicycle to go to church, they'd go with me. If I dodged them they would go to my house, knock on the door, and bother my family. If I got on a bus and managed to shake them, as soon as they realized it, they would have people get off the bus, and two agents would get on and sit in the front, two would get on and sit in the back. Sometimes I would have three, four, or five cars behind me. This would go on for as long as Fidel was out of the country—it happened several times."

The tension surged in early 1999. On February 16 the National Assembly approved a new law that banned introduction into the country of any "subversive" materials, along with equipment that could disseminate such information—a law aimed at squelching the independent Cuban journalists. A fax machine or laptop computer could be declared subversive. Then, two weeks later, the government prepared to put the group of four dissidents, including Vladimiro Roca and Marta Beatriz Roque, on trial behind closed doors. They had been held in prison for nineteen months and were to get a one-day trial on charges of "sedition." The prison sentences were harsh: Roca got five years. To stop any protest outside the trial, state security arrested a hundred dissidents and opposition figures. Both Regis and Tony were detained. State security showed up at Oswaldo's home, ordering him to stay inside. But he had already stepped out, and continued to walk away from them. He was headed off to the university, where he had recently enrolled in classes for a master's degree in bioengineering—professional development, at the behest of his employer, a state enterprise.

One of the officers declared, "You're defying an order from state security! If you don't return home, you're under arrest." Oswaldo responded, "I've already left my home and I won't go back inside. So do what you want." He was detained.

At the university, Oswaldo's teachers called a student meeting to discuss his behavior—without telling him. State security was behind it. They sought to blacken Oswaldo's professional standing, a trick the Stasi had taught. On March 8, he was expelled from the university program for a master's degree.

Nonetheless, Payá saw that a spirit of resistance was alive and well on the streets in the summer of 1999. The pope's visit had encouraged people to act on their own. The signs of civil society were unmistakable in the rise of associations of lawyers, farmers, economists, ecologists, teachers, independent libraries, youth organizations, relatives of political prisoners, and of the blind or otherwise physically disabled. They were spread out across the country, not just in Havana, and the participants were becoming more diverse—youth, women, people of color. The groups were nonviolent, but there was a certain edginess that summer. A forty-day hunger strike was staged at a house in Havana on behalf of freedom of expression and amnesty for political prisoners. The government made no attempt to stop it. Forty-two sympathy fasts broke out across the country. At a Havana market, seven women carried out a sit-in protest, claiming milk rations for children had been denied them. After forty minutes, the city authorities rushed a truck with milk bottles to meet their demands. News about this and other protests was reported by the small but feisty band of independent journalists, whose ranks had grown. Sixteen independent libraries, free of government control and censorship, opened across the island, although state security tried to harass and disrupt them—the thought police were still at work.

Amid all this activity, Oswaldo needed to collect more signatures. The Varela Project had hundreds but not thousands.

Ever since Concilio Cubano was crushed, the idea had lingered that the opposition would be stronger if they worked together. But infighting was chronic and corrosive. To some extent it reflected a society and culture that was by nature individualistic and rebellious. However, some of the divisions were created by state security to undermine the opposition. When a new opportunity arose to work together, Oswaldo grabbed it, and others agreed.

On November 15–16, 1999, Fidel was to play host to the Ninth Ibero-American Summit, attended by the prime ministers of Spain, Portugal, and fourteen Latin American nations, as well as the king and queen of Spain, making it the first visit ever to Cuba by a Spanish monarch. It was also the first Ibero-American Summit held in Havana, a major showcase event for Fidel. The dissidents and opposition leaders concluded: Why not make it a showcase for us, too?

To plan, they called a minisummit of their own at a private house in Havana on November 12. About sixty people were invited. But state security got wind of it, and half of those invited from outside Havana were prevented from traveling. Others were arrested en route. Héctor Palacios, one of the leading dissidents, was taken from his house at 6:00 a.m. Only fourteen of them managed to get to the meeting.

Oswaldo Payá and Elizardo Sánchez took the lead. They drafted a fresh declaration of independence for the opposition. Oswaldo had done this many times before: the movimiento declaration, and manifestos for Foro Cubano, Concilio Cubano, national dialogue, Programa Transitorio, and the Varela Project. Stacks of press releases and manifestos had been issued by others, too, even leaflets dropped from the sky—and nothing happened.

This time they called it *Todos Unidos*, meaning everyone united. The document was a direct call to the principles of the Varela Project. The signers pledged to pursue free elections, freedom of association, freedom of the press, the right to establish private businesses, and freedom for political prisoners. "We, the Cuban people, are the protagonists of our history," Oswaldo wrote. "We are the ones who must create all of these spaces where we, as free men and women, can build a better society." The fourteen who were present signed it, including Héctor's wife, Gisela Delgado Sablón, who noted he was in prison at that time. He was released later.

Oswaldo was named spokesman for Todos Unidos, essentially the leader. He took it quite seriously. One night before the summit, he set up an amateur video handycam at home. Payá was a tinkerer and was very fond of the video camera. He made a focus check, aiming it at his bookshelf. The camera panned across books that had shaped his own views about faith, democracy, and rights—including Félix Varela's seminal volume of letters to his young students in Havana. Then Oswaldo focused the lens on a wood rocking chair next to the bookshelf. He hit Record and sat in the rocking chair. He spoke into the camera for forty-two minutes, nonstop, without notes, as if he were addressing the summit leaders. The sounds of cars honking and dogs barking filtered through the window. Children shouted in a distant hallway.

While Fidel had once claimed to liberate the Cuban people, he said, the truth was different. "They have demanded tribute and adoration of the people. They have demanded unconditional acceptance of power. They have robbed man of his freedom, which is a gift from God.

"We are fighting for pluralism," he declared. "How can one group come and say, 'We are Communists, and we are the only ones who can organize, we are the conscience of the people and we are the leaders of society'? Who said that?"

This lament was based on a recent experience. The Movimiento Cristiano Liberación had applied in October to be legally recognized by the government. The response was silence.

For the opposition, the Havana summit proved to be a smashing success. Oswaldo, along with Sánchez, Palacios, and others, managed to meet nine presidents, prime ministers, and foreign ministers. Spanish prime minister José María Aznar announced at a news conference outside the summit chamber that he had met with the dissidents to defend "aspirations of freedom, human rights, the rule of law and of just laws." They were no longer ignored and isolated.

Todos Unidos took off after the summit. They became the foot soldiers of the Varela Project. Within two years there were one hundred groups working under the umbrella to help collect signatures, including nine independent libraries. It was a rare moment of cohesion and common purpose, and the signature petitions of the Varela Project began to swell.

Six days after the summit, on November 22, a group of fourteen people gathered at water's edge in the early morning darkness in Cárdenas, a city ninety miles east of Havana and not far from the luxury beach at Varadero. It was almost 3:00 a.m. when the group set off in a seventeen-foot aluminum boat with a fifty-horsepower outboard motor. Instead of life jackets, they towed three large inner tubes taken from Russian truck tires. Like so many balseros before them, they left for Florida with high hopes.

The overloaded boat made good headway at first and was within thirty-five miles of the Florida coastline when it was caught in a nasty storm. A huge wave capsized the boat, and then it sank. Eleven people drowned. One couple managed to survive on an inner tube and washed ashore at Key Biscayne, Florida, nearly unconscious, shivering, their skin covered with the bite marks of fish. Separately, a trembling five-year-old boy, Elián González, was rescued bobbing off Fort Lauderdale in one of the black inner tubes on Thanksgiving Day, November 25. His mother, Elizabet Brotons, and her boyfriend, Lázaro Munero, the boatbuilder and leader of the group, were among the lost.

Elián's survival was astonishing. In Miami, he was taken in by his father's uncle, Lázaro González.

Elián's father, Juan Miguel González, who had separated from Elizabet and remained in Cuba, wanted his son back.

The custody dispute exploded into a frenzied tug-of-war between Fidel Castro and the Miami exiles. Demanding that the boy be returned to his father, Fidel staged mass rallies and marches in Cuba. In Miami, exile leaders protested it would be immoral to send Elián back to Communist Cuba, that his mother had paid with her life for him to reach freedom. All the while, Elián raced around the fenced yard, played with a new puppy, and looked shyly at the television cameras.

For Oswaldo, the Elián saga was an unwelcome distraction from the work of fighting for freedom through the Varela Project. All attention turned to Miami. "There are no changes, nor will there be any" from the regime as a result of the Elián affair, he wrote. The furor in Miami served as a reminder of how truly distant he was from the exiles, and they from him.

Miami was a bit of Cuba—without the revolution. Wave after wave of immigrants had come ashore since Fidel took power, on the Pedro Pan airlift in the 1960s, the massive Mariel boatlift in 1980, the balseros exodus of the 1990s, and almost nonstop in between. By the time Elián was rescued, there were 780,000 people of Cuban descent living in Miami-Dade County. Cuban immigrants had largely remade their lives in capitalism and democracy with ingenuity, resourcefulness, and an entrepreneurial spirit. They had become a force to be reckoned with in US politics, their hatred of Castro and support for the US trade embargo a backbone of their beliefs, their political strength amplified by Jorge Mas Canosa and the Cuban American National Foundation (CANF). They were not monolithic; there were 173 exile organizations of many different stripes, and the diaspora was a diverse tapestry of outlooks and ideas. However, an enduring feature of Miami Cubans was the small, hard-line anti-Castro leadership, with influence and economic clout. They had never abandoned the quest for a Cuba without Fidel. Mas Canosa was at the forefront starting in the 1980s and saw himself as a future leader of Cuba, until his death from cancer in November 1997.

Most of the Miami exile leaders were exceedingly wary of anyone who did not subscribe to the overthrow of Fidel and his revolution. They had long feared Castro might try to erect a veneer of democratic practice while keeping his grip on power. They were hostile toward anyone who preached dialogue or engagement, such as Oswaldo, who had already proposed in earlier years a "national dialogue" and often spoke of reconciliation. Oswaldo's model for change was Poland's Solidarity, with a round-table process that led to a peaceful transition. The Miami exile leaders would hear none of it. Their enmity of Fidel was undiminished after four decades. The veterans of the Bay of Pigs still gathered for reunions in Miami. The city had long suffered violent bombings and threats by anti-Castro paramilitaries and vigilantes, targeting those they thought too sympathetic to Fidel. There was no room for compromise, not even for discussion of compromise.

Every day, anti-Castro invective flooded the airwaves from five major Spanish-language radio stations. The most influential broadcaster was Armando Pérez Roura, who directed Radio Mambí, WAQI, 710 on the AM dial, the number one station among the Miami exiles. With a wide smile and a basso voice, he delivered withering denunciations and character assassinations of anyone who dared disagree about Castro. He wrote in 1995 that dialogue with Fidel was a "dirty maneuver" because "any negotiation" would only "perpetuate his bloody dictatorship, his plundering, his murders, his evils, his betrayals and his miseries." He maintained this implacable wall of antagonism for years, assailing dissidents on the island as nothing more than mercenary props for Fidel. Radio Mambí, a fifty-thousand-watt station, played jingles advocating for Fidel's death. Pérez Roura summoned Cubans to march in the streets, to "say 'no' to dialogue and 'yes' to sacred intransigence." Oswaldo and the Varela Project were not spared. Pérez Roura said in later years that the Varela Project was "an arrangement with the government," and added, "We don't believe in any understandings with the Communists, because they will sit and talk to you and do whatever they want." Radio Mambí campaigned the loudest to keep Elián on American soil.

Pérez Roura was flat-out wrong about Oswaldo, who never had any such understandings with Fidel. To the contrary, Oswaldo had resisted Fidel's dictatorship for years, mobilizing people house by house. It was true, certainly, that the Varela Project relied on a provision in the 1976 socialist constitution and that Payá saw a dialogue about transition of power better than violent upheaval. But that was not collaboration with Fidel. Oswaldo sought to leverage the existing laws against Fidel. He drew from the 1940 constitution, Cuba's most democratic ever. The anti-Castro crowd in Miami should have warmly embraced Oswaldo Payá and the Varela Project. His pursuit of democracy and rights for Cubans on the island closely matched their own values. He was the authentic opposition—he was doing, not just talking. Unfortunately, they failed to see this clearly.

Oswaldo's close associate during this time, Regis Iglesias, said another factor was jealousy. Since the exile leaders hadn't conceived of the Varela Project, nor controlled it, they could not accept it. Oswaldo knew of the hostility but was not preoccupied by it, Regis recalled.

In the early morning hours of April 22, President Clinton's attorney general, Janet Reno, ordered federal law enforcement officers to swoop down and seize Elián from the González bungalow in Miami. A terrified Elián was confronted by an officer in full tactical gear, storming the boy's room with his semiautomatic rifle raised threateningly. Elián was flown to Andrews Air Force Base outside of Washington, DC, and entrusted to his waiting father. The Miami relatives argued that the US government should accept an asylum claim submitted on Elián's behalf, but the attorney general refused to do so over the father's objections. Federal courts upheld this decision. The US Supreme Court declined to review the issue, and on June 28, Elián returned to Cuba with his father. The Miami exile community had poured heart and soul into keeping Elián in Florida. The campaign was backed by Mas Canosa's son, Jorge Mas Santos, and the CANF. But in the end, it failed, and changed nothing in Cuba. While battling over Elián, the Miami exile leaders misjudged— or simply missed—a far more consequential effort for democracy and against Fidel, the Varela Project.

In Cuba, Pedro Pablo Álvarez, a union organizer, brought a critical new idea to the Varela Project: to look beyond Havana for signatures. "The real opposition was in the towns," Álvarez told Oswaldo, suggesting that teachers and dockworkers were eager to pitch in. Álvarez, who had been sent to the UMAP camps as a youth and was jailed for trying to organize independent trade unions in late 2000, joined the Varela Project after he was released in 2001.

The Álvarez idea worked. Soon, truckloads of signatures started coming in through his union contacts and through the genuine enthusiasm of Todos Unidos.

"In the middle of this experience," Payá recalled later, "state security stopped me one day, threatened me, and told me that if the opposition in Cuba becomes unified, I'll be imprisoned for so many years—that Todos Unidos was based on destroying the revolution and that they wouldn't allow it."

Oswaldo had been threatened before. However, he took special measures, assisted by a clandestine network of nuns, who concealed the original signatures in convents. Oswaldo also insisted, to avoid counterfeits, that no other activists could print the petitions. They were cranked out on a noisy photocopier given to Oswaldo by Father Juan Rumin, who had let him use it in earlier years. It was now installed in a room in Beba's apartment that became their headquarters. Every petition was imprinted with a unique serial number, for tracking. Every page of ten signatures was laboriously copied, and the original stored with the nuns.

The printing and copying in Beba's little room kicked up a noisy racket day after day. An elderly woman, Beba was always poking her head into the doorway, asking, "Coffee? Water? Bread pudding?"

On the streets, people *wanted* to sign, many more than Oswaldo had imagined. Fredesvinda Hernández personally collected more than one thousand signatures, believed to be the most by any single collector. "First we would approach people we knew," Regis recalled. "Then friends of friends. It was like a staircase. Step by step, it was a chain."

State security harassed the Varela Project collectors all the time. They were threatened with losing their jobs, going to jail, or harm to their families. During the year 2000, hundreds of collectors were arrested; 270 were detained in December alone. But the most remarkable aspect of the Varela Project was that it didn't slow them down. The signatures kept flowing. They came in by the hundreds, and soon by the thousands.

Then Edgar decided on a different approach.

The Stasi handbooks had taught a simple lesson: rather than use brute force, arrests, and violence, it was often much better to subvert, manipulate, and paralyze quietly from within. The Stasi in East Germany had created a vast corps of unofficial informants to infiltrate any corner of society and do the dirty work. In Cuba, state security had embraced these methods and refined them. They knew how to infiltrate, discredit, and figuratively blow up an organization.

Edgar now picked up the handbook.

In Beba's apartment one day, the union organizer Álvarez closely examined a single Varela Project petition carrying ten signatures, addresses, and identification numbers. He scanned the list of names, and a memory flooded back to him from years before.

He had been working in Havana at a seedy twenty-four-room sex motel on the seaside at Malecón where couples checked in for a few hours. Álvarez was the motel manager, manning the front desk. Every person who checked in was required to provide their eleven-digit national identification number. All Cubans had an ID card. Álvarez had learned that each digit in the number had a specific code or meaning.

Now, in Beba's house, Álvarez looked closely at the petition he was holding. He focused on a certain signature, Juana, a woman's name. There was something wrong with the identification number.

He had learned at the motel that each ID contained a single digit that indicated male or female. The men were even, the women were odd.

Juana had a man's number.

He took the page to Oswaldo. They began to look at more petitions.

Oswaldo had a sinking feeling. Hundreds of the signatures were accompanied by ID numbers that were of the opposite gender. The signatures had been falsified.

Edgar and his colleagues in state security had planted a cancer and it was spreading. Oswaldo's efforts—years of hard work—could be ruined.

How had it happened? Oswaldo had instructed the signature collectors to ask for each person's ID card and to make sure the number they gave was correct. But in the torrent of work by Todos Unidos groups, which he did not control, many collectors had skipped this step. They just asked the signer to give an ID number without verifying it on the card, and many signers had given deliberately wrong numbers. The mismatches were not just errors—it was a campaign of subterfuge.

No one knew how many signature petitions were marred this way. Large or small, the very fact of the falsifications might invalidate the whole project. It would give Castro an excuse to dismiss it with a wave of the hand.

For Oswaldo, the falsifications were his worst nightmare. State security was *inside* his network. He had not been tough enough. He was furious. "This was so serious," Regis recalled. "We weren't going to let someone do this to us." Oswaldo concluded that state security had probably twisted the arms—or worse—of the smaller groups in Todos Unidos so that they opened the door to contamination of the signatures. If there was a weakness, state security had figured it out.

In December 2001, when the falsifications were discovered, Oswaldo launched a crash campaign to validate every signature. The movimiento at the time had grown to about 1,000 members across the island. Oswaldo selected the most trusted, about 250, and called them "citizen committees." They were verification brigades. Town by town and village by village, they laboriously rechecked all the signatures, addresses, and ID numbers that had been collected. At the end, every original signature was verified three times. On some petitions of ten signatures, a few that could not be confirmed were marked "void" and the good ones remained. Payá was quiet about it at first. He did not want state security to know that the infiltration had been detected.

On February 4, 2002, Oswaldo and several others met briefly in Havana with President Vicente Fox of Mexico, who was visiting Cuba. Oswaldo told reporters that day the Varela Project had collected the required ten thousand signatures but did not say when they would be submitted to the National Assembly. The verification campaign was still under way, and continued through March.

At the time, state security was turning up the pressure with physical harassment. They detained José Daniel Ferrer, one of the project's leaders in Santiago de Cuba, and about a dozen others. They were beaten up by a roadside, and about 130 signatures were seized. "They were on top of us," Regis recalled. For weeks state security officers with microphones and recording gear shadowed every member of the movimiento who came or left from Beba's house. They walked in telltale pairs around Parque Manila. One night, Oswaldo was driving a VW van, with Regis in the passenger seat. A delivery truck started to follow them, then disappeared. As Oswaldo made a left turn, the delivery vehicle reappeared at the end of a street, then accelerated directly at them down a narrow alley, threatening a head-on collision. It screeched to a halt just an arm's length from Oswaldo's front bumper. It was a warning.

Tony and Oswaldo were working one day in the headquarters room in Beba's house. Tony asked aloud: When would they turn in the signatures? Many of the collectors were getting impatient. When would they see results?

Oswaldo put his fingers to his lips. "Shh!"

Oswaldo suspected that state security had bugged the room.

They both went out to the street and hopped on Tony's motorbike—the safest place they knew to have a confidential discussion.

• • •

On the evening of May 9, 2002, Oswaldo's team gathered in Beba's apartment, in the cramped room that was their headquarters, the walls faded
yellow, the window shutters closed tightly, a small electric fan perched
on an empty chair. The noisy photocopier stood against the wall. Card-
board boxes were piled against another wall. They were labeled "Havana Club," a famous brand of Cuban rum, but inside they contained
signatures brought from the nuns' hiding places. Two of the boxes were
covered on all sides with white paper saying "Project Varela" in English
and *"Proyecto Varela"* in Spanish. In the two boxes were 11,020 verified
signatures.

Oswaldo was excited but tense, trying to avoid giving any hints to
state security that something was going on. He picked this moment with
extreme care. His war of nerves with Edgar had reached a critical moment. If state security attacked Beba's house, they could take away all
the signatures at once and destroy the project.

Payá stood in a circle with eight of his close associates, including
Regis, Tony, Miguel, and José Daniel Ferrer. A much-revered elder was
also with them, Julio Ruiz Pitaluga, who had once been a captain in Fidel's rebel army, later soured on the revolution, and served twenty-three
years as a political prisoner.

Oswaldo spoke aloud, looking up at the ceiling. He said the Varela
Project signatures would be submitted to the National Assembly in *a few
days*—after former president Jimmy Carter arrived in Cuba for a week-
long visit on Sunday, May 12. There would be extensive international
press coverage of Carter's visit, the first by a former US president since
Fidel took power. Fidel was unlikely to want arrests or trouble while
Carter was there.

After Payá spoke, he silently passed around a piece of paper.
Tomorrow, it read. *10:00 a.m.*

The next morning, Tony left home early and went to the National Assembly auxiliary office building, in the Playa district of Havana. Just before 9:00 a.m., Tony approached a door that was used to accept citizen

letters and complaints. An elderly doorman stood there in a light blue shirt and dark trousers.

Tony asked if this was the place to deliver a letter to the parliament.

"Yes, but you have to wait a little bit," he replied, because the office was just opening at 9:00 a.m.

"Oh, that's not a problem," Tony replied. "I didn't bring the letter, I will have to go get it. I'll be back in a little while."

He zipped away on a motorcycle. He then telephoned Beba's house. He said simply that he would be seeing Oswaldo in the afternoon. This was the coded signal.

From Beba's house, CNN and other foreign news organizations were alerted. CNN rushed a camera crew to Calle Peñón. Oswaldo knew that Cuban state television would ignore the Varela Project, but CNN would not. In preparation, he had invited them earlier to shoot footage of the room with the boxes of signatures.

Tony milled around a marketplace, killing time.

At Beba's house, the group gathered. Miguel offered a short prayer, saying everything they had done—and were about to do—was for a free Cuba.

The two boxes containing the signed petitions were placed in the backseat of a red 1957 Chevrolet with a big V-8 gas-guzzling engine that belonged to Jorge Colmenero, who would drive. Regis got in the backseat with the two boxes, while Oswaldo sat up front. Colmenero saw the CNN car pull up and gunned the engine. Pitaluga, Ferrer, and others climbed into a small Volkswagen. They were to be the observation team, standing off to watch and report to the world in case of arrests.

The Chevy accelerated out of the neighborhood, down the sloping Calle Peñón where Oswaldo had once walked to church.

State security was caught off guard. The officers raced to their parked cars and motorcycles. They tried to catch up, but Colmenero had opened up a lead, and the CNN car was close behind him. The observation team was farther behind.

At one point, Colmenero barreled the wrong way down a one-way street, surprising a lone driver coming the other way. Then Oswaldo ordered him to stop, abruptly, on a wide street, Forty-First Avenue. Payá wanted to see what state security would do.

Oswaldo and Regis got out of the car and very casually went over to kick the tires. State security cars, chasing them frantically, almost overshot, and the first officer who got out of the car and came running toward them had a fanny pack—video cameras, most likely.

Oswaldo and Regis scampered back into the Chevy and raced off again for the National Assembly. They stopped momentarily to pick up Tony, who was waiting.

Colmenero pulled to the curb on Forty-Second Street. The entrance for citizens was around a corner, at Twenty-Seventh Avenue. A phalanx of foreign journalists was already waiting there, including CNN, Television Española, and reporters from Associated Press and Reuters, as well as others who had arrived to cover Carter's upcoming visit. There were no Cuban state media.

Regis grabbed one box, Tony the other, and Oswaldo carried a saddlebag with a list of all those who signed, a letter addressed to the president of the National Assembly, Ricardo Alarcón, as well as a press statement.

The journalists shouted questions at Oswaldo as the three of them walked toward the entrance. "We came to present the Varela Project, then we will talk," Oswaldo said. Regis defiantly raised his fist with a thumb and index finger, making the L for "liberation."

The doorman in the blue shirt came down the steps and met them at the street. "How many of you are coming in?" he asked, noticing the gathering crowd. "Three," said Oswaldo. The doorman noticed Tony from earlier and half smiled. He cleared the way for the three of them to carry the boxes inside.

Looking out at the crowd, Tony could see the state security officers were just dismounting from their motorcycles and getting out of their cars. They were beyond the cordon of journalists.

Once through the door, Oswaldo, Tony, and Regis were shown to a small reception room, with a low coffee table and four chairs. They set the boxes down. A woman greeted them, saying she worked for the

Constituent Services Department. Oswaldo explained why they had come, what was in the boxes, made the argument that it was permitted under the constitution, and said he was leaving the signatures and the documents for the president of the National Assembly.

"If you would like to check the signatures in any way—" Tony offered.

"No, that's not necessary," she said coldly.

Oswaldo asked her to stamp a copy of the letter to certify that the materials had been delivered. Visibly nervous, she took it, disappeared, and returned with a stamp and pad. She inked, stamped it, and handed it back to Payá.

Back outside, Oswaldo announced that on this day, 11,020 signatures had been submitted. "A new hope is opened for all Cubans," he said. "We are asking that the people of Cuba be given a voice."

Suddenly Pitaluga, the former political prisoner who was on the observation team watching at a distance, lost his composure. Overcome with emotion, he ran up and embraced Oswaldo, Regis, and Tony. "I have been waiting for this day for forty-two years," he said, his voice cracking.

Oswaldo went to offer a prayer at the chapel of La Inmaculada Concepción in the convent of the Daughters of Charity, in central Havana. A widely known and respected order, especially for their social work, the nuns served in the hospital in Cerro where Oswaldo and his brothers and sisters had been born, and they remained close to Oswaldo and his family. Brave and generous, they had helped protect the Varela Project signatures. They were in prayer when he joined them at the chapel, placing a copy of the Varela Project on the altar.

Later, Regis returned to Beba's house. The phone was jangling. Radio Martí wanted to talk. Florida radio stations and newspapers from around the world wanted to know more. At last they had done it—none of their earlier efforts had ever made it this far.

Regis thought that they might go on to collect 200,000 signatures, or 2 million. "Nothing was going to stop us," he recalled thinking.

They had finally become the protagonists of their own history.

Gustavo Gutiérrez and
his wife, María Vianello,
in his home library, 1940.
Courtesy of Gustavo Ovares Gutiérrez

The mansion, Bellabrisa,
in Havana *Courtesy of
Gustavo Ovares Gutiérrez*

The Capitolio, where the
1940 constitution, Cuba's
most democratic, was
written. Gustavo became
Speaker of the House that
year. *David Almeida/Wolfsonian–
Florida International University*

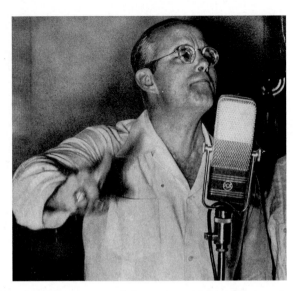

Eduardo Chibás captivated the nation with his radio broadcasts
defending democracy and demanding honest government.

International News Photos/Cuban Heritage Collection, University of Miami

The broom became a Chibás campaign symbol—sweep away
corruption! Enrique Llanos/Cuban Heritage Collection, University of Miami

Oswaldo Payá, early 1960s *Courtesy of Ofelia Acevedo*

Oswaldo, right, with friends in
El Cerro *Courtesy of Ofelia Acevedo*

Home from the forced labor
camp, 1972 *Courtesy of Ofelia Acevedo*

Wedding of Oswaldo and Ofelia, September 13, 1986 *Courtesy of Ofelia Acevedo*

Oswaldo at his day job, working
with hospital equipment
Courtesy of Ofelia Acevedo

Early 1990s, with Ofelia, Rosa María,
Reinaldo, and Oswaldito
Courtesy of Ofelia Acevedo

Archbishop Jaime Ortega
Vincenzo Pinto/Getty Images

El Salvador del Mundo church,
El Cerro *David E. Hoffman*

Pueblo de Dios,
Oswaldo's
newsletter
devoted to
democracy and
truth *Courtesy of
Ofelia Acevedo*

In July 1991, a government-backed mob attacked Oswaldo's house, where he was collecting signatures.
Courtesy of Ofelia Acevedo

In 2006, a wall near Oswaldo's house was painted with a threat warning that dissent is treason. *Courtesy of Ofelia Acevedo*

In 1999, Oswaldo and others created Todos Unidos. Left to right: Pedro Pablo Álvarez, Oswaldo Alfonso, Oswaldo Payá, Vladimiro Roca, Elizardo Sánchez, and Hector Palacios.
Courtesy of Hector Palacios

Oswaldo Payá displays a listening device he found in his home. He was under constant surveillance by state security.
Enrique de al Osa/EPA/Shutterstock

On May 10, 2002, Oswaldo delivered 11,020 Varela Project signatures to the National Assembly. *Jose Goitia/Associated Press/Shutterstock*

Oswaldo at the European Parliament receiving the Sakharov Prize for Freedom of Thought in 2002. *Olivier Morin/AFP/Getty Images*

Ofelia and Rosa María and others pay last respects to Oswaldo Payá, Cristóbal Colón cemetery, Havana, July 24, 2012. *Adalberto Roque/AFP/Getty Images*

PART IV

THE BLACK SPRING

SIXTEEN

THE BLACK SPRING

After years of grueling work, breaking rocks in the quarry, confronting the Church leadership, fighting to publish *Pueblo de Dios*, launching the movimiento, and writing manifestos demanding rights and democracy for the people of Cuba, Oswaldo Payá finally crossed a finish line. The Varela Project was unlike anything that had gone before. He had mobilized thousands of people. He was acting, not just talking.

It was hard to believe, but they had outsmarted Fidel. They managed to collect, verify, and deliver the signatures to the National Assembly right under the nose of state security. "When we submitted the signatures, I think we surprised them," Oswaldo said. "They never thought we'd be able to do it." Payá was not quite sure how or why it worked. Perhaps Castro underestimated them, thinking they were just hot-air agitators who would collect only a few hundred signatures. Perhaps state security had been overconfident about their attempt to sabotage the signatures. Or perhaps the seventy-five-year-old Castro had lost his touch. But that didn't seem likely.

Oswaldo had one worry he could not shake. How would Castro react?

•　　•　　•

Three days after the Varela Project signatures were submitted, on Monday morning, May 13, 2002, Oswaldo strode purposefully to the Santa Isabel Hotel in Old Havana, wearing a crisp, blue button-down dress shirt. Alongside him was Elizardo Sánchez, the former professor turned dissident. Although they had their differences, Payá and Sánchez worked shoulder-to-shoulder on the Concilio Cubano in 1995 and on Todos Unidos in 1999.

They were headed to a private breakfast with former president Jimmy Carter, who had arrived the day before. Foreign journalists crowded into Havana to cover Carter's visit. As president, Carter's early ambitions for better relations with Cuba had run aground. Now, twenty-two years after leaving office, he wanted to improve the human rights situation in Cuba and ease US tensions with Fidel. Carter was the first sitting or former US president to come to Havana since Calvin Coolidge in 1928. He knew his presence could enhance Fidel's prestige. But Carter also hoped to get something for it.

Most importantly, Carter wanted to address the Cuban people directly with a live, uncensored televised speech. Cuban officials agreed, asking Carter in return to tour exhibits of Cuban achievements in agriculture, science, and culture. Jennifer McCoy, who led the Latin America program for the Carter Center, hammered out with Cuban officials every last detail of Carter's visit in advance, including the time of the big speech—6:00 p.m., so people would hear it on television and radio—and the location. She also pressed for free time in Carter's schedule to meet dissidents. The Cubans did not object, as long as Carter would not make them the focal point of his trip.

In Carter's meetings beforehand, the Varela Project came up over and over again. It was raised by the National Democratic Institute, a Washington think tank focused on advancing democracy, and the Cuban American National Foundation, an anti-Castro group in Miami. Both urged Carter to mention the Varela Project in his televised address, since it had been censored in state-controlled news media. Patt Derian, who had served as Carter's assistant secretary of state for human rights, advised Carter, "There is no point in talking to Castro about the Varela Project. The

Cuban people need to hear more about it. Do it gently—and publicly."
Vicki Huddleston, chief of the US Interests Section in Havana, wrote to
Carter that Cubans had really stuck their necks out for democracy in the
Varela Project and it was helping energize a Cuban Spring, so he should
mention it. Huddleston, in a private word with Carter after his arrival in
Havana, urged him to meet Oswaldo personally before giving the speech.

Carter was stepping into a minefield of conflicting pressures; he
sought to navigate them adroitly. When he saw Fidel for their first extended discussion on Sunday evening after a banquet at the Palace of
the Revolution, Carter presented him with a goodwill gesture, a folder
of declassified US documents about Cuba, including his own secret directive, signed just weeks into his presidency, seeking to start a process
toward normalization of relations. Carter never achieved normalization,
but the document showed his early intentions. Carter also forewarned
Fidel about his plan to mention the Varela Project during the television
address. Castro took notes. Carter also met with the Cuban foreign minister, Felipe Pérez Roque, who after the meeting told reporters the Varela Project was "an imported product, a product financed, encouraged
and directed by foreign interests," specifically the United States.

Very early on Monday morning, Oswaldo and Elizardo got a message asking them to come right away to meet Carter at the hotel.

Carter greeted Oswaldo at the colonnaded hotel entrance with an
outstretched hand. "I've heard a lot about you," Carter said.

Payá and Sánchez then joined Carter in a private dining room where
an oval table was set with juice, coffee, and small pastries. Oswaldo didn't
touch a thing. He didn't have time. He began talking. He sketched out
the broad principles of the Varela Project, emphasizing the five points:
free speech, free association, free enterprise, freedom for prisoners, and
free elections. Oswaldo stressed that it was about much more than just
Fidel. He explained how he had fought to collect signatures across the
island. Sánchez hardly got a word in edgewise. He recalled that Oswaldo
underscored his desire "to promote change and reform, from the law to
the law, through the law." Sánchez assured Carter that most of the dissidents on the island supported the Varela Project.

Carter wanted to verify that Oswaldo was not taking money from the United States—it would be exploited by Fidel to discredit the Varela Project. Oswaldo replied that there was no direct assistance from the US government; he knew it would be impossible to succeed if he had taken it. But he added that dissidents on the island had accepted equipment such as faxes, cameras, and laptops on a personal basis, and received remittances from family and friends in the United States. Carter told Oswaldo he would mention the Varela Project in his speech, and Oswaldo thanked him. Carter's staff kept the speech text secret, however, wanting to avoid any last-minute interference from the Cuban government.

On Tuesday, Carter spoke from the podium in the Aula Magna, the cavernous Great Hall at the University of Havana where Pope John Paul II had appeared four years before and where Félix Varela's ashes are held.

Fidel wore a dark suit and tie and sat in the front row.

Carter spoke for twenty minutes, entirely in Spanish, striking a tone of reconciliation and even-handedness, saying he wanted to see better relations between the United States and Cuba after more than four decades of hostility. But after his conciliatory words, Carter grew more pointed in describing the virtues of democracy. His words were broadcast live on radio and television across the island.

"Cuba has adopted a socialist government where one political party dominates, and people are not permitted to organize any opposition movements," Carter said. "Your constitution recognizes freedom of speech and association, but other laws deny these freedoms to those who disagree with the government." Carter acknowledged that the United States was "hardly perfect" in human rights but asserted that its "guaranteed civil liberties offer every citizen an opportunity" to change the laws.

"This fundamental right is also guaranteed to Cubans," he said, noting the provisions in the 1976 constitution that allowed the citizen initiative with ten thousand signatures. "I am informed," he added, "that such an effort, called the Varela Project, has gathered sufficient signatures and has presented such a petition to the National Assembly."

Carter added, "When Cubans exercise this freedom to change laws peacefully by a direct vote the world will see that Cubans, and not foreigners, will decide the future of this country."

This was unprecedented, a demand for genuine democracy in front of Castro, on live television.

In a question-and-answer session, a few students and a professor, selected in advance by the government, sharply assailed the Varela Project and the United States, but Carter responded firmly that democracy meant the right to speak without fear of punishment, to elect one's leaders, organize opposition parties, and confront the government. "Those kind of rights don't exist in Cuba," he said. He appealed for publication of the full text of the Varela Project.

All eyes were on Fidel. Would he object? "I anticipated he would be upset," Carter recalled.

In earlier times, Fidel might have jumped to his feet. But he was calm and remained in his chair. Perhaps mellower, or just careful not to squander the goodwill of Carter's visit, he shook hands with Carter. "I didn't agree with everything you said. But I respect you," Fidel said. "Now let's go to the ball game." At the All-Star game that evening in Havana, Carter threw the ceremonial first pitch.

Oswaldo was at home on Calle Peñón, where he and Regis drank rum on the patio. Then they went inside to watch Carter's speech on television.

Oswaldo listened intently. When Carter mentioned the Varela Project, he was beside himself with joy. He turned to Regis.

"Call a press conference!" he insisted. "Call our people and the accredited agencies!"

Regis was dubious. He replied, "But we've just had a couple of drinks—"

"Get coffee. Wash your face. Call all the international correspondents!"

Regis first called Tony Díaz, who met him at Beba's house. Regis gulped down the coffee that Beba made. They set up a table with a large handmade sign in front of it, *Proyecto Varela*, carrying a drawing of the bespectacled Félix Varela.

Behind the table was a large image of Jesus Christ that hung on Beba's wall. Payá sat at the center, flanked by Regis, Tony, and Pedro Pablo Álvarez, who had been key in uncovering the falsified signatures. The journalists flooded in and a cluster of television cameras and microphones were set up. The small room became stuffy.

Oswaldo was supercharged with enthusiasm. "There's something more important than Carter's comments!" He was referring, he said, to the Varela Project itself, "a liberating gesture that more than ten thousand Cubans, more than twenty thousand Cubans, have dared to say to the government, 'Just a minute!' Ask us, as citizens, if we want economic change! We want our rights!" He added, "It is a constitutional right to have this initiative."

Oswaldo bristled at the suggestions made in *Granma* and by the foreign minister, Pérez Roque, that he was being financed by the United States. "Look, liberation cannot be financed!" he said. "Liberation is born from the soul, through a stroke of lightning that God gives to Cubans. And many Cubans said, 'We want our rights.' This cannot be financed."

He also insisted that the Cuban government publish the Varela Project for all to see. "Unfortunately, the whole world knows about it except the Cuban people."

"Look how short it is!" he said, holding the text. "They're so afraid of it. This little paper, it contains the popular will."

The Communist Party's mouthpiece *Granma* carried a highly sanitized report about Carter's speech on Wednesday. That afternoon, Carter was hosted at a luncheon by Alarcón, the Speaker of the National Assembly and a hard-line ideologue. The National Assembly was a powerless, rubber-stamp body, but the Varela Project would need its approval to proceed. Carter asked Alarcón directly how he planned to handle it. Alarcón replied circuitously that the government hadn't made a decision, but he raised all kinds of problems: legal, technical, and political. And besides, he said, the Varela Project was a subversive plot by the United States. "Inappropriate," he said coldly.

"We tried to convince him that the petitioners deserved a full and open hearing, even if their effort was rejected," Carter recalled.

But Carter had not convinced him, nor Fidel.

On Thursday, in a surprising turnabout, *Granma* printed the entire text of Carter's remarks, including the reference to the Varela Project and the exchange with the students. The newspaper did not, however, publish the text of the Varela Project itself. That day, Carter talked for three and a half hours with twenty-three dissidents and opposition figures, including Oswaldo. Oswaldo presented Carter with a poster depicting Félix Varela. "Something has changed," Payá said afterward. "The Cuban people have met hope."

On May 20, President George W. Bush unveiled his administration's new Cuba policy in a pair of speeches, one in the morning at the White House and another in the afternoon in Miami. He had been in office sixteen months, the last eight dominated by the 9/11 terror attacks. The Cuban exile community in Miami was the anchor of Bush's razor-thin Florida victory in 2000 over Vice President Al Gore. Bush had won more than three-quarters of the Cuban American vote. The exiles generally supported Republicans in the past, but in this election they were also driven by lingering anger at the Clinton administration—and Gore—over returning Elián to Cuba.

The Cuban exile community in Miami was in the throes of change and not single-minded. The descendants of the 1960s and 1970s immigrants were less political and ideological. The recent arrivals—about twenty thousand every year—were more open to differing views, to dialogue, and they were more interested in economic issues. The Cuban American National Foundation, the heavyweight political force created by Jorge Mas Canosa, had also taken a turn toward moderation; his son, Mas Santos, urged Carter to bring up the Varela Project in Cuba. A group of hard-liners, who opposed dialogue and who regarded the Varela Project as collaboration with Castro, quit the foundation and formed a breakaway group, the Cuban Liberty Council. The hard-liners were seated on the stage when Bush spoke in Miami, but he delivered a moderate speech. His younger brother Jeb, running for reelection as Florida governor, was also on the stage. The president blasted Fidel as a "brutal dictator" but stopped short of announcing new sanctions. He called for a "step-by-step" approach to Cuba, saying he would wait and see if Castro allowed free and fair elections in 2003. As anyone in the audience could have told him, Fidel had never held free and fair elections and was unlikely to now. Nevertheless, some responded to Bush with chants of *"¡Cuba si, Castro no!"*

Most importantly for Oswaldo, Bush spoke favorably of the Varela Project, saying the "Cuban people's aspirations for freedom are undiminished. We see this today in Havana, where more than eleven thousand brave citizens have petitioned their government for a referendum on basic freedoms. If that referendum is allowed, it can be a prelude to real change in Cuba."

Oswaldo may have taken some satisfaction at this recognition, but he knew it was dangerous to be too closely associated with the US government. Out of caution, he generally kept aloof from US officials in Havana, although not entirely out of touch. Oswaldo often remarked that Cuba's problems had to be solved by Cubans, at home, not in Miami or Washington. The hard truth was that the Varela Project had grown from the soil of Cuba, from the sweat and tears of Oswaldo and his movement. It could not be anyone's puppet. "A civic campaign conducted amid poverty, where many of those petitions came stuffed between old clothes or a handful of beans, where many mothers, women, young people, elderly women and fathers knew the risks they were taking—no one can finance that," Payá said. "That's the only argument the government has left, claiming that the Cuban people's desire to live as free human beings is financed from abroad. That type of slander does not worry us."

Fidel's silence did worry him, however. Oswaldo had mobilized the masses that Fidel jealously guarded as his own. What would he do about it?

The answer came in June, a month after he submitted the petitions. Castro was bombastic as ever but tried to be clever. The Stasi handbooks had advised that it was better to overwhelm one's opponents with psychological warfare than to physically attack them. The Stasi had recommended "disinforming, disorganizing, paralyzing and crushing" any opposition. Fidel was his own tactician and may have come up with his plan entirely alone. But his response to the Varela Project was exactly what the Stasi rulebook suggested: to disorient and paralyze his adversaries, especially Payá and all those who signed the Varela Project, as well as Bush. Fidel smothered them with the jury of a million, *his* million.

On June 12, he staged a colossal public march across the country. About 1.2 million people were on the streets of Havana. Surrounded by security men and Communist Party officials, Castro walked slowly down the Malecón seaside boulevard for about a mile, then stood on a stage for hours, watching the marchers pass by. Wearing his traditional olive-green uniform and cap, he waved a small Cuban flag as the sea of people passed on the same route he had taken for his 1959 entrance to Havana. "Long live socialism! Down with the lies!" Fidel shouted, apparently answering Bush's speech.

Next, Cuban citizens were asked to support three new amendments to the 1976 constitution, which declared that socialism is "irrevocable," that capitalism "will never return to Cuba," and made it impossible to ever remove the new amendments.

Fidel then called for a snap "referendum" on the amendments. From June 15 to 18, Saturday through Tuesday, signatures were collected across the island. By appropriating the symbols of the Varela Project— signatures, a referendum, the constitution—Fidel sought to bury the Varela Project by confusion and diversion. Oswaldo saw through the gambit but was helpless to stop it. Castro threw the full force of the Committees for the Defense of the Revolution and all the mass organizations that were part of the regime into collecting signatures over three days. The coercion was, literally, door-to-door and person-by-person. "The government set up a table on every block," Oswaldo recalled, "and they went house by house, reminding every family: 'Your child is in college, so it's not a good idea for you not to sign.' 'You have a business fixing shoes, you have a business selling soft drinks, you want to leave the country but we can keep you from doing so.' It is a system of coercion, that worked." While Fidel's frenzied crowds had been genuinely emotional in earlier years, now the exercise seemed stiff and artificial. The results came swiftly: Fidel's referendum was approved by 99 percent of the island's 8.2 million legal voters.

Next, Castro demanded that the National Assembly meet urgently. The regular session was set for July 5, but delegates rushed to Havana to convene on June 24. The government closed schools, offices, and factories so people could follow the sessions, broadcast live on television. The amendments were adopted on June 26. All 559 delegates voted "yes." Not a single "no."

This was Fidel's system at work—one party, one proposal, no competition, no criticism.

On June 27, Oswaldo issued a statement, clear and without fear. "No maneuver can force the people to commit civic suicide," he said. If the constitution's new amendments could never be revoked, as Fidel had dictated, if they were locked up forever, he asked, "Then do we stop being a republic and become a kidnapped people?" Oswaldo, who had been fighting for most of his life against the deprivations of the revolution, was more certain than ever that Cubans were fed up, that they wanted change.

"Let those who want to condemn Cubans to life imprisonment know: the sentence will not be carried out," he said defiantly.

After his moderate May 20 speech, Bush sharply changed course. He abandoned any "step-by-step" approach and ratcheted up pressure on the Castro government. He went all out.

Huddleston, who was leaving her post as chief of mission after four years, believed a détente was developing with Cuba and saw her goal as nurturing it. She was, by her own account, "not a fervent anti-Castro crusader" but wanted to "foster better relations" and bring about change by "empowering the Cuban people." Her signature effort was to distribute hundreds of small radios, allowing Cubans to hear news from overseas, bypassing censorship. But she was wary of going too far, because Castro "would smash our endeavors by throwing me or my officers out of the country or by jailing the dissidents." It was "dangerous," she thought, to "confront the oppressive power of the Cuban state too aggressively." She felt she had walked right up to the edge.

Her successor, James C. Cason, went farther.

Cason had been a career US diplomat for thirty-two years, serving in El Salvador, Venezuela, Uruguay, Panama, Bolivia, Honduras, and Jamaica. He was selected to head what was officially the US Interests Section of the Swiss embassy, the US diplomatic outpost in Havana established in 1977. The position was under the Castro regime's constant watch. The six-story US office building on the Malecón was, on the bottom three floors, run by three hundred Cuban employees: cooks, clerks, drivers, telephone operators, and security guards, any number of them reporting back to state security. Fifty-one employees came from the United States. Many of their offices, homes, and cars were bugged, although the Cubans were not allowed on the top three floors of the interests section, where classified materials were kept.

Cason's marching orders from the Bush administration were explicit: do everything possible to support the opposition except provide money. "I was told, you're not going to be at a mission, you are *on* a mission," he recalled. "The mission is to let the dissidents know we support them. They are not alone." Cason had leeway to act as he saw fit and report to Washington later. Cason took up the task with gusto. Soon after his arrival in September 2002, he invited the dissidents and opposition figures to his residence—including Oswaldo and other leaders of Todos Unidos—and asked how he could help, short of money. Some of them suggested he come to their homes so neighbors would know they had the support of the United States. Cason promised to visit anyone who invited him. They asked for information and means to communicate with each other and to get on the internet, which was inaccessible to most Cubans at the time. Some wanted to learn how to be journalists.

Cason and his staff knew their actions could trigger a backlash from Fidel. They were undeterred; being provocative was their plan. "Our policy was going to be, shake the tree," recalled a diplomat who was there. "It was a desire to trigger a crisis, to ratchet up pressure so high it would create conditions for change."

Cason hit the road. With a driver, he spent several months traversing Cuba's back country. He carried books on democracy, biographies of Gandhi and Martin Luther King, Jr., the just-published memoir of Huber Matos, and copies of the Universal Declaration of Human Rights. He acquired hundreds of packs of Major League Baseball cards featuring players who had fled Cuba. He gave away baseballs, baseball bats, baseball calendars, and shortwave radios by the thousands. The small radios, made by Tecsun of Hong Kong, came in a plastic pouch with rechargeable batteries. People were thrilled with the gifts. Cason stopped and offered rides to hitchhikers or travelers, who were often waiting hours in knots by the roadside, looking for a ride. In the car, he chatted about their lives, asking them who else they knew—*Do you know a nurse we can talk to about the medical system?*—and then dropping them off a safe distance from their destination, so they would not get in trouble. In Havana, he stocked the bookshelves of the US Interests Section with volumes that had been banned. He imported them through the diplomatic pouch, which was not really a "pouch" but a shipping container. There were copies of the 1940 Cuban constitution; George Orwell's *Animal Farm*; Armando Valladares's prison recollections; the works of the renowned Cuban writer Reinaldo Arenas; books about democratic transitions in Poland, Czechoslovakia, and East Germany; and books about Cuban history. One wall was just children's books. He invited dissidents and journalists to help themselves, providing shopping bags to carry them away. He set up two dozen computer terminals so the dissidents could use the internet, and gave them entry passes to come and go. He provided small, blank notepads with sayings by Thomas Jefferson on the cover, and pens emblazoned with slogans such as "Journalism without censorship." In the consular section, copies of *el Nuevo Herald*, the *Miami Herald*'s Spanish-language sister paper, were placed on every chair in the waiting room. He provided journalists and dissidents with equipment and supplies—printers and toner, copying machines, cameras, recorders, and laptops. "We were like a store," Cason recalled.

Cautiously, Payá went to see Cason a few times. Once he took a small, square plastic box with wires hanging out of it. "He said, 'Can you check this out?'" Cason recalled. "I took it and showed it to our people and they said 'Yes, it's a bug. This is a classic.'" The eavesdropping bug wasn't very sophisticated, a microphone connected to a standard telephone wall jack, similar in design to those the Stasi provided Cuba in the late 1970s.

Cuba's nascent civil society seemed to be blossoming anew. "There was a big push for independent everything—independent libraries, independent press," Cason recalled. In the summer of 2002, there was a noticeable bustle at the house of Ricardo González Alfonso, who had pioneered the independent Cubapress agency with the writer Raúl Rivero in the mid-1990s. His house contained the journalism "school" and library they founded—really, just a room. Now the top floor was being renovated into a newsroom, where González was preparing to launch a thoughtful, independent magazine, titled *De Cuba*. He hoped it would resemble the hugely popular *Bohemia* of the 1950s. González had founded a journalists' society in 2001, which had more than a hundred members, and they became the backbone of *De Cuba*. The society won an award from the Cuban Hispanic Foundation, an exile group based in Madrid, and used the proceeds to buy a secondhand computer and other equipment. One of the journalists recalled approaching the computer with awe. "We had never laid our hands on one."

In the first issue, the editors were blunt. They intended to express themselves freely. "No government, not even in an adverse economic situation, should restrict man's freedom of expression and information," they wrote. Their first issue, fifty-two photocopied pages bound with thick brown tape down the spine, was daring and unsparing, probing the dark side of the revolution. One article detailed the miserable health care system in Cuba, including robberies of patients who came into hospitals unconscious, as well as shortages, and bribes to doctors for better treatment. An essay underscored the mediocre state of the island's literary culture and institutions. An article pointed to the revolution's failure to diversify the economy. And the magazine published the story of a state security agent trained to infiltrate opposition groups in his hometown. He was supposed to immerse himself in the Catholic Church, but instead of becoming an informer, he became a believer, and turned on the state. He was sentenced to six years in prison for calling Fidel a liar. He was held in solitary confinement for a year.

For the first issue, they could print only about 250 copies, distributed through the independent libraries. González and Rivero were full of pride. The magazine was built on a "fragile carpentry," Rivero recalled later—"the magazine we wanted to make, the one we thought was needed" in Cuba, which was stuck with the "dense and defeated discourse of the oldest dictatorship in the world."

Oswaldo also felt that, despite Fidel's theatrics in June, there were signs of hope for the Varela Project. Oswaldo's citizen committees—established earlier for the crash verification effort—were now organizing more support, and thousands of signatures were collected. In the past, Oswaldo and his team had photocopied each petition laboriously, a security measure, using the old, wheezing copier. To help speed up the processing, the US Interests Section—Cason's "store"—acquired six scanners that could make digital copies of the petitions, storing them on a laptop. The scanners were badly needed. A US diplomat one day delivered them in boxes to Tony, but as they were unloading from the diplomat's car, state security caught sight of them. Before the curious officers could interfere, Tony took off with the scanners and ducked into a garage. State security pulled up to the garage, thinking they had him cornered. But when they opened the door, there was nothing. Tony had managed to hustle the scanners out the back door of the garage with the help of a friend.

But state security never let up. The Stasi had perfected the art of document forgery to undermine dissidents, and they provided the Cubans with a sophisticated print shop. State security found a letter Oswaldo had written to thank a Varela Project supporter. They forged additional paragraphs, saying the Varela Project would pay cash for signatures, and Oswaldo was the paymaster. Then they distributed the forgery, a sneaky way to smear Payá. He was furious when he found out. "This is false, this is an insult," he protested, a forgery by "the enemies of the people, the enemies of change, the enemies of freedom, the enemies of the Varela Project." He stressed that the Varela Project did not offer money for signatures. "What it offers is the struggle for change and rights in Cuba, and we are going to gain them."

Payá was gaining recognition abroad. In July Czech president Havel nominated him for the Nobel Peace Prize for his work on the Varela Project. In September he was awarded the National Democratic Institute's W. Averell Harriman Democracy Award. Oswaldo found the recognition satisfying but tinged with irony: people around the world were hearing more about the Varela Project than the people inside Cuba. The Varela Project was still censored in Cuba's state-run media. In September, Oswaldo was not permitted to leave Cuba to accept the NDI award. The government strictly controlled who could depart by granting exit permits. Oswaldo told a friend: What better evidence of the dictatorship than the fact they lock the doors?

On October 23, the European Parliament announced that Payá was the recipient of the annual Sakharov Award for Human Rights and Freedom of Thought. The award is one of the most prestigious in the world, established in 1988 and named for the nuclear physicist Andrei Sakharov, a courageous dissident and champion of human rights in the Soviet Union.

Oswaldo was thrilled with the honor but had no hope of actually accepting the award in person. The regime never granted him permission to leave for such events. "Leaving the country was not a right," recalled Ofelia. "We didn't think that they were going to let him go for this prize. We were really happy about the recognition. But it never went through our minds that they would let him go."

Spanish prime minister José María Aznar and European Parliament president Pat Cox pressed Castro to allow Payá to accept the award in Strasbourg, France, seat of the European Parliament. The ceremony was set for December 17. But the outlook was not very encouraging. On Thursday, December 12, it seemed unlikely he could go. Payá had not packed a suitcase. He asked his brother Carlos Alberto, in exile in Spain, to stand in for him and collect the award.

On Friday morning, Oswaldo and Ofelia were getting the children ready for school. Oswaldo, ready to leave for work, went to the front door and pushed it open. But it was stuck. It would not budge. Then he noticed, under the door, red paint seeping through the crack.

He pushed the door again; still tight as a drum.

He saw a passerby on the street and shouted out the window: Would he look at the door?

The passerby said it was lashed shut with electrical cord. Another neighbor helped untie the door. When Oswaldo stepped into the street, he saw that state security had plastered the house with paint and posters calling him a gusano, or worm, and a CIA agent. It was like the acto de repudio in 1991, but this time without the mob.

On the side of the house, Payá noticed state security had erected a banner of Alpha 66, a militant anti-Castro exile group formed in the early 1960s and viewed as a terrorist organization by the Cuban govern-ment. It still existed in Florida, but not in Cuba. Oswaldo, a nonviolent civic campaigner, had never had anything to do with them or their meth-ods. Now Fidel was signaling that Oswaldo should be regarded as the enemy. He had always been an outsider, never inside the revolution, but this took it to another level.

The children and Ofelia were still in the house. Oswaldo stepped over the paint and walked into the street. He began screaming at the top of his lungs.

"Where are you?" he demanded of the state security officers, as-suming they were observing from nearby buildings. "I'm here, I see you! Who did this?"

Oswaldo glimpsed his children at the door. They looked frightened, and that set him off even more, shouting again. Ofelia had never seen such fury.

She took the children to school. Oswaldo called foreign correspon-dents he knew and asked them to come witness what had been done. Early that afternoon, Ofelia doubled back to school, just to make sure the children were all right. "We were afraid—what if they're capable of doing something to our kids? I went to see if they were well, if somebody had come to see them at school." They were shaken, but unharmed.

That night, Oswaldo and Ofelia talked nervously. They could not sleep. Saturday was the last moment Oswaldo could catch a flight to make it to Strasbourg for the prize ceremony. They felt the walls were

closing in. "We didn't know how it was going to end, but we were seriously worried," Ofelia recalled. "What does this mean? What is going to
be their next step? When are they going to stop?"

After midnight, Oswaldo's aunt Beba knocked on their door. They
were startled to see her. Beba said she had received a phone call from the
French embassy. The caller said Oswaldo should go to the authorities in
the morning and pick up his exit visa. He was free to leave.

It now dawned on them what happened: under pressure from the
Europeans, the Cuban government had given in and allowed him to
leave; but first they had to terrorize him and his family.

Ofelia held her breath. On Saturday morning, she waited until Oswaldo had the exit visa and airline tickets in hand before packing a small
suitcase. She saw him off at the airport. "Be careful," she said. "Be very
careful."

Oswaldo flew first to Madrid, where he was reunited at the airport with
two of his brothers, Óscar and Carlos Alberto, and his sister Rosa, who
had once held his hand walking to church. Oswaldo shared with them
his excitement about the Varela Project and what might come in the
future. Their reunion was filled with loud talk and good food, his nieces
and nephews all about. They had bought Oswaldo a light blue suit to
wear in official meetings abroad, and Rosa tailored the pant legs. Carlos
Alberto recalled that at one point he spotted Oswaldo alone, engrossed
in watching *Casablanca*, which he had never seen, on Spanish television.
Carlos Alberto worked feverishly on their travel plans. Óscar was, by his
own account, worried about Oswaldo's safety back in Cuba. "I was always alerting him that he should always do everything within his ability
to stop risking his safety. Not to give them any reason to imprison him."

In Strasbourg, at 7:00 a.m. on the day of the ceremony, Oswaldo
slipped away to attend Mass. Unprepared for the cold weather, he wore
no coat. When he got back, Carlos Alberto noticed that he was chilled
and shivering.

For the award ceremony, the 626-seat chamber of the European Parliament was packed. Along with Carlos Alberto, Payá was accompanied

by Francisco de Armas, a spokesman and translator, whose father was one of Oswaldo's cousins. Francisco had flown in from Puerto Rico, where his family lived, carrying a navy blue wool suit, white shirt, and dark blue tie with gold flecks, borrowed from his father, for Oswaldo to wear on his big day.

It was quite a moment. This was only the second time Oswaldo had been outside of Cuba; he had never set foot in Europe. Just days before, he was standing outside his house in Havana, red paint on his soles, electric cord dangling from the door, screaming in anger at state security. Now, taking the podium at the heart of European democracy, he looked distinguished.

The Sakharov award was presented by Pat Cox, the European Parliament president, an Irish politician and onetime television journalist. "You represent for many Cubans today what Andrei Sakharov represented in the 1980s for many Soviet citizens," Cox said in presenting the award. "You represent hope."

In his speech, Oswaldo paid tribute to all those who had struggled alongside him. "In my country there are thousands of men and women fighting for the rights of all Cubans in the midst of persecution," he said. "Hundreds of them are imprisoned simply for proclaiming and defending these rights, and I am therefore accepting this award on behalf of them." He said he did not want the world to take sides for or against the Cuban government, but he appealed for support of rights, openness, and use of the ballot box to bring about change, to build a "democratic, fair and free society."

Oswaldo recalled Cuba's turbulent political history and warned that violence was not the answer. "The heroic Cuban civic fighters, the citizens who sign the Varela Project, are not carrying arms," he said. "We do not have a single weapon."

They had pencils, a petition, and a wheezing old photocopy machine.

Payá never mentioned Fidel Castro by name, but he directly condemned the revolution. It had taken away their rights, he said, and for what? For poverty and misery? There was no justification for this deprivation, he insisted, certainly not the tattered claim that the revolution would bring about social justice and equality. "The hands of the citizens are tied," he lamented, "neutralizing the Cubans' enormous potential for creativity and hard work. That is the main cause of our poverty.

"This reality," he added, "cannot be justified by claiming that the Cubans freely choose this system."

He noted that Cubans had lived under, and suffered with, different political and economic models—capitalism and communism. "We know today," he said, "that any method or model which, in a supposed quest for justice, development or efficiency, places itself above human beings and cancels out any of their fundamental rights, leads us to some form of oppression, of exclusion, and brings disaster to the people."

This was Oswaldo's bedrock conviction: rights are endowed by God and cannot be taken away by the state. "We Cubans are simple folk," he said, "and we simply wish to live in peace and to move forward with our work, but we are not able and we do not wish to live without freedom."

The parliamentarians responded with a standing ovation.

Not a word of Oswaldo's speech appeared in the Cuban state media.

The Sakharov prize came with $15,000, which Oswaldo pledged to devote to the Varela Project. After the ceremony, he began a whirlwind overseas tour that stretched into January 2003. He saw Pope John Paul II in a general audience at the Vatican; he met Havel in Prague; he met three times with the Spanish prime minister, Aznar, one of the most steadfast champions of the Varela Project; and he met President Vicente Fox in Mexico. Payá flew to Washington and met with Secretary of State Colin Powell, members of Congress, the White House National Security Council, and the National Democratic Institute, which presented him with the Harriman award in person—at last.

He stopped for an hour at the editorial board of the *Washington Post* on January 6. He was asked: What's the use of a petition campaign seeking a legal referendum in a country where there is no rule of law?

Payá hesitated, smiled ruefully, rubbed his forehead, and said, "Let me try to explain." In gentle and melodic Spanish, he talked about the relentless persecution he and his family had suffered; the pervasive fear in Cuba; and the courage it took for people to affix a signature, address, and identity card number to a Varela Project petition. The deputy editorial editor, Jackson Diehl, who had covered the rise of Solidarity in Poland, wrote afterward that many people still had trouble understanding how totalitarian regimes survive with arbitrary brutality and everyday fear, and how vulnerable these regimes are to people who reject both fear and violence. Payá was one such person, he said, "instantly recognizable to anyone who met the democratic revolutionaries of the old Soviet bloc, the seemingly isolated and powerless intellectuals and workers who used to field all the same questions . . . people who challenge their fellow citizens to join them in establishing independent movements that forswear violence and lay the groundwork for democracy."

"Each small piece of paper represents bravery and courage," Oswaldo told the editors. "Every signature is an act of liberation."

His next undertaking was one of the most difficult. Oswaldo flew to Miami on January 11 for what was his first real introduction to the Cuban exile community and the influential hard-liners who shaped its thinking. They had never seen Oswaldo clearly nor understood his fight. In the past few months, in particular, Miami's anti-Castro Spanish radio stations had been blasting away at the Varela Project because it sought democratic change through Fidel's socialist 1976 constitution.

In an empty office building on a Sunday, Oswaldo sat down with Representative Lincoln Díaz-Balart, his brother Representative Mario Díaz-Balart, and Representative Ileana Ros-Lehtinen, all three Miami Republicans and prominent exile community leaders. Ileana's father, Enrique Ros, a prolific author critical of the revolution, was also present. Lincoln Díaz-Balart, who hosted the meeting, recalled having serious doubts about Payá and the Varela Project. "The wariness initially felt toward him was understandable," he said, a fear that Castro "may attempt to fool the international community with an illusory democratic transition."

Oswaldo, who had done so much to challenge the Castro regime, confronted their doubts head-on. He insisted he was not giving legitimacy to Fidel. He described the acto de repudio in Havana before his departure and asked, if he was a collaborator with the regime, would they have done that? He assured them he was using the 1976 constitution as a lever to mobilize people and undermine Fidel's grip on power, not to reinforce it. Lincoln Díaz-Balart was concerned that the Varela Project did not explicitly legalize political parties, which he felt was essential to break the regime's monopoly on power. "I was worried that the dictatorship might allow a few independents into its sham parliament and point to that illusory political opening as being genuine," he recalled. He told Oswaldo that a transition must not go from the existing Communist rule to a Fidel-dominated "corporatist" structure that would still lack independent political parties.

Oswaldo agreed that political parties were important. But in the gritty reality of Cuba at that moment, they could not survive. In 1988, Ricardo Bofill had made an ill-fated attempt to create one and was immediately blocked by Fidel.

In the car after the meeting, Oswaldo asked Orlando Gutiérrez, the trip organizer, what Díaz-Balart meant by "corporatist." He had never heard the term. Gutiérrez, who led a human rights group in Miami, explained that it was the use of a powerful state apparatus to organize people into associations, such as unions, that claim to be their sole representative, suppressing and demobilizing independent civil society groups. The Franco dictatorship in Spain had done this. Oswaldo certainly understood the power of the state. Díaz-Balart's point about creating independent political parties left an impression on him.

That evening, Oswaldo attended Mass at La Ermita de la Caridad, a sanctuary that honors Cuba's patron saint and is a touchstone for the Miami Cuban community. A large mural in the chapel features images of Varela and Martí, among others. The Mass was packed. People in the pews recognized Oswaldo, whose presence was announced near the end. The chapel echoed with thunderous applause. Oswaldo called on the exiles to join him in seeking peaceful change on the island. "This is where the other half of the heart of the Cuban people is," he said of Miami, "and when a heart is divided, both parts suffer." He added, "Help me, this is a task for all of us."

Over four days in Miami, Oswaldo tried to build bridges. He answered detailed questions about the Varela Project before an invitation-only crowd of about a hundred at the Félix Varela Room in the complex at La Ermita. A portrait in the back of the hall honors Eduardo Boza Masvidal, the last priest to walk up the gangplank to the *Covadonga* when Fidel expelled the Catholic clergy in 1961. Oswaldo also met with *plantados*, the long-term political prisoners released from Castro's prisons, and with veterans of the Bay of Pigs. Oswaldo recalled that the meetings were "very intense, very contentious." There was no large public rally or speech, out of security concerns; Gutiérrez was worried about possible violence by Castro infiltrators.

Oswaldo didn't persuade everyone. Ten exile groups issued a statement during his visit, expressing skepticism about the Varela Project. Ninoska Pérez-Castellón, a spokeswoman for the Cuban Liberty Council and prominent radio commentator, said, "If you accept these baby steps, you are legitimizing the system. They are steps but in the wrong direction." At the same time, the Cuban American National Foundation took out a full-page newspaper advertisement in support of the Varela Project.

An intrigued and attentive group listened to Oswaldo in a poolside reception at the elegant home of Carlos Saladrigas, who led the Cuba Study Group, a business association, and was an advocate for more US engagement with Cuba. Saladrigas described Payá as a visionary for using Cuba's existing laws to press for democracy and rights. He felt that the Miami exile community had run into a dead end. They needed someone who would capture the world's imagination for the cause of a free Cuba, in the way that Walesa and Havel had done. "I thought Payá had the best chance of doing that," he said.

In his remarks, Oswaldo liked to recall the promise he and Ofelia had made to each other many years before. "I said, my children are not going to leave Cuba. They are going to live freely in this country."

At a meeting with *Miami Herald* editors, he was asked what lay ahead for the Varela Project. "A change in scale," he replied. Thousands had signed it so far, but now he wanted millions of signatures. He was determined not to stop.

Oswaldo's visit was a watershed for him and the Miami Cuban community. Some critics began to take the Varela Project more seriously. The exiles "got to know that Payá was a democrat who truly wanted Cuba to be free," said Díaz-Balart. "That's what the exiles want as well."

When he returned to Havana on February 2, 2003, Oswaldo's family embraced him at the airport. "Our Varela Project continues," Oswaldo told waiting journalists. "It's a campaign from the Cuban people and we will continue until all Cubans achieve their rights."

But in his absence, dark clouds had gathered.

In December, the Constitution and Legal Affairs Committee of the National Assembly rejected the Varela Project, saying it was illegal and unconstitutional. When Fidel was asked about the Varela Project in January, he replied, "Let's talk about serious things, not silliness."

More dispiriting news came from Tony Díaz. Todos Unidos, the umbrella group that had proven so important in collecting signatures, was shifting its goals and could abandon the Varela Project. "They are sawing the floor out from under us," he warned Oswaldo.

He was right. While Oswaldo was overseas, the other leaders of Todos Unidos had grown restless. They felt they had given their all to the Varela Project, but now it was time to address many of their other unfulfilled ideas for change—projects they considered just as worthy. Elizardo Sánchez raised the prospect of a larger effort, with the Varela Project as a component. "We can't put all our eggs in one basket," Sánchez said. He and the others made a list of thirty-six additional goals they wanted to pursue, including increased salaries and pensions, the right to own a home and open a private business, the right to travel freely outside of Cuba, the legalization of independent labor unions, and elimination of mandatory military conscription. These were all important ideas, and there were many more. The full list was published in February in the second issue of *De Cuba* by the independent journalists Ricardo González Alfonso and Raúl Rivero. The issue was as provocative as the first, with a focus on the Varela Project. A political essayist and social democrat, Manuel Cuesta Morúa, wrote that the Varela Project had already had an "immense" impact in Cuba, demonstrating that there was an alternative to the revolution. The magazine printed the complete text of the Varela Project petition, alongside the thirty-six new goals sought by Sánchez and the others in Todos Unidos.

Oswaldo saw trouble. He stubbornly resisted any shift in strategy and soon was arguing with the others. The tension boiled over in a meeting late one weekday afternoon in February at the home of Héctor Palacios, one of the original founders of Todos Unidos. He had a sizable living room where they could hash things out. Oswaldo came to the meeting with Álvarez. Also at the table were Sánchez and the dissident Vladimiro Roca.

Sánchez said they should use Todos Unidos to branch out. The Varela Project was not the only way to bring about change, he argued.

Oswaldo objected, steadfastly. The Varela Project, he insisted, was the only effort that had ever accomplished a real mobilization for democracy and rights. It *worked*. They must be patient and stick with it—collecting more signatures would eventually pay off.

An undercurrent of jealousy ran through the room. Oswaldo had won international acclaim with the Sakharov prize. He accepted it with humility and tried to share the credit with all. But the leaders of Todos Unidos were restive and agitated.

Oswaldo was also headstrong. He had worked so long and hard to reach this point that it had left him with a certain lone-wolf callousness, a determination to get his way. He had little patience for those who wanted to chase their pet projects. "He thought that the nexus of the changes was the Varela Project," recalled Palacios. "And we felt that we had to do the Varela Project *and many other things*. Oswaldo, a very dignified, very honest, very intelligent man and a very good friend, was a bit authoritarian. He felt that you didn't need to expand all these stages." Oswaldo's attitude was, "You do things the way I say, or I'm not going to participate."

Twilight settled in the Palacios living room. Sánchez and the others demanded that Oswaldo give up his post as the spokesman for Todos Unidos and rotate the position among them. Further, they insisted that he should be subordinate to them when it came to planning the next steps for the Varela Project. Oswaldo felt insulted and isolated. He did not want to take orders from them.

Payá picked up his papers and stalked out of the house. Álvarez was on his heels. The door slammed behind them.

Suddenly the unity of purpose in Todos Unidos—the essential key to the Varela Project's success—was shattered.

In Oswaldo's mind, the breakup was not entirely spontaneous. He knew from long experience that state security tried to infiltrate and splinter every opposition group. He had seen enough of their dirty tricks to recognize that state security might well have a hand in the breakup. He was right to be suspicious; in fact, state security was preparing yet another attempt to undermine him.

The previous summer, Oswaldo had taken his family on a brief vacation to Varadero, the most luxurious of Cuba's beaches, a strip of white sand along the island's northern coast favored by foreign tourists. Oswaldo often complained that Varadero was off-limits to poor Cubans, who were barred from the fancy hotels and could never afford them. He was determined to go there and enjoy it; the beach belonged to all Cubans. Oswaldo and his family rose at dawn in Havana and took the train. He was joined at the beach by Tony Díaz and his family. Oswaldo did not stay in a hotel but squeezed the family into a spare room in the parish church, courtesy of the priest. They enjoyed the serenity and beauty. Oswaldo dove off a bobbing skiff into the turquoise waters.

He was being watched the entire time by state security, photographing Payá in his swim trunks.

On February 24, James Cason personally went to the home of Marta Beatriz Roque, one of the "Group of Four" dissidents who had been imprisoned a few years earlier. She was forming a new opposition group, and Cason's presence was an unusual gesture of support from the United States. A few foreign correspondents were present when Cason spoke. "Sadly, the Cuban government is scared," he said, "scared of freedom of conscience, scared of freedom of expression, scared of human rights."

This remark irritated Fidel personally. He began to turn the screws. An order went out to stop Cason from freely driving around the country. Then a container of books being imported through the US diplomatic pouch was seized by the Cuban authorities. The shipment included Spanish translations of such titles as John Steinbeck's *Grapes of Wrath* and comedian Groucho Marx's *Memoir of a Mangy Lover*. Cason was scornful. "It's fear of losing control," he said. "That's how Groucho Marx . . . can suddenly become subversive." On March 6, Fidel, elected to a sixth term by the National Assembly, called Cason a "dandy with diplomatic immunity."

Fidel could not ignore the reality: bold, independent journalists were openly writing negative stories about the revolution. A group of dissidents openly threatened to derail a trade agreement between Cuba and Europe. Books about democracy were flooding the island. The Varela Project was still expanding. Oswaldo had organized citizen committees in 112 of Cuba's 168 municipalities. These committees were collecting signatures. On top of that, Oswaldo had accepted the Sakharov prize from the European Parliament with a speech that lacerated the revolution.

Something snapped. Fidel had had enough.

On the morning of March 18, from his second-floor apartment window, Pedro Pablo Álvarez noticed a state security officer walking into the Committee for the Defense of the Revolution on the first floor. For weeks, state security officers had been harassing Álvarez. They pressed him to split from Oswaldo, to become an informer. He refused, but was unsettled. He left home that morning for a meeting with Oswaldo at the Dutch embassy, to tell them about the Varela Project.

At the same time, Regis Iglesias telephoned Beba's house, checking in. Was he needed that day? Another member of the movimiento, Ernesto "Freddy" Martini, who was in the office at that moment, told Regis to hurry over. "They are detaining our people!" Calls from journalists were coming in, asking about arrests. At first Regis was puzzled. Who? Why? When he arrived at Beba's, he noticed state security cars snaking up and down Calle Peñón.

At about 6:00 p.m., Álvarez returned home. Within minutes, about twenty state security officers swarmed into his apartment. They searched everything, including his library of books, one by one, looking for any hidden papers. The search went on past midnight, while he watched.

That evening, Tony Díaz gathered up a cache of signed Varela Project petitions he had stored at home. He and his wife, Gisela, rode his German-made MZ-250 motorcycle to drop off the petitions with the nuns for safekeeping. After delivering the petitions, his motorcycle got a flat tire and they laboriously pushed it home. Tony told Gisela to keep their meager savings concealed in a blouse pocket; she probably would not be searched if state security came after him. "They could come at any moment," he warned her. Tony heard on his small shortwave radio that President Bush was about to order the invasion of Iraq.

At about 4:00 a.m. on March 19, Álvarez was handcuffed and taken to the interrogation cells at state security headquarters, Villa Marista.

Throughout that day, Regis answered phone calls at Beba's house. Tony fixed the motorcycle flat tire; then he and Oswaldo sped off, first to the Swedish embassy, then to the European Union offices, appealing for diplomatic pressure on Castro to halt the arrests. In the afternoon, they visited Álvarez's family. His wife told them state security brought in a video camera and filmed everything, including photographs of their four grandchildren in frames on the wall.

Tony and Oswaldo looked drained and exhausted when they finally returned to Beba's house. Oswaldo said, "You should all be aware that we all run the risk of being arrested at any time now."

Tony left for home, worried about his wife and children.

Oswaldo and Regis went to Payá's home. Regis had planned to take Oswaldo's two boys to the baseball stadium for a game—to divert them from all the tension. But then a phone call came. It was Tony's older daughter, Jenny.

"Regis!" she cried. "They've just taken my father. These people have searched our house and taken my father!"

Tony had been handcuffed and driven to Villa Marista.

Regis bunked down at Beba's house overnight, just to be safe. The

next day, he and Oswaldo went to see Tony's family. They took a city
bus. A state security car followed the bus, then an officer boarded, standing silently next to them in the aisle. Next, Regis and Oswaldo went to
the embassy of the Netherlands, pleading for help. The diplomats there
promised to condemn the arrests in the European Parliament.

Alone, Oswaldo and Regis left the embassy and walked, taking a
meandering path through Havana, the two of them trying to figure out
what to do. Oswaldo suggested that they should gather several dozen
members of the movement outside Villa Marista and demand the release of the detainees. Regis said it would just get them all arrested at
once.

"Look, this is against *us*," Regis said. "It's clear they want to finish
us off."

At the Spanish embassy, they were invited into the secure communications room. With the help of the Spanish ambassador, Oswaldo spoke
by phone to the prime minister, Aznar, and to the president of the European Parliament, Pat Cox. Again, Oswaldo appealed for help to pressure
the regime to halt the crackdown and free those detained.

Then Oswaldo and Regis went out walking again, enveloped in a
gathering gloom. They stopped at Cristo Rey, a parish church half a mile
from Oswaldo's house. They knelt in prayer. "What I wanted, what I
hoped, was that this would all stop," Regis recalled. "Other times, when
they conducted a raid, they would start letting us free after seventy-two
hours. I hoped they would start freeing our friends. Because if they
didn't, it was going to be a long haul."

Back home, Oswaldo urged Regis to stay with him. But Regis
wanted to reassure his own family. He telephoned for a taxi. When the
service asked the name of the passenger, Regis said coyly, "Miguel Jag-
ger." When a taxi came down Calle Peñón, it was intercepted by a state
security officer and turned away. Regis called again, and this time gave
his real name. A taxi crawled up to Oswaldo's door. Regis and Freddy
Martini got in. The taxi pulled away. Regis felt tense, as if everything
were unfolding in slow motion.

He took out a mobile phone that he used only rarely. He found the speed-dial entry for Oswaldo and left it on the screen, without pressing Send.

Regis noticed that they were being followed. Then the taxi driver turned the wrong way and pulled into a parking lot. State security cars blocked them front and rear. The officers demanded Regis get out of the taxi. He pressed the button on the phone, and as he stepped out, he threw it on the street, under the taxi, hoping that Oswaldo would figure out what was going on.

Regis was taken to Villa Marista.

The arrests over three days struck at the heart of Oswaldo's movimiento. Of the seventy-five people arrested, twenty-two were from the movimiento, among them the national, provincial, and municipal leaders who had worked on the Varela Project. At least twenty more, including independent librarians and other civil society activists, had been involved in the Varela Project campaign in some way, and many were coordinators of the citizen committees. Still more were independent journalists.

Ricardo González Alfonso was in the first wave of journalists to be taken. He was working upstairs on the next edition of *De Cuba* when his fifteen-year-old son, David, knocked on the door. "Don't have a heart attack," he said, "but state security is downstairs."

While the house was being searched, the son announced he was going out to buy bread. He grabbed the family's savings from a cubbyhole and vanished. He bought a loaf of bread, hid the money inside, and went to tell Rivero.

Meanwhile, González was handcuffed, put in a squad car, and taken to Villa Marista.

On March 20, Raúl Rivero's apartment was searched and he was detained. The two most daring and prominent journalists of the Cuban Spring were now locked up.

Victor Rolando Arroyo, who had first given the Varela Project petitions to Fredesvinda Hernández, was arrested.

Alejandro González Raga, who had carried his dying friend in his arms in Camagüey before joining the Varela Project, was arrested.

José Daniel Ferrer, who had been one of the small group with Oswaldo at Beba's house the night before the submission of the Varela Project's signatures, was arrested.

Héctor Palacios was arrested. His house, where the Todos Unidos schism had opened, was searched and state security carted off some two thousand books.

Elizardo Sánchez, who had met with former president Carter along with Oswaldo, had packed a little bag, and expected to be arrested at any moment. When Rivero, the writer, was taken, Elizardo telephoned the foreign correspondents in Havana to alert them. Suddenly the wave of arrests stopped; Elizardo was not detained.

"Every day, a different person fell," Payá later recalled. "I felt like they were going to come for me very quickly. Every day, I waited for them. At home, my family waited for them." They didn't come. One explanation is that, as the winner of the Sakharov award, his arrest might trigger a large international outcry. Another explanation is that Fidel had a different kind of punishment in mind.

Jimmy Carter phoned Havana. Fidel said he didn't want to speak on the phone and urged Carter to send a personal envoy. A team went, including Jennifer McCoy, who had organized Carter's visit the year before, and John Hardman, director of the Carter Center. In their meeting with Castro, every time they tried to bring up a point, Fidel interrupted them with a diatribe. They never got their concerns across.

Then McCoy and Hardman went to see Oswaldo at home. They saw a state security car parked out front, officers watching who came and left. They sat at the kitchen table with Ofelia, who recalled, "Imagine how he felt. They had taken all his friends to jail and he was left alone." Oswaldo looked grim, McCoy recalled. "He was demoralized, dejected, and worried."

In cell 19, Tony had a pounding headache. He was prisoner 690 at Villa Marista, jailed with three suspected drug dealers. On his arrival, state security took away his eyeglasses, leaving him nearly blind; his head was throbbing. Breakfast was six ounces of sugar water and a piece of stale bread. Lunch was rice, soup or stew, and a hot dog or piece of chicken. Dinner was the same. Time seemed suspended. On Sunday, May 23, nearing midnight, he was awakened by guards shouting, "Six ninety, get ready!"

In the hall, the guard commanded, "Face the wall, grab your card, and show it to the officer!"

Tony couldn't tell which was his card—he couldn't see. He informed the guard, who told him to shut up. "It turns out they took away my sight, asked me to use it, and then didn't want me to tell them I couldn't see," he later wrote. His journey into the absurd was just beginning.

He was marched up and down the hallways. If another prisoner was coming, he was forced to put his hands behind his back, stop, turn, and face the wall, so as not to see the other. He was hauled into and out of cell 19 at all hours for interrogations over the next two weeks. They sometimes quizzed him in small rooms with the air-conditioning on high, chilling him to the bone.

Tony was stubborn. He lectured them on the Varela Project and insisted he had broken no laws.

"Listen to what I am going to tell you," one of the interrogators finally told him. "The revolution has been tolerant for a long time, but the opposition is done for. There mustn't be any opposition here because the entire nation is with us."

At last, Tony got his glasses back. He was interrogated again and again about the US Interests Section. All the questions seemed to center on the United States and whether Tony was working for some masters in Washington. "How many receptions at Cason's house have you been to?" None, he said, but he went there twice when Huddleston was chief of mission. Why did he have a permanent pass for the Interests Section? It allowed him to go online two hours a week, he said, which was impossible for most people in Cuba.

Then he was presented a draft of a "confession" that said he had a "close collaboration" with the United States. Tony read the document in another freezing interrogation room. He handed it back, his hand shaking from the cold. "This is full of lies!" he said, refusing to sign.

Yet another interrogator pressed him about Oswaldo.

"How long have you known Payá?" he said.

"For about fifteen years," Tony replied.

"Don't think you can fool us," the interrogator warned. "We know perfectly well who you are and everything you've done against the revolution. I know all of you better than you can imagine, and I've known Payá since he was a mustachioed stick of a man whom nobody had heard of."

The questions finally ended, and he learned a trial was set for April 3. Tony's family hired a lawyer, Carlos Navarro, whom he met only the night before the trial. The lawyer had just received the file for the first time. "I am totally innocent of the crime they're accusing me of," Tony told him. "I also know that I'll be sentenced to twenty years, because this trial is nothing but a farce." He instructed the lawyer to demand acquittal, nothing else.

The next day, the guards lined up Tony and four other defendants, including Regis, outside the courtroom. A panel of five judges would hear the case. A guard warned them that they could not talk except when called upon. "You cannot look behind you. You cannot yell anything out."

In the courtroom, a table in the center displayed items seized by state security. It included the small Tecsun radio receivers, some magazines, books, office supplies, a video camera, and a small handheld tape recorder.

Tony was accused of violating Article 91 of the Criminal Code, which provides that "Anyone who, in the interests of a foreign State, commits an act with the intent of harming the independence of the Cuban State or the integrity of its territory shall be punished with imprisonment for a period of ten to twenty years or death."

When it came his turn to speak, Tony denied that he had done any such thing. The Varela Project, he said, was protected by Article 88(g) of the Cuban constitution, and it was the only reason for his arrest. He had simply sought to change society for the better. He said he had never received money or direction from the United States. He did get a small shortwave radio, and he listened to channels from all over the world. It was a standard radio receiver, "not prohibited in our country." He explained that his permanent pass to the US Interests Section allowed him to go online for two hours once a week. The charges, he concluded, are "nothing more than a political vendetta by the Cuban government for my work on the Varela Project."

When it came time for the prosecutor, a military lieutenant, to address the judges, he went over the same territory as the interrogations, accusing Tony of working for and being paid by the United States.

Tony's lawyer jumped to his feet.

"Officer, you've just said verbatim that my defendant, Antonio Díaz, has received sums of money from US officials. Is that correct?"

"Affirmative," the lieutenant replied.

"So can you tell us which officials? How much money? Where and when did they give him the money that you've mentioned?"

"No, I can't."

So it went for the rest of the day. The trial was following a script that had been written beforehand. Regis was accused of having in his home such "counterrevolutionary literature" as the magazine *De Cuba*, and magazines from abroad. State security also unearthed color photos showing Regis and Oswaldo delivering the Varela Project signatures to the National Assembly. This submission of signatures, envisioned in Cuba's constitution under a provision conceived by Gustavo Gutiérrez decades before as a bulwark against dictatorship, was now turned into evidence of a crime.

All of the defendants, and their lawyers, asked for acquittal. They had not used guns or bombs to threaten the independence or territorial integrity of Cuba. They were not guilty of any violation under Article 91. They had wielded only pencils and paper. But their fate was not decided by the law, or by the five judges. The law was Fidel.

They were all convicted.

Tony was sentenced to twenty years in prison.

Regis was sentenced to eighteen years.

Pedro Pablo Álvarez got twenty-five years.

The two journalists, González and Rivero, were sentenced to twenty years each.

Arroyo, who had given the Varela Project petitions to Fredesvinda, was sentenced to twenty-five years.

González Raga, who joined after his friend died in the raft accident, drew fourteen years.

Ferrer, who helped submit the signatures, was sentenced to twenty-five years.

Palacios, a founder of Todos Unidos, was sentenced to twenty-five years.

Roque, the economist, dissident, and the only woman arrested, got twenty years.

These days came to be known as the "Black Spring" of 2003. Of the total seventy-five prisoners, one was sentenced to six years, while all the rest received ten to twenty-eight years in jail. The sentences were a devastating setback to Oswaldo's movimiento and a shock to the families. Oswaldo tried to drum up financial support for relatives of the prisoners. He didn't like the term "Black Spring," coined by the wife of one prisoner—Oswaldo was always optimistic about the "Cuba Spring" of democracy—but these months were overwhelmingly dark and painful. He had been the organizer and champion of the Varela Project, but his supporters and friends were paying the price. "He took it hard," recalled Ehrenberg, the Swedish democracy activist who had often visited Oswaldo.

"The true leader of the secret political police was Fidel," said Elizardo Sánchez, who, like Oswaldo, had not been arrested. "The interior minister, the chief of police, followed the orders of Fidel Castro. In the Soviet Union it was the same in the time of Stalin." Castro, he added, "followed the scheme which said that for the leaders, you had to cut their nails, for the followers, you cut off their hands." Fidel had reserved for Oswaldo the Stasi treatment, or Zersetzung. By not arresting Oswaldo, Fidel was raising suspicions about him, leaving him twisting in the wind. State security deliberately fanned the question: *Why was he spared?*

A few weeks after the trials, Oswaldo's oldest son, Oswaldito, then fifteen years old, heard an interesting story from a schoolmate, Julio, who said there was a printing press in Cerro run by state security.

"How do you know?" Oswaldito asked. Julio said his stepfather worked there.

One day, Julio's stepfather brought home a colorful book just off the press, titled *Los disidentes*, or *The Dissidents*. When no one was looking, Julio snatched the book from his father's desk, slipped it into a bag, and brought it to Oswaldito. "Tell your dad to read it quick!" Julio told him. Oswaldito hustled it home and showed it to his father.

The 227-page book would have made the Stasi proud. It was a fine specimen of defamation and disinformation. Filled with photographs, the book purported to be the tale of twelve state security officers who had carried out undercover work, spying on dissidents, opposition, and journalists. Their big revelation? That the dissidents were puppets of the United States. The "evidence" was partly drawn from the interrogations and show trials, such as Tony's permanent pass for going online. The book was written breathlessly, but the details were mundane and proved nothing. In one photograph, Cason is standing off to the side at a press conference in which Roque is speaking, and the caption reads, "The Boss ensures that his orders are carried out . . ." In another, Cason is pictured with Ricardo González Alfonso and another journalist. "The mercenaries and their leader," the caption says.

Oswaldo and the Varela Project were mentioned frequently. One of the undercover officers claimed, yet again, that Oswaldo was paying cash for signatures on the Varela Project. Two pages stung Oswaldo personally. They displayed color photographs taken surreptitiously of Oswaldo at the beach, in his swim trunks. "Oswaldo Payá, in Varadero, enjoying the money from his 'awards,'" the caption said. Under photographs of Oswaldo jumping off the skiff, the book said, "A sequence, taken during his 'discreet' vacation."

The smear, like those earlier by state security, suggested Payá was motivated by personal greed.

Oswaldo returned the book to his son, who stuffed it in a bag and quickly hustled it back to his schoolmate.

Oswaldo was already stressed out by the arrests. He could march up to the printing house and shout at them from the street, but what good would that do? He decided the best course of action was to surprise the regime by exposing the book before it was published. On June 5 he released a long statement, calling the book a "desperate" attempt to justify the Black Spring arrests. He went on at length about the absurdities in the book: "the lies, the clumsiness, the hatred, the desperation." He said he was not ashamed about taking his family to the beach. The real scandal, he said, was how many Cuban government officials had enough money to stay at those fancy hotels in Varadero, who are "stealing from the people" while shouting "socialism or death!"

"Throughout the book," he added, "they talk dozens of times about the Varela Project, but they do not dare publish it because they are afraid that the people will know there is a path to liberation, to peaceful change, to reconciliation, to lifting the people of Cuba out of this mud in which the regime has submerged them."

The book, he added, would only "awaken interest in the truth." And he declared, "We are not afraid."

Three weeks later, the government published the book. Later in 2003, a similar volume, devoted entirely to an attempt to smear Sánchez, was also published.

In October, Oswaldo again carried boxes of Varela Project signatures to the National Assembly, this time submitting 14,384, for a total of 25,404. Although Fidel and the parliament had refused to act, Oswaldo wanted to keep the pressure on. Ofelia joined him in carrying the boxes to the National Assembly door. Thousands more signatures had been collected but not submitted. Some remained hidden by the nuns. Others had been confiscated by state security in the wave of arrests.

With independent journalists Ricardo González Alfonso and Raúl Rivero in prison, the remaining journalists at the freethinking magazine *De Cuba* decided to publish an emergency edition about the Black Spring. "The outlook was bleak," recalled Claudia Márquez, the deputy editor, whose husband, Oswaldo Alfonso, was among the seventy-five prisoners. "Most of our journalist friends were in jail.

"We began to imagine how to edit a third issue without a computer, printer, much less a photocopier." All had been confiscated by state security. But they remembered that in his journalism classes Rivero had taught them to persevere. With help from foreign embassies, they managed to print twelve hundred copies, and distributed them hand-to-hand across the island. This was the third and last edition of *De Cuba*. The cover displayed mug shots of those imprisoned after the April show trials. "Cubans are suffering the greatest wave of repression of the last decade," the editors wrote. "Cuba is now the largest prison for journalists in the world."

The cover also displayed a photograph of women, mostly wives, mothers, and daughters of the Black Spring prisoners, marching in protest in Havana. They gathered at St. Rita's church in the Miramar neighborhood and walked silently, all dressed in white. Soon they had formed a new movement, Ladies in White.

Cason, head of the US Interests Section, kept up the pressure after the seventy-five arrests. Around Havana, when he went for a walk, he wore a hat or football jersey with "75" emblazoned on it. The United States awarded twenty thousand visas a year to Cubans, and Cason made sure to add another seventy-five. With donations from the United States, a thirty-foot-high model of the Statue of Liberty was created and smuggled in through the diplomatic pouch—"more like a truck," said a diplomat—and erected at Cason's residence for a July Fourth celebration. The flame had "75" illuminated in lights. Cason invited dissidents to contribute to a time capsule he buried on the residence grounds, saying it would be raised the day before Cuba had its first genuinely free election. Each person was asked to write something to be read aloud when it was opened. Cason also displayed a mockup of a prison cell made from a shipping container, to highlight the plight of the prisoners. In the US Interests Section, printing was ramped up to produce a daily stapled booklet of news reports from around the world—news that might not be available in Cuba. An unmarked van was used to distribute everything around Havana, including more and more books.

Oswaldo's torment deepened in the summer and fall. The prisoners of the Black Spring were being treated harshly. Tony was being held in Holguín, 620 miles from Havana, in a cell not three steps long and one arm's length wide. Family visits were permitted only once in three months. In October, Gisela had brought him a parcel of food, clothing, and soap. She was told the food was limited to thirty pounds, but prison guards subtracted the weight of the other items from the total, leaving only eight pounds of food. Tony, furious at this indignity, rejected the package. The guards threw it onto the road outside the prison. José Daniel Ferrer, who was from Santiago de Cuba in the far eastern end of the island, was incarcerated in Piñar del Río, in the west, where the inmates were constantly hungry.

Regis was in a prison cell infested with insects in Camagüey. The building was crumbling, and smelly sewer pipes ran up the walls, which were crawling with rats. "When the sun would go down, you'd have a cloud of mosquitoes coming in," he said. Days were blisteringly hot, nights freezing. They were allowed to walk outside for an hour a day.

Once a week, Regis could make a few phone calls from prison, a total of about seven minutes. He usually called his family and Oswaldo.

Once, a forlorn Oswaldo took the call, in his kitchen. He played the Beatles and the Bee Gees from a tape recorder over the scratchy phone line, hoping to lift the spirits of his imprisoned friend.

SEVENTEEN

UNDER SIEGE

In his small living room on a corner table, Oswaldo kept a white plaster obelisk, a sculpture three feet tall, depicting hands reaching ever higher, with one defiant fist at the top clutching a scrolled Varela Project petition. Wrapped in a skein of barbed wire and adorned with photographs of the Black Spring prisoners, the sculpture was a constant reminder of his friends behind bars. He was pained that so many who put their trust in him were paying such a high price. He couldn't shake the feeling that he should have been among them. He was free, but not free—always in the regime's crosshairs. Elizardo Sánchez said that Oswaldo remained Fidel's number one enemy in the years after the Varela Project. State security applied almost constant pressure on Payá and his family. Every once in a while, someone would approach Oswaldo on the street, usually a man he didn't know, and say, "You will not outlive Fidel." Different people would bring the message, but the words were always the same.

In the summer of 2006, Fidel was approaching his eightieth birthday, on August 13. He was not well.

• • •

The Black Spring arrests dealt a heavy blow to the Varela Project. Oswaldo's top lieutenants were locked up in prisons scattered across the island, as well as many of the citizen committee leaders who had organized and verified the petitions. Some ten thousand signatures remained hidden away by the nuns, but the second submission, in October 2003, had been ignored by the National Assembly. The arrests weakened the Varela Project in another way: the prisoners became the focus instead of the project itself.

Oswaldo, who had often picked himself up after defeat and failure, would not let the ideas behind the Varela Project die. After the arrests, he organized a new project called the National Dialogue, which led in 2006 to a sweeping blueprint for a democratic Cuba. Called *Todos Cubanos*, or All Cubans, it promised that in a democratic Cuba "all universally recognized fundamental economic, political and social rights" would be "expressly enshrined." The plan proposed a sprawling, progressive new constitution, much in the spirit of the 1940 constitution. It guaranteed the rights of all Cubans to work, education, health care, and housing, social needs that were woven into the 1940 document and had been at the forefront of the revolution. But Todos Cubanos also demanded release of the political prisoners, a new electoral law, a new law on associations, and contained a detailed plan for the transition to democracy, including the right to create political parties, as Lincoln Díaz-Balart had urged. Oswaldo announced the proposals in a press conference at his house on May 10, the fourth anniversary of the first Varela Project submission.

Oswaldo still worried about the dangers of unrest. Cuba must have a peaceful transition, "from the law to the law," he said. He told the Swedish activist Henrik Ehrenberg, "You never know when the change or transition comes. When is the moment in time when we actually do this?. . . The spark—you cannot predict it, really." Ehrenberg recalled that Payá "was afraid of that turning point; he didn't want to see violence or criminal elements or the security . . . take control of the transition." Oswaldo's fears were heightened by what Václav Havel told him in a personal letter about the Velvet Revolution. "We were caught by surprise at how fast the exhausted Communist system collapsed, and we were not prepared for an immediate takeover of power," Havel recalled. In a private conversation, Oswaldo told a US diplomat that Cubans had a great deal of pent-up rage. Any transition must calm the fury, not ignite new fires. "Let's face it," he said, "the people are brainwashed, compromised, traumatized, held hostage . . . however you want to say it. They're messed up, and we need a solution that doesn't mess them up further."

This led to a new line of thinking in Todos Cubanos. Oswaldo wanted Cuba to avoid the wild crony capitalism that engulfed Russia and the former Soviet bloc in the 1990s. He believed that Fidel's state socialism must be terminated, and a market economy established, allowing for private enterprise and free trade, but without the extremes of post-Soviet Russia. He did not want to replace Castro's regime with a new one made up of cutthroat oligarchs.

The voluminous Todos Cubanos plan—174 pages, including the complete text of a new constitution—was the culmination of Payá's thinking and writing over many years. His speech "Faith and Justice" had been more than two decades earlier. He had authored his first bulky transition plan fourteen years before. Now he hoped to show that, despite the Black Spring, the spirit of the Varela Project was alive.

Out of the blue, Oswaldo was blindsided by President George W. Bush. The president had created a group in 2003 called the Commission for Assistance to a Free Cuba, partly a gesture to the Miami anti-Castro community and chaired by Secretary of State Colin Powell. In 2004, the commission called for boosting US spending on prodemocracy programs aimed at Cuba from $7 million a year to $29 million, while tightening travel and remittances to the island. The commission also detailed a wide array of proposals for a transition to democracy and the naming of a "transition coordinator" in the State Department—a term that implied it was the United States that would be determining Cuba's future. In 2006, the commission came out with a second report recommending the United States begin preparations for the period after Castro, including the creation of an $80 million fund to promote democracy and aid a transitional government. The second report, under Secretary of State Condoleezza Rice and Secretary of Commerce Carlos

Gutiérrez, a Cuban American, appeared to be a blueprint for regime change. The Cuban government, predictably, reacted as if it were another Bay of Pigs. "This is a true threat of aggression," said Alarcón, the Speaker of the parliament. "We have the right to think about an attempt to assassinate Fidel, or war."

When Oswaldo heard the news of the Bush proposal in 2006, he was absolutely livid. Why was it necessary for the United States to surface a transition plan for Cuba, playing right into Fidel's hands? Why do it just weeks after Oswaldo presented a genuine, comprehensive blueprint for transition to democracy, written in Cuba by Cubans? The answer, he knew, was that Bush was pandering to the Miami exiles. He was distressed. Oswaldo had told a US diplomat in May, speaking of any US government program on democracy, "We certainly don't want our group linked to any such . . . announcement."

Oswaldo also had to deal with state security tightening the screws.

On Sunday morning, July 9, 2006, he and his family left their house on Calle Peñón and walked to church. They descended the hill, crossed the Calzada, strolled into the square with the spreading ceiba tree, and entered the church with the circular bell tower. Oswaldo's two sons raced ahead on their bicycles and rushed to pull vestments over their dungarees. The priest, just getting ready for Mass, looked knowingly out of the corner of his eye at the two Payá altar boys, who were late.

On the way home, walking up the hill, Oswaldo saw what at first looked like a street festival near his house, in Parque Manila. But as he drew closer, the sights and sounds were ominous. He saw police patrol cars, officers in uniform, and neighbors whom he knew were informants for state security and who had long kept an eye on him from their windows. A crowd gathered, many wielding long-handled brushes for gluing up posters, others carrying paint brushes, and still others gesturing at him menacingly. State security officers were out with their cameras. Payá realized this was another acto de repudio. Within sight of his front door, a large painted caricature was raised and affixed to a wall, portraying smiling and jeering Cubans facing off against Bush and the United States trade embargo. The caricature, about six feet square, depicted Bush as a hotheaded tool of the US military. Under Bush was a gusano, or worm, Fidel's epithet for Cuban exiles. The cartoon blared the message that Oswaldo was on the side of the United States and thus an enemy of the revolution. The assembled crowd painted a slogan in huge letters on a nearby stone wall: *En una plaza sitiada la disidencia es traición*, a motto of the Jesuit founder Ignacio de Loyola, "In a besieged fortress, dissidence is treason." It was a favored slogan of Fidel—all those outside the revolution were traitors and worms. Oswaldo saw the slogan as a direct threat against him.

Oswaldo told a diplomat that the Cuban government had been "not at all pleased" about Todos Cubanos. That could be the reason for the pressure. Three weeks later, at nightfall, state security returned to Oswaldo's house, set up tables and loudspeakers in the street, and a group of Communist Party stalwarts shouted denunciations at Payá. Then they sang the socialist "Internationale," which Oswaldo thought was a fossil of political anthems.

But why just then? Oswaldo knew, from past experience, that when state security grew more aggressive and intrusive, it usually meant something was up with Fidel.

Two days later, Oswaldo heard words that gave him a fright.

At 8:15 p.m. on state television, Fidel's assistant read a statement in which Castro announced his health had been "broken" by "days and nights of continuous work with hardly any sleep." He revealed he was suffering from an "acute intestinal crisis with sustained bleeding" that required surgery, so he was turning over his presidential powers to Raúl and a handful of trusted ministers.

Since most of Fidel's private life was secret, Oswaldo assumed the worst, that Fidel's condition was grave and death might be near.

That night, Oswaldo could not sleep. He spent the whole night in a rocking chair, worried and writing down his concerns. "They didn't explain what was wrong with Fidel," Ofelia recalled. "Was he dead or alive? You can expect anything." Ringing in Oswaldo's ears was the threat that state security had made so many times before: *You will not outlive Fidel.*

The next evening, another statement was read on television. Fidel said he was "stable" but he could not divulge more because his health must be treated as a "state secret."

But "my spirit is perfectly fine," he reassured the public.

What was not perfectly fine was Fidel's condition. He was suffering severe inflammation of the large intestine, a condition known as diverticulitis in which abnormal bags in the inflamed intestine become infected and bleed. On the operating table, the surgeon had removed part of the large intestine. But Fidel did not heal. The infection persisted and his bodily functions were interrupted.

In a second operation, doctors cleaned and drained the affected area and removed the entire large intestine.

Oswaldo heard about the second operation. He had good sources in the hospitals in Havana, and knew Fidel was being treated at an elite facility, the Centro de Investigaciones Médicas Quirúrgicas, or CIMEQ. He told a US diplomat in August about Fidel's medical troubles, including the second operation, and that "the dictator's long-term health prospects did not look good."

The second operation was not revealed to the public. Fidel was shown on television, talking on the phone and walking, but he did not appear in person. On December 2, he failed to show at a parade, postponed from August, to celebrate his eightieth birthday. The US Interests Section sent a cable to the State Department saying Fidel's absence "is the best indicator that he is probably near death."

Throughout the autumn of 2006, Oswaldo felt unnerved and under siege. When a US diplomat in Havana asked the dissident Marta Beatriz Roque about the worries of the opposition, she did not mince words. She had many differences with Oswaldo. But she told the diplomat that, in the event of Fidel's death, "Oswaldo Payá said the order to kill us has already been issued, and I believe him." State security was now stationed around Oswaldo's house full-time. The cars were curbside at Parque Manila. Every person who came to Oswaldo's door on Calle Peñón was later stopped and interrogated. One day a member of the movimiento, Wilfredo Martínez Soto, from Piñar del Río Province in western Cuba, came to Oswaldo's home and left with a Todos Cubanos brochure. At the bus stop, a plainclothes state security officer grabbed him, hustled him into a patrol car, drove him to a police station for interrogation, threatened him, and took his money as well as the brochure.

Oswaldo also discovered that state security was methodically harassing every person who signed the Varela Project, going down the lists of names, addresses, and identification numbers. They demanded cooperation, and if the signatories balked, they were threatened with losing their jobs, being expelled from school, or other penalties. They were frequently pressed to retract their signature. If they did, state security then demanded they sign a second, false statement that Oswaldo had paid cash to get them to sign, or offered them a way to flee the country. Oswaldo believed thousands of people had been threatened in this way. Fortunately, he heard only a handful of people had acquiesced, and the regime never surfaced them in propaganda, suggesting the pressure tactics had not worked well. But the fact of it was infuriating to Oswaldo. He began to realize that the onslaught against the Varela Project went well beyond the Black Spring arrests.

In the town of Las Tunas in eastern Cuba, one of the Varela Project citizen committees had been led by a physician, José Luis García Paneque, a plastic surgeon specializing in burn injuries. He had turned to independent journalism after losing his hospital job over his political views. One of the seventy-five Black Spring prisoners, he was sentenced to twenty-four years. His wife, Yamilé Llánez Labrada, who was trained as a lawyer, worried about his deteriorating condition in prison. They had four children between ages seven and fifteen.

On August 3, just after Fidel's illness was announced, Yamilé was hosting a dozen Catholic youthful pilgrims who were passing through town. They sang songs in the house and brightened her day at a time of uncertainty and sadness.

Suddenly a cacophony of shouts echoed through the front window. "Down with the worm! Long live Fidel!" More than a hundred people bombarded the house with stones and waved sticks, while a local Communist Party secretary bellowed insults. Yamilé ran away from the window and hugged her terrified children. Outside there were cries of "terrorists" and "murderers" and someone yelled, "Let's set the house on fire and burn the worms!"

She saw the young religious pilgrims, huddled in a corner, in tears. The acto de repudio went on for two hours.

Fredesvinda Hernández had been the champion collector of Varela Project signatures. She lived in López Peña, in Piñar del Río Province, once a "captive town" where people were prohibited from leaving. Fredesvinda had not been arrested in the Black Spring. As a sign of solidarity, she had placed a sign on the door of her house promoting the Varela Project, along with a sample of the petition. She was told by state security to remove them. She refused.

She woke up one morning with the door covered in human and animal excrement.

Oswaldo came home from work every day and asked Ofelia, "Where are the kids?" He enjoyed using the handycam to record family moments—the kids dancing with their friends on the back porch on New Year's or celebrating holidays and events at the church. He lectured them on compassion. He told them never to give up on someone. If they came home after a fight or conflict with another student at school, Oswaldo urged them to think about the other person's life, saying, for example, "They don't have a dad; put yourself in their shoes."

Oswaldo never had much money. His currency was his faith, his family, and his cause. His small house was half owned by the nuns. His Volkswagen was cobbled together with spare parts.

He devoted enormous amounts of his time and energy to the movimiento. Another Swedish activist, Annika Rigö, was amazed by his stamina, pulled one way to help families of the Black Spring prisoners, in another direction for the movimiento, plus his day job and family time. "I thought, this guy, when does he sleep? When does he do something only for fun? He had this tremendous energy."

Once, a group of seminarians invited the older two children, Rosa María and Oswaldito, to join them on an overnight beach outing. He was fourteen and she was thirteen. The distant beach was rustic and rocky.

Oswaldo was protective of his children and reluctant to let them go. He relented but insisted that the youngest, Reinaldo, would stay home.

On the beach, Rosa María was peeling potatoes for a cookout when she looked up and, in shock, saw her father approaching the campsite, with Reinaldo, who had prodded him incessantly to let him go too. Oswaldo didn't want his young son to miss out but he was also worried about the older two.

"We were jumping from a ledge ten or fifteen meters into the water before he came," Rosa María recalled. "I was afraid he would say it was too dangerous." But when he arrived, he challenged them to do it. "You cannot be afraid," he said.

Oswaldo knew his family had suffered because of his work. "Every single member of my family has been bothered by state security, which has threatened and attempted to coerce everybody," he told Ehrenberg. They showed up at Rosa María's quinceañera, menacing the family from the perimeter. They put wiretaps in his aunt Beba's house and in his own. And when his mother, Iraida, was dying of cancer in 2000, his brother Óscar, who lived in Madrid, asked for permission to return to Cuba. Óscar had left Cuba legally but because he was Oswaldo Payá's brother, he was refused entry to say farewell to his mother. Oswaldo blamed himself.

"Cars sit in front of my house," he said, "and my children have been able to identify state security cars since they were very young. Several state security agents go to the church that I go to, every Sunday. They do it to intimidate. If someone comes to talk to me, they pull them aside later and say 'you!'" Sitting with Ehrenberg one day in 2004, Oswaldo said, "The real threats against my life, my family's lives, and our imprisoned colleagues aren't mere intimidation." He felt burdened by it, he said, and did not take the dangers lightly. "I see very few chances of getting out alive."

On December 13, 2006, Michael Parmly, who succeeded Cason as the US chief of mission in Havana, visited Oswaldo at his house. Oswaldo said he was worried about his safety in the event of Fidel's death, adding, "People aren't taking seriously enough the threat that they'd liquidate me."

Every day, Oswaldo maintained and repaired medical equipment in Havana's hospitals. Over time, he became a specialist in respiratory systems. Most of the hospitals had intensive care and neonatal wards, his main areas of responsibility. He was rewarded by helping save lives, but he also thrived on the technical challenges.

On December 18, Oswaldo was dispatched to a clinic in the San Miguel de Padrón borough of Havana. He was told the clinic was having trouble with its oxygen system. Oswaldo figured out that a valve was stuck and needed to be closed. When he gripped it, the metal valve broke and sliced through his hand. Despite the pain, he grasped it tightly to keep the oxygen from leaking, knowing that if it enriched the air, it could create an explosive mixture. Fortunately, someone else managed to shut off the flow. Shards of metal penetrated his hand, but he averted a potential disaster.

He had surgery the next day to remove the metal from his hand.

No one ever was sure whether it was an accident or something more sinister, but it frightened Ofelia. She wondered if someone had laid a trap for Oswaldo, who was always exceedingly careful in his work.

Fidel was not doing well after the second operation. His abdomen had not healed, he was losing fluids and nutrients, and he required intravenous feeding. When a Spanish doctor visited him in December, Fidel's condition was so fragile that the doctor had doubts about whether he could survive another surgery.

For the next year, Fidel was in a long, slow recovery. Finally, in February 2008, Castro notified the National Assembly that he would not run for reelection as president. It was the end of an era, but not of the revolution. Raúl was his handpicked successor. If the past was any guide, Raúl would be every bit as ruthless as Fidel. He had been in control of state security for nearly two decades.

One evening in early 2008, Oswaldo, Ofelia, and the children left a friend's house in Oswaldo's Volkswagen minivan, held together by a makeshift collection of spare parts. That night, another family squeezed into the van as well. Altogether there were four parents and six children.

As they departed, they saw a Lada in the dark turn on its lights and scoot away.

Then, as Oswaldo drove, he heard a rumbling from the wheels. He got out and inspected them. Someone had unfastened, almost to the end, five lug nuts that held a wheel in place. It had clearly happened while he was visiting his friends—there had been no rumbling on the way over. If he had driven longer and a little faster, the tire would have come off and he might have lost control of the van. Oswaldo concluded that someone intended to cause a serious accident. A few days afterward he emailed the Swedish activist Rigö, "As you can see, the regime has moved on to concrete actions against our lives. These are no longer threats."

Every Sunday, the Ladies in White gathered at Santa Rita church in Miramar. After Mass, they walked ten blocks in silence along Quinta Avenida carrying gladioli, a single stem each, shouting "¡Libertad!" at the end, demanding freedom for the seventy-five Black Spring prisoners. Marta Beatriz Roque, the only woman imprisoned in the Black Spring, was released in 2004 due to declining health, and formed another dissident group, Agenda for the Transition. Every year, more than a dozen new independent libraries sprung up, while thousands of small protests, vigils, prayer sessions, and fasts were held.

In the middle of all this activity, a Cuban Spring that stretched through the 2000s, Oswaldo wanted to create a newspaper to demonstrate what a free press could be like. Ehrenberg liked the idea, and obtained funding for what became *La Primavera*, a tabloid-size paper. At first Oswaldo wanted to have complete control over it, to make it the voice of the movimiento. Ehrenberg said that, given the source of funding, it could not support just one organization. Oswaldo reacted sharply; it was either all or nothing. He threw up his hands and let go of the project. Nevertheless, *La Primavera* came alive, with journalists writing from Cuba, edited in Stockholm, and printed elsewhere. It was filled with articles and opinions about the Cuban Spring, in which Payá was often featured. The newspaper was ferried in to Cuba by volunteers and distributed by independent journalists on the island. Ehrenberg hoped to garner more international attention for Oswaldo and had written a 167-page book, *Cuba from Within*, based on their long conversations. The newspaper carried an excerpt under the headline, "A Movement Toward Liberation." *La Primavera* cast light on civil society and its struggles, including the tireless protests of the Ladies in White. It also published accounts of violent detention of peaceful dissidents, and it occasionally prodded the opposition to take more concerted action. The reports in *La Primavera* reflected an unpleasant reality: Cuba's opposition was deeply fragmented. Had they all organized a single, concerted effort, they might have had more power and impact. But as it was, the regime held the upper hand, and the opposition was atomized.

Oswaldo's long years of effort and disappointment had left him wary, his judgment hardened. He became more of a loner, more certain of his own path. He was upset when *La Primavera* published an unsigned editorial calling for more "unity." He also disliked hearing this word from visitors from Europe and the United States. Ehrenberg said Oswaldo was scarred by what happened with Todos Unidos. "Every time we spoke with him about this problem—he often returned to: 'See what happened last time? I am not going to all that effort and all that work, compromising, just to see it explode!' He felt very betrayed by what happened after the European prize."

At the same time, Oswaldo was acutely aware that splits hurt their cause. He tried to grapple with this, without success. When he sat down in 2005 to write about the problem, the words came out vague and stale. He urged "unity in diversity," a "pluralism" of opposition, a "family with a common destiny." He did not have a solution. He knew that a splintered opposition was exactly what Fidel wanted. In April 2007, Oswaldo drafted, and the other opposition leaders and dissidents signed, a statement of unity over goals. But it said little about cooperation in tactics. Oswaldo saw value in everyone working in the same direction, but not in compromising his vision. He was strong-willed, and so were they. The splits festered.

At the same time, Fidel's regime climbed out of the lows of the special period. In October 2000, Cuba struck a deal with Venezuela to import up to fifty-three thousand barrels of oil a day at a fixed, reduced price, while offering Venezuela the services of its medical brigades. After President Hugo Chavez was briefly ousted in 2002, Castro personally mentored Chavez on how to respond; when Chavez came back to power, he turned to Fidel's security services to help protect him. A few years later, Cuba's oil imports from Venezuela reached ninety-six thousand barrels a day. After Raúl took over from Fidel, he allowed some Cubans to operate private businesses and work outside the state-controlled economy, which gave it another boost. To some extent, the regime had survived the 1990s.

But the new digital age and the rise of blogs brought fresh voices demanding more freedom. A trailblazer was Yoani Sánchez, who had been a Havana teenager during the special period and who had graduated from the University of Havana with a degree in philology, the study of words. She had immigrated to Switzerland in 2002, planning to start a new life, but returned two years later to Havana. "I promised myself that I would live in Cuba as a free person, and accept the consequences," she wrote. Sánchez, who had picked up some computer skills, began blogging in April 2007. She named her blog Generation Y, referring to the popularity of "Y" as the first letter in the names of her generation. Why was it so common? As she explained it, her parents and their friends felt hemmed in during the tightly controlled years of the 1970s and 1980s, but one "small area of freedom" was selecting names for children. They chose an exotic Y, such as Yoandri or Yuniesky. Yoani's generation reached puberty when the Berlin Wall fell.

Sánchez dressed as a tourist and, pretending to speak only German, sneaked into the handful of hotel internet cafés to post blog entries. Her accounts were acerbic, poignant, and defiant. She had an authentic way of describing everyday life, such as the ever-present black market. "I try to imagine an incredible twenty-four hours in which I wouldn't have to rely on the black market," she wrote. "I can't conceive of a day without going to the black market to buy eggs, cooking oil or tomato paste. Even to buy peanuts, I must cross the line into illegality." That journey from shortage to illegality was how the regime had clung to power for so long—everyone had to go to the black market, anyone could be arrested at any time.

The internet was beyond reach for most Cubans. The hotel internet cafés were expensive, costing as much as $8 an hour, in a country where the average monthly income was $15 to $30, and the connections were slow. The early bloggers numbered only a few dozen. Their writing had a wider audience abroad than in Cuba, but the blogs were important as a new type of independent journalism. When the government began to allow consumer sales of mobile phones in 2008, text messaging offered another way to communicate and mobilize people. Despite the limitations, Sánchez demonstrated that blogging and text messages could break the regime's monopoly on information. In the summer of 2008, bloggers campaigned for the release of a popular rocker, Gorki Águila, who had been arrested August 27 by state security on the vague charge of "dangerousness." Gorki performed in underground concerts in and around Havana and his lyrics were scathing, ear-splitting tirades about the powers that be, such as a song about Fidel, "The Comandante":

The Comandante wants me to work for a pitiful salary
He wants me to applaud after he spouts his delirious shit
You, sir, are a tyrant and no country's people could stand you

The day after the arrest, a small group protesting with hand-painted signs were beaten by state security. Blogs and texts rapidly circulated word of the attack, and more protests were mobilized. Gorki was put on trial in a sham proceeding with a new charge, "disobedience," and then he was abruptly fined and freed. Yoani attended the trial, and exulted with her friends on the street when he was let go. They had prevailed "thanks to the strength and the cry of thousands of citizens, organized spontaneously and confronting a machinery that is not accustomed to give ground."

What had so frustrated Oswaldo, the rigid controls on information, was starting to crack. In the summer of 2009, he appealed to the bloggers to use their megaphone on behalf of millions of Cubans who did not have a computer or access to the internet. These were the people, he wrote, "who cannot express themselves freely because, before they speak—simply speak—they have to look to the side, because they are watched. In Cuba, the word is also a prisoner."

Sánchez's blog grew in popularity, and she expanded to Twitter. "It occurs to me," she wrote on October 19, "to take advantage of the cutting edge of this new world, sharper than a machete, to slaughter authoritarianism and censorship." She said she wanted to launch a call for:

Freedom of opinion
Freedom of access to the internet
Freedom to enter and leave Cuba
Freedom of association
Freedom for prisoners of conscience
Freedom for Cuba.

These were Oswaldo's principles too. He fought for them over the years with smudgy handbills, such as *Pueblo de Dios*, and with the Varela Project. The bloggers were not involved in Oswaldo's quest for signatures, which came years before. But in pioneering a new world, some of them took up the same ideals. Oswaldo's view of them was complex. In private, he wished they would do more. He worried that, from their "advantageous" and "secure" positions, they were not forceful enough in demanding freedom. Some were more outspoken, some not. The regime noticed this new digital restlessness and soon created its own propaganda bloggers to muddy the waters.

Then, on November 6, Sánchez was on the street in Havana with three friends, including Orlando Luis Pardo Lazo, a dissident writer whose works were banned in Cuba but circulated on blogs. A black car pulled up, and three plainclothes thugs attempted to force Yoani and Orlando into the car. She screamed that they were being kidnapped. One of the thugs warned onlookers, "Don't mess with it, these are counterrevolutionaries." Yoani and Orlando were pummeled and forced into the backseat. The car pulled away. Yoani yelled at the thugs; Orlando later recalled, "I heard her scream with the vehemence of the freest being on the planet," even though she was pushed head-down toward the floor, her feet flailing. Orlando recalls one of them saying, "Tell Yoani to shut up!"

Later they were ejected onto the street. Aching and bruised, they embraced. She started to sob.

Yoani wondered how she would explain to her young son that "his mother has been beaten up on a public street for writing a blog."

Orlando wrote the next day on his blog that "Tell Yoani to shut up!" was a good summary of "the whole obsolete and obscene scene in this country."

In June 2010, after seven years behind bars, Regis Iglesias was asked by the prison warden to come to the office for a phone call. On the line was Jaime Ortega, now a cardinal, who informed Regis that he and the government of Spain were negotiating with Raúl Castro for the release of the Black Spring prisoners on the condition they would immediately go into exile in Spain.

Regis replied, "I have no interest in going to Spain."

"Well," Ortega added, "you can leave with all the family that you want."

Regis again declined. He went back to his cell. No, no, no, he insisted to the other prisoners.

Then he called Oswaldo, who said it was better to leave prison than to stay. Regis disagreed. "They said they were going to set us free, so I'm going to wait for them to set us *free*," he said. But when he called his family, his daughters begged him to reconsider. They wanted to leave. One of them pleaded, "Dad, are you crazy?" Regis melted. He and his family went to Spain.

Tony Díaz had spent the seven years in prisons far from Havana. He scratched out a memoir, a raw and unsettling account of his arrest and incarceration that was smuggled out and published in Stockholm in 2006, thanks to Ehrenberg and his group. In 2010, Díaz was transferred to Combinado del Este Prison outside Havana. In early July he was brought to a prison office with a phone off the hook. It was Ortega, who said he had negotiated Tony's freedom, with a ticket to Spain. Tony said he had no family in Spain, didn't want to travel anywhere, and hung up. But Tony's family begged him to go. He was released on July 22 and put immediately on a night flight to Madrid.

Eventually, all the Black Spring prisoners were released in 2010 or early 2011. Some had been freed earlier for sickness or other reasons, but the Ortega negotiation brought freedom for fifty-two of them. Of the original seventy-five, only about nine remained in Cuba, the others largely forced into exile. Ortega's involvement in their release was essential, a humanitarian move but also a gesture of reconciliation to Oswaldo. Ortega had been spurred on by a direct appeal from the Ladies in White, desperate and determined to get their husbands and sons out of prison.

In Madrid, the arrival of the freed prisoners, in small groups, caused a stir each time they stepped off the plane. Oswaldo's brother Carlos Alberto tried to help them get resettled, raising money for their needs, taking them to doctors' appointments, giving them each a telephone. Meanwhile, the prisoners' stories captured the imagination of a young, ambitious political organizer, Ángel Carromero of the youth wing of Spain's ruling Partido Popular, or People's Party. In 2010, Carromero organized a conference on Cuba outside Madrid. He recruited sixteen of the exiled Cubans to speak, as well as young people from Spain who had gone to Cuba. For his generation, all born after Spain's transition to democracy in the 1970s and brought up in years of prosperity, the bleak accounts of prison life and Castro's dictatorship were disturbing. "We weren't born during the Spanish dictatorship. We didn't live through the Spanish Civil War," Carromero said. "So for us to see people . . . that live in a country that are forced to leave their country for thinking certain things, it's really shocking. We wanted to understand them. How could they risk their physical safety and that of their family for an idea?" He couldn't forget their stories.

One of the last prisoners to be set free was Héctor Maseda Gutiér-rez, an engineer with a degree in nuclear physics who had been forced out of his government job because of his political views. He had turned to independent journalism in 1995, establishing a news agency, Grupo de Trabajo Decoro. Héctor wrote a series of articles exposing brutality in Cuban prisons—which he then experienced personally. In the Black Spring trials, he was sentenced to twenty years. He was released in February 2011, after nearly eight years.

His wife, Laura Pollán, was the leader of the Ladies in White, which had protested the unjust Black Spring sentences, week after week, for years. "At first it seemed a tiny, disjointed movement," Yoani Sánchez later recalled, "given the long miles separating one woman from another. But the ladies' indignation functioned as a unifying element. . . . One voice stood out among them, that of a diminutive blue-eyed woman who taught Spanish and literature to teenagers." That was Pollán, short and blond, a mother, housewife, and teacher. Her small house in central Havana became a headquarters of resistance. Under a slowly turning ceiling fan, the living room walls were hung with lists of the names of the Black Spring prisoners and their photos. Prisoners' wives and daughters crowded in for monthly literary teas; once she squeezed seventy-two women from all over the island into the room. The Ladies in White were strictly nonviolent, sometimes tossing out pencils labeled *Derechos Humanos* and *Damas de Blanco* as they marched. The regime roughed them up constantly. Mobs of other women were sometimes bused in to attack them during the Sunday marches, scratching them, yanking them by the hair, and piercing their skin with needles.

Pollán was lacerated and beaten in an attack on September 24, 2011, as she left her house to attend Mass. She fell ill and was hospitalized. Óscar Elías Biscet, a doctor and one of the Black Spring prisoners, said she appeared to be suffering from dengue fever. A dengue epidemic in Cuba was minimized by the government so as not to alarm tourists. According to Biscet, Pollán was misdiagnosed as suffering from a respiratory virus. Her family was kept in the dark and not allowed to see her. When her daughter was finally admitted, state security officers surrounded the bed and monitored the doctors. She died on October 14, at sixty-three years old.

It was a strange, sad death, one that no one could explain. "There's no way of proving this for sure, but the government was scared of my mother. They knew she could move people," said her daughter, Laura.

In May 2012, Annika Rigö, the Latin America director of the Christian Democratic International Center (KIC) in Stockholm, went to Cuba to help Oswaldo. She and Ehrenberg had devoted many years to supporting him and the Varela Project. They had once rented a car together and driven Oswaldo the 540 miles to Santiago de Cuba, taking turns at the wheel, utterly exhausted. She remembered how Oswaldo knew every town, and could pick out state security cars and officers by sight.

In El Cerro, too, Rigö felt close to Oswaldo's family. She joined them at their kitchen table and swapped family stories and photographs. She spent hours listening to Oswaldo. He was an earnest tutor. "He had very elaborate explanations for everything," Rigö recalled. "He was more of a preacher, or even a teacher. He took a lot of time trying to explain."

On this visit, Oswaldo talked of rebuilding. His latest campaign was the Heredia Project, which sought to claim rights formally held by Cubans but not respected in practice, including the right to travel freely. He told her that he had seventy different groups joining the movimiento in the provinces, even if some of them were just a few people. He took Rigö to meet a youth group that his daughter Rosa María was organizing. The youth gathered at Los Pasionistas, a beautiful, spired white church in Havana, where the priest was sympathetic. At the church, Rigö met Harold Cepero, a curly-haired young man with a boyish smile. Cepero was expelled from veterinary school in Camagüey for openly supporting the Varela Project. Later, he spent years at a seminary, thinking he would become a priest, but quit. He had found his calling as Oswaldo's right-hand man. Over the years, Oswaldo recruited a number of assistants after Regis and Tony were imprisoned. Invariably, they moved on. Cepero was the latest, a committed protégé who, with Rosa María, was searching for ways to connect with young people. The movimiento did not have a youth organization—Oswaldo was always protective of young people, hesitant to expose them to danger—but Rosa María and

Harold were planning a new youth magazine, *Somos Liberación*, almost ready to print.

Cepero displayed an irrepressible charm. "He had a twinkle in his eye, and it was easy to connect with him," Rigö remembered. But Oswaldo was shadowed by something, a darkness. The tension was taking a toll. He confessed to Annika, "I'm not the strong one. Ofelia is the strong one."

On June 2, at about 7:00 p.m., Oswaldo was driving his Volkswagen van with Ofelia in the front passenger seat. They were headed to her mother's house in the La Lisa section of Havana. The streets were slick with rain. Oswaldo drove down the Calzada del Cerro, a main city street near their home, and he approached an intersection with the much broader Avenida de la Independencia. Oswaldo saw the light was green so he kept driving. Almost through the intersection, there was a thunderous crash, and the van tipped over on the driver's side. Oswaldo was trapped and could not see what hit them. It was another car, which had been going fast. Oswaldo's elbow hit the pavement when the van tipped over and he was injured. Ofelia was taken out of the wreck through the passenger-side door, now facing the sky. Oswaldo had to be extracted through the windshield. They were taken to Albarrán Hospital, where Oswaldo was given a chest X-ray and other tests. He had no other injuries. Ofelia was uninjured.

Then the driver who hit them showed up at the hospital and blamed Oswaldo for the accident. He claimed to have a witness. "I'll see you in court," he said, and walked out.

Although police came to the hospital to take down basic information, they did not ask Oswaldo for his version of the accident. He offered to give a statement, and they put him off. Only four days later, when he went to the police station on his own, did someone take down his account. He said the light was green for him; he had plenty of time to cross the intersection. The other driver was at fault.

Then Oswaldo was summoned to court as the defendant. He was being accused of causing the wreck.

The strange events were exactly what Ofelia had feared, a mysterious accident that would now be blamed on Oswaldo.

Rigö froze in fear when she heard. She had been reasonably confident the regime would not arrest Oswaldo for political reasons—he was too well known. But now they had a pretext, the kind of "accident" that state security would choreograph.

"I was sure he would go on trial, and be sentenced," she said. "This was the plan to get rid of him."

Oswaldo's opposition to Fidel's dictatorship was deeply ingrained, and he refused to play the game of *simulación*, or conformism. He had taken risks and faced dangers from state security for many years. But fear was seeping into Oswaldo's soul. He and Ofelia received threats, sometimes whispered by state security officers they didn't know, approaching them on the street, that if Oswaldo did not stop his activity, harm would come to their children. The threats had escalated in the past year. Oswaldo's longtime friend Rolando Sabin recalled, "This tore him apart."

"They knew that our most vulnerable point was our children," Ofelia recalled. "We were panicked. We were afraid that one day they might put some drugs into Oswaldito's book bag at school and then accuse him. And then he would end up in prison as a drug trafficker. Anything can happen. They do the same thing to young girls. It's not just that they would take you and put you in jail, but inside the jail they could do anything to you. They can sexually molest you. They can pay somebody to physically harm you. They can do anything. The state security let us know they didn't care—and that the children could pay the price for this.

"We were trying to find ways to get the children out. We saw it was not just threats—things started to happen.

"Oswaldo at first wanted me to leave with them. I said no. Rosa María and Oswaldito were already over twenty years old, they were independent, they knew how to take care of themselves, and they could study. We had taught them well. They had to take a path on their own."

After taking exams, the two were planning to leave in August for the University of Amsterdam, to study business and economics.

Reinaldo was just twenty years old. Spain had approved a law in which grandchildren of Spanish citizens could apply for citizenship. Oswaldo, whose grandfather had come to Cuba from Spain, applied successfully for a passport for himself and for his youngest son. "I really insisted," Ofelia recalled. "Oswaldo and I decided that we had to get the kids out of Cuba."

Oswaldo's friends abroad witnessed the Black Spring and the ever-tightening vise of state security and did what they could to help. An important source of support was the National Democratic Institute in Washington, which organized a visit to Havana in November 2005 that included Janusz Onyzkiewicz, a vice president of the European Parliament and spokesman for Solidarity in Poland. Oswaldo was thrilled to meet a leader of Solidarity—his model from way back. He asked searching questions: How did Solidarity handle the transition from communism to democracy, especially the difficult part, such as who owned the property? Onyzkiewicz urged him to instead devote all his effort to gaining "political space" for the opposition. That notion—"political space"—hardly existed after the Black Spring, and more than ever before, Oswaldo was desperate for support in Europe and the United States. After this visit, NDI and the KIC in Stockholm established a small one-person office in Miami, open for several years, serving as a sort of base camp to help Oswaldo and his causes.

From Sweden, the activists from KIC were also a lifeline. Ehrenberg recalled they had first worked to build democracy in Eastern and Central Europe, and when that seemed well on its way, "We said to ourselves, where do we have more communism in the world, where we can find Christian Democrats?" The answer was Cuba.

The Swedish activists had earned Oswaldo's trust. He was impatient with visitors who came for the "spectacle," as he called it, a photo opportunity and a press release. The KIC returned year after year, carrying know-how, resources, and equipment. Rigö had visited six times; Ehrenberg made fourteen visits.

In late 2011, Rigö was looking for someone new to make the voyage. She wanted a fresh face, someone who would not be recognized by state security. Also, part of her job was to generate interest in Sweden in the cause of a democratic Cuba, so she sought new people to spread the word. She approached Aron Modig, who was president of the youth wing of the Swedish Christian Democratic Party. The youth wings of European parties were stepping-stones to greater political ambitions, and Modig was a rising star. The son of teachers, he had earned bachelor's and master's degrees in business at the University of Gothenberg and was an ardent Democrat and free marketeer. He was twenty-seven years old, tall, a triathlon competitor, somewhat taciturn, bright, and adventuresome. The year before, he had climbed Mount Kilimanjaro.

Modig had already been on overseas training missions. As an undergraduate, he was an exchange student in authoritarian Singapore, and for his master's degree he worked in Kenya, studying the coffee market and international economics. Then he returned to Kenya, sponsored by the party's youth wing, holding seminars on democracy and building political parties. Next, he taught in Cambodia. In late 2009, he made a trip to Cuba to support independent journalists, including those from *La Primavera*, bringing them laptops, recorders, blank CDs, and sharing his experiences. That trip was sponsored by the KIC. He was a natural choice for the next trip to Cuba.

Originally the trip was envisioned for the spring of 2012 but was delayed until summer. One goal was to train Cubans to use social media. Modig did not speak Spanish, so he needed someone who did. Also, the plan was to rent a car and drive Oswaldo to meet with his followers in the movimiento. But Modig did not have a driver's license.

In early July, Modig attended Sweden's annual week-long political jamboree held on the Baltic island of Gotland. The week was intense, with hundreds of workshops and seminars. When it was over and he returned to Stockholm, Modig still had no idea who would accompany him to Cuba.

He went to see Rigö for a briefing on what to expect. She gave him a copy of Ehrenberg's book on Oswaldo. She explained the practical issues, such as currency exchange. She told Modig there were always risks, although she and Ehrenberg had made the journey many times without incident. If arrested, Rigö said, just be honest about what you are doing. "If they try to make you feel bad about seeing Oswaldo, you shouldn't, because he's not a criminal. This is a tactic they use." She told Modig that if something seemed dangerous, listen to Oswaldo. She encouraged him to drive Oswaldo around, outside Havana.

Rigö had expected a long briefing, but Modig said he had no questions, and it was over quickly.

The Nuevas Generaciones youth wing of the Spanish ruling party, Partido Popular, had contacted Rigö, wanting closer cooperation with Sweden's Christian Democrats. Sweden's KIC had a representative in Madrid, Cayetana Muriel. When word went out that KIC was looking for someone to go to Cuba, Ángel Carromero raised his hand and went to see Muriel. He had what was needed: a driver's license and Spanish. He got the job.

Carromero was twenty-six years old, vice secretary general of Nuevas Generaciones and its leader in Madrid's elegant Salamanca district, where he reveled in the political fray. He was a law graduate, a committed conservative, and a fierce debater who embraced the ideals of capitalism and democracy. His father was a businessman, and Carromero recalled reading the economics and business sections of the newspaper when other boys were reading the sports pages. He signed up for party work when he was just sixteen years old. He once considered a career in nuclear physics, but now, with a top-drawer education, bounding ambition, and a dash of good looks, he was striding into Spain's national politics. On his mobile phone was a recent snapshot, standing next to former prime minister Aznar.

Carromero had a second preparatory meeting with Muriel. This time, she brought Oswaldo's younger brother Carlos Alberto, who had left Cuba in 1986. An architect and building project manager, he represented the movimiento in Madrid for many years. At this meeting, Carromero recalled he was given a mobile phone to use in Cuba with three speed-dial numbers: Carlos, Muriel, and Oswaldo. Carromero was urged to use special code words in text messages—Oswaldo was to be referred to as "father." Muriel would be "mom." Muriel handed over the air tickets, and Carlos gave Carromero medicine to be given to Oswaldo for distribution in Cuba. Carlos said his only role was to help Carromero connect with Oswaldo, telling him, "Call this number, and I'm going to let him know you are going to call." At this meeting, Carromero recalled he was also given a packet of cash for Oswaldo.

Meanwhile, Modig was exceptionally busy. In mid-July he flew from Stockholm to Tbilisi, Georgia, for democracy training sessions with young politicians. He went back to Stockholm on July 17, then flew the next day to Madrid to meet Carromero. When he reached the hotel in Madrid, he had a sore throat, fever, and was exhausted. They met for the first time at dinner, both striving politicos, but very different personalities. Modig was reserved and a bit wary, in part because he was sick; Carromero was brash. He smoked a lot.

On July 19, they got tourist visas for Cuba at the airport and flew to Havana. Although Rigö had advised them to be truthful if interrogated, they both took precautions against being discovered. On the plane they agreed that if asked they would say they were college pals on a vacation. They divided the €8,000 Carromero had been given, as well as the medicine for Catholic charities that Oswaldo would distribute in Cuba. "We were thinking, two different things could happen," Carromero later recalled. "They could catch both of us or they could only catch one of us." Two Czech politicians had been arrested a year earlier. But Modig and Carromero were undeterred. Carromero, in particular, wanted the firsthand experience and to meet those who were resisting Fidel.

On arrival, Carromero grew jittery. Modig was delayed for what seemed like forever in customs. Carromero smoked to calm himself. Finally they reached the Hotel Seville, once a grande dame of Havana luxury hotels but now faded.

When Modig awoke on Friday morning, July 20, Carromero had gone to find a rental car. Modig had abandoned the idea of teaching Cubans about using social media; he doubted they had sufficient internet access, and he did not write up a workshop training plan. Instead, he and Carromero decided to repeat what Ehrenberg and Rigö had often done, driving Oswaldo to meet with his movimiento followers.

At the hotel, the rental car desk was in a rear hallway. Carromero saw a long line of people. He waited. Finally, no longer able to contain himself, he went to the front of the line and asked, Are there any cars available? "No," the clerk replied.

Carromero bolted to the street, checking out nearby hotels. Five hotels had rental car desks but not one had cars.

Back at the Seville, he found Modig at breakfast. "We have lots of problems!" he said, exasperated.

They were supposed to drive Payá around, but they had nothing to drive. Modig was calm; it was only 10:00 a.m. They turned to a hustler on the front steps of the hotel. In a taxi, the hustler took them to more car rental offices, but no cars. Then they were taken to the Miramar district, stopping at what looked like an open-air bar, next to a construction hut that served as a rental office. Inside the hut, with the air-conditioning on full blast, Carromero found one car available—the very last—but it was being repaired. The car had been inundated in a rainstorm and had a flat tire, he was told. They would have to wait. When he was given the price, Carromero swore to himself—*crooks!*—but he had no options.

The blue 2010 Hyundai Accent automatic was finally brought to them. The red license plate, T-31402, marked it as a tourist vehicle. The man who gave Carromero the keys said to keep the windows open and the smell would disappear.

The car was sluggish, Carromero complained as they drove away. They gave the hustler some money to get lost.

When they met Oswaldo later that day, Modig recalled he came across as "just an ordinary guy," calm and soft-spoken, waiting for them on a street curb. But they noticed Oswaldo was practiced in evading surveillance by state security. He slipped into the backseat and gave directions for them to drive and park near the Malecón. They walked on the windy seaside, where Oswaldo felt safe from wiretapping.

He said there was a misunderstanding: he expected them to arrive later and stay longer. During the next week, July 26 was a major revolution holiday, marking the anniversary of Fidel's attack on the Moncada

Barracks. If Oswaldo was going to travel to Santiago de Cuba in the coming days, as he wanted, state security would be watching his every move. Oswaldo said they would have to get one step ahead and leave quickly, on Sunday.

When they stopped in a sports bar for a drink, both Oswaldo and Rosa María, who had joined them, took the batteries out of their cellphones as a security precaution and sat far in the back, where they could not easily be seen. When Oswaldo took them to meet Harold Cepero at a church in central Havana, he first looked around nervously, and asked them to wait in the car while he scouted inside. After five minutes, he signaled it was safe. When Oswaldo took them to meet another activist in the movimiento, the mother of a political prisoner, he instructed Carromero and Modig to stay some steps behind him while walking on the street; foreigners and a Cuban together might attract unwanted attention. Once inside the apartment, the mother, Rosa María Rodríguez Gil, told them her son was being held by state security in retaliation for her refusal to become an informer against Oswaldo. Carromero felt his throat tighten. "I discovered a broken mother's pain," he recalled.

As Carromero and Modig drove away, they suspected they were being followed. They had felt confident at first that they were unnoticed—just two college pals on vacation. Now they were not so sure.

To help Oswaldo, they agreed to exchange the euros they had brought into Cuban hard currency, convertible pesos. The exchange point was a narrow shack wedged between two buildings, with a burly overseer, and a line that stretched to the street corner. Carromero and Modig each took half the cash. Once at the teller window, Carromero showed his Spanish identification card, but Modig was turned away for some reason. The teller said Carromero could exchange money for both if he would say what they were doing with it.

"Going to Varadero," Carromero said—the beach. The fib worked. She handed him a thick wad of notes.

Later, they met Rosa María to talk about Cuba and their own experiences in youth politics. She took them to Playita de 16, a "little beach" that was a barren plaza at the edge of the sea, scattered with hard concrete benches, bleached by sun and salt. Not a tree or bush grew there, no white sand lined the water. But the playita held a special place in the imagination of generations of Cuban youth. It was a favored hangout for teenagers, hippies, punks, and lovers. Rosa María, twenty-three years old, her voice filled with a crackling energy, was soon to leave for study in Amsterdam. She told them state security could not eavesdrop here, with crashing waves and steady wind.

Her father's quest, she told them, meant putting everything on the line. None of us knows, she said, what will happen tomorrow. She told them that reports of "reform" under Raúl Castro were overblown; she called it *cambio fraude*, or phony change. She tried to impress on them how overwhelmingly difficult it was to fight the regime every day. Oswaldo could not meet more than a few people at a time. Their home was wiretapped. A few years earlier, a bricklayer hired by Oswaldo to repair their house was picked up by state security. They tried to persuade him to place microphones in the walls. Carromero and Modig listened attentively. Rosa María brought home the stress and tension in a way they had not fully grasped before. Modig asked about social media. Rosa María reminded him that few people in Cuba had a home internet connection. In addition to the hotels, there were now scattered access points in parks, but they were expensive. The Swedish and Czech embassies allowed Rosa María to go online a few hours at a time, but for most people, the digital age had not yet dawned.

Carromero was astounded. In Madrid, he had never known a day without being connected. Two hours went by on the seaside, and the sun was setting. Carromero realized that he had been standing, out of nervousness, the whole time.

Oswaldo asked them to pick him up early Sunday morning. In Santiago de Cuba, he was planning to push ahead with *Pasos para el Cambio*, or Paths for Change, another blueprint he had written to advance the spirit of the Varela Project. He also planned more organizing and training to mobilize citizens. He had told the Varela Project coordinator in Santiago de Cuba that he was coming with Harold Cepero and two young people from Spain and Sweden to conduct democracy training for youth. Oswaldo was rushing to get there before the July 26 holiday. He always was trying to stay one step ahead of state security.

Back at the hotel on Saturday night, Carromero was engulfed by doubt. The drive would be ten hours or more. What if there were roadblocks? In a lighthearted tone that betrayed his unease, he said to Modig, "Let me see. The car is going to break down, and we are going to be stuck in the middle of the road, and the police are going to find us with two dissidents in the back?" Modig, calmer, reminded him what Rigö had said: it was up to them to make the final decision whether to accept Oswaldo's requests for driving.

Adding to their worry was something Payá mentioned. He and Cepero would have to sleep in churches in Santiago, to avoid state security. Carromero and Modig would be on their own.

Then Payá told them of the wreck a month earlier, when his Volkswagen van had been rammed.

Carromero worried. Could it happen to them?

The only Wi-Fi connection at the Seville was in the lobby, and outrageously expensive, 10 euros for 15 minutes. Carromero could not resist. He sent concerned messages to a friend in Madrid, saying they were being followed. Next, using WhatsApp, he messaged Cayetana Muriel, the KIC office director in Madrid, who had handled the logistics. He asked her to find them a hotel in Santiago de Cuba.

Carromero used the agreed-upon codes. Payá was to be called "father."

Carromero: "Did you know that on June 2, my father had a traffic accident? Nothing serious happened to him, but, as always, they are trying to use it against him."

Muriel: "Yes, how is he? Is everything okay in that sense?" She added, "I hope you are helping your father in whatever you can."

"Sure. Kisses," Carromero signed off. He did not feel so sure. She had told him to do whatever he could. Carromero went back to see

Modig and declared, yes, he would go ahead and drive. "We're not on vacation," he said. But he felt way over his head.

That weekend, Oswaldo wrote yet another political declaration. An election season was approaching in Cuba, starting with municipal assemblies. None of the elections was competitive or democratic; the Communist Party was the only legal party. Little had changed since Oswaldo was excluded from running for the parliament in 1992.

Across the top of the page he wrote, "There are no free elections if there are no free men and women."

In Cuba, he wrote, there is no democracy and the "government does not respect the political rights of its citizens." The "lack of freedom of association, of expression and of free elections . . . prevents the political participation of the people."

"The people know that they cannot decide."

"What oppresses us is fear and intolerance, and one powerful group's determination to keep its absolute grip on power."

"If there is no pluralism, there are no elections."

"Let's take the people's way," he wrote, "which is democracy."

He did not publish the declaration just yet. Perhaps he was thinking of more to say. He wrote at the bottom: "July 20, 2012."

Ofelia was away, visiting her parents. On their nightstand, Oswaldo and Ofelia kept a small book of meditations by the Jesuit bishop Carlo Maria Martini, *Por los Caminos del Señor*, or *In the Ways of the Lord*, which they read aloud to each other at night before bed. Oswaldo had read Alexander Solzhenitsyn's *Gulag Archipelago* in earlier years, and he was just finishing *Solzhenitsyn*, a 1972 biography of the dissident writer; the book was by his bedside.

He sent a text message to his brother Carlos Alberto in Madrid. "I'm going on a long trip," he said. "I'll call you later."

Before dawn on Sunday, Carromero and Modig roused themselves at the Hotel Seville, which was dark and slumbering. Carromero tried to quietly close the door on their way out, but it creaked loudly in the wood frame. They hurried through the deserted lobby. Both carried small backpacks, stuffed with a two-day change of clothes.

Modig, in a T-shirt with navy and white stripes and blue shorts, looked dubiously at Carromero. "You're driving in flip-flops?"

The blue Hyundai still smelled musty. They drove cautiously in the dark to El Cerro and picked up Oswaldo and Harold at 6:15 a.m.

Oswaldo carried a single mobile phone; Cepero carried two, one personal, the other to contact members of the movement in Santiago de Cuba.

Two hours earlier, a progovernment blogger believed to be aligned with state security and going by the name Yohandry Fontana, posted a mocking and ominous message on Twitter. Carromero and Modig did not see it at the time. The message said,

> Oswaldo Payá está de vacaciones para Varadero. Este negocio de la disidencia en #Cuba es un relajo. No dejaron guardia en Twitter.

Or,

> Oswaldo Payá is going on vacation to Varadero. This business of being a dissident in #Cuba is a joke. They left Twitter unguarded.

"Varadero" was what Carromero told the clerk at the currency exchange.

In the calm of the Sunday morning, few cars were on the road as the Hyundai left Havana. Before lunch, they were shadowed by a red Lada. They stopped twice for gas.

At lunch they bought a Beatles CD and played music. Oswaldo was singing. Modig fell asleep.

Then Carromero noticed the other car tailing them.

Oswaldo told Carromero to hold steady, not to do anything to give a reason to stop them.

They were driving down a long straightaway on Route 152, already past Las Tunas, and heading south toward Bayamo, which lay sixteen miles ahead. They were surrounded by farms. Trees and an irrigation channel ran parallel to the road on the right side, and beyond, a rice field. Although Carromero thought the Hyundai rental car was sluggish in Havana, they had made good time on the road, traveling 442 miles in about 7½ hours, or around 58 miles per hour. But with three stops, their road speed was probably greater.

The road was flat. A construction sign directed traffic going in their direction to move left, since the far right was being repaved and was covered with gravel. Carromero shifted to the left.

At about 1:50 p.m., as they drove through the construction zone, the car that had been following them leaped forward and hit the Hyundai in the rear. Carromero felt the push and lost control of the rental car. Barreling ahead, it began to drift to the right. It skidded on the loose gravel of the lane under construction, kicked up a cloud of dust, and kept drifting to the right, off the road.

Modig had been dozing in the front seat, but suddenly he was awake. He was wearing a seat belt. He pulled his legs up toward his chest in a protective fetal position.

The car twisted and crashed into a tree on the side of the road, according to the official Cuban government account. The tree, a species known as the Manila tamarind, caved in the driver's side passenger door and part of the roof, right where Oswaldo was sitting, the official account says.

Questions about what exactly happened in these critical moments have never been satisfactorily answered. Who was driving the car that rammed the Hyundai? If that vehicle was state security—and Oswaldo believed it was—why carry out the attack in a remote countryside? To avoid being seen? Who gave the orders?

Were the state security officers trying to harass Oswaldo?

Were they trying to show Oswaldo that they had spotted him?

Were they trying to kill him?

In the Hyundai, Carromero blacked out. Modig also lost consciousness.

When Carromero awoke, two "brawny" Cuban men were pulling him from the car, he later recalled in a memoir. They rushed him to a blue van with a sliding door. Carromero remembered walking on solid ground, no smoke or shards of glass. "There weren't any people around either. Just the van I was being dragged over to. I couldn't look back. There was no noise or anyone talking."

Carromero asked them, "Who are you, and what are you doing to us?" They didn't answer.

Once in the van, Carromero leaned forward. He grabbed the headrest of the front passenger seat, trying to see the two men in the front more clearly. He was hit with something—a "blow"—and lost consciousness again.

Modig woke in an ambulance, lying on his back.

Again, unanswered questions linger. Where did the blue van and ambulance come from? What explains the ambulance and van showing up so quickly in the middle of nowhere? Were they already in position—because someone knew what was about to happen?

What was the condition of Oswaldo and Harold after the crash?

In the ambulance, Modig's mind was foggy. There was blood on his shirt, pants, hands, and arms. He touched his head and realized he was injured. A man in a white shirt, probably a medic's uniform, was looking at him. They could not understand each other. Modig reached into the right pocket of his shorts, looking for his cell phone. The pockets were shallow, and the phone often slipped out. But he was relieved to find it there.

At 2:13 p.m., he sent a text message to his girlfriend, Sara Rydefjärd, in Stockholm.

Modig: "Are you there? Something has happened. I'm bleeding from my head. I don't know what. I have hit my head. Is serious."

Sara: "Oh no, where is it bleeding? Are you feeling nauseous?"

Modig: "My head. Am I in Cuba? With whom? Seriously."

Sara: "You are in Cuba with a Spaniard. Don't know his name. Is there anyone close by? Do you know what has happened?"

Modig: "Don't remember anything. Can you tell Cayetana at KIC that something has happened? Don't recall anything."

Carromero only regained consciousness when the van reached the Carlos Manuel de Céspedes Hospital in Bayamo, about seventeen miles southeast of the crash site. "I was stunned and afraid," he later recalled. He resisted being laid down on a stretcher. "I wanted to know what was going on." He realized there was an open wound on the right side of his head, where he was hit in the van. Finally, he lay down on a gurney and was taken to a hospital admissions area. He did not have his backpack or his mobile phone.

A uniformed officer arrived, a woman from the Ministry of Interior, who interrogated him. "Another car charged at us, and ran us off the road," he replied. He told her that he lost control of the Hyundai. She took notes, then asked him to sign the statement, and he did.

When she left, Carromero badgered the nurses for information about the others in his car, including Oswaldo and Harold. At first they said there were four people in the car, and all were coming to the hospital. He was slightly relieved. If he was hospitalized first, he thought, he must have been the most seriously hurt. The others would be along soon and would be fine. Then a nurse told him only three were brought to the hospital. Carromero plunged anew into worry and anxiety.

Meanwhile, still in the ambulance, Modig sent more messages to Sara. His head clearing, he wrote at 2:32 p.m. that he was in "some medical place. What am I doing here?"

Sara: "Is it possible you were in a car crash? Trying to reach KIC."

Modig: "Probably. Tell her."

He added, "We have crashed with our car. In the ambulance now. Don't have my passport. Doesn't seem like it is that serious."

Sara replied at 2:46, "Good. You likely fainted when you crashed, hence the confusion and memory lapse. It will be all okay. Hugs."

At the hospital, Modig was wheeled into the same room with Carromero. Modig searched for someone who spoke English, who could at least tell him where they were. An orderly gave him the name of the hospital and helped Modig spell it out on his phone. He sent the message to Sara and added, "Ángel is here and he's okay."

Carromero asked him to send a quick text to Sara and others

explaining what happened. Modig wrote, "Ángel is saying that someone tried to force us off the road."

Sara: "Information is good, I will pass it on."

Modig: "Only three people were found in the car. There were four of us."

Carromero was agitated.

"Oh my God," he said. "They ran at us from behind and ran us off the road. They're going to kill us."

Modig was calmer, but he was frightened too. In the ambulance he had thought, *We are in a dictatorship and we did something illegal. This is not going very well.*

He loaned his phone to Carromero, who called Muriel in Madrid and said they were in a hospital and the situation was serious. The connection was bad, the call brief.

While together in the admissions area, Modig handed Carromero two mobile phones, which had belonged to Cepero. How did he get the phones? At the time, Carromero didn't ask. Modig didn't volunteer anything. Modig could not explain it later, but confirmed that he had the phones and gave them to Carromero.

Carromero tried to use the phones, but no calls would go through. He put them in his pants pocket.

The two young men were moved deeper into the hospital, assigned to the same room, but separated about forty feet apart, Carromero shielded by a screen. They could not see each other. Both were given blood tests and taken out for X-rays.

Carromero asked a nurse for more information on the others in the car. She replied that the nurses were now forbidden to speak with him.

Then he saw a nurse put a sedative into the drip. He felt exhausted, and struggled against sleep. He was pondering how to get out of the hospital.

A group of uniformed soldiers, and a few men in civilian dress, surrounded his bed. One of them spoke sternly right away. There was no collision, he said. No other car crashed into the Hyundai. Whatever Carromero had told the Ministry of Interior officer earlier simply had not happened.

Carromero was groggy, but alert enough to catch the drift. He had already given an accurate account to the female officer. He replied that what happened was not an accident, but "a blatant attack."

The soldier slapped him in the face, he recalled. Then, in a calmer tone, he told Carromero, "You are too young to remain on the island for years; you must decide whether or not to cooperate. We can treat you well or poorly, but only you will decide. Your future depends on your confession."

Another officer identified himself as a government "expert." He told Carromero not to be a fool—if he cooperated he would be safe. He then recited a version of what happened: that Carromero was speeding, braked because of a pothole, lost control of the vehicle, and the car slid down an embankment. No mention of the other car, no mention of being hit from behind. He asked Carromero to repeat it several times.

The officer tore up Carromero's first statement and demanded he sign the new version. Carromero signed, but with an exaggerated signature, larger than his usual one. He thought maybe it would be recognized as a sign of protest.

Then another officer turned on a video camera. Before returning his backpack, they demanded that Carromero list every item inside. They tossed the backpack to the side of the bed, and interrogated him further about the trip and his relationship with Modig. Carromero said they had been on vacation. At this point, he didn't think state security knew who they really were, and why they had come.

Heavily sedated, Carromero fell asleep. When he woke, there was a new guard, a woman. He asked to speak to Modig. She said no. Then he begged her to ask Modig for his mobile phone—their only link with the outside world—so he could send a message to his mother. She relented, and fetched the phone.

Carromero wrote a text message to Muriel.

"Help," he wrote.

She answered, "Call! What's going on?"

"Surrounded by military," he messaged back. He didn't say any more. Then he erased the message from Modig's phone and gave it back.

Carromero remembered that he still had the two mobile phones that Modig had given him in his pockets. The phones had belonged to Cepero. Carromero did not want the contents of the phones, including lists of members of the movimiento, to fall into the hands of state security. He asked to go to the bathroom.

In the bathroom, Carromero looked at a small window. If he threw the phones out the window, they would certainly be found. The only answer was the toilet. He opened the back of each phone, took out the SIM cards, and dropped them into the toilet. He then tried to flush, but the toilet handle was broken. With few options left, he reached into the toilet bowl and pushed the cards down as far as he could. He dried his arm off with toilet paper and went back to bed. He put his head under the sheet, turned on the phones, and erased everything. Then he put the empty phones in his backpack.

Across the room, Modig got a message from Rigö in Stockholm, urging him to walk by Carromero's bedside—behind the screen—and make sure he was safe. Modig was still connected to the intravenous tube, and repeatedly jumped up, apologetically saying he had to go to the bathroom.

In Havana, Ofelia's cellphone rang at about 3:00 p.m. The call was from Regis Iglesias, who was in Madrid. Obliquely, Regis asked if she had heard anything about two young men—"some friends"—visiting Havana. He told Ofelia that he heard they had run into problems on the road in eastern Cuba. She knew nothing but said she would try to find out.

A few minutes later, Regis called again. This time he said one of the passengers had a head injury and asked her, "Where is Oswaldo?"

Ofelia said Oswaldo was not with her. Both she and Regis knew state security might wiretap such calls, and were naturally cautious. She immediately dialed Oswaldo's cell phone, but there was no answer.

Then at 3:18 p.m. came a text message from Regis. He conveyed what he knew, that four people were in the car but only three in the hospital, one unaccounted for. Of the two "friends," he said one was unconscious. Then he added, "They were hit and wrecked off on a deserted road." In the text message, he asked again, "Who was in the car?"

Regis once again called Ofelia. "Who were these other two people traveling with the friends?" he pressed her.

Oswaldo Payá and Harold Cepero, she said.

Ofelia hung up and called Oswaldo's phone again—no answer.

Her heart began to sink. Oswaldo had told her so many times before that the regime would come after him.

An hour ticked by, with no new information.

Rosa María called her father's cell phone at 4:16 p.m. and someone answered.

"Papa?" she asked.

"No, no, no," said a man, his voice shaky and nervous.

"Where is the owner of this cellphone?" Rosa María demanded.

The man said he was a traffic officer, at the scene of an accident. He didn't answer any of Rosa María's insistent questions. He handed the phone to a woman, who was identified as a medical examiner. She didn't respond either, just started firing questions back at Rosa María: "Who are you looking for? Is the person a foreigner? How old?"

Rosa María demanded: Is he alive or not? Where is the owner of this phone?

Then she appealed to the woman, urgently, "Tell me if he is alive or not. Tell me where he is. Tell me where you found this cellphone!"

The woman would not answer, just kept repeating her useless questions.

Finally, the woman admitted, "Okay, there is one person who is deceased."

Meanwhile, Oswaldo's eldest son, Oswaldito, reached the hospital in Bayamo by telephone. They told him three people from an accident were in the hospital, but the dead man had not arrived yet.

Oswaldito asked, "Who is the deceased?"

"Oswaldo Payá."

From Havana, Ofelia telephoned two friends who lived in Bayamo, Teresa Amador and her husband, Juan Fernández. She asked them to rush to the hospital, to be her eyes and ears until she could get there.

At 6:00 p.m., they called. Cepero had died in the hospital.

Ofelia went quickly to the Havana airport, where two flights were soon departing, one to Santiago de Cuba, the other to Holguín. From either destination she could get to Bayamo. Ofelia implored the authorities to give her a seat. They said the planes were booked. The next flights, at 6:00 a.m., were also sold out. Ofelia returned home at about 8:00 p.m. and rapidly packed, planning to drive through the night to Bayamo, as hazardous as it would be. Then the phone rang. An officer from state security said he could provide transportation to Bayamo. Ofelia said she didn't need it—annoyed, because obviously the officers were listening to all her earlier telephone calls.

Her Bayamo friends called again from the hospital. It was hot, the middle of summer, and they reported that the cold storage in the morgue had failed. They were worried about the condition of Oswaldo's corpse. The director of the hospital took Juan Fernández into the morgue to prove the refrigeration systems were not working. Juan saw Oswaldo's body, laying out on a gurney. He noticed a syringe in his groin. He had his shoes on, his shirt. There was blood everywhere, and "his head was a little tilted to the side, and he had some blood on him. His arms were spread out."

The hospital wanted to conduct an autopsy soon. The Bayamo friends recommended it also. By telephone from Havana, Ofelia gave permission to the hospital director for the autopsy.

Afterward, the Bayamo friends were shown to a small, dark room. They found Oswaldo's body there. They dressed him with the clothes he had tucked in the backpack that morning. But they noticed something very odd. Oswaldo's head was badly injured. It felt so soft under the hair that they were afraid to touch it, fearing it might disintegrate.

Carefully, the friends lifted his body into a coffin. They were told not to go near Cepero's corpse, wrapped in a sheet nearby.

Teresa and Juan asked the police for Oswaldo's possessions from the crash site. The police brought his backpack and started to remove everything, taking an inventory aloud. "Toothbrush." "Underwear." They wrote it all down. They found money that Carromero had given

Oswaldo. An officer spread the money out like a fan, without comment. They found the medicine from Madrid. They took apart Oswaldo's wallet. Then they found a list of movimiento members from Santiago de Cuba and began reading the names out loud. When finished, they handed the backpack to Teresa and Juan.

Later, Teresa was waiting in another room at the hospital, filled with police officers, who seemed to be agitated, milling about. An officer appeared, and spoke up, unsolicited. He was Captain Fulgencio Medina, an investigator, who had gone to the scene of the wreck. Unprompted, he said, "I am going to tell you how it happened."

He gave an account from two people who said they were nearby, on the road, when the crash happened. One was on a bicycle, another on a tractor. They offered nothing about what preceded the crash and did not mention a car ramming the Hyundai from behind. The bicycle rider saw dust when the Hyundai veered off the road. They both stopped. On closer inspection they said the Hyundai had apparently spun and hit a tree, then fallen into a ditch. They recalled a passing red Lada had halted to help the wounded. According to Captain Medina, when the passengers from the red Lada went to help, one person in the backseat of the Hyundai was already dead, the other gravely wounded, crying in pain. The foreigners in the front seat were taken out of the wreck first, according to Medina, and one of them said, "Who are you, and why did you do this to us?" Then a blue van arrived and took one of the foreigners away. An ambulance arrived very soon thereafter.

At the hospital, at about 2:00 a.m., the bodies of Payá and Cepero were put into separate vehicles and began the long journeys home— Oswaldo to Havana, and Cepero to the village of Chambas, in Ciego de Ávila Province. The car bearing Oswaldo was followed by the Bayamo friends and a priest all the way.

At 1:00 p.m. on Monday, Ofelia went with Rosa María and her younger son, Reinaldo, to the Institute of Forensic Medicine, the government facility in Havana that handled corpses from violent deaths.

Ofelia noticed that everyone there was watching them intently. She and Rosa María were escorted to a small office, where a young man in a black police uniform introduced himself as Sánchez, a forensic officer from Bayamo. He had traveled from there overnight. Another man stood to the side of the room and recorded everything with a handheld video camera. Ofelia filled out paperwork. Then Sánchez said, "I will give you an explanation" of the crash, and added that he would provide a diagram to help them understand.

"I'm an engineer, I can understand perfectly well," Ofelia responded.

Sánchez said the roadway was under construction. The Hyundai was seen by a tractor driver and bicycle rider. They saw a large cloud of dust.

"And it looks like the car is going at a high speed, that it is going at a higher speed than permitted," Sánchez said. Rosa María interrupted. "The car was sluggish," she said.

"We have witnesses," Sánchez replied.

"Do you have witnesses who measured the speed?" she asked.

"No," he admitted, "but that's what the witnesses said."

"The witnesses could not know what speed they were going," Ofelia interjected.

Sánchez implored them, *Please, just listen to me.* He took out a blank sheet of paper and began to sketch the roadway with a pen. He said the driver lost control of the car "because of the conditions of the road and because of the speed—primarily the speed." With his hands slicing the air, Sánchez tried to illustrate the car leaving the lane, cutting through gravel, hitting a tree, and bouncing from the tree. He said nothing about the car being hit from behind.

"My husband," Ofelia declared, "is Oswaldo Payá Sardiñas. He's an opposition leader. He has received death threats innumerable times."

Sánchez, growing pensive, folded his hands tightly on the desk.

"Put yourself in our place," Ofelia added, her voice beginning to crack. "If you can, even a little bit, put yourself in our place so that you know this is the reality. This is the reality of the person whose body you've just brought—a body that left on this trip in good health. I know that an accident can happen to anyone at any time, but I have every right to think that there could be something more than an accident that happened here."

"I would not be a human being if I were to lie to you," Sánchez replied.

Ofelia said she wasn't criticizing his work as an investigator. "I'm sure you've done what you can."

"We have reasons to believe this was not an accident," Rosa María said.

Sánchez stiffened. He stood, opened his arms, then nervously rubbed his hands together. "I respect you a lot," he said, "but the revolution does not assassinate." He repeated it several times. *La Revolución no asesina.*

"My husband has been threatened with death," Ofelia added.

"The revolution does not assassinate," Sánchez insisted.

At the funeral home, Funeraria la Nacional in El Cerro, Oswaldo's body was taken into a back room, where the employees were to prepare it for the funeral. Ofelia and her son Reinaldo were joined there by Pedro Ferreiro, a doctor and longtime friend of Oswaldo, and Segundo Lima, a member of the movimiento. She asked them to take the fresh clothes she had brought and to dress Oswaldo in a white linen guayabera and black pants. They slipped away into the other room. Ofelia was relieved; she did not want Reinaldo to see his father's broken body.

Soon, a few strangers arrived and disappeared quickly into the back of the funeral home. She did not know them. She waited for a long time.

At last, the door opened.

Ofelia was stricken with grief, but the sight of Oswaldo was a shock. It was not his face. Not his expression. She leaned closer to kiss him good-bye, and when she reached to touch his head, Ferreiro warned her away. She wondered to herself why his head was so badly smashed. Ofelia could only kiss his sewn lips. She was terribly frightened, unable to grasp his hand. She stood there, with her son, silent, stunned.

The funeral home gave her a small, stamped ticket recording Oswaldo's death—his name, the date, his national identification number. Under cause of death, it read: "Injury to the nervous system." Nothing more.

On leaving, she wanted to tip the undertakers, but Ferreiro intervened. He had discovered they were not employees of the funeral home but state security, sent to keep an eye on her. They had stood in for the funeral home's regular workers.

In Bayamo, the day after the car wreck, Carromero and Modig were taken from the hospital to be interrogated separately by police. Carromero was jailed in a cell with a man he assumed was an informer for state security, who told Carromero he should cooperate. In the interrogation, the police insisted that Carromero take full responsibility for the accident and admit that he was speeding recklessly. He was not to mention the car that rammed the Hyundai. Deeply uncertain and fearing for his life, Carromero relented, and before a video camera delivered the confession they wanted. When he failed to repeat their lines exactly, they made him do it again and again for the camera, finally writing out the precise text. He repeated their words. Next, they presented a written confession, which he signed, but deliberately scrambled the signature, his silent protest.

He and Modig were then flown separately to Havana for more questioning.

Under an afternoon sun on Monday, a crowd gathered near the ceiba tree in front of El Salvador del Mundo church in El Cerro. The bells tolled slowly. The lilting voices of the choir floated through the plaza. The vehicle bearing the coffin backed up to the church front door. Looming above was the circular bell tower from which Oswaldo had once, daringly, strung a *Feliz Navidad* greeting. The casket was carried through the foyer where parish families had gathered every Sunday after Mass for lively, informal debates that inspired his early political awakening.

The casket then entered the nave, where, as a teenager, Oswaldo once prayed in solitude on a weekday afternoon. The sight of his casket, laden with roses and ribbons, unleashed a spontaneous outpouring among friends and supporters who had packed shoulder-to-shoulder to say good-bye, including the Ladies in White. A rhythmic clapping swelled from the pews and did not stop. The sound chased away the silence and soothed the sorrows. It was not out of tradition or a plan;

it just happened. Sustained chants of *"¡Libertad!"* echoed through the old stone church. The writer Orlando Luis Pardo Lazo recalled it was "a farewell to our hopes for a life in truth. It was a clapping from the soul."

For hours, mourners filed by to pay their last respects. State security was there too, staying in the background, watching.

On Tuesday morning, two days after the car wreck, a funeral Mass was celebrated in the church, the pews packed, heads up in the baking summer heat, craning to see and listen, some holding cameras aloft. Ofelia was weak with grief and sadness, and as she sat in a chair, Rosa María comforted her. Oswaldito and Reinaldo stood at their sides.

Cardinal Jaime Ortega eulogized Oswaldo as a man of faith on a political mission. While they did not always agree, there had been respect and dignity. Ortega expressed understanding about what drove Payá. "Oswaldo lived the heartrending role of being a Christian layman with a political choice, in total faithfulness to his ideas, without ceasing to be faithful to the Church until the very last day of his life," Ortega said. "He was kind and attentive to his bishop, whom he always wanted to respect, and it was true that he did. His faith and his love for the Church were constant. In light of that faith he professed, we bid him farewell today. And knowing that death does not have the last word, we place him in the merciful hands of God."

Rosa María rose to speak for the family, defiant yet compassionate, in the same way that her father had fought to free Cuba. Oswaldo "devoted his life to the cause of freedom and rights for the Cuban people," she said. "We will uncover the truth and seek justice for the violent death of my father and our young friend Harold. We do not seek vengeance. We do not act out of hate, because, as my father said, 'The first victory we can claim is that we have no hate in our hearts,' but instead out of a thirst for justice and a desire for liberation.

"My father has already shown us the path to liberation, and it is a path of hope."

The crowd again began to applaud, unceasingly. Then Ofelia stood at the head of the casket, her children and family surrounding her, along with some members of the movement. The crowd fell quiet.

She read a statement from the movimiento that Oswaldo had founded, her voice pained and creased by loss, but her message un-bowed.

"Only the people of Cuba can define and make decisions about the changes that our society needs, and carry out our national project," she said. "But for Cuban citizens to truly design, decide and construct their future, their rights must be guaranteed by the law and an atmosphere of trust and respect for all must be achieved."

She vowed that Oswaldo's movimiento would continue "to fight for the rights of the Cuban people."

The casket was then taken to the sprawling Cristóbal Colón Cemetery, where many of Cuba's most prominent are interred, among them Gustavo Gutiérrez and Eddy Chibás. A crowd solemnly accompanied the casket from the gate to the graveside, then stood among the white stone tombstones, including the nuns who had protected the Varela Project signatures, and young men holding their hands high in the movement's "L" sign—for *Liberación*.

As Oswaldo was laid to rest, they all broke into a mournful hymn, "Death Is Not the End," by the Spanish priest and composer Cesáreo Gabaráin. They sang from their hearts and from their souls to the man who wanted them to live free.

Tú nos dijiste que la muerte
no es el final del camino,
que aunque morimos no somos,
carne de un ciego destino.

Tú nos hiciste, tuyos somos,
nuestro destino es vivir,
siendo felices contigo,
sin padecer ni morir.

Siendo felices contigo,
sin padecer ni morir.

You told us that death
is not the end of the road,
that though we die, we are not
flesh for a blind fate.

You made us. We are yours.
Our destiny is to live,
being happy with you,
without suffering or dying.

Epilogue

After the crash, Aron Modig remembered almost nothing about it. Dozing, he had awakened suddenly, reflexively drawing his knees toward his chin in a split second of fear. He could not remember why. He was knocked unconscious and came to only later in the ambulance.

When he was later flown to Havana, the authorities brought him to a small villa, with pink walls and a small bed. He was still wearing the same navy-blue shorts and striped T-shirt, now covered with dried blood, he had when leaving the Hotel Seville. They resumed interrogating him, in front of a video camera. They zeroed in on his purpose in coming to Cuba. "Who sent you?" he recalled being asked. "What is your assignment and who told you to carry it out?" Whom did you meet, and where, and why? The interrogators became agitated when they found in Modig's luggage a business card from the International Republican Institute, a prodemocracy organization based in Washington, DC. Modig had received the card from an activist in Tbilisi, Georgia, just before he flew to Cuba. He had considered throwing it away but decided to keep it. The minute they discovered it, Modig knew it was trouble. His interrogator thought he had found a link to the United States and the Republican Party—enemies of the revolution. The interrogators printed photos they found on his phone, including of Ángel and Rosa María; printed copies of columns he had written on Christian democratic politics in Sweden; and scrutinized his Twitter feed. "This was interspersed with outright scolding because what I had come to Cuba to do was strictly prohibited by Cuban law," he recalled. "I shouldn't have come to Cuba and meddle in their internal affairs, I was told."

The authorities then demanded Modig give a press conference and apologize. Although his interrogators didn't say so directly, he concluded that if he apologized, he could depart sooner. He was eager to go home. "I think the hardest thing for me" was the apology, he reflected later. "I came there with a purpose—and then I apologize for actually coming there with that purpose? But I saw it as obvious that if I do this, I will most probably get out of here sooner, to be honest."

At the press conference, on July 30, he told reporters he had come to meet with Oswaldo, to meet with young people in the movimiento, and to help Payá with his travel. He admitted to carrying €4,000 for Oswaldo. These activities "are not legal here in Cuba, and I want to apologize for doing such activity.

"I don't remember there being another car involved in this accident," he said.

Cuban state television broadcast his remarks, and snippets of his interrogation in the villa.

By that evening, helped by Swedish diplomats, Modig was on his way to the airport. He had a nagging fear he might be detained again. Even after he was allowed to board the flight, which was delayed on the tarmac, "I sat there for over an hour, on high alert, just waiting for the police to enter the aircraft and arrest me again."

Modig said the Cuban authorities never insisted that he remain silent. But he nevertheless did so when he returned home. Much of what happened in the car wreck was a blank in his memory, he said, perhaps out of shock. Besides, he did not want to say anything that could jeopardize Carromero, who had been left behind in Cuba.

Ángel Carromero was held for two months at Cien y Aldabó Prison in Havana. He was then flown back to Bayamo for a trial on October 5 before the Popular Provincial Court of Granma. He was seated in the center of the courtroom, his defense to his right, the prosecutor to the left, five judges directly before him, and eight or nine rows of spectators behind. The press was watching on a closed-circuit television from another room. He had pleaded not guilty to charges of vehicular homicide and vehicular assault. He was represented by a Cuban lawyer, and advised by a lawyer from Madrid who had come for the trial.

The lawyers told Carromero their defense strategy was to pick apart the official government version that held Carromero responsible for the wreck. They would not attempt to lay out in full what actually happened, that a state security car had rammed him from behind. Carromero recalled they told him, "We can't say the truth, but let's all play with their fabricated version. They put it together so poorly and it has so many black holes, so we're going to try to pick it apart."

Carromero was outwardly calm, but inwardly in turmoil. In a brief exchange, he told the Madrid lawyer that his sanity and mental stability were stretched to the breaking point and he had contemplated suicide. He wanted desperately to go home. The lawyer promised he would go home, perhaps by the end of the year.

On the day of the trial, the courthouse was surrounded by a police cordon. Rosa María, Oswaldito, and Reinaldo Payá stood outside but were not admitted to the trial.

The first witness was Wilber Rondon Barrero, the tractor driver who was on the road that day. He said the Hyundai was speeding, kicked up a cloud of dust, then hit a tree. He went to help. He said he saw one person dead in the backseat, one injured, but neither of the two in the front seat were in distress. The next witness, Lazaro Miguel Parra Arjona, said he was driving toward Bayamo when he was overtaken by the Hyundai. He estimated it was speeding but could not say how fast. He, too, recalled seeing the cloud of dust, which obscured the wreck. The third witness, José Antonio Duque de Estrada Pérez, was riding a bicycle when the Hyundai passed him, and he too saw the cloud of dust. The bicycle rider said he helped three people who were alive at the scene, and a fourth was dead.

Those were the only witnesses called to testify who were at the scene at the time of the wreck. They said nothing about seeing a car with blue government plates hit the Hyundai.

Carromero noticed that all three carried papers with their testimony written out beforehand in pen. He sensed something was missing. His lawyers were not permitted to call their own expert witnesses. But they did cross-examine the government witnesses. "Not one of them could explain who else was at the scene, what car had taken us to the hospital, whether or not the police or the army were there," Carromero recalled later in a memoir. A traffic policeman who arrived afterward, Yoandris Rodriguez González, testified that one person was dead at the scene but said nothing about who else was there.

As the trial went on, a representative of the car rental company testified the Hyundai was in perfect working condition. The road contractor testified that the construction warning signs were properly in place. A botanist testified that the wood of the tree, Manila tamarind or sweet inga, was very strong and could have caused the deep contusion in the side of the Hyundai where Oswaldo was sitting. A forensics expert testified the car violently hit the tree after traveling more than a hundred kilometers per hour, or sixty-two miles per hour. Medical reports describing the injuries suffered by Oswaldo and Harold were introduced into the record.

The prosecution displayed photographs from the scene of the smashed-up car. But the photographs looked odd, as if the car had been moved. Carromero noticed that one photo showed the car perpendicular to the highway, in another it was nearly fallen into a watery ditch. A fender was hanging off in one, it was gone in another. No explanations were given for the anomalies.

During the trial, Carromero was examined and cross-examined by the prosecution and defense. Asked if he was speeding, he responded, "The last time that I looked at my speedometer, I was not going faster than eighty or ninety kilometers per hour." He expressed "profound sorrow" over the crash. "I have lost a lot during this time, and I'm going to lose even more, but nothing in comparison with the pain felt by the families involved," he told the court.

His videotaped statement in Bayamo was played for the trial—the session in which the police had handwritten the script. This was the official version of events: that he was solely responsible, that he lost control of the car after it hit the construction zone, and then he was knocked unconscious.

Previously, Carromero had described the Hyundai being hit from behind. He told it to the first investigator in the hospital; he had texted it in the messages from the hospital; he had questioned the burly guys who hustled him away from the scene.

But he also signed a different document, a confession to the official version, and he gave the videotaped statement. These became the basis of the government's case.

Carromero said later in an interview that his lawyers told him that "everything was fixed" before the trial, even the terms of the sentence. "You know what my body was crying out for me to do? Get to the trial and tell them everything. And have it end with me shouting and they would grab me and have to take me away." He added, "That's not what I did. I was terrified and I wanted to come home. That's basically it. The lawyer said it's all fixed." So Carromero did not raise the ramming of the car from behind.

On October 12, Carromero was convicted on the vehicular homicide charge, and the assault charge was dropped. He was sentenced to four years in prison. The verdict declared the deaths were caused "by the excess of speed with which the defendant was driving . . ."

The verdict added, "At the time the crime was committed, there were no attenuating, aggravating, or exculpatory circumstances."

A few days after Payá's death, state security began to follow his eldest son, Oswaldito, when he drove his father's car. The officers then approached Oswaldito's girlfriend and demanded she break up with him, and they threatened the girlfriend's mother. They telephoned Ofelia at dawn, hinting darkly that they could arrest Rosa María. They pressured the University of Havana to revoke approval of a biophysics research position for her that had been previously arranged. They telephoned threatening messages to Oswaldo's aunt Beba, whose apartment had been headquarters for the Varela Project. The Payás understood that the harassment and intimidation were attempts to force them to remain silent about Oswaldo's death.

Ofelia recalled that Oswaldo had once told her, "If they imprison me or kill me, you have to immediately leave the country with the children because they are going to come for you." In December, six months after his death, she decided it was time to go. Her son Oswaldito went first, alone, to the United States. "Oswaldo had not been wrong," Ofelia recalled. "The persecution against us grew immediately after his death."

Ofelia arranged for Oswaldo's body to be transferred to the mausoleum of the Daughters of Charity and Vincentian Fathers in Colón Cemetery. The nuns had been at his side in life, and their shelter would provide a protected final resting place. Then, on June 6, 2013, Ofelia and her family departed for Miami. They left behind a gaping hole in their lives. They never got closure for Oswaldo's death. The Carromero trial raised more questions than it answered. On the day of the trial, Ofelia raced back and forth between the hospital and police offices in Bayamo, trying to obtain a copy of the autopsy report. No one would give it to her. At day's end, a hospital director promised her it would be mailed. It never was. Ofelia had no confidence that the autopsy would reveal the truth. But she hoped it might provide a clue, or at least bear a doctor's signature—someone who, someday, could be questioned about what really happened.

Under a treaty between Spain and Cuba, Ángel Carromero was repatriated to Spain on December 29, 2012, to serve out his sentence. He was later released on a monitored parole.

In March 2013, Carromero spoke out in an interview with the *Washington Post*, saying he had been coerced to give the videotaped and written confessions in Cuba, and describing how the Hyundai was hit from behind. "The trial in Bayamo was a farce, to make me the scapegoat," he said. Members of Congress and the Payá family demanded an independent international investigation into Oswaldo's death. It never happened. No one in Cuba was ever held to account. The family asked a Spanish court to order a credible and independent investigation, but the request was dismissed. In a memo to the UN high commissioner for human rights, the Cuban government repeated the Bayamo trial testimony and said no other vehicle had hit the Hyundai. The government claimed, "There has not been one single extrajudicial, summary, or arbitrary execution in Cuba since 1959."

In Miami, Rosa María founded Cuba Decide, an initiative devoted to the cause of democracy that her father had fought for. She returned to Havana often, and in March 2016 joined several others to deliver a box to the door of the National Assembly. Inside were ten thousand more signatures for the Varela Project, which had been kept in hiding by nuns.

Ofelia tried in October 2017 to return to Cuba, hoping to obtain the autopsy report. She was refused entry at the Havana airport and forced to return home. She never received the report.

Long ago, in the 1950s, the church in El Cerro echoed with the voices of the sprawling Payá clan. The catechism classes were almost entirely Payá children. "We were a huge family that didn't even fit in the photo," recalled Oswaldo's brother Carlos Alberto. "And now there is no one left. We have only tombs in Cuba."

Oswaldo Payá fought long and hard for democracy and respect for basic human rights. His dreams were not achieved in his lifetime; the Castro dictatorship remained entrenched. But an important legacy of Oswaldo's quest was that gradually, painstakingly, despite all the obstacles and hardships, Cubans began to lose their fear and raise their voice against despotism.

And on one sultry summer afternoon, they became the protagonists of their own history.

After Fidel Castro died in 2016, and Raúl went into retirement, their handpicked successor, Miguel Díaz-Canel, proclaimed, "We are continuity." He meant continuity with the revolution, but for many Cubans, the revolution was a faded relic. A younger generation had become more connected, daring, entrepreneurial, and restless.

In November 2020, a group of artists and intellectuals known as the San Isidro Movement, tired of constant harassment and pressure, demanded the same freedoms that Oswaldo had sought. They bravely organized a public protest one evening in front of the government's Ministry of Culture and hundreds came in support. One of the young artists stood in the dusky twilight and held up a defiant thumb and forefinger in an "L," the signature of Oswaldo's movimiento, for "Liberation."

That was only the beginning. The 2020 global coronavirus pandemic destroyed tourism and sunk Cuba's economy, already weakened by Venezuela's collapse. Electric power blackouts rolled across the island. Food shortages and hunger became more widespread. After a year of relatively low infection rates, the virus surged in July 2021. At a hospital in Cárdenas, in Matanzas Province, sick patients piled up in hospitals, some lying on benches, on floors, or in the street. The hospital system was near collapse.

By this time, mobile internet service had come to Cuba. It was patchy and expensive, but enough to spread the word. Agonizing scenes from the Cárdenas hospital began to ricochet around the island on social media. This was a powerful means to reach people that Oswaldo had never known in his days of smudgy handbills.

On Sunday, July 11, a crowd gathered in San Antonio de los Baños, a small town southwest of Havana. Through their pandemic face masks, they chanted *"¡Patria y Vida!,"* homeland and life, the title of a hugely popular protest song that had become an anthem of discontent, a play on Fidel's old war cry of *"patria o muerte,"* homeland or death. The lyrics of the new song declare, "No more lies, my people ask for freedom." The crowd marched into the hot sun, and more shouts erupted: *"¡Libertad!* Down with dictatorship! We are not afraid!" Everywhere, smartphones were being held high. Yoan de la Cruz, twenty-six, captured a forty-nine-minute video and uploaded it on Facebook.

Then Cuba exploded. The Facebook video was widely seen and shared. In the largest spontaneous antigovernment demonstration since Fidel took power in 1959, tens of thousands— then a hundred thousand or more people in thirty cities and towns—expressed fury over shoddy medical care, electricity blackouts, hunger, and the regime's political straitjacket. A sudden and vast outpouring of discontent, it was authentic grassroots anger, a cry from within, and an almost entirely peaceful protest.

The dictatorship responded with force. The internet was interrupted.

On state television, Diaz-Canel declared, "The order for combat has been given," and "We are calling on all the revolutionaries of the country, all the Communists, to take to the streets." State security sent plainclothes thugs to beat demonstrators with metal rods. One protester was killed in a clash with police. Soon a wave of arrests began. In the Black Spring, seventy-five were sent to prison. This time, more than 1,300 people were detained, including teenagers. Many reported physical abuse after they were arrested, including jailhouse beatings with batons. Most had done nothing more than shout "*¡Libertad!*" Among those arrested was Yoan de la Cruz, who uploaded the Facebook video, and was later sentenced to six years in prison. Eight months after the protests, 726 people were still incarcerated, and sham trials held for more than 260, many threatened with long prison sentences.

As Oswaldo had learned, change is hard. A totalitarian state does not simply flutter and faint. The Cuban regime still commands an army and vast security forces; it controls the airwaves, the borders, and the economy, and it monopolizes all politics. But Oswaldo Payá showed—and the events of July 11 proved again—that no state, no matter how dictatorial, can imprison an idea forever. The quest for liberty runs free.

In the year before his death, Oswaldo took advantage of quiet moments at the house on Calle Peñón to pull a chair up to the small table in his bedroom. For years he had thought about writing a book, to collect all his ideas. In the late 1980s, he had set it all down in a manuscript titled *Souls of Rebellion*. But back then there were periodic searches by state security, so Oswaldo hid his papers at the house of his friend Ramón Antúnez. One day, facing another scare, Oswaldo wrapped the manuscript in a big yellow plastic bag and concealed it in a friend's barnyard. The bag got soaked by rain and the manuscript was ruined. Ofelia insisted that he try again. Oswaldo often had flashes of inspiration, writing down on scraps of paper what he wanted to address and how to say it. Finally he started over.

He wrote furiously and with great passion, the words tumbling out. It was as if all he had experienced and fought for was still in his memory, and he raced to set it down. He wrote very much as he spoke, his explanations earnest, his tone urgent, his pace impatient.

"Those in power want to deprive the people of the right to design, plan, and build their future, because they know that future is a future of freedom," he wrote. "In Cuba, they are forbidding us from preparing for that future, from working now during the night to be ready for the next morning, because someone has said that the night will never end. But this night will not be eternal, its time is running out. Yes, the sun will rise and there will be a new day. For that matter, let's hurry, dawn is already breaking."

"The protagonist of change in Cuba," he declared, "must be the Cuban people."

Acknowledgments

Mylena Vazquez, a dedicated and tenacious investigator, was the primary researcher for this book. While searching at the Cuban Heritage Collection of the University of Miami one day, she discovered the text of Gustavo Gutiérrez's first draft for a citizen initiative. I let out a whoop—and broke the strict rules for quiet. From then until the end of the project, Mylena kept coming back with more.

I benefited enormously from Myriam Marquez's translations and counsel about Cuba and the Cuban American community in Miami. Her high standards were upheld by Eloisa Echazabal in Miami, Pamela Rolfe in Madrid, and Ashley Caja in Washington. Terri Shaw translated dozens of audio and video recordings, and Mónica Klien translated *Ecos del Sínodo* and *Pueblo de Dios*. This is the third book for which Maryanne Warrick accurately transcribed hundreds of hours of interviews and provided valuable feedback on the manuscript. I thank them all.

Gustavo Ovares Gutiérrez provided copious insights about his grandfather, Gustavo Gutiérrez. He also generously shared a draft of his own memoir, photographs, and family documents. His mother, Yolanda Gutiérrez Ovares, offered rich recollections of her father.

Michael Bustamante steered me smartly through the history of Cuba, always finding time to respond to questions. Ilan Ehrlich, biographer of Eddy Chibás, guided me through the intricate byways of the Cuban Republic. I am grateful for their critiques of the manuscript. Petra Kuivala of the Faculty of Theology at the University of Helsinki shared her groundbreaking research on the Catholic Church in Cuba and critiqued the manuscript.

I am indebted to Oswaldo's friends, Ramón Antúnez, Santiago Cardenas, and Rolando Sabin for their recollections. Dr. Sabin was a dedicated and constant adviser. I am also grateful to Humberto León and Andrés Cárdenas Machado for reaching deep into their memories of the forced labor camps.

My research would have been impossible without the help of many who worked with Oswaldo in the Movimiento Cristiano Liberación. Regis Iglesias tirelessly connected me to others and contributed his deep well of recollections. I am deeply grateful to Tony Díaz, Pedro Pablo Álvarez, Jose Miguel Martinez, Ernesto Martini, Miguel Saludes, Osmel Rodriguez, Jesus Mustafa, Andrés Chacón, Fredesvinda Hernández, Jorge Colmenero, Minerva Chil Siret, Alejandro González Raga, and Julio Rodriguez. Julio Hernández, who served as the movimiento's international representative, was extremely helpful, as was Francisco de Armas, who accompanied Oswaldo to receive the Sakharov prize in 2002.

Raúl Rivero and Ricardo González Alfonso described their struggle to teach and practice journalism. Elizardo Sánchez and Héctor Palacios filled in the story of Todos Unidos. Andrés Solares recounted his pursuit of signatures for a new party and the arrest and imprisonment that followed. Orlando Gutiérrez helped me with important context and delivered an armful of *Steps to Freedom*, the journal that meticulously chronicled the grassroots stirring of the 1990s.

Ángel Carromero and Aron Modig provided lengthy interviews about the car wreck and its aftermath.

Rebecca De Mar was indispensable, sharing recollections and helping analyze archival material. Carl Gershman framed my thinking about democracy in Cuba. Ricardo Zuñiga, a foreign service officer in Havana during key years covered by the book, provided extremely useful analysis, as well as a critique of the manuscript. Jennifer McCoy carefully filled me in on the Carter trip to Havana. I am also grateful for interviews and materials from Leonel Morejón Almagro, Genaro Arriagada, Daniel Aviles, Vanessa Bauza, Tomas Bilbao, Ricardo Bofill, Phil Brenner, Frank

Calzon, Juan Manuel Cao, James Cason, Jeffrey DeLaurentis, Pablo Díaz, Sor Elvira Garcia, Felice Gorodo, Julio Cesar Guanche, Lillian Guerra, Luis Hernández, Kelly Keiderling, Elena Larrinaga, Maria Letunic, Erica Morawski, Nick Miroff, Francisco Mueller, Orlando Rivero-Valdes, Father José Conrado Rodriguez, Rafael Rojas, Cindy Romero, Father Juan Rumin, Carlos Saladrigas, Omar Rodriguez Saludes, John Suarez, Jim Swigert, Dagoberto Valdés, and Aimel Rios Wong. Kate Thorp created the map that opens the book.

Henrik Ehrenberg, who helped Oswaldo on behalf of KIC, the Kristdemokratiskt Internationellt Center, or Christian Democratic International Center, in Stockholm, was a valued source of recollections and provided transcripts of his interviews in 2004 for *Cuba from Within*. Annika Rïgo of KIC shared poignant memories of working with Oswaldo.

In Berlin, independent researcher Jorge L. García Vázquez, a member of the Movimiento Cristiano Liberación, guided me through the relationship between the East German Stasi and Cuba's state security. I am especially grateful for his assistance with the Stasi archives and for sharing his research report, "Havana-Berlin Connection: State Secrets and Notes on Collaboration Between the Stasi and Ministry of Interior." Kerstin Schädler executed my archive search with great skill. Dr. Jochen Staadt provided guidance on Stasi methods and past contacts with Cuban state security. Nicola Duemler superbly translated documents from the archives.

Glenn Frankel stands above all others in helping me overcome deficits in my writing over the years; no one has been more generous and patient. Phil Bennett challenged my assumptions and set demanding standards for the narrative that made it far better. Marie Arana gave me early encouragement and a valuable reading of the manuscript. Steve Fainaru and Charles Lane, colleagues over many years at the *Washington Post*, added to my understanding of Cuba and carefully read drafts. Christopher Schroeder was a much-needed sounding board, reader, and adviser. W. Ross Newland was a source of astute counsel.

Maria Lipman posed tough questions on every page, as she has over and over again through four books.

Fred Hiatt, editor of the editorial page of the *Post*, and Jackson Diehl, deputy editor, grasped the Payá story from the outset and encouraged my efforts to dig into it. Their leadership kept the *Post* at the forefront of voices defending human rights and democracy around the world.

I thank the helpful staff of the Cuban Heritage Collection at the University of Miami, a researcher's dream. The Library of Congress is a temple to knowledge and I thank whoever had the foresight to preserve eight-decade-old texts from Cuba, some of them falling apart, held together only by a string. Tom Blanton and Svetlana Savranskaya of the National Security Archive at George Washington University shared their own experiences in Cuba and their considerable expertise as historians.

I am deeply grateful to Rosa María Payá for her commitment to this project, including long hours of intense conversations over almost a decade that helped me understand her father's quest and his sense of mission. Ofelia Acevedo Maura was exceptionally open and generous, revealing her private conversations with Oswaldo and sharing vivid, poignant reminiscences. On my visits to the Payá home in Miami, Rosa María pulled out old flash drives bulging with Oswaldo's files while Ofelia brought yellowed, handwritten texts to the table and all of us pored over family albums, videos, and memorabilia. Oswaldito and Reinaldo Payá were welcoming and helpful, as was María Ofelia Maura. Oswaldo's brothers Alejandro, Óscar, and Carlos Alberto, and his sister Marlene, provided illuminating interviews.

Esther Newberg, my agent, waited patiently, read enthusiastically, and represented brilliantly. There is no one better and more dedicated to an author's success.

Mindy Marques of Simon & Schuster saw the promise of Oswaldo's story from the very first minute. She edited superbly with a deep well of understanding about Cuba. Also at Simon & Schuster, my thanks to Hana Park, for her steady hand in steering the ship; to Elisa Rivlin for a careful review; to Yvette Grant for overseeing production with such grace and patience; to William Drennan, Hercilia Mendizabal, and Linda Sawicki for exacting scrutiny of every line; to Jackie Seow for such a striking cover; to Ruth Lee-Mui for skillfully creating and shepherding interior design and layout; and Amanda Mulholland for making sure it all came together like an orchestra.

Our sons Daniel and Benjamin have been eager voyagers in every sense, a source of great pride and joy. This book is dedicated to my wife, Carole, who tolerated the long hours, but did so with constant encouragement. She was the first and strongest advocate for the Payá story, and joined me in Havana, retracing the steps of Oswaldo Payá around Parque Manila, down Calle Peñón to El Salvador del Mundo, then on to the Gutiérrez Castillo Bellabrisa in Miramar and to the gleaming, restored Capitolio, where the 1940 constitution was born. I could not have done it without you.

Notes

THE PAYÁ COLLECTION
The author drew from a large collection of handwritten and typed documents, audio recordings, video recordings, and photographs shared by Ofelia Acevedo Maura and Rosa María Payá Acevedo. A selection of these documents are online at the author's website, www.davidehoffman.com. Other valuable references are posted by the Movimiento Cristiano Liberación at https://mcliberacion.org.

PROLOGUE
xii *hurtling into the darkness:* Ofelia Acevedo Maura, interviews with author, August 11, 2017, December 3, 2017, January 21, 2018, June 5, 2021, Miami, Florida.

xiv *she admonished him:* Rosa María Payá Acevedo, "Prólogo," in *Muerte bajo sospecha: Toda la verdad sobre el caso* (Madrid: Oberon, 2014), pp. 17–36, and Rosa María Payá Acevedo, interviews with author, August 11, 2017, January 20, 2018.

xv *a neighborhood of luxury villas:* Dick Cluster and Rafael Hernández, *The History of Havana* (New York: OR Books/Counterpoint Press, 2018), p. 52.

xv *painted a threatening slogan:* "En una plaza sitiada la disidencia es traición." The graffiti was painted when Fidel underwent surgery July 31, 2006, and turned his duties over to Raúl.

xvi *Carromero was nervous:* Ángel Carromero, *Muerte*, and interview with author, September 13, 2017, Madrid; Aron Modig, interviews with author, December 9 and 13, 2018, Stockholm, and unpublished memorandum, October 2012, provided to author. Payá's comments are based on the recollections of Modig and Carromero.

xvii *"the threat that they'd liquidate me":* U.S. Interests Section Havana to Department of State, December 14, 2006, HAVANA 023602, WikiLeaks.org.

xvii   *"I see very few chances of getting out alive"*: Oswaldo Payá, interviews with Henrik Ehrenberg, 2004, for *Cuba from Within* (Stockholm: Samhällsgemenskaps Förlag, 2007). Interview transcripts provided to author, courtesy Ehrenberg.

xviii *salaries paltry, food and goods scarce:* Richard Feinberg, "Cuba's Economy after Raúl Castro: A Tale of Three Worlds" (Washington, DC: Brookings Institution, 2018). Feinberg notes growth in self-employed, or *cuentapropistas*, under Raúl, and the relative vibrancy of the private economy, but adds: "Cuban agriculture is a disaster. . . . For many crops, including sugar, coffee, tobacco, citrus, and fisheries, pre-revolutionary production levels far exceeded today's harvests."

ONE. AGONY OF THE REPUBLIC

3   *"black and white in speech and action"*: Berta Gutiérrez Montalvo, *El hombre olvidado*, pamphlet, July 1994, courtesy Gustavo Ovares Gutiérrez, 2019, and Berta Montalvo Papers, CHC0297, Cuban Heritage Collection, University of Miami, Coral Gables, Florida. Throughout, Gustavo Gutiérrez's family history and insights into his thinking were drawn from Gustavo Ovares Gutiérrez, *Despite the Oaths of Angels*, unpublished manuscript, and "El Estadista Olvidado," unpublished monograph, both by permission, conversations with Ovares Gutiérrez, 2019–2021, and posts from his blog, https://drgustavoguti errez.blogspot.com.

4   *from justice to freedom:* Carlos Miguel de Céspedes, *Republica de Cuba: Libro del Capitolio* (Havana: Talleres tip. De P. Fernández y Cía, 1933), p. 359. Also, author photographs and visit, March 2019.

4   *a vast stream of migration:* Louis A. Pérez Jr., *Cuba Under the Platt Amendment, 1902–1934* (Pittsburgh: University of Pittsburgh Press, 1986), p. 10. Manuel Moreno Fraginals estimated that from 1868 to 1898 a total 464,503 civilians and 535,495 soldiers arrived, almost a million people, of whom about 700,000 remained. Moreno, "Spain in Cuba," in *The Cuba Reader: History, Culture, Politics*, ed. Aviva Chomsky, Barry Carr, Alfredo Prieto, and Pamela María Smorkaloff, 2nd ed. (Durham, NC, and London: Duke University Press, 2019), p. 155.

4   *to fight with the rebel army:* The first battle of the war occurred at Jobito, May 13, 1895. John Lawrence Tone, *War and Genocide in Cuba, 1895–1898* (Chapel Hill: University of North Carolina Press, 2006), p. 56. On Machado, see Hugh Thomas, *Cuba: The Pursuit of Freedom* (New York: Harper & Row, 1971), p. 567.

5   *solicitors, court clerks, and scribes:* Some 80 percent of the *peninsular* population were qualified to vote, compared to only 24 percent of the Cuban population. Three-fourths of all mayors on the island were peninsulares. In Güines, thirty miles southeast of Havana, pop. 13,000, some 500 were Spanish. But

the electoral census counted 400 Spaniards and only 32 Cubans. Pérez, *Cuba Under*, pp. 17–18.

5   *"everything must be destroyed"*: A portion of the Gómez letter, dated May 25, 1896, is reproduced in Grover Flint, *Marching with Gómez* (Boston: Lamson, Wolfee, 1896), p. 190; Tone, *War and Genocide*, p. 60.

5   *sharpshooters in the rebel ranks*: John Lawrence Tone, "The Machete and the Liberation of Cuba," *Journal of Military History*, no. 62 (January 1998): 7–28, and Tone, *War and Genocide*, p. 127.

5   *joined the rebel army en masse*: Hudson Strode, *The Pageant of Cuba* (New York: Harrison Smith and Robert Haas, 1934), pp. 119–120; Aline Helg, *Our Rightful Share: The Afro-Cuban Struggle for Equality, 1886–1912* (Chapel Hill: University of North Carolina Press, 1995).

6   *"wrapped in the stillness of death"*: In 1896, yellow fever killed 1 of every 200 people in Havana. Raymond Leslie Buell, *Problems of the New Cuba: Report of the Commission on Cuban Affairs* (New York: Foreign Policy Association, 1935), p. 103; W. Adolfe Roberts, *Havana: The Portrait of a City* (New York: Coward-McCann, 1953), pp. 113, 119–120; Tone, *War and Genocide*, pp. 210, 223. Calhoun said, "The countryside outside the military posts was practically depopulated. Every house had been burned, banana trees cut down, cane fields swept by fire, and everything in the shape of food destroyed. . . . I did not see a house, man, woman, or child, a horse, mule or cow, nor even a dog. . . ."

6   *a smoking ruin, but not yet entirely free*: Louis A. Pérez Jr., *Cuba: Between Reform and Revolution* (Oxford: Oxford University Press, 1988), p. 213; Thomas, *Cuba*, p. 423; Tone, *War and Genocide*, p. 9.

7   *Carlos Finlay's discovery*: The cause of yellow fever, spread by female mosquitoes, was not discovered until 1901. When mosquitos were properly fought, it was completely stamped out. Buell, *Problems*, p. 103. On schools, Cuba had only 541 schools on the island during the war, but the US military government left with 3,474 schools and 163,348 registered students. A still-larger share, some 191,583 students, did not attend. José R. Álvarez Díaz, chairman, Cuban Economic Research Project, *A Study on Cuba: The Colonial and Republican Periods, the Socialist Experiment* (Coral Gables, FL: University of Miami Press, 1965), p. 181, and Thomas, *Cuba*, p. 446.

7   *ordered Cuban schools reorganized*: Thomas, *Cuba*, p. 445.

7   *He looked down upon them*: Thomas, *Cuba*, p. 445.

7   *"not ready for self-government"*: Thomas, *Cuba*, p. 445. Also see Pérez, *Cuba Under*, pp. 32–33 and n. 15, p. 347. The letter was April 12, 1900.

7   *"These men are all rascals"*: Pérez, *Cuba Under*, pp. 40–41. Wood letter to Root, December 23, 1900.

7   *In newspaper cartoons*: John J. Johnson, "U.S. Cartoonists Portray Cuba," in Chomsky et al., *The Cuba Reader*, pp. 132–135.

7 *The rebel army . . . not even acknowledged:* Franklin Matthews, "The Reconstruction of Cuba," *Harper's Weekly* 49 (May 27, 1899): 520–521; William E. Biederwolf, *History of the One Hundred and Sixty-First Regiment, Indiana Volunteer Infantry* (Logansport, IN: Wilson, Humphreys, 1899–1900), pp. 154–155. The US occupation attempted to lure army officers and soldiers away from the rebel army with offers to exchange jobs for arms. Public works programs pulled many out of the force. By mid-1899, several thousand veterans had abandoned the army for civilian employment. In the end, the United States offered to fund the army's demobilization, with each veteran receiving a bonus of $75 upon surrendering arms. By the end of the summer of 1899, the army had been dissolved. Louis A. Pérez Jr., "Supervision of a Protectorate: The United States and the Cuban Army, 1898–1908," *Hispanic American Historical Review* 52, no. 2 (May 1972): 250–271.

8 *Cuba's 1901 Constitution:* The new constitution was promulgated May 20, 1901. The US military occupation ended a year later.

8 *Tobacco rebounded quickly after the war:* Tobacco exports boomed, and exceeded sugar in value for 1901–1902. Álvarez Díaz, *A Study on Cuba,* pp. 176–177. A small advertisement published in *United States Tobacco Journal,* a weekly in New York, said: "Miguel Gutiérrez y Gutiérrez, Packers of Santa Clara, Vuelto Abajo and Patidos Tobaccos." The advertisement provided an address in a commercial section of Havana and added: "English spoken." The ad appeared in the February 15, 1908, edition, p. 15.

8 *Havana . . . had fared better in the war:* Thomas, *Cuba,* p. 433.

9 Partido Independiente de Color: Helg, *Our Rightful Share;* Thomas, *Cuba,* pp. 514–524.

9 *A friend later wrote:* Montalvo, *El hombre olvidado.*

9 *the schools of law and medicine:* Jaime Suchlicki, *University Students and Revolution in Cuba, 1920–1968* (Coral Gables, FL: University of Miami Press, 1969), p. 18. From 1925 to 1930, the law school graduated 891 students; the medical, dental, pharmacy, and veterinary schools, 1,537 students; and the remaining, consisting primarily of engineering professions with agriculture, 402 students. Buell, *Problems,* p. 154.

9 *no-show professors on the payroll:* Russell H. Fitzgibbon, *Cuba and the United States: 1900–1935* (Menasha, WI: George Banta, 1935), pp. 49–50. Also, Charles E. Chapman, *A History of the Cuban Republic: A Study in Hispanic American Politics* (New York: Macmillan, 1927), p. 595.

9 *Gustavo graduated in 1916:* The Cuban system merged undergraduate and graduate education; Gustavo's university study included liberal arts as well as law. The author is grateful to Orlando Rivero-Valdes for this explanation.

10 *They married in 1918:* Ovares Gutiérrez, *Despite the Oaths of Angels.*

10 *Conrado Massaguer, a caricaturist, illustrator, and satirist: Social* popularized an

Art Deco aesthetic, a sense of the Avant Garde, and Massaguer celebrated women as independent and freethinking with drawings of American flappers. But his drawings also reflected the disenchantment of Gustavo's generation. In 1923, he depicted the republic as a young and sad girl, dressed in worn and threadbare clothes. In another, a young Cuban contemplates tombstones in a cemetery where civic conscience, idealism, sacrifice, Cubanism, patriotism, and nationalism are all buried. María Luisa Lobo Montalvo and Zoila Lapique Becali, "The Years of *Social*," trans. Narciso G. Menocal and Edward Shaw, *The Journal of Decorative and Propaganda Arts*, no. 22 (1996): 105–131. Also, Jorge Mañach, "Los Minoristas Sabáticos eschuchan al gran Titta," *Social* 9, no. 2 (February 1924): 23.

11 *"we magnificently lived out our remarkable youth"*: Andrés Nuñez Olano, "Rubén," *Lunes de Revolución*, Havana, January 23, 1961, p. 16.

11 *"the stillbirth rather than the birth of a republic"*: Lillian Guerra, *The Myth of José Martí: Conflicting Nationalisms in Early Twentieth-Century Cuba* (Chapel Hill: University of North Carolina Press, 2005), p. 3.

11 *expected to put the bribes*: Roberts, *Havana*, p. 128.

11 *substantial stealing by his friends and relatives*: Chapman, *A History*, p. 395. On January 29, 1919, Carlos Mendieta, a prominent politician who had become editor-in-chief of *El Heraldo de Cuba*, wrote in a column: "Menocal has converted Cuba into a factory that is a theatre of caprices, dilapidations, and madness. He has usurped the power, and has wronged his compatriots. His work of decomposition is almost impossible to repair. He has relaxed public customs, with a governmental regime contrary to every precept of economy, and has enthroned the desire for lucre in official circles." Mendieta was promptly hauled into court and fined $500 for insulting the president. Chapman, p. 396, quoting the article in *El Heraldo de Cuba* of January 29, 1919. Chapman said the criticism "may not have been too severe."

12 *fresh waves of Spanish immigrants surged to Cuba*: Pérez, *Cuba Under*, p. 61, and Thomas, *Cuba*, p. 202.

12 *"Graft, bribery and embezzlement"*: Pérez, *Cuba Under*, pp. 215–217.

12 *election campaigns celebrated as the "second harvest,"*: Luis E. Aguilar, *Cuba 1933: Prologue to Revolution* (Ithaca: Cornell University Press, 1972), pp. 33–34.

12 *botellas, or no-show jobs and sinecures*: Charles E. Chapman, a University of California professor who chronicled this period of Cuba's history, found that "so firmly rooted is the Spanish colonial practice of 'government for the sake of the office-holders' that almost no social stigma is involved in graft, and there is hardly any need for concealment." Chapman, *A History*, pp. 396, 565. Also see Buell, *Problems*, pp. 1–4.

12 *"Cuban society is disintegrating"*: Fernando Ortiz, *The Cuban Decadence*, lecture to the Sociedad Económica de Amigos del País, February 23, 1924, pamphlet.

12 *a culture of impunity:* Pérez, *Cuba Under,* p. 218; Ortiz, "The Cuban Decadence."

13 *In the professions, Black presence was very small:* Thomas, *Cuba,* pp. 430, 514–524; Pérez, *Cuba Under,* p. 212.

13 *"by the people and for the people":* Gustavo Gutiérrez, "La desintegración de la nación cubana," address to the Cuban Society of International Law, Havana, January 30, 1919, in *Anuario de la Sociedad Cubana de Derecho Internacional 3* (1919): 285–300.

14 *dance of the millions:* Sugar prices went from 9⅛ cents a pound in February to 12 cents in March, to a peak of 22½ cents in May. Thomas, *Cuba,* p. 543; Aguilar, *Cuba 1933,* p. 43; Leland Hamilton Jenks, *Our Cuban Colony: A Study in Sugar* (New York: Vanguard Press, 1928), pp. 218–219.

14 *speculation, price-fixing, bank manipulation, and credit pyramids:* Banco Nacional de Cuba, seemingly invincible, with $194 million in deposits and 121 branches and offices, symbolized the new prosperity. The majority shareholder was a Havana hustler, José Lopez Rodriguez, an immigrant from Galicia who profited off government contracts for school supplies, public works, and sanitation, and later spun a fortune in land and sugar. He reportedly was allowed to carry a $25 million overdraft. Speculators flocked to Cuba from abroad to buy up sugar properties at ridiculously inflated prices. Some fifty mills, about one-quarter of the total, were acquired by new owners between 1919 and 1920. Bank credit to sugar producers was cheap and almost unlimited. Cuban farmers who had taken out one loan were begged by competing banks to borrow more and more. By the peak, $80 million in loans were made on sugar with valuation set at 22 cents a pound. Jenks, *Our Cuban Colony,* pp. 211, 214; Chapman, *A History,* pp. 398–399; Strode, *The Pageant,* pp. 245–246. Also see Álvarez Díaz, *A Study on Cuba,* p. 248, and Pérez, *Cuba Under,* p. 225.

14 *a dizzying expansion of credit:* Jenks, *Our Cuban Colony,* p. 207; Strode, *The Pageant,* pp. 236–254; and Tom Gjelten, *Bacardi and the Long Fight for Cuba: The Biography of a Cause* (New York: Viking, 2008), pp. 109–110.

14 *Then it all crashed:* Prices fell to 3¾ cents a pound in December. Planters and mill owners had excess sugar stocks that could not be sold and debts that could not be serviced. Trade and commerce seized up. A run on banks broke out in early October 1920. The government forestalled panic by imposing a temporary moratorium on debts, effective October 11, suspending all debt payments until December 1, a deadline extended until January 1 and then February 1. Eighteen banks went under in 1921. On April 9, Banco Nacional closed its doors. Eight banks with 123 branches failed in May, three more in June. The government had $12 million stuck in Banco Nacional and was facing imminent bankruptcy. Two banks that met their obligations and remained open were both foreign: the National City Bank of New York and the Royal Bank of Canada. Jenks, *Our Cuban Colony,* pp. 244–245, 248.

14   *unemployment, strikes, and shortages:* Aguilar described these years as a period
     "of continuous decline of the moral and political standards of the island."
     He added: "In the background, the mass of the population took refuge in an
     attitude of irreverence toward everything that had any national or spiritual
     value. This popular reaction, a mixture of disillusion and drollery, of bitter-
     ness and biting humor, called *choteo criollo,* became a national characteristic,
     a psychological escape from unpleasant social realities." Aguilar, *Cuba 1933,*
     p. 29.

14   *more than 76 percent were in foreign banks:* Aguilar, *Cuba 1933,* p. 43.

14   *sugar mills were taken over by US banks:* Thomas, *Cuba,* p. 551; Jenks, *Our Cuban
     Colony,* p. 285.

14   *Sugar demanded land, labor, and capital:* In 1919 some 20,000 immigrants ar-
     rived from Haiti and Jamaica to cut sugarcane, and 34,000 in 1920. The in-
     flux halted later when sugar prices and exports fell. The length of the season
     varied over the years. In 1909, the harvest went 250 days, from December to
     September. But by 1926, it was only 135 days, and it fell to only 66 days by
     1933. The curtailed season was part of a futile effort to prop up prices. Barry
     Carr, "Mill Occupations and Soviets: The Mobilisation of Sugar Workers in
     Cuba 1917–1933," *Journal of Latin American Studies* 28, no. 1 (February 1996):
     129–158. Also see Ramiro Guerra y Sánchez, *Sugar and Society in the Carib-
     bean,* Caribbean Series 7 (New Haven: Yale University Press, 1964), p. xxxiv,
     including Sidney W. Mintz's foreword to this edition. The book comprises
     newspaper accounts originally published in Cuba in 1927. Translated from
     Spanish by Marjory M. Urquidi.

15   *For capital, the main source was the United States:* Álvarez Díaz, *A Study on Cuba,*
     p. 238.

15   *US interests also controlled the railroads:* Ortiz, "The Cuban Decadence"; Jenks,
     Our Cuban Colony, pp. 281–302.

15   *a faded revolutionary martyr:* Alfred J. Lopez, *José Martí and the Future of Cuban
     Nationalisms* (Gainesville: University Press of Florida, 2006), pp. 20–23.

15   *a famous poet and educator, Rafael Mendive:* López, *José Martí,* pp. 1–6, 26–44.

15   *he saw the horrors of political imprisonment in Cuba:* Jorge Mañach, *Martí: Apos-
     tle of Freedom* (in Spanish, *Martí, el apóstol,* Madrid: Espasa-Calpe, 1933), repr.,
     Coley Taylor, trans. (New York: Devin-Adair, 1950), pp. 40–41.

16   *Martí laid the foundations:* Carlos Ripoll, *Jose Martí Thoughts: On Liberty, Social
     Justice, Government, Art and Morality* (New York: Editorial Dos Ríos, 1995), p.
     6. This work is drawn from Ripoll's *José Martí: Thoughts/Pensamientos: A Bilin-
     gual Anthology* (New York: Unión de Cubanos en el Exilio, 1980).

17   *Martí wrote a long letter to Gómez:* Mañach, *Martí,* p. 230.

17   *"One does not establish a people, General, the way one commands a military camp.":*
     Tone, *War and Genocide,* p. 34.

17 *an intense, slight man, with quiet magnetism:* López, *José Martí: A Revolutionary Life,* pp. 52–65; C. A. M. Hennessy, "The Roots of Cuban Nationalism," *International Affairs* 39, no. 3 (July 1963): 345–359; Thomas, *Cuba,* pp. 293–309.

18 *to plan the course of the new war:* Maceo said in a proclamation in 1885, "Liberty is not begged for, it is conquered." See Philip S. Foner, *Antonio Maceo: The "Bronze Titan" of Cuba's Struggle for Independence* (New York: Monthly Review Press, 1977), p. 126. The disagreement had lingered between them for years. Maceo was killed in action December 7, 1896.

18 *Martí had been through weeks of hard marching in the Cuban bush:* López, *Jose Martí: A Revolutionary Life,* p. 305.

18 *"I lived in the monster":* The letter was to his old friend from Mexico, Manuel Mercado. Jose Martí, *Obras Completas* (Havana: Editorial de Ciencias Sociales, second printing, 1991), p. 167; Thomas, *Cuba,* p. 310; López, *José Martí: A Revolutionary Life,* p. 316.

18 *Martí, on horseback, was shot and killed:* López, *Jose Martí: A Revolutionary Life,* pp. 316–328.

19 *the Martí story sparked imagination and curiosity:* Mañach, who took part in the café debates with Gustavo, later wrote a popular biography titled *Martí: Apostle of Freedom.*

19 *Martí's prescient warning of domination by the United States:* Ripoll, *José Martí,* p. 41.

19 *Crowder became a proconsul:* Jenks, *Our Cuban Colony,* pp. 238–239.

19 *lengthy memorandums to Zayas:* The memos were written between February 24 and August 15, 1922. Russell H. Fitzgibbon, *Cuba and the United States, 1900–1935* (Menasha, WI: George Banta, 1935), p. 172; Thomas, *Cuba,* p. 554.

20 *"could not have been more offensive to Cuban sovereignty":* Gustavo Gutiérrez, "La misión del general Crowder en Cuba desde el punto de vista del derecho internacional," *Anuario de la Sociedad Cubana de Derecho Internacional, Sociedad Cubana de Derecho Internacional* 6 (1923): 364–417.

20 *wave of nationalism was rising in Cuba:* Aguilar, *Cuba 1933,* pp. 11, 68, 71; Pérez, *Cuba Under,* p. 246.

20 *depth and breadth of corruption:* Pérez, *Cuba Under,* p. 246; Chapman, *A History,* pp. 561–562. However, Gustavo and his generation admired philosopher Enrique José Varona, who had long championed freedom, sovereignty, and independence. Varona was vice president of the republic from 1913 to 1917 and professor of philosophy at the University of Havana. Carlos Ripoll, *La generación del 23 en Cuba* (New York: Las Américas, 1968), and Medardo Vitier, "La lección de Varona," *Jornadas,* vol. 31 (Mexico City: Colegio de Mexico, 1945), pp. 1–74.

20 *a plethora of voices:* Pérez, *Cuba Under,* pp. 234–235; Chapman, *A History,* pp. 596–603. The estimate of thirty-seven papers was made in 1917, which

Chapman says compares favorably to the number of newspapers in New York City at the time. The Cuban papers were quite frequently given pay-offs from government for political purposes and controlled by members of Congress, or they hired the members as editorial writers since they enjoyed immunity from prosecution and could say whatever they pleased without consequences. Chapman noted criticisms of Zayas's corruption over a three-week span not only in *Heraldo de Cuba*, the largest Havana paper, but also in *El Comercio, Diario de la Marina, La Discusión, El Heraldo, El Mundo, La Noche, El País*, the *Havana Post, El Sol, La Tarde*, and *El Triunfo*. Chapman, *A History*, pp. 497–498, on the period between November 15 and December 4, 1924, near the end of Zayas's term.

21 *El Grupo Minorista:* On March 18, after lunch, a group of them went to hear a visiting writer from Uruguay, Paulina Luisi, give a talk. This was a formal literary event at the Academy of Sciences. She was to be introduced by the justice minister in the Zayas government, Erasmo Regüeiferos Bodet, who had signed a corrupt contract to buy the Santa Clara Convent for an inflated price. At the event, Rubén Martínez Villena stood up abruptly in front of everyone and loudly protested the sleazy deal, a "repellant and clumsy business." He and his group of artists then walked out, and the next day they published a manifesto titled "Protest of the Thirteen," declaring they were fed up with Zayas and his corruption. Aguilar, *Cuba 1933*, pp. 69–70. Also see Ana Cairo Ballester, *El grupo minorista y su tiempo* (Havana: Editorial de Ciencias Sociales, 1978), and Thomas, *Cuba*, pp. 566–567. In a subsequent edition of *Social*, Gutiérrez was pictured prominently on a page of photos of the members in "Nuestros colaboradores: Los minoristas," *Social* 11, no. 1 (January 1926): 34. Days after the protest, the secretary of justice filed a legal complaint against the Thirteen, for the crime of insulting him, seeking 180 days in jail. But the secretary resigned at the end of March 1923, and the case was dismissed in mid-1924. See http://www.cubaliteraria.cu/monografia/grupo_minorista/memoria2.html.

21 *time for a complete overhaul:* The Cuban Committee of National and Civic Restoration published the manifesto on April 2, 1923. Chapman, *A History*, pp. 466–467.

21 *a student protest:* Chapman, *A History*, p. 596.

21 *the University Students Federation, or FEU:* Thomas, *Cuba*, p. 565; Jaime Suchlicki, *University Students and Revolution in Cuba, 1920–1968* (Coral Gables, FL: University of Miami Press, 1969), pp. 21–22. Gustavo knew Mella and once had been his coach on a rowing team competition trip to Mexico. Mella went on to champion social revolution in Latin America and cofounded Cuba's first Communist Party. "Wall Street must be destroyed!" he wrote in a pamphlet. Mella, approximately 1925, "Cuba: Un pueblo que jamás ha sido

libre," in *Mella: Documentos y artículos* (Havana: Editorial de Ciencias Sociales, Instituto Cubano del Libro, 1975), pp. 174–183.

21   *the Veterans and Patriots Association:* The group was led by a former general and diplomat, Carlos García Vélez, who was Cuba's ambassador to London and son of the famous independence war general Calixto García. Chapman, *A History*, 468–474; Pérez, *Cuba Under*, 246–247.

21   *resisted his suggestion:* On September 18, Gutiérrez proposed that the Veterans and Patriots become an official political party, to channel its popularity into a more formal—and constitutional—process for seeking change. But militancy was in the air; his proposal fell flat. Cairo Ballester, *El grupo minorista*, pp. 53–54; also see Cairo Ballester, *El movimiento de veteranos y patriotas* (Havana: Editorial Arte y Literatura, 1976). In October 1923, Zayas responded to the rebellion. Leaders of the Veterans and Patriots were harassed, meetings disrupted, and printing shops publishing its propaganda were closed. Zayas issued an order prohibiting the group from holding public meetings. On October 14, a thousand people defied him, crowding into the Fausto Theater in Havana, to hear scorching denunciations of the president. Then the Zayas government attempted to arrest the leadership; some twenty were imprisoned, although not Gustavo. Others fled abroad. Chapman, *A History*, pp. 474–475. In early 1924, some members of the group attempted an armed uprising in Las Villas province. However, the revolt collapsed quickly, marking the end of the movement. They had won no concrete reforms.

22   *becoming a successful vice president:* He was vice president of Cuban Electric, the Havana subsidiary of the Electric Bond and Share Company, a large holding company for electric stocks that was controlled by J. P. Morgan & Co. Thomas, *Cuba*, p. 569; Carleton Beals, *The Crime of Cuba* (Philadelphia: J. B. Lippincott, 1933), p. 242; Pérez, *Cuba Under*, p. 257. "Secretary of *Gobernación*" was equivalent to "interior minister," providing him experience in controlling political machinery and electric light and power concessions, which he dished out right and left, including to himself. Beals, *The Crime of Cuba*, p. 242.

22   *a personal fortune with other companies:* These included a sugar mill, a construction company, a paint factory, two newspapers, *El País* and *Excelsior*, Banco del Comercio, a shoe company, a market, and the Moulin Rouge theater showing pornographic films. Pérez, *Cuba Under*, p. 261. On the court records, see Beals, *The Crime of Cuba*, pp. 241–242.

22   *the Liberal Party nominated Machado:* Thomas, *Cuba*, p. 570; Strode, *The Pageant*, p. 269.

22   *Politicians shifted allegiances:* Gustavo was invited to join the Liberal Party by Cuba's second president, José Miguel Gómez. Gómez was defeated by Zayas in a tainted election in 1920. Gómez fell ill and died June 13, 1921. In Cuba, it was said he died of a broken heart. His funeral procession was the largest

Havana had ever seen. Emilio Roig de Leuchsenring, *Social* 10, no. 9 (September 1925): 7–8.

22 *reelection was seen as the first step toward dictatorship:* Aguilar, *Cuba 1933*, pp. 62–63. The quote not "one single day longer" is from Fitzgibbon, *Cuba and the United States*, p. 187.

22 *He had backing from the United States:* Beals, *The Crime of Cuba*, p. 243, reports that the president of the electric company, Henry Catlin, gave Machado a half-million-dollar campaign contribution, and "affiliated" interests put up another half million. Beals does not identify where the money came from but says Machado's "hand-in-glove" relationship with Catlin and US interests was a "fundamental reason" for his election. Thomas says "it seems probable" the first contribution occurred, p. 570. Fitzgibbon says Machado's statements about the Platt Amendment were "designed for home consumption," p. 185.

22 *No one expected him to be totally clean:* He reportedly made a deal with the outgoing president, Zayas, for help in the election. There are differing accounts; some say Machado offered Zayas three cabinet positions in the new government, others that he offered a lucrative share of lottery collectorships.

22 *Machado won five of the six provinces:* Strode, *The Pageant*, p. 264, says: "Despite falsifications, bribery, and official coercion, Machado was 'honestly' elected. Beyond doubt he was the people's choice."

22 *Two leaders of the Veterans and Patriots:* Pérez, *Cuba Under*, p. 249. He identifies the two Veterans and Patriots figures as Rogelio Zayas Bazán, who became secretary of *Gobernación*, and Enrique Hernández Cartaya, who became secretary of the treasury.

22 *just completed a book about the League of Nations:* Gustavo Gutiérrez y Sánchez, *¿Es la guerra susceptible de represión?: Examen del problema que trata de resolver la Sociedad de la Naciones* (Havana: El Siglo XX, 1925). Bustamante, his mentor, was appointed to the Permanent Court of International Justice, provided for in the Covenant of the League of Nations.

23 *profile a new generation of Cuban intellectuals:* Emilio Roig de Leuchsenring, "Notas del director literario," *Social* 10, no. 9 (September 1925): 7–8, and Gustavo Gutiérrez, "La necesidad de un mundo nuevo," p. 13.

23 *Machado was probusiness:* Thomas, *Cuba*, p. 572.

23 *the most ambitious public works program ever seen in Cuba:* Strode, *The Pageant*, p. 275. They built the road at a cost of $120,000 per mile, while Strode says it could have been done for $50,000 a mile.

23 *a new national capitol:* Machado had put Carlos Miguel de Céspedes in charge of public works. He wore round, bookish eyeglasses like Machado and threw lavish parties at his oceanfront mansion in Havana, a spread that featured an artificial island made of local coral and a menagerie and botanical garden, with monkeys, flamingos, macaws, iguanas, two lions, a bear, and exotic

flora. Céspedes and his business partners owned casinos, cabarets, bars, and hotels in Havana.

23 *a huge overrun:* Roberts, *Havana,* p. 134.

23 *an imposing symbol of Cuban statehood:* Joseph R. Hartman, *Dictator's Dreamscape: How Architecture and Vision Built Machado's Cuba and Invented Modern Havana* (Pittsburgh: University of Pittsburgh Press, 2019), pp. 29, 38–43, 80–88. Also see Carlos Miguel de Céspedes, *Republica de Cuba.*

23 *Hotel Nacional:* Erica N. Morawski, "Negotiating the Hotel Nacional de Cuba: Politics, Profits and Protest," *Journal of the Society of Architectural Historians* 78, no. 1 (March 2019): 90–108.

24 *connections with US banks, architects, and engineers:* Gustavo Ovares Gutiérrez, communications with author, 2019, 2021.

24 *a mansion in Miramar:* Visit by author, March 2019; Ovares Gutiérrez, *Despite the Oaths,* and communications with author, 2019–2020.

TWO. TO TYRANNY AND BACK

25 *the most popular president:* Thomas, *Cuba,* p. 582; Aguilar, *Cuba 1933,* p. 57.

25 *shot and killed while turning the key to his front door:* Beals, *The Crime of Cuba,* p. 273; Aguilar, *Cuba 1933,* p. 59; and Strode, *The Pageant,* p. 270. Thomas, *Cuba,* p. 574, says: "The evidence suggested that the police had been responsible, and that they were acting on Machado's orders."

26 *Machado's forces had killed no fewer than 147 people:* Thomas, *Cuba,* p. 584.

26 *Machado hinted at something sensitive to discuss:* This account is based on María Vianello's unpublished written recollections, courtesy Gustavo Ovares Gutiérrez. Machado also met with Crowder for the same purpose in February 1927. Pérez, *Cuba Under,* p. 270.

26 Machado was "savoring of dictatorship.": Thomas, *Cuba,* p. 584.

26 *The United States decided to look the other way:* In a cable May 13, 1927, Secretary of State Frank B. Kellogg informed Crowder that as a policy matter the department "does not consider that in the circumstances it would be justified in raising any objections" to proposed constitutional amendments to prolong the president's term. See *Papers Relating to the Foreign Relations of the United States, 1927,* vol. 2 (Washington, DC: U.S. Govt. Printing Office, 1942), p. 522. On a visit to Washington in April 1927, Machado told President Coolidge that he would remain in office longer. Coolidge was noncommittal. "Memorandum by the Chief of the Division of Latin American Affairs (Morgan)" notes from the Coolidge meeting with Machado, April 23, 1927. See *Papers Relating to the Foreign Relations of the United States, 1927,* vol. 2, p. 526.

27 *shark-infested waters:* Beals, *The Crime of Cuba,* p. 270.

27 *making the Cuban president's term six years instead of four:* Aguilar, *Cuba 1933,* pp. 62–67, 86.

27   *Gustavo was bitterly disappointed:* Gustavo Gutiérrez, *Constitución de la República de Cuba* (Havana: Editorial Lex, 1941), pp. 31–34. Gustavo wrote: "Public opinion appeared to be prepared to undertake a Constitutional reform to eliminate those precepts that were considered the cause of some of our evils—presidential reelection, the excessive power of the executive branch, the lack of minority representation in the Senate, undue parliamentary immunity, the adulteration of the municipal regime, the lack of guarantees for the individual rights recognized by the Constitution, etc.—and introduce in the Constitution new ideas—such as a woman's right to vote, corporate representation, and a more technical public administration—as well as the long-standing yet constantly rekindled yearning for a parliamentary system. . . . However, when that time came, the political entities charged with making the reform a reality added an unpopular amendment that extended the powers of public officials in elected positions at the time of the reform, and they tanked the proposals that had been languishing in the legislative bodies, until 1927." On Bustamante: Jaime Suchlicki, *Historical Dictionary of Cuba*, 2nd. ed. (Lanham, MD: Scarecrow Press, 2001), p. 537.

27   *Gustavo had business ties to the government:* On August 16, 1929, Gutiérrez was involved in signing land deeds for the new Hotel Nacional. A photo shows a group of about two dozen businessmen and Cuban government officials crowded into an underground bunker, known as the Santa Clara Battery, a fortification dating from colonial times, on a hill overlooking the sea at Havana's Vedado district. A table in front of them was strewn with legal documents, stamps, and seals. Gutiérrez, in his white linen dril cien, stood in the center of the group, close to the public works secretary, Carlos Miguel de Céspedes, maestro of Machado's grandiose and expensive building boom. The meeting was to sign the papers for land—adjacent to the bunker—on which the magnificent hotel would be constructed. The $300 million hotel was to be marked by luxury, a self-congratulatory monument to Machado. The plans required an opulent suite for the president's guests of honor. Gustavo's presence shows that he was still working closely with the Machado government, most likely helping to facilitate the contracts with the National Cuban Hotel Corporation, a conglomerate of US firms that handled the financing, engineering, design, and construction, all under Machado's careful watch. Photo courtesy Gustavo Ovares Gutiérrez.

28   *a farce, not democracy:* The elections "were fraudulent in that the returns were prepared without regard to any votes cast and that nobody, or practically nobody, voted at the polls," wrote a US consul in Cuba. The chargé d'affaires at the US Embassy, C. B. Curtis, reported that events indicated "more and more that President Machado has developed into a Latin-American dictator of a type not far removed from the worst." Pérez, *Cuba Under*, p. 278.

28 *a bronze bas-relief square panel*: The role of Enrique García Cabrera is noted by Alberto Camacho, "El Capitolio Nacional," *Colegio de Arquitectos*, Havana, May 1929, pp. 9–32. The brass panels were forged by Richard Struyf of Belgium, who contributed other works as well.

28 *He and María traveled extensively*: María estimated they made fifty-one overseas trips together in Gustavo's lifetime. Vianello, unpublished recollections, courtesy Gustavo Ovares Gutiérrez.

28 *"catch up to that car of progress and modernity that has gotten a little ahead of us"*: Gutiérrez made the remark in 1933 at his swearing-in as secretary of justice. Courtesy Gustavo Ovares Gutiérrez.

28 *"Toward a Culture in Pursuit of Truth"*: Gutiérrez became the journal's director, and he assembled prominent board members, including the poet Rubén Martínez Villena, novelist Alejo Carpentier, and the historian Ramiro Guerra, whose book *Sugar and Society in the Caribbean*, exposing the big business of sugar plantations on the island, had shaped the thinking of Gustavo and his friends. *Revista* was published at the same time as *Avance*, a literary journal begun by five writers in 1927, also serving as a megaphone for the young intellectuals.

29 *speed, elegance, simplicity*: Revista de La Habana I, no. 1 (January 1930): 1–7.

29 *many were jobless and deeply frustrated*: Pérez, *Cuba Under*, p. 253, 257; Buell, *Problems*, pp. 52–54. The population estimates are for 1931.

29 *armed thugs invaded*: Beals, *The Crime of Cuba*, p. 245.

30 *The closure of the university*: "Política," *Revista de La Habana* IV, no. 12 (December 1930): 317–330.

30 *Military censors gagged the newspapers*: On October 17, 1930, Cuban journalists wrote an open letter to Machado, published in Gustavo's journal. They said *La Voz*, a newspaper, had been banned "due to the strange allegation that it slandered the President of the Republic when it had not even gone to print." The police smashed the printing press before the first edition could be run. Machado's police ransacked newsrooms and confiscated print runs. The letter said censorship was pervasive in Cuba. Newspapers were constantly having to redraw their pages to account for articles rejected by the censors. This was wrong, they declared, in a country that had sacrificed so much for "the sublime ideals of democracy and freedom." Gustavo added, at the bottom: The *Revista* agreed. "From the Press Association to the President of the Republic," *Revista de La Habana* IV, no. 11 (November 1930): 190.

30 *They killed, assaulted, and tortured*: Strode, *The Pageant*, pp. 288–289.

31 *"Don't shoot"*: Ruby Hart Phillips, *Cuba: Island of Paradox* (New York: McDowell, Obolensky, 1959), p. 8. This book builds on Phillips's *Cuban Sideshow* (Havana: Cuban Press, 1935).

31 *The thugs beat and slashed them savagely*: Beals, *The Crime of Cuba*, pp. 285–287.

31   *a fragmented opposition:* It included students, the *directorio*, and a leftist splinter group, Ala Izquierda Estudiantil, or Student Left Wing; Communists; and the odd-couple pair of Menocal, the former president, and Mendieta, the newspaper columnist who had once called him a vulgar dictator. The old-guard politicians tried to launch an armed rebellion against Machado in August 1931 but were quickly crushed. See Aguilar, *Cuba 1933*, pp. 107–111.

31   *a clandestine organization known as ABC:* Strode, *The Pageant*, p. 287. The murder was carried out by seven men sent by Arsenio Ortiz, chief of military police in Havana, one of Machado's most terrifying extrajudicial killers.

31   *Havana echoed with bomb blasts:* Beals, *The Crime of Cuba*, p. 312; Phillips, *Cuba*, p. 49.

32   *a long shadow over Cuba:* Strode, *The Pageant*, p. 294.

32   *A decision that is difficult to explain:* Vianello, unpublished recollections; "Speech Given by Dr. Gustavo Gutiérrez on June 26, 1933, on the Occasion of Being Sworn In as Secretary of Justice," courtesy Gustavo Ovares Gutiérrez. Gustavo's thinking was described by his daughter Yolanda and Gustavo Ovares Gutiérrez, communication with author, January 19, 2021.

32   *Assistant Secretary of State Sumner Welles:* Benjamin Welles, *Sumner Welles: FDR's Global Strategist* (New York: St Martin's Press, 1997), pp. 158–164.

33   *Havana was gripped by fear:* Strode, *The Pageant*, p. 301.

33   *officers told him he must resign:* Phillips, *Cuba*, p. 37, recounts an interview with Capt. Torres Menier, a witness. Also see Thomas, *Cuba*, pp. 623–625; Aguilar, *Cuba 1933*, pp. 149–150; and Strode, *The Pageant*, pp. 305–307.

33   *Hungry looters ransacked:* "Wild Disorder in Havana," *New York Times*, August 13, 1993, p. 1. Also see Strode, *The Pageant*, pp. 304–309; Thomas, *Cuba*, pp. 630–631.

33   *Mobs began a violent spasm of revenge:* Armando de Córdova y Quesada, "La neurosis colectiva consecutiva a la caída del gobierno del general Machado," in *La locura en Cuba* (Havana: Seoane, Fernández, 1940), pp. 105–118.

34   *defaced with deep, angry slash marks:* Alberto Camacho, "El Capitolio Nacional," *Revista Mensual de Arquitectura* 13, no. 5 (May 1929): 932. According to Hartman, *Dictator's*, p. 37, the scenes were created largely by Cabrera, portraying Cuba's national history and ex-presidents. Also, author's observations, March 2019, and discussions with staff of Capitolio restoration project.

34   *professors were ousted from the University of Havana:* Vianello, unpublished recollections; Ovares Gutiérrez, *Despite the Oaths* and communications with author. Bustamante was reinstated in 1936.

34   *María kept their spirits lifted:* Ovares Gutiérrez, *Despite the Oaths* and interviews with author. On sale of the house, Montalvo collection, Cuban Heritage Collection, University of Miami, Coral Gables, Florida.

35   *Two distinct forces rose to take power:* Frank Argote-Freyre, *Fulgencio Batista:*

From Revolutionary to Strongman (New Brunswick, NJ: Rutgers University Press, 2006); Aguilar, *Cuba 1933*, p. 172; Thomas, *Cuba*, pp. 634–649; Strode, *The Pageant*, p. 315.

35 *Céspedes was removed in a bloodless coup:* Argote-Freyre, *Fulgencio Batista*, p. 74.

36 *the revolution of 1933:* Aguilar, *Cuba 1933*, pp. 174–182; Thomas, *Cuba*, pp. 650–657; Argote-Freyre, *Fulgencio Batista*, pp. 91–94.

36 *Grau's rapid-fire decrees led to near anarchy:* Aguilar, *Cuba 1933*, p. 178.

36 *deposed army officers staged an armed uprising:* Thomas, *Cuba*, pp. 658–665; Argote-Freyre, *Fulgencio Batista*, p. 100.

37 *the Auténticos:* Ilan Ehrlich, "Old and New Politics in Cuba: Revisiting Young Eddy Chibás, 1927–1940," *Cuban Studies* 45, no. 1 (2017): 227–250; "The Chargé in Cuba (Matthews) to the Secretary of State," Doc. No. 376, *Foreign Relations of the United States, Diplomatic Papers, 1934, The American Republics* 5 (January 22, 1934).

37 *recognized by the United States:* Telegram, "The Secretary of State to the Personal Representative of the President (Caffery)," *Foreign Relations of the United States, Diplomatic Papers, 1934, The American Republics* 5 (January 23, 1934).

37 *Three men held the office of Cuba's president:* They were Carlos Mendieta, Miguel Mariano Gómez, and Federico Laredo Brú.

37 *the army had taken control:* Louis A. Pérez Jr., *Army Politics in Cuba: 1898–1958* (Pittsburgh: University of Pittsburgh Press, 1976), pp. 101–115. On the fractured politics, see Russell H. Fitzgibbon and H. Max Healey, "The Cuban Elections of 1936," *American Political Science Review* 30, no. 4 (August 1936): 724–735. Also see Argote-Freyre, *Fulgencio Batista*, on Batista's rule through these provisional presidents.

37 *suppressing a general strike:* Thomas, *Cuba*, p. 750. Argote-Freyre, *Fulgencio Batista*, p. 175, says reports of a larger death toll from the strike, in the hundreds, which appeared at the time, are not true.

37 *confronted and killed Antonio Guiteras:* Guiteras had been active in the student *directorio* that fought Machado, and formed Joven Cuba to bring radical change to Cuba, creating a "revolutionary dictatorship," with land reform, nationalizations, and more attention to education and literacy. In April 1935, he organized the kidnapping of Eutimio Falla Bonet, scion of a wealthy and prominent Cuban family, and planned to use some of the ransom money, which he received, to organize a force of trained guerrillas and fight Batista. He was encircled and shot May 8, 1935, by the army when preparing to escape to Mexico. Argote-Freyre, *Fulgencio Batista*, pp. 178–185, notes that some have lionized Guiteras as a brave revolutionary and others described him as a gangster.

38 *"how far Cuba was from anything resembling democracy":* Argote-Freyre, *Fulgencio Batista*, p. 231.

38 *saw clearly the horrors of Machado's despotism:* Gutiérrez wrote this reflection

August 5, 1937, in a preface to the printed text of "La nueva ruta," a keynote speech to the Liberal Party convention.

38   *climb back into the political arena:* On January 10, 1934, Gustavo bluntly warned the Machado exile crowd in Miami—the old Liberals—not to return. He went to Miami, accompanied by Juan Antonio Vázquez Bello, brother of the slain Senate president Clemente Vázquez Bello. Both Gustavo and Juan Antonio were from the old Liberal Party, which at that point had been banned by a Grau decree, but Gustavo was clearly thinking about the future. The two men surprised a gathering of exiles from the Machado regime. Gutiérrez spoke to them bluntly, delivering a "truth, difficult and cruel," as a journalist put it. Gutiérrez said the Liberals "did not want anything to do at all" with the old bosses. They should not come home soon, Gustavo insisted. They weren't wanted anymore. The reaction from the exiles was not friendly. Unsigned, "La moral del Machadismo en el exilio," *Bohemia*, March 4, 1934, p. 18.

38   *he began to write a new constitution for Cuba:* Ramón Vasconcelos and Gustavo Gutiérrez, *El Partido Liberal al pueblo de Cuba*, Havana, November 5, 1934. The author surmises the quoted passages were written by Gustavo, based on similarity with his other writings, but Vasconcelos may also have drafted it.

39   *Ramón Vasconcelos:* Vasconcelos was at the time compiling columns he wrote in *El País* about the Machado era into a book, *Dos años bajo el terror: Revolución y desintegración* (Havana: Cultural, 1935.)

39   *sending back reports on radical student exiles:* Vasconcelos's activity was described by Chibás in documents made public in 1945. See Luis Conte Agüero, *Eduardo Chibás: El adalid de Cuba* (Miami, FL: La Moderna Poesia, 1987), pp. 341–347. Also see Thomas, *Cuba*, p. 820.

39   *the Liberal Party, but reduced in size and influence:* A decree prohibited some high-ranking members of the Machado regime from taking part in politics, but not Gustavo. Law No. 169, imposed by decree of President Carlos Mendieta, May 23, 1935, barred from politics members of the Congress that approved the Machado amendment, members of the 1928 Constituent Assembly that approved the Machado power grab, and some high-ranking officials of that period. The law did not name specific individuals. The list did not cover cabinet members like Gustavo. See Fitzgibbon and Healy, "The Cuban Elections," p. 727, and *Gaceta oficial de la República de Cuba, Edición Extraordinaria*, no. 66 (May 23, 1935).

39   *Gustavo's draft constitution:* In preparation, he also studied constitutions from the Soviet Union, 1918 and 1936; Germany, 1919; Austria, 1920; Spain, 1931; and Uruguay and Brazil, 1934. He took from these the need to add sections on guaranteeing social rights. Gustavo Ovares Gutiérrez, communication with author, January 19, 2021.

39   *The right of legislative initiative:* Vasconcelos and Gutiérrez, *El Partido Liberal,* p. 28.

39   *reduced the number of required signatures for a citizen initiative to one thousand people:* Gustavo Gutiérrez y Sánchez, "La convención constituyente y la Constitución de 1940," in *Historia de la Nación Cubana,* vol. 8, ed. Ramiro Guerra y Sánchez et al. (La Habana: Editorial Historia de la Nación Cubana, S. A., 1952), p. 178.

40   *the requirement for a citizen initiative was ten thousand signatures:* Andrés M. Lazcano y Mazón, *Las constituciones de Cuba* (Madrid: Ediciones Cultura Hispánica, 1952), p. 801.

40   *Gustavo was elected to the House:* The midterm election May 3, 1938, was to fill one-half the seats in the House. After the vote, the Liberal Party held twenty-five of the eighty-three seats in the chamber. Dieter Nohlen, ed., *Elections in the Americas: A Data Handbook,* vol. 1 (Oxford: Oxford University Press, 2005), pp. 195–222.

40   *Batista proceeded to transform himself:* Argote-Freyre, *Fulgencio Batista,* pp. 230–274, and Irwin F. Gellman, *Roosevelt and Batista* (Albuquerque: University of New Mexico Press, 1973), pp. 172–173. Also, Pérez, *Army Politics in Cuba,* p. 117, notes that "to a considerable extent, Batista relied on the old *machadista* machines," including some former members of Congress under Machado.

41   *the fairest in the history of the Cuban republic:* Argote-Freyre, *Fulgencio Batista,* pp. 262–264; Thomas, *Cuba,* pp. 716–723; Gellman, *Roosevelt,* pp. 159–183.

41   *Grau's forces won a victory over Batista:* The vote was 514,343 for Batista's coalition to 529,7000 for Grau's. Candidates from the Liberal Party, led by Vasconcelos and with Gutiérrez's active participation, won 179,239 votes, the largest single amount in Batista's group. Gellman, *Roosevelt,* p. 173. Overall, voters were asked to pick 76 delegates from a field of 816 candidates put up by eleven parties. "Cubans Set to Elect New Assembly Today," *New York Times,* November 15, 1939, p. 9.

41   *resigned from the army:* Argote-Freyre, *Fulgencio Batista,* p. 264, says: "Military noninterference in a national election was a singular accomplishment in Cuban history up to that point. Since the beginning of the Cuban republic in 1902, the armed forces had played a crucial role in rigging virtually every national election. This election was different, and there was great hope throughout Cuba that the presidential elections would be carried out in a similar fashion."

41   *"a melting pot come to a boil":* Gutiérrez y Sánchez, "La convención," pp. 138–39.

41   *the public gallery was packed:* Gellman, *Roosevelt,* p. 180.

41   Bohemia, *published a running chronicle:* "En la Asamblea Constituyente," *Bohemia,* February 18, 1940, pp. 28–29.

41 *an atmosphere of high-mindedness:* Carlos Márquez Sterling, "Perspectiva histórica de la Constituyente de 1940," in Néstor Carbonell Cortina, *Grandes debates de la Constituyente Cubana de 1940* (Miami: Ediciones Universal, 2001), pp. 39–62. Also, Constituent Assembly proceedings in *Diario de sesiones de la Convención Constituyente* 1 and 2 (1940).

42 *"This assembly represents the destiny of Cuba":* Diario de sesiones de la Convención Constituyente 1, no. 3 (February 14, 1940): 5.

42 *Jorge Mañach:* Diario de sesiones de la Convención Constituyente 1, no. 1 (February 9, 1940): 7–9.

42 *José Manuel Cortina:* Diario de sesiones de la Convención Constituyente 1, no. 1 (February 9, 1940): 9–13.

42 *a seventeen-member umbrella coordinating committee, led by Cortina:* Diario de sesiones de la Convención Constituyente 1, no. 19 (March 25, 1940): 12.

42 *"Cuban politics is pretty rotten":* Argote-Freyre, *Fulgencio Batista*, p. 270; Gellman, *Roosevelt*, p. 181.

42 *When Grau tried to resign in protest, it was rejected:* "Un alto ejemplo de democracia," *Noticias de Hoy*, March 24, 1940.

43 *a "formal and irrevocable" resignation:* Diario de sesiones de la Convención Constituyente 1, no. 40 (May 17, 1940): 11.

43 *José Manuel Cortina rose to the moment:* Diario de sesiones de la Convención Constituyente 1, no. 40 (May 17, 1940): 1, 11–13.

43 *written expressly to limit the power of the executive:* Wyatt MacGaffey and Clifford R. Barnett, *Twentieth Century Cuba: The Background of the Castro Revolution* (New York: Anchor, 1965), p. 131.

43 *debated the death penalty, habeas corpus, equality before the law:* Carbonell Cortina, *Grandes Debates.*

43 *Cuba had been awash in Nazi propaganda:* According to Phillips, there were thousands of Spaniards in Cuba who were sympathetic to Franco and the Nazis and Nazi propaganda was distributed by Cuba's Communists. Phillips, *Cuba*, p. 197.

43 *outlaw organizations with "totalitarian tendencies":* Diario de sesiones de la Convención Constituyente 1, no. 34 (May 10, 1940): 5–23. The vote was quite narrow, 26–25. The provision became Article 37.

43 *the right of people to resist with force:* Diario de sesiones de la Convención Constituyente 1, no. 28 (May 3, 1940): 24–25; summary, 1, no. 33 (May 9, 1940): 3–4.

43 *The Assembly rushed to finish:* Gutiérrez y Sánchez, "La Convención," pp. 179–80.

43 *included 61 sections:* Gellman, *Roosevelt*, p. 181.

44 *the power of initiative:* Leónel-Antonio de la Cuesta, *Constituciones cubanas: Desde 1812 hasta nuestros días* (New York: Ediciones Exilio, 1974), p. 272. Gutiérrez said key debates occurred within the *secciones* and there were

disagreements on texts with the Coordinating Committee, but records of those deliberations have never been made public. Article 135 passed through Sección VI, Organización del Estado, which was chaired by Joaquín Martínez Sáenz, of the ABC party. According to Gutiérrez, the assembly spent only one session on Sección VI, Organización del Estado. The provision for ten thousand signatures does not appear to have been altered at any point during the process. Gutiérrez y Sánchez, "La Convención," pp. 147–148, 179–180.

44 *the throngs gathered at the Capitolio:* "Ante una nutrida concurrencia popular fue promulgada la nueva carta constitucional," *Hoy,* July 6, 1940, p. 1; "Promulgada la nueva Constitución," *Bohemia,* July 14, 1940, p. 35.

45 *a genuine blueprint:* Gustavo Gutiérrez y Sánchez, *Constitucion de la república de cuba: Promulgada el día 5 de julio de 1940. Sus antecedentes históricos. Su espíritu. Estudio crítico sobre sus más fundamentales principios* (Havana: Editorial Lex, 1941), pp. 44–87. Of the 286 articles, 61 covered economic and social matters. Gutiérrez was dissatisfied with provisions of the new constitution that would allow its guarantees to be suspended for a national security emergency. He feared it could be misused. Section II of Title IV said in cases where the security of the state requires it, the constitution's guarantees can be suspended for a period of not more than forty-five days. Title XVIII allows for a state of emergency in which the government can exercise extraordinary powers if external security or domestic order of the nation is in danger (Articles 281–284.) See International Commission of Jurists, *Cuba and the Rule of Law* (Geneva: ICJ, 1962), pp. 79, 82. For more on the political structure of the new constitution, see MacGaffey and Barnett, *Twentieth Century Cuba,* pp. 125–165.

45 *the Constitution of 1940 formally promulgated:* Diario de sesiones de la Convención Constituyente 11, no. 84 (July 5, 1940): pp. 1–4.

46 *Batista won, defeating Grau:* The vote was 805,125 to 583,526, according to Gellman, *Roosevelt,* p. 183. "Cuban Congress Elects: Mendieta, Ex-Mayor of Havana, Chosen to Preside in Senate," *New York Times,* November 22, 1940, p. 7.

46 *he drafted and introduced an electoral code:* Gutiérrez submitted the draft to the House in April 1941. It was signed into law May 31, 1943. On direct election, see Rafael Rojas, *Historia mínima de la revolución cubana* (Madrid: Turner, 2015), p. 14; for an analysis, see Gustavo Gutiérrez Sánchez, *Código electoral* (Havana: Editorial Lex, 1943).

46 *Batista did little:* Batista did make one important contribution: he began to gradually assert civilian control over the military, which had enjoyed such dominance in the 1930s. Pérez, *Army Politics in Cuba,* p. 121.

46 *Disenchanted, he stepped down:* Gustavo resigned as Speaker but kept his House seat through the term. A reason for the poor attendance in 1941 was a political deal struck the year before that allowed half of the old Congress to serve out their remaining terms as well as install the new members elected

after adoption of the new constitution. This created an inflated membership in the chamber, and many members simply didn't show up. "Cuban's Resignation Accepted," *New York Times*, October 28, 1941, p. 10; Gellman, Roosevelt, pp. 177–178; Ovares Gutiérrez, *Despite the Oaths*. A writer for the magazine *Carteles* observed: "He could not obtain a 'quorum' for any constructive, essential, or establishing law. The President was tired of sending messages to Congress about laws that were urgent or vital, many of which concerned the Cuban economy or international affairs. . . . It wasn't long before the President of the House resigned due to the impossibility of getting the body to meet to study and vote on the laws that the Republic urgently called for." Montalvo, "The Forgotten Man," citing Alfredo T. Quílez, *Carteles*, October 18, 1941.

47 *Gustavo's proposed global bill of rights:* Gustavo Gutiérrez, *La carta magna de la comunidad de las naciones* (Havana: Editorial Lex, 1945), pp. 474–491. At the time the book was published, Gustavo took part in a major international conference of twenty Latin American governments and the United States in Mexico City on February 21, 1945. Gustavo's proposals were advanced by the Cuban delegation at the conference. On February 12, 1946, the Cuban delegation proposed to the U.N. General Assembly that it create a Declaration on Human Rights. The Cuban draft had twenty-two points, sixteen of which were similar to Gustavo's proposal in *La carta magna*. Both Gustavo's ideas and the Cuban draft were reflected in the final Universal Declaration of Human Rights. Cuba's chief delegate, Guy Pérez Cisneros, praised the final declaration in a speech December 10, 1948, and Cuba can rightly claim to have provided early impetus to the declaration. On the drafts, see Evelina Skagerlind, *Cuba Made the First Draft in the Making of the Universal Declaration of Human Rights* (term paper, Lund University, Spring 2019). Later, when the drafting was underway, seven private drafts were among those considered, including Gustavo's. See https://drgustavogutierrez.blogspot.com/. On the Cisneros speech, see https://www.cubanet.org/htdocs/ref/dis/05200202 .html. Samuel Moyn, in *The Last Utopia: Human Rights in History* (Cambridge: Belknap Press, 2010), notes that the 1948 declaration was overshadowed by the global competition of the Cold War that followed and human rights came to the fore only in the 1970s.

47 *he felt the constitution was in danger of becoming "ineffective":* In 1941, Gustavo wrote of the new constitution: ". . . the people must be its most zealous guardian." He added: "Cuba's problem, Cuba's great problem, is a problem of faith. All of us who are influenced by that feeling must join a great crusade to overcome whatever difficulties cross our paths to resolve those problems that have afflicted Cuba since it achieved its independence. Those who have lost faith in the country's destiny should move out of the way, because, as citizens, the smallest sacrifice they could make for the good of the Republic

is to not hinder a period of revitalization in which the nation's highest and most essential interests are at stake." Gutiérrez y Sánchez, *Constitución de la República*, pp. 61–62. On June 9, 1944, Gustavo made a presentation at a conference sponsored by the Institute of Spanish-Cuban Culture, titled "The Ineffective Constitution," at which he lamented the lack of action. A conference report published by the institute quoted Gustavo as saying, "The four years [the constitution] has been in effect are enough to bring light to a serious problem that has begun to develop, which could nullify a great deal of the essential text: the lack of complementary legislation and the tendency of the three branches of the State—the Executive, the Legislature, and the Judiciary—to shirk their new constitutional duties . . . it must be acknowledged that, despite its merits, the new Constitution hardly works at all. It is truly ineffective." He pointed out that the semi-parliamentary system so carefully drafted to prevent excessive presidential action had hardly been used; in four years there had not been a single case in which the apathetic Congress had tried to check the president's power. Nor had Congress passed the legislation to enable the social goals of the constitution, such as the minimum wage. The new electoral code was not passed until two years after Gutiérrez introduced it.

THREE. "BITE, ROOSTER!"

48   *his outrage building and spilling out onto the pages:* Luis Conte Agüero, *Eduardo Chibás: El adalid de Cuba* (Mexico City: Editorial Jus, 1955; repr., Miami: La Moderna Poesia, 1987), pp. 340–341, 363. Conte Agüero was a friend of Chibás and secretary of the Ortodoxos Party. Also see Charles D. Ameringer, *The Cuban Democratic Experience: The Auténtico Years, 1944–1952* (Gainesville: University Press of Florida, 2000), p. 42.

49   *He had one preoccupation: to clean up Cuba's soiled politics and dysfunctional government:* Ilan Ehrlich, *Eduardo Chibás: The Incorrigible Man of Cuban Politics* (Lanham, MD: Rowman & Littlefield, 2015), is an excellent work on Chibás, especially the Ortodoxo years, 1947–1951. Also see Ehrlich, "Old and New Politics in Cuba: Revisiting Young Eddy Chibás, 1927–1940," *Cuba Studies*, no. 45 (2017): 227–250. During the 1940 Constituent Assembly, Chibás proposed an amendment to guarantee that radio broadcasts could not be interrupted on air, to enjoy the same free press protections as, say, newspapers. But other delegates thought this would give radio a special status, and it was rejected. In the end, the constitution stated: "All persons shall have freedom to express their thoughts by speech, writing, or any other graphic or oral means of expression without prior censure" and "utilizing for this purpose any and all means of dissemination available." That included radio. *Diario de sesiones de la Convención Constituyente* 1, no. 28 (May 3, 1940): 18–24.

49 *Cubans got far more news, culture, and entertainment from radio:* Michael B. Salwen, *Radio and Television in Cuba: The Pre-Castro Era* (Ames: Iowa State University Press, 1994). By 1959, Cuba had 176 receivers per 1,000 population, second only to Uruguay, with 189, p. 70. On radio vs. newspapers, see table 2.1, p. 24.

50 *cheering him on with whoops of "¡Pica, gallo!" or "Bite, rooster!":* Ehrlich, *Eduardo Chibás,* pp. 20–21.

51 *"Let there be candy for everyone.":* Mary Speck, "Let There Be Candy for Everyone: Reform, Regulation, and Rent-Seeking in the Republic of Cuba, 1902–1952," Association for the Study of the Cuban Economy, November 30, 2002; Jorge I. Domínguez, *Cuba: Order and Revolution* (Cambridge, MA: Harvard University Press, 1978), p. 108.

51 *a thirty-minute program on CMQ radio:* Salwen, *Radio and Television in Cuba,* p. 71.

51 *"What have you done, bandit":* Lillian Guerra, *Heroes, Martyrs and Political Messiahs in Revolutionary Cuba, 1946–1958* (New Haven: Yale University Press, 2018), pp. 44–45.

51 *he denounced cabinet members for profiteering:* Ehrlich, *Eduardo Chibás,* pp. 13–14.

51 *a cool $19 million:* Ehrlich, *Eduardo Chibás,* p. 83; Thomas, *Cuba,* p. 758.

52 *Chibás broke with Grau entirely:* Ehrlich, *Eduardo Chibás,* pp. 12–16. The letter was dated January 19, 1947. Ehrlich, *Eduardo Chibás,* p. 10. A portion of the text is reproduced in Conte Agüero, *Eduardo Chibás,* pp. 476–478. *Diario de la Marina* published the text in its entirely on January 21, 1947.

52 *apostle of the black market, botellas, and corruption:* Ameringer, *Auténtico Years,* p. 69.

52 *The Cuban People's Party, known as the Ortodoxos:* Ehrlich, *Eduardo Chibás,* p. 23.

52 *His name was Fidel Castro:* Ehrlich, *Eduardo Chibás,* p. 18.

52 *He came in third, with 16.4 percent of the vote:* Guerra, *Heroes,* pp. 60–61.

52 *demolished all formal barriers between candidate and voter:* Ehrlich, *Eduardo Chibás,* p. 78.

53 *difficult for him to distinguish between liberty and license:* Thomas, *Cuba,* p. 759.

53 *The files and the thieves were never found:* Ameringer, *Auténtico Years,* pp. 111–112; Ehrlich, "Eduardo Chibás: The Incorrigible Man of Cuban Politics" (PhD dissertation, City University of New York, 2009), pp. 331–339.

53 *small, murderous squads:* In 1947, two leaders of the action groups, both Grau police appointees, confronted each other in a bloody shootout in Orfila, a prosperous neighborhood in the Marianao section of Havana. As bullets rained for hours, a radio reporter conveyed live accounts and a news cameraman captured the bloodshed. Although the authorities tried to hush up the film, Chibás managed to sneak a screening and on his radio show courageously described the horrifying scenes, including that of one leader,

supposedly a police official, who surrendered with $14,000 inside his shoes. Ehrlich, *Eduardo Chibás*, pp. 30–31.

54   *loosely implicated in several assassination attempts:* Accounts differ on Castro's involvement. Jonathan M. Hansen, *Young Castro: The Making of a Revolutionary* (New York: Simon & Schuster, 2019), says that Castro was framed for the killing of Manolo Castro by gangster Rolando Masferrer and that after Fidel was arrested and given a paraffin test, which proved negative, he was released. Hansen quotes others as saying Castro had nothing to do with it. Robert E. Quirk, *Fidel Castro: The Full Story of his Rise to Power, His Regime, His Allies, and His Adversaries* (New York: W. W. Norton, 1993), p. 25, says that Fidel "had been seen in the area at the time of the assassination, and although he was arrested and taken into custody, he was never charged. The police allegedly could find no evidence that linked him directly to the crime." Antonio Rafael de la Cova, *The Moncada Attack: Birth of the Cuban Revolution* (Columbia: University of South Carolina Press, 2007), pp. 18–19, 26, 31, says Fidel was a "triggerman" in several attempted murders, arrested and released for the homicides of Manolo de Castro and Óscar Fernández Caral, but never convicted; cases were dropped for lack of evidence. Some accounts also say Fidel shot a gang leader, Leónel Gómez, who was injured but not killed, but others claim that is not correct. See Enrique Ovares, interview with Antonio de la Cova, April 8, 1990, p. 11, http://www.latinamericanstudies.org/ovares/Ovares.pdf.

54   *more a foot soldier than chieftain:* Quirk, *Fidel*, p. 29. "In the 'gangster' groups he tagged along, was at no time one of the leaders."

54   *a violent mass protest in Bogotá:* Quirk, *Fidel*, p. 27.

54   *Fidel created a political splinter group, Acción Radical Ortodoxo:* Leycester Coltman, *The Real Fidel Castro* (New Haven: Yale University Press, 2003), p. 51.

54   *"I don't like people to see me with a gangster":* Ameringer, *Auténtico Years*, p. 45.

54   *Fidel campaigned for Chibás in 1948:* Rolando E. Bonachea and Nelson P. Valdés, *Cuba in Revolution* (Garden City, NY: Anchor, 1972), pp. 26–29.

54   *his wealthy father controlled valuable votes in Oriente:* Ilan Ehrlich, communication with author, August 1, 2019.

55   *Chibás dove headfirst:* Ehrlich, *Eduardo Chibás*, p. 61.

55   *the most powerful opposition voice in Cuba:* A political brawler, Chibás also fought at least nine duels with those who challenged him. Duels were prohibited by law, but that had not stopped politicians and journalists from defending their honor with swords or pistols, usually outside Havana, and if someone was injured, the newspaper accounts said they were hurt "while examining weapons." A room in the Capitolio, largely hidden, was used for fencing. A professor in charge of the room had presided over hundreds of duels. Phillips, *Cuba: Land of Paradox*, p. 209.

55 *when Chibás was at the microphone, those present included the admiring young Fidel:* A photo published in *Bohemia* documents one such occasion.

55 *Prío responded with censorship:* Prío had also closed the Communist Party newspaper *Hoy* in August 1950. Ameringer, *Auténtico Years*, p. 114. The radio decree was No. 2273, originally hatched by Communications Minister Sergio Clark and Justice Minister Óscar Gans to curry favor with Prío, who was looking for a new mechanism for suppressing media criticism. Ehrlich, *Eduardo Chibás*, p. 179. On the Prío promise, see Ehrlich, *Eduardo Chibás*, p. 199. When Masferrer was to speak, the Ortodoxos summoned followers to CMQ studios on Sunday, February 18, to block him. The Ortodoxos cited Article 40 of the constitution, which said that "adequate resistance" was legitimate to protect constitutional rights. Police cordoned off a five-block radius around the studios. Chibás addressed his followers from a news truck, urging them to stay calm and refrain from violence. A confrontation ensued between Ortodoxo supporters and police in which one person was killed and thousands roughed up or injured. Eventually, Masferrer was permitted to speak on the radio. Chibás furiously blamed Prío on the air, saying he had attempted to rob him of his airtime, protected by the constitution. The affair was a serious blunder by Prío. Román Vasconcelos, who was a friend of Gutiérrez and served in the Prío cabinet, resigned over the government's attacks on free expression. See Ehrlich, *Eduardo Chibás*, pp. 197–204.

56 *"This is my last knock on your conscience!":* Conte Agüero, *El adalid*, p. 784.

56 *the suicide has never been fully explained:* Quirk, *Fidel*, p. 33: "Cynics observed that if a man plans to die, he aims at his heart or his head. Chibás had shot himself in the abdomen. They supposed that he had wanted to provide a spectacular drama that would galvanize the people, but not imperil his life."

57 *Fidel prepared five separate speeches, one for each station:* Quirk, *Fidel*, p. 33.

FOUR. THE FIREBRAND

61 *erase the taint of his gangster past:* In a 1956 article for *Bohemia*, Castro denied an association with the gangsters in earlier years. "Every time my adversaries tried the vile and selfish procedure of involving me with gangsterism, I stood resolutely against their slander," he wrote, adding: "It is extraordinary, cynical, and shameful that the sponsors, protectors and subsidizers of gangsterism should use this argument in attacking me. They could not be more barefaced!" Castro, "¡Frente a todos!," *Bohemia*, January 8, 1956, p. 81. Fidel appears to have started distancing himself from the gangsters while still at the university. He tried in the autumn of 1949 to join a group, known as the Committee of 30th of September, which sought to eliminate the influence of gangsters on the university campus. The founders of the group included Max Lesnick, who was incredulous: Fidel was one of the gangsters; now he

wanted to fight them? Fidel wanted to join so badly that he promised to no longer carry a gun on campus, to sign the group's declaration against gangsterism, and to gather up specific details about the gangs and a pact they struck with Prío, in which they pledged to refrain from violence in exchange for money and no-show jobs. According to Lesnick, a meeting was held at the university at which thirteen presidents of the different schools were present as well as several hundred others. Fidel publicly revealed the details about the pact with the gangsters. Lesnick says as a result of this disclosure, Fidel was threatened by gangsters and had to go into hiding for a while. Lesnick, interview with author Tad Szulc, Cuban Heritage Collection, University of Miami, Coral Gables, Florida. On November 13, 1949, *Bohemia* magazine termed the committee's efforts "laughable" because some members had come from the gangs and "lived harmoniously" with them. Fidel was not named, but the criticism certainly applied to him. See "En Cuba," *Bohemia*, November 13, 1949, p. 81. Coltman, in *The Real Fidel Castro*, pp. 51, 56–57, recounts the story and says the 1952 attack on Prío was a "rehash" but nevertheless caused a "considerable stir." In 1948, Fidel had married Mirta Díaz-Balart, from a prominent family, and their son, Fidelito, was born September 1, 1949, just as Fidel was approaching the committee.

61   *Fidel sifted through land records:* Fidel discovered a farm with ownership linked to Prío had expanded from 166 acres to 1,944 acres since he became president in 1948. The wealthy businessman had been charged and convicted of rape in 1944. The businessman's sentence was delayed by appeals. Prío granted a full pardon in August 1950. Fidel unearthed evidence that the businessman had transferred farms he owned to a company controlled by Prío as a payoff.

61   *in the daily newspaper* Alerta: *Alerta* was now edited by Vasconcelos, who had once headed the Liberal Party with Gutiérrez.

62   *directly from the presidential palace to each of sixty gangs:* On Fidel's muckraking against Prío, see Ameringer, *Auténtico Years*, pp. 176–177; Lionel Martin, *The Early Fidel: Roots of Castro's Communism* (Secaucus, NJ: Lyle Stuart, 1978), pp. 85–92; Szulc, *Fidel Castro*, pp. 204–206; Thomas, *Cuba*, pp. 820–821; Georgie Anne Geyer, *Guerrilla Prince: The Untold Story of Fidel Castro* (Boston: Little Brown, 1991), pp. 96–97; and Quirk, *Fidel*, p. 34.

62   *A leadership vacuum enveloped Cuba:* This weakness existed throughout the years of the republic. None of the parties "had evolved as a consistently strong contender in national or local elections, and none had developed a clear ideology of its own," concluded a CIA historical study. "Conservatives of one day would run on the ticket of the Liberals the following day. . . . Opportunism was the trademark of Cuban politics. . . . Parties were not tied rigidly to a narrow ideology, and therefore new parties could be created and old ones discarded without damage to the politicians or the political system.

It was a candidate's personal charm and rhetorical skill, not the party he represented, that were important factors in an election." Central Intelligence Agency, *Cuba, Its Institutions and Castro*, October 1974, declassified October 22, 2003, p. 35.

62 *a vigorous grassroots campaign:* Quirk, *Fidel*, p. 32; Geyer, *Guerrilla Prince*, pp. 94–95; Martin, *The Early Fidel*, pp. 87–93; Hansen, *Young Castro*, pp. 141–142.

63 *a fighter with a temper:* Fidel Castro and Ignacio Ramonet, *Fidel Castro: My Life* (New York: Scribner, 2006), pp. 46–60; Hansen, *Young Castro,* pp. 53–63; De la Cova, *Moncada*, pp. 1–31.

64 *Alexander the Great:* Georgie Anne Geyer, in *Guerrilla Prince*, pp. 41-44, wrote that Fidel was attracted to leaders of strong states who liquidated the corrupt and unruly old democracies. Brian Latell, in *History Will Absolve Me: Fidel Castro: Life and Legacy* (New York: Rosetta Books, 2016), Kindle edition, loc. 1035, says Castro's childhood warrior hero was Alexander the Great. When he changed his name after his father legitimatized his birth, Fidel chose Alejandro for a middle name, which he also used as a nom de guerre in the Sierra Maestra. Cuban intelligence officials often used it as his alias, and Fidel named three of his sons after his hero.

64 *opened the family safe:* Geyer, *Guerrilla Prince*, pp. 33, 42. Latell found that Fidel never expressed admiration for any democratic leaders. *History Will Absolve Me*, Kindle edition, loc. 197.

64 *"Those of us who did not have anything to do went to law school":* Quirk, *Fidel*, p. 20.

64 *loaned him money for the rent:* Hansen, *Young Castro*, p. 133. On Fidel's childhood, in addition to Hansen, see Bonachea and Valdés, *Revolutionary Struggle*, pp. 3–6; Martin, *The Early Fidel*, pp. 19–55; Szulc, *Fidel Castro*, pp. 91–203; Jules Dubois, *Fidel Castro: Rebel—Liberator or Dictator?* (Indianapolis: Bobbs-Merrill, 1959), p. 15; Quirk, *Fidel*, pp. 3–30; Geyer, *Guerrilla Prince*, pp. 3–53; Thomas, *Cuba*, pp. 803–807; Patrick Symmes, *The Boys from Dolores: Fidel Castro's Classmates from Revolution to Exile* (New York: Pantheon, 2007), pp. 79–80; and De la Cova, *Moncada*, pp. 6–7. These accounts differ in some respects on Ángel's family history. They agree that Ángel married a schoolteacher, María Argota. De la Cova gives the date as March 1911. They had two children, Lidia and Pedro Emilio. Thomas doesn't say what happened to her. Quirk says she died. De la Cova says in 1936 María left Manacas with the two children and went to Santiago de Cuba, then to Havana. Hansen agrees. De la Cova adds that Ángel became a naturalized citizen September 19, 1941, filed for divorce from María ten days later, and then married Lina Ruz on April 23, 1943, when he was sixty-seven years old. He recognized all the children with Lina on December 11, 1943.

64 *"We were growing accustomed to living within the Constitution.":* This appeared

in a mimeographed paper, *Al Acusador*, March 13, 1952, text reprinted in Bonachea and Valdés, *Revolutionary Struggle*, pp. 147–148.

64   *Prío began to implement some neglected provisions of the 1940 Constitution:* Álvarez Díaz, *A Study on Cuba*, pp. 417–418, says Prío represented "the period of the greatest volume of congressional legislation, not only as to quantity but also as to quality of laws passed."

64   *deepened public cynicism:* Pérez, *Cuba Under*, p. 288; Thomas, *Cuba*, p. 790.

65   *the highest penetration of TV sets per household in Latin America:* Salwen, *Radio and Television*; Yeidy M. Rivero, *Broadcasting Modernity: Cuban Commercial Television, 1950–1960* (Durham, NC: Duke University Press, 2015).

65   *Newspapers and magazines were also plentiful:* Kirby Smith and Hugo Llorens, "Renaissance and Decay: A Comparison of Socioeconomic Indicators in Pre-Castro and Current-Day Cuba," in *Cuba in Transition*, vol. 8, ed. Association for the Study of the Cuban Economy (Papers and proceedings, 8th Annual Meeting, Miami, August, 1998), pp. 247–259; Wyatt MacGaffey and Clifford R. Barnett, *Cuba: Its People, Its Society, Its Culture* (New Haven: Human Relations Area Files Press, 1962), pp. 221–222.

66   *a sense of duty:* Gustavo Ovares Gutiérrez, communication with author, based on recollections of Gustavo's daughter Yolanda.

66   *Batista's forces seized radio and television:* Quirk, *Fidel*, pp. 38–39; Phillips, *Cuba*, pp. 259–260; Thomas, *Cuba*, pp. 784–786.

67   *stimulate growth with government subsidies:* Michael P. McGuigan, "Fulgencio Batista's Economic Policies, 1952–1958" (PhD dissertation, University of Miami, Coral Gables, Florida, August 2012).

67   *suspended the 1940 constitution:* Batista's statute, the Constitutional Act of 1952, was issued April 4. The forty-five-day suspensions were used almost constantly after Fidel's landing in 1956 and until Batista fled Cuba at the end of December 1958. See International Commission of Jurists, *Cuba and the Rule of Law*, pp. 84–85.

67   *an eighty-member "consultative council":* Thomas, *Cuba*, pp. 784, 790.

67   *"It has been murdered.":* On April 4, some two hundred students interred a copy of the constitution before a bust of Martí in Havana. Thomas, *Cuba*, p. 794.

68   *the time had come to overthrow Batista:* De la Cova, *Moncada*, p. 32; Hansen, *Young Fidel*, p. 157.

69   *a caravan of cars packed with the fighters pulled out of the farm onto the dirt road toward the city:* This account is based on De la Cova, *Moncada*; Bonachea and Valdés, *Revolutionary Struggle*, and their text of Fidel's manifesto/speech, "History Will Absolve Me," pp. 164–221; and a parallel translation, "History Will Absolve Me" (Havana: Editorial de Ciencias Sociales, 1975). Also see

Geyer, *Guerrilla Prince*, pp. 111–129; Thomas, *Cuba*, pp. 824–844; Quirk, *Fidel*, pp. 53–59; and Ramón L. Bonachea and Marta San Martín, *The Cuban Insurrection, 1952–1959* (New Brunswick, NJ: Transaction, 1974).

70   *he went looking for Fidel:* De la Cova, *Moncada*, p. 153.

70   *a repressive "public order" law:* Phillips, *Cuba*, p. 270. The law was partially repealed on May 4, 1954. Philip W. Bonsal, former ambassador, recalls that Batista "had allowed freedom of the press until the time of Fidel Castro's assault on the Moncada barracks," in *Cuba, Castro and the United States* (Pittsburgh: University of Pittsburgh Press, 1971), p. 12.

71   *Fidel delivered an expansive defense:* Fidel claimed that his deputy, Abel Santamaría, had an eye gouged out in prison and it was presented to his horrified sister Haydée in an adjacent cell. Some historians and witnesses have called this claim of torture into question. De la Cova, *Moncada*, p. 165, says it is a legend, quoting Manuel Bartolomé, who was the funeral director who retrieved the rebel dead, including Abel Santamaría, and said he saw no sign of it. Hansen, *Young Castro*, p. 184, also suggests the story may have been exaggerated. Lillian Guerra, in *Heroes*, p. 128, reports conversations with Carlos Franqui, who was a TV reporter filming gruesome scenes at Moncada and who "confirmed the singular horror" of the account of torture.

71   *the Constitution of 1940 as the supreme law of the state:* Castro, "History Will Absolve Me," in Bonachea and Valdés, *Revolutionary Struggle*, pp. 184–185, also (Havana: Editorial de Ciencias Sociales, 1975).

73   *sentenced to fifteen years in prison:* Fidel and the others were not held in the infamous circular panopticon jail, but rather in a prison infirmary.

73   *sent many letters to Naty Revuelta:* On the Castro letters to Revuelta, see Hansen, *Young Castro*, pp. 213–263. At one point in prison, letters Castro wrote to his wife, Mirta, and his love interest Naty crossed and each received the other's letter, which produced sparks. Castro learned from a radio broadcast after this that his wife was also on the Interior Ministry payroll, which infuriated him, and they divorced. Fidel spent ten days with Naty in the summer of 1954 before leaving for Mexico. She gave birth to their daughter nine months later.

73   *the long, embellished version of his courtroom speech:* Mario Mencía, *The Fertile Prison: Fidel Castro in Batista's Jails* (Melbourne, Australia: Ocean Press, 1993), p. 107, an English translation of Mencía's original in Spanish, *La prisión fecunda*. On Fidel's reading list, see pp. 46–48.

73   *"enough time later to crush all the cockroaches together":* Ann Louise Bardach and Luis Conte Agüero, *The Prison Letters of Fidel Castro* (New York: Nation Books, 2007), p. 16, originally published in Spanish as *Cartas del presidio* (Havana: Editorial Lex, 1959).

FIVE. THE GUERRILLA

74   *he established a base on a secluded ranch outside Mexico City:* Batista sent agents
     to Mexico to spy on the guerrillas. They planned to assassinate Fidel but
     failed due to his precautions, so they urged Mexico's federal police to arrest
     them instead. Fidel was arrested June 21, and forty of his men were arrested
     June 26 at the ranch and held incommunicado on charges of illegal weapons
     possession and violating an immigration law prohibiting conspiracy against
     other governments. The men were beaten and badly treated before being
     released on July 25. Then, in late November, Mexico's federal police seized a
     weapons cache. Castro was tipped off to move quickly or he, too, would be
     arrested. Fidel ordered his men to scramble to Tuxpan. Bonachea and Valdés,
     Revolutionary Struggle, pp. 80–81.

75   *people did not rise up, and País was arrested:* "En Cuba: Santiago de Cuba," *Bo-
     hemia,* December 9, 1956, pp. 56–60; Steve Cushion, *A Hidden History of the
     Cuban Revolution: How the Working Class Shaped the Guerrilla's Victory* (New
     York: Monthly Review Press, 2016), p. 125.

76   *a tiny band in a remote wilderness:* Of the 82 men who landed from the *Granma,*
     21 made it to the mountains, 21 were killed by the army, 21 imprisoned,14
     managed to escape entirely and joined Fidel's movement elsewhere, and 5
     were unaccounted for, probably murdered, according to Tony Perrottet, cit-
     ing a detailed study by Cuban historian Heberto Norman Acosta. See Per-
     rottet, *¡Cuba Libre!: Che, Fidel, and the Improbable Revolution that Changed World
     History* (New York: Blue Rider Press, 2019), p. 110.

76   *Fidel wanted a journalist from the United States:* Phillips's husband, James Doyle
     Phillips, known as Phil, had been the correspondent initially. While on vaca-
     tion, they were in a car wreck outside of Pomona, California, on August 23,
     1937. He was killed. Ruby Hart Phillips returned to Havana for many years as
     the *Times* correspondent.

77   *"we are fighting for a democratic Cuba":* Herbert L. Matthews, "Cuban Rebel Is
     Visited in Hideout; Castro Is Still Alive and Still Fighting in Mountains," *New
     York Times,* February 24, 1957.

78   *to negotiate a political settlement:* This was the Civic Dialogue, a series of con-
     ferences between the moderate opposition and the president. The opposi-
     tion wanted a promise of free elections with guarantees for all participants.
     Batista refused. He may have been overly complacent, given Cuba's thriving
     economy. Also, at the time he enjoyed the backing of the United States. Ba-
     tista was a regional ally against the Soviet Union in the gathering Cold War.

78   *students stepped forward and led a violent opposition:* Pérez, *Cuba Under,* p. 290.

78   *Echeverría, twenty-four years old, was every bit as persuasive and charismatic as
     Fidel:* They met once while Fidel was still in Mexico, pledging joint efforts,

but in fact Echeverría had a totally different idea. Echeverría wanted to directly decapitate the regime.

79 *The attack had utterly failed:* Echeverría's fighters arrived at the presidential palace at 3:20 p.m. in a civilian truck labeled "Fast Delivery," then made their way to Batista's office. He wasn't there; they roamed the corridors looking to kill him. Batista was eating lunch in a private study they didn't know about. Meanwhile, police and troops arrived to repulse the intruders, and the army soon rolled tanks into the center of Havana. Echeverría went to Radio Reloj, in the Radiocentro building. He announced that Batista was dead and called on people to take up arms. Unbeknownst to him, the broadcast cut off just after he said Batista was dead. The audience never heard the call to arms.

79 *"a long, toilsome expedition":* Robert Taber, *M-26: The Biography of a Revolution* (New York: Lyle Stuart, 1961), p. 135.

79 *"the Batista regime, too, is confused, disorganized":* Taber, *M-26,* p. 136.

79 *"They won't be able to defeat us":* Szulc, *Fidel Castro,* p. 420. Celia Sánchez and her father had placed a bust of Jose Martí at the mountain peak many years earlier. Taber, *M-26,* p. 11; Wendell L. Hoffman, "Yo condeno el terrorismo," *Bohemia,* May 26, 1957, pp. 70–72, 97–98; Manuel Márquez Sterling with R. Rembert Aranda, *Cuba: 1952–1959, the True Story of Castro's Rise to Power* (Wintergeen, VA: Klieopatria Digital Press, 2009), p. 111.

80 *"All guns, all bullets, and all supplies to the Sierra":* Szulc, *Fidel Castro,* p. 422; Julia Sweig, *Inside the Cuban Revolution* (Cambridge, MA.: Harvard University Press, 2002), pp. 12, 45.

80 *an indispensable coordinator for Castro:* Szulc, *Fidel Castro,* p. 422; Sweig, *Inside,* pp. 12, 45.

80 *"in the gloom of the virgin jungle":* "Raúl Chibás en la Sierra Maestra," *Bohemia,* July 14, 1957, pp. 72–73.

80 *"Sierra Manifesto":* Quirk, *Fidel,* p. 143. Sweig says that while Fidel may have been the principal author, the timing, ideas, and message of moderation were not entirely his and reflected input from others. Sweig, *Inside,* p. 33. Szulc quotes Raúl Chibás as saying Castro drafted the manifesto "totally by himself," without influence from the others. Che Guevara later wrote that it was a moderate, compromise document that he was not satisfied with but saw as necessary, given the position they were in—not particularly strong at that moment. Szulc, *Fidel Castro,* p. 425.

81 *Havana was still the moneyed playground of glitz:* Phillips, *Cuba,* p. 283.

81 *brothels multiplied through the early 1950s:* Pérez, *Cuba Under,* p. 305.

81 *more Cadillacs per capita than any other city in the world:* Ramon Eduardo Ruiz, *Cuba: The Making of a Revolution* (New York: Norton, 1970), p. 9.

82 *a city of light and luxury:* Phillips, *Cuba,* p. 335.

82   *"Fabulous casinos, nightclubs, and bordellos"*: T. J. English, *Havana Nocturne* (New York: HarperCollins, 2008), pp. 289–290.

82   *Sugar's power and curse still gripped Cuba*: McGuigan, "Fulgencio Batista's Economic Policies, 1952–1958," pp. 21–38.

82   *sense of prosperity concealed a hidden trap*: Pérez, *Cuba Under*, p. 299.

82   *the sugar harvest hit a ceiling*: An exception was a record crop of 7 million tons in 1952. Álvarez Díaz, *A Study on Cuba*, p. 481. The official price in cents per pound was 4.18 in 1948 and 4.18 in 1958.

82   *Gutiérrez . . . had devoted more and more time to economics*: Gustavo Ovares Gutiérrez, communication with author, January 20, 2021.

83   *Batista . . . was unwilling to break the sugar barony*: McGuigan, "Fulgencio Batista's Economic Policies," pp. 239–242.

83   *mirrored in every phase of Cuban life*: Thomas G. Paterson, *Contesting Castro* (Oxford: Oxford University Press, 1994), p. 41; Phillips, *Cuba*, p. 357.

83   *A stark disparity separated bustling Havana and destitute rural Cuba*: Marianne Ward and John Devereux, "The Road Not Taken: Pre-revolutionary Cuban Living Standards in Comparative Perspective," *Journal of Economic History* 72, no. 1 (2012): 104–33. Also see Francis Adams Truslow, *Report on Cuba* (Washington, DC: International Bank for Reconstruction and Development, 1951), pp. 403–449. This report offers a valuable snapshot of Cuba's development in 1950–1951 based on a fact-finding mission. Also see Kirby Smith and Hugo Llorens, "Renaissance and Decay: A Comparison of Socioeconomic Indicators in Pre-Castro and Current-Day Cuba," in Association for the Study of the Cuban Economy, ed., *Cuba in Transition*, 8: 247–259, and Pérez, *Cuba Under*, pp. 301–302.

84   *he gave the Cuban Communists room to operate*: Guerra, *Heroes*, pp. 198–217.

84   *a growing army of anonymous clandestine foes*: Guerra, *Heroes*, pp. 224–226; Sweig, *Inside*, pp. 42, 98. Also see Michelle Chase, *Revolution within the Revolution: Women and Gender Politics in Cuba, 1952–1962* (Chapel Hill: University of North Carolina Press, 2015).

84   *Batista tried to smash the underground*: Dubois, *Rebel*, p. 255.

85   *Press freedom, another pillar of democracy, withered*: When Catholic Church leaders prepared a statement suggesting Batista resign, the presidential palace applied pressure on every newspaper in Havana not to publish it. Jules Dubois, a correspondent for the *Chicago Tribune*, recalled visiting *Diario de la Marina*, one of the most influential papers, a semi-official organ of the church, and found editors there equivocating. They decided to wait a day and then printed a watered-down "clarification." Batista's pressure had worked. "A story which would have ordinarily merited an eight-column banner line on page one was given a two-column headline in some newspapers and a one-column headline in others, and played below the fold or on an inside page," Dubois wrote. Dubois, *Rebel*, p. 218.

85   *numbered Swiss bank accounts:* Pérez, *Cuba Under*, p. 303. The issue date was
       May 26, 1957.

85   *Batista deposited millions of dollars:* McGuigan, "Fulgencio Batista's Economic
       Policies," p. 235; English, *Havana*, p. 133, says some estimates were that Ba-
       tista garnered nearly $10 million a year from the hotel-casino boom.

85   *"Not to be rich was a humiliation":* Paterson, *Contesting Castro*, p. 27.

85   *Gustavo was thoroughly disgusted:* Gutiérrez wrote to his daughter Yolanda that he
       was "at ease" about his role in the Batista government. He had frequently pro-
       tested Batista's poor decisions. He added: "The regime's economic policy was
       good in that it extraordinarily increased revenues, gross national product, invest-
       ments, and employment and wage levels, but it was bad in the way the money
       was used. The responsibility lies primarily with Batista and the small privileged
       circle." Gutiérrez, letter from Buenos Aires to Yolanda Ovares, February 4, 1959,
       reproduced in Berta Gutiérrez Montalvo, "Exilio," unpublished monograph,
       Cuban Heritage Collection, University of Miami, Coral Gables, Florida.

85   *discontent spread through the ranks:* Pérez, *Cuba Under*, p. 294.

85   *suspension of arms shipments to Batista:* Dubois, *Rebel*, p. 243.

86   *"more important to us at the time than a military victory":* Guerra, *Heroes*, p. 245,
       says: "To put it mildly, foreign journalists were Castro's secret weapon." Also
       see Lillian Guerra, "Searching for the Messiah: Staging Revolution in the Sie-
       rra Maestra, 1956–1959," in *The Revolution from Within: Cuba, 1959–1980*, eds.
       Michael J. Bustamante and Jennifer L. Lambe (Durham, NC: Duke University
       Press, 2019), pp. 67–94. This article includes some of the remarkable photo-
       graphs made by St. George.

86   *amplified Fidel's message that his intention was to preserve Cuba's democracy:* An-
       drew St. George, "Cuban Rebels," *Look*, February 4, 1958, p. 30, reproduced
       in Bonachea and Valdés, *Revolutionary Struggle*, p. 369.

86   *"The single word most expressing our aim and spirit is simply—freedom":* Andrew
       St. George, "A Visit with a Revolutionary," *Coronet*, February 1958, pp. 74–80;
       Fidel Castro, "Why We Fight," *Coronet*, February 1958, pp. 80–86.

86   *growth and expansion of the rebel army:* Dubois, *Rebel*, p. 212.

87   *the rebels sought to manage their own image as a superior moral force:* Thomas,
       Cuba, p. 998. Fidel may also have considered it was cheaper to release them
       than to hold them.

87   *Raúl, however, took no prisoners:* Quirk, *Fidel*, p. 218.

87   *"these rebels with a cause":* Guerra, *Heroes*, p. 278.

87   *there was a darker side:* See Guerra's superb account, *Heroes*, pp. 224–278.

87   *the work of Huber Matos:* Huber Matos, *Cómo llegó la noche* (Barcelona: Tus-
       quets Editores, 2002), pp. 75–85.

88   *the strike . . . was a dud:* The plans included using militia cells in the under-
       ground to create havoc, downing power lines, blowing up gas mains, lobbing

grenades at police, and cutting off communications. Sweig, *Inside*, pp. 131–135. The 26th of July Movement and the underground Civic Resistance Movement issued a joint warning to people: keep supplies on hand, such as candles and first aid; stay off the buses; when you hear the call, sabotage your workplace and leave; block the streets with junk, garbage cans and bottles; assemble Molotov cocktails; throw oil and tacks on the streets; and more. Dubois, *Rebel*, pp. 243–244. But after the "total war" statement, Batista was on alert and carried out bloody preemptive raids against suspected underground militants. Castro's movement estimated that some two hundred of its members were killed in the aftermath. After this, Fidel took direct charge of the entire guerrilla war. Still, Sweig has shown how the underground played an indispensable role in Fidel's advance. Sweig, *Inside*, pp. 135–136; Dubois, *Rebel*, p. 253.

88 *Batista was losing ground:* Thomas, *Cuba*, pp. 997–998.

88 *army was disintegrating:* Thomas, *Cuba*, p. 1019.

88 *he resigned and headed for the airport:* Thomas, *Cuba*, p. 1027.

SIX. "JURY OF A MILLION"

89 *eloquent blend of counselor, father, and rebel:* Thomas, *Cuba*, p. 1051.

89 *"absolute freedom of the press and all individual rights in the country":* In Spanish, http://www.cuba.cu/gobierno/discursos/1959/esp/f010159e.html. In English, http://lanic.utexas.edu/project/castro/db/1959/19590103.html.

90 *"no more censorship":* Associated Press, "Crowds Hail Castro on Trip to Havana," *Washington Post*, January 6, 1959, p. 6.

90 *his face creased with fatigue:* Quirk, *Fidel*, pp. 218–219.

90 *"Not permitting that any dictatorship":* See https://www.youtube.com/watch?v=kjpnfDwWd7Y. Also see Tony Perrottet, "When Fidel Castro Charmed the United States," *Smithsonian*, January 24, 2019, https://www.smithsonianmag.com/history/when-fidel-castro-charmed-united-states-180971277/, and the Sullivan website, http://www.edsullivan.com/fidel-castro-interview-on-the-ed-sullivan-show/. Sullivan compliments Castro as "in the great tradition of George Washington." When the show aired, Sullivan said he thought that Fidel would lead Cuba toward democracy.

91 *as honest, incorruptible and youthful:* Central Intelligence Agency, *Cuba, Its Institutions*, p. 27.

91 *"exceptionally gifted man" with "tenacious commitment":* Enrique Pérez Serantes, "Vida nueva," January 3, 1959, in *La voz de la Iglesia en Cuba, 100 documentos episcopales* (Mexico City: Conferencia de Obispos Católicos de Cuba, 1995). On the rosaries, Geyer, *Guerrilla Prince*, pp. 204–205, says they were distributed by a nonbeliever, Ramiro Valdés, a survivor of the *Granma* landing who went on to become Fidel's intelligence and security service chief.

91 *Fidel appeared at Camp Columbia:* Geyer, *Guerrilla Prince*, p. 207.

91 *embassies were swamped with requests for asylum from Batista's aides:* Paul D. Bethel, *The Losers: The Definitive Account by an Eyewitness of the Communist Conquest of Cuba and the Soviet Penetration in Latin America* (New Rochelle, NY: Arlington House, 1969), pp. 103–104.

92 *a frequent target of Castro's 26th of July movement:* Sweig, *Inside*, p. 17.

93 *He would never see Cuba again:* Ovares Gutiérrez, *Despite the Oaths.* On the airport scene: Associated Press, "Giant Rally Supports Executions in Cuba," *Orlando Sentinel*, January 17, 1959, p. 3A. Gutiérrez landed in Buenos Aires, where he fell gravely ill with cancer. He underwent an operation but suffered complications. He remained in a hospital for two months, not healing well. On May 26, 1959, he wrote to his daughter Yolanda, who was still in Havana: "I repudiate any relationship with Batista's people and I don't correspond with any of them, neither of the past, nor of the present or the future. I know my political responsibility for the positions I held, but I accept only those matters in which I was personally involved. Castro's government is a disaster and could lead the country into economic chaos, but I think there is no doubt that it has the backing of the great masses of people." The letter is reproduced in Montalvo, "Exilio." Gutiérrez went to Miami for further medical treatment, where he died July 17, 1959. He was buried in Havana's Colón Cemetery.

93 *obsessed with eliminating the "underdevelopment" of Cuba:* Szulc, *Fidel Castro*, pp. 537–538.

93 *"liberty with bread, bread without terror":* Loree Wilkerson, *Fidel Castro's Political Programs from Reformism to "Marxism-Leninism"* (Gainesville: University of Florida Press, 1965), p. 55. Fidel said he would be "different from capitalism and from communism" on May 21, 1959, on *Ante la Prensa*, CMQ television, quoted in "No se reconsiderará la reforma agraria, dijo Fidel Castro," *Diario de la Marina*, May 22, 1959, section A, pp. 1, 6. Carlos Franqui describes these slogans in *Family Portrait with Fidel* (New York: Random House, 1984), pp. 37, 50.

94 *"What Fidel was thinking no one knew":* Franqui, *Family Portrait*, p. 21.

94 *shocking photographs of mutilated bodies:* Bohemia, January 11 and 18, 1959. On the *Bohemia* publication and its impact, see Lillian Guerra, *Visions of Power in Cuba: Revolution, Redemption, and Resistance, 1959–1971* (Chapel Hill: University of North Carolina Press, 2012), pp. 42-43. On the actual death toll, Michele Chase suggests it was two to three thousand. Chase, "The Trials: Violence and Justice in the Aftermath of the Cuban Revolution," in *A Century of Revolution: Insurgent and Counterinsurgent Violence During Latin America's Long Cold War*, eds. Greg Grandin and Gilbert M. Joseph (Durham, NC: Duke University Press, 2010), p. 167.

95 *the trials were carried out in a spirit of rage and revenge:* International Commission of Jurists, *Cuba and the Rule of Law*, pp. 166–167.

95 *mowed down by rebel forces with machine guns:* The Associated Press on January 12 reported that seventy-five had been killed by a firing squad and buried in a mass grave in Santiago de Cuba. Ambassador Bonsal said "there was reason to believe" that they were "mowed down by rebel soldiers at the command of Raúl Castro and bulldozed underground without any semblance whatsoever of a trial." Bonsal, *Cuba, Castro,* p. 36. Jon Lee Anderson, in *Che Guevara: A Revolutionary Life* (New York: Grove Press, 1997), p. 388, writes that Raúl "directed a mass execution of over 70 captured soldiers by bulldozing a trench, standing the condemned men in front of it, and mowing them down with machine guns." Coltman, in *The Real Fidel Castro,* p. 148, puts the toll at seventy-one.

95 *tried and executed:* Larry Allen, Associated Press, "Cuba Continues Executions As Toll Hits 180," *Washington Post,* January 15, 1959, p. A8.

96 *"two hundred thousand gringos dead":* R. Hart Phillips, "Castro Says Cuba Wants Good Ties with Washington," *New York Times,* January 16, 1959, p. 1. Phillips said Castro made the remark to a crowd, but he later regretted it was reported by journalists.

96 *"Cuban women demand execution of murderers":* Thomas, *Cuba,* p. 1087.

96 *a look of pleased astonishment:* Guerra, *Visions,* p. 49, reproduces the photo.

96 *"Fidel's popularity bordered on madness":* Franqui, *Family Portrait,* p. 36.

96 *"I say that this is democracy":* In Spanish, "Discurso pronunciado por el comandante Fidel Castro Ruz, en la magna concentración popular, en el Palacio Presidencial, el 21 de enero de 1959," http://www.cuba.cu/gobierno/discursos/1959/esp/f210159e.html. In English, http://lanic.utexas.edu/project/castro/db/1959/19590121.html.

96 *a show trial:* Bonsal, who had just arrived in Cuba, said the Cuban public had been fed the myth that Batista's army killed twenty thousand people; the televised extravaganza was intended to respond to demands for revenge. When it was over, Fidel ordered no more televised trials. In Havana, prosecutions were moved to the La Cabaña fortress and put under the supervision of Guevara. Chase suggests this marked a transition from the period of revolutionary justice aimed at Batista-era veterans to using tribunals for prosecuting those suspected of counterrevolutionary activity. Chase, "The Trials," p. 186. See Bonsal, *Cuba, Castro,* p. 36; Szulc, *Fidel,* pp. 482–484; Geyer, *Guerrilla Prince,* pp. 212–213; and Anderson, *Che,* pp. 386–387.

97 *about 550 Batista officers and soldiers had been executed:* Chase says in total "perhaps between 300 and 700 people were executed." See Chase, "The Trials," p. 186. Alex Von Tunzelmann, *Red Heat: Conspiracy, Murder, and the Cold War in the Caribbean* (New York: Henry Holt, 2011), p. 129, says the White House estimate of the total executed in 1959 was 600, while Fidel put it at 550. A US Embassy official, Daniel M. Braddock, estimated in a cable to the State

Department on February 25, 1959: "Over 300 persons have been executed by sentence of those courts, as well as an indeterminate number sentenced to long imprisonment, and the trials are continuing." Braddock, "Dispatch from the Embassy in Cuba to the Department of State: Political Conditions in Cuba," in *Foreign Relations of the United States, 1958–1960*, vol. 6, *Cuba*, ed. John P. Glennon (Washington, DC: Office of the Historian, Bureau of Public Affairs, United States Department of State), Doc. 257, pp. 410–420, February 25, 1959.

97 *charges against forty-five members of the Batista air force:* Francisco José Moreno, "Justice and Law in Latin America: A Cuban Example," *Journal of Interamerican Studies and World Affairs* 12, no. 3 (July 1970): 367–378. Also see Associated Press, "43 Batista Fliers Get Long Terms," March 8, 1959, *Washington Post*, March 9, 1959, p. A7; Thomas, *Cuba*, pp. 1202–1203; Geyer, *Guerrilla Prince*, p. 213; and Matos, *Cómo llegó*, p. 316.

97 *a cabinet of moderates:* This first cabinet included Roberto Agramonte of the Ortodoxos, as foreign minister; Manuel Ray Rivero, an engineer active in the urban underground, as secretary of public works; and Rufo López-Fresquet, as minister of finance. MacGaffey and Barnett, *Twentieth Century Cuba*, p. 295.

98 *to hold elections within eighteen months:* Bethel, *The Losers*, p. 99, quoting from Fidel's January 9, 1959, appearance on the Cuban version of *Meet the Press*.

98 *the whole democratic process—were nowhere in evidence:* The International Commission of Jurists' *Cuba and the Rule of Law* is a comprehensive account of the changes made to Cuba's political structure in early 1959. See pp. 85–98. Urrutia, a judge for thirty-one years, knew what he was doing. In his 1964 memoir from exile, he said the decisions in January were a "judicious adaptation" of the 1940 Constitution "that took into account the exigencies of the Revolutionary period." He claimed that his goal was to put the constitution into effect and that he was against "arbitrary rule." But the actions of his cabinet led to precisely that. Manuel Urrutia Lleó, *Fidel Castro & Co., Inc.: Communist Tyranny in Cuba* (New York: Frederick A. Praeger, 1964), p. 35.

98 *Revolution or counterrevolution had never been considered a crime punishable by death:* Phillips, *Cuba*, p. 410.

98 *property could be seized from anyone:* International Commission of Jurists, *Cuba and the Rule of Law*, pp. 98–99.

99 *abolition of constitutional guarantees of personal freedom:* International Commission of Jurists, *Cuba and the Rule of Law*, pp. 89–90. The 1940 Constitution prohibited the establishment of special courts outside the regular judiciary. Unfortunately, this provision was consistently flouted by the use of *tribunales de urgencia*, emergency courts, which were despised as instruments of political repression. These tribunals had existed since the 1930s and permitted rapid-fire trials, often based only on oral testimony, and were originally

conceived for terrorism cases. They remained in place after 1940. During Batista's final years they were used to try anti-government activity. Urrutia presided over a tribunal in 1957 when he declared that violent insurrection was a legitimate form of protest, and Fidel's fighters were freed. Instead of implementing the 1940 Constitution, Urrutia's cabinet suspended the provision entirely, to make way for Castro's revolutionary tribunals. MacGaffey and Barnett, *Cuba*, p. 115; Ehrlich, "Eduardo Chibás," p. 268.

99 *Batista had arranged a similar structure:* In his April 1952 statutes, Batista did away with Congress and created a council of ministers that would appoint the president. The International Commission of Jurists notes that such a closed system was a target of ridicule by Fidel Castro in his Moncada trial speech, "History Will Absolve Me." International Commission of Jurists, *Cuba and the Rule of Law*, p. 96. Batista also had claimed his revolution was a legitimate source of law and once he got things straightened out he would return to elected government. See *Constituciones cubanas: Desde 1812 hasta nuestros días*, p. 330, the preliminary declaration to the Constitutional Law of April 4, 1952. Also see L. B. Klein, "The Socialist Constitution of Cuba (1976)," *Columbia Journal of Transnational Law* 17 (1978): 456. Batista reinstated the 1940 Constitution in a short-lived period in 1955–1956 but suspended it again for most of the period from Fidel's landing in 1956 until the end of Batista's rule.

99 *a feverish, revolutionary spirit:* Thomas, *Cuba*, p. 1085.

100 *a revolutionary movement would approve its own laws:* Rufo López-Fresquet, the finance minister who attended Urrutia's cabinet meetings, recalled that the revisions in law were supposed to be temporary, lasting only until a new government was established by popular election. In fact, such elections were never held and such a government never materialized. López-Fresquet, *My Fourteen Months with Castro* (Cleveland: World Publishing, 1966), p. 78.

100 *Gustavo's provision for a citizen initiative:* It became Article 122 (f) in the Fundamental Law, under "Initiation and Enactment of Laws, Their Sanction and Promulgation." The provision said citizens could propose laws. "In this case it shall be indispensable that the initiative be exercised by at least ten thousand citizens who are qualified to vote."

100 *his habits were maddening:* Franqui, *Family Portrait*, p. 5; Coltman, *The Real*, p. 144; Teresa Casuso, *Cuba and Castro*, trans. Elmer Grossberg (New York: Random House, 1961), pp. 164–166.

101 *"disorganization, amateurishness, and incompetence":* Herbert L. Matthews, *Castro: A Political Biography* (London: Allen Lane, 1969), p. 140. Matthews quotes a letter to his wife July 4, 1959. Theodore Draper later observed that "the Cuban regime has operated on the basis of a proliferation of decrees rather than a legislative process governed by a written constitution." See Theodore Draper, "On the Cuban Constitutional Problem," in *Constitutions of the*

Communist Party-States, ed. Jan F. Triska (Stanford, CA: Hoover Institution Publications, 1968), p. 256.

101 *hated facing up to the responsibilities of running a country:* Quirk, *Fidel*, p. 231.

102 *"by the people and for the people":* "Discurso pronunciado por el comandante Fidel Castro Ruz, primer ministro del Gobierno Revolucionario, en el aniversario del ataque al palacio presidencial," March 13, 1959, http://www.cuba.cu/gobierno/discursos/1959/esp/c130359e.html.

102 *council of ministers was not representative:* The council of ministers used this constituent power twenty-two times between January 1, 1959, and August 23, 1961, each time to modify the Fundamental Law, which the revolution had itself created. These modifications "reveal a single purpose, namely to concentrate arbitrary power in the hands of the ruling group." Draper, "On the Cuban Constitutional Problem," p. 286.

103 *Cuba's Communist Party:* "Dispatch from the Embassy in Cuba to the Department of State," in *Cuba*, Glennon, ed., Doc. 278, April 14, 1959, pp. 458–466, drafted by Braddock, James A. Noel, Francis J. Donahue, and Bethel. Also see Guerra, *Heroes*, p. 209. "The party attempted to deceive Cubans into believing that many of their institutions, publications and activities were not financed, sponsored, or subsidized by the Soviet Union when in fact they were." Also see Pérez, *Cuba Under*, p. 288.

103 *the Communists sensed a new day:* "Dispatch," *Cuba*, Glennon, ed., Doc. 278, April 14, 1959, pp. 458–466.

103 *"Against Communism":* "Contra el comunismo," *Bohemia*, January 11, 1959, p. 95. The editorial is unsigned but probably was written by Quevedo.

104 *"the free press is the first enemy of dictatorship":* Szulc, *Fidel*, p. 489.

104 *Castro met . . . Vice President Richard Nixon:* Richard Nixon, *RN: The Memoirs of Richard Nixon* (New York: Grosset & Dunlap, 1978), p. 202. The full memo was released in volume 3 of the CIA history *Official History of the Bay of Pigs Invasion:* Jack B. Pfeiffer, *Evolution of CIA's Anti-Castro Policies, 1959–January 1961*, December 1979, appendix F.

104 *Fidel met in a hotel room with Gerry Droller, the CIA's top Latin America expert:* Geyer, *Guerrilla Prince*, pp. 240–241. Droller's cover name, Frank Bender, is used by Geyer. The SNIE is quoted in Pfeiffer, *Evolution of CIA's Anti-Castro Policies*, p. 23, declassified in 1998. The deputy director's testimony, p. 27.

105 *Secretary of State Christian Herter:* "Memorandum Prepared in the Department of State: Unofficial Visit of Prime Minister Castro of Cuba to Washington— a Tentative Evaluation," in *Cuba*, Glennon, ed., Doc. 292, April 23, 1959, pp. 482–483. The evaluation was attached to a covering memo from Herter to Eisenhower. The incessant questions about communism exasperated Castro. On his return to Havana, he insisted in a TV appearance, "Our revolution is not red, but olive green, the color of the rebel army that emerged from the

heart of the Sierra Maestra." "No se reconsiderará la reforma agraria, dijo Fidel Castro," *Diario de la Marina*, May 22, 1959, pp. 1, 6.

105 *He was primarily a nationalist and a social reformer:* Franqui, in *Family Portrait*, p. 14, wrote: "I couldn't help thinking that the struggle and the war were carried on and won because of the truth. But power is made out of lies. Why, when we were weak, did we use the truth, and now that we were strong, did we lie?"

105 *conferred secretly with Blas Roca:* Some rank-and-file Communists tried to stoke resistance to Batista. Steve Cushion, *A Hidden History of the Cuban Revolution: How the Working Class Shaped the Guerrillas' Victory* (New York: Monthly Review Press, 2016), p. 200, notes the "work of ordinary rank-and-file Communists, who risked their lives distributing a constant stream of leaflets and underground newspapers, which contributed to maintaining and building a level of working-class discontent" that rallied to Fidel in January 1959.

105 *remnants of the old political parties:* Central Intelligence Agency, *Cuba, Its Institutions*, p. 35.

105 *The Cuban Communists were the answer:* MacGaffey and Barnett, *Twentieth Century Cuba*, p. 301.

106 *"I needed them":* Thomas, *Cuba*, p. 1233.

106 *Raúl Castro was closer to the Communists:* Accounts differ on Raúl's past. Franqui said Raúl was an "orthodox Communist, both by training and military temperament," described him as "Moscow's man," and said he was the "point of entry" of the Communists into the revolution. Franqui, *Family Portrait*, pp. 22, 50. Aleksandr Fursenko and Timothy Naftali, in *"One Hell of a Gamble": Khrushchev, Castro and Kennedy, 1958–1964* (New York: W. W. Norton, 1997), p. 15, say Raúl had read Marx while at the university, secretly joined the Communist youth league and the PSP in the 1950s, and kept his membership secret from his brother, but it was known in Moscow. A CIA report identified Raúl as "a hard-core Communist." Pfeiffer, *Evolution of CIA's Anti-Castro Policies*, p. 24. The report on Raúl was prepared by Rudolph Gómez, deputy chief of the Western Hemisphere division of the CIA.

106 *They became friends while sailing to North America:* Fursenko and Naftali, *"One Hell of a Gamble,"* p. 57.

106 *a secret request for Soviet military advisers:* The emissary was Lázaro Peña. Fursenko and Naftali, *"One Hell of a Gamble,"* pp. 11–12. The authors say Raúl requested Spanish Communist officers who had graduated from the Soviet military academy to act as advisers and for intelligence work. The Soviet Presidium approved the request April 23, 1959; two Spaniards were sent, followed by a group of fifteen.

106 *Che Guevara was a Marxist:* Andrew St. George, "A Revolution Gone Wrong," *Coronet*, July 1960, p. 111.

106 *hidden blueprint, or was he just making it up:* A substantial unanswered question is whether Fidel had been or planned to become a Marxist from the outset or he got there by improvising and reacting to events. Some who knew him from his early years, such as José Ignacio Rasco, have stated that Fidel was a Communist from early on and deceived the Cuban people, revealing it only later. Others say Fidel was not so inclined at the outset but navigated his way there as he struggled to steer the revolution. Archival evidence has not settled the question. See Jorge Macle Cruz, "Writing the Revolution's History out of Closed Archives? Cuban Archival Laws and Access to Information," in *The Revolution from Within: Cuba 1959–1980*, eds. Michael Bustamante and Jennifer Lambe (Durham, NC: Duke University Press, 2019), pp. 47–63.

106 *the powerful trio of Fidel, Raúl, and Che:* The core decisions were made by a small junta that met weekly, while the council of ministers was convened primarily when decisions needed the form of law. The junta was Fidel, Raúl, Che, and a few others. MacGaffey and Barnett, *Twentieth Century Cuba*, p. 308. Szulc, writing in the *New York Times*, observed: "As often as not, the full cabinet and President Osvaldo Dorticós are merely called upon by Premier Castro and his brain trust to approve plans." Szulc, "A Super-Cabinet Rules over Cuba," *New York Times*, December 18, 1959, p. 1.

106 *two plans were secretly drafted:* The tactics are described by Franqui, in *Family Portrait*, p. 37. When Fidel was fighting in the mountains, he had promised to give land to those who tilled it. The rebel army's Law No. 3 in October 1958 suggested a massive land redistribution. But the plan that emerged from the beach house was much different. It nationalized the largest plantations, including those foreign owned, distributing some land to small farmers but placing the bulk in the hands of new, large "cooperatives" to be run by the state. Two years later, there were 662 sugarcane cooperatives. A second Agrarian Reform Law was enacted in 1963, impacting medium-sized landowners, bringing 70 percent of the lands under direct state control. José Álvarez, "Transformations in Cuban Agriculture after 1959," Doc. No. FE481, Institute of Food and Agricultural Sciences Extension, University of Florida, August 2009, pp. 2–5. Sorí Marín, a veteran of the Sierra Maestra campaign, where he was a lawyer drafting laws to govern the rebel army, resigned from the cabinet in 1959 and became part of the exile group fighting the revolution. Infiltrated back into Cuba by the CIA before the Bay of Pigs to lead resistance efforts, he was caught and executed in 1961. According to the State Department's 1961 "white paper" on Cuba, of the nineteen members of the original cabinet in January 1959, nearly two-thirds were either in exile, in prison, or dead two years later.

106 *"We are not doing so.":* Matos, *Cómo llegó*, p. 322.

107 *"blockbuster reality television":* Jennifer Lambe, "The Medium Is the Message:

The Screen Life of the Cuban Revolution, 1959–1962," *Past and Present* 246, issue 1 (February 2020): 227–267.

107   *The TV age amplified Fidel:* R. Hart Phillips, "Castro Reaches 95% of Cubans with Radio-TV Exhortations," *New York Times*, August 6, 1959, p. 9.

108   *a significant redistribution of income:* Pérez, *Cuba Under*, pp. 319–320.

108   *six-week political indoctrination courses with a Marxist tone:* The schooling was mentioned in the CIA's daily intelligence bulletin for June 22, 1959. Bethel, *The Losers*, p. 193, says the schools were preparatory for officers being trained as guerrillas to be sent abroad as instructors. In an April 1959 cable, "Growth of Communism in Cuba," Braddock observed: "Much of the strength of the Communist effort in Cuba is directed toward infiltration of the Armed Forces. La Cabaña appears to be the main Communist center, and its Commander, Che Guevara, is the most important figure whose name is linked with Communism. Guevara is definitely a Marxist if not a Communist. He is a frequent guest speaker before the Communist front organizations. Political indoctrination courses have been instituted among the soldiers under his command at La Cabaña. Material used in these courses, some of which the Embassy has seen, definitely follows the Communist line. Guevara enjoys great influence with Fidel Castro and even more with the Commander-in-Chief of the Armed Forces of the Revolution, Commander Raúl Castro, who is believed to share the same political views as Che Guevara." In *Cuba*, Glennon, ed., Doc. 278, pp. 458–466.

109   *defected to the United States:* Díaz Lanz's testimony infuriated Fidel and grabbed headlines, although he was not that well informed and made errors. He confused membership in the 26th of July Movement and in the PSP. Carla Anne Robbins, *The Cuban Threat* (New York: McGraw-Hill, 1983), p. 89.

109   *a speech in Camagüey:* Matos, *Cómo llegó*, p. 326.

109   *he sent in his resignation letter:* Matos, *Cómo llegó*, pp. 332–352. Also see Thomas, *Cuba*, pp. 1244–1245, and Quirk, *Fidel*, pp. 264–279.

110   *He was actually a KGB officer:* Sergo Mikoyan, *The Soviet Cuban Missile Crisis: Castro, Mikoyan, Kennedy, Khrushchev, and the Missiles of November*, ed. Svetlana Savranskaya (Washington, DC: Woodrow Wilson Center Press, 2012), pp. 53–59; Fursenko and Naftali, *"One Hell of a Gamble,"* pp. 20–34. Interestingly, Gómez, deputy head of the CIA's Western Hemisphere division, was in Havana from October 15 to 18. His purpose was to encourage the CIA station to make stronger efforts to penetrate the Cuban Communist Party. He probably did not detect that a KGB man was meeting with Fidel—it would have been an intelligence scoop had he found out. Pfeiffer, *Evolution of CIA's Anti-Castro Policies*, p. 25.

111   *Castro was enraged:* Szulc, *Fidel Castro*, p. 505, says Fidel feared that other

officers would follow, testing the loyalty of the military. See Quirk, *Fidel*, p. 277, on Fidel's statement at the trial.

111 *"All I wanted was to save the revolution"*: Szulc, "A Super-Cabinet Rules over Cuba," p. 1.

111 *Camilo was pained by it all*: Matos, *Cómo llegó*, p. 344.

111 *Matos was taken into custody*: Quirk, *Fidel*, p. 268.

111 *"we do not want communism"*: "Telegram from the Embassy in Cuba to the Department of State," in *Cuba*, Glennon, ed., Doc. 373, October 21, 1959, p. 631.

111 *rolled out the red carpet*: R. Hart Phillips, "Cuba Convention: Havana Will Roll Out the Red Carpet for Travel Agents Convention," *New York Times*, October 11, 1959, p. X27.

112 *piloted by Díaz Lanz*: The plane has been described variously. This is how it appeared in the draft of a US diplomatic note, according to Bethel, *The Losers*, p. 196.

112 *shaken travel agents left for home*: Carlos Hall, the State Department's intelligence officer, who visited Cuba, wrote after visiting: "Cuba's tourist trade went to pot after the 'bombing' of Habana and Fidel's subsequent virulent attack on the US by television. . . . Steamship and airplane cancellations, as well as those of cruises, flowed in at once. The Habana Hilton and the Caribe [hotels] are almost empty, as is the Nacional which has 600 employees, none of which can be dismissed. On November 6 the Havana Riviera, with 750 employees, had 16 guests. The casinos are practically deserted." Carlos Hall, "Memorandum from the Director of the Office of Intelligence Research and Analysis for American Republics (Hall) to the Director of Intelligence and Research (Cumming)," in *Cuba*, Glennon, ed., Doc. 395 (November 18, 1959), pp. 672–675.

112 *Castro delivered a vitriolic attack on the United States*: Quirk, *Fidel*, p. 268; Phillips, "Castro Charges Planes from U.S. Bombed Havana," *New York Times*, October 24, 1959, p. 1; also see "Telegram from the Embassy in Cuba to the Department of State," in *Cuba*, Glennon, ed., Doc. 374 (October 22, 1959), pp. 632.

113 *The bombing was like Pearl Harbor*: According to Bethel, within days the public relations department of the Ministry of Foreign Affairs issued a pamphlet claiming that the leaflet drop was "Our Pearl Harbor," stating that the dead and injured "were felled by the shrapnel of the plane." For good measure it threw in some pictures of Batista "war criminals" and their victims. Bethel, *The Losers*, pp. 195–196.

113 *"To the wall!"*: Quirk, *Fidel*, p. 270.

113 *Camilo's plane never arrived in Havana*: López-Fresquet told Bonsall on November 8 that he heard "after Camilo's plane took off from Camagüey on the

evening of Oct. 28 a Sea Fury took off in pursuit." The minister said peasants had witnessed the shootdown of Camilo's plane and it fell into the sea; a crew from the Camagüey base was currently in jail, he added. See "Memorandum of a Conversation between the Ambassador in Cuba (Bonsal) and the Cuban Minister of Finance (López-Fresquet) Havana, November 8, 1959," in *Cuba*, Glennon, ed., Doc. 389, pp. 660–663. Quirk says that the Cuban air force base near Camagüey received a report that a plane, possibly from the United States, was firebombing cane fields. A Cuban Sea Fury fighter with four 20mm cannons was ordered to intercept it. The pilot returned some time later saying his mission was accomplished; he had shot down the intruder. Quirk, *Fidel*, pp. 271–272. The disappearance of the plane was followed by Fidel putting on a show of leading the search for Camilo, "monopolizing the television cameras, the radio waves, and headlines of the newspapers," recalled Bethel, the former US embassy press attaché, who asserts that few believed the conclusion of Fidel and other searchers that the plane got lost and crashed. See Bethel, *The Losers*, pp. 201–202.

113 *the influence of the Communists:* "Telegram from the Embassy in Cuba to the Department of State," in *Cuba*, Glennon, ed., Doc. 302, May 6, 1959, pp. 503–504.

113 *"very little else was being talked about":* Bethel, *The Losers*, p. 164.

114 *a call for a national conference:* Margaret E. Crahan suggests moments of crisis can provoke loyalty to the church that does not always manifest itself otherwise. The turnout may have been an example of this. Crahan, "Salvation Through Christ or Marx: Religion in Revolutionary Cuba," *Journal of Interamerican Studies and World Affairs* 21, no. 1 (February 1979): p. 158.

114 *larger than any audience assembled by Castro:* "Telegram from the Embassy in Cuba to the Department of State," in *Cuba*, Glennon, ed., Doc. 401 (November 30, 1959), pp. 682–683; Ruby Hart Phillips, "Cuban Catholics Counter Red Aim," *New York Times*, November 30, 1959, p. 12; Harold K. Milke, Associated Press, "Communism Scorned at Huge Rally in Cuba," *Washington Post*, November 30, 1959, p. A11; Ignacio Uría, *Church and Revolution in Cuba: Enrique Pérez Serantes (1883–1968), the Bishop Who Saved Fidel Castro* (Madrid: Encuentro Editions, 2011).

114 *He needed to buy time:* Fursenko and Naftali, *"One Hell of a Gamble,"* p. 34.

114 *Matos went on trial:* Quirk, *Fidel*, pp. 264–279.

SEVEN. THE SILENCING

116 *new civilian militias:* R. Hart Phillips, "Tread of Militia Resounds in Cuba," *New York Times*, January 17, 1960, p. 1; Guerra, *Heroes*, pp. 118–119, including the St. George photo of the children's militia.

116 *The Communists captured the professional associations:* R. Hart Phillips, "Cuba

Unions Oust Anti-Red Leaders," *New York Times*, January 25, 1960, p. 1. Also see Wilkerson, *Fidel Castro's Political Programs*, p. 63; MacGaffey and Barnett, *Twentieth Century Cuba*, pp. 306–307. In a healthy system, these associations, part of civil society, function as an autonomous intermediary between state and society; they are the sinews connecting the rulers and the ruled. The Communists, allied with Castro, acted as an instrument of the regime to liquidate independent civil society. For more on civil society and its importance in democracy, see Larry Diamond, "Toward Democratic Consolidation," *Journal of Democracy* 5, no. 3 (July 1994): 4–17.

117 *Pedro Luis Boitel:* Boitel was imprisoned for more than a decade. He earned a reputation in prison for advocating nonviolent resistance, staging hunger strikes and other protests. He died May 25, 1972, during a prison hunger strike; a guard suffocated him with a pillow. Carl Gershman, "Pedro Luis Boitel and the Future of Freedom in Cuba," an address at the presentation of the Ninth Annual Pedro Luis Boitel Freedom Award, September 24, 2009, Miami.

117 *Havana is a hive of Communist and Communist-front activity:* St. George, "A Revolution Gone Wrong," p. 111.

118 *"You can't publish these!"* The AP article quoted Sen. Prescott Bush (R-Conn.). The UPI article quoted Rep. H. Allen Smith (R-Calif.), who had issued a statement saying, "Let us make no mistake: Fidel Castro is the Achilles' heel of our national security. We cannot allow Moscow to gain an established position too close to our coastline." He added that the United States should be displeased "with the growing Communist infiltration and, in some areas, Communist guidance. These facts should give the United States great care, lest Cuba become a Soviet stronghold on our own doorstep." Allen said Fidel may not be a Communist but described Che as "a promoter of dictatorship."

119 *The* coletillas *were a wedge of subterfuge:* Bethel, *The Losers*, pp. 179–180; *Información*, Cuban Heritage Collection, University of Miami, Coral Gables, Florida. Also see Guerra, *Visions*, pp. 122–133; Guerra, "To Condemn the Revolution Is to Condemn Christ: Radicalization, Moral Redemption, and the Sacrifice of Civil Society in Cuba, 1960," *Hispanic American Historical Review* 89, no. 1 (February 1, 2009): 73–109; Salwen, *Radio and Television*, pp. 146–147.

119 *At the end of the editorial, a* coletilla: *Información*, January 17, 1960, Cuban Heritage Collection, University of Miami, Coral Gables, Florida.

119 *newspapers eagerly accepted subsidies:* MacGaffey and Barnett, *Cuba*, pp. 221–222.

119 *censorship was punitive and used selectively:* Bethel, *The Losers*, p. 152.

119 *"bloody money from tyranny.":* "Castro Gives First of Friday Series," Havana FIEL Network, Castro remarks May 14, 1960, Latin American Network

Information Center, Castro Speech Database, http://lanic.utexas.edu/proj ect/castro/db/1960/19600516.html.

119 *"a rank and file soldier in this great struggle"*: Guerra, *Visions*, p. 123. The "disappearance" of Cuba's "flourishing and diverse" national press had wider ramifications, Guerra suggests. "The state's call to defend the Revolution by ending all public criticism of state policies and its leaders ensured that the autonomy not only of the press but also of two other groups would collapse: unionized labor and the historically significant sector of Cuban university students."

120 *the independent afternoon newspaper* Avance *fell*: Jorge Zayas, "Castro Is Accused of Stifling Press," *Miami Herald*, reprinted in the *New York Times* January 24, 1960, p. 9. Earlier that month, in an editorial in *Avance* on January 7, he wrote: "One can easily prove that absolute freedom of expression exists in Cuba simply by reading all of the insults, vexations and gross statements launched in unison by the official press against those who dare to dissent." United Press International, "Cuban Editor Hits at Press 'Liberty,'" *New York Times*, January 8, 1960, p. 8.

120 *By April, there were only four remaining*: Salwen, *Radio and Television*, p. 147.

120 Diario de la Marina: Guerra, *Visions*, p. 132. Also see Salwen, *Radio and Television*, p. 148; Bethel, *The Losers*, p. 181; and Associated Press, "Castro Unions Seize Cuba's Oldest Paper," May 11, 1960, *Washington Post*, May 12, 1960, p. A10.

121 Diario de la Marina *had been struggling*: Guerra, *Visions*, p. 132. Also see Salwen, *Radio and Television*, p. 148; Bethel, *The Losers*, p. 181; and Associated Press, "Castro Unions Seize Cuba's Oldest Paper," p. A10.

121 *"The people will not cry"*: "Castro Gives First of Friday Series," Havana FIEL Network, Castro remarks May 14, 1960, via LANIC Castro Speech Database, http://lanic.utexas.edu/project/castro/db/1960/19600516.html.

121 *"There will be no disagreeing voices"*: Luis Aguilar, "Los que construyen y los que destruyen," *Prensa Libre*, Havana, November 24, 1959, reprinted in translation in Bonachea and Valdés, *Cuba in Revolution*, pp. 147–149.

122 Información *died by the end of the year*: Salwen, *Radio and Television*, pp. 148–149.

122 Conte Agüero . . . *had been close to Fidel*: Castro letter to Conte Agüero from the Isle of Pines prison, December 12, 1953. Fidel Castro, *The Prison Letters of Fidel Castro* (New York: Nation Books, 2006), p. 9. The book was originally published in Havana in 1959 with an introduction by Luis Conte Agüero, but this edition contains an epilogue by him expressing bitter regret for helping Fidel.

122 *squads of Communist toughs*: The mob was commanded by Manuel Piñeiro, known as "Red Beard," who was playing a key role in building Fidel's secret police. Thomas, *Cuba*, p. 1273.

123 *All television and radio were then merged by decree into a state network:* Salwen, *Radio and Television,* p. 158.

123 *one year, or eighteen months, or two years:* He made the one-year promise in the Sierra Maestra Manifesto, 1958. He said "approximately eighteen months" in a televised appearance in Havana January 9, 1959. See Bethel, *The Losers,* p. 99.

124 *only fraud in the past:* Fidel had made a similar argument in private to Nixon, who wrote afterward that Fidel emphasized "the people did not want elections because the elections in the past had produced bad government." Nixon memo, April 19, 1959, in Pfeiffer, Official History of the Bay of Pigs Operation, Vol. III, *Evolution of CIA's Anti-Castro Policies,* appendix F, p. 337.

124 *"We already voted for Fidel!":* In Spanish, http://www.cuba.cu/gobierno/dis cursos/1960/esp/f010560e.html. A summarized version in English: http:// lanic.utexas.edu/project/castro/db/1960/19600501.html.

124 *it was all "yes,":* If Fidel had conducted early elections, he undoubtedly would have won. His popularity was genuine. He could also have created a political party and would likely have built legitimacy while also fulfilling his promises of democracy. His claim that elections had failed in the past and therefore should not be tried is simplistic and glib. The Cuban republic did suffer a flawed democracy, but he could have tried to make it better. More likely, Fidel did not want elections because of his aversion to sharing power or having to cede it. He did not want elections out of fear they would lead to compromises that could change the character of the revolution. He saw himself as a messiah, a savior, backed by the "jury of a million," and concluded: Why bother with elections?

124 *"unmistakably going wrong":* St. George, "A Revolution Gone Wrong," p. 111.

124 *willfully gave up their rights:* Guerra, *Visions,* p. 9, argues: "Willingly and even joyfully, millions of Cubans surrendered their rights, including rights to public protest, an autonomous press, and free assembly."

124 *delayed trade exhibition:* Fidel went to the exhibit and was unimpressed by the Russian products, which appeared inferior to the US goods he was accustomed to, according to Fidel's first treasury minister, Rufo López-Fresquet, in *My 14 Months with Castro,* p. 174. He says that Fidel "belittled everything we saw at the exhibit" in front of Mikoyan.

124 *exploded in Havana Harbor:* St. George, "A Revolution Gone Wrong"; Quirk, *Fidel,* pp. 292–295; Mikoyan, *Soviet Cuban Missile Crisis,* pp. 65–88; Fursenko and Naftali, *"One Hell of a Gamble,"* pp. 38–39.

124 *begin a covert action:* Eisenhower approved a program to train "resistance forces" but at this stage did not envision an invasion. Pfeiffer, *Evolution of CIA's Anti-Castro Policies,* p. 75.

126   *Cuba took over 382 large private enterprises:* Thomas, *Cuba*, p. 1297; Pérez, *Cuba
       Under*, p. 326; Andrés Suárez, *Cuba: Castroism and Communism, 1959–1966*
       (Cambridge, MA: MIT Press, 1967), p. 98.

126   *"This is a revolution betrayed":* Thomas, *Cuba*, p. 1292.

126   *Enrique Pérez Serantes, the archbishop of Santiago de Cuba:* Ignacio Uría, *Church
       and Revolution in Cuba: Enrique Pérez Serantes (1883–1968), the Bishop Who Saved
       Fidel Castro* (Madrid: Encuentro Editions, 2011), loc. 3396. On Sardiñas, see Luis
       Hernández Serrano, "Father Guillermo Sardiñas Spent 18 Months in the Sierra
       Maestra as Chaplain of the Rebel Army," *Juventud Rebelde*, December 21, 2014,
       http://www.juventudrebelde.cu/cuba/2014-12-20/el-altar-en-la-mochila.

127   *enthusiastically backed Fidel's rebel army:* Bohemia, "Catolicismo: La Cruz y El
       Diablo," January 18, 1959, pp. 98-100.

127   *religious education in public schools:* "Exposición del episcopado cubano: A los
       delegados a la asamblea constituyente," February 6, 1940, in *La voz de la igle-
       sia en Cuba, 100 documentos episcopales* (Mexico City: Conferencia de Obispos
       Católicos de Cuba, 1995), Doc. 4. The church requested that the 1940 Con-
       stituent Assembly "agree on the compulsory education of religion in the pub-
       lic schools, respecting the freedom of conscience of those who do not wish
       it." The assembly rejected this, and instead, the constitution, Art. 55, says that
       public education shall be secular, but private schools are guaranteed the right
       to carry out religious education.

127   *the "Catholic Church supports the revolution":* Diario de la Marina, April 18, 1959,
       p. 8B.

127   *eight Havana priests: Diario de la Marina,* "Piden los sacerdotes cubanos cesen
       polémicas infecundas," March 7, 1959, p. 1.

128   *questions about loyalty of Spanish clerics:* Leslie Dewart, *Christianity and Revo-
       lution: The Lesson of Cuba* (New York: Herder and Herder, 1963), says that
       early in 1960 a document was circulated for signature among the Spanish
       clergy in Cuba asking them to reaffirm their loyalty to Franco. "The mean-
       ing of this gesture could not escape anyone in Cuba, where the memory of
       the Spanish civil war is more alive than anywhere else in the world outside
       of Spain itself. The document amounted to a condemnation of Castro on
       the grounds that, as the Republican government had supposedly once done
       in Spain, Castro was now culpably betraying the revolution to communism.
       This explains in part why only a few months later Castro's favorite epithet
       for the clergy would be *cura falangista*—loosely, 'Franco-following-priest,'"
       pp. 154–155. Fidel did frequently voice such criticism. Pérez Serantes denied
       any connection to Franco in his pastoral "Ni traidores ni parias," September
       24, 1960. The priests, Pérez Serantes said, were not bound to Franco, "with
       whom we have never maintained relationships of any kind," and "whoever
       claims otherwise is wrong."

128 *regularly observant:* According to a statistical survey from the Batista years, published in 1956 by the Catholic University Association of Havana, in a population of about 6 million 72.5 percent claimed to be Catholic. Of them, three-quarters said they were not practicing Catholics, and of the remaining 25 percent, only 11 percent said they received the sacraments regularly, which amounts to 2 percent of the overall population. Raúl Gómez Treto, *The Church and Socialism in Cuba* (Maryknoll, NY: Orbis Books, 1988), p. 12. But Crahan offers an important caveat: Cubans identified themselves as Christian even if they had little or no contact with a church. "The so-called weakness of religion in pre-revolutionary Cuba was primarily institutional rather than cultural," she wrote. Crahan, "Salvation Through Christ or Marx," p. 159.

128 *white, middle, and the wealthy upper classes:* Dewart, *Christianity and Revolution,* pp. 97–99.

128 *chronically short of priests:* Dewart says that middle- and upper-class Cubans shunned vocations and the hope of building a native Cuban clergy "simply did not materialize." He added: "Relatively few city dwellers in Cuba had as much as seen the Cuban countryside . . . the country parishes were indigent." Dewart, *Christianity and Revolution,* p. 99. On Pérez Serantes, see Uría, *Iglesia y revolución en Cuba,* location 4820, Kindle edition. According to Gómez Treto, in 1959 there were three minor seminaries in Havana, Santiago de Cuba and Matanzas with a total of 114 seminarians, and one major seminary in Havana with 19. *The Church and Socialism in Cuba,* p. 11.

128 *churn out leaflets and small publications:* Petra Kuivala, *Never a Church of Silence: The Catholic Church in Revolutionary Cuba, 1959–1986* (Helsinki: University of Helsinki, 2019). Kuivala had unparalleled access to church archives and found them stuffed with hundreds of examples of church publications.

129 *the great enemy of Christianity is Communism:* Pérez Serantes, "Por Dios y por Cuba," May 1960, in *La voz de la Iglesia en Cuba, 100 documentos episcopales* (Mexico City: Conferencia de Obispos Católicos de Cuba, 1995) Doc. 27.

129 *"the state has no right to control all means of expression":* United Press International, "Cuban Catholic Prelate Raps Totalitarianism," *Washington Post,* June 2, 1960, p. B2. For more on Boza Masvidal's views, see Eduardo Boza Masvidal, *Revolución cristiana en Latinoamérica* (Santiago de Chile: Editorial del Pacífico, S.A., 1963), pp. 34–39.

129 *The G-2 secret police:* Fursenko and Naftali, in *"One Hell of a Gamble,"* p. 64, citing Soviet intelligence archives, say that Fidel purged the entire Cuban security apparatus in September 1960 after it was discovered that dissident officers in the service were tapping Raúl's phone lines and those of some PSP leaders, and they also intercepted calls between Fidel and Raúl.

129 *Manuel Artime was working with the CIA:* Artime had fought with the rebel army against Batista but left Cuba in December 1959 to become a key figure

in the CIA plan to overthrow Castro, including the Bay of Pigs. Haynes Johnson et al., *The Bay of Pigs: The Leaders' Story of Brigade 2506* (New York: W. W. Norton, 1964), pp. 24–26.

129 *José Ignacio Rasco:* The Lincoln or Lenin comment is from Rasco, "El V Congreso Internacional de la Democracia Cristiana," *Bohemia*, December 6, 1959, p. 38, 114–115. Also see Uría, *Iglesia y revolución.* Further details about the movement are contained in a paper Rasco wrote in exile, "The Catholic Opinion of Commander Fidel Castro's Regime," date unknown but approximately 1961, files of Rasco, Cuban Heritage Collection, University of Miami, Coral Gables, Florida. Rasco's conversation with Fidel is recounted in interviews with Sylvia Pedraza of the University of Michigan that Rasco included in *Acuerdos, desacuerdos y recuerdos* (Miami: Ediciones Universal, 2012), pp. 142–143, and also in Manny Hildago, "Catholic Social Justice Deferred: The Church's Struggle for Reform the Republic of Cuba," Florida International University, Cuban Research Institute, June 1998, which Rasco reviewed. Rasco collection, CHC5219, Cuban Heritage Collection, University of Miami, Coral Gables, Florida. Rasco became a member of the CIA-backed Frente Revolucionario Democratico, a group formed in 1960 to be a united exile front to overthrow Castro. "Memorandum from the Assistant Secretary of State for Inter-American Affairs (Mann) to the Secretary of State, Subject: President's Inquiry Regarding Cuban Opposition Groups," in *Cuba*, Glennon, ed., Doc. 599 (October 28, 1960), pp. 1104–1105.

130 *the opposition was "defeating its own purpose":* Daniel M. Braddock, "Dispatch from the Embassy in Cuba to the Department of State," in *Cuba*, Glennon, ed., Doc. 617 (December 6, 1960), pp. 1149–1163.

130 *the whole Catholic leadership spoke with one voice:* "Text of Cuban Pastoral Message," *New York Times*, August 8, 1960, p. 2.

131 *subvert the Catholic hierarchy from within:* Fidel may have toyed with the idea of creating a separate, national church, promoted by a lone priest, but never went ahead with it. There is little documentary evidence. For more on the priest who advanced this idea, Germán Lence, see Uría, *Iglesia y revolución,* location 5620, Kindle edition.

131 *The pastoral letters were resonating:* "From the Journal of S.M. Kudryavtsev, 'Record of a Conversation with Prime Minister of Cuba Fidel Castro Ruz, 21 January 1961,'" February 15, 1961, History and Public Policy Program Digital Archive, AVP RF, F. 0104. Op. 17, P. 118, D. 3. ll. 48–52, obtained by James G. Hershberg and translated by Gary Goldberg, https://digitalarchive .wilsoncenter.org/document/177859.

131 *a speech on the balcony of the presidential palace:* Text, http://lanic.utexas.edu /project/castro/db/1960/19600928.html and https://www.marxists.org/his tory/cuba/archive/castro/1960/09/29.htm.

132 *they were named Committees for Defense of the Revolution:* Although the idea was seemingly impromptu, Richard R. Fagen says it had been gestating ever since the *La Coubre* explosion March 4, 1960, as Fidel and his regime faced "the growing need for some form of urban-based civil defense against sabotage and counterrevolutionary terror." Further, Fagen says that at a mass rally in August the crowd was asked to dedicate themselves to a list of commitments that included increasing revolutionary vigilance at home, at work, and on the streets, a precursor of the September 28 announcement, suggesting it was premeditated. Richard R. Fagen, *The Transformation of Political Culture in Cuba* (Stanford, CA: Stanford University Press, 1969), p. 70. Also see Josep M. Colomer, "Watching Neighbors: The Cuban Model of Social Control," *Cuban Studies 31* (Pittsburgh: University of Pittsburgh Press, 2000): pp. 118–138; and Quirk, *Fidel*, pp. 344–345. Colomer points out that the Soviet and Chinese systems were not identical to what Castro built. The Soviet system relied on the KGB secret police but was based more on the workplace, while the Chinese system was based on groups of not more than fifteen people at schools or party and government offices.

132 *"a hand grasping onto their neck":* Silvia Pedraza, *Political Disaffection in Cuba's Revolution and Exodus* (Cambridge: Cambridge University Press, 2007), p. 89.

133 *a secret assassination plan:* Howard Jones, *The Bay of Pigs* (Oxford: Oxford University Press, 2008), p. 21. Also see the CIA's *Official History of the Bay of Pigs Operation*, especially volume 3, Pfeiffer, *Evolution of CIA's Anti-Castro Policies*.

133 *a propaganda radio station:* Quirk, *Fidel*, p. 368.

134 *a growing feeling of discontent:* Phillips, "Anti-Castro Forces Make Some Gains in Cuba," *New York Times*, August 14, 1960, p. E4.

134 *Santa Claus, whom Fidel had banned:* Quirk, *Fidel*, p. 352. Fidel saw Santa Claus as a foreign symbol imported into Cuba. The revolution replaced Santa Claus with "Don Feliciano," a Cuban peasant from colonial days, with a long, drooping mustache, a beard in two thin strands, wearing a straw hat, a guayabera, and baggy trousers. "Now we have Don Feliciano in place of Santa Claus and this shows that the Cuban Christmas will really be Cuban," Castro declared. See "Don Feliciano, a Native, Replaces Santa in Cuba," *New York Times*, December 21, 1959, p. 9.

134 *Thousands applied for visas:* CIA director Allan Dulles told a National Security Council meeting January 5, 1961, that there were fifty thousand outstanding applications for visas. *Foreign Relations of the United States, 1961–1963*, vol. 10, *Cuba, January 1961–September 1962*, ed. Louis J. Smith, no. 11, editorial note (Washington, DC: Office of the Historian, Bureau of Public Affairs, United States Department of State), p. 178.

134 *Operation Pedro Pan:* The exodus may have been prompted in part by murky rumors, promoted by the CIA's propaganda station, Radio Swan, that the Cuban

government had a plan to seize parental rights, or *patria potestad*, over children and subject them to Communist indoctrination. The Cuban government denied the rumors. Even without hearing the rumors, many Cubans were well aware that Marxist indoctrination was already underway in schools. Victor Andrés Triay, *Fleeing Castro: Operation Pedro Pan and the Cuban Children's Program* (Gainesville: University Press of Florida, 1998), pp. 12–20; Yvonne M. Conde, *Operation Pedro Pan: The Untold Exodus of 14,048 Cuban Children* (New York: Routledge, 1999). María de los Angeles Torres, *The Lost Apple: Operation Pedro Pan, Cuban Children in the U.S., and the Promise of a Better Future* (Boston: Beacon Press, 2003), p. 89, describes the rumor as part of a CIA propaganda campaign.

134 *Miami swelled:* Pérez, *Cuba Under*, p. 343. Of about 85,000 professionals in Cuba, an estimated 20,000 left through the end of 1962. More than 3,000 physicians from a total of 6,000 departed, and 700 dentists of almost 2,000.

134 *"Kick them out!":* Quirk, *Fidel*, pp. 353–354.

135 *"An open battle against the religion of Christ":* "Prelate Attacks Cuban Reds Again," *New York Times*, January 15, 1961, p. 1.

135 *"to poison the minds of our children":* "Raúl Castro Declares Priests Call for Strike by Students," *New York Times*, February 8, 1961, p. 8.

135 *the worst-kept secret:* Fursenko and Naftali, in *"One Hell of a Gamble,"* pp. 67–70, report that Fidel, by mid-October 1960, was bracing for an imminent invasion, a "war scare" based on faulty information. In January, the G-2 sent an intelligence report that identified the CIA training activity in Guatemala. Although it vastly overestimated the size of the trainee force as six thousand and was partly based on news articles, the report broadly outlined the invasion preparations, and many specifics were clearly not hard for Castro to discover. "Cuban G-2 (Military Intelligence), 'Report on Mercenary Camps and Bases in Guatemala, Nicaragua, and Florida' (Forwarded to Cuban President Osvaldo Dorticós Torrado)," January 12, 1961, History and Public Policy Program Digital Archive, released by Cuban government for March 22–24, 2001, conference, "Bay of Pigs: 40 Years After," in Havana, trans. by National Security Archive, http://digitalarchive.wilsoncenter.org/document/115184.

135 *"Anti-Castro Force":* Paul P. Kennedy, "U.S. Helps Train an Anti-Castro Force at Secret Guatemalan Air-Ground Base," *New York Times*, January 10, 1961, p. 1.

135 *Kennedy told his press secretary:* Jones, *The Bay of Pigs*, p. 68.

136 *a thirty-two-page "white paper" on Cuba:* The paper, titled "Cuba," released April 3, 1961, was initially drafted in the Bureau of Inter-American Affairs but was extensively revised in the White House by Arthur Schlesinger, with the assistance of Richard Goodwin. President Kennedy carefully reviewed the final draft. The white paper said Castro had delivered his country "to the Sino-Soviet bloc" and was mounting an attack on the entire inter-American system. Editorial note 79 in Smith, ed., *Cuba*, p. 451.

136 *a serious miscalculation:* A CIA memo in early January stated: "It is expected that these operations will precipitate a general uprising throughout Cuba and cause the revolt of large segments of the Cuban Army and Militia. . . . A general revolt in Cuba, if one is successfully triggered by our operations, may serve to topple the Castro regime within a period of weeks." "Memorandum from the Chief of WH/4/PM, Central Intelligence Agency (Hawkins) to the Chief of WH/4 of the Directorate for Plans (Esterline)," in Smith, ed., *Cuba,* p. 165. In a separate memo, a CIA official cautioned that Castro's strong position at home was reinforced by "effective controls over daily life in Cuba and by the increasing effectiveness of its security forces." Quirk, *Fidel,* p. 360. This was stated in a memo from Sherman Kent, chairman of the agency's Board of National estimates, to director Allen Dulles.

136 *thousands of people who could be contacted:* A CIA memo dated April 12 stated: "On the latest estimate there are nearly 7,000 insurgents responsive to some degree of control through agents with whom communications are currently active. About 3,000 of these are in Havana itself, over 2,000 in Oriente, about 700 in Las Villas in central Cuba. For the most part, the individual groups are small and very inadequately armed. Air drops are currently suspended because available aircraft are tied up in the movement of troops from their training area to the staging base. After D-Day when it is hoped that the effectiveness of the Castro air force will be greatly reduced, it is planned to supply these groups by daytime air drops. Every effort will be made to coordinate their operations with those of the landing parties. Efforts will be made also to sabotage or destroy by air attack the microwave links on which Castro's communication system depends. The objective is of course to create a revolutionary situation, initially perhaps in Oriente and Las Villas Provinces, and then spreading to all parts of the island." Smith, ed., *Cuba,* pp. 504–509.

137 *"We cannot hold.":* Jones, *The Bay of Pigs;* Johnson et al., *The Bay of Pigs;* the CIA's *Official History of the Bay of Pigs Operation,* especially vol. 3, Pfeiffer, *Evolution of CIA's Anti-Castro Policies.* Szulc in *Fidel* reports that Cuba lost 161 dead, p. 554. Johnson, writing two decades earlier, quoted Cuban doctors as saying Cuba lost 1,250 dead, but he acknowledges this was a guess, p. 179.

137 *"How could I have been so stupid?":* Quirk, *Fidel,* p. 374.

138 *rule by fear and intimidation:* Thomas, *Cuba,* p. 1365. Robert Berrellez of the Associated Press interviewed a civilian who overheard police officials discuss 147,500 arrested, but that estimate may have been too high. Berrellez, Associated Press, "G-2 Agents in Havana Jailed over 147,000," *Washington Post,* May 20, 1961, p. A8. Berrellez was detained for twenty-five days in the roundup. Castro's mass detentions did put a damper on internal opposition. See Pérez, *Cuba Under,* p. 331.

138 *the Kennedys did not cease:* Fursenko and Naftali, *"One Hell of a Gamble,"*

pp. 132–148. After the Bay of Pigs came another anti-Castro effort, Operation Mongoose, in late 1961. It generated a host of harebrained schemes, most of which were shelved. But it did create espionage networks on the island and eleven sabotage teams were deployed. The intelligence effort resulted in early reports of the Soviet missile deployments that led to the Cuban Missile Crisis, but the operation was no more successful in sparking a popular rebellion in Cuba or overthrowing Castro than earlier efforts. See Max Boot, *The Road Not Taken: Edward Landsdale and the American Tragedy in Vietnam* (New York: Liveright, 2018), pp. 376–399; and John Prados and Arturo Jimenez-Bacardi, *"Kennedy and Cuba: Operation Mongoose,"* Briefing Book No. 687, National Security Archive, October 3, 2019.

138 *a Latin cross in the center:* An image of the shoulder patch is reproduced in *Playa Girón: Derrota del imperialismo,* vol. 2 (Havana: Ediciones R, 1961).

138 *"Christian and Catholic":* Dewart, *Christianity and Revolution,* p. 166. Dewart notes that the whole brigade was not Catholic, but a sizable portion was.

138 *a wave of repression at the church:* Uría, *Iglesia y revolución,* location 6594, Kindle edition. Uría says that militiamen in Camagüey were tried and sentenced to three years in prison for the excesses, but released once the sentences had been widely reported.

139 *Pérez Serantes . . . forced to accept a military escort:* Uría, *Iglesia y revolución,* location 6642, Kindle edition.

139 *Pérez Serantes was summoned one evening by Raúl:* Uría, *Iglesia y revolución,* location 6693, Kindle edition. Pérez Serantes died April 18, 1968, in Santiago de Cuba, and the city came to a halt at his funeral procession as a sign of great respect. Gómez Treto, *The Church and Socialism in Cuba,* pp. 66–67.

140 *"there was not a single priest executed.":* Fidel Castro and Ignacio Ramonet, *Fidel Castro: A Spoken Autobiography,* trans. Andrew Hurley (New York: Scribner, 2006), p. 236.

141 *"the 1940 Constitution is already too outdated and too old for us":* "Discurso pronunciado por el comandante Fidel Castro Ruz, primer ministro del Gobierno Revolucionario de Cuba, resumiendo los actos del Día Internacional del Trabajo," May 1, 1961, via government of Cuba: http://www.cuba.cu/gobierno/discursos/1961/esp/f010561e.html, and Havana International Service, "Castro Proclaims Socialist Cuba," May 2, 1961, Latin American Network Information Center, Castro Speech Data Base. Also see Associated Press, "Castro Rules Out Elections in Cuba," *New York Times,* May 2, 1961, p. 1.

141 *"Down with communism!":* Richard Eder, "4,000 Protest in Havana; Shots Disperse Throngs," *New York Times,* September 11, 1961; also see Uría, *Iglesia y revolución.*

142 *Now he ordered their formal expulsion:* Richard Eder, "Havana Deports 135 Priests and Accused Bishop to Spain," *New York Times,* September 18, 1961,

p. 1. According to Boza Masvidal, 46 of those deported were Cuban born and the total expelled on this date was 132. Boza Masvidal, *Revolución*, pp. 69–70.

142 *about two hundred priests remained in Cuba:* This estimate is from the ENEC final report, section 1.8. Other estimates are as low as 130 remaining. By comparison, in 1955 there were 681 priests in Cuba, including 220 diocesan priests, of whom 95 were Cuban and the remainder Spanish. Of another 461 priests in male religious orders, 30 were Cuban. Gómez Treto, *The Church and Socialism in Cuba*, p. 11. By 1972, there remained a scarcity of pastors. Crahan reports that year there were 211 priests in Cuba, of whom 102 were in Havana.

142 *"sullen resentment":* Ruby Hart Phillips, "Castro Tightens His Hold on Cubans," *New York Times*, March 26, 1961, p. E8.

142 *subversive, decadent, and undermined the revolution:* Joel del Río, *Estudos avançados* 25, no. 72, São Paulo, May/August 2011, http://dx.doi.org/10.1590/S0103-40142011000200013.

142 *"Within the revolution, everything":* Quirk, *Fidel*, pp. 382–385. The first meeting was June 16 and the last one, where Fidel spoke, on June 30.

143 *modeled on Soviet communism:* Several accounts have claimed that this evolution was underway earlier. Fursenko and Naftali report that Fidel confessed he was a Communist at a meeting with PSP members on November 8, 1960, at the offices of the newspaper *Hoy*. According to the authors, who cite the reports of Alekseev to Moscow, Fidel said, "I have been a Marxist from my student days and have pulled together all the fundamental works of Marxism." He claimed to have introduced Marxist literature to Raúl, too; Alekseev added: "Fidel is convinced that he deserves credit for the formation of Raúl's views." Fidel also said that morning that he saw no other course for Cuba but socialism and said in the speech that "Moscow is our brain and our great leader, and we must pay attention to its voice." The authors say Fidel's remarks were widely distributed among the Soviet leadership and that it may be Fidel was trying to send them a signal of his support. But when looking at evidence of Castro's youth supplied by the PSP, "Moscow could conclude only that Fidel Castro was fantasizing, or was playing the role of supplicant, when he claimed to have been a Communist all along." Fursenko and Naftali, *"One Hell of a Gamble,"* p. 71. Fidel contributed to this revisionism about his conversion to communism. On December 22, 1961, he told a school class in Havana that he had concealed that he was a Marxist-Leninist while in the Sierra Maestra. Referring to the highest peak in the range, where he had climbed, Fidel said, "If, while we were on Turquino Peak, at a time when we were *cuatro gatos*"—an idiomatic expression meaning "when there were only a very few of us"—"we had said we are Marxist-Leninists, it is possible we would never have been able to descend to the lowlands from Turquino

Peak. So we called it something else. We did not present that theme. We presented others that people were able to understand easily." United Press International, "Castro Affirms He Concealed Marxism-Leninism in Revolt," *New York Times*, December 23, 1961, p. 7.

EIGHT. THE SECRET LIBRARY

147 *The two brothers were well known:* This account is based on interviews with Alejandro Payá, August 12, 2017; Óscar Payá, September 14, 2017; Marlene Payá, February 6, 2019; Carlos Alberto Payá, April 29, 2021; Ofelia Acevedo Maura, August 11, 2017, October 28 and December 3, 2018, and June 6, 2021; and numerous interviews with Rosa María Payá Acevedo, 2017–2021.

149 *Oswaldo stood fast, and the gang retreated:* Alejandro Payá, interview with author, August 12, 2017, Miami.

149 *Oswaldo was nicknamed* el Chivo: Santiago A. Cárdenas, *Payá: El Chivo, el Hombre, el Profeta* (Miami, FL: Instituto de la Memoria Histórica Cubana contra el Totalitarismo, 2013), p. 10.

149 *"a very strong and individualist kind of personality"*: Carlos Alberto Payá, interview with Pamela Rolfe, April 29, 2021, Madrid.

150 *"Give them the keys!"*: Marlene Payá, interview with author, February 6, 2019, Miami.

150 *"debris of the past."*: Quirk, *Fidel*, p. 520.

150 *Iraida's eight brothers and sisters:* Iraida had nine siblings, but one died as a baby.

150 *"Science has shown that Jesus Christ did not exist."*: Oswaldo Payá, *La noche no será eterna* (Miami: Editorial Hypermedia, 2018), p. 85.

151 *hundreds poured into the port to embark:* The government said departees must register. A total of 2,979 people left while the port remained open. See https://media.defense.gov/2020/Jul/02/2002356759/-1/-1/0/CAMARIOCA1965.PDF. The surge proved so embarrassing that Cuba stopped accepting applications in May 1966. But under an agreement with the United States, three to four thousand could leave by air every month, and the waiting lists were full for years afterward. See Quirk, *Fidel*, pp. 530–533. Also see Central Intelligence Agency, *Cuba, Its Institutions*.

151 *Payá family's oasis:* Rolando Sabin, *El Salvador del Cerro*, CreateSpace, July 24, 2013, in Spanish. Sabin says the church was probably not named for Christ the savior, but rather a popular Spanish captain general, Salvador de Muro y Salazar. For the same reason, Sabin said, there are San Salvador and Salvador streets in the neighborhood. The captain general, he writes, "who had arrived in Havana in 1799, was an exceptional politician who knew how to win the sympathy of the wealthy Creoles, mainly because he refused to put into effect Spain's orders to prevent foreign trade."

151 *For decades, the parish had been home to people of renown:* The *parroquia* is about

four square miles. Martí lived at No. 32, Calle Tulipán, in 1878, when his son was born. Finlay had a laboratory on Calle Tulipán and, as a religious man, may have attended Mass at the church. Sabin, *El Salvador del Cerro*. The square in front of the church was named Plaza Galicia in 1993.

152 *We can't be scared:* Ramón Antúnez, interview with author, November 30, 2017, Miami.

152 *"You have to yield—in order to triumph":* Carlos Alberto Payá, interview with Pamela Rolfe.

153 *called to the front of his classroom:* Rolando Sabin, communication with author, February 7, 2020.

153 *Alejo got a job at a state-run printing house:* Óscar Payá, interview with author, September 14, 2017, Madrid.

154 *the hammer fell on what remained of small businesses:* Quirk, *Fidel*, p. 592.

154 *improvising parts for cars:* Paul Hofmann, "Spare-Part Lack Tantalizes Cuba," *New York Times*, March 12, 1965, p. 12. The US trade embargo was partly to blame for such shortages, as well as the inefficient socialist economy.

154 *revolutionary offensive:* Carmelo Mesa-Lago, "The Revolutionary Offensive," *Trans-action* 6 (April 1969): 22–29. He says that 52 percent of retail trade had been collectivized or bought into the state system by 1962, but by 1968 it was 100 percent.

154 *"triumph of the revolution":* Paul Kidd, "The Price of Achievement under Castro," *Saturday Review*, May 3, 1969, p. 25; Quirk, *Fidel*, pp. 592–594.

155 *Alfredo Petit Vergel:* Cárdenas, *Payá: El Chivo*, p. 19.

155 *open and free discussions:* On the parish mood, Sabin, communication with author, February 7 and 9, 2020. On the Vikings, Sabin, *El Salvador del Cerro*, and Cárdenas, *Payá: El Chivo*. On the renegades, Oswaldo's brother Alejandro, interview with author, June 6, 2021, Miami, and Oswaldo Payá comments in *Cuba libre*, a film directed by Mateo J. Juez and produced by N. C. Yuma, Richter Scale Media, 2006.

155 *"a totally repressive situation":* Jose Yglesias, "Cuba Report: Their Hippies, Their Squares," *New York Times Magazine*, January 12, 1969, p. 25.

156 *"They thought Fidel had gone mad":* Latell, *History Will Absolve Me*, Kindle edition, location 659.

156 *a secret speech:* James G. Blight and Philip Brenner, *Sad and Luminous Days: Cuba's Struggle with the Superpowers after the Missile Crisis* (New York: Rowman & Littlefield, 2002), p. 67. The authors provide new information from declassified documents about Castro's disenchantment with Moscow after the missile crisis. He delivered a secret speech to his own politburo in January 1968 about the events, portions of which are reproduced by the authors.

157 *"There was no way out":* Reinaldo Arenas, *Before Night Falls: A Memoir*, trans. Dolores M. Koch (New York: Penguin, 1993), p. 125.

157 *outraged by the crushing of the Prague Spring:* Regis Iglesias Ramírez, communication with author, March 29, 2018, and March 26, 2021; Antúnez, interview with author.

157 *"youths who have gone wrong":* "Castro Speaks at Havana Province CDR Rally," September 28, 1968, Latin American Network Information Center, Castro Speech Database, http://lanic.utexas.edu/project/castro/db/1968 /19680929.html.

157 *they were all outsiders:* Humberto León, interview with author, January 23, 2018, Coral Gables, Florida. A similar account is provided by Jesús Hernández Cuéllar, "Cuba: Una historia de trabajos forzados," *Contacto Magazine,* May 26, 2003. An expanded version is posted on the website oswaldopaya.org.

158 *Oswaldo could not keep quiet:* Iglesias, communication with author, March 29, 2018, based on what Payá told him of the protest.

158 *Unidades Militares de Ayuda a la Producción:* Supposedly, Fidel invented the name. Gerardo Rodríguez Morejón, "UMAP: Forja de ciudadanos útiles a la sociedad," *El Mundo,* April 14, 1966, p. 5. The estimate of thirty-five thousand is from November 1965 to July 1968. See Abel Sierra Madero, " 'El trabajo os hará hombres': Masculinización nacional, trabajo forzado y control social en Cuba durante los años sesenta," *Cuban Studies,* no. 44 (2016): pp. 309–349. Also, Joseph Tahbaz, "Demystifying las UMAP: The Politics of Sugar, Gender and Religion in 1960s Cuba," *Delaware Review of Latin American Studies* 14, no. 2 (December 31, 2013).

158 *In raids carried out in October 1961:* The detainees were put in striped uniforms with a huge *P* across the back, standing for *prostitutas* (prostitutes), *proxenetas* (pimps), and *pájaros* (queers). The raids grabbed a far broader circle of people than just those described in the three *Ps.* The police invaded private homes without warning or legality; a prominent gay writer, Virgilio Piñera, was dragged from his house at midnight. Franqui, *Family Portrait,* p. 140.

159 *new men through work:* Sierra Madero, " 'El trabajo,' " p. 328. In this revealing study, Sierra Madero points out that camps were first applied to social rehabilitation of criminals in 1962. Also see Rachel Hynson, *Laboring for the State: Women, Family, and Work in Revolutionary Cuba, 1959–1971* (Cambridge: Cambridge University Press, 2019), p. 203.

159 *Fidel loved the metaphor of the steel forge:* Sierra Madero, "El trabajo," p. 315.

159 *"not by the dancers of twist or rock and roll":* Sierra Madero, "El trabajo," p. 317. Heberto Padilla wrote in a memoir that the camps were the invention of Raúl, who got the idea while on a trip to Bulgaria. Padilla, *Self-Portrait of the Other: A Memoir* (New York: Farrar, Straus and Giroux, 1990), p. 129.

159 *A clandestine system was set up:* Many of the students were first purged from their schools by the Young Communist League. Also, a clandestine system allowed anyone to secretly identify "deviants" by calling a "National

Information Center." Sierra Madero in "El trabajo" reproduces a card with instructions to informants, p. 323.

159 *"turning them into useful men in society":* Enrique Ros, *La UMAP: El gulag castrista* (Miami: Ediciones Universal, 2004), p. 45, quoting Luis Báez, *Granma,* April 14, 1966. The draft was imposed in 1963, covering young men fourteen and older, although they were not called to service until age seventeen.

159 *barracks that resembled cattle pens:* Paul Kidd, United Press International, November 9, 1966. The UPI dispatch includes a haunting photograph of the inside of the barracks. In 1969, Kidd wrote a longer piece that included similar observations about the camps, "The Price of Achievement under Castro," *Saturday Review,* May 3, 1969, pp. 23–25, 45–48.

160 *forced laborers were depicted as heroic field workers:* P. E. Cabrera, "Las brigadas de las UMAP," *Verde Olivo* 8, no. 19 (May 15, 1967): 36.

160 *a serious shortfall of agricultural workers:* For insight into how the UMAP system fit into Fidel's economic goals, see Tahbaz, "Demystifying las UMAP."

160 *Father Petit was sent to the camps:* Antonio Rodríguez, "The Auxiliary Bishops of Havana IV," *Palabra Nueva,* Havana, July 2, 2020, https://palabranueva .net. Petit was released in 1967 under a program to free those in the UMAP older than twenty-seven. He was assigned to El Cerro after that.

160 *stripped naked, tied up, and strapped to a fence:* Ros, *La UMAP,* pp. 136–138. Tahbaz says in "Demystifying las UMAP" that the Jehovah's Witnesses were "victims of the worst brutality of the UMAP camps."

160 *sticks between their legs:* Ros, *La UMAP,* p. 112.

160 *winched by his hands up a flagpole:* José Luis Llovio-Menéndez, *Insider: My Hidden Life as a Revolutionary in Cuba* (New York: Bantam, 1988), p. 153.

160 *"You are going to rot here":* Ros, *La UMAP,* p. 134, quoting Emilio Izquierdo.

160 *a can of sardines:* Ros, *La UMAP,* pp. 166–167, quoting Silvio Mancha.

160 *secreting scraps in his pocket:* Humberto León, interview with author, August 12, 2017, Miami, and January 23, 2018, Coral Gables, Florida.

160 *tied to fences, left to the mercy of giant mosquitoes:* Ros, *La UMAP,* p. 189.

161 *"Work will make you men":* Sierra Madero, "El trabajo," p. 329. The sign said: "El trabajo os hará hombres." The sign echoed one over the gate at Auschwitz: *"Arbeit macht frei,"* or "Work sets you free."

161 *"as if they were Elvis":* Lee Lockwood, *Castro's Cuba, Cuba's Fidel* (New York: Vintage, 1969), p. 107. Also see Fidel Castro Ruz, "Discurso en la clausura del acto conmemorativo del VI aniversario del asalto al Palacio Presidencial, en la escalinata de la Universidad de La Habana," 1963, http://www.cuba.cu /gobierno/discursos/1963/esp/f130363e.html.

161 *barbaric attempts to modify their behavior:* Many homosexuals had wires attached and were shocked with alternating currents while being shown pictures of naked men, in the theory that they would reject them and become

heterosexual. See Sierra Madero, "'El trabajo,'" p. 358, interview with María Elena Solé Arrondo, one of the psychologists who were there. Novelist Norberto Fuentes, who was once close to Fidel and later fled into exile, claimed there were 72 deaths in the camps from torture and ill treatment, 180 deaths by suicide, and 507 hospitalized for psychiatric treatment. Norberto Fuentes, *Dulces Guerreros Cubanos* (Barcelona: Editorial Seiz Barral, 1999, 2017), p. 337. No official estimates or data exist on deaths and injuries in the camps.

161 *other reports began to tumble out:* Kidd was expelled from Cuba on September 9, 1966. According to his account, the foreign ministry claimed he had an "incorrect attitude toward the revolution" and photographed an anti-aircraft gun emplacement visible from the grounds of his Havana hotel. He admitted to snapping a photo but said he stopped when an officer asked him to. He went to Camagüey after that and was expelled on his return to Havana. See Paul Kidd, "Cuba Expels Reporter," *Edmonton Journal*, September 10, 1966, p. 1. He was awarded the 1966 Maria Moors Cabot award for journalism from Columbia University.

161 *the men worked harvesting sugarcane twelve hours a day:* "Hard-Labor Units in Cuba Described," *New York Times*, June 25, 1967, p. 30. Another escapee, Juan Antonio Ortega, who was rescued at sea, described three hard-labor camps on the Isle of Pines. "Prison Isle Holds 10,000, Cuban Says," *New York Times*, December 4, 1966, p. 33.

161 *"real concentration camps":* Inter-American Commission on Human Rights, Organization of American States, *Report on the Situation of Human Rights in Cuba*," April 7, 1967, ch. 1, section F, "Concentration Camps." Tahbaz in "Demystifying las UMAP" takes issue with the description "concentration camps," saying that "torture was not systematically practiced at the camps" and that there was approximately one death at each camp over two and a half years, "not quite 'Cuba's concentration camps.'"

161 *"No, the revolution does not mean slave labor":* Fidel Castro speech to the Twelfth CTC Congress, August 29, 1966, Latin American Network Information Center, http://lanic.utexas.edu/project/castro/db/1966/19660830.html.

162 *"our miniature version of Stalinism":* Guerra, *Visions*, p. 354, says Padilla was part of a backroom committee at the writers and artists union that protested the imprisonment of artists and intellectuals in the UMAP camps. Padilla's essay was published in *El caimán barbudo*, no. 19 (1968). This was the literary supplement of the Cuban magazine *Juventud Rebelde*. In 1966, five prominent artists were called up to the UMAP and as a result of protests by other intellectuals Castro apologized to them. "Cuba: Revolution and the Intellectual: The Strange Case of Heberto Padilla," Index on Censorship, June 1, 1972.

162 *a "moral mistake":* Graham Greene wrote two articles that appeared in the *Weekend Telegraph* in London in December. "Shadow and Sunlight in Cuba," the

second article, was published December 9, 1966, and is reproduced in Greene, *Reflections* (New York: Penguin, 1990), p. 245. The first, a profile of Fidel, was published in the magazine December 2, 1966, and is reproduced in Greene's *Collected Essays* (New York: Viking, 1969), p. 405. Greene was influenced by the fact that several of his best friends in Cuba's cultural sphere were well-known homosexuals, including Piñera, who had been arrested in "Operation P" in 1961, according to Christopher Hull, *Our Man Down in Havana: The Story behind Graham Greene's Cold War Spy Novel* (New York: Pegasus, 2019), p. 263.

162 *a canny tactician:* In June, the youth organization of the Communist Party announced the creation of a new agricultural labor force, known as the Centennial Youth Column, designed to channel young people, especially from small towns, into the fields. The youth column was somewhat different from the UMAP, without the barbed wire and providing pay and technical training for teenagers who had shown some kind of unruly behavior or were maladjusted. They were organized in military-type squads, platoons, and companies and did the same back-breaking work in the sugar harvest.

162 *Sugarcane stalks:* This account of work in the sugarcane fields in 1969 is based on Payá's recollections to Regis Iglesias Ramírez, who recounted them in interviews with author; Pamela Rolfe interview with Carlos Alberto Payá; author's interviews with León; author's interview with Andrés Cárdenas Machado, September 12, 2018, Tampa, Florida; and the account of Jesús Hernández Cuéllar, "Cuba: A History of Forced Labor," *Contacto* magazine, Los Angeles, May 26, 2003.

163 *the "atomic bomb of sugar":* Pérez, *Cuba*, pp. 339–340. The sugar harvest of 1970 never reached Fidel's goal of 10 million tons but still, at about 8.5 million, was high for Cuba. The rest of the economy was nearly ruined in pursuit of the goal.

163 *a large "10 million" emblazoned on one side:* An image of the card, in Payá collection.

163 *the Isle of Pines:* Morton D. Winsberg, "The Isle of Pines, Cuba: A Geographic Interpretation" (PhD dissertation, University of Florida, June 1958), p. 1. Also see the valuable work by Michael E. Neagle, *America's Forgotten Colony: Cuba's Isle of Pines* (Cambridge: Cambridge University Press, 2016). He estimates 934 square miles.

163 *When the tower is darkened:* See https://www.atlasobscura.com/places/presidio-modelo.

164 *Oswaldo escaped to nearby hills:* Alejandro Payá, interview with author, June 5, 2021, Miami.

164 *"The Star-Spangled Banner" played:* Carlos Alberto Payá, interview with Pamela Rolfe.

164 *units were shifted to other projects:* Humberto León, communication with author, February 13, 2020. León says the other work was largely construction

and they were permitted civilian clothes. Upon completion of the three-year term, all had to report to the regional military committee in order to be officially discharged.

165 *played in a popular rock band, Los Kents:* Humberto León, communication with author, February 16, 2020.

165 *cleaned the pews:* On the repairs to the church and visit of the party bigwig, León and Cárdenas Machado interviews. Nuestra Señora de los Dolores is Our Lady of Sorrows.

166 *hundreds of books considered subversive or prohibited in Cuba:* Neagle, *America's Forgotten Colony*, pp. 8–9, 258–284. Settlers from the United States had set down roots there at the end of the Spanish colonial era, establishing citrus farms, purchasing 90 percent of the arable land, building a dozen towns, a school, and a community that reached a peak of two thousand people by 1910. The community dwindled as Fidel's agrarian reforms led to confiscation of large landholdings. The American Central School closed its doors in 1961, and remaining landholders hastily packed their bags to return to the United States. The books and music in the library were probably abandoned by the school, or the wealthy families, or both. León told the author that the group was aware of possible risks to talking about politics in the room, in case it was bugged, and they were cautious, but they did talk when they were free.

167 *the regime secretly decided to ban all books by foreign and domestic authors who took up Padilla's cause:* Guerra, *Visions*, pp. 353–362.

167 *with totalitarian ambitions:* Anne Applebaum, *Iron Curtain: The Crushing of Eastern Europe* (New York: Doubleday, 2012), pp. xxi–xxii. The term was coined by Giovanni Amendola, a journalist and politician prominent in the opposition to Mussolini. He first used the term in 1923; two years later, Mussolini embraced it. See Abbott Gleason, *Totalitarianism: The Inner History of the Cold War* (Oxford: Oxford University Press, 1995), pp. 13–20.

168 *totalitarian regimes had at least five common elements:* Carl J. Friedrich and Zbigniew Brzezinski, *Totalitarian Dictatorship and Autocracy* (New York: Praeger, 1956, 1965), p. 22.

NINE. DEFIANCE

169 *"You have failed":* Andrés Cárdenas Machado, interview with author, September 12, 2018, Tampa, Florida.

170 *"tovarishch!" or "comrade!" in Russian:* Quirk, *Fidel*, p. 682.

170 *a long interrogation:* This account is based on Payá, interviews with Ehrenberg.

171 *"they assigned other Communist youth to work on you":* León, interview with author.

171 *If anyone is going to leave Cuba:* Humberto León, interview with author, January 23, 2018, Miami.

172   *Fidel did not resign:* Quirk, *Fidel,* p. 644. Fidel spoke July 26, 1970, at the Plaza
      of Revolution. Quirk notes that by August 8 Fidel was saying he didn't intend
      to resign.

172   *made even the most minor decisions:* See Quirk, *Fidel,* pp. 618–629. A 1974 analytical
      study by the CIA concluded that Fidel "indulged in the luxury of government
      by whim" and added: "With the country suffering from an extremely serious
      housing shortage, for example, Castro spent millions on prize cattle flown in
      from Canada and housed them and their offspring in expensive 'show case'
      barns equipped with air conditioning and piped-in music." Central Intelligence
      Agency, *Cuba, Its Institutions,* p. 9. Castro explained the air-conditioned barns in
      remarks January 30, 1969, at the "Niña Bonita" experimental farm, Cangrejera.
      http://www.cuba.cu/gobierno/discursos/1969/esp/f300169e.html.

172   *a more formal political structure:* Fidel's interest also seemed to shift. Between
      November 1971 and October 1973, he spent long periods abroad, visiting
      twenty countries, several of them twice. Central Intelligence Agency, *Cuba,
      Its Institutions,* p. 5.

172   *Soviet Union . . . pressed Fidel to delegate more decision-making:* Carmelo Mesa-
      Lago, *Cuba in the 1970s: Pragmatism and Institutionalization* (Albuquerque: Uni-
      versity of New Mexico Press, 1974), p. 17.

173   *a third were taken almost verbatim:* Leónel-Antonio de la Cuesta, "The Cuban
      Socialist Constitution: Its Originality and Role in Institutionalization," *Cuban
      Studies* 6, no. 2 (July, 1976): 15–30. Also see Georgetown University, Edmund
      A. Walsh School of Foreign Service, Center for Latin American Studies Pro-
      gram, Political Database of the Americas, Republic of Cuba, Political Consti-
      tution of 1976, in Spanish and English.

173   *a brief window for a genuinely democratic electoral system:* Szulc, *Fidel Castro,*
      pp. 642–643. Also see Jorge I. Domínguez, *Cuba: Order and Revolution* (Cam-
      bridge, MA: Harvard, Belknap Press, 1978), appendix D, pp. 528–530.

173   *Fidel remained Cuba's undisputed leader:* Quirk, *Fidel,* p. 728. Szulc, *Fidel Castro,*
      p. 644, says the new constitution set Cuba's future "in granite."

174   *One of them was Gustavo's citizen initiative, based on ten thousand signatures:* It
      was Article 135 in the 1940 Constitution and Article 122 in the Fundamental
      Law of 1959. The 1976 charter was modified in 1992 so that this provision
      became Article 88 (g).

174   *a nascent human rights organization was formed clandestinely:* Alex Anton, "The
      Rise of the Cuban Human Rights Movement," in Reinaldo Bragado Bretaña,
      La Fisure: Los Derechos Humanos en Cuba, vol. 1 (Miami: Cátedra del Pensam-
      iento Libre, 1998), pp. 389–405.

175   *he freed about four thousand political prisoners:* Castro agreed in late 1978 to
      release about four thousand political prisoners including several hundred so-
      called *plantados* serving since the early 1960s on condition they immigrate to

the United States. Many did so, but the process was interrupted by the chaos of the Mariel boatlift of 1980 and many of the released prisoners were subsequently stranded in Cuba. See Jorge Valls, *Twenty Years and Forty Days: Life in a Cuban Prison* (New York: Americas Watch, 1986), pp. 107–109.

175 *More than one hundred thousand exiles returned for visits:* For an account of the negotiations, see Robert M. Levine, *Secret Missions to Cuba: Fidel Castro, Bernardo Benes, and Cuban Miami* (New York: Palgrave, 2001). On the return, see Michael Bustamante, *Cuban Memory Wars: Retrospective Politics in Revolution and Exile* (Chapel Hill: University of North Carolina Press, 2021), pp. 179–214.

176 *the Mariel boatlift:* Geyer, *Guerrilla Prince*, pp. 368–371; Kuivala, *Never a Church of Silence*, p. 237. On the prisoners, Fidel's onetime bodyguard Juan Reinaldo Sánchez recalled witnessing Fidel select the prisoners personally. Sánchez with Axel Glydén, *The Double Life of Fidel Castro: My 17 Years as Personal Bodyguard to El Líder Máximo* (New York: St. Martin's, 2014), p. 163.

176 *first we would liberate Cuba:* Payá, interviews with Ehrenberg.

177 *Carlos Alberto realized he needed to act:* Payá, interviews with Ehrenberg; Carlos Alberto Payá, interview with Pamela Rolfe.

177 *Andrés Solares had an inspiration:* This account is based on the author's interview with Solares, October 30, 2018, Miami, and documents on his case provided by Solares; Solares, *Cuba: The Disaster of Castro's Revolution* (Xlibris: 2010), pp. 9–17; Charles J. Brown and Armando M. Lago, *The Politics of Psychiatry in Revolutionary Cuba* (New Brunswick, NJ: Transaction, 1991), pp. 92–94; and Jennifer L. Lambe, *Madhouse: Psychiatry and Politics in Cuban History* (Chapel Hill: University of North Carolina Press, 2017).

178 *He decided to establish a new political party in Cuba:* The original copy of the party goals was seized in the raid of Solares's home, and documents were destroyed after his trial. However, he reconstructed it from memory in prison and provided it to the author. A summary is included in an appendix to his book.

179 *handcuffed to a nervous young man:* Juan Manuel Cao, interview with author, September 10, 2018, Miami.

180 *Havana Psychiatric Hospital, known as Mazorra:* For a history of Mazorra, see Lambe, *Madhouse*.

180 *Solares was convicted:* "Courtroom of Crimes against the Security of the State," Havana, Sentence No. 23, 3 pp., May 13, 1982.

TEN. "FAITH AND JUSTICE"

181 *Oswaldo Payá greeted Christmas every year with a special joviality:* Rolando Sabin, communication with author, February 8, 2020.

183 *My relationship is directly with God:* Santiago A. Cárdenas, *Payá: El Chivo*, pp.

27–28, and Cárdenas, interview with author, November 9, 2019, Hialeah, Florida. Santería is a syncretic religion rooted in the religious practices of the Yoruba people, who were brought as slaves to Cuba from the Congo Basin and West Africa. Kirsten Lavery, "The Santería Tradition in Cuba," Fact sheet, United States Commission on International Religious Freedom, February 2021.

183 *the rights of man are bestowed by God, not the state:* Payá, interviews with Ehrenberg.

184 *The French scholar Jean Gerson:* Dan Edelstein, *On the Spirit of Rights* (Chicago: University of Chicago Press, 2019), p. 15.

184 *crystalized many of the ideas in natural law:* Jacques Maritain, *Christianity and Democracy,* trans. Doris C. Anson (London: Centenary Press, 1945).

184 *Christian Democratic movements:* "Christian Democracy: Principles and Policy-Making," Konrad-Adenauer-Stiftung, Berlin, 2001, p. 9. Christian democracy broadly endorses market capitalism and private property, but with regulation of the market and emphasizing that social responsibility comes with private ownership.

184 *also spread to Latin America:* "The Christian Democratic Movement in Latin America," Central Intelligence Agency, November 6, 1964.

184 *revolution had snuffed it out:* A Christian Democratic movement founded in Havana by José Ignacio Rasco in late 1959 attracted students and young professionals but disappeared after his flight into exile the following year.

184 *Payá would have been at home with all these ideas:* Sabin, communication with author, and interviews with Ofelia Acevedo Maura.

185 *Oswaldo earned a degree in electrical engineering:* Ofelia Acevedo Maura, interview with author, August 11, 2017. Payá received the degree in electrical engineering on July 15, 1983.

186 *In a wrenching conversation:* León, interviews with author.

186 *archbishop of Havana:* Jaime Ortega Alamino, "Everything Is Nothing, Only God," a statement written before his death July 26, 2019, published posthumously in Havana, www.palabranueva.net. Also see Katharine Q. Seelye, "Cardinal Jaime Ortega Is Dead at 82; Helped Cuba and U.S. Restore Ties," *New York Times,* July 27, 2019, p. A22, and Ortega, *Te basta mi gracia* (Madrid: Palabra, 2002).

187 *All the church's institutions were gone:* José Conrado, interview with author, January 23, 2018, Miami.

187 *"still live in the catacombs today":* Pope Paul VI, "Visit to the Roman Catacombs," text of homily, Sunday, September 12, 1965, http://www.vatican.va /content/paul-vi/it/homilies/1965/documents/hf_p-vi_hom_19650912 _catacombe.html.

187 *Cuba was such a country:* Kuivala, *Never a Church of Silence.* The author is grateful to Kuivala for sharing her conclusions and insights from groundbreaking

archival research in Cuba on the history of the church in this period. For estimates on 1957, see J. Lloyd Mecham, *Church and State in Latin America: A History of Politico-Ecclesiastical Relations* (Chapel Hill: University of North Carolina Press, 1966), p. 303. The estimate of nuns and priests attending multiple churches is from *Encuentro nacional eclesial cubano*, the final report of the conference of February 1986 in Havana, p. 63.

188 *resources were so scarce:* Kuivala, *Never a Church of Silence*, p. 231.

188 *transformed the attitudes of the church:* John Witte Jr. and Frank S. Alexander, eds., *Christianity and Human Rights: An Introduction* (Cambridge: Cambridge University Press, 2010), pp. 24–25.

189 *to reject liberation theology:* The pope urged bishops to think of liberation "that in the framework of the Church's proper mission is not reduced to the simple and narrow economic, political, social or cultural dimension, and is not sacrificed to the demands of any strategy, practice or short-term solution." Address of Pope John Paul II, Puebla, Mexico, Sunday, January 28, 1979, http://www .vatican.va/content/john-paul-ii/en/speeches/1979/january/documents /hf_jp-ii_spe_19790128_messico-puebla-episc-latam.html. Also see Daniel H. Levine, ed., *Churches and Politics in Latin America* (Beverly Hills, CA: Sage, 1979), p. 24.

189 *The Puebla texts did not reflect Cuba's reality:* Luis Báez and Pedro de la Hoz, *Monseñor Carlos Manuel se confiesa* (Havana: Ediciones Abril, 2015), p. 157. Céspedes died in 2014.

189 *alarmed that both clergy and laity were thinking of leaving:* On the church and Mariel, Kuivala, *Never a Church of Silence*, pp. 235–236. Azcárate made the proposal at a meeting in July 1979, held at El Cobre, the national sanctuary of Cuban Catholics, home to the shrine to La Virgen de la Caridad, Cuba's patron saint.

189 *Pope John Paul II's pilgrimage to his native Poland:* George Weigel, *Witness to Hope: The Biography of Pope John Paul II* (New York: HarperCollins, 1999), pp. 303–325.

190 *The church could make peace with Castro:* Antonio G. Chizzoniti, *Agostino Casaroli: Lo sguardo lungo della Chiesa* (Milan: Vita e Pensario-Largo A. Gemelli, 2015), p. 46. Cesare Zacchi, the apostolic nuncio in Cuba, representing the Holy See, also carried out the *Ostpolitik* approach toward Fidel.

191 *no longer ostracized:* Kuivala, *Never a Church of Silence*, p. 245, quoting a draft press release announcing Ortega's appointment as archbishop of Havana, reports that "Ortega called for recognition of lay people's difficulties in social and economic life: the prejudice, pressure and rejection experienced by Catholics at schools, universities and workplaces."

191 *Oswaldo was well suited:* Ofelia Acevedo Maura, interviews with author, October 28, 2018, and December 3, 2017, Miami.

191   *the letter from Ortega on July 9, 1984:* Payá collection.

192   *a key decision made by Ortega:* Kuivala, *Never a Church of* Silence, pp. 247–249, and communication with author April 28, 2020.

192   *unleashed a flood of restiveness:* Kuivala, *Never a Church of Silence,* pp. 247–253.

193   *"Who is that?" "Oswaldo Payá":* Ofelia Acevedo Maura, interviews with author, and Cárdenas, *Payá.*

194   *Castro's views of religion:* Fidel Castro, *Fidel and Religion: Castro Talks on Revolution and Religion with Frei Betto* (New York: Simon & Schuster, 1987), originally published as *Fidel y la religión* (Havana: Oficina de Publicaciones del Consejo de Estado, 1985).

194   *Oswaldo received another letter:* Payá collection. On the committee and presidency, the process is described in *Encuentro nacional eclesial cubano.*

195   *a wary embrace:* Kuivala found church documents that described these contacts between the bishops and Fidel as the "normal course of work between the Catholic Church and the Cuban State." Kuivala, *Never a Church of Silence,* p. 272. However, she notes, this normalcy was a change after many years without any direct sustained relations between the episcopate and the revolutionary leadership. Ortega told the Associated Press there had been a "quiet but sustained dialogue" with the government for some time and "we hope it will be intensified and that it can be carried out at the highest level." George Gedda, Associated Press, "Archbishop Reports Negotiation with Marxist Government," July 31, 1985.

195   *touched off a sensation:* Kuivala, *Never a Church of Silence,* p. 280; William R. Long, "Cuba and Church—a Thaw Starts," *Los Angeles Times,* April 12, 1986, p. 1.

196   *the right to speak out:* This account is primarily based on interviews with Ofelia Acevedo Maura, who witnessed the talk, and Ramón Antúnez. No text of this speech could be located.

196   *Everybody was in shock at that moment:* Dagoberto Valdes, interview with author, February 8, 2019, Homestead, Florida.

197   *"This cannot be allowed":* Conrado, interview with author and *Sueños y pesadillas de un cura en Cuba: ¿El futuro de la Iglesia en Cuba?* (Miami: Ediciones Universal, 2017), pp. 24–25.

197   *sent an intermediary:* The intermediary was José Navarro Campo of Santiago de Cuba, who was a member of the presidency, the council created to oversee the conference.

198   *Fidel was being given an advance look:* Báez and de la Hoz, *Monseñor Carlos Manuel se confiesa,* pp. 156–162.

198   *Oswaldo spoke up:* Payá, interviews with Ehrenberg. The conversation with Pironio is based on a confidential source. The author could not determine whether the pope responded. Pironio also met with Fidel on the trip. Cuban

International Radio, February 23, 1986, Office of Research and Policy, Radio Martí Program, *Cuba Annual Report: 1986* (New Brunswick, NJ: Transaction, 1990), p. 160.

200 *continued to serve on Ortega's pastoral council:* Payá collection.

201 *the chauffeur and limousine disappeared:* Ofelia Acevedo Maura, interviews with author, August 11, 2017, December 3, 2017, and October 28, 2018, and photographs, Payá collection.

201 *Carlos Alberto left for Spain:* Carlos Alberto Payá, interview with Pamela Rolfe.

201 *shortwave radio broadcasts:* Rolando Sabin, communication with author, February 8–9, 2020.

201 *"a free, critical point of view":* Payá, interviews with Ehrenberg.

202 *"He caused learning to become vital":* Joseph and Helen M. McCadden, *Félix Varela: Torch Bearer from Cuba* 2nd. rev. ed. (New York: Félix Varela Foundation, 1984), pp. 1–37. Also, "Félix Varela y Morales," Cuban Studies Institute, January 7, 2021.

203 *Varela's political goals were democratic, and nonviolent:* McCadden and McCadden, *Félix Varela*, pp. 38–71. The assassination plot, pp. 59–60.

203 *what had they achieved:* Ortega, *Te basta*, pp. 329–337. This is Ortega's homily on the first anniversary of the ENEC, delivered February 18, 1987.

203 *whether lay people could act independently of local bishops:* Robert Suro, "Pope Opens Synod of Bishops on Role of the Laity," *New York Times*, October 2, 1987. The synod's 232 participants represented 101 national bishops' conferences from around the world.

204 *words of steel:* The next week, Payá was more direct, insisting that lay people not waste time looking for points of agreement with socialism. Rather, he declared, "We must discover the joy of truth that makes us free, casting aside the willingness to accommodate, freeing our hearts and our minds from prejudice, selfishness, and fear, and bearing witness with a stance that is both free and liberating." *Ecos del Sínodo*, no. 1, courtesy Rolando Sabin; nos. 2, 3, 4, 5, Payá collection. A complete collection is also posted at www.mcliberacion .org.

ELEVEN. THE MOVEMENT

206 *the outlawed Solidarity labor movement led renewed strikes and protests:* Prices on approximately half of Polish goods and services were raised February 1, triggering protests and strikes in April. Svetlana Savranskaya, Thomas Blanton, and Vladislav Zubok, *Masterpieces of History: The Peaceful End of the Cold War in Europe, 1989* (Budapest: Central European University Press, 2010), pp. xxxii–xxxiii.

206 *Spanish-language issues of* Sputnik: Regis Iglesias Ramírez, communication with author, April 11, 2020. *Sputnik*, a colorful magazine, was printed

in Finland, published by the Soviet news agency Novosti in Spanish, German, English, French, Portuguese, and Russian. The Spanish edition was titled *Sputnik: Selecciones de la prensa soviética*. See https://ufdc.ufl.edu /AA00048425/00100/allvolumes.

206   *The couple vowed they would not leave Cuba and that their children would live in a free country:* Ofelia Acevedo Mauro, interviews with author.

207   *could they create a Solidarity labor movement:* Santiago Cárdenas, *Payá: El Chivo*, pp. 39–40.

207   *The plight of political prisoners:* Armando Valladares, *Against All Hope: The Prison Memoirs of Armando Valladares*, trans. Andrew Hurley (New York: Knopf, 1986), p, 198; Valls, *Twenty Years and Forty Days*.

208   *folded the lists into tiny paper packets:* Andrés Solares, interview with author, October 30, 2018, Miami, and Solares, *Cuba*.

208   *Their plight inspired Oswaldo:* Oswaldo J. Payá Sardiñas, "To All Cuban Political Prisoners, Past and Present," October 1987, Movimiento Cristiano Liberación, www.oswaldopaya.org.

209   *an elite military unit in El Salvador:* Mark Danner, *The Massacre at El Mozote* (New York: Vintage, 1994), p.10.

209   *Reagan saw the world first and foremost through the Cold War prism:* Ronald Reagan, *The Reagan Diaries* (New York: HarperCollins, 2007), pp. 50, 132–133. This singular focus on fighting communism in the region led to the Iran-Contra scandal, in which Reagan defied Congress to provide aid to the Nicaraguan rebels fighting the Marxist Sandinista government. The scandal was just breaking open in late 1986.

209   *Reagan appeared with former political prisoner Valladares:* W. Dale Nelson, "Reagan Calls Marchenko a 'Martyr,' Assails Soviet Rights Abuses," Associated Press, December 10, 1986.

209   *a personal letter of encouragement to Bofill:* Dan Williams, "Actions Provoke Regime's Wrath; Rare Dissident Challenges Cuba over Human Rights," *Los Angeles Times*, August 4, 1987, p. 1.

209   *"massive violations of human rights":* Statement by Ambassador Vernon Walters, U.S. Mission to the United Nations, November 26, 1986. Also see Tony Platt, "Cuba and the Politics of Human Rights," *Social Justice* 15, no. 2 (summer 1998): 38–54. In a 1969 report, Americas Watch said "there is no evidence" to support charges of 10,000 or 15,000 political prisoners at that time. But the group said widespread human rights violations existed in Cuba, including denial of rights to privacy, assembly, and freedom of speech and thought. See Americas Watch, "Human Rights in Cuba," January 1969, p. 4. No one knew exactly how many political prisoners there were. Amnesty International, in a 1986 report, "Political Imprisonment in Cuba," reported up to one hundred long-term political prisoners, or *plantados*, first arrested in the 1960s were still

held. Some were prisoners of conscience, including Solares. Valls listed 126 *plantados* in his memoir as of April 1986. Valls, *Twenty Years and Forty Days*, pp. 113–120. When Cardinal John O'Connor of New York came to Cuba in April 1988, the government produced a list of 429 Cubans that it said included all political prisoners. But the lowest independent estimate at the time was 1,000. Julia Preston, "Cuban Dissident Tries to Form Party," *Washington Post*, July 28, 1988, p. A23. A decade earlier, in 1978, a deputy Cuban interior minister, Enio Leyva Fuentes, visiting East Germany, said the number had reached a peak of 18,000 in 1965 but declined to about 3,200 "counterrevolutionaries," of whom 2,300 were "genuine counterrevolutionaries" and the remainder sentenced for trying to escape the island. A large number of those mentioned by Leyva Fuentes were released in 1979. Gerhard Ehlert, Jochen Staadt, and Tobias Voigt, "Die Zusammenarbeit Zwischen dem Ministerium für Staatssicherheit de DDR (MfS) und dem Ministerium des Innern Kubas (MININT)," Research Association SED State, Free University of Berlin, Working Paper No. 33/2002, June 2002, p. 31. On the availability of information, Orlando Gutiérrez, communication with author, June 4, 2020.

209   *the rising power of Jorge Mas Canosa:* Born in 1939, Mas Canosa was the son of an army veterinarian from Santiago de Cuba. He fled Cuba in 1960 to Miami. He took part in the Bay of Pigs invasion, though his unit never disembarked on the Cuban coast. He later become a wealthy construction magnate in South Florida. In 1981, he and a handful of wealthy exiles launched CANF, which had a political action committee and lobbying arm and was said to have been modeled on the pro-Israel lobbying group, the American Israel Political Action Committee. CANF became very influential in the Reagan years. Christopher Marquis, "Jorge Mas Canosa dead at 58," *Miami Herald*, November 24, 1997; John Newhouse, "Socialism or Death," *The New Yorker*, April 27, 1992, pp. 52–83. Radio Martí went on the air May 20, 1985, under the supervision of the Voice of America and in the first years gained an audience on the island. AM reception was sometimes accompanied by an annoying hum but not jammed altogether, and the station was also broadcast loud and clear on shortwave from transmitters on Marathon Key. More intensive jamming of the radio station came after the 1990 decision to launch TV Martí. The audience is hard to calculate. Telephone surveys from 2003–2008 found that fewer than 2 percent of Cuban adults in households with landline phones listened to the radio or watched television on a weekly basis, but the low response may have been due to fear of acknowledging they were listening or watching. In 2010, 661 immigrants were interviewed within six months of leaving Cuba and 40 percent of respondents reported hearing Radio Martí and 6 percent of respondents reported seeing TV Martí at least once a week on average during their last year on the island. But again, the method may

have skewed the results—those leaving may have been more likely to listen. The author was told by many who worked on the Varela Project that they periodically heard reports on Radio Martí. U.S. Government Accountability Office, "Cuba Broadcasting Strategy," GAO-12-243R, December 13, 2011, p. 10; George Gedda, Associated Press, "Cuba Extends Jamming of Radio Martí Past Sunrise," April 24, 1990.

210 *Castro had resisted:* The United States pressed for a resolution on Cuba before the U.N. Human Rights Commission in 1987. The text then did not refer to political prisoners but condemned deprivation of rights to a fair trial, freedom from arbitrary arrest and detention, and freedom of expression. This resolution was defeated on a procedural motion 19–18. The administration redoubled the effort at the 1988 session, which resulted in the compromise of a delegation visit. The NBC interview was February 24, 1988. Valladares was appointed to the commission by Reagan in November 1987 and given ambassadorial rank in his capacity as head of the delegation for the 1988 meeting in Geneva. See https://www.reaganlibrary.gov/archives/speech/nominations-and-appointments-march-4-1988.

210 *sought retribution against Bofill:* Voice of America, United States Information Agency, Office of Research and Policy, Radio Martí Program, *Cuba Annual Report: 1988* (New Brunswick, NJ: Transaction, 1991), pp. 407–418.

210 *a special supplement to* Granma: February 29, 1988; Voice of America, *Cuba Annual Report*, p. 406.

211 *"Something has to be done":* Antúnez, interview with author.

211 *The first issue: Pueblo de Dios:* Editions 1–7, Payá collection.

212 *Sabin told his friends:* Sabin, communication with author, February 9, 2020.

212 *Who put so many strange and wrong ideas in your head?:* Cárdenas, El Chivo, p. 38.

213 *Andrés Solares learned he would be released:* Andrés Solares, interview with author, October 30, 2018.

214 *she found Bofill in his darkened, hot apartment:* Julia Preston, "Cuban Dissident Tries to Form Party; Castro Issues Stern Warnings against Alternatives to Communists," *Washington Post*, July 27, 1988, p. A23, and Preston, communication with author, April 19, 2020.

215 *"only one party here":* "Discurso pronunciado por el comandante en jefe Fidel Castro Ruz, primer secretario del Comité Central del Partido Comunista de Cuba y presidente de los Consejos de Estado y de Ministros, en el acto central por el XXXV aniversario del asalto al Cuartel Moncada, efectuado en la plaza Antonio Maceo, de Santiago de Cuba, el 26 de julio de 1988," http://www.cuba.cu/gobierno/discursos/1988/esp/f260788e.html.

215 *"Fidel would not tolerate it":* Ricardo Bofill, interview with author, September 14, 2018, Miami.

215 *Gorbachev presided over a party congress:* Savranskaya et al., *Masterpieces*, p. xxxiii.

The Gorbachev-Reagan summit was May 29–June 1. Gorbachev's speech was June 28 to the XIX All-Union Conference of the Communist Party. David Remnick, "Gorbachev Proposes Presidential System," *Washington Post*, June 29, 1988, p. A1.

215   *stories of glasnost and perestroika:* Julia Preston, "For Castro's Cloistered Realm, No Glasnost Yet," *Washington Post*, July 31, 1988, p. A1.

215   *"We must not play or flirt with capitalist things":* Preston, "For Castro's Cloistered Realm."

215   *an emerging interest in human rights:* Preston, "For Castro's Cloistered Realm."

216   *something more ambitious:* Payá, interviews with Ehrenberg.

216   *"opened up a world of ideas":* Sabin, communication with author, February 9, 2020.

216   *letters Varela wrote from New York and Madrid:* Félix Varela, *Cartas a Elpidio, Sobre la impiedad, la superstición y el fanatismo en sus relaciones con la Sociedad,* vols. 1 and 2 (Havana: University of Havana, 1944).

216   *stay on the high road:* McCadden and McCadden, *Félix Varela*, pp. 94–98.

216   *"we had to do something concrete":* Antúnez, interview with author.

217   *"I feel a cold that paralyzes me":* Cárdenas, *El Chivo*, p. 41.

217   *The movement was born:* Cárdenas, *El Chivo*, p. 42, and Antúnez, interview with author. The other two present were Dagoberto Capote, who voted no, and Fernando Avedo, an engineer who knew Oswaldo from work and voted yes.

218   *"Nosotros los Cubanos":* Oswaldo Payá, "Liberación," handwritten copy, Payá collection.

219   *just a few people:* Antúnez, interview with author.

219   *the visit by the U.N. Human Rights Commission:* United Nations Commission on Human Rights, 45th Session, "Consideration of the Report of the Mission Which Took Place in Cuba in Accordance with the Commission Decision 1988/106," E/CN.4/1989/46, February 21, 1989, 55 pp. plus 32 annexes.

220   *human rights concerns had not disappeared:* The delegation reported in February 1989, but without a strong recommendation. Instead, they simply published statements they had gathered, both from the government and from complainants. Many of the government statements were ridiculous, such as the claim that members of the National Assembly were elected by a "free, equal and secret vote." See p. 40.

220   *the struggle to mobilize people and collect signatures:* Bofill, interview with author.

220   *the ouster of . . . Pinochet:* Eugene Robinson, "Chile's Pinochet Beaten in Plebiscite on Rule; Voters Reject Bid for 8 More Years in Power," *Washington Post*, October 6, 1988, p. 1.

221   *"That man is crazy":* Tanya Rodriguez was the lead singer in Monte de Espuma. "Este hombre esta loco" was on side B of their 1987 record, *Latino*, Areito, Havana.

221 "*Signs of crisis*": Stasi Records Archive, Federal Commissioner for the Stasi Records (BStU), Berlin, MfS HAI 13937, November 1988. On transmission to Honecker, see Ehlert et al., "Die Zusammenarbeit," pp. 64–65.

TWELVE. THE STASI LESSONS

223 *intelligence was their means of survival:* Piñeiro, who died in 1998, made this remark to a foreign diplomat, who recounted it to the author.

223 *one of the half-dozen best foreign intelligence agencies in the world:* Brian Latell, *Castro's Secrets: Cuban Intelligence, the CIA and the Assassination of John F. Kennedy* (New York: Palgrave Macmillan, 2012), p. 2.

223 *double agents:* Latell, *Castro's Secrets*, p. 10, says "more than four dozen Cubans, recruited by the CIA as spies, were actually doubles" working for Cuba's intelligence directorate. After defector Florentino Aspillaga revealed the long-running deception to the CIA in 1987, the official Cuban media identified twenty-seven. A former US intelligence officer interviewed by the author said there were twenty-eight.

223 *planted a mole, Ana Belén Montes:* Montes was arrested September 21, 2001 and charged with espionage. She pleaded guilty and was sentenced to twenty-five years in prison.

223 *informants on every block:* On the CDRs, see Josep M. Colomer, "Watching Neighbors: The Cuban Model of Social Control," *Cuban Studies* 31 (2000): 118–138. On the size of state security, little reliable information is available; the estimate of ten to fifteen thousand staff is from DIA's *Handbook of the Cuban Armed Forces*, DDB-2680-62-79, April 1979, pp. 1–12. On state security's reach, see Sánchez, *The Double Life of Fidel Castro*, p. 158. On the cells at Villa Marista, see Adolfo Rivero Caro, "How to Survive in Villa Marista," https://cubanitoweb.wordpress.com/2010/06/02/como-sobrevivir-en-villa -marista/. Rivero Caro was a former political prisoner and human rights activist. The U.N. Human Rights Commission delegation that visited in September 1988 was shown a cell at Villa Marista that was 4 by 4.5 meters, freshly painted.

224 *sailing in a sea of difficulties:* Fred Bruning and Larry Rohter, "Cuba: Castro's Sea of Troubles," *Newsweek*, March 3, 1980, p. 39.

224 *an operational technique known as Zersetzung. It meant "decomposition":* The author is indebted to Jorge Luis García Vázquez for generous help on this section, including documents, advice, and personal reflections. Details of Stasi methods are drawn from: Stasi Records Archive, Federal Commissioner for the Stasi Records (BStU), Berlin (as of June 17, 2021, the Stasi Records Archive became part of Germany's Federal Archive); the Stasi Museum, House 1 on the former grounds of the headquarters of the Ministry of State Security, Berlin; the Stasi prison memorial, Berlin-Hohenschönhausen; also David Childs and Richard Popplewell, *The Stasi: The East German Intelligence and*

Security Service (London: Macmillan, 1996). On SOUD, see Andrei Soldatov, "Догнать и перегнать 'Эшелон'!," *Segodnya*, Moscow, November 19, 1999.

224   *a drab campus that could not be found on any list of higher educational institutions:* The school used "Juristische Hochschule Potsdam" or "Potsdam University of Law" in external correspondence and on documents and exam certificates to conceal the link to the Stasi. Internally, it was called the University of the Ministry of State Security, according to Günther Forester, "The Dissertations at the 'Law School' of the MfS: An Annotated Bibliography," Department of Education and Research, Federal Commissioner for the Records of the State Security Service of the former German Democratic Republic, 1997, pp. 5, 16. Also see Leónie Kayser, *Der Universitätscampus Golm* (Potsdam: Potsdam University Press, 2019). The young recruits just out of high school were added in 1984, according to Forester.

225   *had studied in Pennsylvania in the 1960s:* Ehlert et al., "Die Zusammenarbeit," p. 28. Also, "Jacinto Valdes-Dapena," Philadelphia's Central High School yearbook, 1960, p. 113.

225   *the latest methods of East Germany's secret police:* Cuba's Ministry of Interior requested the berth at Golm for Valdés-Dapena in January 1981, and officials corresponded about his progress and his dissertation over the next three years. See BStU, MfS, JHS 21952. According to Forester in "The Dissertations at the 'Law School' of the MfS," Valdés-Dapena was one of only five foreigners among more than four hundred doctoral students at the school over its history. He and two other Cubans got degrees there, plus two from the Soviet KGB. The title of his thesis and the document: BStU, MfS JHS 255/83.

226   *the technical aspects of surveillance:* Childs and Popplewell, *The Stasi*, p. 91; Stasi Museum, Berlin.

226   *assassination by staging a car wreck:* Childs and Popplewell, in *The Stasi*, p. 62, say the key factor in the shift was Stalin's death and Nikita Khrushchev's secret speech in 1956 revealing some details of repressions. After that, "there could be no recourse to the violent repression of the years 1945–1953." However, the Stasi did plan for and sometimes carry out assassinations and its training manuals included methods of ambush of individuals. Among others, they tried to poison the former political prisoner Wolfgang Welsch. Although it was never proven, there are suspicions that the Stasi also was involved in the death of professional soccer player Lutz Eigendorf on March 5, 1983. He had played for a Stasi-sponsored soccer club and defected to the West; the killing may have been revenge. In November 1987, the former East German dissidents Freya Klier and Stefan Krawczyk had a mysterious car wreck. Klier wrote in a book published in 2021 that an aging former Stasi officer had confessed to her that the car had been tampered with by the Stasi so that the steering would fail on a curve. They hit a bridge pillar. Freya Klier, *Under*

Mysterious Circumstances: The Political Murders of the State Security (Freiburg, Germany: Verlag Herder, 2021). Thomas Auerbach, a Stasi archives historian, reports that the Stasi had the will to carry out political murders, but only a few cases can be proven because orders were not written down or preserved. Training manuals, however, referred to "faked suicides or accidents" as one method. Auerbach, "Liquidierung = Mord? Zur vieldeutigen Semantik des Begriffs in den MfS-Unterlagen," *Horch un Guch*, no. 59 (2008): 4–7. Also see Jens Gieseke, *The History of the Stasi: East Germany's Secret Police, 1945–1990*, trans. David Burnett (New York: Berghahn Books, 2014), p. 144.

226 *an army of unofficial workers:* The 189,000 estimate includes about 33,000 people in a second group known as "societal collaborators for security," or GMS, who dealt more at established levels and not with dissidents. Together, the IM and GMS dwarfed the regular workforce of the Stasi, about 100,000. Stasi Museum display; Childs and Popplewell, *The Stasi*, p. 176. Another historian, Ilko-Sascha Kowalczuk, in 2013 stated the earlier estimates of IM were too high and put the number at about 109,000. See Kowalczuk, *Stasi Konkret. Überwachung und Repression in der DDR* (Munich: C. H. Beck, 2013).

227 *guidelines and handbooks:* Ministry of State Security, German Democratic Republic, *Richtlinie Nr. 1/79 für die Arbeit mit Inoffiziellen Mitarbeitern (IM) und Gesellschaftlichen Mitarbeitern für Sicherheit (GMS)*, Stasi Records Archive, Federal Commissioner for the Stasi Records (BStU), Berlin.

227 *operational psychology:* Forester, "The Dissertations at the 'Law School' of the MfS," p. 19.

227 *core of the Stasi:* Thomas Auerbach, Matthias Braun, Bernd Eisenfeld, Gesine von Prittwitz, and Clemens Vollnhals: "Department XX: State Apparatus, Block Parties, Churches, Culture, 'Political Underground,'" in *Anatomie der Staatssicherheit: Geschichte, Struktur und Methoden MfS-Handbuch* [in German] (Berlin: Federal Commissioner for the Stasi Records, 2008), an online publication. See: https://www.stasi-unterlagen-archiv.de/informationen-zur-stasi/publikationen/publikation/hauptabteilung-xx/.

228 *crushing any hostility:* The undercover IM operatives belonged to several divisions: "IMS" worked at a broad level to survey the political situation and spot potential dangers; "IMB" were for rapid deployment against suspected hostile persons and organizations; "IME" handled delicate special operations; "IMK" oversaw a chain of secret apartments for Stasi meetings; and "FIM" were IM who were leaders of other IM.

228 *to make them come apart at the seams: Die Qualifizierung der politisch-operativen Arbeit des MfS zur vorbeugenden Verhinderung und Bekämpfung der gegen die Staats- und Gesellschchaftsordnung der DDR gerichteten politischen Untergrundtätigkeit* [The qualification of the political-operative work of the MfS to prevent and combat underground political activity directed against the state

and social order of the GDR], March 1979, JHS 001 Nr. 200/79, Stasi Records Archive, Federal Commissioner for the Stasi Records, Berlin, BStU MfS JHS Nr. 21886.

229 *radioactive tracking material: Die Qualifizierung*, section 6.5, p. 663; also see Bernd Eisenfeld, Thomas Auerbach, Gudrun Weber, and Dr. Sebastian Pflugbeil, Project Report, "Radiation. Use of X-rays and Radioactive Substances by the MfS against Opposition Members—Fiction or Reality?," Ed. BStU, Berlin, 2002.

230 *raising doubts among friends of his mental condition:* The story of the campaign against "Traitor" is described at the Stasi Museum, Berlin. Templin is not named there but has been identified elsewhere as the target of "Traitor" and since the fall of the Berlin Wall has publicly discussed the campaign against him. He was an IM for the Stasi from 1973 to 1975, then turned against them and became a dissident. In 1985, he became spokesman for the dissident Peace and Human Rights Initiative and the Stasi-launched operation "Traitor." Roy Gutman, "East Germany's Internal Insecurity Force: How Country Spied on 800,000 of Its Own," *Newsday*, February 23, 1992, p. 3.

230 *when the first signs of politically subversive activity appear:* Jacinto Valdés-Dapena Vivanco, *Die konterrevolutionären Pläne und Absichten des USA-Imperialismus zur Schaffung und Inspirierung feindlicher Stützpunkte und einer inner Oppositionsbewegung in der Republik Kuba* [The counterrevolutionary plans and intentions of US imperialism to create and inspire enemy bases and an internal opposition movement in the Republic of Cuba], Juristischen Hochschule Potsdam, BStU MfS JHS 21952 or JHS 20053, 210 pp.

231 *to absorb lessons from the Stasi:* The dissertation defense came in tense months of the Cold War, including the US invasion of Grenada, which expelled Cuban troops from the island, and deployment of US intermediate-range ballistic missiles and ground-launched cruise missiles in Europe, accompanied by a "war scare" over a US NATO military exercise, "Able Archer." See David E. Hoffman, *The Dead Hand: The Untold Story of the Cold War Arms Race and Its Dangerous Legacy* (New York: Doubleday, 2009).

231 *infiltrate the minds of targets:* Capt. Jacinto Valdés-Dapena, "The Author's Referat," DGCI, Ministry of Interior, Cuba, in Spanish, attendance sheet at the defense, and six reviewers' comments.

231 *"alien and hostile to socialism":* Paul Kienberg, commentary on the thesis, Berlin, November 24, 1983, 9 pages. Kienberg was appointed head of HA XX in 1964.

232 *Stasi warned about people who plan, prepare or carry out "collections of signatures":* JHS 001, no. 200/79, BStU MfS JHS Nr. 21886, section 6.2.3., pp. 410–412.

232 *every Cuban into a potential informant:* Colomer, "Watching Neighbors," p. 123.

232 *Fidel yearned for more:* Kristie Macrakis, *Seduced by Secrets: Inside the Stasi's Spy-Tech World* (Cambridge: Cambridge University Press, 2008), pp. 168, 278.

233   *stole communications ciphers:* Ehlert et al., "Die Zusammenarbeit," pp. 45–46.

233   *"religious activists with positions contrary to the Revolution":* "Tarea técnico operativa del sistema de información biográfica del Ministerio del Interior [Technical-operational task for the Ministry of Interior biographical information system]," no date but approximately 1983–84, BStU MfS ZAIG 50175, 30 pages.

THIRTEEN. REBELLION OF THE SOULS

234   *police arrested Václav Havel:* Michael Zantovsky, *Havel* (London: Atlantic Books, 2014), pp. 280-285; Victor Sebestyen, *Revolution 1989: The Fall of the Soviet Empire* (New York: Pantheon Books, 2009), p. 244; Savranskaya, *Masterpieces,* pp. xxxvi–xxxvii. The Soviet election was March 26. Solidarity was legalized April 17.

234   *Castro insisted that Cuba could not follow Gorbachev's example:* Susanne Sternthal, United Press International, "Castro Says Soviet Reforms Would be 'Absurd' for Cuba," April 5, 1989.

235   *no independent thinking:* Andrés Oppenheimer, *Castro's Final Hour: The Secret Story behind the Coming Downfall of Communist Cuba* (New York: Simon & Schuster, 1992), pp. 125–129.

235   *Raúl and the military would call the shots:* Frank O. Mora, "Cuba's Ministry of Interior: The FAR's Fifth Army," *Bulletin of Latin American Research* 26, no. 2 (2007): 222–237.

236   *from the law to the law:* Iglesias, interview with author; Rolando Sabin, communication with author, April 1, 2021.

236   *"to give voice": Pueblo de Dios,* editions no. 6 and 7, Payá collection.

236   *a moment of panic:* Sabin, communication with author, February 9, 2020.

237   *warned that if the rebelliousness continued:* Cárdenas, *Payá: el Chivo,* p. 39; Rolando Sabin, communication with author, February 12, 2021; Ofelia Acevedo Maura, interview with author, June 5, 2021, Miami.

238   *the school in Potsdam closed:* The last doctoral defense was in December 1989; the final teaching took place in January 1990, and the school was officially dissolved March 31, 1990. Forester, "The Dissertations at the 'Law School' of the MfS," p. 6.

238   *"Giving up is for cowards":* Reuters, "Castro Attacks Reforms and Promises to Fight On," December 9, 1989; "President Castro Dedicates Cienfuegos School," November 6, 1989, Havana Cubavision Television, Latin American Network Information Center, http://lanic.utexas.edu/project/castro/db/1989/19891030.html.

238   *a purge of the Cuban security services:* Mora, "Cuba's Ministry," p. 230.

239   *concealed it under bedsheets:* Ofelia Acevedo Maura, interview with author, August 11, 2017.

239 *They all promptly ignored the warning:* Cárdenas, *Payá: el Chivo*; Sabin, communication with author February 8, 2020; Payá, interviews with Ehrenberg.

240 *initial gathering of signatures by the movimiento:* Iglesias, interview with author.

241 *a hard-to-find photocopy machine:* Juan Rumin, interview with author, November 7, 2019, Key West, Florida.

241 *called for creating a "round table":* There are two versions of this text, roughly similar. One is titled "Proposición de diálogo nacional," with a heading "Movimiento Cristiano 'Liberación,'" and signed by Payá, undated, Payá collection. The second is titled "Texto de proyecto de ley que convoca al diálogo nacional, decreta amnistía política y llama a elecciones para la nueva asamblea constituyente," November 20, 1990, courtesy Regis Iglesias.

241 *met with stony silence:* The interrogation dates are in a declaration by MCL covering the events of 1990 and 1991 and signed by Payá and others, courtesy Regis Iglesias.

241 *"They don't want any communication":* Audio recording of Payá telephone call from Havana to contacts in Miami, March 21, 1992, cassette No. 16, Payá collection.

242 *"rebellion of the souls":* Ofelia Acevedo Maura, interview with author, October 28, 2018, Miami.

242 *lines and shortages:* Lee Hockstader, "Castro Says Cuba Faces Hard Times," *Washington Post*, April 7, 1990, p. 1.

242 *a scathing letter that called for a more open political system:* Mimi Whitefield, "Critical Letter from Bishops Reportedly Needled Castro," *Miami Herald*, May 11, 1990. George Weigel writes in his biography of Pope John Paul II that the bishops urged Castro to "give up dictatorial power" and that Fidel "flew into a rage" as a result. *Witness to Hope*, p. 806.

243 *"kill each other over a slice of bread":* Oswaldo Payá, "Mensaje por el día de la caridad; A todos los cubanos," September 8, 1990, Payá collection.

243 *a handbill that for the first time openly appealed to the public:* Oswaldo Payá, "Te invitamos a que firmes la petición legal de transición pacífica," Payá collection.

243 *Twenty or more people a day began to show up:* Iglesias, interview with author.

244 *"we've been under pressure":* Julio Hernández, interview with author, November 29, 2017, Doral, Florida; "Phone Conversation with Oswaldo Payá." July 8, 1991, transcript, Christian Democratic Party of Cuba (PDC), Puerto Rico Delegation, San Juan, P.R., courtesy Hernández.

245 *"You need to be finished off!":* This account is drawn from Payá's complaint to the Popular Municipal Court of Cerro, asking for an investigation, August 19, 1991, and photographs, Payá collection.

245 *The mob had arrived on a bus:* Undated declaration by MCL, courtesy Regis Iglesias.

245 *"Now, Freedom!":* "The Cobre Appeal," September 8, 1991, Payá collection. On the bicycle incident, Cárdenas, *Payá: el Chivo,* p. 49.

246 *"socialism—at any price":* John Rice, Associated Press, "Castro Vows Steadfast Socialism Despite Collapse Elsewhere," October 15, 1991.

248 *Fidel Castro must go:* "Programa transitorio," 46 pages, courtesy Julio Hernández.

248 *"a way to remove their mask":* Payá read the text of his announcement and discussed it in a phone call to Miami on March 21, 1992. Audio cassettes No. 15 and 16, Payá collection. Also, Cárdenas, *Payá: el Chivo,* p. 50.

249 *"putting the government on the spot":* News conference with journalists in Miami, March 25, 1992, audio cassettes No. 35 and 36, Payá collection.

249 *Then the police came:* Michael B. Wise, "Cuban Constitutionalism: Will There Be Changes?," *Duquesne Law Review* 51 (2013): p. 482. Also, Payá, interviews with Ehrenberg.

249 *distributing "enemy propaganda.":* "Harassment of People Linked to the Liberation Movement," press release, June 10, 1992, and "Statement from Oswaldo Payá," June 16, 1992, Payá collection.

FOURTEEN. RAFTS OF DESPAIR

250 *There was nothing else:* Kevin F. Hayes, "The Only Solution . . . Leave the Country Now; Desperation Drives Cubans to Sea in Rafts," *Hartford Courant,* September 4, 1994, p. A1. Also, Ofelia Acevedo Maura, communication with author, June 13, 2020; Payá, interviews with Ehrenberg; Payá family photographs.

251 *Trade collapsed. The economy shriveled:* Suzanne Leigh Wilson, "When Disorder Is the Order: Cuba during the Special Period" (PhD dissertation, University of California, Berkeley, 2011), p. 17; Berta Esperanza Hernández Truyol, "Out in Left Field: Cuba's Post–Cold War Strikeout," *Fordham International Law Journal* 18, no. 1 (1994).

251 *neurologic damage, including impaired eyesight:* Pedro Coutin-Churchman, "The 'Cuban Epidemic Neuropathy' of the 1990s: A Glimpse from inside a Totalitarian Disease," *Surgical Neurology International* 5 (June 4, 2014), https://doi.org/10.4103/2152-7806.133888. Also see Centers for Disease Control and Prevention, "International Notes Epidemic Neuropathy—Cuba, 1991–1994," *Morbidity and Mortality Weekly Report* 43, no. 10 (March 18, 1994): p. 183, 189–92.

251 *"We're hungry!":* Anne-Marie O'Connor, "Cuba Fed Up, Not Taking It Anymore; Hunger, Despair Provoke the Unthinkable—Protest," *Atlanta Journal and Constitution,* August 8, 1993.

251 *food rations were reduced sharply:* Wilson, "When Disorder," p. 17.

251 *"steak" made from grapefruit rind:* Pablo Alfonso, "Cocinero inventa bisté de toronja en Período Especial," *el Nuevo Herald,* March 7, 1991.

251 *All mammals are edible: El libro de la familia* (Cuba: Verde Olivo, 1991). Also see Elzbieta Sklodowska, *Invento, luego resisto: El Período Especial en Cuba como experiencia y metáfora (1990–2015)* (Santiago de Chile: Editorial Cuarto Propio, 2016), pp. 213–214. A similar book, *Con nuestros propios esferzos*, which contained reader-submitted ideas, was published by Verde Olivo in December 1992.

252 *Bicycles:* Richard Boudreaux, "In Cuba, Hardships Only Grow: Residents of One of the Last Communist Bastions Are Squeezed by Shortages of Food and Fuel. Some See It as a Test of Their Resolve, but Frustration Deepens," *Los Angeles Times*, September 4, 1990, p. 1.

252 *"There is discontent, uncertainty, despair in the population":* Jaime Ortega et al., "El amor todo lo espera: Mensaje de la Conferencia de obispos católicos de Cuba," September 8, 1993.

252 *Church attendance in Cuba was surging:* Ortega was elevated to a cardinal October 30, 1994, by Pope John Paul II, only the second in Cuba's history. On church attendance, Douglas Farah, "Religious Activity Increases As Cuban Economy Declines," *Washington Post*, April 3, 1994, p. A21.

253 *"Castro's government is in acute distress":* Brian Latell, US National Intelligence Officer for Latin America, "Statement on Cuba, Senate Select Committee on Intelligence," July 29, 1993; "CIA Official Sees Cuba in Crisis," *New York Times*, July 30, 1993, p. A3. The project on potential future leadership of Cuba was described to the author by a confidential source.

253 *While Cubans suffered, Fidel did not:* Juan Reinaldo Sánchez, *The Double Life of Fidel Castro*, pp. 11–18.

254 *These were the* balseros—*the rafters:* Hayes, "The Only Solution . . ."

254 *"We have nothing left to lose":* Carlos Batista, Inter Press Service, "Cuba: Embassy Occupations End Peacefully," July 2, 1994; Antonio Raluy, Agence France-Presse, "Cubans in Ambassadors Residence Reject Dialogue," June 1, 1994; John Rice, Associated Press, "Asylum-Seekers Invade German Embassy," June 13, 1994; "Eight Cubans Leave Chilean Consulate Voluntarily," BBC Summary of World Broadcasts, June 25, 1994.

254 *stepped aboard a tugboat, the* 13 *de marzo:* Inter-American Commission on Human Rights, Report No. 47/96, Case 11.436, "Victims of the Tugboat 13 de marzo v. Cuba," October 16, 1996, http://hrlibrary.umn.edu/cases/1996/cuba47-96.htm.

255 *González jumped into the dark waters:* Frank González Vázquez, "They Forced Me to Endorse a False Truth," interview transcript, in "Orgullosamente balseros cubanos" (1994), Dora Plavetic Collection, Cuban Heritage Collection, University of Miami, Coral Gables, Florida.

255 *"We are not opposed to . . . letting those who want to leave, leave":* Report by Lisbet Barrera, "NTV" newscast, Havana Tele Rebelde and Cuba Vision

Networks, via FBIS-LAT-94-152 Daily Report, August 6, 1994, Latin American Network Information Center, http://lanic.utexas.edu/project/castro /db/1994/19940806.html.

256 *more than thirty-two thousand people fled Cuba:* See http://balseros.miami .edu/.

256 *she began to play "The Star-Spangled Banner":* Myriam Márquez, "Cuban Refugees at Guantanamo Caught in Web of Hopelessness," *Orlando Sentinel,* November 7, 1994. Also see https://www.nbcmiami.com/news/local/lizbet-mar tinez-violin-teacher-milam-k8/6280/ and https://www.youtube.com/watch?v =828OscG11jA.

256 *"trying to get Oswaldo to make a mistake":* Ofelia Acevedo Maura, communication with author, January 2020.

257 *to train his members in civic activism:* In June 1994, Payá sent a handwritten letter, smuggled by a nun, to Rasco. Payá implored him to find couriers to keep in touch, noting that it was often difficult, and added: "Please send us any material that you have on Christian democratic thought." He also wrote: "Professor, now I want to ask you a favor: please recommend a program to train people, and, within your abilities, try to send us materials to develop them. You're uniquely able to help us with that." Letter from Payá to Rasco, June 1, 1994, files of Rasco, Cuban Heritage Collection, University of Miami, Coral Gables, Florida. On Payá's friends, Sabin, communication with author, June 20, 2020; Antúnez, communication with author, January 6, 2021.

257 *a rebellious young man, Regis Iglesias Ramírez:* Iglesias, interview with author.

259 *Antonio Díaz Sánchez also was driven toward Payá:* Antonio Ramón Díaz Sánchez, *690: Vivencias de terribles pesadillas* (Stockholm: Samhällsgemenskaps Förlags AB, 2006), pp.135–136; Díaz Sánchez, interview with author, December 2, 2017, Miami, Florida.

260 *he called it Foro Cubano:* "Llamamiento a Foro Cubano," March 25, 1994, and auxiliary document, 6 pages, Payá collection.

261 *dungeons of the station were known as El Tanque:* Miguel Salvatierra, "España se limitará a protestar a través de su Embajada por la detención de opositores," *ABC,* Madrid, November 23, 1994, p. 40; Ofelia Acevedo Maura, communication with author, January 18, 2020.

262 *to teach and practice journalism:* Ricardo González Alfonso, interview with author, September 15, 2017, Madrid.

262 *an independent news agency:* By 1995, five independent news agencies existed in Cuba: CubaPress, Habana Press, Patria, Círculo de Periodistas de La Habana, and Asociación de Periodistas Independientes de Cuba (APIC). APIC was founded in 1989 by Yndamiro Restano Díaz, a journalist, dissident, and founding member of the Movimiento de Armonía (MAR) political group. Restano was arrested in December 1991 and given a ten-year prison sentence

on charges of "rebellion" for his work with MAR. He was released in 1995 and founded the Buró de Prensa Independiente de Cuba (BPIC), an umbrella group that encompassed Habana Press, Patria, and Círculo de Periodistas de la Habana. See "Cuba: Government Crackdown on Dissent," Amnesty International, April 1996; Sarah Beaulieu, "Los orígenes del periodismo independiente: Yndamiro Restano," *Cubaencuentro*, October 4, 2014; "Notorious Cuban Agent-'Journalist' Dies," Voice of America, October 29, 2009. Also see: Michael Ranneberger, testimony June 27, 1996, before the House Subcommittee on International Operations and Human Rights and the House Subcommittee on the Western Hemisphere, Committee on International Relations, House of Representatives, 104th Congress, Second Session, Appendix, p. 67.

263 *"we worked with a lot of passion"*: Raúl Rivero, interview with author, September 13, 2018, Miami.

263 *"This is our first Cuban spring"*: Dagoberto Valdés, interview with author, February 8, 2019.

264 *Concilio Cubano*: Leonel Morejón Almagro, interview with Mylena Vazquez, January 20, 2021. The organizers of the Concilio—about a dozen people—debated at one point about whether the 1976 Constitution should be a starting point for a legal transition to democracy, as in Chile and Spain. This was Oswaldo's preference, and he had previously advocated it in the National Dialogue. Elizardo Sánchez backed him. But they were outvoted, 10–2, by others who wanted nothing to do with the legal system of the Castro regime. So the published declaration did not mention Fidel or the constitution. Pablo Alfonso, "Cita en La Habana de coalición disidente," *el Nuevo Herald*, December 6, 1995, p. 1.

265 *"It would be a miracle if they allowed it"*: Anita Snow, Associated Press, "Bruised by Crackdown, Cuban Opposition Vows to Fight On," March 24, 1996; Pablo Alfonso, "Cita en La Habana de coalición disidente," *el Nuevo Herald*, December 6, 1995, p. 1; Juan O. Tamayo, "Cuban Dissidents Create New Coalition; Castro Question Has Group Deadlocked," *Miami Herald*, December 11, 1995, p. 10A.

265 *a "dirty deal,"*: Leonel Morejón Almagro, interview with Mylena Vazquez, March 19, 2021.

266 *"You are the inspiration!"*: Payá, interviews with Ehrenberg.

266 *State security swung into action*: Pablo Alfonso, "Cuba Disrupts Opposition Meeting, 3 Held," *Miami Herald*, February 16, 1996, p. 14.

266 *Morejón was summarily tried and convicted*: Michael Ranneberger, Office of Cuban Affairs, U.S. Department of State, "The Crackdown on Concilio Cubano," in written statement submitted to the U.S. House Subcommittee on International Relations and Human Rights, June 27, 1996; also see John Rice, Associated Press, "Dissidents Sentenced in Crackdown," February 23, 1996. In 1997, Morejón was one of two Cuban lawyers given the International

Human Rights Award by the American Bar Association's litigation section, but he was refused permission to attend the ceremony in person. Reuters, "Cuba Thwarts 2 from Accepting Human Rights Honor," *Chicago Tribune*, August 6, 1997, p. 10.

267   *The shootdowns were cold-blooded killings:* Lily Prellezo and José Basulto, *Seagull One: The Amazing True Story of Brothers to the Rescue* (Gainesville: University Press of Florida, 2010).

FIFTEEN. THE VARELA PROJECT

268   *Oswaldo looked up and handed Tony the paper:* Tony Díaz, interview with author, December 2, 2017, Miami.

270   *Oswaldo had a completely different idea:* Henrik Ehrenberg, interview with author, November 8, 2018, Washington, DC.

270   *naming it the "Varela Project":* Miguel Saludes, interview with author, January 22, 2018, Miami.

270   *people connected with the Concilio were either interrogated, detained, or jailed*: United States Department of State, "U.S. Department of State Country Report on Human Rights Practices 1996—Cuba," January 30, 1997, section 1.d, https://www.refworld.org/docid/3ae6aa23e.html.

270   *"There was a lot of fear":* Payá, interviews with Ehrenberg.

270   *the arrest on July 16, 1997, of four dissidents:* In May and June before the arrests, the group held two press conferences for foreign journalists, presenting the paper at the second. They had become an important center of political activity. Pablo Alfonso, "Police Arrest Four Opposition Leaders in Havana," *Miami Herald*, July 17, 1997.

271   *Oswaldo endured a personal crisis:* Cynthia Corzo, "Cardenal Ortega intercedió por Payá," *el Nuevo Herald*, April 3, 1997. Also, Rolando Sabin, communication with author, March 23, 2021; Ofelia Acevedo Maura, communication with author, April 13, 2021; and Oswaldo Payá Acevedo, interview with author, August 11, 2017, Miami.

272   *Ten members of the* movimiento: Oswaldo Payá, "Nota informativa," listing the candidates and their home districts; "Petición ciudadana a la Asamblea Nacional del Poder Popular," December 10, 1997; "A la opinión pública," December 22, 1997, all in Payá collection.

273   *John Paul stole the show:* Weigel, *Witness to Hope*, pp. 790–792, 809–814. This account is partially drawn from Weigel. Payá's comments are from his interviews with Ehrenberg. For the pope's arrival remarks, see "Discurso del Santo Padre," January 21, 1998, http://www.vatican.va/content/john-paul-ii/es/speeches/1998/january/documents/hf_jp-ii_spe_19980121_lahavana-arrival.html (in Spanish).

273   *the principal agents of your own history:* "Homily of John Paul II," Camagüey,

Cuba, January 23, 1998. See https://w2.vatican.va/content/john-paul-ii/en/homilies/1998/documents/hf_jp-ii_hom_19980123_camaguey.html.

274 *the essence of all that Oswaldo believed in:* Payá had written those words in *Pueblo de Dios*, no. 7 (September 1989). Oswaldo had nursed a hope that John Paul—who had done so much for Solidarity in Poland—might say something about the opposition in Cuba. He did not, nor did he address Fidel directly during the visit. Ariel Hidalgo, "Los cambios tenemos que hacerlos nosotros," March 5, 1998, an interview of Payá by Hidalgo, director of the Information Bureau of the Cuban Human Rights Movement, Miami.

274 *The pope paid tribute to Félix Varela:* "Address of John Paul II," University of Havana, January 23, https://w2.vatican.va/content/john-paul-ii/en/speeches/1998/january/documents/hf_jp-ii_spe_19980123_lahavana-culture.html.

274 *an authentically Cuban system of freedom:* Weigel, *Witness to Hope*, p. 811.

275 *"The pope is free and wants us all to be free":* Payá, interviews with Ehrenberg. "Homilía del Santo Padre," José Martí Plaza, Havana, in Spanish. See http://www.vatican.va/content/john-paul-ii/es/homilies/1998/documents/hf_jp-ii_hom_19980125_lahabana.html. Also, "Ending His Stay amid Chants of 'Freedom!' Pontiff Preaches Change at Havana Mass," *Miami Herald*, January 26, 1998, p. A1. Before the pope arrived in Cuba, a Vatican security team, sent in advance, discovered that state security placed a listening device in a room he would stay in, according to Sabin, who was a medical doctor assigned to the Vatican staff. Sabin, communication with author, March 5, 2021. The discovery was reported by *El País* of Madrid, which said the Vatican had threatened to reconsider the visit because of it. When Cubans protested that the listening device dated from Batista's day, the Vatican officials did not believe them, *El País* said. Associated Press, "Discovery of Bug Reportedly Jeopardized Visit," *Los Angeles Times*, January 11, 1998, p. A12.

275 *"Varela Project. Citizen Petition":* Payá collection.

276 *"like keeping our hands tied while the ship sinks":* Hidalgo, "Los Cambios."

278 *dreaming of escape on a raft:* Alejandro González Raga, interview with author, September 12, 2017, Madrid.

278 *grew up on an isolated farm:* Fredesvinda Hernández, interview with author, January 19, 2018, Hialeah, Florida.

279 *"captive towns":* Lillian Guerra, "Beyond Paradox: Counterrevolution and the Origins of Political Culture in the Cuban Revolution, 1959–2009," in Grandin and Joseph, *A Century of Revolution*, pp. 199–235.

279 *taught anatomy in medical school:* Andrés Chacón, interview with author, January 17, 2018, Miami.

282 *"multiple tools to aim at you":* Ricardo Zuñiga, interview with author, October 30, 2019.

282 *"I know they are tracking me"*: Ehrenberg, interview with author.

282 *on a higher state of alert:* Payá, interviews with Ehrenberg.

283 *declared subversive:* Anita Snow, Associated Press, "Cuba Cracks Down on Political Opponents, Common Crime," February 17, 1999.

283 *The prison sentences were harsh:* Gómez and Bonne got four years and Beatriz Roque three years. Anita Snow, Associated Press, "Risking Condemnation, Cuba Sentences Dissidents to Prison," March 15, 1999.

283 *"I won't go back inside":* Payá, interviews with Ehrenberg.

283 *expelled from the university program:* Carmelo Díaz Fernández, "Expulsado de la universidad Oswaldo Payá Sardiñas," APSIC, April 5, 1999, oswaldopaya .org.

283 *a spirit of resistance was alive:* Janisset Rivero-Gutiérrez, Orlando Gutiérrez, and Omar López Montenegro, *Pasos a la libertad, 1999,* Directorio Revolucionario Democrático Cubano, and Centro de Estudios para una Opción Nacional, August 2000, and *Steps to Freedom, 2000,* March 2001.

285 *a minisummit of their own:* Juan Zamorano, Associated Press, "Cuban Opposition Leaders Meet," November 12, 1999; Juan O. Tamayo, "Dissidents Get a Castro Warning," *Miami Herald,* November 12, 1999, p. 3A; Alfonso Chardy, "Cuban Dissidents Grab Moment on World Stage," *Miami Herald,* November 13, 1999, p. 1A; "Twenty Dissident Organizations Meet for the First Time despite Recent Arrests," citing Spanish newspaper *La Vanguardia,* BBC Summary of World Broadcasts, November 13, 1999.

285 Todos Unidos, *meaning "Everyone united":* Declaration of *Todos Unidos,* November 12, 1999, Payá collection.

286 *the Movimiento Cristiano Liberación had applied in October to be legally recognized:* The first application by MCL was made in March 1995, under the Cuban law on associations, which required a minimum of 30 members to be named. Oswaldo proposed 31 members. The second request was made October 6, 1999, with 241 members. In both cases, no response was received, according to Payá and Iglesias. The government preferred leaving the movimiento in limbo, the classic tactic of dictatorship, saying neither yes nor no, to keep them off-balance. They were not legal, but not illegal.

286 *the Havana summit proved to be a smashing success:* Mark Fineman, "Cuban Dissidents Emerge at Last," *Los Angeles Times,* via *Newsday,* November 21, 1999, and "Dissent and Diplomacy," *The Economist,* November 20, 1999.

286 *there were one hundred groups:* In October 2001, a message to the Eleventh Ibero-American Summit was signed by one hundred groups.

286 *they left for Florida with high hopes:* Ann Louise Bardach, *Cuba Confidential: Love and Vengeance in Miami and Havana* (New York: Random House, 2002), pp. 3–35, 71–100.

287 *how truly distant he was from the exiles:* Oswaldo Payá et al., "El momento del

pueblo cubano," *Diario de las Américas*, July 12, 2000. Oswaldo argued that the important business was in Cuba, giving people a voice in their destiny.

288   *173 exile organizations:* Elaine de Valle, "Former Members of CANF Regroup," *Miami Herald*, October 10, 2001. The 173 estimate came from Joe García, executive director of CANF.

288   *suffered violent bombings and threats:* Bardach, *Cuba Confidential*, pp. 101–125.

288   *dialogue with Fidel was a "dirty maneuver":* Armando Pérez Roura, *Tome nota*, self-published essay collection. See "Otra vez el diálogo," January 14, 1995, pp. 179–183.

289   *jingles advocating Fidel's death:* Deborah Hastings, Associated Press, "Radio Mambí: News, Opinion, and Insults," January 21, 2000.

289   *"say no to dialogue":* Myriam Márquez, "No Dialogue: Anti-Castro Hard-Liners Defile Dignity," *Orlando Sentinel*, April 1, 2003, p. A11.

289   *"an arrangement with the government":* Armando Pérez Roura, comments at a forum on Cuba June 12, 2009.

289   *Oswaldo knew of the hostility:* Regis Iglesias Ramírez, communication with author, October 29, 2020.

290   *Elián returned to Cuba:* Larry M. Eig, "The Case of Elián González: Legal Basics," Congressional Research Service, RS20450, September 12, 2000. Also see Ruth Ellen Wasem, "Cuban Migration to the United States: Policy and Trends," Congressional Research Service, R40566, June 2, 2009, p. 16.

290   *Pedro Pablo Álvarez, a union organizer:* Álvarez, interview with author, December 2, 2017, Miami, Florida.

290   *"I'll be imprisoned":* Payá, interviews with Ehrenberg.

290   *a unique serial number:* Iglesias, interview with author.

291   *the most by any single collector:* Regis Iglesias Ramírez, communication with author, July 21, 2020.

291   *hundreds of collectors were arrested:* Oswaldo Payá, Elizardo Sánchez, Héctor Palacios, and Oswaldo Alfonso, "Llamamiento desde La Habana," January 16, 2001. See: https://mcliberacion.org/2001/01/todos-unidos-llamamiento-desde-la-habana/.

292   *a crash campaign to validate every signature:* This account of the falsifications is based on interviews with Iglesias, Álvarez, and Díaz.

293   *the Varela Project had collected the required ten thousand:* Payá, "Información a la opinión pública," press release, March 25, 2002, Payá collection.

293   *about 130 signatures were seized:* Oswaldo Payá and Miguel Saludes, "Repression against the Varela Project during the First Three Months of 2002," press release, March 13, 2002.

293   *threatening a head-on collision:* Iglesias, interview with author.

293   *when would they turn in the signatures?:* Díaz, interview with author.

294   *eight of his close associates:* The others in the room were Oswaldo Alfonso,

Ernesto Martín Fonseca, Efrén Fernández, and Jorge Colmenero. This account is based on interviews with Iglesias, Díaz, and Colmenero; Iglesias Ramirez, *Como un eco en el destierro* (Miami, FL: Editorial Voces de Hoy, 2018) and Díaz, *690 vivencias de terribles pesadillas.*

296　*phalanx of foreign journalists was already waiting:* Regis Iglesias Ramírez, communication with author, January 12, 2021.

SIXTEEN. THE BLACK SPRING

301　*"I think we surprised them":* Payá, interviews with Ehrenberg.

302　*Carter also hoped to get something:* Fidel may have hoped the visit would help him gain admission to the Cotonou Agreement, a trade and cooperation pact signed by the European Union and seventy-eight developing nations in 2000 in Cotonou, Benin's largest city. Most of the signatories were former colonies of European nations. Cuba wanted to join but faced opposition from some European countries, including Britain and Sweden, because of human rights concerns.

302　*Carter wanted to address the Cuban people:* Jennifer McCoy, interview with author, June 4, 2018, Atlanta; Jimmy Carter, "President Carter's Cuba Trip Report," cartercenter.org, May 20, 2002. The dissident meetings were left off Carter's official schedule.

302　*the Varela Project came up over and over again:* McCoy, interview with author. Vicki Huddleston, *Our Woman in Havana: A Diplomat's Chronicle of America's Long Struggle with Castro's Cuba* (New York: Overlook Press, 2018), p. 222. Huddleston feared Carter might neglect the Varela Project in his speech, so she urged him to meet Oswaldo beforehand. However, Carter had already decided to include the Varela Project in his speech, according to McCoy. The meeting was arranged at the last minute. See Deutsche Presse-Agentur, "Carter Meets with Political Dissidents in Cuba," May 13, 2002.

303　*the document showed his early intentions:* The documents Carter presented to Fidel included his presidential directive, NSC-6, March 15, 1977, setting in motion an exploratory process for normalizing relations with Cuba. The documents were assembled by Carter's former Latin America director on the National Security Council, Robert Pastor, who accompanied him to Havana in 2002. The directive was published online by the National Security Archive at George Washington University on May 15, 2002. William M. LeoGrande and Peter Kornbluh, *Back Channel to Cuba: The Hidden History of Negotiations between Washington and Havana* (Chapel Hill: University of North Carolina Press, 2014), p. 155.

303　*Carter also forewarned Fidel:* Carter, "President Carter's Cuba Trip Report," cartercenter.org. On Pérez Roque, see Deutsche Presse-Agentur, "Carter Meets with Political Dissidents."

303   *Payá and Sánchez then joined Carter:* McCoy, interview with author; Carter, "President Carter's Trip Report"; John Hardman, director of the Carter Center, notes of meeting, via McCoy; Elizardo Sánchez, interview with author, October 27, 2018, Miami. For Carter's greeting, see: https://youtu.be /mogsm3iITEo.

304   *Carter wanted to verify:* On meeting details, Hardman, notes; Jennifer McCoy, recollections and notes.

304   *Carter spoke for twenty minutes, entirely in Spanish:* "Remarks by Former U.S. President Jimmy Carter at the University of Havana, Cuba, Tuesday May 14, 2002," cartercenter.org; Carter, "President Carter's Trip Report"; Hardman, notes; LeoGrande and Kornbluh, *Back Channel to Cuba,* pp. 352–253; "It is necessary to find the ways for understanding, tolerance and peace," *Granma,* May 16, 2002, via online edition, https://www.granma.cu/gran mad/2002/05/16/nacional/articulo14.html.

305   *"Call a press conference!":* Adrián Ley from the movimiento also joined Oswaldo at the press conference, as well as Osvaldo Alfonso, president of the Liberal Democratic Party and a manager of the Varela Project.

306   *"They're so afraid of it!":* Iglesias, interview with author; video of the press conference, May 14, 2002, Payá collection.

306   *a subversive plot by the United States:* Carter, "President Carter's Trip Report"; McCoy, interview with author; "May We Become Friends and Respect Each Other," *Granma,* May 15, 2002, via online edition, https://www.granma.cu /granmad/2002/05/15/nacional/articulo09.html.

307   Granma *printed the entire text:* David Gonzalez, "Party Organ in Cuba Prints Speech by Carter," *New York Times,* May 17, 2002, p. 7; "It is necessary to find," *Granma,* May 16, 2002.

307   *"The Cuban people have met hope.":* Kevin Sullivan, "Carter Meets Activists in Cuba; Ex-president Puts Focus on Dissidents," *Washington Post,* May 17, 2002, p. A17; Anthony Boadle, Reuters, "Carter Meets Cuban Dissidents Pushing for Reforms," May 16, 2002; Anita Snow, Associated Press, "Former U.S. President Carter Meets Cuban Dissidents," May 16, 2002.

307   *lingering anger at the Clinton administration:* Jules Whitcover, "Florida's Cuban vote," *Baltimore Sun,* Oct. 1, 2004: https://www.baltimoresun.com/news/bs -xpm-2004-10-01-0410010234-story.html.

307   *in the throes of change:* Guillermo Grenier and Hugh Gladwin, "The 2000 FIU Cuba Poll," *Cuba Poll, 6,* Cuban Research Institute, Institute for Public Opinion Research, Center for Labor Research and Studies, Florida International University, 2000. One finding of the survey was that over 51 percent of the respondents said they would support dialogue with Cuba's government. See https://digitalcommons.fiu.edu/cuba_poll/6/.

307   *a moderate speech:* President Bush, "Remarks on the 100th Anniversary of

Cuban Independence in Miami, Florida," Public Papers of the Presidents, May 27, 2002. Bardach reports that the Cuban Liberty Council had hoped for more stringent actions in the speech, but Bush didn't deliver anything on their wish list. Bardach, *Cuba Confidential*, p. 350.

308 *he generally kept aloof from US officials in Havana:* "The United States is our neighbor, our friend, the country has defended human rights in Cuba. The Americans are not the people who have to solve the Cuban problem or carry out the transition in Cuba." Payá, interviews with Ehrenberg.

308 *"A civic campaign conducted amid poverty . . . no one can finance that":* Alberto Mueller, "Exclusive Interview with Oswaldo Payá about the Varela Project," *Diario Las Américas,* June 4, 2002, p. 7-B. The interview was conducted May 25, 2002. Payá did receive some help from friends abroad. Often it involved equipment such as laptop computers. His overseas supporters included Christian Democrats in Chile and Sweden, especially the Kristdemokratiskt Internationellt Center, or Christian Democratic International Center, in Stockholm. Henrik Ehrenberg of KIC made more than a dozen visits to Cuba. Others supporting the Varela Project included Dutch, Spanish, and US organizations, among them NDI. Payá, interviews with Ehrenberg.

309 *exactly what the Stasi rulebook suggested: Richtlinie Nr. 1/79 für die Arbeit mit Inoffiziellen Mitarbeitern (IM) und Gesellschaftlichen Mitarbeitern für Sicherheit (GMS)* [Guideline no. 1/79 for the work with unofficial employees (IM) and social workers for safety (GMS)], Ministry of State Security, German Democratic Republic, Stasi Records Archive, Federal Commissioner for the Stasi Records (BStU), Berlin.

309 *a colossal public march:* Vivian Sequera, Associated Press, "Castro Leads Hundreds of Thousands in March Supporting Cuba's Socialist State," June 12, 2002.

310 *Fidel's referendum was approved by 99 percent:* Associated Press International, "Cuba Announces Victory in Its Signature Gathering Drive in Support of 'Untouchable' Socialism," June 18, 2002.

310 *Not a single "no.":* Anita Snow, Associated Press, "Reform Activist Says Massive March Shows Government's Fear of Reform Referendum," June 13, 2002; Anita Snow, Associated Press, "Democratic Reform Organizer Calls on Cubans to Regroup after Pro-socialism Campaign," June 19, 2002; Anita Snow, "Cuban Lawmakers Argue for Making Socialist System Sacrosanct," June 25, 2002; Anthony Boadle, Reuters, "Cuba, Defying Bush, Carves Communism in Stone," June 26, 2002.

310 *"a kidnapped people?":* Oswaldo Payá, "Declaration of the Citizens Committee Managing the Varela Project," June 27, 2002, Havana, Payá collection.

310 *Huddleston . . . believed a détente was developing:* Huddleston, *Our Woman in Havana,* pp. 192, 209–210, 217.

311 *"you are on a mission"*: James Cason, interview with author, October 31, 2018, Coral Gables, Florida; Amb. James C. Cason, interviewed by Charles Stuart Kennedy, November 13, 2009, in Association for Diplomatic Studies & Training, *Foreign Affairs Oral History Project*, pp. 89–94, online at: https://adst.org /OH%20TOCs/Cason-James-C..pdf.

311 *a desire to trigger a crisis*: US diplomat who asked not to be identified by name, interview with author.

312 *"We were like a store"*: On the book titles, Frank Calzón, former director of the Center for a Free Cuba, communication with author, September 5, 2020; Cason, interview with author. Both before Cason and after, the United States funded programs to support democracy in Cuba. From 1996 to April 2000, the USAID Cuba Program made grant awards totaling $6.4 million to fifteen US nongovernmental organizations and three universities. See "Evaluation of the USAID Cuba Program," United States Agency for International Development, 2000. The pace quickened after Cason's arrival. According to the U.S. Government Accountability Office, by 2005 the U.S. Interests Section distributed over 269,000 books, magazines, articles, pamphlets, and other materials. The annual volume of shipments increased between 2000 and 2005 by about 200 percent—from about 51,000 to 155,000 pounds. See U.S. Government Accountability Office, "U.S. Democracy Assistance for Cuba Needs Better Management and Oversight," GAO-07-147, November 2006, p. 24.

312 *eavesdropping bug*: Photo of the eavesdropping device; Stasi devices on display at the Stasi Museum in Berlin. The Stasi provided the Cubans with installation instructions; see Ehlert et al., "Die Zusammenarbeit," Document 8, pp. 139–158.

313 *"There was a big push for independent everything"*: González Alfonso, interview by author; Luis Cino Álvarez, "The Price of Trying to Be Free in a Dictatorship," December 19, 2017, www.cubanet.org; Anita Snow, Associated Press, "Official Tolerance for Cuba's Unsanctioned Journalists Slowly Improves," March 17, 2003.

313 *In the first issue*: De Cuba, no. 1 (December 2002), Magazine of the Manuel Márquez Sterling Journalists Association.

314 *the magazine we wanted to make*: Raúl Rivero, "La verdad siempre regresa," in publication by Reporters Without Borders, www.rsf.org, November 2005.

314 *thousands of signatures were collected*: The author was unable to locate records, but Iglesias estimated about eight thousand more signatures were collected in 2002 after the first submission in May.

314 *Tony took off with the scanners*: Díaz, interview with author; US diplomat, interview with author.

314 *a sneaky way to smear Payá*: Oswaldo Payá, "Message from Payá to Varela Project Signatories," October 16, 2002, Payá collection.

315   *nominated him for the Nobel Peace Prize:* Oswaldo was nominated multiple times but never awarded the prize. The Havel nomination underscored growing international awareness of Oswaldo's work and his close relationship with Havel and his ideals.

315   *no hope of actually accepting:* Ofelia Acevedo Maura, interview with author, August 11, 2017.

316   *a banner of "Alpha 66":* The reasons for the "Alpha 66" banner have been open to debate; some family members saw it as a veiled warning of the dangers Oswaldo might face from extremists in the United States.

317   *"Be very careful":* Ofelia Acevedo Maura, interviews with author; Payá, interviews with Ehrenberg. Also see Nancy San Martín, "Dissident in Cuba Wins Key Rights Award," *Miami Herald*, October 24, 2002, p. 1.

317   *worried about Oswaldo's safety:* Óscar Payá, interview with author, September 14, 2017, Madrid.

318   *navy blue wool suit:* Francisco de Armas, communication with author, September 2, 2020. His father, José de Armas, was Oswaldo's godfather.

318   *a "democratic, fair and free society.":* "Award of the Sakharov Prize for 2002," European Parliament translation to English, December 17, 2002, www.europarl.europa.eu. Also see "Cuban Dissident Leader Wins Human Rights Prize from European Parliament," U.S. Department of State, Washington File, October 23, 2002; and Constant Brand, Associated Press, "Cuba's Payá Awarded EU's Top Human Rights Prize," December 17, 2002.

319   *Not a word:* Carol J. Williams, "Voices for Change in Cuba Find Achieving Harmony Difficult; the Regime's Rhetoric Drowns Out Opposition Parties As They Squabble about Effecting Change," *Los Angeles Times*, January 5, 2003.

319   *a whirlwind overseas tour:* Francisco de Armas, correspondence with author, September 2, 2020; National Democratic Institute, schedule of Oswaldo Payá in Washington. Oswaldo's general audience with the pope on January 8, rather than a private meeting, was the pope's decision "because the church did not wish to provoke a negative reaction from the Cuban government," a Vatican diplomat told a US diplomat. "Payá Visits Pope; FM Tauran May Reciprocate," January 16, 2003, cable from US embassy at Vatican City to the State Department, WikiLeaks.org.

320   *Every signature is an act of liberation:* Jackson Diehl, "Solidarity, Cuban-Style," *Washington Post*, January 13, 2003, p. A21.

320   *blasting away at the Varela Project:* Myriam Márquez, "No Dialogue: Anti-Castro Hardliners Defile Dignity," *Orlando Sentinel*, April 1, 2003, p. A11.

320   *"an illusory democratic transition":* Lincoln Díaz-Balart, communication with author, October 26, 2020. The Díaz-Balarts are sons of Rafael Díaz-Balart, who served as deputy secretary of interior in Batista's post-1952 regime. Rafael's sister, Mirta, was Fidel Castro's first wife.

321 *"corporatist" structure:* Mexico was the leading example in Latin America of corporatist authoritarianism. The Varela Project had not explicitly authorized political parties but had sought freedom of association. The project stated among its demands: "That the necessary changes are made to the laws so that the common good and respect for universally recognized human rights and human dignity are guaranteed to citizens . . .The right to associate freely according to their interests and ideas, so that they can legally form social, political, economic, cultural, trade union, student, religious, humanitarian and other associations and organizations, respecting the principle of pluralism and the diversity of ideas present in society."

321 *"half of the heart of the Cuban people":* Orlando Gutiérrez, communications with author, September 28, 29, 2020; John-Thor Dahlburg, "Plea for Unity among Cuban Exiles," *Los Angeles Times,* January 14, 2003.

322 *"very intense, very contentious":* Payá, interviews with Ehrenberg; Nancy San Martín, "Wary Exiles a Challenge for Dissident's Project," *Miami Herald,* January 10, 2003; Dahlburg, "Plea for Unity"; Oscar Corral and Andrés Viglucci, "Dissident Makes Progress in Building Consensus," *Miami Herald,* January 14, 2003.

322 *"Payá had the best chance":* Carlos Saladrigas, interview with author, January 17, 2018, Miami.

322 *"my children are not going to leave Cuba":* Elaine De Valle, "Payá Asks for Exile's Support," *Miami Herald,* January 14, 2003, pp. 1, 14.

322 *"A change in scale":* Interview with the editorial board of the *Miami Herald,* published January 19, 2003.

323 *take the Varela Project more seriously:* Lincoln Díaz-Balart, communication with author, October 30, 2020.

323 *"we will continue":* Mar Román, Associated Press, "Cuban Dissident Oswaldo Payá Returns Home," February 2, 2003.

323 *rejected the Varela Project:* Vanessa Bauza, "Cuban Government Rejects Varela Project Call for Referendum," *Orlando Sun-Sentinel,* January 24, 2003.

323 *"Let's talk about serious things":* Anita Snow, Associated Press, "Castro, Millions of Cubans Vote in Elections Dissidents Call a Farce," January 19, 2003.

323 *a list of thirty-six additional goals:* The leaders of Todos Unidos issued a statement of the thirty-six points while Oswaldo was in Europe. Anita Snow, Associated Press, "Leading Cuban Opponents Propose Wide-Reaching Reforms," December 19, 2002. Also, Díaz, interview with author; Elizardo Sánchez, interview with author; Héctor Palacios, interview with author, January 22, 2018. The full text of the thirty-six-point proposal was published in *De Cuba,* no. 2 (February 2002).

323 *an "immense" impact:* Manuel Cuesta Morúa, "Proyecto Varela: Pértiga a la democracia," *De Cuba,* no. 2 (February 2002): 18–19.

324 *tension boiled over in a meeting:* This account is based on Payá, interviews with Ehrenberg; interviews by author with Sánchez, Palacios, Díaz, and Iglesias.

325 *insulted and isolated:* Iglesias, interview with author.

325 *a brief vacation to Varadero:* Payá, interviews with Ehrenberg.

325 *an unusual gesture of support:* Cason, interview with author, and Andrea Rodríguez, Associated Press, "America's Top Diplomat in Havana Visits Dissidents, Says Cuba Fears Freedom," February 24, 2003.

326 *"That's how Groucho Marx . . . can suddenly become subversive.":* Anita Snow, Associated Press International, "Cuba Seizes Book Shipment Ordered by American Mission," February 27, 2003.

326 *"dandy with diplomatic immunity.":* Patricia Grogg, Inter Press Service, "Cuba-U.S.: Dozens Arrested for 'Subversion'; Castro Accuses Envoy," March 20, 2003.

326 *bold, independent journalists:* On March 14, Cason opened his residence for a seminar on media ethics attended by thirty independent journalists. The U.S. Interests Section had been urged to hold it by a number of Cuban activists, including Manuel David Orrio, who they thought was an independent journalist. The Cuban government, which regarded the independent journalists as counterrevolutionaries, then lambasted Cason personally, saying his activities—such as the seminar—were "truly offensive." In fact, Orrio was neither independent nor a journalist. He was working for state security. He had used the seminar to give the government a pretext to assail Cason and the United States. Rosa Miriam Elizalde and Luis Báez, *The Dissidents: Cuban State Security Agents Reveal the True Story* (Havana: Editoria Politica, 2003), pp. 67–92. Orrio confesses he was working for state security for years while posing as a journalist. Also, Marc Frank, Reuters, "Cuban Government Minister Lambastes Bush Envoy," March 14, 2003.

326 *derail a trade agreement:* The dissidents called on the European Union to reject Cuba's bid for membership in a trade agreement known as the Cotonou pact between the European Union and seventy-eight developing countries. The dissidents involved were those Oswaldo had been at odds with—Elizardo Sánchez and Marta Beatriz Roque. Their statement was a poke in the eye at Fidel. Cuba needed the EU pact to help its troubled economy. Reuters, "Cuban Dissidents Oppose More EU Cooperation," March 12, 2003. Such a protest would hurt Cuba's chances; Castro had withdrawn a previous bid to join the trade pact in 2000 in protest over the demands from Europe for progress on human rights. Cuba reapplied in 2002. Paul Ames, Associated Press, "Cuba-EU Trade Pact Wins Support," March 7, 2003. Also see BBC, "Dissidents Lobby EU against Cuba," March 13, 2003, and Joaquin Roy, "The European Union's Perception of Cuba: From Frustration to Irritation," in *Reinventing the Revolution: A Contemporary Cuba Reader*, eds. Philip Brenner,

Marguerite Rose Jiménez, John M. Kirk, and William M. LeoGrande (Lanham, MD: Rowman & Littlefield, 2008), pp. 254–261. The European Union froze Cuba's bid for entry on May 1, 2003, after the events detailed in this chapter.

326   *Oswaldo had organized citizen committees:* Regis Iglesias, communication with author, September 12, 2020.

326   *"They are detaining our people!":* This account is based on interviews with Álvarez, Iglesias, Díaz, González Alfonso, and Rivero; interviews with Ofelia Acevedo Maura; and Payá, interviews with Ehrenberg.

328   *the embassy of the Netherlands:* Regis Iglesias, communication with author, January 13, 2021.

329   *struck at the heart of Oswaldo's movimiento:* Regis Iglesias, communication with author, September 12, 2020.

330   *Elizardo was not detained:* Sánchez, interview with author.

330   *"demoralized, dejected, and worried":* McCoy, interview with author.

330   *Tony had a pounding headache:* This account is based on Díaz's memoir, *690*, pp. 87–225, by permission. Also see Frank Hernández-Trujillo and Juan F. Benemelis, *Juicios a opositores pacíficos en Cuba: Terrorismo de estado* (Miami, FL: Grupo de Apoyo a la Democracia, 2004), a compilation of sentencing documents, including Díaz and Iglesias, pp. 99–113. Also see Organization of American States, Report No. 67/06, Case 12.476.

332   *Article 91 of the Criminal Code:* Organization of American States, Report No. 67/06, p. 5.

334   *for the followers, you cut off their hands:* Sánchez, interview with author.

335   Los disidentes: Oswaldo Payá Jr., interview with author, August 11, 2017; Elizalde and Báez, *The Dissidents*; Oswaldo Payá, "La verdad sobre el libro Los disidentes," a written statement, June 5, 2003, Payá collection. The book aimed at Sánchez was titled *El Camaján* (The freeloader) and asserted that Sánchez was a government informant for six years, which he strongly denied. Sánchez told the author that he had begun talks with Cuban security officials that he thought were worthwhile in 1997, but it was a trap in which they were collecting photographs and video of him to use against him later. "They had thousands of photographs," he said. "Fidel Castro was in charge of everything."

336   *Oswaldo wanted to keep the pressure on:* Kevin Sullivan, "Cuban Democracy Drive Adds 14,000 Names," *Washington Post*, October 4, 2003, p. A13; Payá, interviews with Ehrenberg; Payá, letter to Ricardo Alarcón, October 3, 2003, Payá collection.

336   *"The outlook was bleak":* Claudia Márquez, "The Third Edition," in publication by Reporters Without Borders, www.rsf.org, November 2005.

337   *the largest prison for journalists in the world:* The Committee to Protect Journalists reported at the end of 2003 that China had the most imprisoned

journalists, thirty-nine, and Cuba was second, with twenty-nine. See https://
cpj.org/reports/2004/03/attacks-on-the-press-in-2003-journalists-in-prison/.

337 *Ladies in White: De Cuba*, no. 3. (September 2003), journal of the Society of
Journalists Manuel Márquez Sterling.

337 *Cason . . . kept up the pressure:* Cason, interview with author.

337 *The prisoners of the Black Spring were being treated harshly:* Oswaldo Payá, "Biena-
venturados los prisioneros de la primavera de Cuba porque tienen hambre y
sed de justicia," written statement, October 20, 2003, Payá collection.

338 *a forlorn Oswaldo took the call:* Iglesias, interview with author.

SEVENTEEN. UNDER SIEGE

339 *Oswaldo remained Fidel's number one enemy:* Sánchez, interview with author.

340 *a sweeping blueprint for a democratic Cuba:* Oswaldo Payá, "Programa todos
cubanos," 174 pages, May 10, 2006, Havana. Payá believed "to open the way
for other political parties, you need the structure and support of laws. Right
now, those laws do not exist." U.S. Interests Section Havana to Department
of State, "Political Pluralism Key to Cuba's Future, Says Payá," April 26, 2006,
HAVANA 009342, WikiLeaks.org.

340 *"The spark—you cannot predict it":* Ehrenberg, interview with author.

340 *"We were caught by surprise":* Havel letter to Payá, November 17, 2003, *Journal
of Democracy* 15, no. 2 (April 2004): 169. Havel added: "We were thus forced
to make all essential decisions, under pressure of circumstances, in a matter
of days—sometimes even hours. But it was precisely the first moments in
the transfer of power that were the most important. At that time, decisions
were made that would affect the fate of the country for years to come. Whatever we did not deal with at the beginning we had to catch up on later, with
much greater difficulty. We ran up against the fact that we had not prepared
a shadow cabinet, and that we had not selected competent people who could
be presented to the public as credible replacements for the old dysfunctional
parliament. It turned out that, for the most part, we had not prepared the
basic legislation for nascent democratic structures and for securing the country's economy during the coming months. Without clear laws, the quickest to
come to the fore were . . . those for whom any system serves merely as a veil
for their own ambitions, crooks capable of anything and who have economic
advantages based on the functions they previously held."

341 *"They're messed up, and we need a solution that doesn't mess them up further.":* U.S.
Interests Section Havana to Department of State, "Political Pluralism Key to
Cuba's Future, says Payá," April 26, 2006, HAVANA 009342, WikiLeaks.org.

341 *without the extremes of post-Soviet Russia:* Payá, "Programa todos cubanos."
Also see Payá, "The Unstoppable Cuban Spring," *Washington Post*, July 1,
2006, p. A25. On the oligarchy, Payá, interviews with Ehrenberg.

341 *boosting US spending on prodemocracy programs: Commission for Assistance to a Free Cuba: Report to the President*, May 2004, chairman Colin L. Powell, Washington, DC; *Commission for Assistance to a Free Cuba, Report to the President*, July 2006, chairman Condoleezza Rice, Washington, DC; Anita Snow, Associated Press, "Cuba Says U.S. Transition Proposal for Island is Plan for Regime Change," July 6, 2006.

342 *absolutely livid:* Ofelia Acevedo Maura, interview with author, January 21, 2018; U.S. Interests Section Havana to State Department, May 11, 2006, HAVANA 010078.

342 *two sons raced ahead on their bicycles:* Oswaldo Payá, "In Cuba, in the Face of Pogroms and Lies, We Sow Hope," unpublished article, August 11, 2006, and "While Cuba Dawns," unpublished essay, April 28, 2008, Payá collection.

342 *acto de repudio:* Francisco de Armas, Christian Liberation Movement, press release, September 8, 2006, Payá collection; photographs of the caricature and painted slogans, Payá collection. Sabin, communication with author, April 1, 2021, said Payá was deeply irritated by the slogan, using the words of the Jesuit founder against him, since he greatly admired Saint Ignacio de Loyola and the life of his followers.

343 *Oswaldo told a diplomat:* U.S. Interests Section Havana to State Department, May 11, 2006, HAVANA 010078.

343 *Oswaldo heard words that gave him a fright:* Payá recalled his nervousness over this moment to many friends and family.

343 *turning over his presidential powers to Raúl:* Anita Snow, Associated Press, "Extent of Fidel Castro's Illness Unknown," August 1, 2006.

343 *Fidel's private life was secret:* At the time, Cubans knew little of Fidel's second wife, Dalia Soto del Valle, with whom he had five sons.

344 *"my spirit is perfectly fine":* Vanessa Arrington, Associated Press, "Cuba Again Says Castro's Health Stable," August 2, 2006.

344 *In a second operation:* Oriol Güell and Ana Alfageme, "A Chain of Failed Medical Actions Aggravated Castro's Condition," *El País*, January 15, 2007.

344 *the dictator's long-term health prospects did not look good:* U.S. Interests Section Havana to Department of State, "Cuba Human Rights Roundup August 11, 2006," HAVANA 016023, August 11, 2006, WikiLeaks.org.

344 *he is probably near death:* U.S. Interests Section Havana to Department of State, "Scenesetter for Codel Flake: Fidel Ebbing Away," HAVANA 023588, December 12, 2006, WikiLeaks.org.

344 *"Oswaldo Payá said the order to kill us has already been issued, and I believe him":* U.S. Interests Section Havana to Department of State, "Repression in Cuba Worse under Raúl, Say Activists," HAVANA 020774, October 6, 2006, WikiLeaks.org.

345 *a plainclothes state security officer grabbed him:* "Siege against Members of the

Christian Liberation Movement," Christian Liberation Movement press release, November 3, 2006; Payá told a US diplomat December 13 that in the previous seven days state security had "detained a number of people who visited or were trying to visit his house." U.S. Interests Section Havana to Department of State, HAVANA 023602, December 14, 2006.

345   *the onslaught against the Varela Project:* Oswaldo Payá, "El Proyecto Varela y el eslabón perdido," unpublished article, April 24, 2005, Payá collection. Also see Movimiento Cristiano Liberación, "Represión contra miembros del MCL, 'Los prisioneros de la primavera de Cuba,' firmantes del Proyecto Varela y participantes en el Diálogo Nacional desde agosto del 2004," undated, but recording events after August 2004.

345   *"Down with the worm! Long live Fidel!":* U.S. Interests Section Havana to Department of State, HAVANA 023588, December 12, 2006.

346   *the door covered in human and animal excrement:* Movimiento Cristiano Liberación, *"Represión contra."*

346   *Oswaldo never had much money:* Ofelia Acevedo Maura and Rosa María Payá Acevedo, interviews with author.

346   *"this guy, when does he sleep?":* Annika Rigö, interview with author, December 12, 2018, Stockholm.

347   *"You cannot be afraid":* Rosa María Payá Acevedo, interview with author, January 16, 2018.

347   *"I see very few chances of getting out alive.":* Payá, interviews with Ehrenberg.

347   *"People aren't taking seriously enough the threat that they'd liquidate me.":* U.S. Interests Section Havana to Department of State, December 14, 2006, HAVANA 023602, WikiLeaks.org.

348   *the metal valve broke and sliced through his hand:* Ministerio de Salud Pública, Havana, record of anesthesia, X-rays, Oswaldo Payá, December 19, 2006, Payá collection; Ofelia Acevedo Maura, interview with author, December 3, 2017.

348   *Fidel's condition was so fragile:* Güell and Alfageme, "A Chain of Failed Medical Actions."

348   *Raúl was his handpicked successor:* Oswaldo issued a statement saying that Fidel's replacement must be a "sovereign people," who wanted to "begin a new stage of their lives." Oswaldo Payá, "Comunicado del Movimiento Cristiano Liberación sobre la renuncia de Fidel Castro," February 19, 2007.

349   *"These are no longer threats":* Oswaldo Payá, statement about the incident, January 30, 2008; Payá, email to Annika Rigö, February 3, 2008.

349   *the Ladies in White:* The group was honored with the 2005 Sakharov Prize.

349   *a Cuban Spring that stretched through the 2000s:* A comprehensive account of civil society activities from 2000 to 2008 is contained in the series of reports *Steps to Freedom,* by the Cuban Democratic Directorate, Hialeah, Florida, and

the Center for the Study of a National Option, with funding from the International Republican Institute, Washington, DC.

349　*filled with articles and opinions about the Cuban Spring: La Primavera* 1, no. 2 (December 2006) through vol. 5, no. 25 (December 2011). For example, in an editorial in March 2009, headlined *"Romper la inercia,"* the paper gently scolded Oswaldo's proposed National Dialogue, saying it needed to be tested on the ground and shown to be "politically sound." *La Primavera* 3, no. 14, p. 1.

350　*the opposition was atomized:* At one point, Oswaldo suggested all the opposition and the government meet together, like the roundtable in Poland that had eventually led to Solidarity's rise to power. He called his proposal the Cuban Forum, but the talks never materialized. The Cuban Forum campaign was announced June 24, 2007. See press release, "Press Statement for the Cuban Forum Campaign," and "Cuban Forum Campaign" text, Christian Liberation Movement, June 24, 2007, Payá collection.

350　*The splits festered:* For the 2005 comments, see "Babel or Pentecost? A Challenge and a Task for the Cuban people," statement by MCL Coordinating Council, August 30, 2005. The 2007 joint declaration "Unity for Freedom" was signed April 15, 2007, by Payá, Elizardo Sánchez, Vladimiro Roca, Marta Beatriz Roque, Laura Pollán, and Héctor Palacios, among others. Ehrenberg, interview with author. An additional attempt at joint efforts came in 2011 with the signing of a democracy plan titled *"El camino del pueblo,"* which echoed the Varela Project, and added guarantees for political parties. In addition to Payá, the signatories included Roque, Sánchez, and Pollán. See *"El camino del pueblo,"* July 13, 2011.

351　*the regime had survived the 1990s:* Brian Fonseca and John Polga-Hecimovich, "Two Nations, One Revolution: The Evolution of Contemporary Cuba-Venezuela Relations," in *Venezuela and Cuba: The Ties That Bind*, Wilson Center, Latin American Program, Washington, DC, 2020. On Raúl and the economy, Richard E. Feinberg concluded that over the decade from 2008 to 2018 the private economy took off, providing jobs and income to as many as four out of ten Cubans of working age. Feinberg, "Cuba's Economy after Raúl Castro: A Tale of Three Worlds," Brookings Institution, 2018.

351　*"I promised myself that I would live in Cuba as a free person":* Yoani Sánchez, *Havana Real: One Woman Fights to Tell the Truth about Cuba Today* (Brooklyn: Melville House, 2011), pp. ix–xv, 1–3.

352　*bloggers campaigned for the release of a popular rocker, Gorki Águila:* Yoani Sánchez, "Brief Chronology of a Victory," pp. 11–17, in *Steps to Freedom, 2007–2008*, Cuban Democratic Directorate and Center for the Studies of a National Option, Hialeah, Florida, 2009. Also, Marc Lacy, "Punk Rocker Takes On the Castros," *New York Times*, September 5, 2008.

353   *"In Cuba, the word is also a prisoner"*: Oswaldo Payá statement, June 1, 2009, Havana.

353   *Oswaldo's view of them was complex*: Regis Iglesias, communication with author, March 31, 2021; Payá statement, June 1, 2009.

354   *"Tell Yoani to shut up!"*: Orlando Luis Pardo Lazo, blog post, http://orland oluispardolazo.blogspot.com/2009/11/abuse-your-desillusion.html; also see Yoani Sánchez, *Havana Real*, pp. 170–173.

354   *"They said they were going to set us free, so I'm going to wait for them to set us free"*: Iglesias, interview with author.

354   *a raw and unsettling account of his arrest*: Díaz, 690.

355   *put immediately on a night flight to Madrid*: Antonio Ramón Díaz Sánchez, communication with author, October 12, 2020.

355   *the prisoners' stories captured the imagination of a young, ambitious political organizer*: Ángel Carromero, interview with author, September 13, 2017, Madrid; Carromero, *Muerte*, pp. 42–43; Carlos Alberto Payá, interview with Pamela Rolfe.

357   *strange, sad death*: "Laura Pollán," obituary, *The Economist*, October 29, 2011; Yoani Sánchez, "The Legacy of Laura Pollán," *Washington Post*, October 16, 2011; Tim MacGabhann, "Cuba: Remember Founder of Ladies in White Movement," Al Jazeera, April 9, 2016; Mary Anastasia O'Grady, "A Dissident's Mysterious Death in Havana," *Wall Street Journal*, October 24, 2011; Óscar Elías Biscet, blog post, November 2, 2011, https://oscareliasbiscet.blogspot .com/2011/11/un-analisis-medico-de-la-muerte.html.

357   *His latest campaign was the Heredia Project*: It sought to support the right of Cubans to travel and move freely and protections for those who requested travel visas or exit visas, including protection against their house and assets being seized, which was common practice. The project demanded that Cuban citizens be able to move to and live in whatever part of the country they wished, without fear of being detained or deported; that Cubans have the right to stay at hotels that had been reserved exclusively for tourists; that Cubans living abroad should not have to request permission to reenter their own country, among other things. See https://mcliberacion.org/iniciativas -y-documentos/ley-de-reencuentro-nacional-proyecto-heredia/.

358   *The tension was taking a toll*: Rigö, interview with author.

359   *"This was the plan to get rid of him"*: Oswaldo Payá, "Choque," notes on the accident, Payá collection; Rigö, interview with author and email correspondence with Payá. Oswaldo wrote to her: "On June 2, while I was going to my mother-in-law's house, with our VW, a car hit us and overturned ours. By a miracle, it didn't kill us." But the VW was "destroyed."

359   *fear was seeping into Oswaldo's soul*: Ofelia Acevedo Maura, interviews with author, January 20, 2018, and October 28, 2018, Miami; Rosa María Payá Acevedo, multiple interviews.

360 *Oswaldo was desperate for support in Europe and the United States:* "Cuba Trip Report," National Democratic Institute, November 21, 2005. NDI was created in 1983 as one of the four core institutes of the National Endowment for Democracy, established by Congress that year to promote democracy around the world. NDI's sources of funding include the US government and others; it is loosely affiliated with the Democratic Party.

360 *"where we can find Christian Democrats?":* Ehrenberg, interview with author.

360 *KIC returned year after year:* Rigö, Ehrenberg, interviews with author.

360 *looking for someone new to make the voyage:* Modig, interview with author, December 9, 2018.

362 *Rigö had expected a long briefing:* Rigö, interview with author, December 12, 2018.

362 *a second preparatory meeting:* Carromero, interview with author; and Carromero, *Muerte.* Carlos said that he had nothing to do with the cash, phones, or code words.

363 *They met for the first time:* The account that follows is based on Carromero, interview with author, and *Muerte.* Modig's recollections are taken from an unpublished memorandum about the trip that he wrote in October 2012 and provided to the author and an interview with the author, December 9–10, 2018, Stockholm.

365 *She took them to Playita de 16:* This account of the conversation is based on interviews with Rosa María Payá Acevedo, Modig, and Carromero.

366 *to place microphones in the walls:* On the listening devices, the author viewed one example, removed from the apartment. It had been affixed to a telephone line jack, not to tap the line, but to pick up sound in the room, Payá collection. On the bricklayer, see Ehrenberg, *Cuba from Within,* p. 71.

366 *he was planning to push ahead with* Pasos para el cambio: The proposal was announced July 13, 2011. For text, see https://mcliberacion.org/iniciativas-y -documentos/el-camino-del-pueblo/. Ofelia Acevedo Maura, with author, December 3, 2017; Andrés Chacón, interview with author, January 17, 2018.

368 *Oswaldo wrote yet another political declaration:* Oswaldo Payá, "There Are No Free Elections If There Are No Free Men and Women," July 20, 2012, Payá collection.

368 *he was just finishing up Solzhenitsyn:* Ofelia Acevedo Maura, communication with author, April 2, 2020; David Burg and George Feifer, *Solzhenitsyn: A Biography* (New York: Stein and Day, 1972).

368 *"I'm going on a long trip":* Carlos Alberto Payá, interview with Pamela Rolfe.

369 *"Oswaldo Payá is going on vacation to Varadero. This business of being a dissident in #Cuba is a joke.":* See https://mcliberacion.org/2019/07/cronologia -de-los-sucesos-del-22-de-julio-de-2012/. It is not clear why it was put out so early in the morning, but that does suggest that state security knew Oswaldo

was going somewhere. The blogger may have been more than one person—a group of state security officers.

370 *the official Cuban government account:* Popular Provincial Court of Granma, First Criminal Court, Verdict No. 573/2012, October 12, 2012, Bayamo, Cuba.

370 *"Were they trying to kill him?":* In photographs published after the accident by the Cuban authorities, no airbags are evident. The car, an Accent, model year 2010, was probably distributed through Mexico to Cuba. Hyundai cars sold in Mexico did not require airbags until 2019. The Highway Loss Data Institute of the Insurance Institute for Highway Safety has published data for the 2010 Accent that give it a poor rating for safety in a side-impact crash. The group's report shows that a side curtain airbag where Oswaldo was sitting in the car could have significantly protected his head. See Test CES0635, Insurance Institute for Highway Safety, http://www.iihs.org/iihs/ratings/vehicle/v/hyundai/accent-4-door-sedan/2010/.

370 *Carromero blacked out. Modig also lost consciousness:* This account is drawn from Carromero, interview with author, and email communications, 2013–2014; Carromero, *Muerte*, pp. 1–3, 58–59, 95–99; multiple screenshots of text messages, in Spanish, English, and Swedish, Payá collection.

371 *"Are you there? Something has happened":* Modig, unpublished memorandum.

373 *"This is not going very well":* Modig, unpublished memorandum.

373 *confirmed that he had the phones, and gave them to Carromero:* The author pressed Modig about this. He said, "I think I gave him the phones, but I don't know where I got them from. They were not our phones." Harold was sitting behind him in the car. He speculated that after the crash "maybe they were in the car on the floor" and medics "took them and gave them to me." Asked whether Cepero perhaps gave him the phones for safekeeping before the crash, at lunch or perhaps in the car during those minutes when state security was bearing down on them, he replied, "No, I don't think so." Modig, interview with author.

374 *if he cooperated he would be safe:* Javier El-Hage and Roberto C. González, *The Case of Oswaldo Payá* (New York: Human Rights Foundation, July 22, 2015), p. 42, interview of Ángel Carromero, August 26, 2013. Also, Carromero, interview with author and *Muerte*, pp. 115–119.

375 *Ofelia's cell phone rang about 3:00 p.m.:* Ofelia Acevedo Maura, memorandum recounting events of July 22–24, 2012, undated, including screenshots, Payá collection; Acevedo Maura, interviews with author, August 11, 2017, December 3, 2017, January 20–21, 2018, Miami; Regis Iglesias, interview with author, November 28, 2017, Miami.

376 *"Okay, there is one person who is deceased":* Rosa María Payá Acevedo, interviews with author, August 11, 2017, December 3, 2017, January 20–21, 2018,

Miami; also see: El-Hage and González, *The Case of Oswaldo Payá*, p. 29, interview with Rosa María Payá Acevedo, November 1, 2013.

378 *"I am going to tell you how it happened"*: Medina's account of the crash was described by the friends from Bayamo when they arrived in Havana and met with Rosa María; audio recording of their description, July 23, 2012, Payá collection. Rosa María also gave an account of Captain Medina's report in a press conference August 1 in Havana.

379 *a forensic officer from Bayamo*: Ofelia Acevedo Maura, memorandum; also, video recording of the meeting, courtesy Rosa María Payá Acevedo, translated by Myriam Márquez.

380 *At the funeral home*: Ofelia Acevedo Maura, memorandum, and interviews.

380 *a small, stamped ticket*: "Servicios necrológicos, Ciudad de La Habana," a photograph of the paper, Payá collection.

381 *Under an afternoon sun*: This account is based on video courtesy of Orlando Luis Pardo Lazo.

EPILOGUE

385 *After the crash, Aron Modig remembered almost nothing about it*: Modig, unpublished memorandum, and interviews with author, December 9 and 13, 2018. Modig's comment that "I don't remember there being another car involved in this accident" is from "The Case of Oswaldo Payá: Legal Report," Human Rights Foundation, New York, July 22, 2013, p. 23.

386 *Ángel Carromero was held for two months*: This account is based on Carromero, interview with author; Verdict No. 573/2012, Popular Provincial Court of Granma, First Criminal Court, October 12, 2012; Carromero, *Muerte*; and Agence France-Presse, "Trial Begins for Spaniard Involved in Fatal Cuba Crash," October 5, 2012.

389 *"I was terrified"*: Carromero, interview with author.

389 *to force them to remain silent*: Ofelia Acevedo Maura, communication with author, March 19, 2021.

390 *"The trial in Bayamo was a farce"*: "I Only Wish They Were Nightmares, and Not Memories," *Washington Post*, March 6, 2013, p. A17.

391 *a group of artists and intellectuals known as the San Isidro Movement*: Carlos Manuel Álvarez, "A Group of Cuban Artists Is Daring to Live in Democracy," *Washington Post*, November 22, 2020. Also, photographs of the protest.

392 *sick patients piled up in hospitals, some lying on benches, on floors*: Atahualpa Amerise, EFE, "Cuba Facing Worst Health Crisis of the Pandemic," July 7, 2021. Also see Laura Tedesco and Rut Diamint, "The Cuban Crackdown," *Foreign Affairs*, August 30, 2021.

392 *The crowd marched into the hot sun*: The Facebook video is at https://www .youtube.com/watch?v=0L8A0_BAm7Q. "Patria y Vida" is at https://www

.youtube.com/watch?v=pP9Bto5lOEQ. On Yoan de la Cruz, see 14yMedio, July 26, 2021. For more on the protests, see the coverage of 14yMedia.com, an independent online news outlet.

393 *"The order for combat has been given"*: See https://www.youtube.com/watch?v=O_ewAUfSUyc&t=473s and https://www.youtube.com/watch?v=9vPZWMXikRE. Also, Anthony Faiola, "Cubans Take to the Streets for Biggest Anti-government Protests in Decades," *Washington Post*, July 12, 2021, p. A14; Agence France-Presse, July 12, 2021; BBC, July 11, 2021, https://www.bbc.com/news/world-latin-america-57799852.

393 *beatings with batons:* "Case Descriptions of Protestors Detained by the Cuban Government, July 2021," Human Rights Watch, October 19, 2021, https://www.hrw.org/video-photos/interactive/2021/10/19/case-descriptions-protestors-detained-cuban-government-july#.

393 *726 people were still incarcerated:* A list of those arrested has been maintained by Cubalex, a nonprofit association that "seeks the restoration of democracy and the rule of law in Cuba." The list is at bit.ly/3r8AomN. The estimate of 260 trials is by US Asst. Secretary of State Brian Nichols, Jan. 20, 2022. See https://twitter.com/WHAAsstSecty/status/1484164057192144903. Also see www.Cubalex.org.

394 *"dawn is already breaking"*: Oswaldo Payá, *La noche no será eterna* (Miami: Editorial Hypermedia, 2018), p. 234. On the earlier effort, *Souls of Rebellion*, Ofelia Acevedo Maura, interview with author, December 3, 2017.

Index

Straits of Florida

Gulf of Mexico

Havana
Camarioca
Port of Mariel
Matanzas
Cárdenas
Artemisa
Colón
Güines
Camajuaní
Pinar
del Río
López
Peña
Santa Clara

**Payá route
July 22, 2012**

Sancti
Spíritus
Escambray

Cienfuegos

Bay of Pigs

Nueva
Gerona

Isle of
Pines

Trinidad

Caribbean Sea

Havana

0   0.5   1 Mile
0   0.5   1 Kilometer

Gulf of Mexico

VÍA MONUMENTAL

**Hotel
Nacional**

MALECÓN

MALECÓN

LÍNEA

AVE. DE LOS PRESIDENTES

AVE. PASEO

CALLE 23

**University
of Havana**

**Plaza
Vieja**

EL PRADO

Havana
Harbor

AVE. SALVADOR
ALLENDE

AVE. SIMÓN
BOLÍVAR

El Capitolio

Colón
Cemetery

**Plaza de la
Revolución**

AVE. 26

AVE. DE LA INDEPENDENCIA

El Cerro

Detail

CERRO

CALZADA DEL

AVE. 51

**El Salvador
del Mundo
church**

Oswaldo's neighborhood

Beba's house
Varela Project HQ

TALLERES

**Payá
childhood
home**

MARQUÉS

Parque
Manila

PEÑÓN

MONASTERIO

**Payá
family
home**

AYUNTAMIENTO

MANILA

0   200 Feet
0   50 Meters

Maps by Kate Thorp